America's Top-Rated Cities: a Statistical Handbook

Volume I
Southern Region

1998
6th Edition

Rhoda Garoogian, *Managing Editor*
Andrew Garoogian, *Research Editor*
Patrice Walsh Weingart, *Assistant Editor*

Universal Reference Publications

Copyright © 1998 by Universal Reference Publications. All Rights Reserved.

America's Top-Rated Cities: A Statistical Handbook 1998
ISBN 1-881220-38-7 (4 volume set)
ISBN 1-881220-40-0 (Vol. 1 - South)
ISBN 1-881220-41-9 (Vol. 2 - West)
ISBN 1-881220-42-7 (Vol. 3 - Central)
ISBN 1-881220-43-5 (Vol. 4 - East)

Printed and bound in the United States of America.

Preface

This revised and expanded 1998 edition of *America's Top-Rated Cities* is intended to provide the user with a current and concise statistical profile of 76 "top" U.S. cities with populations over 100,000, based on latest census data and/or current estimates. These cities, selected on the basis of their rankings in various surveys (*Money, Fortune, Entrepreneur, Home Office Computing, Site Selection* and others) were found to be the "best" for business and/or living, during 1997.

There are now four regional guides in the series: Southern, Western, Central and Eastern. Designed with ease of use in mind, each handbook is arranged alphabetically by city and divided into two sections: the business environment and the living environment. Rankings and evaluative comments follow a brief overview. Information is then presented under such topics as cost of living, finances, taxes, population, employment and earnings, commercial real estate, education, major employers, media, crime, climate and more. Where appropriate, comparisons with Metropolitan Statistical Areas (MSA) and U.S. figures are included.

There is also a section listing Chambers of Commerce, economic development groups, and State Departments of Labor/Employment Security, that the reader may wish to contact for further information.

In addition to material provided by public/private agencies/organizations, numerous library sources were also consulted. Also utilized were various web sites on the Internet. Tables and charts are properly cited with the appropriate reference to the source of the data. Those tables which are based on the 1990 Census of Population & Housing: Summary Tape File 3C contain sample data to represent the total population.

Although every effort has been made to gather the most current and most accurate information, discrepancies may occur due to the changing nature in the way private and governmental agencies compile and interpret statistical data.

Information in previous editions should not be compared with data in this edition since some historical and forecast data have been revised.

The *America's Top-Rated Cities* series has been compiled for individuals considering relocating, business persons, general and market researchers, real estate consultants, human resource personnel, urban planners as well as students and others who use public, school, academic and special libraries.

The editors wish to thank all of those individuals who responded to our requests for information. Especially helpful were the many Chambers of Commerce, economic development organizations, labor market information bureaus and city school districts. Their assistance is greatly appreciated.

The mission of Universal Reference Publications is to develop a series of comprehensive but reasonably priced statistical reference handbooks about America's "best" cities. Towards that end we have also published *America's Top-Rated Smaller Cities, Health & Environment in America's Top-Rated Cities* and *Crime in America's Top-Rated Cities*.

We welcome your comments and suggestions for improving the coverage and presentation of data in future editions of these handbooks.

The Editors

Table of Contents

Abilene, Texas

Atlanta, Georgia

Austin, Texas

Brownsville, Texas

Corpus Christi, Texas

Dallas, Texas

Fort Lauderdale, Florida

Fort Worth, Texas

Houston, Texas

Jacksonville, Florida

Knoxville, Tennessee

Mobile, Alabama

Nashville, Tennessee

New Orleans, Louisiana

Orlando, Florida

San Antonio, Texas

Tallahassee, Florida

Tampa, Florida

Comparative Statistics

Abilene, Texas

Background

The westward progress of the Texas and Pacific Railroad led to the founding of Abilene. The area was originally home to the Native Americans of the Plains, including the Comanche. After January 1876, when one of the last engagements occurred, large numbers of settlers began to arrive and to develop communities.

When the railroad was considering two possible routes through west Texas, a group of ranchers led by Col. C.W. Merchant and his twin brother met with railway officials and persuaded them to choose the route which went through Abilene. In 1880 the merchants named the town after the famous Kansas shipping point.

In February of 1881, the first official train arrived. In March of the same year, town lots were auctioned. 317 lots were sold in two days and Abilene was officially "born".

On January 2, 1883, Abilene was incorporated when the town boasted two newspapers, several churches and a public school. On October 23, 1883 it was voted to move the county seat from Buffalo Gap to Abilene. The vote was immediately challenged by the people from the Gap who leveled charges that train passengers were encouraged to leave the train, vote, and then partake of a barrel of whiskey set up in a nearby lumberyard. The battle escalated until the two opposing groups brought six-shooters into the court session where the challenge was to be heard. A confrontation was avoided and Abilene was named the new county seat.

Regional agricultural products are primarily cattle, dry-land cotton, and field crops. The city's economy, originally based solely on livestock and agriculture, has expanded to include industry. Petroleum and natural gas are produced in a multicounty area, of which Abilene is the center. The city's manufactures include light machinery, aerospace structures, and band instruments.

Abilene has undergone some economic expansion recently with the opening of a new telemarketing facility by Sitel. the city is also widening its international trade focus under the North American Free Grade Agreements. *Site Selection, Dec. 1997/Jan. 1998.*

Located in north central Texas in the midst of rolling plains, Abilene is 1,750 feet above sea level. The city lies on the boundary between the humid east Texas climate and the semi-arid west and northwest Texas climate. Severe storms, occurring mostly in the spring, are infrequent. The summer generally has high temperature days and cool nights. Fair, mild weather is typical for the winters. Cold weather periods are short lived.

General Rankings and Evaluative Comments

■ Abilene was ranked #92 out of 300 cities by *Money's* 1997 "Survey of the Best Places to Live." Criteria used: health services, crime, economy, housing, education, transportation, weather, leisure and the arts. The city was ranked #46 in 1996 and #106 in 1995. *Money, July 1997; Money, September 1996; Money, September 1995*

■ *Ladies Home Journal* ranked America's 200 largest cities based on the qualities women care about most. Abilene ranked 137 out of 200. Criteria: low crime rate, good public schools, well-paying jobs, quality health and child care, the presence of women in government, proportion of women-owned businesses, size of the wage gap with men, local economy, divorce rates, the ratio of single men to single women, whether there are laws that require at least the same number of public toilets for women as men, and the probability of good hair days. *Ladies Home Journal, November 1997*

■ Abilene was ranked #48 out of 219 cities in terms of children's health, safety, and economic well-being. Criteria: total population, percent population change, birth rate, child immunization rate, infant mortality rate, percent low birth weight infants, percent of births to teens, physician-to-population ratio, student-to-teacher ratio, dropout rate, unemployment rate, median family income, percent of children in poverty, violent and property crime rates, number of juvenile arrests for violent crimes as a percent of the total crime index, number of days with pollution standard index (PSI) over 100, pounds toxic releases per 1,000 people and number of superfund sites. *Zero Population Growth, Children's Environmental Index 1997*

■ According to *Working Mother,* "This year, the Texas Licensed Child Care Association lobbied heavily against proposed standards that would have improved the adult-to-child ratios in many programs. Unfortunately, it prevailed. Lawmakers delayed adoption of the new rules.

Texas may finally get statewide resource and referral services, however, with new federal funds coming into the state. In addition to helping parents find care, R&Rs may handle both caregiver training and consumer education—a positive development.

Providers across the state may also get low-interest loans to buy new equipment, upgrade their facilities and do other things to improve the quality of care, under a bill pending in the state legislature that looked likely to pass as we went to press." *Working Mother, July/August 1997*

Business Environment

STATE ECONOMY

State Economic Profile

"The Texas economy remains among the strongest in the nation....

Overall, Texas gained over 141,000 people last year through in-migration. While this is down from the three-year average of over 170,000, it still represents 43% of the Texas population increase. By far, throughout this decade, California has been the largest domestic source of in-migrants into Texas. With the California economy rebounding, in-migration to Texas is slowing.

The slowdown in household growth, coupled with solid residential construction, is creating a slight oversupply throughout the state. As a result, house price growth is decelerating. New residential permits have yet to slow, with new permits up by 14% last year—nearly twice the national increase. The slowdown in population and household growth cannot sustain such robust growth in permits, and as a result, new permits will slow this year.

The Texas economy shows no major imbalances. Although the important computer-chip industry remains moribund, the economy continues to expand solidly. The turnaround in computer memory prices will help the state continue to expand. Texas' growth is becoming increasingly supported by in-migrants. With an increasing presence in high-tech, an attractive business environment, and close proximity to Mexico, Texas will continue to expand faster than the nation and lure workers from other locales. In addition, as an attractive destination for retirees, Texas will continue to experience solid population and household growth as the population ages. Texas is ranked above average for short-and long-term growth." *National Association of Realtors, Economic Profiles: The Fifty States, July 1997*

IMPORTS/EXPORTS

Total Export Sales

Area	1993 ($000)	1994 ($000)	1995 ($000)	1996 ($000)	% Chg. 1993-96	% Chg. 1995-96
MSA[1]	n/a	n/a	n/a	n/a	n/a	n/a
U.S.	464,858,354	512,415,609	583,030,524	622,827,063	34.0	6.8

Note: (1) Metropolitan Statistical Area - see Appendix A for areas included; n/a not available
Source: U.S. Department of Commerce, International Trade Association, Metropolitan Area Exports: An Export Performance Report on Over 250 U.S. Cities, October 1997

Imports/Exports by Port

Type	Cargo Value			Share of U.S. Total	
	1995 (US$mil.)	1996 (US$mil.)	% Change 1995-1996	1995 (%)	1996 (%)
Imports	0	0	0	0	0
Exports	0	0	0	0	0

Source: Global Trade Information Services, WaterBorne Trade Atlas 1997

CITY FINANCES

City Government Finances

Component	FY92 ($000)	FY92 (per capita $)
Revenue	63,621	588.02
Expenditure	66,011	610.11
Debt Outstanding	65,160	602.24
Cash & Securities	87,854	811.99

Source: U.S. Bureau of the Census, City Government Finances: 1991-92

City Government Revenue by Source

Source	FY92 ($000)	FY92 (per capita $)	FY92 (%)
From Federal Government	1,979	18.29	3.1
From State Governments	1,358	12.55	2.1
From Local Governments	136	1.26	0.2
Property Taxes	12,575	116.22	19.8
General Sales Taxes	12,264	113.35	19.3
Selective Sales Taxes	4,340	40.11	6.8
Income Taxes	0	0.00	0.0
Current Charges	10,397	96.09	16.3
Utility/Liquor Store	11,101	102.60	17.4
Employee Retirement[1]	1,748	16.16	2.7
Other	7,723	71.38	12.1

Note: (1) Excludes "city contributions," classified as "nonrevenue," intragovernmental transfers.
Source: U.S. Bureau of the Census, City Government Finances: 1991-92

City Government Expenditures by Function

Function	FY92 ($000)	FY92 (per capita $)	FY92 (%)
Educational Services	1,075	9.94	1.6
Employee Retirement[1]	1,099	10.16	1.7
Environment/Housing	12,695	117.33	19.2
Government Administration	3,778	34.92	5.7
Interest on General Debt	4,808	44.44	7.3
Public Safety	14,275	131.94	21.6
Social Services	1,579	14.59	2.4
Transportation	5,574	51.52	8.4
Utility/Liquor Store	9,702	89.67	14.7
Other	11,426	105.60	17.3

Note: (1) Payments to beneficiaries including withdrawal of contributions.
Source: U.S. Bureau of the Census, City Government Finances: 1991-92

Municipal Bond Ratings

Area	Moody's	S & P
Abilene	A1	n/a

Note: n/a not available; n/r not rated
Source: Moody's Bond Record, 2/98; Statistical Abstract of the U.S., 1997;
Governing Magazine, 9/97, 3/98

POPULATION

Population Growth

Area	1980	1990	% Chg. 1980-90	July 1996 Estimate	% Chg. 1990-96
City	98,312	106,665	8.5	108,476	1.7
MSA[1]	n/a	119,655	n/a	122,130	2.1
U.S.	226,545,805	248,765,170	9.8	265,179,411	6.6

Note: (1) Metropolitan Statistical Area - see Appendix A for areas included
Source: 1980/1990 Census of Housing and Population, Summary Tape File 3C;
Census Bureau Population Estimates

Population Characteristics

| Race | City | | | | | MSA[1] | |
| | 1980 | | 1990 | | % Chg. 1980-90 | 1990 | |
	Population	%	Population	%		Population	%
White	83,437	84.9	88,067	82.6	5.5	100,488	84.0
Black	6,632	6.7	7,418	7.0	11.9	7,464	6.2
Amer Indian/Esk/Aleut	332	0.3	379	0.4	14.2	407	0.3
Asian/Pacific Islander	1,032	1.0	1,358	1.3	31.6	1,394	1.2
Other	6,879	7.0	9,443	8.9	37.3	9,902	8.3
Hispanic Origin[2]	12,281	12.5	16,099	15.1	31.1	17,014	14.2

Note: (1) Metropolitan Statistical Area - see Appendix A for areas included;
(2) people of Hispanic origin can be of any race
Source: 1980/1990 Census of Housing and Population, Summary Tape File 3C

Ancestry

Area	German	Irish	English	Italian	U.S.	French	Polish	Dutch
City	19.6	18.0	15.3	1.4	8.6	3.5	0.9	2.7
MSA[1]	19.7	18.6	15.2	1.4	8.9	3.5	0.9	2.8
U.S.	23.3	15.6	13.1	5.9	5.3	4.2	3.8	2.5

Note: Figures are percentages and include persons that reported multiple ancestry (eg. if a person reported being Irish and Italian, they were included in both columns); (1) Metropolitan Statistical Area - see Appendix A for areas included
Source: 1990 Census of Population and Housing, Summary Tape File 3C

Age

| Area | Median Age (Years) | Age Distribution (%) | | | | | | |
		Under 5	Under 18	18-24	25-44	45-64	65+	80+
City	29.6	8.3	27.1	14.0	31.1	16.2	11.6	3.0
MSA[1]	30.2	8.1	27.2	13.1	30.9	16.8	11.9	3.1
U.S.	32.9	7.3	25.6	10.5	32.6	18.7	12.5	2.8

Note: (1) Metropolitan Statistical Area - see Appendix A for areas included
Source: 1990 Census of Population and Housing, Summary Tape File 3C

Male/Female Ratio

Area	Number of males per 100 females (all ages)	Number of males per 100 females (18 years old+)
City	93.9	90.7
MSA[1]	94.1	91.0
U.S.	95.0	91.9

Note: (1) Metropolitan Statistical Area - see Appendix A for areas included
Source: 1990 Census of Population, General Population Characteristics

INCOME

Per Capita/Median/Average Income

Area	Per Capita ($)	Median Household ($)	Average Household ($)
City	11,857	24,725	32,120
MSA[1]	11,791	24,661	31,840
U.S.	14,420	30,056	38,453

Note: all figures are for 1989; (1) Metropolitan Statistical Area - see Appendix A for areas included
Source: 1990 Census of Population and Housing, Summary Tape File 3C

Household Income Distribution by Race

Income ($)	City (%)					U.S. (%)				
	Total	White	Black	Other	Hisp.[1]	Total	White	Black	Other	Hisp.[1]
Less than 5,000	7.4	6.3	16.6	12.5	12.6	6.2	4.8	15.2	8.6	8.8
5,000 - 9,999	10.1	9.6	11.3	14.0	14.0	9.3	8.6	14.2	9.9	11.1
10,000 - 14,999	11.4	11.1	12.8	13.7	13.7	8.8	8.5	11.0	9.8	11.0
15,000 - 24,999	21.6	21.5	23.2	22.2	24.2	17.5	17.3	18.9	18.5	20.5
25,000 - 34,999	17.7	17.5	17.4	21.2	20.2	15.8	16.1	14.2	15.4	16.4
35,000 - 49,999	15.8	16.5	13.3	10.6	10.5	17.9	18.6	13.3	16.1	16.0
50,000 - 74,999	10.7	11.7	5.3	4.0	4.2	15.0	15.8	9.3	13.4	11.1
75,000 - 99,999	2.9	3.3	0.0	1.4	0.7	5.1	5.5	2.6	4.7	3.1
100,000+	2.3	2.6	0.2	0.5	0.0	4.4	4.8	1.3	3.7	1.9

Note: all figures are for 1989; (1) people of Hispanic origin can be of any race
Source: 1990 Census of Population and Housing, Summary Tape File 3C

Effective Buying Income

Area	Per Capita ($)	Median Household ($)	Average Household ($)
City	12,708	27,010	35,710
MSA[1]	13,015	27,639	36,177
U.S.	15,444	33,201	41,849

Note: data as of 1/1/97; (1) Metropolitan Statistical Area - see Appendix A for areas included
Source: Standard Rate & Data Service, Newspaper Advertising Source, 2/98

Effective Household Buying Income Distribution

Area	% of Households Earning						
	$10,000 -$19,999	$20,000 -$34,999	$35,000 -$49,999	$50,000 -$74,999	$75,000 -$99,000	$100,000 -$124,999	$125,000 and up
City	20.8	27.4	16.8	13.5	3.7	0.8	1.7
MSA[1]	20.2	26.6	17.4	14.0	4.0	0.9	1.7
U.S.	16.5	23.4	18.3	18.2	6.4	2.1	2.4

Note: data as of 1/1/97; (1) Metropolitan Statistical Area - see Appendix A for areas included
Source: Standard Rate & Data Service, Newspaper Advertising Source, 2/98

Poverty Rates by Race and Age

Area	Total (%)	By Race (%)				By Age (%)		
		White	Black	Other	Hisp.[2]	Under 5 years old	Under 18 years old	65 years and over
City	15.3	12.0	24.6	33.7	32.4	22.7	19.3	14.7
MSA[1]	15.4	12.5	24.5	34.1	32.8	23.1	19.4	16.1
U.S.	13.1	9.8	29.5	23.1	25.3	20.1	18.3	12.8

Note: figures show the percent of people living below the poverty line in 1989. The average poverty threshold was $12,674 for a family of four in 1989; (1) Metropolitan Statistical Area - see Appendix A for areas included; (2) people of Hispanic origin can be of any race
Source: 1990 Census of Population and Housing, Summary Tape File 3C

EMPLOYMENT

Labor Force and Employment

Area	Civilian Labor Force			Workers Employed		
	Dec. '95	Dec. '96	% Chg.	Dec. '95	Dec. '96	% Chg.
City	53,903	53,630	-0.5	51,879	51,920	0.1
MSA[1]	60,896	60,603	-0.5	58,713	58,759	0.1
U.S.	134,583,000	136,742,000	1.6	127,903,000	130,785,000	2.3

Note: Data is not seasonally adjusted and covers workers 16 years of age and older;
(1) Metropolitan Statistical Area - see Appendix A for areas included
Source: Bureau of Labor Statistics, http://stats.bls.gov

Unemployment Rate

Area	1997											
	Jan.	Feb.	Mar.	Apr.	May	Jun.	Jul.	Aug.	Sep.	Oct.	Nov.	Dec.
City	4.5	4.6	4.8	4.2	4.4	5.0	4.6	4.2	3.8	3.6	3.7	3.2
MSA[1]	4.3	4.4	4.6	4.0	4.2	4.7	4.4	4.0	3.7	3.4	3.5	3.0
U.S.	5.9	5.7	5.5	4.8	4.7	5.2	5.0	4.8	4.7	4.4	4.3	4.4

Note: Data is not seasonally adjusted and covers workers 16 years of age and older; All figures are percentages; (1) Metropolitan Statistical Area - see Appendix A for areas included
Source: Bureau of Labor Statistics, http://stats.bls.gov

Employment by Industry

Sector	MSA[1]		U.S.
	Number of Employees	Percent of Total	Percent of Total
Services	19,200	34.1	29.0
Retail Trade	12,200	21.7	18.5
Government	10,100	17.9	16.1
Manufacturing	3,200	5.7	15.0
Finance/Insurance/Real Estate	2,400	4.3	5.7
Wholesale Trade	2,700	4.8	5.4
Transportation/Public Utilities	2,500	4.4	5.3
Construction	2,300	4.1	4.5
Mining	1,700	3.0	0.5

Note: Figures cover non-farm employment as of 12/97 and are not seasonally adjusted;
(1) Metropolitan Statistical Area - see Appendix A for areas included
Source: Bureau of Labor Statistics, http://stats.bls.gov

Employment by Occupation

Occupation Category	City (%)	MSA[1] (%)	U.S. (%)
White Collar	60.8	59.7	58.1
Executive/Admin./Management	11.3	10.9	12.3
Professional	16.5	15.7	14.1
Technical & Related Support	4.1	4.0	3.7
Sales	13.3	13.3	11.8
Administrative Support/Clerical	15.6	15.7	16.3
Blue Collar	20.9	21.9	26.2
Precision Production/Craft/Repair	10.0	10.6	11.3
Machine Operators/Assem./Insp.	3.9	4.0	6.8
Transportation/Material Movers	4.2	4.4	4.1
Cleaners/Helpers/Laborers	2.9	2.9	3.9
Services	16.8	16.3	13.2
Farming/Forestry/Fishing	1.5	2.1	2.5

Note: figures cover employed persons 16 years old and over;
(1) Metropolitan Statistical Area - see Appendix A for areas included
Source: 1990 Census of Population and Housing, Summary Tape File 3C

Occupational Employment Projections: 1993 - 2000

Occupations Expected to have the Largest Job Growth (ranked by numerical growth)	Fast-Growing Occupations[1] (ranked by percent growth)
1. Home health aides	1. Home health aides
2. Nursing aides/orderlies/attendants	2. Personal and home care aides
3. Child care workers, private household	3. Health service workers
4. Farmers	4. Recreation workers
5. Cashiers	5. Computer systems analysts
6. Registered nurses	6. Cleaners/servants, private home
7. Food preparation workers	7. Child care workers, private household
8. General office clerks	8. Corrections officers & jailers
9. Licensed practical nurses	9. Housekeeper supervisors, institutional
10. Salespersons, retail	10. Teachers, special education

Projections cover Brown, Callahan, Coleman, Comanche, Eastland, Fisher, Haskell, Jones, Kent, Knox, Mitchell, Nolan, Runnels, Scurry, Shackelford, Stephens, Stonewall, Taylor and Throckmorton Counties.
Note: (1) Includes occupations with absolute job growth of 100 or more
Source: Texas Employment Commission, Texas Employment Projections Reporting System, Statewide and Regional Projections 1993-2000, Ver. 1.0

Average Wages

Occupation	Wage	Occupation	Wage
Professional/Technical/Clerical	$/Week	**Health/Protective Services**	$/Week
Accountants III	672	Corrections Officers	-
Attorneys III	-	Firefighters	-
Budget Analysts III	-	Nurses, Licensed Practical II	-
Buyers/Contracting Specialists II	-	Nurses, Registered II	-
Clerks, Accounting III	-	Nursing Assistants II	-
Clerks, General III	349	Police Officers I	-
Computer Operators II	-	**Hourly Workers**	$/Hour
Computer Programmers II	-	Forklift Operators	7.91
Drafters II	-	General Maintenance Workers	7.75
Engineering Technicians III	-	Guards I	6.50
Engineering Technicians, Civil III	-	Janitors	4.96
Engineers III	842	Maintenance Electricians	-
Key Entry Operators I	-	Maintenance Electronics Techs II	-
Personnel Assistants III	-	Maintenance Machinists	-
Personnel Specialists III	-	Maintenance Mechanics, Machinery	-
Secretaries III	488	Material Handling Laborers	-
Switchboard Operator-Receptionist	256	Motor Vehicle Mechanics	-
Systems Analysts II	-	Shipping/Receiving Clerks	8.98
Systems Analysts Supervisor/Mgr II	-	Tool and Die Makers	-
Tax Collectors II	-	Truckdrivers, Tractor Trailer	9.30
Word Processors II	-	Warehouse Specialists	-

Note: Wage data includes full-time workers only for 12/93 and cover the Metropolitan Statistical Area (see Appendix A for areas included). Dashes indicate that data was not available.
Source: Bureau of Labor Statistics, Occupational Compensation Survey

TAXES

Major State and Local Tax Rates

State Corp. Income (%)	State Personal Income (%)	Residential Property (effective rate per $100)	Sales & Use		State Gasoline (cents/ gallon)	State Cigarette (cents/ 20-pack)
			State (%)	Local (%)		
None[a]	None	n/a	6.25	2.0	20	41

Note: Personal/corporate income tax rates as of 1/97. Sales, gasoline and cigarette tax rates as of 1/98; (a) Texas imposes a franchise tax of 4.5% of earned surplus
Source: Federation of Tax Administrators, www.taxadmin.org; Washington D.C. Department of Finance and Revenue, Tax Rates and Tax Burdens in the District of Columbia: A Nationwide Comparison, June 1997; Chamber of Commerce

Total Taxes Per Capita and as a Percent of Income

Area	Per Capita Income ($)	Per Capita Taxes ($)			Taxes as Pct. of Income (%)		
		Total	Federal	State/Local	Total	Federal	State/Local
Texas	24,145	8,118	5,538	2,580	33.6	22.9	10.7
U.S.	26,187	9,205	6,127	3,078	35.2	23.4	11.8

Note: Figures are for 1997
Source: Tax Foundation, Web Site, www.taxfoundation.org

COMMERCIAL REAL ESTATE

Data not available at time of publication.

COMMERCIAL UTILITIES

Typical Monthly Electric Bills

Area	Commercial Service ($/month)		Industrial Service ($/month)	
	12 kW demand 1,500 kWh	100 kW demand 30,000 kWh	1,000 kW demand 400,000 kWh	20,000 kW demand 10,000,000 kWh
City	121	2,265	28,631	819,777
U.S.	162	2,360	25,590	545,677

Note: Based on rates in effect July 1, 1997
Source: Edison Electric Institute, Typical Residential, Commercial and Industrial Bills, Summer 1997

TRANSPORTATION

Transportation Statistics

Avg. travel time to work (min.)	14.3
Interstate highways	I-20
Bus lines	
In-city	CityLink, 10 city buses
Inter-city	6
Passenger air service	
Airport	Abilene Regional
Airlines	2
Aircraft departures	n/a
Enplaned passengers	n/a
Rail service	No Amtrak service
Motor freight carriers	14
Major waterways/ports	None

Source: OAG, Business Travel Planner, Summer 1997; Editor & Publisher Market Guide, 1998; FAA Airport Activity Statistics, 1996; Amtrak National Time Table, Northeast Timetable, Fall/Winter 1997-98; 1990 Census of Population and Housing, STF 3C; Chamber of Commerce/Economic Development 1997; Jane's Urban Transport Systems 1997-98; Transit Fact Book 1997

Means of Transportation to Work

Area	Car/Truck/Van		Public Transportation			Bicycle	Walked	Other Means	Worked at Home
	Drove Alone	Car-pooled	Bus	Subway	Railroad				
City	80.9	11.7	0.5	0.0	0.0	0.5	3.1	1.1	2.3
MSA[1]	80.7	11.9	0.5	0.0	0.0	0.5	3.0	1.0	2.4
U.S.	73.2	13.4	3.0	1.5	0.5	0.4	3.9	1.2	3.0

Note: figures shown are percentages and only include workers 16 years old and over;
(1) Metropolitan Statistical Area - see Appendix A for areas included
Source: 1990 Census of Population and Housing, Summary Tape File 3C

BUSINESSES

Major Business Headquarters

Company Name	1997 Rankings	
	Fortune 500	Forbes 500

No companies listed.

Note: Companies listed are located in the city; Dashes indicate no ranking
Fortune 500: companies that produce a 10-K are ranked 1 - 500 based on 1996 revenue
Forbes 500: private companies are ranked 1 - 500 based on 1996 revenue
Source: Forbes 12/1/97; Fortune 4/28/97

HOTELS & MOTELS

Hotels/Motels

Area	Hotels/ Motels	Rooms	Luxury-Level Hotels/Motels		Average Minimum Rates ($)		
			♦♦♦♦	♦♦♦♦♦	♦♦	♦♦♦	♦♦♦♦
City	16	1,689	0	0	50	84	n/a

Note: n/a not available; Classifications range from one diamond (budget properties with basic amenities) to five diamond (luxury properties with the finest service, rooms and facilities).
Source: OAG, Business Travel Planner, Summer 1997

CONVENTION CENTERS

Major Convention Centers

Center Name	Meeting Rooms	Exhibit Space (sf)
Abilene Civic Center	9	43,000

Source: Trade Shows Worldwide 1997

Living Environment

COST OF LIVING

Cost of Living Index

Composite Index	Housing	Utilities	Groceries	Health Care	Trans-portation	Misc. Goods/ Services
93.5	87.3	101.6	88.4	99.2	104.8	95.2

Note: U.S. = 100
Source: ACCRA, Cost of Living Index, 3rd Quarter 1997

HOUSING

Median Home Prices and Housing Affordability

Area	Median Price[2] 3rd Qtr. 1997 ($)	HOI[3] 3rd Qtr. 1997	Afford-ability Rank[4]
MSA[1]	n/a	n/a	n/a
U.S.	127,000	63.7	–

Note: (1) Metropolitan Statistical Area - see Appendix A for areas included; (2) U.S. figures calculated from the sales of 625,000 new and existing homes in 195 markets; (3) Housing Opportunity Index - percent of homes sold that were within the reach of the median income household at the prevailing mortgage interest rate; (4) Rank is from 1-195 with 1 being most affordable; n/a not available
Source: National Association of Home Builders, Housing Opportunity Index, 3rd Quarter 1997

Average New Home Price

Area	Price ($)
City	118,800
U.S.	135,710

Note: Figures are based on a new home with 1,800 sq. ft. of living area on an 8,000 sq. ft. lot.
Source: ACCRA, Cost of Living Index, 3rd Quarter 1997

Average Apartment Rent

Area	Rent ($/mth)
City	497
U.S.	569

Note: Figures are based on an unfurnished two bedroom, 1-1/2 or 2 bath apartment, approximately 950 sq. ft. in size, excluding all utilities except water
Source: ACCRA, Cost of Living Index, 3rd Quarter 1997

RESIDENTIAL UTILITIES

Average Residential Utility Costs

Area	All Electric ($/mth)	Part Electric ($/mth)	Other Energy ($/mth)	Phone ($/mth)
City	107.85	--	--	15.19
U.S.	109.40	55.25	43.64	19.48

Source: ACCRA, Cost of Living Index, 3rd Quarter 1997

HEALTH CARE

Average Health Care Costs

Area	Hospital ($/day)	Doctor ($/visit)	Dentist ($/visit)
City	398.25	48.86	60.00
U.S.	392.91	48.76	60.84

Note: Hospital - based on a semi-private room. Doctor - based on a general practitioner's routine exam of an established patient. Dentist - based on adult teeth cleaning and periodic oral exam.
Source: ACCRA, Cost of Living Index, 3rd Quarter 1997

Distribution of Office-Based Physicians

| Area | Family/Gen. Practitioners | Specialists | | |
		Medical	Surgical	Other
MSA[1]	32	61	66	44

Note: Data as of 12/31/96; (1) Metropolitan Statistical Area - see Appendix A for areas included
Source: American Medical Assn., Physician Characteristics & Distribution in the U.S., 1997-1998

Hospitals

Abilene has 3 general medical and surgical hospitals. *AHA Guide to the Healthcare Field 1997-98*

EDUCATION

Public School District Statistics

District Name	Num. Sch.	Enroll.	Classroom Teachers[1]	Pupils per Teacher	Minority Pupils (%)	Current Exp.[2] ($/pupil)
Abilene ISD	42	19,649	1,428	13.8	n/a	n/a
Wylie ISD	6	2,562	155	16.5	n/a	n/a

Note: Data covers the 1995-1996 school year unless otherwise noted; (1) Excludes teachers reported as working in school district offices rather than in schools; (2) Based on 1993-94 enrollment collected by the Census Bureau, not the enrollment figure shown in column 3; SD = School District; ISD = Independent School District; n/a not available
Source: National Center for Education Statistics, Common Core of Data Survey; Bureau of the Census

Educational Quality

School District	Education Quotient[1]	Graduate Outcome[2]	Community Index[3]	Resource Index[4]
Abilene	82.0	90.0	87.0	68.0

Note: Nearly 1,000 secondary school districts were rated in terms of educational quality. The scores range from a low of 50 to a high of 150; (1) Average of the Graduate Outcome, Community and Resource indexes; (2) Based on graduation rates and college board scores (SAT/ACT); (3) Based on the surrounding community's average level of education and the area's average income level; (4) Based on teacher salaries, per-pupil expenditures and student-teacher ratios.
Source: Expansion Management, Ratings Issue 1997

Educational Attainment by Race

| Area | High School Graduate (%) | | | | | Bachelor's Degree (%) | | | | |
	Total	White	Black	Other	Hisp.[2]	Total	White	Black	Other	Hisp.[2]
City	76.0	78.8	73.5	49.2	46.9	22.0	24.3	9.7	7.9	5.6
MSA[1]	75.4	78.0	73.3	48.2	45.9	20.7	22.6	9.6	7.5	5.4
U.S.	75.2	77.9	63.1	60.4	49.8	20.3	21.5	11.4	19.4	9.2

Note: figures shown cover persons 25 years old and over; (1) Metropolitan Statistical Area - see Appendix A for areas included; (2) people of Hispanic origin can be of any race
Source: 1990 Census of Population and Housing, Summary Tape File 3C

School Enrollment by Type

| Area | Preprimary | | | | Elementary/High School | | | |
| | Public | | Private | | Public | | Private | |
	Enrollment	%	Enrollment	%	Enrollment	%	Enrollment	%
City	1,324	62.1	808	37.9	17,930	96.3	693	3.7
MSA[1]	1,444	62.6	863	37.4	20,549	96.3	799	3.7
U.S.	2,679,029	59.5	1,824,256	40.5	38,379,689	90.2	4,187,099	9.8

Note: figures shown cover persons 3 years old and over;
(1) Metropolitan Statistical Area - see Appendix A for areas included
Source: 1990 Census of Population and Housing, Summary Tape File 3C

School Enrollment by Race

Area	Preprimary (%)				Elementary/High School (%)			
	White	Black	Other	Hisp.[1]	White	Black	Other	Hisp.[1]
City	78.7	9.9	11.4	14.9	75.2	9.1	15.7	24.5
MSA[2]	80.1	9.2	10.7	14.0	77.5	7.9	14.5	22.6
U.S.	80.4	12.5	7.1	7.8	74.1	15.6	10.3	12.5

Note: figures shown cover persons 3 years old and over; (1) people of Hispanic origin can be of any race; (2) Metropolitan Statistical Area - see Appendix A for areas included
Source: 1990 Census of Population and Housing, Summary Tape File 3C

SAT/ACT Scores

Area/District	1997 SAT				1997 ACT	
	Percent of Graduates Tested (%)	Average Math Score	Average Verbal Score	Average Combined Score	Percent of Graduates Tested (%)	Average Composite Score
Abilene ISD	60	504	512	1,016	29	20.9
State	49	501	494	995	30	20.2
U.S.	42	511	505	1,016	36	21.0

Note: Math and verbal SAT scores are out of a possible 800; ACT scores are out of a possible 36
Caution: Comparing or ranking states/cities on the basis of SAT/ACT scores alone is invalid and strongly discouraged by the The College Board and The American College Testing Program as students who take the tests are self-selected and do not represent the entire student population.
Source: Abilene ISD, Office of Administration, 1997; American College Testing Program, 1997; College Board, 1997

Classroom Teacher Salaries in Public Schools

District	B.A. Degree		M.A. Degree		Ph.D. Degree	
	Min. ($)	Max ($)	Min. ($)	Max. ($)	Min. ($)	Max. ($)
Abilene	20,948	41,600	21,945	42,833	n/a	n/a
Average[1]	26,120	39,270	28,175	44,667	31,643	49,825

Note: Salaries are for 1996-1997; (1) Based on all school districts covered; n/a not available
Source: American Federation of Teachers (unpublished data)

Higher Education

Two-Year Colleges		Four-Year Colleges		Medical Schools	Law Schools	Voc/ Tech
Public	Private	Public	Private			
1	1	0	3	0	0	5

Source: College Blue Book, Occupational Education 1997; Medical School Admission Requirements, 1998-99; Peterson's Guide to Two-Year Colleges, 1997; Peterson's Guide to Four-Year Colleges, 1997; Barron's Guide to Law Schools 1997

MAJOR EMPLOYERS

Major Employers

ABCO Industries (boilers)
First National Bank of Abilene
Merchants of Texas (trucking)
Reporter Publishing Co.

Allied Staffing (employment agency)
Hendrick Medical Center
Pride Refining
West Texas Utilities

Note: companies listed are located in the city
Source: Dun's Business Rankings 1997; Ward's Business Directory, 1997

PUBLIC SAFETY

Crime Rate

Area	All Crimes	Violent Crimes				Property Crimes		
		Murder	Forcible Rape	Robbery	Aggrav. Assault	Burglary	Larceny -Theft	Motor Vehicle Theft
City	5,213.8	6.1	57.6	110.0	348.4	978.0	3,499.7	213.9
Suburbs[1]	2,874.0	8.1	56.7	8.1	291.5	995.8	1,489.6	24.3
MSA[2]	4,986.0	6.3	57.5	100.1	342.9	979.7	3,304.0	195.5
U.S.	5,078.9	7.4	36.1	202.4	388.2	943.0	2,975.9	525.9

Note: Crime rate is the number of crimes per 100,000 pop.; (1) defined as all areas within the MSA but located outside the central city; (2) Metropolitan Statistical Area - see Appendix A for areas incl.
Source: FBI Uniform Crime Reports 1996

RECREATION

Culture and Recreation

Museums	Symphony Orchestras	Opera Companies	Dance Companies	Professional Theatres	Zoos	Pro Sports Teams
2	1	1	3	2	1	0

Source: International Directory of the Performing Arts, 1996; Official Museum Directory, 1998; Chamber of Commerce/Economic Development 1997

Library System

The Abilene Public Library has one branch, holdings of 190,072 volumes and a budget of $1,357,588 (1995-1996). The Big Country Library System has no branches, holdings of 29,784 volumes and a budget of $340,062 (1995-1996). *American Library Directory, 1997-1998*

MEDIA

Newspapers

Name	Type	Freq.	Distribution	Circulation
Abilene Reporter News	General	7x/wk	Area	44,000

Note: Includes newspapers with circulations of 500 or more located in the city; Source: Burrelle's Media Directory, 1998 Edition

AM Radio Stations

Call Letters	Freq. (kHz)	Target Audience	Station Format	Music Format
KTAE	1260	Hispanic	M/S/T	Country/Easy Listening/Spanish
KEAN	1280	General	M/S	Country
KYYD	1340	General	S/T	n/a
KBBA	1470	Hispanic	M	Spanish
KMXO	1500	Religious	E/M/N/T	Christian/Spanish

Note: Stations included broadcast in the Abilene metro area; n/a not available
Station Format: E = Educational; M = Music; N = News; S = Sports; T = Talk
Source: Burrelle's Media Directory, 1998 Edition

FM Radio Stations

Call Letters	Freq. (mHz)	Target Audience	Station Format	Music Format
KGNZ	88.1	Religious	M/N	Adult Contemporary/Christian
KACU	89.7	General	M	Adult Contemporary/Classical/Jazz
KBCY	99.7	Religious	M	Country
KORQ	100.7	General	M	Adult Contemporary
KCWS	102.7	n/a	M/N	Country
KCDD	103.7	General	M	Contemporary Top 40
KEAN	105.1	General	M	Country
KHXS	106.3	General	M	Big Band/Easy Listening
KEYJ	107.9	General	M/N/S	AOR

Note: Stations included broadcast in the Abilene metro area; n/a not available
Station Format: E = Educational; M = Music; N = News; S = Sports; T = Talk
Music Format: AOR = Album Oriented Rock; MOR = Middle-of-the-Road
Source: Burrelle's Media Directory, 1998 Edition

Television Stations

Name	Ch.	Affiliation	Type	Owner
KACB	9	NBC	Commercial	Abilene Radio & TV
KRBC	9	NBC	Commercial	Abilene Radio & TV
KTXS	12	ABC	Commercial	Abilene-Sweetwater Broadcasting
KTAB	32	CBS	Commercial	Shooting Star Broadcasting/KTAB L.P.

Note: Stations included broadcast in the Abilene metro area
Source: Burrelle's Media Directory, 1998 Edition

CLIMATE

Average and Extreme Temperatures

Temperature	Jan	Feb	Mar	Apr	May	Jun	Jul	Aug	Sep	Oct	Nov	Dec	Ann
Extreme High (°F)	88	89	97	99	107	109	110	107	106	103	92	89	110
Average High (°F)	55	60	68	78	84	91	95	94	87	78	66	58	76
Average Temp. (°F)	44	48	56	65	73	80	84	83	76	66	54	46	65
Average Low (°F)	31	36	43	53	61	69	72	72	65	54	42	34	53
Extreme Low (°F)	-1	-7	9	25	36	47	57	55	38	28	14	-7	-7

Note: Figures cover the years 1948-1990
Source: National Climatic Data Center, International Station Meteorological Climate Summary, 3/95

Average Precipitation/Snowfall/Humidity

Precip./Humidity	Jan	Feb	Mar	Apr	May	Jun	Jul	Aug	Sep	Oct	Nov	Dec	Ann
Avg. Precip. (in.)	0.9	1.1	1.1	2.1	3.4	2.7	2.3	2.4	2.8	2.5	1.3	1.0	23.6
Avg. Snowfall (in.)	2	1	1	0	0	0	0	0	0	Tr	1	1	5
Avg. Rel. Hum. 6am (%)	72	73	69	72	79	78	73	73	77	76	73	71	74
Avg. Rel. Hum. 3pm (%)	44	44	37	38	43	41	38	37	43	43	42	43	41

Note: Figures cover the years 1948-1990; Tr = Trace amounts (<0.05 in. of rain; <0.5 in. of snow)
Source: National Climatic Data Center, International Station Meteorological Climate Summary, 3/95

Weather Conditions

Temperature			Daytime Sky			Precipitation		
10°F & below	32°F & below	90°F & above	Clear	Partly cloudy	Cloudy	0.01 inch or more precip.	0.1 inch or more snow/ice	Thunderstorms
2	52	102	141	125	99	65	4	43

Note: Figures are average number of days per year and covers the years 1948-1990
Source: National Climatic Data Center, International Station Meteorological Climate Summary, 3/95

AIR & WATER QUALITY

Maximum Pollutant Concentrations

	Particulate Matter (ug/m³)	Carbon Monoxide (ppm)	Sulfur Dioxide (ppm)	Nitrogen Dioxide (ppm)	Ozone (ppm)	Lead (ug/m³)
MSA[1] Level	n/a	n/a	n/a	n/a	n/a	n/a
NAAQS[2]	150	9	0.140	0.053	0.12	1.50
Met NAAQS?	n/a	n/a	n/a	n/a	n/a	n/a

Note: (1) Metropolitan Statistical Area - see Appendix A for areas included; (2) National Ambient Air Quality Standards; ppm = parts per million; ug/m³ = micrograms per cubic meter; n/a not available
Source: EPA, National Air Quality and Emissions Trends Report, 1996

Pollutant Standards Index

Data not available. *EPA, National Air Quality and Emissions Trends Report, 1996*

Drinking Water

Water System Name	Pop. Served	Primary Water Source Type	Number of Violations in Fiscal Year 1997	Type of Violation/ Contaminants
City of Abilene	106,654	Surface	None	None

Note: Data as of January 16, 1998
Source: EPA, Office of Ground Water and Drinking Water, Safe Drinking Water Information System

Abilene tap water is alkaline, hard and not fluoridated.
Editor & Publisher Market Guide, 1998

Atlanta, Georgia

Background

When one thinks of the South, one may imagine images of antebellum gentility and how Atlanta might fit that picture. However Atlanta was borne of a rough and tumble past: first as a natural outgrowth of a thriving railroad network in the 1840's; and second, as a resilient go-getter that proudly rose again above the rubble of the Civil War.

Blanketed over the rolling hills of the Piedmont Plateau, at the foot of the Blue Ridge Mountains, Georgia's capital stands 1,000 miles above sea level. Atlanta is located in the northwest corner of Georgia where the terrain is rolling to hilly and slopes downward to the east, west and south.

Atlanta proper begins at the "terminus", or zero mile mark, of the now defunct Western and Atlantic Railroad Line. However its metropolitan area, comprised of twenty counties that include Fulton, DeKalb, and Clayton, extends as far as 30 miles from its origin. Perhaps Atlanta's Chamber of Commerce is not exaggerating when it calls its city, "The City Without Limits".

Indeed, Atlanta may be called "The City Without Limits" in other ways. Its diversified economy allows for employment in a variety of sectors such as manufacturing (transportation equipment and textiles), retail, and the government. Also noteworthy is Atlanta's position as the headquarters or branch office to many corporations and institutions including; Cable News Network, Coca-Cola, and The Centers for Disease Control.

These accomplishments are the result of an involved city government that seeks to work closely with its business community. This may be largely due to a change in its Charter in 1974, when greater administrative powers were vested in the Mayoral Office. 1974 also marked the inauguration of its first black mayor.

Atlanta, after the 1996 Olympics, must face the complex issue of where it plans to move as an urban center in light of the conflict between the city and its surroundings. Middle-class residents, both white and black have increasingly moved to the suburbs separating themselves from Atlanta's old downtown and possibly any sense of responsibility for its future.
New York Times, 6/23/96

While schools in the city remain predominantly black and schools in its suburbs remain predominantly white, Atlanta can still boast of a racially progressive climate. The Martin Luther King, Jr. Historic District, Auburn Avenue, a street of black middle-class enterprises, and a consortium of black colleges that includes Morehouse College and the Interdenominational Theological Center testify to the city's appreciation for a people who have always been one-third of Atlanta's population.

The Appalachian chain of mountains, the Gulf of Mexico and the Atlantic Ocean influence the Atlanta climate. Temperatures are moderate throughout the year. Prolonged periods of hot weather are unusual and 100-degree-heat is rarely experienced. Atlanta winters are mild with a few, short-lived cold spells. Summers can be humid.

General Rankings and Evaluative Comments

■ Atlanta was ranked #159 out of 300 cities by *Money's* 1997 "Survey of the Best Places to Live." Criteria used: health services, crime, economy, housing, education, transportation, weather, leisure and the arts. The city was ranked #115 in 1996 and #252 in 1995. *Money, July 1997; Money, September 1996; Money, September 1995*

■ Atlanta appeared on *Fortune's* list of "North America's Most Improved Cities" Rank: 9 out of 10. The selected cities satisfied basic business-location needs and also demonstrated improvement over a five- to ten-year period in a number of business and quality-of-life measures.

"...With little to set it apart from the competition back in the 1960s, Atlanta declared itself the 'Capital of the New South.' Sure enough, it became just that....

Today few could question Atlanta's right to assert itself on the international stage....More than 586,000 new jobs have been created here in the past decade....In the past three years alone, more than 688 companies moved to Atlanta. In spite of the influx, it continues to offer competitive wages and a relatively low cost of living.

...if there is one entity that symbolizes Atlanta's boom, it's Hartsfield Airport. In 1978 there was no nonstop international air service from Atlanta. Now it is home to the world's second-busiest airport, following Chicago's O'Hare, serving over 63 million passengers last year....

Recently the city has developed telecommunications prowess....Atlanta is the transmission hub for the nation's two largest fiber-optic trunk routs and also boasts $200 million in pre-Olympics telecom infrastructure improvements, which has been a boon to business since the games....

Lots of Olympics money was also invested in sprucing up the downtown area, most notably by building Centennial Park in what was once an abandoned warehouse district....Yet, as people move farther into the suburbs, traffic and the resulting air pollution remain problems.

...Atlantans are determined to overcome such obstacles...." *Fortune, 11/24/97*

■ *Ladies Home Journal* ranked America's 200 largest cities based on the qualities women care about most. Atlanta ranked 43 out of 200. Criteria: low crime rate, good public schools, well-paying jobs, quality health and child care, the presence of women in government, proportion of women-owned businesses, size of the wage gap with men, local economy, divorce rates, the ratio of single men to single women, whether there are laws that require at least the same number of public toilets for women as men, and the probability of good hair days. *Ladies Home Journal, November 1997*

■ Atlanta was ranked #211 out of 219 cities in terms of children's health, safety, and economic well-being. Criteria: total population, percent population change, birth rate, child immunization rate, infant mortality rate, percent low birth weight infants, percent of births to teens, physician-to-population ratio, student-to-teacher ratio, dropout rate, unemployment rate, median family income, percent of children in poverty, violent and property crime rates, number of juvenile arrests for violent crimes as a percent of the total crime index, number of days with pollution standard index (PSI) over 100, pounds toxic releases per 1,000 people and number of superfund sites. *Zero Population Growth, Children's Environmental Index 1997*

■ Atlanta appeared on *Ebony's* list of the best cities for African-Americans. Rank: 1 out of 4. The cities were selected based on a survey of the 100 Most Influential Black Americans. They were asked which city offered the best overall experience for African-Americans, and which dream city they would select if they could live anywhere they wanted to. *Ebony* also asked opinion-makers which cities offered the best cultural experiences, the best schools and the most diversity.

"If you thought Atlanta's appeal among African-Americans was fading, that it was no longer the land of milk and honey for Blacks, think again. Georgia's capital continues to be the No. 1 city for African-Americans....

...Atlanta is overwhelmingly considered to be the best city for Blacks, the city with the most employment opportunities for Blacks, the most diverse city, and the city with the best schools and most affordable housing for African-Americans....

While still suffering from many big-city ills like high crime and poverty rates, Atlanta's job market, business climate, small-town atmosphere and relatively low cost of living continue to be attractive...." *Ebony, 9/97*

- Atlanta is among the 20 most livable cities for gay men and lesbians. The list was divided between 10 cities you might expect and 10 surprises. Atlanta was on the cities you would expect list. Rank: 4 out of 10. Criteria: legal protection from antigay discrimination, an annual gay pride celebration, a community center, gay bookstores and publications, and an array of organizations, religious groups, and health care facilities that cater to the needs of the local gay community. *The Advocate, June 1997*

- *Yahoo! Internet Life* selected "America's 100 Most Wired Cities & Towns". 50 cities were large and 50 cities were small. Atlanta ranked 2 out of 50 large cities. Criteria: Internet users per capita, number of networked computers, number of registered domain names, Internet backbone traffic, and the per-capita number of Web sites devoted to each city. Atlanta was highlighted as having the most web sites per person. *Yahoo! Internet Life, March 1998*

- *Reader's Digest* non-scientifically ranked the 12 largest U.S. metropolitan areas in terms of having the worst drivers. The Atlanta metro area ranked number 5. The areas were selected by asking approximately 1,200 readers on the *Reader's Digest* Web site and 200 interstate bus drivers and long-haul truckers which metro areas have the worst drivers. Their responses were factored in with fatality, insurance and rental-car rates to create the rankings. *Reader's Digest, March 1998*

- Interface (commercial-carpet manufacturer), headquartered in Atlanta, is among the "100 Best Companies to Work for in America." Criteria: trust in management, pride in work/company, camaraderie, company responses to the Hewitt People Practices Inventory, and employee responses to their Great Place to Work survey. The companies also had to be at least 10 years old and have a minimum of 500 employees. *Fortune, January 12, 1998*

- According to *Working Mother,* "No state does a better job of funding prekindergarten than Georgia, thanks to its lottery, which pays for the program. Last year, the state allocated $211 million to provide care for about 62,000 children. And now the state has created a formal agency the Office of School Readiness, to oversee prekindergarten initiatives across the state. Eventually, every four-year-old in Georgia will have free prekindergarten education.

  As we went to press, state lawmakers had just begun to consider changes in Georgia's child care licensing laws. Most important, the proposals would impose safety standards on more providers.

  The state also decided to use federal funds to pay for a public awareness campaign on the need for quality child care. State officials are asking communities around the state to identify one person—a local elected official, a parent, a caregiver—who can be a champion for child care in that community. Those designated will be given materials and support to advocate for the expansion and improvement of child care. This sounds like a good model to inspire community activism." *Working Mother, July/August 1997*

Business Environment

STATE ECONOMY

State Economic Profile

"Georgia's economy continues to expand at well above the national pace, albeit at a considerably more moderate one than during the Olympic build-up. The greatest deceleration is occurring in the services and construction industries.

Georgia's economy has now entered into a period of slower growth. Trade industries and construction are expected to contribute less to growth this year, as retail space and residential construction will slow following a protracted period of tremendous, and in some places, excessive building activity.

An important stimulant to Georgia's economic growth has been its above-average population expansion. Since 1992, population growth has exceeded 2% annually, more than twice the national average. Strong in-migration flows account for nearly two-thirds of last year's population growth. The incomes of those moving into Georgia exceed the incomes of those moving out, indicating that the quality of jobs being created in Georgia is improving.

Despite the strong economy, the number of bankruptcy filings per household in Georgia remains far higher than the national rate. Georgia ranks second in the nation, after Tennessee, in the incidence of household bankruptcy filings, about two for every one hundred households.

Georgia will maintain its above average economic performance through the end of the century. The state's highly competitive manufacturing base and diverse service and transportation center of Atlanta will continue to propel the economy forward. Job opportunities, a mild climate, and a moderate cost of living will continue to draw in-migrants to the state. Long-term risks to Georgia include the dependence on military bases for many smaller metro areas and the large presence of the contracting apparel industries. Another liability for the state is its relatively high business costs compared to other states in the South." *National Association of Realtors, Economic Profiles: The Fifty States, July 1997*

IMPORTS/EXPORTS

Total Export Sales

Area	1993 ($000)	1994 ($000)	1995 ($000)	1996 ($000)	% Chg. 1993-96	% Chg. 1995-96
MSA[1]	3,870,589	4,739,124	5,811,439	5,891,451	52.2	1.4
U.S.	464,858,354	512,415,609	583,030,524	622,827,063	34.0	6.8

Note: (1) Metropolitan Statistical Area - see Appendix A for areas included
Source: U.S. Department of Commerce, International Trade Association, Metropolitan Area Exports: An Export Performance Report on Over 250 U.S. Cities, October 1997

Imports/Exports by Port

Type	Cargo Value			Share of U.S. Total	
	1995 (US$mil.)	1996 (US$mil.)	% Change 1995-1996	1995 (%)	1996 (%)
Imports	0	0	0	0	0
Exports	0	0	0	0	0

Source: Global Trade Information Services, WaterBorne Trade Atlas 1997

CITY FINANCES

City Government Finances

Component	FY92 ($000)	FY92 (per capita $)
Revenue	810,963	2,045.85
Expenditure	766,514	1,933.71
Debt Outstanding	1,433,054	3,615.22
Cash & Securities	1,874,189	4,728.08

Source: U.S. Bureau of the Census, City Government Finances: 1991-92

City Government Revenue by Source

Source	FY92 ($000)	FY92 (per capita $)	FY92 (%)
From Federal Government	55,486	139.98	6.8
From State Governments	9,683	24.43	1.2
From Local Governments	72,714	183.44	9.0
Property Taxes	122,556	309.18	15.1
General Sales Taxes	0	0.00	0.0
Selective Sales Taxes	68,136	171.89	8.4
Income Taxes	0	0.00	0.0
Current Charges	209,484	528.47	25.8
Utility/Liquor Store	60,911	153.66	7.5
Employee Retirement[1]	55,397	139.75	6.8
Other	156,596	395.05	19.3

Note: (1) Excludes "city contributions," classified as "nonrevenue," intragovernmental transfers.
Source: U.S. Bureau of the Census, City Government Finances: 1991-92

City Government Expenditures by Function

Function	FY92 ($000)	FY92 (per capita $)	FY92 (%)
Educational Services	18,757	47.32	2.4
Employee Retirement[1]	60,929	153.71	7.9
Environment/Housing	141,995	358.22	18.5
Government Administration	54,684	137.95	7.1
Interest on General Debt	96,468	243.36	12.6
Public Safety	129,441	326.55	16.9
Social Services	437	1.10	0.1
Transportation	136,428	344.17	17.8
Utility/Liquor Store	81,845	206.47	10.7
Other	45,530	114.86	5.9

Note: (1) Payments to beneficiaries including withdrawal of contributions.
Source: U.S. Bureau of the Census, City Government Finances: 1991-92

Municipal Bond Ratings

Area	Moody's	S & P
Atlanta	Aa3	AA

Note: n/a not available; n/r not rated
Source: Moody's Bond Record, 2/98; Statistical Abstract of the U.S., 1997;
Governing Magazine, 9/97, 3/98

POPULATION

Population Growth

Area	1980	1990	% Chg. 1980-90	July 1996 Estimate	% Chg. 1990-96
City	425,022	394,017	-7.3	401,907	2.0
MSA[1]	2,138,231	2,833,511	32.5	3,541,230	25.0
U.S.	226,545,805	248,765,170	9.8	265,179,411	6.6

Note: (1) Metropolitan Statistical Area - see Appendix A for areas included
Source: 1980/1990 Census of Housing and Population, Summary Tape File 3C;
Census Bureau Population Estimates

Population Characteristics

Race	City 1980 Population	%	City 1990 Population	%	% Chg. 1980-90	MSA[1] 1990 Population	%
White	138,235	32.5	122,363	31.1	-11.5	2,021,586	71.3
Black	283,158	66.6	264,213	67.1	-6.7	735,477	26.0
Amer Indian/Esk/Aleut	610	0.1	626	0.2	2.6	6,176	0.2
Asian/Pacific Islander	2,001	0.5	3,327	0.8	66.3	49,965	1.8
Other	1,018	0.2	3,488	0.9	242.6	20,307	0.7
Hispanic Origin[2]	5,842	1.4	7,640	1.9	30.8	54,318	1.9

Note: (1) Metropolitan Statistical Area - see Appendix A for areas included;
(2) people of Hispanic origin can be of any race
Source: 1980/1990 Census of Housing and Population, Summary Tape File 3C

Ancestry

Area	German	Irish	English	Italian	U.S.	French	Polish	Dutch
City	6.2	5.3	8.1	1.0	4.3	1.5	0.8	0.5
MSA[1]	15.1	15.5	15.8	2.5	9.5	2.9	1.6	1.9
U.S.	23.3	15.6	13.1	5.9	5.3	4.2	3.8	2.5

Note: Figures are percentages and include persons that reported multiple ancestry (eg. if a person reported being Irish and Italian, they were included in both columns); (1) Metropolitan Statistical Area - see Appendix A for areas included
Source: 1990 Census of Population and Housing, Summary Tape File 3C

Age

Area	Median Age (Years)	Age Distribution (%) Under 5	Under 18	18-24	25-44	45-64	65+	80+
City	31.4	7.6	24.1	13.0	34.7	16.8	11.3	2.9
MSA[1]	31.4	7.7	25.9	10.7	37.8	17.7	7.9	1.6
U.S.	32.9	7.3	25.6	10.5	32.6	18.7	12.5	2.8

Note: (1) Metropolitan Statistical Area - see Appendix A for areas included
Source: 1990 Census of Population and Housing, Summary Tape File 3C

Male/Female Ratio

Area	Number of males per 100 females (all ages)	Number of males per 100 females (18 years old+)
City	91.0	87.8
MSA[1]	94.7	91.5
U.S.	95.0	91.9

Note: (1) Metropolitan Statistical Area - see Appendix A for areas included
Source: 1990 Census of Population, General Population Characteristics

INCOME

Per Capita/Median/Average Income

Area	Per Capita ($)	Median Household ($)	Average Household ($)
City	15,279	22,275	37,882
MSA[1]	16,897	36,051	44,968
U.S.	14,420	30,056	38,453

Note: all figures are for 1989; (1) Metropolitan Statistical Area - see Appendix A for areas included
Source: 1990 Census of Population and Housing, Summary Tape File 3C

Household Income Distribution by Race

Income ($)	City (%)					U.S. (%)				
	Total	White	Black	Other	Hisp.[1]	Total	White	Black	Other	Hisp.[1]
Less than 5,000	14.8	5.7	20.7	18.3	13.3	6.2	4.8	15.2	8.6	8.8
5,000 - 9,999	11.6	7.2	14.5	11.5	10.7	9.3	8.6	14.2	9.9	11.1
10,000 - 14,999	9.9	7.0	11.7	13.0	11.1	8.8	8.5	11.0	9.8	11.0
15,000 - 24,999	17.8	14.9	19.7	17.3	20.4	17.5	17.3	18.9	18.5	20.5
25,000 - 34,999	13.1	13.1	13.2	10.7	13.9	15.8	16.1	14.2	15.4	16.4
35,000 - 49,999	12.5	15.1	10.8	15.2	14.6	17.9	18.6	13.3	16.1	16.0
50,000 - 74,999	10.1	15.1	6.8	8.5	6.9	15.0	15.8	9.3	13.4	11.1
75,000 - 99,999	3.9	7.1	1.7	2.2	2.4	5.1	5.5	2.6	4.7	3.1
100,000+	6.3	14.7	0.9	3.3	6.7	4.4	4.8	1.3	3.7	1.9

Note: all figures are for 1989; (1) people of Hispanic origin can be of any race
Source: 1990 Census of Population and Housing, Summary Tape File 3C

Effective Buying Income

Area	Per Capita ($)	Median Household ($)	Average Household ($)
City	16,720	26,038	42,362
MSA[1]	17,633	39,042	47,409
U.S.	15,444	33,201	41,849

Note: data as of 1/1/97; (1) Metropolitan Statistical Area - see Appendix A for areas included
Source: Standard Rate & Data Service, Newspaper Advertising Source, 2/98

Effective Household Buying Income Distribution

Area	% of Households Earning						
	$10,000 -$19,999	$20,000 -$34,999	$35,000 -$49,999	$50,000 -$74,999	$75,000 -$99,000	$100,000 -$124,999	$125,000 and up
City	18.2	21.5	13.5	12.4	5.2	2.4	4.6
MSA[1]	12.4	22.5	19.9	21.6	8.2	2.8	3.1
U.S.	16.5	23.4	18.3	18.2	6.4	2.1	2.4

Note: data as of 1/1/97; (1) Metropolitan Statistical Area - see Appendix A for areas included
Source: Standard Rate & Data Service, Newspaper Advertising Source, 2/98

Poverty Rates by Race and Age

Area	Total (%)	By Race (%)				By Age (%)		
		White	Black	Other	Hisp.[2]	Under 5 years old	Under 18 years old	65 years and over
City	27.3	9.8	35.0	35.5	30.5	47.1	42.9	25.1
MSA[1]	10.0	5.4	22.4	14.4	16.2	15.5	13.9	14.3
U.S.	13.1	9.8	29.5	23.1	25.3	20.1	18.3	12.8

Note: figures show the percent of people living below the poverty line in 1989. The average poverty threshold was $12,674 for a family of four in 1989; (1) Metropolitan Statistical Area - see Appendix A for areas included; (2) people of Hispanic origin can be of any race
Source: 1990 Census of Population and Housing, Summary Tape File 3C

EMPLOYMENT

Labor Force and Employment

Area	Civilian Labor Force			Workers Employed		
	Dec. '95	Dec. '96	% Chg.	Dec. '95	Dec. '96	% Chg.
City	216,314	222,211	2.7	201,998	211,163	4.5
MSA[1]	2,015,113	2,091,518	3.8	1,941,078	2,029,140	4.5
U.S.	134,583,000	136,742,000	1.6	127,903,000	130,785,000	2.3

Note: Data is not seasonally adjusted and covers workers 16 years of age and older;
(1) Metropolitan Statistical Area - see Appendix A for areas included
Source: Bureau of Labor Statistics, http://stats.bls.gov

Atlanta was listed among the top 20 metro areas (out of 114 major areas) in terms of projected job growth from 1997 to 2002 with an annual percent change of 2.2%.
Standard & Poor's DRI, July 23, 1997

Unemployment Rate

Area	1997											
	Jan.	Feb.	Mar.	Apr.	May	Jun.	Jul.	Aug.	Sep.	Oct.	Nov.	Dec.
City	6.3	6.4	6.4	5.5	5.7	6.7	6.2	6.0	6.3	5.6	4.9	5.0
MSA[1]	3.6	3.8	3.7	3.3	3.4	4.0	3.8	3.6	3.8	3.4	3.0	3.0
U.S.	5.9	5.7	5.5	4.8	4.7	5.2	5.0	4.8	4.7	4.4	4.3	4.4

Note: Data is not seasonally adjusted and covers workers 16 years of age and older; All figures are percentages; (1) Metropolitan Statistical Area - see Appendix A for areas included
Source: Bureau of Labor Statistics, http://stats.bls.gov

Employment by Industry

Sector	MSA[1]		U.S.
	Number of Employees	Percent of Total	Percent of Total
Services	599,900	29.6	29.0
Retail Trade	376,900	18.6	18.5
Government	259,500	12.8	16.1
Manufacturing	221,600	10.9	15.0
Finance/Insurance/Real Estate	131,600	6.5	5.7
Wholesale Trade	168,400	8.3	5.4
Transportation/Public Utilities	169,200	8.3	5.3
Construction	99,200	4.9	4.5
Mining	1,700	0.1	0.5

Note: Figures cover non-farm employment as of 12/97 and are not seasonally adjusted;
(1) Metropolitan Statistical Area - see Appendix A for areas included
Source: Bureau of Labor Statistics, http://stats.bls.gov

Employment by Occupation

Occupation Category	City (%)	MSA[1] (%)	U.S. (%)
White Collar	60.2	65.7	58.1
Executive/Admin./Management	12.8	15.6	12.3
Professional	16.0	13.6	14.1
Technical & Related Support	3.6	4.0	3.7
Sales	11.5	13.9	11.8
Administrative Support/Clerical	16.2	18.5	16.3
Blue Collar	20.7	22.4	26.2
Precision Production/Craft/Repair	6.8	10.2	11.3
Machine Operators/Assem./Insp.	4.9	4.8	6.8
Transportation/Material Movers	4.2	3.8	4.1
Cleaners/Helpers/Laborers	4.7	3.7	3.9
Services	17.9	10.9	13.2
Farming/Forestry/Fishing	1.2	1.1	2.5

Note: figures cover employed persons 16 years old and over;
(1) Metropolitan Statistical Area - see Appendix A for areas included
Source: 1990 Census of Population and Housing, Summary Tape File 3C

Occupational Employment Projections: 1994 - 2005

Occupations Expected to have the Largest Job Growth (ranked by numerical growth)	Fast-Growing Occupations[1] (ranked by percent growth)
1. General managers & top executives	1. All other computer scientists
2. Cashiers	2. Systems analysts
3. Waiters & waitresses	3. Computer engineers
4. Salespersons, retail	4. Electronic pagination systems workers
5. Marketing & sales, supervisors	5. Computer support specialists
6. Secretaries, except legal & medical	6. Database administrators
7. Systems analysts	7. Occupational therapists
8. General office clerks	8. Occupational therapy assistants
9. All other helper, laborer, mover	9. Manicurists
10. Receptionists and information clerks	10. Personal and home care aides

Projections cover Cherokee, Clayton, Cobb, DeKalb, Douglass, Fayette, Forsythe, Fulton, Gwinett, Henry, Rockdale and Spaulding Counties (EDR #3).
Note: (1) Based on 1994 employment greater than 100
Source: Georgia Department of Labor, Labor Information Systems, OES Industry-Occupation Matrix, 1994 Average Annual and 2005 Projected Employment, EDR #3

Average Wages

Occupation	Wage	Occupation	Wage
Professional/Technical/Clerical	$/Week	**Health/Protective Services**	$/Week
Accountants III	789	Corrections Officers	391
Attorneys III	1,158	Firefighters	532
Budget Analysts III	832	Nurses, Licensed Practical II	-
Buyers/Contracting Specialists II	654	Nurses, Registered II	-
Clerks, Accounting III	462	Nursing Assistants II	-
Clerks, General III	-	Police Officers I	521
Computer Operators II	469	**Hourly Workers**	$/Hour
Computer Programmers II	591	Forklift Operators	10.60
Drafters II	558	General Maintenance Workers	10.68
Engineering Technicians III	601	Guards I	6.62
Engineering Technicians, Civil III	536	Janitors	6.58
Engineers III	942	Maintenance Electricians	-
Key Entry Operators I	351	Maintenance Electronics Techs II	18.58
Personnel Assistants III	554	Maintenance Machinists	17.73
Personnel Specialists III	786	Maintenance Mechanics, Machinery	14.92
Secretaries III	551	Material Handling Laborers	-
Switchboard Operator-Receptionist	372	Motor Vehicle Mechanics	17.17
Systems Analysts II	892	Shipping/Receiving Clerks	-
Systems Analysts Supervisor/Mgr II	1,342	Tool and Die Makers	-
Tax Collectors II	558	Truckdrivers, Tractor Trailer	15.59
Word Processors II	-	Warehouse Specialists	-

Note: Wage data includes full-time workers only for 3/96 and cover the Metropolitan Statistical Area (see Appendix A for areas included). Dashes indicate that data was not available.
Source: Bureau of Labor Statistics, Occupational Compensation Survey, 10/96

TAXES

Major State and Local Tax Rates

State Corp. Income (%)	State Personal Income (%)	Residential Property (effective rate per $100)	Sales & Use		State Gasoline (cents/ gallon)	State Cigarette (cents/ 20-pack)
			State (%)	Local (%)		
6.0	1.0 - 6.0	2.04	4.0	3.0	7.5	12

Note: Personal/corporate income tax rates as of 1/97. Sales, gasoline and cigarette tax rates as of 1/98.
Source: Federation of Tax Administrators, www.taxadmin.org; Washington D.C. Department of Finance and Revenue, Tax Rates and Tax Burdens in the District of Columbia: A Nationwide Comparison, June 1997; Chamber of Commerce

Total Taxes Per Capita and as a Percent of Income

Area	Per Capita Income ($)	Per Capita Taxes ($)			Taxes as Pct. of Income (%)		
		Total	Federal	State/Local	Total	Federal	State/Local
Georgia	25,370	8,393	5,666	2,727	33.1	22.3	10.8
U.S.	26,187	9,205	6,127	3,078	35.2	23.4	11.8

Note: Figures are for 1997
Source: Tax Foundation, Web Site, www.taxfoundation.org

Estimated Tax Burden

Area	State Income	Local Income	Property	Sales	Total
Atlanta	2,416	0	2,700	666	5,782

Note: The numbers are estimates of taxes paid by a married couple with two kids and annual earnings of $65,000. Sales tax estimates assume they spend average amounts on food, clothing, household goods and gasoline. Property tax estimates assume they live in a $225,000 home.
Source: Kiplinger's Personal Finance Magazine, June 1997

COMMERCIAL REAL ESTATE

Office Market

Class/Location	Total Space (sq. ft.)	Vacant Space (sq. ft.)	Vac. Rate (%)	Under Constr. (sq. ft.)	Net Absorp. (sq. ft.)	Rental Rates ($/sq.ft./yr.)
Class A						
CBD	14,064,658	1,163,579	8.3	0	n/a	15.25-26.00
Outside CBD	28,461,527	1,797,924	6.3	2,875,069	n/a	18.50-32.50
Class B						
CBD	3,133,517	749,567	23.9	0	n/a	14.50-22.50
Outside CBD	20,888,378	1,793,826	8.6	1,905,401	n/a	14.00-22.00

Note: Data as of 10/97 and covers Atlanta; CBD = Central Business District; n/a not available;
Source: Society of Industrial and Office Realtors, 1998 Comparative Statistics of Industrial and Office Real Estate Markets

"Speculative development will occur in six submarkets: Buckhead (1.1 million sq. ft.), North Fulton (840,000) sq. ft.), Northeast (326,000 sq. ft.), Northwest (1.3 million sq. ft.), Peachtree Corners (142,000 sq. ft.), and Perimeter Central (725,000 sq. ft.). Preleasing has not been strong with initial numbers indicating 18 percent to date. SIOR's numbers indicating 18-percent to date. SIOR's reporter does not think this will immediately slow down the number of announced starts as optimism seems to be at an all time high. Vacancies and landlord concessions should increase due to the volume of speculative construction. Sales will likely slow this year in response to the aggressive nature of the past year's investment activity. Atlanta has been hot, and many feel that it may be getting a bit overpriced." *Society of Industrial and Office Realtors, 1998 Comparative Statistics of Industrial and Office Real Estate Markets*

Industrial Market

Location	Total Space (sq. ft.)	Vacant Space (sq. ft.)	Vac. Rate (%)	Under Constr. (sq. ft.)	Net Absorp. (sq. ft.)	Gross Lease ($/sq.ft./yr.)
Central City	28,324,000	5,300,000	18.7	80,000	217,000	2.00-4.50
Suburban	311,476,000	41,200,000	13.2	13,485,000	12,106,000	2.75-6.50

Note: Data as of 10/97 and covers Atlanta; n/a not available
Source: Society of Industrial and Office Realtors, 1998 Comparative Statistics of Industrial and Office Real Estate Markets

"Absorption levels should remain just above 12 million sq. ft. averting a sharp increase in the vacancy rate. Look for modest increases in lease and sales prices. Suburban markets will benefit at the cost of the CBD as several companies will vacate the Atlanta Redevelopment Park in favor of suburban locations. Such firms as Suzuki, Toys 'R Us (one million sq. ft.), and Circuit City (300,000 sq. ft.) were located in the park for 10 years, and now that tax incentives are expiring they are planning moves." *Society of Industrial and Office Realtors, 1998 Comparative Statistics of Industrial and Office Real Estate Markets*

Retail Market

Shopping Center Inventory (sq. ft.)	Shopping Center Construction (sq. ft.)	Construction as a Percent of Inventory (%)	Torto Wheaton Rent Index[1] ($/sq. ft.)
76,638,000	1,303,000	1.7	14.43

Note: Data as of 1997 and covers the Metropolitan Statistical Area - see Appendix A for areas included; (1) Index is based on a model that predicts what the average rent should be for leases with certain characteristics, in certain locations during certain years.
Source: National Association of Realtors, 1997-1998 Market Conditions Report

"An estimated 1.5 million visitors to the Summer Olympics spent over $1.2 billion at Atlanta hotels, restaurants, and retail shops. Now that the Games are over, people are watching the Atlanta retail market. The area's retail rent index increased nearly 6% in 1997 and is above the South's average of $13.79 per square foot. The area's population growth is expected to average 1.7% per year through 1998. The Buckhead and northern retail markets should benefit from the continued growth. Strong net absorption is likely to persist since new centers are mostly pre-leased." *National Association of Realtors, 1997-1998 Market Conditions Report*

COMMERCIAL UTILITIES

Typical Monthly Electric Bills

Area	Commercial Service ($/month)		Industrial Service ($/month)	
	12 kW demand 1,500 kWh	100 kW demand 30,000 kWh	1,000 kW demand 400,000 kWh	20,000 kW demand 10,000,000 kWh
City	200	2,431	25,234	473,591
U.S.	162	2,360	25,590	545,677

Note: Based on rates in effect July 1, 1997
Source: Edison Electric Institute, Typical Residential, Commercial and Industrial Bills, Summer 1997

TRANSPORTATION

Transportation Statistics

Avg. travel time to work (min.)	24.2
Interstate highways	I-20; I-75; I-85
Bus lines	
In-city	Metropolitan Atlanta Rapid Transit Authority, 704 vehicles
Inter-city	1
Passenger air service	
Airport	Hartsfield Atlanta International
Airlines	33
Aircraft departures	345,714 (1995)
Enplaned passengers	27,556,894 (1995)
Rail service	Amtrak
Motor freight carriers	95
Major waterways/ports	None

Source: OAG, Business Travel Planner, Summer 1997; Editor & Publisher Market Guide, 1998; FAA Airport Activity Statistics, 1996; Amtrak National Time Table, Northeast Timetable, Fall/Winter 1997-98; 1990 Census of Population and Housing, STF 3C; Chamber of Commerce/Economic Development 1997; Jane's Urban Transport Systems 1997-98; Transit Fact Book 1997

A survey of 90,000 airline passengers during the first half of 1997 ranked most of the largest airports in the U.S. Hartsfield Atlanta International ranked number 9 out of 36. Criteria: cleanliness, quality of restaurants, attractiveness, speed of baggage delivery, ease of reaching gates, available ground transportation, ease of following signs and closeness of parking. *Plog Research Inc., First Half 1997*

Means of Transportation to Work

Area	Car/Truck/Van		Public Transportation			Bicycle	Walked	Other Means	Worked at Home
	Drove Alone	Car-pooled	Bus	Subway	Railroad				
City	61.2	11.6	16.7	2.9	0.1	0.3	3.8	1.2	2.4
MSA[1]	78.0	12.7	3.5	1.0	0.1	0.1	1.5	1.0	2.2
U.S.	73.2	13.4	3.0	1.5	0.5	0.4	3.9	1.2	3.0

Note: figures shown are percentages and only include workers 16 years old and over;
(1) Metropolitan Statistical Area - see Appendix A for areas included
Source: 1990 Census of Population and Housing, Summary Tape File 3C

BUSINESSES

Major Business Headquarters

Company Name	1997 Rankings	
	Fortune 500	Forbes 500
Bellsouth	53	-
Coca-Cola	58	-
Coca-Cola Enterprises	188	-
Cox Enterprises	-	31
Delta Air Lines	106	-
Genuine Parts	250	-
Georgia-Pacific	100	-
Home Depot	50	-
National Distributing	-	193
Printpack	-	266
RaceTrac Petroleum	-	128
Riverwood International	-	143
Southern	133	-
Suntrust Banks	336	-
United Parcel Service	37	3
Watkins Associated Industries	-	335

Note: Companies listed are located in the city; Dashes indicate no ranking
Fortune 500: companies that produce a 10-K are ranked 1 - 500 based on 1996 revenue
Forbes 500: private companies are ranked 1 - 500 based on 1996 revenue
Source: Forbes 12/1/97; Fortune 4/28/97

Fast-Growing Businesses

According to *Inc.*, Atlanta is home to three of America's 100 fastest-growing private companies: Gearon & Co., SQL Financials and Capricorn Systems. Criteria for inclusion: must be an independent, privately-held, U.S. corporation, proprietorship or partnership; sales of at least $200,000 in 1993; five-year operating/sales history; increase in 1997 sales over 1996 sales; holding companies, regulated banks, and utilities were excluded. *Inc. 500, 1997*

Atlanta is home to one of *Business Week's* "hot growth" companies: K&G Men's Center. Criteria: sales and earnings, return on capital and stock price. *Business Week, 5/26/97*

Atlanta was ranked #5 out of 24 (#1 is best) in terms of the best-performing local stocks in 1996 according to the Money/Norby Cities Index. The index measures stocks of companies that have headquarters in 24 metro areas. *Money, 2/7/97*

Women-Owned Businesses: Number, Employment, Sales and Share

Area	Women-Owned Businesses in 1996				Share of Women-Owned Businesses in 1996	
	Number	Employment	Sales ($000)	Rank[2]	Percent (%)	Rank[3]
MSA[1]	117,900	222,100	29,812,600	13	36.6	27

Note: (1) Metropolitan Statistical Area - see Appendix A for areas included; (2) Calculated on an averaging of number of businesses, employment and sales and ranges from 1 to 50 where 1 is best; (3) Ranges from 1 to 50 where 1 is best
Source: The National Foundation for Women Business Owners, 1996 Facts on Women-Owned Businesses: Trends in the Top 50 Metropolitan Areas, March 26, 1997

Women-Owned Businesses: Growth

Area	Growth in Women-Owned Businesses (% change from 1987 to 1996)				Relative Growth in the Number of Women-Owned and All Businesses (% change from 1987 to 1996)			
	Num.	Empl.	Sales	Rank[2]	Women-Owned	All Firms	Absolute Difference	Relative Difference
MSA[1]	112.7	187.2	279.0	16	112.7	78.1	34.6	1.4:1

Note: (1) Metropolitan Statistical Area - see Appendix A for areas included; (2) Calculated on an averaging of the percent growth of number of businesses, employment and sales and ranges from 1 to 50 where 1 is best
Source: The National Foundation for Women Business Owners, 1996 Facts on Women-Owned Businesses: Trends in the Top 50 Metropolitan Areas, March 26, 1997

Minority Business Opportunity

Atlanta is home to two companies which are on the Black Enterprise Industrial/Service 100 list (largest based on gross sales): H.J. Russell & Co. (construction, property mgmt., airport concessions, real estate devel.); Gourmet Companies Inc. (food services, golf course mgmt.). Criteria: 1) operational in previous calendar year; 2) at least 51% black-owned; 3) manufactures/owns the product it sells or provides industrial or consumer services. Brokerages, real estate firms and firms that provide professional services are not eligible. *Black Enterprise, July 1997*

Six of the 500 largest Hispanic-owned companies in the U.S. are located in Atlanta. *Hispanic Business, June 1997*

Small Business Opportunity

Atlanta was included among *Entrepreneur* magazines listing of the ''20 Best Cities for Small Business.'' It was ranked #12 among large metro areas. Criteria: risk of failure, business performance, economic growth, affordability and state attitude towards business. *Entrepreneur, 10/97*

According to *Forbes*, Atlanta is home to two of America's 200 best small companies: Aaron Rents, K&G Men's Center. Criteria: companies must be publicly traded, U.S.-based corporations with latest 12-month sales of between $5 and $350 million. Earnings must be at least $1 million for the 12-month period. Limited partnerships, REITs and closed-end mutual funds were not considered. Banks, S&Ls and electric utilities were not included. *Forbes, November 3, 1997*

HOTELS & MOTELS

Hotels/Motels

Area	Hotels/Motels	Rooms	Luxury-Level Hotels/Motels		Average Minimum Rates ($)		
			♦♦♦♦	♦♦♦♦♦	♦♦	♦♦♦	♦♦♦♦
City	100	25,651	3	2	86	125	150
Airport	31	6,517	0	0	n/a	n/a	n/a
Suburbs	88	10,694	0	0	n/a	n/a	n/a
Total	219	42,862	3	2	n/a	n/a	n/a

Note: n/a not available; Classifications range from one diamond (budget properties with basic amenities) to five diamond (luxury properties with the finest service, rooms and facilities).
Source: OAG, Business Travel Planner, Summer 1997

CONVENTION CENTERS

Major Convention Centers

Center Name	Meeting Rooms	Exhibit Space (sf)
Atlanta Exposition Center	5	160,000
Atlanta Hilton & Towers	87	41,000
Atlanta Market Center/INFORUM	41	376,000
Cobb Galleria Center	n/a	n/a
Emory Conference Center Hotel	20	5,600
Georgia World Congress Center	70	350,000
Hyatt Regency Atlanta	38	66,500
Omni Hotel at CNN Center	n/a	40,000
Sheraton Gateway Hotel	25	125,000
Southern Conference Center at Colony Square Hotel	14	36,000
Westin Peachtree Plaza	41	55,000
Georgia International Convention Center	35	112,000
Lakewood Exhibit Center	n/a	114,000

Note: n/a not available
Source: Trade Shows Worldwide 1997

Living Environment

COST OF LIVING

Cost of Living Index

Composite Index	Housing	Utilities	Groceries	Health Care	Trans-portation	Misc. Goods/ Services
100.5	98.9	97.8	100.8	106.9	99.2	101.7

Note: U.S. = 100
Source: ACCRA, Cost of Living Index, 3rd Quarter 1997

HOUSING

Median Home Prices and Housing Affordability

Area	Median Price[2] 3rd Qtr. 1997 ($)	HOI[3] 3rd Qtr. 1997	Afford-ability Rank[4]
MSA[1]	125,000	73.1	65
U.S.	127,000	63.7	--

Note: (1) Metropolitan Statistical Area - see Appendix A for areas included; (2) U.S. figures calculated from the sales of 625,000 new and existing homes in 195 markets; (3) Housing Opportunity Index - percent of homes sold that were within the reach of the median income household at the prevailing mortgage interest rate; (4) Rank is from 1-195 with 1 being most affordable
Source: National Association of Home Builders, Housing Opportunity Index, 3rd Quarter 1997

It is projected that the median price of existing single-family homes in the metro area will increase by 13.9% in 1998. Nationwide, home prices are projected to increase 6.6%.
Kiplinger's Personal Finance Magazine, January 1998

Average New Home Price

Area	Price ($)
City	136,627
U.S.	135,710

Note: Figures are based on a new home with 1,800 sq. ft. of living area on an 8,000 sq. ft. lot.
Source: ACCRA, Cost of Living Index, 3rd Quarter 1997

Average Apartment Rent

Area	Rent ($/mth)
City	589
U.S.	569

Note: Figures are based on an unfurnished two bedroom, 1-1/2 or 2 bath apartment, approximately 950 sq. ft. in size, excluding all utilities except water
Source: ACCRA, Cost of Living Index, 3rd Quarter 1997

RESIDENTIAL UTILITIES

Average Residential Utility Costs

Area	All Electric ($/mth)	Part Electric ($/mth)	Other Energy ($/mth)	Phone ($/mth)
City	--	57.38	39.77	22.75
U.S.	109.40	55.25	43.64	19.48

Source: ACCRA, Cost of Living Index, 3rd Quarter 1997

HEALTH CARE

Average Health Care Costs

Area	Hospital ($/day)	Doctor ($/visit)	Dentist ($/visit)
City	343.40	51.67	73.60
U.S.	392.91	48.76	60.84

Note: Hospital - based on a semi-private room. Doctor - based on a general practitioner's routine exam of an established patient. Dentist - based on adult teeth cleaning and periodic oral exam.
Source: ACCRA, Cost of Living Index, 3rd Quarter 1997

Distribution of Office-Based Physicians

Area	Family/Gen. Practitioners	Specialists		
		Medical	Surgical	Other
MSA[1]	532	2,155	1,708	1,670

Note: Data as of 12/31/96; (1) Metropolitan Statistical Area - see Appendix A for areas included
Source: American Medical Assn., Physician Characteristics & Distribution in the U.S., 1997-1998

Hospitals

Atlanta has 10 general medical and surgical hospitals, 4 psychiatric, 1 obstetrics and gynecology, 1 alcoholism and other chemical dependency, 1 other specialty, 1 children's general, 1 children's psychiatric. *AHA Guide to the Healthcare Field 1997-98*

According to *U.S. News and World Report,* Atlanta has 1 of the best hospitals in the U.S.: **Emory University Hospital**, noted for ophthalmology; *U.S. News and World Report, "America's Best Hospitals", 7/28/97*

EDUCATION

Public School District Statistics

District Name	Num. Sch.	Enroll.	Classroom Teachers[1]	Pupils per Teacher	Minority Pupils (%)	Current Exp.[2] ($/pupil)
Atlanta City School District	102	60,209	n/a	n/a	93.4	6,924
Fulton County School District	55	56,338	3,567	15.8	49.3	5,522

Note: Data covers the 1995-1996 school year unless otherwise noted; (1) Excludes teachers reported as working in school district offices rather than in schools; (2) Based on 1993-94 enrollment collected by the Census Bureau, not the enrollment figure shown in column 3; SD = School District; ISD = Independent School District; n/a not available
Source: National Center for Education Statistics, Common Core of Data Survey; Bureau of the Census

Educational Quality

School District	Education Quotient[1]	Graduate Outcome[2]	Community Index[3]	Resource Index[4]
Atlanta City	106.0	52.0	116.0	149.0

Note: Nearly 1,000 secondary school districts were rated in terms of educational quality. The scores range from a low of 50 to a high of 150; (1) Average of the Graduate Outcome, Community and Resource indexes; (2) Based on graduation rates and college board scores (SAT/ACT); (3) Based on the surrounding community's average level of education and the area's average income level; (4) Based on teacher salaries, per-pupil expenditures and student-teacher ratios.
Source: Expansion Management, Ratings Issue 1997

Educational Attainment by Race

Area	High School Graduate (%)					Bachelor's Degree (%)				
	Total	White	Black	Other	Hisp.[2]	Total	White	Black	Other	Hisp.[2]
City	69.9	86.7	59.8	62.1	54.4	26.6	51.9	11.1	34.6	21.7
MSA[1]	79.5	82.6	70.3	72.7	69.8	26.8	29.7	16.6	32.3	24.5
U.S.	75.2	77.9	63.1	60.4	49.8	20.3	21.5	11.4	19.4	9.2

Note: figures shown cover persons 25 years old and over; (1) Metropolitan Statistical Area - see Appendix A for areas included; (2) people of Hispanic origin can be of any race
Source: 1990 Census of Population and Housing, Summary Tape File 3C

School Enrollment by Type

Area	Preprimary				Elementary/High School			
	Public		Private		Public		Private	
	Enrollment	%	Enrollment	%	Enrollment	%	Enrollment	%
City	3,898	59.8	2,621	40.2	55,393	90.3	5,935	9.7
MSA[1]	28,793	49.6	29,303	50.4	437,891	92.0	37,989	8.0
U.S.	2,679,029	59.5	1,824,256	40.5	38,379,689	90.2	4,187,099	9.8

Note: figures shown cover persons 3 years old and over;
(1) Metropolitan Statistical Area - see Appendix A for areas included
Source: 1990 Census of Population and Housing, Summary Tape File 3C

School Enrollment by Race

Area	Preprimary (%)				Elementary/High School (%)			
	White	Black	Other	Hisp.[1]	White	Black	Other	Hisp.[1]
City	26.6	71.9	1.5	1.5	13.8	84.6	1.6	1.9
MSA[2]	72.8	25.3	1.9	1.5	64.8	32.0	3.2	2.0
U.S.	80.4	12.5	7.1	7.8	74.1	15.6	10.3	12.5

Note: figures shown cover persons 3 years old and over; (1) people of Hispanic origin can be of any race; (2) Metropolitan Statistical Area - see Appendix A for areas included
Source: 1990 Census of Population and Housing, Summary Tape File 3C

SAT/ACT Scores

Area/District	1997 SAT				1997 ACT	
	Percent of Graduates Tested (%)	Average Math Score	Average Verbal Score	Average Combined Score	Percent of Graduates Tested (%)	Average Composite Score
Atlanta PS	52	423	427	850	n/a	n/a
State	63	481	486	967	16	20.2
U.S.	42	511	505	1,016	36	21.0

Note: Math and verbal SAT scores are out of a possible 800; ACT scores are out of a possible 36
Caution: Comparing or ranking states/cities on the basis of SAT/ACT scores alone is invalid and strongly discouraged by the The College Board and The American College Testing Program as students who take the tests are self-selected and do not represent the entire student population.
Source: Atlanta Public Schools, Department of Research & Evaluation, 1997; College Board, 1997; American College Testing Program, 1997

Classroom Teacher Salaries in Public Schools

District	B.A. Degree		M.A. Degree		Ph.D. Degree	
	Min. ($)	Max. ($)	Min. ($)	Max. ($)	Min. ($)	Max. ($)
Atlanta	29,544	39,396	32,760	43,728	40,452	53,844
Average[1]	26,120	39,270	28,175	44,667	31,643	49,825

Note: Salaries are for 1996-1997; (1) Based on all school districts covered; n/a not available
Source: American Federation of Teachers (unpublished data)

Higher Education

Two-Year Colleges		Four-Year Colleges		Medical Schools	Law Schools	Voc/ Tech
Public	Private	Public	Private			
2	2	2	10	2	3	23

Source: College Blue Book, Occupational Education 1997; Medical School Admission Requirements, 1998-99; Peterson's Guide to Two-Year Colleges, 1997; Peterson's Guide to Four-Year Colleges, 1997; Barron's Guide to Law Schools 1997

MAJOR EMPLOYERS

Major Employers

BellSouth Telecommunications	Coca-Cola
Delta Air Lines	Equifax (credit reporting)
Food Services Management	Fulton DeKalb Hospital Authority
Georgia Baptist Health Care System	Georgia Power
Home Depot	Northside Hospital
Piedmont Hospital	St. Joseph's Hospital of Atlanta
Turner Broadcasting	United Parcel Service
Georgia-Pacific Corp.	Genuine Parts (motor vehicle parts)
Cable News Network	

Note: companies listed are located in the city
Source: Dun's Business Rankings 1997; Ward's Business Directory, 1997

PUBLIC SAFETY

Crime Rate

Area	All Crimes	Violent Crimes				Property Crimes		
		Murder	Forcible Rape	Robbery	Aggrav. Assault	Burglary	Larceny -Theft	Motor Vehicle Theft
City	17,070.2	47.4	94.9	1,163.1	2,010.5	2,534.6	8,981.3	2,238.3
Suburbs[1]	6,375.1	4.9	28.9	175.3	229.9	1,065.0	4,107.7	763.4
MSA[2]	7,647.7	9.9	36.8	292.8	441.8	1,239.9	4,687.7	938.9
U.S.	5,078.9	7.4	36.1	202.4	388.2	943.0	2,975.9	525.9

Note: Crime rate is the number of crimes per 100,000 pop.; (1) defined as all areas within the MSA but located outside the central city; (2) Metropolitan Statistical Area - see Appendix A for areas incl.
Source: FBI Uniform Crime Reports 1996

RECREATION

Culture and Recreation

Museums	Symphony Orchestras	Opera Companies	Dance Companies	Professional Theatres	Zoos	Pro Sports Teams
17	3	1	6	12	1	3

Source: International Directory of the Performing Arts, 1996; Official Museum Directory, 1998; Chamber of Commerce/Economic Development 1997

Library System

The Atlanta-Fulton Public Library has 32 branches, holdings of 1,950,552 volumes and a budget of $18,073,787 (1996). *American Library Directory, 1997-1998*

MEDIA

Newspapers

Name	Type	Freq.	Distribution	Circulation
Atlanta Bulletin	n/a	1x/wk	Local	50,000
Atlanta Constitution	n/a	7x/wk	Local	330,885
The Atlanta Inquirer	Black	1x/wk	Area	61,082
Atlanta Journal	General	7x/wk	Area	189,332
Atlanta Voice	Black	1x/wk	Area	133,000
The Georgia Bulletin	Religious	1x/wk	Area	56,400
Mid-De Kalb Neighbor	General	1x/wk	Local	48,100
The Sandy Springs Neighbor	General	1x/wk	Local	27,475
The Stone Mountain-De Kalb Neighbor	General	1x/wk	Local	48,100

Note: Includes newspapers with circulations of 25,000 or more located in the city; n/a not available
Source: Burrelle's Media Directory, 1998 Edition

AM Radio Stations

Call Letters	Freq. (kHz)	Target Audience	Station Format	Music Format
WKHX	590	General	M/N	Country
WGST	640	General	N/T	n/a
WCNN	680	n/a	N/T	n/a
WSB	750	n/a	N/T	n/a
WQXI	790	General	M/T	Oldies
WAEC	860	Religious	M	Christian
WNIV	970	Religious	N/S/T	n/a
WGKA	1190	General	M	Classical
WFOM	1230	General	N/T	n/a
WTJH	1260	General	M	Christian
WXLL	1310	Religious	M/N/T	Christian
WALR	1340	General	M	R&B
WAOK	1380	Black	M/N/S	Christian
WAZX	1550	Hispanic	M/N/S	Spanish
WSSA	1570	n/a	M/N/S	Christian/Country

Note: Stations included broadcast in the Atlanta metro area; n/a not available
Station Format: E = Educational; M = Music; N = News; S = Sports; T = Talk
Source: Burrelle's Media Directory, 1998 Edition

FM Radio Stations

Call Letters	Freq. (mHz)	Target Audience	Station Format	Music Format
WJSP	88.1	General	M/N/T	Classical/Jazz
WPPR	88.3	General	M/N/T	Classical/Jazz
WRAS	88.5	n/a	M/N/S	Alternative
WRFG	89.3	Black	E/M/T	Jazz/R&B/Urban Contemporary
WDCO	89.7	General	M/N/T	Classical/Jazz
WXVS	90.1	General	M/N/T	Classical
WABE	90.1	General	M/N	Classical/Jazz
WJWV	90.9	General	M/N/T	Classical/Jazz
WREK	91.1	General	M/N/S/T	n/a
WABR	91.1	General	M/N/T	Classical/Jazz
WWET	91.7	General	M/N/T	n/a
WUNV	91.7	General	M/N/T	Classical/Jazz
WCLK	91.9	General	M/S/T	Christian/Jazz/Oldies
WZGC	92.9	General	M/N/S	Classic Rock
WSTR	94.1	General	M	Contemporary Top 40
WPCH	94.9	General	M/N	Adult Contemporary
WKZJ	95.7	Black	M	Oldies/Urban Contemporary
WKLS	96.1	General	M/N/S	AOR
WFOX	97.1	General	M	Oldies
WSB	98.5	n/a	M/N	Adult Contemporary
WNNX	99.7	n/a	M/N/S	Alternative
WKHX	101.5	General	M/N/S	Country
WLKQ	102.3	General	M	Oldies
WVEE	103.3	General	M/N/S	Urban Contemporary
WALR	104.7	General	M/N/S	R&B
WGST	105.7	Men	N/T	n/a
WYAY	106.7	n/a	M	Country

Note: Stations included broadcast in the Atlanta metro area; n/a not available
Station Format: E = Educational; M = Music; N = News; S = Sports; T = Talk
Music Format: AOR = Album Oriented Rock; MOR = Middle-of-the-Road
Source: Burrelle's Media Directory, 1998 Edition

Television Stations

Name	Ch.	Affiliation	Type	Owner
WSB	2	ABC	Commercial	Cox Enterprises Inc.
WAGA	5	Fox	Commercial	New World Communications
WGTV	8	PBS	Public	Georgia Public Telecommunications Commission
WXIA	11	NBC	Commercial	Gannett Company Inc.
WTBS	17	n/a	Commercial	Turner Broadcasting System Inc.
WPBA	30	PBS	Commercial	Atlanta Board of Education
WATL	36	WB	Commercial	Qwest Broadcasting
WGNX	46	CBS	Commercial	Tribune Broadcasting Co.
WCI	67	Telemundo	Commercial	James Sim
WUPA	69	UPN	Commercial	VSC Communications, Inc.

Note: Stations included broadcast in the Atlanta metro area
Source: Burrelle's Media Directory, 1998 Edition

CLIMATE

Average and Extreme Temperatures

Temperature	Jan	Feb	Mar	Apr	May	Jun	Jul	Aug	Sep	Oct	Nov	Dec	Ann
Extreme High (°F)	79	80	85	93	95	101	105	102	98	95	84	77	105
Average High (°F)	52	56	64	73	80	86	88	88	82	73	63	54	72
Average Temp. (°F)	43	46	53	62	70	77	79	79	73	63	53	45	62
Average Low (°F)	33	36	42	51	59	66	70	69	64	52	42	35	52
Extreme Low (°F)	-8	5	10	26	37	46	53	55	36	28	3	0	-8

Note: Figures cover the years 1945-1990
Source: National Climatic Data Center, International Station Meteorological Climate Summary, 3/95

Average Precipitation/Snowfall/Humidity

Precip./Humidity	Jan	Feb	Mar	Apr	May	Jun	Jul	Aug	Sep	Oct	Nov	Dec	Ann
Avg. Precip. (in.)	4.7	4.6	5.7	4.3	4.0	3.5	5.1	3.6	3.4	2.8	3.8	4.2	49.8
Avg. Snowfall (in.)	1	1	Tr	Tr	0	0	0	0	0	0	Tr	Tr	2
Avg. Rel. Hum. 7am (%)	79	77	78	78	82	83	88	89	88	84	81	79	82
Avg. Rel. Hum. 4pm (%)	56	50	48	45	49	52	56	57	56	51	52	55	52

Note: Figures cover the years 1945-1990; Tr = Trace amounts (<0.05 in. of rain; <0.5 in. of snow)
Source: National Climatic Data Center, International Station Meteorological Climate Summary, 3/95

Weather Conditions

Temperature			Daytime Sky			Precipitation		
10°F & below	32°F & below	90°F & above	Clear	Partly cloudy	Cloudy	0.01 inch or more precip.	0.1 inch or more snow/ice	Thunder-storms
1	49	38	98	147	120	116	3	48

Note: Figures are average number of days per year and covers the years 1945-1990
Source: National Climatic Data Center, International Station Meteorological Climate Summary, 3/95

AIR & WATER QUALITY

Maximum Pollutant Concentrations

	Particulate Matter (ug/m³)	Carbon Monoxide (ppm)	Sulfur Dioxide (ppm)	Nitrogen Dioxide (ppm)	Ozone (ppm)	Lead (ug/m³)
MSA[1] Level	60	4	0.022	0.027	0.14	0.03
NAAQS[2]	150	9	0.140	0.053	0.12	1.50
Met NAAQS?	Yes	Yes	Yes	Yes	No	Yes

Note: (1) Metropolitan Statistical Area - see Appendix A for areas included; (2) National Ambient Air Quality Standards; ppm = parts per million; ug/m³ = micrograms per cubic meter; n/a not available
Source: EPA, National Air Quality and Emissions Trends Report, 1996

Pollutant Standards Index

In the Atlanta MSA (see Appendix A for areas included), the Pollutant Standards Index (PSI) exceeded 100 on 12 days in 1996. A PSI value greater than 100 indicates that air quality would be in the unhealthful range on that day. *EPA, National Air Quality and Emissions Trends Report, 1996*

Drinking Water

Water System Name	Pop. Served	Primary Water Source Type	Number of Violations in Fiscal Year 1997	Type of Violation/ Contaminants
Atlanta	649,836	Surface	1	Lead & copper rule[1]

Note: Data as of January 16, 1998; (1) System failed to use appropriate sampling procedures, collect the required number of samples, ensure proper analysis of samples, or submit information on time.
Source: EPA, Office of Ground Water and Drinking Water, Safe Drinking Water Information System

Atlanta tap water is neutral, soft.
Editor & Publisher Market Guide, 1998

Austin, Texas

Background

Austin is the legacy of bloody raids, dusty stampedes, and charging bayonets in the glaring sun of the territorial expansion age of the United States. Starting out as a peaceful Spanish mission in 1730, on the north bank of the Colorado River in south central Texas, the area we know today as Austin soon engaged in an imbroglio of territorial wars. This began when the "Father of Texas", Stephen F. Austin, annexed the territory from Mexico in 1833 as his own. Later, the Republic of Texas named the territory "Austin" in honor of the colonizer, and conferred state capital status. Challenges to this decision ensued, ranging from an invasion by the Mexican government to reclaim its land, to Sam Houston's call that the capital ought to move from Austin to Houston.

During peaceful times, however, Austin has been called the "City of the Violet Crown". Coined by the short story writer, William Sydney Porter or O'Henry, the "Violet Crown" refers to the purple mist that circles the surrounding hills of the Colorado River Valley.

Because of its desirable location along the Colorado River, many recreational activities and public facilities center around water. Austin boasts of being one of the first cities to operate its own hydroelectric plant. Therefore it is not surprising that a city of such technological innovation is home to a strong computer and aerospace industry.

When deciding upon a home for its first U.S. semiconductor manufacturing plant, the high-tech company of Samsung Electronics of South Korea settled on Austin. This Texas city was chosen because of its background in semiconductors, its educated labor market, access to "high-quality suppliers, supportive local government and an existing fabrication facility specifically built for the semiconductor industry." *World Trade, 3/96*

Austin is another one of those hot U.S. high-tech centers with numerous high-tech companies undergoing major expansions in 1998. Solectron and Applied Materials have both expanded their facilities by 50 percent. 3M is adding a new customer center to its research and development complex, and Tokyo Electron and Dell Computer are also expanding. Austin recently landed Samsung Electronics' $1.3 billion computer chip plant.

This city's high-tech growth has also been beneficial to the air cargo business, making Austin Texas' third-largest air cargo market. In addition a new 20 million air cargo facility opened in 1997 at Austin-Bergstrom International, and will be ready for passenger traffic in 1999. *Site Selection, Dec. 1997/Jan. 1998.*

With growth has come the problem of increased traffic especially on Interstate 35, the main highway linking the U.S. and Mexico.

But Austinites still see the city as special, and corporate executives still think of relocating their companies there along with others looking for a good place to live. *New York Times 1/31/98.*

In addition to its technological orientation, Austin seeks to be a well-rounded leader in cultural activities. As the hard-fought capital of Texas, Austin takes pride in its support of its cultural institutions.

The climate of Austin is humid subtropical with hot summers. Winters are mild, with below-freezing temperatures occurring on an average of 25 days a year. Cold spells are of short duration, seldom lasting two days. Daytime temperatures in summer are hot, but summer nights are usually pleasant.

General Rankings and Evaluative Comments

■ Austin was ranked #44 out of 300 cities by *Money's* 1997 "Survey of the Best Places to Live." Criteria used: health services, crime, economy, housing, education, transportation, weather, leisure and the arts. The city was ranked #8 in 1996 and #35 in 1995.
Money, July 1997; Money, September 1996; Money, September 1995

■ *Ladies Home Journal* ranked America's 200 largest cities based on the qualities women care about most. Austin ranked 29 out of 200. Criteria: low crime rate, good public schools, well-paying jobs, quality health and child care, the presence of women in government, proportion of women-owned businesses, size of the wage gap with men, local economy, divorce rates, the ratio of single men to single women, whether there are laws that require at least the same number of public toilets for women as men, and the probability of good hair days. *Ladies Home Journal, November 1997*

■ Austin was ranked #44 out of 219 cities in terms of children's health, safety, and economic well-being. Criteria: total population, percent population change, birth rate, child immunization rate, infant mortality rate, percent low birth weight infants, percent of births to teens, physician-to-population ratio, student-to-teacher ratio, dropout rate, unemployment rate, median family income, percent of children in poverty, violent and property crime rates, number of juvenile arrests for violent crimes as a percent of the total crime index, number of days with pollution standard index (PSI) over 100, pounds toxic releases per 1,000 people and number of superfund sites. *Zero Population Growth, Children's Environmental Index 1997*

■ Sun City Georgetown, located 30 miles north of Austin, is among America's best retirement communities. Criteria: communities must have state-of-the-art facilities, newly built homes for sale, and give you the most value for your money in every price range. Communities must also welcome newcomers of all races and religions. *New Choices, July/August 1997*

■ Austin is among the 20 most livable cities for gay men and lesbians. The list was divided between 10 cities you might expect and 10 surprises. Austin was on the cities you wouldn't expect list. Rank: 3 out of 10. Criteria: legal protection from antigay discrimination, an annual gay pride celebration, a community center, gay bookstores and publications, and an array of organizations, religious groups, and health care facilities that cater to the needs of the local gay community. *The Advocate, June 1997*

■ Austin was selected by *Swing* magazine as being one of "The 10 Best Places to Live" in the U.S. It was also named the "Best Place to Work in Technology".
The cities were selected based on census data, cost of living, economic growth, and entertainment options. Swing also read local papers, talked to industry insiders, and interviewed young people. *Swing, July/August 1997*

■ *Conde Nast Traveler* polled 37,000 readers in terms of travel satisfaction. Cities were ranked based on the following criteria: people/friendliness, environment/ambiance, cultural enrichment, restaurants and fun/energy. Austin appeared in the top thirty, ranking number 22, with an overall rating of 60.3 out of 100 based on all the criteria. *Conde Nast Traveler, Readers' Choice Poll 1997*

■ *Yahoo! Internet Life* selected "America's 100 Most Wired Cities & Towns". 50 cities were large and 50 cities were small. Austin ranked 4 out of 50 large cities. Criteria: Internet users per capita, number of networked computers, number of registered domain names, Internet backbone traffic, and the per-capita number of Web sites devoted to each city. *Yahoo! Internet Life, March 1998*

■ Austin was among "The 10 Hotbeds of Entrepreneurial Activity" in 1996 with 1.62 start-ups per 100 people. Rank: 3 out of 200 metro areas. *Inc., The State of Small Business 1997*

■ Whole Foods Market (natural-foods supermarket chain), headquartered in Austin, is among the "100 Best Companies to Work for in America." Criteria: trust in management, pride in work/company, camaraderie, company responses to the Hewitt People Practices Inventory, and employee responses to their Great Place to Work survey. The companies also had to be at least 10 years old and have a minimum of 500 employees. *Fortune, January 12, 1998*

■ According to *Working Mother,* "This year, the Texas Licensed Child Care Association lobbied heavily against proposed standards that would have improved the adult-to-child ratios in many programs. Unfortunately, it prevailed. Lawmakers delayed adoption of the new rules.

Texas may finally get statewide resource and referral services, however, with new federal funds coming into the state. In addition to helping parents find care, R&Rs may handle both caregiver training and consumer education—a positive development.

Providers across the state may also get low-interest loans to buy new equipment, upgrade their facilities and do other things to improve the quality of care, under a bill pending in the state legislature that looked likely to pass as we went to press." *Working Mother, July/August 1997*

Business Environment

STATE ECONOMY

State Economic Profile

"The Texas economy remains among the strongest in the nation....

Overall, Texas gained over 141,000 people last year through in-migration. While this is down from the three-year average of over 170,000, it still represents 43% of the Texas population increase. By far, throughout this decade, California has been the largest domestic source of in-migrants into Texas. With the California economy rebounding, in-migration to Texas is slowing.

The slowdown in household growth, coupled with solid residential construction, is creating a slight oversupply throughout the state. As a result, house price growth is decelerating. New residential permits have yet to slow, with new permits up by 14% last year—nearly twice the national increase. The slowdown in population and household growth cannot sustain such robust growth in permits, and as a result, new permits will slow this year.

The Texas economy shows no major imbalances. Although the important computer-chip industry remains moribund, the economy continues to expand solidly. The turnaround in computer memory prices will help the state continue to expand. Texas' growth is becoming increasingly supported by in-migrants. With an increasing presence in high-tech, an attractive business environment, and close proximity to Mexico, Texas will continue to expand faster than the nation and lure workers from other locales. In addition, as an attractive destination for retirees, Texas will continue to experience solid population and household growth as the population ages. Texas is ranked above average for short-and long-term growth." *National Association of Realtors, Economic Profiles: The Fifty States, July 1997*

IMPORTS/EXPORTS

Total Export Sales

Area	1993 ($000)	1994 ($000)	1995 ($000)	1996 ($000)	% Chg. 1993-96	% Chg. 1995-96
MSA[1]	1,721,514	2,128,774	2,929,208	2,743,135	59.3	-6.4
U.S.	464,858,354	512,415,609	583,030,524	622,827,063	34.0	6.8

Note: (1) Metropolitan Statistical Area - see Appendix A for areas included
Source: U.S. Department of Commerce, International Trade Association, Metropolitan Area Exports: An Export Performance Report on Over 250 U.S. Cities, October 1997

Imports/Exports by Port

Type	Cargo Value			Share of U.S. Total	
	1995 (US$mil.)	1996 (US$mil.)	% Change 1995-1996	1995 (%)	1996 (%)
Imports	0	0	0	0	0
Exports	0	0	0	0	0

Source: Global Trade Information Services, WaterBorne Trade Atlas 1997

CITY FINANCES

City Government Finances

Component	FY92 ($000)	FY92 (per capita $)
Revenue	1,130,427	2,261.65
Expenditure	1,112,679	2,226.14
Debt Outstanding	3,189,676	6,381.59
Cash & Securities	1,541,196	3,083.47

Source: U.S. Bureau of the Census, City Government Finances: 1991-92

City Government Revenue by Source

Source	FY92 ($000)	FY92 (per capita $)	FY92 (%)
From Federal Government	8,470	16.95	0.7
From State Governments	22,018	44.05	1.9
From Local Governments	3,768	7.54	0.3
Property Taxes	98,147	196.36	8.7
General Sales Taxes	55,401	110.84	4.9
Selective Sales Taxes	18,466	36.94	1.6
Income Taxes	0	0.00	0.0
Current Charges	232,264	464.69	20.5
Utility/Liquor Store	500,130	1,000.61	44.2
Employee Retirement[1]	69,967	139.98	6.2
Other	121,796	243.68	10.8

Note: (1) Excludes "city contributions," classified as "nonrevenue," intragovernmental transfers.
Source: U.S. Bureau of the Census, City Government Finances: 1991-92

City Government Expenditures by Function

Function	FY92 ($000)	FY92 (per capita $)	FY92 (%)
Educational Services	8,188	16.38	0.7
Employee Retirement[1]	22,975	45.97	2.1
Environment/Housing	179,041	358.21	16.1
Government Administration	20,629	41.27	1.9
Interest on General Debt	99,995	200.06	9.0
Public Safety	88,567	177.20	8.0
Social Services	142,961	286.02	12.8
Transportation	37,281	74.59	3.4
Utility/Liquor Store	478,325	956.98	43.0
Other	34,717	69.46	3.1

Note: (1) Payments to beneficiaries including withdrawal of contributions.
Source: U.S. Bureau of the Census, City Government Finances: 1991-92

Municipal Bond Ratings

Area	Moody's	S & P
Austin	Aa2	AA

Note: n/a not available; n/r not rated
Source: Moody's Bond Record, 2/98; Statistical Abstract of the U.S., 1997;
Governing Magazine, 9/97, 3/98

POPULATION

Population Growth

Area	1980	1990	% Chg. 1980-90	July 1996 Estimate	% Chg. 1990-96
City	345,544	465,577	34.7	541,278	16.3
MSA[1]	536,688	781,572	45.6	1,041,330	33.2
U.S.	226,545,805	248,765,170	9.8	265,179,411	6.6

Note: (1) Metropolitan Statistical Area - see Appendix A for areas included
Source: 1980/1990 Census of Housing and Population, Summary Tape File 3C;
Census Bureau Population Estimates

Population Characteristics

Race	City 1980 Population	%	City 1990 Population	%	% Chg. 1980-90	MSA[1] 1990 Population	%
White	263,618	76.3	329,309	70.7	24.9	601,163	76.9
Black	42,108	12.2	57,675	12.4	37.0	71,959	9.2
Amer Indian/Esk/Aleut	1,516	0.4	1,768	0.4	16.6	2,906	0.4
Asian/Pacific Islander	4,127	1.2	13,939	3.0	237.8	18,341	2.3
Other	34,175	9.9	62,886	13.5	84.0	87,203	11.2
Hispanic Origin[2]	64,766	18.7	105,162	22.6	62.4	157,866	20.2

Note: (1) Metropolitan Statistical Area - see Appendix A for areas included;
(2) people of Hispanic origin can be of any race
Source: 1980/1990 Census of Housing and Population, Summary Tape File 3C

Ancestry

Area	German	Irish	English	Italian	U.S.	French	Polish	Dutch
City	20.7	12.6	13.7	2.3	2.7	3.6	1.6	1.5
MSA[1]	23.7	14.2	14.7	2.3	3.3	3.9	1.7	1.7
U.S.	23.3	15.6	13.1	5.9	5.3	4.2	3.8	2.5

Note: Figures are percentages and include persons that reported multiple ancestry (eg. if a person reported being Irish and Italian, they were included in both columns); (1) Metropolitan Statistical Area - see Appendix A for areas included
Source: 1990 Census of Population and Housing, Summary Tape File 3C

Age

Area	Median Age (Years)	Under 5	Under 18	18-24	25-44	45-64	65+	80+
City	28.9	7.5	23.1	17.2	38.7	13.6	7.4	1.8
MSA[1]	29.4	7.7	25.3	14.9	38.1	14.4	7.3	1.7
U.S.	32.9	7.3	25.6	10.5	32.6	18.7	12.5	2.8

Note: (1) Metropolitan Statistical Area - see Appendix A for areas included
Source: 1990 Census of Population and Housing, Summary Tape File 3C

Male/Female Ratio

Area	Number of males per 100 females (all ages)	Number of males per 100 females (18 years old+)
City	99.9	98.4
MSA[1]	99.8	97.8
U.S.	95.0	91.9

Note: (1) Metropolitan Statistical Area - see Appendix A for areas included
Source: 1990 Census of Population, General Population Characteristics

INCOME

Per Capita/Median/Average Income

Area	Per Capita ($)	Median Household ($)	Average Household ($)
City	14,295	25,414	33,947
MSA[1]	14,521	28,474	36,754
U.S.	14,420	30,056	38,453

Note: all figures are for 1989; (1) Metropolitan Statistical Area - see Appendix A for areas included
Source: 1990 Census of Population and Housing, Summary Tape File 3C

Household Income Distribution by Race

Income ($)	City (%)					U.S. (%)				
	Total	White	Black	Other	Hisp.[1]	Total	White	Black	Other	Hisp.[1]
Less than 5,000	8.9	7.4	14.8	13.4	10.2	6.2	4.8	15.2	8.6	8.8
5,000 - 9,999	9.5	8.5	12.4	12.5	11.5	9.3	8.6	14.2	9.9	11.1
10,000 - 14,999	10.6	9.5	12.9	14.7	13.6	8.8	8.5	11.0	9.8	11.0
15,000 - 24,999	20.3	19.3	23.6	23.2	23.7	17.5	17.3	18.9	18.5	20.5
25,000 - 34,999	16.1	16.2	16.4	15.2	16.7	15.8	16.1	14.2	15.4	16.4
35,000 - 49,999	15.6	16.7	10.8	12.9	14.2	17.9	18.6	13.3	16.1	16.0
50,000 - 74,999	11.6	13.2	6.9	6.3	7.9	15.0	15.8	9.3	13.4	11.1
75,000 - 99,999	4.0	4.9	1.3	1.2	1.4	5.1	5.5	2.6	4.7	3.1
100,000+	3.5	4.4	1.0	0.6	0.8	4.4	4.8	1.3	3.7	1.9

Note: all figures are for 1989; (1) people of Hispanic origin can be of any race
Source: 1990 Census of Population and Housing, Summary Tape File 3C

Effective Buying Income

Area	Per Capita ($)	Median Household ($)	Average Household ($)
City	17,494	31,362	42,133
MSA[1]	17,880	35,778	46,175
U.S.	15,444	33,201	41,849

Note: data as of 1/1/97; (1) Metropolitan Statistical Area - see Appendix A for areas included
Source: Standard Rate & Data Service, Newspaper Advertising Source, 2/98

Effective Household Buying Income Distribution

Area	% of Households Earning						
	$10,000 -$19,999	$20,000 -$34,999	$35,000 -$49,999	$50,000 -$74,999	$75,000 -$99,000	$100,000 -$124,999	$125,000 and up
City	17.1	23.7	16.8	16.2	6.4	2.6	2.9
MSA[1]	14.9	21.9	17.2	18.8	8.3	3.2	3.3
U.S.	16.5	23.4	18.3	18.2	6.4	2.1	2.4

Note: data as of 1/1/97; (1) Metropolitan Statistical Area - see Appendix A for areas included
Source: Standard Rate & Data Service, Newspaper Advertising Source, 2/98

Poverty Rates by Race and Age

Area	Total (%)	By Race (%)				By Age (%)		
		White	Black	Other	Hisp.[2]	Under 5 years old	Under 18 years old	65 years and over
City	17.9	13.5	26.5	30.2	27.4	23.4	21.5	11.7
MSA[1]	15.3	11.8	26.2	27.7	26.3	19.1	17.4	13.0
U.S.	13.1	9.8	29.5	23.1	25.3	20.1	18.3	12.8

Note: figures show the percent of people living below the poverty line in 1989. The average poverty threshold was $12,674 for a family of four in 1989; (1) Metropolitan Statistical Area - see Appendix A for areas included; (2) people of Hispanic origin can be of any race
Source: 1990 Census of Population and Housing, Summary Tape File 3C

EMPLOYMENT

Labor Force and Employment

Area	Civilian Labor Force			Workers Employed		
	Dec. '95	Dec. '96	% Chg.	Dec. '95	Dec. '96	% Chg.
City	354,750	356,386	0.5	342,933	346,014	0.9
MSA[1]	640,276	643,741	0.5	621,407	626,991	0.9
U.S.	134,583,000	136,742,000	1.6	127,903,000	130,785,000	2.3

Note: Data is not seasonally adjusted and covers workers 16 years of age and older;
(1) Metropolitan Statistical Area - see Appendix A for areas included
Source: Bureau of Labor Statistics, http://stats.bls.gov

Austin was listed among the top 20 metro areas (out of 114 major areas) in terms of projected job growth from 1997 to 2002 with an annual percent change of 2.6%.
Standard & Poor's DRI, July 23, 1997

Unemployment Rate

Area	1997											
	Jan.	Feb.	Mar.	Apr.	May	Jun.	Jul.	Aug.	Sep.	Oct.	Nov.	Dec.
City	3.8	3.6	3.6	3.1	3.1	3.8	3.6	3.6	3.4	3.3	3.2	2.9
MSA[1]	3.4	3.3	3.3	2.9	2.9	3.5	3.3	3.2	3.1	2.9	2.9	2.6
U.S.	5.9	5.7	5.5	4.8	4.7	5.2	5.0	4.8	4.7	4.4	4.3	4.4

Note: Data is not seasonally adjusted and covers workers 16 years of age and older; All figures are percentages; (1) Metropolitan Statistical Area - see Appendix A for areas included
Source: Bureau of Labor Statistics, http://stats.bls.gov

Employment by Industry

Sector	MSA[1]		U.S.
	Number of Employees	Percent of Total	Percent of Total
Services	167,000	28.7	29.0
Retail Trade	103,300	17.8	18.5
Government	129,100	22.2	16.1
Manufacturing	77,800	13.4	15.0
Finance/Insurance/Real Estate	30,200	5.2	5.7
Wholesale Trade	23,300	4.0	5.4
Transportation/Public Utilities	19,200	3.3	5.3
Construction	30,800	5.3	4.5
Mining	1,200	0.2	0.5

Note: Figures cover non-farm employment as of 12/97 and are not seasonally adjusted;
(1) Metropolitan Statistical Area - see Appendix A for areas included
Source: Bureau of Labor Statistics, http://stats.bls.gov

Employment by Occupation

Occupation Category	City (%)	MSA[1] (%)	U.S. (%)
White Collar	69.3	68.4	58.1
Executive/Admin./Management	15.3	15.6	12.3
Professional	19.0	17.9	14.1
Technical & Related Support	5.5	5.3	3.7
Sales	11.4	11.6	11.8
Administrative Support/Clerical	18.1	18.0	16.3
Blue Collar	15.9	17.5	26.2
Precision Production/Craft/Repair	7.5	8.5	11.3
Machine Operators/Assem./Insp.	3.4	3.8	6.8
Transportation/Material Movers	2.3	2.5	4.1
Cleaners/Helpers/Laborers	2.6	2.7	3.9
Services	13.8	12.7	13.2
Farming/Forestry/Fishing	1.0	1.4	2.5

Note: figures cover employed persons 16 years old and over;
(1) Metropolitan Statistical Area - see Appendix A for areas included
Source: 1990 Census of Population and Housing, Summary Tape File 3C

Occupational Employment Projections: 1993 - 2000

Occupations Expected to have the Largest Job Growth (ranked by numerical growth)	Fast-Growing Occupations[1] (ranked by percent growth)
1. General office clerks	1. Flight attendants
2. Salespersons, retail	2. Computer systems analysts
3. Waiters & waitresses	3. Title examiners and abstractors
4. Child care workers, private household	4. Computer scientists
5. Food preparation workers	5. Computer engineers
6. General managers & top executives	6. Home health aides
7. Corrections officers & jailers	7. Human services workers
8. Guards	8. Detectives/investigators, private
9. Computer systems analysts	9. Lawn maintenance workers
10. Secretaries, except legal & medical	10. Personal and home care aides

Projections cover Bastrop, Blanco, Burnet, Caldwell, Fayette, Hays, Lee, Llano, Travis and Williamson Counties.
Note: (1) Includes occupations with absolute job growth of 200 or more
Source: Texas Employment Commission, Texas Employment Projections Reporting System, Statewide and Regional Projections 1993-2000, Ver. 1.0

Average Wages

Occupation	Wage	Occupation	Wage
Professional/Technical/Clerical	**$/Week**	**Health/Protective Services**	**$/Week**
Accountants III	-	Corrections Officers	-
Attorneys III	-	Firefighters	-
Budget Analysts III	-	Nurses, Licensed Practical II	-
Buyers/Contracting Specialists II	-	Nurses, Registered II	722
Clerks, Accounting III	442	Nursing Assistants II	-
Clerks, General III	387	Police Officers I	-
Computer Operators II	407	**Hourly Workers**	**$/Hour**
Computer Programmers II	653	Forklift Operators	10.75
Drafters II	520	General Maintenance Workers	8.39
Engineering Technicians III	609	Guards I	6.26
Engineering Technicians, Civil III	-	Janitors	5.42
Engineers III	-	Maintenance Electricians	17.77
Key Entry Operators I	294	Maintenance Electronics Techs II	16.49
Personnel Assistants III	-	Maintenance Machinists	-
Personnel Specialists III	-	Maintenance Mechanics, Machinery	13.47
Secretaries III	517	Material Handling Laborers	7.15
Switchboard Operator-Receptionist	325	Motor Vehicle Mechanics	15.03
Systems Analysts II	908	Shipping/Receiving Clerks	8.65
Systems Analysts Supervisor/Mgr II	-	Tool and Die Makers	-
Tax Collectors II	-	Truckdrivers, Tractor Trailer	10.52
Word Processors II	-	Warehouse Specialists	-

Note: Wage data includes full-time workers only for 8/95 and cover the Metropolitan Statistical Area (see Appendix A for areas included). Dashes indicate that data was not available.
Source: Bureau of Labor Statistics, Occupational Compensation Survey, 12/95

TAXES

Major State and Local Tax Rates

State Corp. Income (%)	State Personal Income (%)	Residential Property (effective rate per $100)	Sales & Use State (%)	Sales & Use Local (%)	State Gasoline (cents/ gallon)	State Cigarette (cents/ 20-pack)
None[a]	None	n/a	6.25	2.0	20	41

Note: Personal/corporate income tax rates as of 1/97. Sales, gasoline and cigarette tax rates as of 1/98; (a) Texas imposes a franchise tax of 4.5% of earned surplus
Source: Federation of Tax Administrators, www.taxadmin.org; Washington D.C. Department of Finance and Revenue, Tax Rates and Tax Burdens in the District of Columbia: A Nationwide Comparison, June 1997; Chamber of Commerce

Total Taxes Per Capita and as a Percent of Income

Area	Per Capita Income ($)	Per Capita Taxes ($)			Taxes as Pct. of Income (%)		
		Total	Federal	State/Local	Total	Federal	State/Local
Texas	24,145	8,118	5,538	2,580	33.6	22.9	10.7
U.S.	26,187	9,205	6,127	3,078	35.2	23.4	11.8

Note: Figures are for 1997
Source: Tax Foundation, Web Site, www.taxfoundation.org

Estimated Tax Burden

Area	State Income	Local Income	Property	Sales	Total
Austin	0	0	5,175	701	5,876

Note: The numbers are estimates of taxes paid by a married couple with two kids and annual earnings of $65,000. Sales tax estimates assume they spend average amounts on food, clothing, household goods and gasoline. Property tax estimates assume they live in a $225,000 home.
Source: Kiplinger's Personal Finance Magazine, June 1997

COMMERCIAL REAL ESTATE

Office Market

Class/Location	Total Space (sq. ft.)	Vacant Space (sq. ft.)	Vac. Rate (%)	Under Constr. (sq. ft.)	Net Absorp. (sq. ft.)	Rental Rates ($/sq.ft./yr.)
Class A						
CBD	3,441,509	344,150	10.0	n/a	142,846	20.00-23.00
Outside CBD	4,944,949	148,348	3.0	700,000	465,629	20.00-24.50
Class B						
CBD	3,565,897	427,907	12.0	n/a	208,682	13.00-19.00
Outside CBD	9,742,170	584,530	6.0	n/a	435,231	15.50-19.00

Note: Data as of 10/97 and covers Austin; CBD = Central Business District; n/a not available;
Source: Society of Industrial and Office Realtors, 1998 Comparative Statistics of Industrial and Office Real Estate Markets

"Seven new buildings slated for completion by the end of 1997 are adding 700,000 sq. ft. of suburban Class 'A' space. They will take only some of the pressure off the market since a good deal of the space has already been leased. During 1998, 1.3 million sq. ft. of new construction is planned in the northwest and southwest suburban markets. However, if current trends continue this space will be 65 percent pre-leased very early in construction and will not reverse the trend of CBD backfilling during 1998. Our SIOR reporters expect another year of strong absorption. Insurance companies and commercial banks are supplying most of the mortgage funds for new developments." *Society of Industrial and Office Realtors, 1998 Comparative Statistics of Industrial and Office Real Estate Markets*

Industrial Market

Location	Total Space (sq. ft.)	Vacant Space (sq. ft.)	Vac. Rate (%)	Under Constr. (sq. ft.)	Net Absorp. (sq. ft.)	Lease ($/sq.ft./yr.)
Central City	n/a	n/a	n/a	n/a	n/a	n/a
Suburban	19,800,935	1,322,335	6.7	1,232,041	1,662,362	4.20-4.80

Note: Data as of 10/97 and covers Austin; n/a not available
Source: Society of Industrial and Office Realtors, 1998 Comparative Statistics of Industrial and Office Real Estate Markets

"During 1998, a significant increase in speculative development of larger lease deals closed during 1997. Demand from vendors and suppliers related to the semiconductor industry is expected to continue in 1998. New construction is anticipated in most of the industrial areas around Austin, with a heavy concentration near the new airport. Our SIOR reporter projects solid increases in absorption during 1998 with all industrial categories approximately six to 10 percent above the levels observed in 1997. More than 1.2 million sq. ft. of additional space is under construction with additional projects in the planning stages. Rising land prices and the shortages of space in the market will likely lead to increases in lease prices during 1998 but the increases are not expected to be more than five percent." *Society of Industrial and Office Realtors, 1998 Comparative Statistics of Industrial and Office Real Estate Markets*

Retail Market

Shopping Center Inventory (sq. ft.)	Shopping Center Construction (sq. ft.)	Construction as a Percent of Inventory (%)	Torto Wheaton Rent Index[1] ($/sq. ft.)
19,509,000	630,000	3.2	15.90

Note: Data as of 1997 and covers the Metropolitan Statistical Area - see Appendix A for areas included; (1) Index is based on a model that predicts what the average rent should be for leases with certain characteristics, in certain locations during certain years.
Source: National Association of Realtors, 1997-1998 Market Conditions Report

"Between 1994 and 1996, Austin registered a blistering 6.0% average annual rate of employment growth, which slowed somewhat in 1997. Nonetheless, such strong employment and population growth have caused vacancy rates to drop and the rent index to soar 56% since 1994. A large amount of retail activity has been centered in the Golden Triangle area near Research Boulevard, Loop 360, and North MoPac Expressway. Development has also been found in the I-35-35 area. Expect population and real income growth to decelerate somewhat over the next few years which, will likely put downward pressure on the retail rent index." *National Association of Realtors, 1997-1998 Market Conditions Report*

COMMERCIAL UTILITIES

Typical Monthly Electric Bills

Area	Commercial Service ($/month)		Industrial Service ($/month)	
	12 kW demand 1,500 kWh	120 kW demand 30,000 kWh	1,000 kW demand 400,000 kWh	20,000 kW demand 10,000,000 kWh
City[1]	98	2,498	22,842	528,500
U.S.[2]	162	2,360[a]	25,590	545,677

Note: (1) Based on rates in effect January 1, 1997; (2) Based on rates in effect July 1, 1997; (a) Based on 100 kW demand and 30,000 kWh usage.
Source: Memphis Light, Gas and Water, 1997 Utility Bill Comparisons for Selected U.S. Cities; Edison Electric Institute, Typical Residential, Commercial and Industrial Bills, Summer 1997

TRANSPORTATION

Transportation Statistics

Avg. travel time to work (min.)	19.1
Interstate highways	I-35
Bus lines	
In-city	Capital Metro, 300 vehicles
Inter-city	2
Passenger air service	
Airport	Robert Mueller Austin Municipal
Airlines	10
Aircraft departures	39,823 (1995)
Enplaned passengers	2,638,039 (1995)
Rail service	Amtrak
Motor freight carriers	20
Major waterways/ports	None

Source: OAG, Business Travel Planner, Summer 1997; Editor & Publisher Market Guide, 1998; FAA Airport Activity Statistics, 1996; Amtrak National Time Table, Northeast Timetable, Fall/Winter 1997-98; 1990 Census of Population and Housing, STF 3C; Chamber of Commerce/Economic Development 1997; Jane's Urban Transport Systems 1997-98; Transit Fact Book 1997

Means of Transportation to Work

Area	Car/Truck/Van		Public Transportation			Bicycle	Walked	Other Means	Worked at Home
	Drove Alone	Car-pooled	Bus	Subway	Railroad				
City	73.6	13.3	4.8	0.0	0.0	0.8	3.3	1.3	2.8
MSA[1]	75.3	13.9	3.2	0.0	0.0	0.5	2.9	1.2	3.0
U.S.	73.2	13.4	3.0	1.5	0.5	0.4	3.9	1.2	3.0

Note: figures shown are percentages and only include workers 16 years old and over;
(1) Metropolitan Statistical Area - see Appendix A for areas included
Source: 1990 Census of Population and Housing, Summary Tape File 3C

BUSINESSES

Major Business Headquarters

Company Name	1997 Rankings	
	Fortune 500	Forbes 500

No companies listed.

Note: Companies listed are located in the city; Dashes indicate no ranking
Fortune 500: companies that produce a 10-K are ranked 1 - 500 based on 1996 revenue
Forbes 500: private companies are ranked 1 - 500 based on 1996 revenue
Source: Forbes 12/1/97; Fortune 4/28/97

Fast-Growing Businesses

According to *Inc.*, Austin is home to two of America's 100 fastest-growing private companies: Evolutionary Technologies International and Progressive System Technologies. Criteria for inclusion: must be an independent, privately-held, U.S. corporation, proprietorship or partnership; sales of at least $200,000 in 1993; five-year operating/sales history; increase in 1997 sales over 1996 sales; holding companies, regulated banks, and utilities were excluded. *Inc. 500, 1997*

Women-Owned Businesses: Number, Employment, Sales and Share

Area	Women-Owned Businesses in 1996				Share of Women-Owned Businesses in 1996	
	Number	Employment	Sales ($000)	Rank[2]	Percent (%)	Rank[3]
MSA[1]	35,000	50,800	6,077,300	50	36.0	32

Note: (1) Metropolitan Statistical Area - see Appendix A for areas included; (2) Calculated on an averaging of number of businesses, employment and sales and ranges from 1 to 50 where 1 is best; (3) Ranges from 1 to 50 where 1 is best
Source: The National Foundation for Women Business Owners, 1996 Facts on Women-Owned Businesses: Trends in the Top 50 Metropolitan Areas, March 26, 1997

Women-Owned Businesses: Growth

Area	Growth in Women-Owned Businesses (% change from 1987 to 1996)				Relative Growth in the Number of Women-Owned and All Businesses (% change from 1987 to 1996)			
	Num.	Empl.	Sales	Rank[2]	Women-Owned	All Firms	Absolute Difference	Relative Difference
MSA[1]	79.2	171.3	227.3	30	79.2	55.4	23.8	1.4:1

Note: (1) Metropolitan Statistical Area - see Appendix A for areas included; (2) Calculated on an averaging of the percent growth of number of businesses, employment and sales and ranges from 1 to 50 where 1 is best
Source: The National Foundation for Women Business Owners, 1996 Facts on Women-Owned Businesses: Trends in the Top 50 Metropolitan Areas, March 26, 1997

Minority Business Opportunity

One of the 500 largest Hispanic-owned companies in the U.S. are located in Austin.
Hispanic Business, June 1997

Austin was listed among the top 25 metropolitan areas in terms of the number of Hispanic-owned companies. The city was ranked number 22 with 13,496 companies. *Hispanic Business, May 1997*

Small Business Opportunity

According to *Forbes*, Austin is home to two of America's 200 best small companies: National Instrument, Prime Medical Services. Criteria: companies must be publicly traded, U.S.-based corporations with latest 12-month sales of between $5 and $350 million. Earnings must be at least $1 million for the 12-month period. Limited partnerships, REITs and closed-end mutual funds were not considered. Banks, S&Ls and electric utilities were not included. *Forbes, November 3, 1997*

HOTELS & MOTELS

Hotels/Motels

Area	Hotels/ Motels	Rooms	Luxury-Level Hotels/Motels		Average Minimum Rates ($)		
			◆◆◆◆	◆◆◆◆◆	◆◆	◆◆◆	◆◆◆◆
City	48	7,752	2	0	69	133	176
Airport	14	2,500	0	0	n/a	n/a	n/a
Suburbs	3	240	0	0	n/a	n/a	n/a
Total	65	10,492	2	0	n/a	n/a	n/a

Note: n/a not available; Classifications range from one diamond (budget properties with basic amenities) to five diamond (luxury properties with the finest service, rooms and facilities).
Source: OAG, Business Travel Planner, Summer 1997

CONVENTION CENTERS

Major Convention Centers

Center Name	Meeting Rooms	Exhibit Space (sf)
Austin Convention Center	29	400,000
City Coliseum	n/a	64,924
Lakeway Inn	10	n/a
Palmer Auditorium	13	60,000

Note: n/a not available
Source: Trade Shows Worldwide 1997

Living Environment

COST OF LIVING

Cost of Living Index

Composite Index	Housing	Utilities	Groceries	Health Care	Trans- portation	Misc. Goods/ Services
98.9	103.2	86.3	88.1	108.1	97.8	102.1

Note: U.S. = 100
Source: ACCRA, Cost of Living Index, 3rd Quarter 1997

HOUSING

Median Home Prices and Housing Affordability

Area	Median Price[2] 3rd Qtr. 1997 ($)	HOI[3] 3rd Qtr. 1997	Afford- ability Rank[4]
MSA[1]	127,000	57.1	160
U.S.	127,000	63.7	–

Note: (1) Metropolitan Statistical Area - see Appendix A for areas included; (2) U.S. figures calculated from the sales of 625,000 new and existing homes in 195 markets; (3) Housing Opportunity Index - percent of homes sold that were within the reach of the median income household at the prevailing mortgage interest rate; (4) Rank is from 1-195 with 1 being most affordable
Source: National Association of Home Builders, Housing Opportunity Index, 3rd Quarter 1997

It is projected that the median price of existing single-family homes in the metro area will increase by 8.6% in 1998. Nationwide, home prices are projected to increase 6.6%.
Kiplinger's Personal Finance Magazine, January 1998

Average New Home Price

Area	Price ($)
City	130,220
U.S.	135,710

Note: Figures are based on a new home with 1,800 sq. ft. of living area on an 8,000 sq. ft. lot.
Source: ACCRA, Cost of Living Index, 3rd Quarter 1997

Average Apartment Rent

Area	Rent ($/mth)
City	843
U.S.	569

Note: Figures are based on an unfurnished two bedroom, 1-1/2 or 2 bath apartment, approximately 950 sq. ft. in size, excluding all utilities except water
Source: ACCRA, Cost of Living Index, 3rd Quarter 1997

RESIDENTIAL UTILITIES

Average Residential Utility Costs

Area	All Electric ($/mth)	Part Electric ($/mth)	Other Energy ($/mth)	Phone ($/mth)
City	–	61.81	28.08	15.06
U.S.	109.40	55.25	43.64	19.48

Source: ACCRA, Cost of Living Index, 3rd Quarter 1997

HEALTH CARE

Average Health Care Costs

Area	Hospital ($/day)	Doctor ($/visit)	Dentist ($/visit)
City	389.33	48.20	75.00
U.S.	392.91	48.76	60.84

Note: Hospital - based on a semi-private room. Doctor - based on a general practitioner's routine exam of an established patient. Dentist - based on adult teeth cleaning and periodic oral exam.
Source: ACCRA, Cost of Living Index, 3rd Quarter 1997

Distribution of Office-Based Physicians

Area	Family/Gen. Practitioners	Specialists		
		Medical	Surgical	Other
MSA[1]	290	501	428	460

Note: Data as of 12/31/96; (1) Metropolitan Statistical Area - see Appendix A for areas included
Source: American Medical Assn., Physician Characteristics & Distribution in the U.S., 1997-1998

Hospitals

Austin has 6 general medical and surgical hospitals, 4 psychiatric, 3 rehabilitation, 1 other specialty, 2 children's psychiatric. *AHA Guide to the Healthcare Field 1997-98*

EDUCATION

Public School District Statistics

District Name	Num. Sch.	Enroll.	Classroom Teachers[1]	Pupils per Teacher	Minority Pupils (%)	Current Exp.[2] ($/pupil)
Austin ISD	103	74,772	4,502	16.6	61.1	5,062
Eanes ISD	8	6,865	481	14.3	n/a	n/a
Lake Travis ISD	4	2,649	195	13.6	n/a	n/a

Note: Data covers the 1995-1996 school year unless otherwise noted; (1) Excludes teachers reported as working in school district offices rather than in schools; (2) Based on 1993-94 enrollment collected by the Census Bureau, not the enrollment figure shown in column 3; SD = School District; ISD = Independent School District; n/a not available
Source: National Center for Education Statistics, Common Core of Data Survey; Bureau of the Census

Educational Quality

School District	Education Quotient[1]	Graduate Outcome[2]	Community Index[3]	Resource Index[4]
Austin	96.0	103.0	126.0	59.0

Note: Nearly 1,000 secondary school districts were rated in terms of educational quality. The scores range from a low of 50 to a high of 150; (1) Average of the Graduate Outcome, Community and Resource indexes; (2) Based on graduation rates and college board scores (SAT/ACT); (3) Based on the surrounding community's average level of education and the area's average income level; (4) Based on teacher salaries, per-pupil expenditures and student-teacher ratios.
Source: Expansion Management, Ratings Issue 1997

Educational Attainment by Race

Area	High School Graduate (%)					Bachelor's Degree (%)				
	Total	White	Black	Other	Hisp.[2]	Total	White	Black	Other	Hisp.[2]
City	82.3	88.7	69.6	58.4	57.9	34.4	40.0	16.5	18.4	13.8
MSA[1]	82.5	87.3	70.0	58.5	56.8	32.2	35.9	16.9	17.8	13.1
U.S.	75.2	77.9	63.1	60.4	49.8	20.3	21.5	11.4	19.4	9.2

Note: figures shown cover persons 25 years old and over; (1) Metropolitan Statistical Area - see Appendix A for areas included; (2) people of Hispanic origin can be of any race
Source: 1990 Census of Population and Housing, Summary Tape File 3C

School Enrollment by Type

Area	Preprimary				Elementary/High School			
	Public		Private		Public		Private	
	Enrollment	%	Enrollment	%	Enrollment	%	Enrollment	%
City	4,815	52.7	4,328	47.3	62,838	93.4	4,472	6.6
MSA[1]	8,688	52.4	7,888	47.6	119,826	94.2	7,318	5.8
U.S.	2,679,029	59.5	1,824,256	40.5	38,379,689	90.2	4,187,099	9.8

Note: figures shown cover persons 3 years old and over;
(1) Metropolitan Statistical Area - see Appendix A for areas included
Source: 1990 Census of Population and Housing, Summary Tape File 3C

School Enrollment by Race

Area	Preprimary (%)				Elementary/High School (%)			
	White	Black	Other	Hisp.[1]	White	Black	Other	Hisp.[1]
City	73.9	11.0	15.1	20.9	58.1	18.2	23.8	33.8
MSA[2]	80.3	7.7	12.0	18.3	69.7	12.2	18.2	28.3
U.S.	80.4	12.5	7.1	7.8	74.1	15.6	10.3	12.5

Note: figures shown cover persons 3 years old and over; (1) people of Hispanic origin can be of any race; (2) Metropolitan Statistical Area - see Appendix A for areas included
Source: 1990 Census of Population and Housing, Summary Tape File 3C

SAT/ACT Scores

Area/District	1997 SAT				1997 ACT	
	Percent of Graduates Tested (%)	Average Math Score	Average Verbal Score	Average Combined Score	Percent of Graduates Tested (%)	Average Composite Score
Austin ISD	54	531	524	1,055	17	21.4
State	49	501	494	995	30	20.2
U.S.	42	511	505	1,016	36	21.0

Note: Math and verbal SAT scores are out of a possible 800; ACT scores are out of a possible 36
Caution: Comparing or ranking states/cities on the basis of SAT/ACT scores alone is invalid and strongly discouraged by the The College Board and The American College Testing Program as students who take the tests are self-selected and do not represent the entire student population.
Source: Austin Independent School District, 1997; American College Testing Program, 1997; College Board, 1997

Classroom Teacher Salaries in Public Schools

District	B.A. Degree		M.A. Degree		Ph.D. Degree	
	Min. ($)	Max ($)	Min. ($)	Max. ($)	Min. ($)	Max. ($)
Austin	25,110	39,760	25,930	40,580	25,930	40,580
Average[1]	26,120	39,270	28,175	44,667	31,643	49,825

Note: Salaries are for 1996-1997; (1) Based on all school districts covered; n/a not available
Source: American Federation of Teachers (unpublished data)

Higher Education

Two-Year Colleges		Four-Year Colleges		Medical Schools	Law Schools	Voc/ Tech
Public	Private	Public	Private			
1	1	0	4	0	1	6

Source: College Blue Book, Occupational Education 1997; Medical School Admission Requirements, 1998-99; Peterson's Guide to Two-Year Colleges, 1997; Peterson's Guide to Four-Year Colleges, 1997; Barron's Guide to Law Schools 1997

MAJOR EMPLOYERS

Major Employers

Austin State Hospital
National Instruments
St. David's Health Care System
Barton Creek Resort & Clubs
Daughters of Charity Health System

Continuum Inc. (computer programming)
Sematech Inc. (research)
Tracor Inc. (aircraft parts)
J.C. Evans Construction
Pharmaco International (medical labs)

Note: companies listed are located in the city
Source: Dun's Business Rankings 1997; Ward's Business Directory, 1997

PUBLIC SAFETY

Crime Rate

Area	All Crimes	Violent Crimes				Property Crimes		
		Murder	Forcible Rape	Robbery	Aggrav. Assault	Burglary	Larceny -Theft	Motor Vehicle Theft
City	7,865.9	7.4	50.2	256.0	397.2	1,409.3	5,058.2	687.5
Suburbs[1]	3,760.7	3.0	30.3	42.7	225.6	871.6	2,408.3	179.3
MSA[2]	5,960.0	5.4	41.0	157.0	317.6	1,159.7	3,827.9	451.5
U.S.	5,078.9	7.4	36.1	202.4	388.2	943.0	2,975.9	525.9

Note: Crime rate is the number of crimes per 100,000 pop.; (1) defined as all areas within the MSA but located outside the central city; (2) Metropolitan Statistical Area - see Appendix A for areas incl.
Source: FBI Uniform Crime Reports 1996

RECREATION

Culture and Recreation

Museums	Symphony Orchestras	Opera Companies	Dance Companies	Professional Theatres	Zoos	Pro Sports Teams
14	2	1	1	4	1	0

Source: International Directory of the Performing Arts, 1996; Official Museum Directory, 1998; Chamber of Commerce/Economic Development 1997

Library System

The Austin Public Library has 18 branches, holdings of 1,324,784 volumes and a budget of $n/a (1995-1996). The Westbank Community Library has no branches, holdings of 31,979 volumes and a budget of $210,318 (1995-1996). Note: n/a means not available. *American Library Directory, 1997-1998*

MEDIA

Newspapers

Name	Type	Freq.	Distribution	Circulation
Austin American-Statesman	n/a	7x/wk	Area	175,000
Austin Chronicle	n/a	1x/wk	Local	80,000
Austin Sun	Black	1x/wk	Local	15,000
The Catholic Spirit	Religious	1x/mo	Regional	27,500
The Daily Texan	n/a	5x/wk	Campus & community	30,000
El Mundo	Hispanic	1x/wk	Local	20,000
Lake and Country Living	General	1x/wk	Local	15,000
La Prensa-Austin	Hispanic	1x/wk	Local	10,000

Note: Includes newspapers with circulations of 10,000 or more located in the city; n/a not available
Source: Burrelle's Media Directory, 1998 Edition

AM Radio Stations

Call Letters	Freq. (kHz)	Target Audience	Station Format	Music Format
KLBJ	590	n/a	N/T	n/a
KIXL	970	Religious	E/M/N/T	Christian
KFIT	1060	Black/Hisp	M/N/T	Christian
KVET	1300	General	N/S/T	n/a
KJCE	1370	General	M	R&B
KELG	1440	Hispanic	M	Contemporary Top 40
KFON	1490	General	S	n/a
KTXZ	1560	Hispanic	M	n/a

Note: Stations included broadcast in the Austin metro area; n/a not available
Station Format: E = Educational; M = Music; N = News; S = Sports; T = Talk
Source: Burrelle's Media Directory, 1998 Edition

FM Radio Stations

Call Letters	Freq. (mHz)	Target Audience	Station Format	Music Format
KNLE	88.1	n/a	M/N/S	Adult Contemporary/Alternative/Christian
KAZI	88.7	Black/Relig	E/M/N/S/T	Christian/Jazz/Oldies/R&B/Urban Contemporary
KMFA	89.5	n/a	E/M	Classical
KUT	90.5	General	E/M/N	n/a
KOOP	91.7	General	E/M/N/T	n/a
KVRX	91.7	General	E/M/N/S/T	Alternative/Classical/Country/Jazz/Spanish
KKLB	92.5	Hispanic	M	Contemporary Top 40/Spanish
KAJZ	93.3	General	M	Adult Contemporary/Jazz
KLBJ	93.7	General	M/N/S	AOR
KPTY	94.7	General	M/N/T	Adult Contemporary/Alternative
KKMJ	95.5	General	M	Adult Contemporary
KHFI	96.7	General	M	Contemporary Top 40
KVET	98.1	General	M/N/S	Country
KJFK	98.9	General	T	n/a
KASE	100.7	General	M	Country
KROX	101.5	General	M	Alternative
KPEZ	102.3	General	M/S	Classic Rock
KEYI	103.5	General	M	Oldies
KHLR	103.9	n/a	M	Adult Contemporary/Alternative
KGSR	107.1	General	M	Alternative

Note: Stations included broadcast in the Austin metro area; n/a not available
Station Format: E = Educational; M = Music; N = News; S = Sports; T = Talk
Music Format: AOR = Album Oriented Rock; MOR = Middle-of-the-Road
Source: Burrelle's Media Directory, 1998 Edition

Television Stations

Name	Ch.	Affiliation	Type	Owner
KTBC	7	Fox	Commercial	Fox Television Stations Inc.
KXAM	14	NBC	Commercial	Lin Broadcasting
KLRU	18	PBS	Public	Capital of Texas Public Telecommunications
KVUE	24	ABC	Commercial	Gannett Company Inc.
KXAN	36	NBC	Commercial	Lin Broadcasting
KEYE	42	CBS	Commercial	Granite Broadcasting Corporation
KNVA	54	n/a	Commercial	54 Broadcasting Inc.

Note: Stations included broadcast in the Austin metro area
Source: Burrelle's Media Directory, 1998 Edition

CLIMATE

Average and Extreme Temperatures

Temperature	Jan	Feb	Mar	Apr	May	Jun	Jul	Aug	Sep	Oct	Nov	Dec	Ann
Extreme High (°F)	90	97	98	98	100	105	109	106	104	98	91	90	109
Average High (°F)	60	64	72	79	85	91	95	96	90	81	70	63	79
Average Temp. (°F)	50	53	61	69	75	82	85	85	80	70	60	52	69
Average Low (°F)	39	43	50	58	65	72	74	74	69	59	49	41	58
Extreme Low (°F)	-2	7	18	35	43	53	64	61	47	32	20	4	-2

Note: Figures cover the years 1948-1990
Source: National Climatic Data Center, International Station Meteorological Climate Summary, 3/95

Average Precipitation/Snowfall/Humidity

Precip./Humidity	Jan	Feb	Mar	Apr	May	Jun	Jul	Aug	Sep	Oct	Nov	Dec	Ann
Avg. Precip. (in.)	1.6	2.3	1.8	2.9	4.3	3.5	1.9	1.9	3.3	3.5	2.1	1.9	31.1
Avg. Snowfall (in.)	1	Tr	Tr	0	0	0	0	0	0	0	Tr	Tr	1
Avg. Rel. Hum. 6am (%)	79	80	79	83	88	89	88	87	86	84	81	79	84
Avg. Rel. Hum. 3pm (%)	53	51	47	50	53	49	43	42	47	47	49	51	48

Note: Figures cover the years 1948-1990; Tr = Trace amounts (<0.05 in. of rain; <0.5 in. of snow)
Source: National Climatic Data Center, International Station Meteorological Climate Summary, 3/95

Weather Conditions

Temperature			Daytime Sky			Precipitation		
10°F & below	32°F & below	90°F & above	Clear	Partly cloudy	Cloudy	0.01 inch or more precip.	0.1 inch or more snow/ice	Thunder-storms
< 1	20	111	105	148	112	83	1	41

Note: Figures are average number of days per year and covers the years 1948-1990
Source: National Climatic Data Center, International Station Meteorological Climate Summary, 3/95

AIR & WATER QUALITY

Maximum Pollutant Concentrations

	Particulate Matter (ug/m^3)	Carbon Monoxide (ppm)	Sulfur Dioxide (ppm)	Nitrogen Dioxide (ppm)	Ozone (ppm)	Lead (ug/m^3)
MSA[1] Level	32	3	n/a	0.018	0.10	n/a
NAAQS[2]	150	9	0.140	0.053	0.12	1.50
Met NAAQS?	Yes	Yes	n/a	Yes	Yes	n/a

Note: (1) Metropolitan Statistical Area - see Appendix A for areas included; (2) National Ambient Air Quality Standards; ppm = parts per million; ug/m^3 = micrograms per cubic meter; n/a not available
Source: EPA, National Air Quality and Emissions Trends Report, 1996

Pollutant Standards Index

In the Austin MSA (see Appendix A for areas included), the Pollutant Standards Index (PSI) exceeded 100 on 0 days in 1996. A PSI value greater than 100 indicates that air quality would be in the unhealthful range on that day. *EPA, National Air Quality and Emissions Trends Report, 1996*

Drinking Water

Water System Name	Pop. Served	Primary Water Source Type	Number of Violations in Fiscal Year 1997	Type of Violation/ Contaminants
Austin Water & Wastewater	548,000	Surface	None	None

Note: Data as of January 16, 1998
Source: EPA, Office of Ground Water and Drinking Water, Safe Drinking Water Information System

Austin tap water is alkaline, soft and fluoridated.
Editor & Publisher Market Guide, 1998

Brownsville, Texas

Background

Brownsville was originally settled by hunters and cowboys near a fort named for General Zachary Taylor. The fort, established at the start of the Mexican War in 1846, was subsequently renamed for Major Jacob Brown who was killed in the fort's defense. Brownsville, incorporated in 1850, is situated on the Rio Grande River across from Matamoros, Mexico, around 20 miles west of the Gulf of Mexico.

Located at the southern tip of Texas, Brownsville is a deep-water port and was once a chief port for the Confederacy during the Civil War. Today Brownsville is a trading center for a major ranching, irrigated farming, and citrus-growing area in the lower Rio Grande Valley. It is a hub for international air, rail and highway transportation; as well as headquarters for commercial fisheries, primarily shrimping. Food processing, petrochemical, aircraft parts and electronic equipment manufacturing comprise the leading industries in the area.

The Gulf of Mexico is the dominant influence on local weather. Prevailing southeast breezes off the Gulf provide a humid but generally mild climate. Winds are frequently strong and gusty in the spring. Brownsville weather is generally favorable for outdoor activities and the Rio Grande Valley is a popular tourist area, especially for Texans who come to enjoy the mild winters.

General Rankings and Evaluative Comments

- Brownsville was ranked #71 out of 300 cities by *Money's* 1997 "Survey of the Best Places to Live." Criteria used: health services, crime, economy, housing, education, transportation, weather, leisure and the arts. The city was ranked #43 in 1996 and #83 in 1995.
  Money, July 1997; Money, September 1996; Money, September 1995

- *Ladies Home Journal* ranked America's 200 largest cities based on the qualities women care about most. Brownsville ranked 160 out of 200. Criteria: low crime rate, good public schools, well-paying jobs, quality health and child care, the presence of women in government, proportion of women-owned businesses, size of the wage gap with men, local economy, divorce rates, the ratio of single men to single women, whether there are laws that require at least the same number of public toilets for women as men, and the probability of good hair days. *Ladies Home Journal, November 1997*

- Brownsville was ranked #162 out of 219 cities in terms of children's health, safety, and economic well-being. Criteria: total population, percent population change, birth rate, child immunization rate, infant mortality rate, percent low birth weight infants, percent of births to teens, physician-to-population ratio, student-to-teacher ratio, dropout rate, unemployment rate, median family income, percent of children in poverty, violent and property crime rates, number of juvenile arrests for violent crimes as a percent of the total crime index, number of days with pollution standard index (PSI) over 100, pounds toxic releases per 1,000 people and number of superfund sites. *Zero Population Growth, Children's Environmental Index 1997*

- According to *Working Mother,* "This year, the Texas Licensed Child Care Association lobbied heavily against proposed standards that would have improved the adult-to-child ratios in many programs. Unfortunately, it prevailed. Lawmakers delayed adoption of the new rules.

  Texas may finally get statewide resource and referral services, however, with new federal funds coming into the state. In addition to helping parents find care, R&Rs may handle both caregiver training and consumer education—a positive development.

  Providers across the state may also get low-interest loans to buy new equipment, upgrade their facilities and do other things to improve the quality of care, under a bill pending in the state legislature that looked likely to pass as we went to press." *Working Mother, July/August 1997*

Business Environment

STATE ECONOMY

State Economic Profile

"The Texas economy remains among the strongest in the nation....

Overall, Texas gained over 141,000 people last year through in-migration. While this is down from the three-year average of over 170,000, it still represents 43% of the Texas population increase. By far, throughout this decade, California has been the largest domestic source of in-migrants into Texas. With the California economy rebounding, in-migration to Texas is slowing.

The slowdown in household growth, coupled with solid residential construction, is creating a slight oversupply throughout the state. As a result, house price growth is decelerating. New residential permits have yet to slow, with new permits up by 14% last year—nearly twice the national increase. The slowdown in population and household growth cannot sustain such robust growth in permits, and as a result, new permits will slow this year.

The Texas economy shows no major imbalances. Although the important computer-chip industry remains moribund, the economy continues to expand solidly. The turnaround in computer memory prices will help the state continue to expand. Texas' growth is becoming increasingly supported by in-migrants. With an increasing presence in high-tech, an attractive business environment, and close proximity to Mexico, Texas will continue to expand faster than the nation and lure workers from other locales. In addition, as an attractive destination for retirees, Texas will continue to experience solid population and household growth as the population ages. Texas is ranked above average for short-and long-term growth." *National Association of Realtors, Economic Profiles: The Fifty States, July 1997*

IMPORTS/EXPORTS

Total Export Sales

Area	1993 ($000)	1994 ($000)	1995 ($000)	1996 ($000)	% Chg. 1993-96	% Chg. 1995-96
MSA[1]	1,904,366	2,113,362	2,245,917	2,612,577	37.2	16.3
U.S.	464,858,354	512,415,609	583,030,524	622,827,063	34.0	6.8

Note: (1) Metropolitan Statistical Area - see Appendix A for areas included
Source: U.S. Department of Commerce, International Trade Association, Metropolitan Area Exports: An Export Performance Report on Over 250 U.S. Cities, October 1997

Imports/Exports by Port

Type	Cargo Value			Share of U.S. Total	
	1995 (US$mil.)	1996 (US$mil.)	% Change 1995-1996	1995 (%)	1996 (%)
Imports	155	180	16.73	0.04	0.05
Exports	90	99	10.13	0.04	0.04

Source: Global Trade Information Services, WaterBorne Trade Atlas 1997

CITY FINANCES

City Government Finances

Component	FY92 ($000)	FY92 (per capita $)
Revenue	98,721	852.34
Expenditure	119,602	1,032.62
Debt Outstanding	241,921	2,088.69
Cash & Securities	66,349	572.84

Source: U.S. Bureau of the Census, City Government Finances: 1991-92

City Government Revenue by Source

Source	FY92 ($000)	FY92 (per capita $)	FY92 (%)
From Federal Government	7,181	62.00	7.3
From State Governments	772	6.67	0.8
From Local Governments	231	1.99	0.2
Property Taxes	9,607	82.94	9.7
General Sales Taxes	6,402	55.27	6.5
Selective Sales Taxes	2,057	17.76	2.1
Income Taxes	0	0.00	0.0
Current Charges	14,347	123.87	14.5
Utility/Liquor Store	47,726	412.06	48.3
Employee Retirement[1]	0	0.00	0.0
Other	10,398	89.77	10.5

Note: (1) Excludes "city contributions," classified as "nonrevenue," intragovernmental transfers.
Source: U.S. Bureau of the Census, City Government Finances: 1991-92

City Government Expenditures by Function

Function	FY92 ($000)	FY92 (per capita $)	FY92 (%)
Educational Services	229	1.98	0.2
Employee Retirement[1]	0	0.00	0.0
Environment/Housing	14,205	122.64	11.9
Government Administration	2,635	22.75	2.2
Interest on General Debt	2,030	17.53	1.7
Public Safety	12,642	109.15	10.6
Social Services	1,228	10.60	1.0
Transportation	11,415	98.55	9.5
Utility/Liquor Store	74,209	640.70	62.0
Other	1,009	8.71	0.8

Note: (1) Payments to beneficiaries including withdrawal of contributions.
Source: U.S. Bureau of the Census, City Government Finances: 1991-92

Municipal Bond Ratings

Area	Moody's	S & P
Brownsville	Baa1	A

Note: n/a not available; n/r not rated
Source: Moody's Bond Record, 2/98; Statistical Abstract of the U.S., 1997;
Governing Magazine, 9/97, 3/98

POPULATION

Population Growth

Area	1980	1990	% Chg. 1980-90	July 1996 Estimate	% Chg. 1990-96
City	84,997	98,962	16.4	132,091	33.5
MSA[1]	209,727	260,120	24.0	315,015	21.1
U.S.	226,545,805	248,765,170	9.8	265,179,411	6.6

Note: (1) Metropolitan Statistical Area - see Appendix A for areas included
Source: 1980/1990 Census of Housing and Population, Summary Tape File 3C;
Census Bureau Population Estimates

Population Characteristics

Race	City 1980 Population	%	City 1990 Population	%	% Chg. 1980-90	MSA[1] 1990 Population	%
White	67,491	79.4	83,760	84.6	24.1	214,424	82.4
Black	178	0.2	180	0.2	1.1	903	0.3
Amer Indian/Esk/Aleut	106	0.1	337	0.3	217.9	615	0.2
Asian/Pacific Islander	166	0.2	346	0.3	108.4	643	0.2
Other	17,056	20.1	14,339	14.5	-15.9	43,535	16.7
Hispanic Origin[2]	71,215	83.8	89,186	90.1	25.2	212,592	81.7

Note: (1) Metropolitan Statistical Area - see Appendix A for areas included;
(2) people of Hispanic origin can be of any race
Source: 1980/1990 Census of Housing and Population, Summary Tape File 3C

Ancestry

Area	German	Irish	English	Italian	U.S.	French	Polish	Dutch
City	2.8	1.7	1.7	0.4	1.8	0.7	0.4	0.2
MSA[1]	5.7	3.6	3.9	0.6	2.1	1.1	0.6	0.5
U.S.	23.3	15.6	13.1	5.9	5.3	4.2	3.8	2.5

Note: Figures are percentages and include persons that reported multiple ancestry (eg. if a person reported being Irish and Italian, they were included in both columns); (1) Metropolitan Statistical Area - see Appendix A for areas included
Source: 1990 Census of Population and Housing, Summary Tape File 3C

Age

Area	Median Age (Years)	Under 5	Under 18	18-24	25-44	45-64	65+	80+
City	25.9	9.0	36.6	11.7	28.0	15.1	8.6	1.6
MSA[1]	27.4	8.9	35.4	10.9	27.5	15.7	10.5	1.9
U.S.	32.9	7.3	25.6	10.5	32.6	18.7	12.5	2.8

Note: (1) Metropolitan Statistical Area - see Appendix A for areas included
Source: 1990 Census of Population and Housing, Summary Tape File 3C

Male/Female Ratio

Area	Number of males per 100 females (all ages)	Number of males per 100 females (18 years old+)
City	89.3	82.5
MSA[1]	91.8	86.6
U.S.	95.0	91.9

Note: (1) Metropolitan Statistical Area - see Appendix A for areas included
Source: 1990 Census of Population, General Population Characteristics

INCOME

Per Capita/Median/Average Income

Area	Per Capita ($)	Median Household ($)	Average Household ($)
City	6,284	15,890	23,219
MSA[1]	7,125	17,336	24,858
U.S.	14,420	30,056	38,453

Note: all figures are for 1989; (1) Metropolitan Statistical Area - see Appendix A for areas included
Source: 1990 Census of Population and Housing, Summary Tape File 3C

Household Income Distribution by Race

Income ($)	City (%)					U.S. (%)				
	Total	White	Black	Other	Hisp.[1]	Total	White	Black	Other	Hisp.[1]
Less than 5,000	16.1	16.2	21.1	15.5	17.8	6.2	4.8	15.2	8.6	8.8
5,000 - 9,999	16.4	16.1	0.0	18.1	17.9	9.3	8.6	14.2	9.9	11.1
10,000 - 14,999	15.3	15.7	0.0	13.4	16.3	8.8	8.5	11.0	9.8	11.0
15,000 - 24,999	20.2	20.0	35.1	21.1	19.9	17.5	17.3	18.9	18.5	20.5
25,000 - 34,999	12.8	12.7	0.0	13.6	12.0	15.8	16.1	14.2	15.4	16.4
35,000 - 49,999	9.5	9.2	36.8	11.0	8.8	17.9	18.6	13.3	16.1	16.0
50,000 - 74,999	6.6	6.9	7.0	5.0	5.3	15.0	15.8	9.3	13.4	11.1
75,000 - 99,999	1.8	1.9	0.0	1.6	1.0	5.1	5.5	2.6	4.7	3.1
100,000+	1.3	1.4	0.0	0.8	0.9	4.4	4.8	1.3	3.7	1.9

Note: all figures are for 1989; (1) people of Hispanic origin can be of any race
Source: 1990 Census of Population and Housing, Summary Tape File 3C

Effective Buying Income

Area	Per Capita ($)	Median Household ($)	Average Household ($)
City	7,361	19,372	27,978
MSA[1]	8,600	21,681	31,061
U.S.	15,444	33,201	41,849

Note: data as of 1/1/97; (1) Metropolitan Statistical Area - see Appendix A for areas included
Source: Standard Rate & Data Service, Newspaper Advertising Source, 2/98

Effective Household Buying Income Distribution

Area	% of Households Earning						
	$10,000 -$19,999	$20,000 -$34,999	$35,000 -$49,999	$50,000 -$74,999	$75,000 -$99,000	$100,000 -$124,999	$125,000 and up
City	25.3	22.6	11.6	9.1	3.2	0.9	1.0
MSA[1]	23.7	22.9	13.1	10.4	3.9	1.3	1.3
U.S.	16.5	23.4	18.3	18.2	6.4	2.1	2.4

Note: data as of 1/1/97; (1) Metropolitan Statistical Area - see Appendix A for areas included
Source: Standard Rate & Data Service, Newspaper Advertising Source, 2/98

Poverty Rates by Race and Age

Area	Total (%)	By Race (%)				By Age (%)		
		White	Black	Other	Hisp.[2]	Under 5 years old	Under 18 years old	65 years and over
City	43.9	44.3	16.4	42.0	47.3	54.0	54.3	34.5
MSA[1]	39.7	38.7	24.1	44.4	45.9	50.9	50.7	26.9
U.S.	13.1	9.8	29.5	23.1	25.3	20.1	18.3	12.8

Note: figures show the percent of people living below the poverty line in 1989. The average poverty threshold was $12,674 for a family of four in 1989; (1) Metropolitan Statistical Area - see Appendix A for areas included; (2) people of Hispanic origin can be of any race
Source: 1990 Census of Population and Housing, Summary Tape File 3C

EMPLOYMENT

Labor Force and Employment

Area	Civilian Labor Force			Workers Employed		
	Dec. '95	Dec. '96	% Chg.	Dec. '95	Dec. '96	% Chg.
City	46,450	48,057	3.5	40,580	41,784	3.0
MSA[1]	123,355	127,539	3.4	109,840	113,098	3.0
U.S.	134,583,000	136,742,000	1.6	127,903,000	130,785,000	2.3

Note: Data is not seasonally adjusted and covers workers 16 years of age and older;
(1) Metropolitan Statistical Area - see Appendix A for areas included
Source: Bureau of Labor Statistics, http://stats.bls.gov

Unemployment Rate

Area	1997											
	Jan.	Feb.	Mar.	Apr.	May	Jun.	Jul.	Aug.	Sep.	Oct.	Nov.	Dec.
City	14.9	14.9	14.4	14.0	13.7	16.3	16.3	14.0	13.4	13.4	14.2	13.1
MSA[1]	12.9	13.0	12.5	12.1	11.9	14.2	14.2	12.1	11.6	11.7	12.3	11.3
U.S.	5.9	5.7	5.5	4.8	4.7	5.2	5.0	4.8	4.7	4.4	4.3	4.4

Note: Data is not seasonally adjusted and covers workers 16 years of age and older; All figures are percentages; (1) Metropolitan Statistical Area - see Appendix A for areas included
Source: Bureau of Labor Statistics, http://stats.bls.gov

Employment by Industry

Sector	MSA[1]		U.S.
	Number of Employees	Percent of Total	Percent of Total
Services	28,100	28.2	29.0
Retail Trade	20,300	20.3	18.5
Government	23,400	23.4	16.1
Manufacturing	12,200	12.2	15.0
Finance/Insurance/Real Estate	3,600	3.6	5.7
Wholesale Trade	4,200	4.2	5.4
Transportation/Public Utilities	4,400	4.4	5.3
Construction/Mining	3,600	3.6	5.0

Note: Figures cover non-farm employment as of 12/97 and are not seasonally adjusted;
(1) Metropolitan Statistical Area - see Appendix A for areas included
Source: Bureau of Labor Statistics, http://stats.bls.gov

Employment by Occupation

Occupation Category	City (%)	MSA[1] (%)	U.S. (%)
White Collar	55.1	52.3	58.1
Executive/Admin./Management	9.3	9.8	12.3
Professional	14.6	13.3	14.1
Technical & Related Support	2.3	2.4	3.7
Sales	14.4	13.1	11.8
Administrative Support/Clerical	14.5	13.8	16.3
Blue Collar	26.1	26.7	26.2
Precision Production/Craft/Repair	9.9	10.5	11.3
Machine Operators/Assem./Insp.	7.9	7.3	6.8
Transportation/Material Movers	3.6	4.3	4.1
Cleaners/Helpers/Laborers	4.7	4.6	3.9
Services	16.5	16.9	13.2
Farming/Forestry/Fishing	2.3	4.1	2.5

Note: figures cover employed persons 16 years old and over;
(1) Metropolitan Statistical Area - see Appendix A for areas included
Source: 1990 Census of Population and Housing, Summary Tape File 3C

Occupational Employment Projections: 1993 - 2000

Occupations Expected to have the Largest Job Growth (ranked by numerical growth)	Fast-Growing Occupations[1] (ranked by percent growth)
1. Salespersons, retail	1. Demonstrators/promoters/models
2. Teachers, secondary school	2. Paralegals
3. Cashiers	3. Cleaners/servants, private home
4. Home health aides	4. Human services workers
5. Teachers, elementary school	5. Computer engineers
6. General office clerks	6. Computer systems analysts
7. Food preparation workers	7. Corrections officers & jailers
8. First line supervisor, sales & related	8. Home health aides
9. Registered nurses	9. Concrete and terrazzo finishers
10. General managers & top executives	10. Personal and home care aides

Projections cover Cameron, Hidalgo and Willacy Counties.
Note: (1) Includes occupations with absolute job growth of 100 or more
Source: Texas Employment Commission, Texas Employment Projections Reporting System, Statewide and Regional Projections 1993-2000, Ver. 1.0

Average Wages

Occupation	Wage	Occupation	Wage
White-Collar Occupations	$/Hour	**Blue-Collar Occupations**	$/Hour
Accountants/Auditors	-	Assemblers	-
Bookkeepers	6.80	Carpenters	-
Cashiers	7.02	Electricians	-
Clerks, General Office	7.45	Groundskeepers, except farm	-
Clerks, Order	-	Hand Packers/Packagers	-
Computer Programmers	-	Helpers/Mechanics/Repairers	-
Computer Systems Analysts	-	Machine Operators, Textile Sewing	7.11
Data Entry Keyers	-	Mechanics, Automobile	-
Drafters	-	Plumbers/Pipefitters/Steamfitters	-
Electrical/Electronic Tech.	-	Printing Press Operators	-
Engineers, Mechanical	-	Roofers	-
Managers, Medicine/Health	24.56	Stock Handlers/Baggers	5.63
Managers, Financial	-	Truck Drivers	-
Nurses, Licensed Practical	13.30	**Service Occupations**	
Nurses, Registered	-	Cooks	6.31
Receptionists	-	Health Aides, except nursing	7.46
School Teachers, Secondary	23.45	Janitors/Cleaners	6.02
Secretaries	8.88	Nursing Aides/Orderlies/Attendants	6.49
Social Workers	-	Police/Detectives	-
Teachers' Aides	7.27	Waiters/Waitresses	-

Note: Figures are for May 1997 and cover the Brownsville-Harlingen-San Benito Metropolitan Statistical Area (see Appendix A for areas included). Dashes indicate that data was not available.
Source: Bureau of Labor Statistics, National Compensation Survey, December 1997

TAXES

Major State and Local Tax Rates

State Corp. Income (%)	State Personal Income (%)	Residential Property (effective rate per $100)	Sales & Use		State Gasoline (cents/ gallon)	State Cigarette (cents/ 20-pack)
			State (%)	Local (%)		
None[a]	None	n/a	6.25	2.0	20	41

Note: Personal/corporate income tax rates as of 1/97. Sales, gasoline and cigarette tax rates as of 1/98; (a) Texas imposes a franchise tax of 4.5% of earned surplus
Source: Federation of Tax Administrators, www.taxadmin.org; Washington D.C. Department of Finance and Revenue, Tax Rates and Tax Burdens in the District of Columbia: A Nationwide Comparison, June 1997; Chamber of Commerce

Total Taxes Per Capita and as a Percent of Income

Area	Per Capita Income ($)	Per Capita Taxes ($)			Taxes as Pct. of Income (%)		
		Total	Federal	State/Local	Total	Federal	State/Local
Texas	24,145	8,118	5,538	2,580	33.6	22.9	10.7
U.S.	26,187	9,205	6,127	3,078	35.2	23.4	11.8

Note: Figures are for 1997
Source: Tax Foundation, Web Site, www.taxfoundation.org

COMMERCIAL REAL ESTATE

Data not available at time of publication.

COMMERCIAL UTILITIES

Typical Monthly Electric Bills

Area	Commercial Service ($/month)		Industrial Service ($/month)	
	12 kW demand 1,500 kWh	100 kW demand 30,000 kWh	1,000 kW demand 400,000 kWh	20,000 kW demand 10,000,000 kWh
City	221	2,326	23,116	411,990
U.S.	162	2,360	25,590	545,677

Note: Based on rates in effect July 1, 1997
Source: Edison Electric Institute, Typical Residential, Commercial and Industrial Bills, Summer 1997

TRANSPORTATION

Transportation Statistics

Avg. travel time to work (min.)	16.7
Interstate highways	None
Bus lines	
In-city	Brownsville Urban System
Inter-city	4
Passenger air service	
Airport	South Padre Island International
Airlines	1
Aircraft departures	2,576 (1995)
Enplaned passengers	71,297 (1995)
Rail service	No Amtrak Service
Motor freight carriers	17
Major waterways/ports	Port of Brownsville

Source: OAG, Business Travel Planner, Summer 1997; Editor & Publisher Market Guide, 1998; FAA Airport Activity Statistics, 1996; Amtrak National Time Table, Northeast Timetable, Fall/Winter 1997-98; 1990 Census of Population and Housing, STF 3C; Chamber of Commerce/Economic Development 1997; Jane's Urban Transport Systems 1997-98; Transit Fact Book 1997

Means of Transportation to Work

Area	Car/Truck/Van		Public Transportation			Bicycle	Walked	Other Means	Worked at Home
	Drove Alone	Car-pooled	Bus	Subway	Railroad				
City	67.0	22.6	2.3	0.0	0.0	0.3	3.8	1.6	2.5
MSA[1]	69.3	21.4	1.1	0.0	0.0	0.3	3.3	1.6	3.0
U.S.	73.2	13.4	3.0	1.5	0.5	0.4	3.9	1.2	3.0

Note: figures shown are percentages and only include workers 16 years old and over;
(1) Metropolitan Statistical Area - see Appendix A for areas included
Source: 1990 Census of Population and Housing, Summary Tape File 3C

BUSINESSES

Major Business Headquarters

Company Name	1997 Rankings	
	Fortune 500	Forbes 500

No companies listed.

Note: Companies listed are located in the city; Dashes indicate no ranking
Fortune 500: companies that produce a 10-K are ranked 1 - 500 based on 1996 revenue
Forbes 500: private companies are ranked 1 - 500 based on 1996 revenue
Source: Forbes 12/1/97; Fortune 4/28/97

Minority Business Opportunity

One of the 500 largest Hispanic-owned companies in the U.S. are located in Brownsville. *Hispanic Business, June 1997*

Brownsville was listed among the top 25 metropolitan areas in terms of the number of Hispanic-owned companies. The city was ranked number 24 with 9,945 companies. *Hispanic Business, May 1997*

HOTELS & MOTELS

Hotels/Motels

Area	Hotels/ Motels	Rooms	Luxury-Level Hotels/Motels		Average Minimum Rates ($)		
			♦♦♦♦	♦♦♦♦♦	♦♦	♦♦♦	♦♦♦♦
City	7	943	0	0	n/a	n/a	n/a
Airport	2	299	0	0	n/a	n/a	n/a
Total	9	1,242	0	0	n/a	n/a	n/a

Note: n/a not available; Classifications range from one diamond (budget properties with basic amenities) to five diamond (luxury properties with the finest service, rooms and facilities).
Source: OAG, Business Travel Planner, Summer 1997

CONVENTION CENTERS

Major Convention Centers

Center Name	Meeting Rooms	Exhibit Space (sf)
Jacob Brown Auditorium	n/a	10,944

Note: n/a not available
Source: Trade Shows Worldwide 1997

Living Environment

COST OF LIVING

Cost of Living Index

Composite Index	Housing	Utilities	Groceries	Health Care	Trans-portation	Misc. Goods/Services
94.1	77.6	108.9	95.1	101.4	103.6	100.1

Note: U.S. = 100
Source: ACCRA, Cost of Living Index, 3rd Quarter 1997

HOUSING

Median Home Prices and Housing Affordability

Area	Median Price[2] 3rd Qtr. 1997 ($)	HOI[3] 3rd Qtr. 1997	Afford-ability Rank[4]
MSA[1]	n/a	n/a	n/a
U.S.	127,000	63.7	–

Note: (1) Metropolitan Statistical Area - see Appendix A for areas included; (2) U.S. figures calculated from the sales of 625,000 new and existing homes in 195 markets; (3) Housing Opportunity Index - percent of homes sold that were within the reach of the median income household at the prevailing mortgage interest rate; (4) Rank is from 1-195 with 1 being most affordable; n/a not available
Source: National Association of Home Builders, Housing Opportunity Index, 3rd Quarter 1997

Average New Home Price

Area	Price ($)
City	101,300
U.S.	135,710

Note: Figures are based on a new home with 1,800 sq. ft. of living area on an 8,000 sq. ft. lot.
Source: ACCRA, Cost of Living Index, 3rd Quarter 1997

Average Apartment Rent

Area	Rent ($/mth)
City	483
U.S.	569

Note: Figures are based on an unfurnished two bedroom, 1-1/2 or 2 bath apartment, approximately 950 sq. ft. in size, excluding all utilities except water
Source: ACCRA, Cost of Living Index, 3rd Quarter 1997

RESIDENTIAL UTILITIES

Average Residential Utility Costs

Area	All Electric ($/mth)	Part Electric ($/mth)	Other Energy ($/mth)	Phone ($/mth)
City	117.03	–	–	14.47
U.S.	109.40	55.25	43.64	19.48

Source: ACCRA, Cost of Living Index, 3rd Quarter 1997

HEALTH CARE

Average Health Care Costs

Area	Hospital ($/day)	Doctor ($/visit)	Dentist ($/visit)
City	380.50	49.20	65.40
U.S.	392.91	48.76	60.84

Note: Hospital - based on a semi-private room. Doctor - based on a general practitioner's routine exam of an established patient. Dentist - based on adult teeth cleaning and periodic oral exam.
Source: ACCRA, Cost of Living Index, 3rd Quarter 1997

Distribution of Office-Based Physicians

| Area | Family/Gen. Practitioners | Specialists | | |
		Medical	Surgical	Other
MSA[1]	44	111	79	46

Note: Data as of 12/31/96; (1) Metropolitan Statistical Area - see Appendix A for areas included
Source: American Medical Assn., Physician Characteristics & Distribution in the U.S., 1997-1998

Hospitals

Brownsville has 2 general medical and surgical hospitals. *AHA Guide to the Healthcare Field 1997-98*

EDUCATION

Public School District Statistics

District Name	Num. Sch.	Enroll.	Classroom Teachers[1]	Pupils per Teacher	Minority Pupils (%)	Current Exp.[2] ($/pupil)
Brownsville ISD	42	40,270	2,682	15.0	97.1	4,906

Note: Data covers the 1995-1996 school year unless otherwise noted; (1) Excludes teachers reported as working in school district offices rather than in schools; (2) Based on 1993-94 enrollment collected by the Census Bureau, not the enrollment figure shown in column 3; SD = School District; ISD = Independent School District; n/a not available
Source: National Center for Education Statistics, Common Core of Data Survey; Bureau of the Census

Educational Quality

School District	Education Quotient[1]	Graduate Outcome[2]	Community Index[3]	Resource Index[4]
Brownsville	70.0	51.0	51.0	109.0

Note: Nearly 1,000 secondary school districts were rated in terms of educational quality. The scores range from a low of 50 to a high of 150; (1) Average of the Graduate Outcome, Community and Resource indexes; (2) Based on graduation rates and college board scores (SAT/ACT); (3) Based on the surrounding community's average level of education and the area's average income level; (4) Based on teacher salaries, per-pupil expenditures and student-teacher ratios.
Source: Expansion Management, Ratings Issue 1997

Educational Attainment by Race

| Area | High School Graduate (%) | | | | | Bachelor's Degree (%) | | | | |
	Total	White	Black	Other	Hisp.[2]	Total	White	Black	Other	Hisp.[2]
City	45.5	46.4	60.9	40.3	39.1	12.2	12.7	45.3	9.2	8.7
MSA[1]	50.0	52.1	57.8	39.1	39.3	12.0	12.9	21.5	6.8	7.3
U.S.	75.2	77.9	63.1	60.4	49.8	20.3	21.5	11.4	19.4	9.2

Note: figures shown cover persons 25 years old and over; (1) Metropolitan Statistical Area - see Appendix A for areas included; (2) people of Hispanic origin can be of any race
Source: 1990 Census of Population and Housing, Summary Tape File 3C

School Enrollment by Type

| Area | Preprimary | | | | Elementary/High School | | | |
| | Public | | Private | | Public | | Private | |
	Enrollment	%	Enrollment	%	Enrollment	%	Enrollment	%
City	1,032	76.7	314	23.3	27,286	95.5	1,284	4.5
MSA[1]	3,016	78.3	834	21.7	67,669	96.3	2,573	3.7
U.S.	2,679,029	59.5	1,824,256	40.5	38,379,689	90.2	4,187,099	9.8

Note: figures shown cover persons 3 years old and over;
(1) Metropolitan Statistical Area - see Appendix A for areas included
Source: 1990 Census of Population and Housing, Summary Tape File 3C

School Enrollment by Race

Area	Preprimary (%)				Elementary/High School (%)			
	White	Black	Other	Hisp.[1]	White	Black	Other	Hisp.[1]
City	86.1	0.4	13.4	90.1	84.5	0.3	15.3	94.6
MSA[2]	80.9	0.7	18.4	84.1	80.6	0.3	19.1	91.1
U.S.	80.4	12.5	7.1	7.8	74.1	15.6	10.3	12.5

Note: figures shown cover persons 3 years old and over; (1) people of Hispanic origin can be of any race; (2) Metropolitan Statistical Area - see Appendix A for areas included
Source: 1990 Census of Population and Housing, Summary Tape File 3C

SAT/ACT Scores

Area/District	1996 SAT				1996 ACT	
	Percent of Graduates Tested (%)	Average Math Score	Average Verbal Score	Average Combined Score	Percent of Graduates Tested (%)	Average Composite Score
Brownsville ISD	15	444	429	873	n/a	17.7
State	48	500	495	995	30	20.2
U.S.	41	508	505	1,013	35	20.9

Note: Math and verbal SAT scores are out of a possible 800; ACT scores are out of a possible 36
Caution: Comparing or ranking states/cities on the basis of SAT/ACT scores alone is invalid and strongly discouraged by the The College Board and The American College Testing Program as students who take the tests are self-selected and do not represent the entire student population. 1996 SAT scores cannot be compared to previous years due to recentering.
Source: Brownsville ISD, Research & Evaluation, 1996; College Board, 1996; American College Testing Program, 1996

Classroom Teacher Salaries in Public Schools

District	B.A. Degree		M.A. Degree		Ph.D. Degree	
	Min. ($)	Max. ($)	Min. ($)	Max. ($)	Min. ($)	Max. ($)
Brownsville	n/a	n/a	n/a	n/a	n/a	n/a
Average[1]	26,120	39,270	28,175	44,667	31,643	49,825

Note: Salaries are for 1996-1997; (1) Based on all school districts covered; n/a not available
Source: American Federation of Teachers (unpublished data)

Higher Education

Two-Year Colleges		Four-Year Colleges		Medical Schools	Law Schools	Voc/ Tech
Public	Private	Public	Private			
1	0	1	0	0	0	1

Source: College Blue Book, Occupational Education 1997; Medical School Admission Requirements, 1998-99; Peterson's Guide to Two-Year Colleges, 1997; Peterson's Guide to Four-Year Colleges, 1997; Barron's Guide to Law Schools 1997

MAJOR EMPLOYERS

Major Employers

Trico Technologies Corp. (motor vehicle parts)

Brownsville-Valley Regional Medical Center

Mextile (men's clothing)

Lopez Supermarket

M.C. Fabrication Industries (industrial machinery)

Leonard Electric Products

Eagle Coach Corp. (bus assembly)

Note: companies listed are located in the city
Source: Dun's Business Rankings 1997; Ward's Business Directory, 1997

PUBLIC SAFETY

Crime Rate

Area	All Crimes	Violent Crimes				Property Crimes		
		Murder	Forcible Rape	Robbery	Aggrav. Assault	Burglary	Larceny -Theft	Motor Vehicle Theft
City	8,397.5	9.4	18.7	196.6	754.8	1,130.1	5,881.2	406.8
Suburbs[1]	4,897.1	4.2	5.7	54.3	253.7	1,241.0	3,114.2	224.0
MSA[2]	6,228.1	6.1	10.7	108.4	444.3	1,198.8	4,166.3	293.5
U.S.	5,078.9	7.4	36.1	202.4	388.2	943.0	2,975.9	525.9

Note: Crime rate is the number of crimes per 100,000 pop.; (1) defined as all areas within the MSA but located outside the central city; (2) Metropolitan Statistical Area - see Appendix A for areas incl.
Source: FBI Uniform Crime Reports 1996

RECREATION

Culture and Recreation

Museums	Symphony Orchestras	Opera Companies	Dance Companies	Professional Theatres	Zoos	Pro Sports Teams
1	0	0	0	1	1	0

Source: International Directory of the Performing Arts, 1996; Official Museum Directory, 1998; Chamber of Commerce/Economic Development 1997

Library System

The Brownsville Public Library has no branches, holdings of 66,910 volumes and a budget of $860,334 (1994-1995). *American Library Directory, 1997-1998*

MEDIA

Newspapers

Name	Type	Freq.	Distribution	Circulation
The Brownsville Herald	General	7x/wk	Local	17,745
El Heraldo de Brownsville	Hispanic	7x/wk	Local	18,172

Note: Includes newspapers with circulations of 500 or more located in the city; Source: Burrelle's Media Directory, 1998 Edition

AM Radio Stations

Call Letters	Freq. (kHz)	Target Audience	Station Format	Music Format
KVJY	840	n/a	M	Easy Listening/MOR
KMIL	1330	General	M/N/S	Country
KBOR	1600	Hispanic	M/N	Spanish

Note: Stations included broadcast in the Brownsville metro area; n/a not available
Station Format: E = Educational; M = Music; N = News; S = Sports; T = Talk
Music Format: AOR = Album Oriented Rock; MOR = Middle-of-the-Road
Source: Burrelle's Media Directory, 1998 Edition

FM Radio Stations

Call Letters	Freq. (mHz)	Target Audience	Station Format	Music Format
KHID	88.1	General	M/N/S	n/a
KBNR	88.3	Hispanic	M	Spanish
KMBH	88.9	General	M/N/S	n/a
KZSP	95.3	General	M	Country
KTEX	100.3	General	M	Country
KTJX	105.5	Hispanic	M/N	Spanish
KTJN	106.3	Hispanic	M	Spanish

Note: Stations included broadcast in the Brownsville metro area; n/a not available
Station Format: E = Educational; M = Music; N = News; S = Sports; T = Talk
Source: Burrelle's Media Directory, 1998 Edition

Television Stations

Name	Ch.	Affiliation	Type	Owner
KGBT	4	CBS	Commercial	Draper Communications Inc.
KVEO	23	NBC	Commercial	Communications Corporation of America
KLUJ	44	TBN	Non-Commercial	Community Educational TV Inc.
KMBH	60	PBS	Public	RGV Educational Broadcasting Inc.

Note: Stations included broadcast in the Brownsville metro area
Source: Burrelle's Media Directory, 1998 Edition

CLIMATE

Average and Extreme Temperatures

Temperature	Jan	Feb	Mar	Apr	May	Jun	Jul	Aug	Sep	Oct	Nov	Dec	Ann
Extreme High (°F)	93	94	106	102	102	102	101	102	99	96	97	94	106
Average High (°F)	70	73	78	83	87	91	93	93	90	85	78	72	83
Average Temp. (°F)	60	63	69	75	80	83	84	85	82	76	68	63	74
Average Low (°F)	51	53	59	66	72	75	76	76	73	66	59	53	65
Extreme Low (°F)	19	22	32	38	52	60	67	63	56	40	33	16	16

Note: Figures cover the years 1948-1990
Source: National Climatic Data Center, International Station Meteorological Climate Summary, 3/95

Average Precipitation/Snowfall/Humidity

Precip./Humidity	Jan	Feb	Mar	Apr	May	Jun	Jul	Aug	Sep	Oct	Nov	Dec	Ann
Avg. Precip. (in.)	1.4	1.4	0.6	1.5	2.5	2.8	1.8	2.6	5.6	3.2	1.5	1.1	25.8
Avg. Snowfall (in.)	Tr	Tr	0	0	0	0	0	0	0	0	Tr	Tr	Tr
Avg. Rel. Hum. 6am (%)	88	89	88	89	90	91	92	92	91	89	87	87	89
Avg. Rel. Hum. 3pm (%)	62	60	57	58	60	59	54	55	60	58	59	61	59

Note: Figures cover the years 1948-1990; Tr = Trace amounts (<0.05 in. of rain; <0.5 in. of snow)
Source: National Climatic Data Center, International Station Meteorological Climate Summary, 3/95

Weather Conditions

Temperature			Daytime Sky			Precipitation		
32°F & below	45°F & below	90°F & above	Clear	Partly cloudy	Cloudy	0.01 inch or more precip.	0.1 inch or more snow/ice	Thunder-storms
2	30	116	86	180	99	72	0	27

Note: Figures are average number of days per year and covers the years 1948-1990
Source: National Climatic Data Center, International Station Meteorological Climate Summary, 3/95

AIR & WATER QUALITY

Maximum Pollutant Concentrations

	Particulate Matter (ug/m³)	Carbon Monoxide (ppm)	Sulfur Dioxide (ppm)	Nitrogen Dioxide (ppm)	Ozone (ppm)	Lead (ug/m³)
MSA[1] Level	40	2	0.004	n/a	0.08	0.02
NAAQS[2]	150	9	0.140	0.053	0.12	1.50
Met NAAQS?	Yes	Yes	Yes	n/a	Yes	Yes

Note: (1) Metropolitan Statistical Area - see Appendix A for areas included; (2) National Ambient Air Quality Standards; ppm = parts per million; ug/m³ = micrograms per cubic meter; n/a not available
Source: EPA, National Air Quality and Emissions Trends Report, 1996

Pollutant Standards Index

Data not available. *EPA, National Air Quality and Emissions Trends Report, 1996*

Drinking Water

Water System Name	Pop. Served	Primary Water Source Type	Number of Violations in Fiscal Year 1997	Type of Violation/ Contaminants
Brownsville Public Utility Dist.	130,000	Surface	1	(1)

Note: Data as of January 16, 1998; (1) System failed to report violation of the Surface Water Treatment Rule.
Source: EPA, Office of Ground Water and Drinking Water, Safe Drinking Water Information System

Brownsville tap water is alkaline and medium hard.
Editor & Publisher Market Guide, 1998

Corpus Christi, Texas

Background

On the Roman Catholic feast day of Corpus Christi in the year 1519, the Spanish explorer Alonso de Pineda sailed into a beautiful bay on the Gulf of Mexico. Naming the bay Corpus Christi in honor of the feast day, Pineda claimed the region for Spain and then sailed off to other lands. For more than 300 years, the area was left to the native tribes and the occasional pirate. But in 1838 Henry Lawrence Kinney built a small trading post at the mouth of the Nueces River overlooking the bay. The trading post soon became the unofficial capital of southeastern Texas and the town of Corpus Christi was born.

The early settlers in Corpus Christi helped to build the city and the Republic of Texas, which later became the state of Texas. General Zachary Taylor camped in the town before the beginning of the Mexican-American War in 1846, and during the Civil War the city was bombarded and then occupied by Federal troops. At the turn of the century, railroads made their way to the area. Development was further strengthened by discovering natural gas reserves and the construction of a deep water port. When oil was discovered in 1939, the city's continued growth was assured.

Corpus Christi's basic industries are oil refining, manufacturing and commercial fishing. Surrounding the city are natural gas and oil fields, and large cattle-ranching concerns. Agricultural areas grow cotton, sorghum, flaxseed and truck crops. Products are sent to the port on Corpus Christi Bay, which is the deepest on the Gulf and the seventh largest in the country.

The bay, an inlet of the Gulf of Mexico, provides beauty, sport, commerce, food and even protection for the town. 25 miles long and three to ten miles wide, the town and the bay are protected from Gulf storm surges by Mustang Island, a barrier island running along the bay's eastern side. The bay's deep water harbor protects the shipping that serves the petroleum, chemical and agricultural industries. Oyster shells harvested from its waters are used in Corpus Christi's chemical plants, while the oysters, along with the other seafood caught by the commercial fishing fleets, feed the townspeople and the nation. Resorts catering to fishing, waterfowl hunting, boating and water sports are located along the bay and on the coastal barrier islands, including the Padre Island National Seashore which stretches 113 miles southward almost to Brownsville.

The huge Corpus Christi Naval Air Station , built in 1941, and an Army depot further support the economy, while the Texas A&M University-Corpus Christi campus and Del Mar College provide first class education. But whether hard at work or school, the warm, subtropical weather lends to an informal and relaxed Texas style. While nearly half of the residents are Mexican-American, a wide mix of peoples makes Corpus Christi a cosmopolitan city with a decidedly Tex-Mex flair. With the brilliant Texas sun shining down through the clear coastal air, it's easy to see why Corpus Christi's title is "Sparkling City by the Sea."

General Rankings and Evaluative Comments

■ Corpus Christi was ranked #110 out of 300 cities by *Money's* 1997 "Survey of the Best Places to Live." Criteria used: health services, crime, economy, housing, education, transportation, weather, leisure and the arts. The city was ranked #99 in 1996 and #164 in 1995. *Money, July 1997; Money, September 1996; Money, September 1995*

■ *Ladies Home Journal* ranked America's 200 largest cities based on the qualities women care about most. Corpus Christi ranked 185 out of 200. Criteria: low crime rate, good public schools, well-paying jobs, quality health and child care, the presence of women in government, proportion of women-owned businesses, size of the wage gap with men, local economy, divorce rates, the ratio of single men to single women, whether there are laws that require at least the same number of public toilets for women as men, and the probability of good hair days. *Ladies Home Journal, November 1997*

■ Corpus Christi was ranked #118 out of 219 cities in terms of children's health, safety, and economic well-being. Criteria: total population, percent population change, birth rate, child immunization rate, infant mortality rate, percent low birth weight infants, percent of births to teens, physician-to-population ratio, student-to-teacher ratio, dropout rate, unemployment rate, median family income, percent of children in poverty, violent and property crime rates, number of juvenile arrests for violent crimes as a percent of the total crime index, number of days with pollution standard index (PSI) over 100, pounds toxic releases per 1,000 people and number of superfund sites. *Zero Population Growth, Children's Environmental Index 1997*

■ According to *Working Mother,* "This year, the Texas Licensed Child Care Association lobbied heavily against proposed standards that would have improved the adult-to-child ratios in many programs. Unfortunately, it prevailed. Lawmakers delayed adoption of the new rules.

Texas may finally get statewide resource and referral services, however, with new federal funds coming into the state. In addition to helping parents find care, R&Rs may handle both caregiver training and consumer education—a positive development.

Providers across the state may also get low-interest loans to buy new equipment, upgrade their facilities and do other things to improve the quality of care, under a bill pending in the state legislature that looked likely to pass as we went to press." *Working Mother, July/August 1997*

Business Environment

STATE ECONOMY

State Economic Profile

''The Texas economy remains among the strongest in the nation....

Overall, Texas gained over 141,000 people last year through in-migration. While this is down from the three-year average of over 170,000, it still represents 43% of the Texas population increase. By far, throughout this decade, California has been the largest domestic source of in-migrants into Texas. With the California economy rebounding, in-migration to Texas is slowing.

The slowdown in household growth, coupled with solid residential construction, is creating a slight oversupply throughout the state. As a result, house price growth is decelerating. New residential permits have yet to slow, with new permits up by 14% last year—nearly twice the national increase. The slowdown in population and household growth cannot sustain such robust growth in permits, and as a result, new permits will slow this year.

The Texas economy shows no major imbalances. Although the important computer-chip industry remains moribund, the economy continues to expand solidly. The turnaround in computer memory prices will help the state continue to expand. Texas' growth is becoming increasingly supported by in-migrants. With an increasing presence in high-tech, an attractive business environment, and close proximity to Mexico, Texas will continue to expand faster than the nation and lure workers from other locales. In addition, as an attractive destination for retirees, Texas will continue to experience solid population and household growth as the population ages. Texas is ranked above average for short-and long-term growth.'' *National Association of Realtors, Economic Profiles: The Fifty States, July 1997*

IMPORTS/EXPORTS

Total Export Sales

Area	1993 ($000)	1994 ($000)	1995 ($000)	1996 ($000)	% Chg. 1993-96	% Chg. 1995-96
MSA[1]	186,763	153,571	162,390	241,770	29.5	48.9
U.S.	464,858,354	512,415,609	583,030,524	622,827,063	34.0	6.8

Note: (1) Metropolitan Statistical Area - see Appendix A for areas included
Source: U.S. Department of Commerce, International Trade Association, Metropolitan Area Exports: An Export Performance Report on Over 250 U.S. Cities, October 1997

Imports/Exports by Port

Type	Cargo Value			Share of U.S. Total	
	1995 (US$mil.)	1996 (US$mil.)	% Change 1995-1996	1995 (%)	1996 (%)
Imports	3,710	5,564	49.97	0.95	1.45
Exports	975	1,323	35.72	0.43	0.56

Source: Global Trade Information Services, WaterBorne Trade Atlas 1997

CITY FINANCES

City Government Finances

Component	FY92 ($000)	FY92 (per capita $)
Revenue	213,873	803.50
Expenditure	195,311	733.76
Debt Outstanding	429,337	1,612.97
Cash & Securities	286,614	1,076.78

Source: U.S. Bureau of the Census, City Government Finances: 1991-92

City Government Revenue by Source

Source	FY92 ($000)	FY92 (per capita $)	FY92 (%)
From Federal Government	10,248	38.50	4.8
From State Governments	3,811	14.32	1.8
From Local Governments	1,091	4.10	0.5
Property Taxes	36,325	136.47	17.0
General Sales Taxes	20,690	77.73	9.7
Selective Sales Taxes	13,171	49.48	6.2
Income Taxes	0	0.00	0.0
Current Charges	37,886	142.33	17.7
Utility/Liquor Store	49,861	187.32	23.3
Employee Retirement[1]	0	0.00	0.0
Other	40,790	153.24	19.1

Note: (1) Excludes "city contributions," classified as "nonrevenue," intragovernmental transfers.
Source: U.S. Bureau of the Census, City Government Finances: 1991-92

City Government Expenditures by Function

Function	FY92 ($000)	FY92 (per capita $)	FY92 (%)
Educational Services	2,235	8.40	1.1
Employee Retirement[1]	0	0.00	0.0
Environment/Housing	33,570	126.12	17.2
Government Administration	12,862	48.32	6.6
Interest on General Debt	30,528	114.69	15.6
Public Safety	39,785	149.47	20.4
Social Services	5,389	20.25	2.8
Transportation	19,986	75.09	10.2
Utility/Liquor Store	41,803	157.05	21.4
Other	9,153	34.39	4.7

Note: (1) Payments to beneficiaries including withdrawal of contributions.
Source: U.S. Bureau of the Census, City Government Finances: 1991-92

Municipal Bond Ratings

Area	Moody's	S & P
Corpus Christi	A	A+

Note: n/a not available; n/r not rated
Source: Moody's Bond Record, 2/98; Statistical Abstract of the U.S., 1997;
Governing Magazine, 9/97, 3/98

POPULATION

Population Growth

Area	1980	1990	% Chg. 1980-90	July 1996 Estimate	% Chg. 1990-96
City	231,999	257,453	11.0	280,260	8.9
MSA[1]	326,228	349,894	7.3	384,056	9.8
U.S.	226,545,805	248,765,170	9.8	265,179,411	6.6

Note: (1) Metropolitan Statistical Area - see Appendix A for areas included
Source: 1980/1990 Census of Housing and Population, Summary Tape File 3C;
Census Bureau Population Estimates

Population Characteristics

Race	City 1980 Population	%	City 1990 Population	%	% Chg. 1980-90	MSA[1] 1990 Population	%
White	190,386	82.1	196,500	76.3	3.2	265,685	75.9
Black	11,821	5.1	12,236	4.8	3.5	13,396	3.8
Amer Indian/Esk/Aleut	782	0.3	960	0.4	22.8	1,253	0.4
Asian/Pacific Islander	1,439	0.6	2,305	0.9	60.2	2,524	0.7
Other	27,571	11.9	45,452	17.7	64.9	67,036	19.2
Hispanic Origin[2]	108,229	46.7	128,743	50.0	19.0	180,586	51.6

Note: (1) Metropolitan Statistical Area - see Appendix A for areas included;
(2) people of Hispanic origin can be of any race
Source: 1980/1990 Census of Housing and Population, Summary Tape File 3C

Ancestry

Area	German	Irish	English	Italian	U.S.	French	Polish	Dutch
City	14.2	10.6	9.3	1.2	3.1	2.6	1.1	1.3
MSA[1]	14.1	10.4	9.2	1.1	3.1	2.6	1.1	1.3
U.S.	23.3	15.6	13.1	5.9	5.3	4.2	3.8	2.5

Note: Figures are percentages and include persons that reported multiple ancestry (eg. if a person reported being Irish and Italian, they were included in both columns); (1) Metropolitan Statistical Area - see Appendix A for areas included
Source: 1990 Census of Population and Housing, Summary Tape File 3C

Age

Area	Median Age (Years)	Age Distribution (%) Under 5	Under 18	18-24	25-44	45-64	65+	80+
City	30.5	8.2	30.1	9.7	32.8	17.4	10.0	1.9
MSA[1]	30.5	8.2	30.7	9.6	31.8	17.8	10.0	1.9
U.S.	32.9	7.3	25.6	10.5	32.6	18.7	12.5	2.8

Note: (1) Metropolitan Statistical Area - see Appendix A for areas included
Source: 1990 Census of Population and Housing, Summary Tape File 3C

Male/Female Ratio

Area	Number of males per 100 females (all ages)	Number of males per 100 females (18 years old+)
City	95.2	91.4
MSA[1]	96.0	92.2
U.S.	95.0	91.9

Note: (1) Metropolitan Statistical Area - see Appendix A for areas included
Source: 1990 Census of Population, General Population Characteristics

INCOME

Per Capita/Median/Average Income

Area	Per Capita ($)	Median Household ($)	Average Household ($)
City	11,755	25,773	33,396
MSA[1]	11,065	24,952	32,308
U.S.	14,420	30,056	38,453

Note: all figures are for 1989; (1) Metropolitan Statistical Area - see Appendix A for areas included
Source: 1990 Census of Population and Housing, Summary Tape File 3C

Household Income Distribution by Race

Income ($)	City (%)					U.S. (%)				
	Total	White	Black	Other	Hisp.[1]	Total	White	Black	Other	Hisp.[1]
Less than 5,000	9.6	8.1	20.1	14.1	13.0	6.2	4.8	15.2	8.6	8.8
5,000 - 9,999	10.1	9.4	17.4	11.6	13.0	9.3	8.6	14.2	9.9	11.1
10,000 - 14,999	10.2	9.7	10.8	12.7	12.5	8.8	8.5	11.0	9.8	11.0
15,000 - 24,999	18.8	18.0	23.0	21.7	20.6	17.5	17.3	18.9	18.5	20.5
25,000 - 34,999	15.8	16.0	9.8	16.3	15.5	15.8	16.1	14.2	15.4	16.4
35,000 - 49,999	17.4	18.3	11.0	14.5	14.8	17.9	18.6	13.3	16.1	16.0
50,000 - 74,999	12.3	13.8	6.1	7.0	8.3	15.0	15.8	9.3	13.4	11.1
75,000 - 99,999	3.1	3.6	1.1	1.1	1.5	5.1	5.5	2.6	4.7	3.1
100,000+	2.7	3.1	0.7	1.1	0.8	4.4	4.8	1.3	3.7	1.9

Note: all figures are for 1989; (1) people of Hispanic origin can be of any race
Source: 1990 Census of Population and Housing, Summary Tape File 3C

Effective Buying Income

Area	Per Capita ($)	Median Household ($)	Average Household ($)
City	13,909	30,976	40,284
MSA[1]	13,598	31,004	40,308
U.S.	15,444	33,201	41,849

Note: data as of 1/1/97; (1) Metropolitan Statistical Area - see Appendix A for areas included
Source: Standard Rate & Data Service, Newspaper Advertising Source, 2/98

Effective Household Buying Income Distribution

Area	% of Households Earning						
	$10,000 -$19,999	$20,000 -$34,999	$35,000 -$49,999	$50,000 -$74,999	$75,000 -$99,000	$100,000 -$124,999	$125,000 and up
City	17.2	22.4	17.7	17.0	6.0	1.7	2.2
MSA[1]	17.3	22.2	17.1	17.3	6.4	1.8	2.2
U.S.	16.5	23.4	18.3	18.2	6.4	2.1	2.4

Note: data as of 1/1/97; (1) Metropolitan Statistical Area - see Appendix A for areas included
Source: Standard Rate & Data Service, Newspaper Advertising Source, 2/98

Poverty Rates by Race and Age

Area	Total (%)	By Race (%)				By Age (%)		
		White	Black	Other	Hisp.[2]	Under 5 years old	Under 18 years old	65 years and over
City	20.0	16.8	34.8	29.4	27.9	30.3	27.2	19.1
MSA[1]	21.6	17.9	35.9	32.7	30.5	32.6	29.1	20.4
U.S.	13.1	9.8	29.5	23.1	25.3	20.1	18.3	12.8

Note: figures show the percent of people living below the poverty line in 1989. The average poverty
threshold was $12,674 for a family of four in 1989; (1) Metropolitan Statistical Area - see Appendix A
for areas included; (2) people of Hispanic origin can be of any race
Source: 1990 Census of Population and Housing, Summary Tape File 3C

EMPLOYMENT

Labor Force and Employment

Area	Civilian Labor Force			Workers Employed		
	Dec. '95	Dec. '96	% Chg.	Dec. '95	Dec. '96	% Chg.
City	136,195	135,863	-0.2	125,789	127,830	1.6
MSA[1]	180,604	180,374	-0.1	166,812	169,519	1.6
U.S.	134,583,000	136,742,000	1.6	127,903,000	130,785,000	2.3

Note: Data is not seasonally adjusted and covers workers 16 years of age and older;
(1) Metropolitan Statistical Area - see Appendix A for areas included
Source: Bureau of Labor Statistics, http://stats.bls.gov

Unemployment Rate

Area	1997											
	Jan.	Feb.	Mar.	Apr.	May	Jun.	Jul.	Aug.	Sep.	Oct.	Nov.	Dec.
City	8.7	8.5	8.4	7.5	7.4	8.8	8.1	7.3	7.1	6.5	6.3	5.9
MSA[1]	8.8	8.6	8.5	7.6	7.6	9.0	8.3	7.5	7.2	6.6	6.4	6.0
U.S.	5.9	5.7	5.5	4.8	4.7	5.2	5.0	4.8	4.7	4.4	4.3	4.4

Note: Data is not seasonally adjusted and covers workers 16 years of age and older; All figures are percentages; (1) Metropolitan Statistical Area - see Appendix A for areas included
Source: Bureau of Labor Statistics, http://stats.bls.gov

Employment by Industry

Sector	MSA[1]		U.S.
	Number of Employees	Percent of Total	Percent of Total
Services	48,700	31.1	29.0
Retail Trade	30,900	19.7	18.5
Government	31,300	20.0	16.1
Manufacturing	13,300	8.5	15.0
Finance/Insurance/Real Estate	6,500	4.1	5.7
Wholesale Trade	6,000	3.8	5.4
Transportation/Public Utilities	6,500	4.1	5.3
Construction	11,100	7.1	4.5
Mining	2,400	1.5	0.5

Note: Figures cover non-farm employment as of 12/97 and are not seasonally adjusted;
(1) Metropolitan Statistical Area - see Appendix A for areas included
Source: Bureau of Labor Statistics, http://stats.bls.gov

Employment by Occupation

Occupation Category	City (%)	MSA[1] (%)	U.S. (%)
White Collar	57.3	54.1	58.1
Executive/Admin./Management	10.7	10.1	12.3
Professional	14.1	13.1	14.1
Technical & Related Support	3.7	3.6	3.7
Sales	13.0	12.5	11.8
Administrative Support/Clerical	15.9	14.8	16.3
Blue Collar	25.2	27.3	26.2
Precision Production/Craft/Repair	14.1	14.9	11.3
Machine Operators/Assem./Insp.	3.7	4.1	6.8
Transportation/Material Movers	3.6	4.2	4.1
Cleaners/Helpers/Laborers	3.7	4.1	3.9
Services	16.3	16.4	13.2
Farming/Forestry/Fishing	1.2	2.3	2.5

Note: figures cover employed persons 16 years old and over;
(1) Metropolitan Statistical Area - see Appendix A for areas included
Source: 1990 Census of Population and Housing, Summary Tape File 3C

Occupational Employment Projections: 1993 - 2000

Occupations Expected to have the Largest Job Growth (ranked by numerical growth)	Fast-Growing Occupations[1] (ranked by percent growth)
1. Home health aides	1. General farm workers
2. Child care workers, private household	2. Physical therapy assistants and aides
3. Registered nurses	3. Computer engineers
4. Cashiers	4. Home health aides
5. Food preparation workers	5. Personal and home care aides
6. Waiters & waitresses	6. Health service workers
7. General office clerks	7. Physical therapists
8. Nursing aides/orderlies/attendants	8. Paralegals
9. Salespersons, retail	9. Child care workers, private household
10. Licensed practical nurses	10. Computer systems analysts

Projections cover Aransas, Bee, Brooks, Duval, Jim Wells, Kenedy, Kleberg, Live Oak, McMullen, Nueces, Refugio and San Patricio Counties.
Note: (1) Includes occupations with absolute job growth of 100 or more
Source: Texas Employment Commission, Texas Employment Projections Reporting System, Statewide and Regional Projections 1993-2000, Ver. 1.0

Average Wages

Occupation	Wage	Occupation	Wage
Professional/Technical/Clerical	$/Week	**Health/Protective Services**	$/Week
Accountants III	656	Corrections Officers	403
Attorneys III	809	Firefighters	658
Budget Analysts III	-	Nurses, Licensed Practical II	-
Buyers/Contracting Specialists II	714	Nurses, Registered II	-
Clerks, Accounting III	393	Nursing Assistants II	-
Clerks, General III	295	Police Officers I	595
Computer Operators II	441	**Hourly Workers**	$/Hour
Computer Programmers II	584	Forklift Operators	-
Drafters II	522	General Maintenance Workers	7.70
Engineering Technicians III	-	Guards I	6.49
Engineering Technicians, Civil III	452	Janitors	6.46
Engineers III	936	Maintenance Electricians	14.50
Key Entry Operators I	294	Maintenance Electronics Techs II	-
Personnel Assistants III	376	Maintenance Machinists	18.04
Personnel Specialists III	654	Maintenance Mechanics, Machinery	18.15
Secretaries III	388	Material Handling Laborers	-
Switchboard Operator-Receptionist	306	Motor Vehicle Mechanics	12.06
Systems Analysts II	756	Shipping/Receiving Clerks	10.41
Systems Analysts Supervisor/Mgr II	-	Tool and Die Makers	-
Tax Collectors II	-	Truckdrivers, Tractor Trailer	-
Word Processors II	-	Warehouse Specialists	-

Note: Wage data includes full-time workers only for 9/95 and cover the Metropolitan Statistical Area (see Appendix A for areas included). Dashes indicate that data was not available.
Source: Bureau of Labor Statistics, Occupational Compensation Survey, 2/96

TAXES

Major State and Local Tax Rates

State Corp. Income (%)	State Personal Income (%)	Residential Property (effective rate per $100)	Sales & Use		State Gasoline (cents/ gallon)	State Cigarette (cents/ 20-pack)
			State (%)	Local (%)		
None[a]	None	n/a	6.25	1.5	20	41

Note: Personal/corporate income tax rates as of 1/97. Sales, gasoline and cigarette tax rates as of 1/98; (a) Texas imposes a franchise tax of 4.5% of earned surplus
Source: Federation of Tax Administrators, www.taxadmin.org; Washington D.C. Department of Finance and Revenue, Tax Rates and Tax Burdens in the District of Columbia: A Nationwide Comparison, June 1997; Chamber of Commerce

Total Taxes Per Capita and as a Percent of Income

Area	Per Capita Income ($)	Per Capita Taxes ($)			Taxes as Pct. of Income (%)		
		Total	Federal	State/Local	Total	Federal	State/Local
Texas	24,145	8,118	5,538	2,580	33.6	22.9	10.7
U.S.	26,187	9,205	6,127	3,078	35.2	23.4	11.8

Note: Figures are for 1997
Source: Tax Foundation, Web Site, www.taxfoundation.org

COMMERCIAL REAL ESTATE

Data not available at time of publication.

COMMERCIAL UTILITIES

Typical Monthly Electric Bills

Area	Commercial Service ($/month)		Industrial Service ($/month)	
	12 kW demand 1,500 kWh	100 kW demand 30,000 kWh	1,000 kW demand 400,000 kWh	20,000 kW demand 10,000,000 kWh
City	221	2,326	23,116	411,990
U.S.	162	2,360	25,590	545,677

Note: Based on rates in effect July 1, 1997
Source: Edison Electric Institute, Typical Residential, Commercial and Industrial Bills, Summer 1997

TRANSPORTATION

Transportation Statistics

Avg. travel time to work (min.)	18.8
Interstate highways	I-37
Bus lines	
In-city	Regional Transit Authority
Inter-city	3
Passenger air service	
Airport	Corpus Christi International
Airlines	6
Aircraft departures	11,092 (1995)
Enplaned passengers	487,764 (1995)
Rail service	No Amtrak Service
Motor freight carriers	15
Major waterways/ports	Gulf of Mexico; Port of Corpus Christi

Source: OAG, Business Travel Planner, Summer 1997; Editor & Publisher Market Guide, 1998; FAA Airport Activity Statistics, 1996; Amtrak National Time Table, Northeast Timetable, Fall/Winter 1997-98; 1990 Census of Population and Housing, STF 3C; Chamber of Commerce/Economic Development 1997; Jane's Urban Transport Systems 1997-98; Transit Fact Book 1997

Means of Transportation to Work

Area	Car/Truck/Van		Public Transportation			Bicycle	Walked	Other Means	Worked at Home
	Drove Alone	Car-pooled	Bus	Subway	Railroad				
City	75.8	16.9	1.8	0.0	0.0	0.2	1.9	1.4	1.8
MSA[1]	75.6	17.0	1.5	0.0	0.0	0.3	2.1	1.5	2.0
U.S.	73.2	13.4	3.0	1.5	0.5	0.4	3.9	1.2	3.0

Note: figures shown are percentages and only include workers 16 years old and over;
(1) Metropolitan Statistical Area - see Appendix A for areas included
Source: 1990 Census of Population and Housing, Summary Tape File 3C

BUSINESSES

Major Business Headquarters

Company Name	1997 Rankings	
	Fortune 500	Forbes 500
TRT Holdings		437

Note: Companies listed are located in the city; Dashes indicate no ranking
Fortune 500: companies that produce a 10-K are ranked 1 - 500 based on 1996 revenue
Forbes 500: private companies are ranked 1 - 500 based on 1996 revenue
Source: Forbes 12/1/97; Fortune 4/28/97

Minority Business Opportunity

Corpus Christi was listed among the top 25 metropolitan areas in terms of the number of Hispanic-owned companies. The city was ranked number 25 with 7,695 companies. *Hispanic Business, May 1997*

HOTELS & MOTELS

Hotels/Motels

Area	Hotels/ Motels	Rooms	Luxury-Level Hotels/Motels		Average Minimum Rates ($)		
			♦♦♦♦	♦♦♦♦♦	♦♦	♦♦♦	♦♦♦♦
City	21	3,523	0	0	62	77	n/a
Airport	8	1,185	0	0	n/a	n/a	n/a
Suburbs	1	150	0	0	n/a	n/a	n/a
Total	30	4,858	0	0	n/a	n/a	n/a

Note: n/a not available; Classifications range from one diamond (budget properties with basic amenities) to five diamond (luxury properties with the finest service, rooms and facilities).
Source: OAG, Business Travel Planner, Summer 1997

CONVENTION CENTERS

Major Convention Centers

Center Name	Meeting Rooms	Exhibit Space (sf)
Bayfront Plaza Convention Center	17	104,500
Corpus Christi Memorial Coliseum	1	40,000

Source: Trade Shows Worldwide 1997

Living Environment

COST OF LIVING

Cost of Living Index

Composite Index	Housing	Utilities	Groceries	Health Care	Trans- portation	Misc. Goods/ Services
n/a	n/a	n/a	n/a	n/a	n/a	n/a

Note: U.S. = 100; n/a not available
Source: ACCRA, Cost of Living Index, 3rd Quarter 1997

HOUSING

Median Home Prices and Housing Affordability

Area	Median Price[2] 3rd Qtr. 1997 ($)	HOI[3] 3rd Qtr. 1997	Afford- ability Rank[4]
MSA[1]	n/a	n/a	n/a
U.S.	127,000	63.7	–

Note: (1) Metropolitan Statistical Area - see Appendix A for areas included; (2) U.S. figures calculated from the sales of 625,000 new and existing homes in 195 markets; (3) Housing Opportunity Index - percent of homes sold that were within the reach of the median income household at the prevailing mortgage interest rate; (4) Rank is from 1-195 with 1 being most affordable; n/a not available
Source: National Association of Home Builders, Housing Opportunity Index, 3rd Quarter 1997

Average New Home Price

Area	Price ($)
City	n/a
U.S.	135,710

Note: n/a not available
Source: ACCRA, Cost of Living Index, 3rd Quarter 1997

Average Apartment Rent

Area	Rent ($/mth)
City	n/a
U.S.	569

Note: n/a not available
Source: ACCRA, Cost of Living Index, 3rd Quarter 1997

RESIDENTIAL UTILITIES

Average Residential Utility Costs

Area	All Electric ($/mth)	Part Electric ($/mth)	Other Energy ($/mth)	Phone ($/mth)
City	n/a	n/a	n/a	n/a
U.S.	109.40	55.25	43.64	19.48

Note: n/a not available
Source: ACCRA, Cost of Living Index, 3rd Quarter 1997

HEALTH CARE

Average Health Care Costs

Area	Hospital ($/day)	Doctor ($/visit)	Dentist ($/visit)
City	n/a	n/a	n/a
U.S.	392.91	48.76	60.84

Note: n/a not available
Source: ACCRA, Cost of Living Index, 3rd Quarter 1997

Distribution of Office-Based Physicians

Area	Family/Gen. Practitioners	Specialists		
		Medical	Surgical	Other
MSA[1]	88	197	177	154

Note: Data as of 12/31/96; (1) Metropolitan Statistical Area - see Appendix A for areas included
Source: American Medical Assn., Physician Characteristics & Distribution in the U.S., 1997-1998

Hospitals

Corpus Christi has 6 general medical and surgical hospitals, 2 psychiatric, 1 rehabilitation, 1 children's general. *AHA Guide to the Healthcare Field 1997-98*

EDUCATION

Public School District Statistics

District Name	Num. Sch.	Enroll.	Classroom Teachers[1]	Pupils per Teacher	Minority Pupils (%)	Current Exp.[2] ($/pupil)
Calallen ISD	6	4,767	303	15.7	n/a	n/a
Corpus Christi ISD	62	41,624	2,416	17.2	74.6	4,465
Flour Bluff ISD	6	5,402	345	15.7	n/a	n/a
London ISD	1	166	13	12.8	n/a	n/a
Tuloso-Midway ISD	5	2,884	217	13.3	n/a	n/a
West Oso ISD	5	1,949	138	14.1	n/a	n/a

Note: Data covers the 1995-1996 school year unless otherwise noted; (1) Excludes teachers reported as working in school district offices rather than in schools; (2) Based on 1993-94 enrollment collected by the Census Bureau, not the enrollment figure shown in column 3; SD = School District; ISD = Independent School District; n/a not available
Source: National Center for Education Statistics, Common Core of Data Survey; Bureau of the Census

Educational Quality

School District	Education Quotient[1]	Graduate Outcome[2]	Community Index[3]	Resource Index[4]
Corpus Christi	72.0	71.0	64.0	80.0

Note: Nearly 1,000 secondary school districts were rated in terms of educational quality. The scores range from a low of 50 to a high of 150; (1) Average of the Graduate Outcome, Community and Resource indexes; (2) Based on graduation rates and college board scores (SAT/ACT); (3) Based on the surrounding community's average level of education and the area's average income level; (4) Based on teacher salaries, per-pupil expenditures and student-teacher ratios.
Source: Expansion Management, Ratings Issue 1997

Educational Attainment by Race

Area	High School Graduate (%)					Bachelor's Degree (%)				
	Total	White	Black	Other	Hisp.[2]	Total	White	Black	Other	Hisp.[2]
City	70.9	74.3	61.8	56.1	54.4	17.8	20.2	8.0	8.5	7.8
MSA[1]	67.6	71.6	60.2	50.2	49.7	16.0	18.4	8.0	6.7	6.6
U.S.	75.2	77.9	63.1	60.4	49.8	20.3	21.5	11.4	19.4	9.2

Note: figures shown cover persons 25 years old and over; (1) Metropolitan Statistical Area - see Appendix A for areas included; (2) people of Hispanic origin can be of any race
Source: 1990 Census of Population and Housing, Summary Tape File 3C

School Enrollment by Type

Area	Preprimary				Elementary/High School			
	Public		Private		Public		Private	
	Enrollment	%	Enrollment	%	Enrollment	%	Enrollment	%
City	2,476	56.7	1,894	43.3	52,069	94.0	3,309	6.0
MSA[1]	3,591	61.8	2,216	38.2	73,649	95.2	3,729	4.8
U.S.	2,679,029	59.5	1,824,256	40.5	38,379,689	90.2	4,187,099	9.8

Note: figures shown cover persons 3 years old and over;
(1) Metropolitan Statistical Area - see Appendix A for areas included
Source: 1990 Census of Population and Housing, Summary Tape File 3C

School Enrollment by Race

Area	Preprimary (%)				Elementary/High School (%)			
	White	Black	Other	Hisp.[1]	White	Black	Other	Hisp.[1]
City	75.8	7.2	17.0	43.2	70.5	5.2	24.3	61.7
MSA[2]	75.7	5.6	18.7	46.8	70.4	4.0	25.6	62.9
U.S.	80.4	12.5	7.1	7.8	74.1	15.6	10.3	12.5

Note: figures shown cover persons 3 years old and over; (1) people of Hispanic origin can be of any race; (2) Metropolitan Statistical Area - see Appendix A for areas included
Source: 1990 Census of Population and Housing, Summary Tape File 3C

SAT/ACT Scores

Area/District	1997 SAT				1997 ACT	
	Percent of Graduates Tested (%)	Average Math Score	Average Verbal Score	Average Combined Score	Percent of Graduates Tested (%)	Average Composite Score
Corpus Christi ISD	48	498	496	994	28	19.9
State	49	501	494	995	30	20.2
U.S.	42	511	505	1,016	36	21.0

Note: Math and verbal SAT scores are out of a possible 800; ACT scores are out of a possible 36
Caution: Comparing or ranking states/cities on the basis of SAT/ACT scores alone is invalid and strongly discouraged by the The College Board and The American College Testing Program as students who take the tests are self-selected and do not represent the entire student population.
Source: Corpus Christi ISD, Office of Management Information, 1997; College Board, 1997; American College Testing Program, 1997

Classroom Teacher Salaries in Public Schools

District	B.A. Degree		M.A. Degree		Ph.D. Degree	
	Min. ($)	Max ($)	Min. ($)	Max. ($)	Min. ($)	Max. ($)
Corpus Christi	23,313	37,982	25,395	41,311	26,895	42,811
Average[1]	26,120	39,270	28,175	44,667	31,643	49,825

Note: Salaries are for 1996-1997; (1) Based on all school districts covered; n/a not available
Source: American Federation of Teachers (unpublished data)

Higher Education

Two-Year Colleges		Four-Year Colleges		Medical Schools	Law Schools	Voc/ Tech
Public	Private	Public	Private			
1	0	1	0	0	0	4

Source: College Blue Book, Occupational Education 1997; Medical School Admission Requirements, 1998-99; Peterson's Guide to Two-Year Colleges, 1997; Peterson's Guide to Four-Year Colleges, 1997; Barron's Guide to Law Schools 1997

MAJOR EMPLOYERS

Major Employers

Spohn Health Systems
Nueces County Hospital District
Sam Kane Beef Processors
Energy Industries

Susser Co. (real estate)
Driscoll Childrens Hospital
Central Power & Light
Southwestern Refining Co.

Note: companies listed are located in the city
Source: Dun's Business Rankings 1997; Ward's Business Directory, 1997

PUBLIC SAFETY

Crime Rate

Area	All Crimes	Violent Crimes				Property Crimes		
		Murder	Forcible Rape	Robbery	Aggrav. Assault	Burglary	Larceny -Theft	Motor Vehicle Theft
City	10,628.3	6.3	96.3	169.2	781.8	1,316.2	7,676.7	581.9
Suburbs[1]	2,983.4	4.7	21.8	23.7	248.9	834.0	1,714.5	135.8
MSA[2]	8,574.8	5.9	76.3	130.1	638.6	1,186.7	6,075.1	462.1
U.S.	5,078.9	7.4	36.1	202.4	388.2	943.0	2,975.9	525.9

Note: Crime rate is the number of crimes per 100,000 pop.; (1) defined as all areas within the MSA but located outside the central city; (2) Metropolitan Statistical Area - see Appendix A for areas incl.
Source: FBI Uniform Crime Reports 1996

RECREATION

Culture and Recreation

Museums	Symphony Orchestras	Opera Companies	Dance Companies	Professional Theatres	Zoos	Pro Sports Teams
5	1	0	1	0	0	0

Source: International Directory of the Performing Arts, 1996; Official Museum Directory, 1998; Chamber of Commerce/Economic Development 1997

Library System

The Corpus Christi Public Libraries has four branches, holdings of 358,000 volumes and a budget of $2,626,088 (1994-1995). The South Texas Library System has no branches, holdings of n/a volumes and a budget of $725,538 (1994-1995). Note: n/a means not available. *American Library Directory, 1997-1998*

MEDIA

Newspapers

Name	Type	Freq.	Distribution	Circulation
Corpus Christi Caller-Times	n/a	7x/wk	Area	71,896
South Texas Catholic	Religious	1x/mo	Local	16,500

Note: Includes newspapers with circulations of 1,000 or more located in the city; n/a not available
Source: Burrelle's Media Directory, 1998 Edition

AM Radio Stations

Call Letters	Freq. (kHz)	Target Audience	Station Format	Music Format
KCTA	1030	Religious	M	Christian
KCCT	1150	Hispanic	M/N	Spanish
KSIX	1230	Religious	M/N	Easy Listening
KRYS	1360	General	M	Country
KUNO	1400	Hispanic	M	Spanish
KEYS	1440	General	N/S/T	n/a
KGLF	1510	General	M	Christian
KDAE	1590	General	M/N/S	Easy Listening

Note: Stations included broadcast in the Corpus Christi metro area; n/a not available
Station Format: E = Educational; M = Music; N = News; S = Sports; T = Talk
Source: Burrelle's Media Directory, 1998 Edition

FM Radio Stations

Call Letters	Freq. (mHz)	Target Audience	Station Format	Music Format
KLUX	89.5	General	E/M/N	Easy Listening
KEDT	90.3	General	M/N/S	Classical/Jazz
KVRT	90.7	n/a	M/N	Classical/Jazz
KBNJ	91.7	General	E/M/N/S	Christian
KKBA	92.7	General	M	Country
KMXR	93.9	n/a	M	Adult Contemporary
KBSO	94.7	Hispanic	M	Country
KZFM	95.5	General	M	Contemporary Top 40
KLTG	96.5	General	M	Oldies
KFTX	97.5	General	M/N/S	Country/Oldies
KRYS	99.1	General	M/N/S	Country
KSAB	99.9	Hispanic	M	Spanish
KNCN	101.3	General	M	AOR
KOUL	103.7	General	M/N/T	Country
KMFM	104.9	Hispanic	M	Christian
KRAD	105.5	General	M/N/S	AOR/Classic Rock

Note: Stations included broadcast in the Corpus Christi metro area; n/a not available
Station Format: E = Educational; M = Music; N = News; S = Sports; T = Talk
Music Format: AOR = Album Oriented Rock; MOR = Middle-of-the-Road
Source: Burrelle's Media Directory, 1998 Edition

Television Stations

Name	Ch.	Affiliation	Type	Owner
KIII	3	ABC	Commercial	McKinnon Broadcasting Company
KRIS	6	NBC	Commercial	Gulf Coast Broadcasting Co.
KZTV	10	CBS	Commercial	K-SIX Television Inc.
KEDT	16	PBS	Public	South Texas Public Broadcasting System
KORO	28	Univision	Commercial	Telecorpus Inc.

Note: Stations included broadcast in the Corpus Christi metro area
Source: Burrelle's Media Directory, 1998 Edition

CLIMATE

Average and Extreme Temperatures

Temperature	Jan	Feb	Mar	Apr	May	Jun	Jul	Aug	Sep	Oct	Nov	Dec	Ann
Extreme High (°F)	91	97	102	102	103	101	101	103	103	98	98	91	103
Average High (°F)	66	69	75	81	86	91	93	93	90	84	75	69	81
Average Temp. (°F)	56	60	66	73	78	82	84	85	81	74	65	59	72
Average Low (°F)	46	49	56	63	70	74	75	75	72	64	55	49	63
Extreme Low (°F)	14	18	24	33	47	58	64	64	54	39	29	13	13

Note: Figures cover the years 1948-1992
Source: National Climatic Data Center, International Station Meteorological Climate Summary, 3/95

Average Precipitation/Snowfall/Humidity

Precip./Humidity	Jan	Feb	Mar	Apr	May	Jun	Jul	Aug	Sep	Oct	Nov	Dec	Ann
Avg. Precip. (in.)	1.7	1.9	1.1	2.0	3.1	3.0	2.0	3.2	5.5	3.2	1.6	1.5	29.9
Avg. Snowfall (in.)	Tr	Tr	Tr	0	0	0	0	0	0	0	Tr	Tr	0
Avg. Rel. Hum. 6am (%)	87	88	87	89	92	92	93	92	90	89	86	85	89
Avg. Rel. Hum. 3pm (%)	62	59	57	61	64	62	56	56	60	57	58	60	59

Note: Figures cover the years 1948-1992; Tr = Trace amounts (<0.05 in. of rain; <0.5 in. of snow)
Source: National Climatic Data Center, International Station Meteorological Climate Summary, 3/95

Weather Conditions

Temperature			Daytime Sky			Precipitation		
32°F & below	45°F & below	90°F & above	Clear	Partly cloudy	Cloudy	0.01 inch or more precip.	0.1 inch or more snow/ice	Thunder-storms
6	49	106	84	177	104	76	< 1	27

Note: Figures are average number of days per year and covers the years 1948-1992
Source: National Climatic Data Center, International Station Meteorological Climate Summary, 3/95

AIR & WATER QUALITY

Maximum Pollutant Concentrations

	Particulate Matter (ug/m³)	Carbon Monoxide (ppm)	Sulfur Dioxide (ppm)	Nitrogen Dioxide (ppm)	Ozone (ppm)	Lead (ug/m³)
MSA[1] Level	45	n/a	0.015	n/a	0.10	n/a
NAAQS[2]	150	9	0.140	0.053	0.12	1.50
Met NAAQS?	Yes	n/a	Yes	n/a	Yes	n/a

Note: (1) Metropolitan Statistical Area - see Appendix A for areas included; (2) National Ambient Air Quality Standards; ppm = parts per million; ug/m³ = micrograms per cubic meter; n/a not available
Source: EPA, National Air Quality and Emissions Trends Report, 1996

Pollutant Standards Index

Data not available. *EPA, National Air Quality and Emissions Trends Report, 1996*

Drinking Water

Water System Name	Pop. Served	Primary Water Source Type	Number of Violations in Fiscal Year 1997	Type of Violation/ Contaminants
City of Corpus Christi	270,000	Surface	None	None

Note: Data as of January 16, 1998
Source: EPA, Office of Ground Water and Drinking Water, Safe Drinking Water Information System

Corpus Christi tap water is neutral, hard and fluoridated.
Editor & Publisher Market Guide, 1998

Dallas, Texas

Background

Dallas is one of those cities that offers everything. Founded in 1841 by Tennessee lawyer and trader, John Neely Bryan, Dallas has come to symbolize in modern times, all that is big, exciting, and affluent.

Originally one of the largest markets for cotton in the U.S., Dallas moved on to become one of the largest markets for oil in the country. In the 1930's, oil was struck on the eastern fields of Texas. As a result of that discovery, millionaires and oil companies were made. The face we now associate with Dallas and Texas had emerged.

Today, oil still plays a dominant role in the Dallas economy. Outside of Alaska, Texas holds 75% of the U.S. oil reserves. For that reason, more oil companies choose to headquarter themselves in the glittery silver skyscrapers of Dallas, than in any other U.S. city.

If one is not attracted to oil as a source for making one's fortune, one may work for the Dallas branch of the Federal Reserve Bank, or a host of other banks and investment firms clustering around the Federal Reserve hub. Or, one may consider the wealth of other opportunities offered in the aircraft, advertising, motion picture, and publishing industries.

Finally, one may indulge in Dallas's busy cultural calendar. A host of independent theatre groups is sponsored by Southern Methodist University. The Museum of Fine Arts houses an excellent collection of modern art, especially American paintings. If that is not enough, stroll through one of the many historical districts, such as the Swiss Avenue District, or contemplate the elegant City Hall Building designed by I.M. Pei.

The climate of Dallas is generally temperate. Periods of extreme cold that occasionally occur are short lived and the extremely high temperatures which can sometimes occur in summer usually do not last for extended periods of time.

General Rankings and Evaluative Comments

- Dallas was ranked #40 out of 300 cities by *Money's* 1997 "Survey of the Best Places to Live." Criteria used: health services, crime, economy, housing, education, transportation, weather, leisure and the arts. The city was ranked #65 in 1996 and #144 in 1995.
  Money, July 1997; Money, September 1996; Money, September 1995

- *Ladies Home Journal* ranked America's 200 largest cities based on the qualities women care about most. Dallas ranked 66 out of 200. Criteria: low crime rate, good public schools, well-paying jobs, quality health and child care, the presence of women in government, proportion of women-owned businesses, size of the wage gap with men, local economy, divorce rates, the ratio of single men to single women, whether there are laws that require at least the same number of public toilets for women as men, and the probability of good hair days. *Ladies Home Journal, November 1997*

- Dallas was ranked #156 out of 219 cities in terms of children's health, safety, and economic well-being. Criteria: total population, percent population change, birth rate, child immunization rate, infant mortality rate, percent low birth weight infants, percent of births to teens, physician-to-population ratio, student-to-teacher ratio, dropout rate, unemployment rate, median family income, percent of children in poverty, violent and property crime rates, number of juvenile arrests for violent crimes as a percent of the total crime index, number of days with pollution standard index (PSI) over 100, pounds toxic releases per 1,000 people and number of superfund sites. *Zero Population Growth, Children's Environmental Index 1997*

- *Yahoo! Internet Life* selected "America's 100 Most Wired Cities & Towns". 50 cities were large and 50 cities were small. Dallas ranked 13 out of 50 large cities. Criteria: Internet users per capita, number of networked computers, number of registered domain names, Internet backbone traffic, and the per-capita number of Web sites devoted to each city. *Yahoo! Internet Life, March 1998*

- *Reader's Digest* non-scientifically ranked the 12 largest U.S. metropolitan areas in terms of having the worst drivers. The Dallas-Ft. Worth metro area ranked number 9. The areas were selected by asking approximately 1,200 readers on the *Reader's Digest* Web site and 200 interstate bus drivers and long-haul truckers which metro areas have the worst drivers. Their responses were factored in with fatality, insurance and rental-car rates to create the rankings. *Reader's Digest, March 1998*

- Dallas was among "The 10 Hotbeds of Entrepreneurial Activity" in 1996 with 1.49 start-ups per 100 people. Rank: 8 out of 200 metro areas. *Inc., The State of Small Business 1997*

- Dallas appeared on *Sales & Marketing Management's* list of the 20 hottest domestic markets to do business in. Rank: 8 out of 20. America's 320 Metropolitan Statistical Areas were ranked based on the market's potential to buy products in certain industries like high-tech, manufacturing, office equipment and business services, as well as population and household income growth. The study had nine criteria in all.

  "As the second biggest market on our list, Dallas' economy has undergone some changes in the past five years. The area has shifted to a service-based economy, accounting for 30 percent of jobs, from a manufacturing-based one in the 1980s. This market is perfect for seller to services industries and any office equipment providers." *Sales & Marketing Management, January 1998*

- Southwest Airlines, TD Industries (installs/services air-conditioning and plumbing systems), Texas Instruments and Mary Kay Cosmetics , headquartered in Dallas, are among the "100 Best Companies to Work for in America." Criteria: trust in management, pride in work/company, camaraderie, company responses to the Hewitt People Practices Inventory, and employee responses to their Great Place to Work survey. The companies also had to be at least 10 years old and have a minimum of 500 employees. *Fortune, January 12, 1998*

- Texas Instruments, headquartered in Dallas, is among the "100 Best Companies for Working Mothers." Criteria: pay compared with competition, opportunities for women to advance, support for child care, flexible work schedules and family-friendly benefits. *Working Mother, October 1997*

■ According to *Working Mother,* "This year, the Texas Licensed Child Care Association lobbied heavily against proposed standards that would have improved the adult-to-child ratios in many programs. Unfortunately, it prevailed. Lawmakers delayed adoption of the new rules.

Texas may finally get statewide resource and referral services, however, with new federal funds coming into the state. In addition to helping parents find care, R&Rs may handle both caregiver training and consumer education—a positive development.

Providers across the state may also get low-interest loans to buy new equipment, upgrade their facilities and do other things to improve the quality of care, under a bill pending in the state legislature that looked likely to pass as we went to press." *Working Mother, July/August 1997*

Business Environment

STATE ECONOMY

State Economic Profile

"The Texas economy remains among the strongest in the nation....

Overall, Texas gained over 141,000 people last year through in-migration. While this is down from the three-year average of over 170,000, it still represents 43% of the Texas population increase. By far, throughout this decade, California has been the largest domestic source of in-migrants into Texas. With the California economy rebounding, in-migration to Texas is slowing.

The slowdown in household growth, coupled with solid residential construction, is creating a slight oversupply throughout the state. As a result, house price growth is decelerating. New residential permits have yet to slow, with new permits up by 14% last year—nearly twice the national increase. The slowdown in population and household growth cannot sustain such robust growth in permits, and as a result, new permits will slow this year.

The Texas economy shows no major imbalances. Although the important computer-chip industry remains moribund, the economy continues to expand solidly. The turnaround in computer memory prices will help the state continue to expand. Texas' growth is becoming increasingly supported by in-migrants. With an increasing presence in high-tech, an attractive business environment, and close proximity to Mexico, Texas will continue to expand faster than the nation and lure workers from other locales. In addition, as an attractive destination for retirees, Texas will continue to experience solid population and household growth as the population ages. Texas is ranked above average for short-and long-term growth." *National Association of Realtors, Economic Profiles: The Fifty States, July 1997*

IMPORTS/EXPORTS

Total Export Sales

Area	1993 ($000)	1994 ($000)	1995 ($000)	1996 ($000)	% Chg. 1993-96	% Chg. 1995-96
MSA[1]	4,817,639	5,679,711	6,870,414	7,096,879	47.3	3.3
U.S.	464,858,354	512,415,609	583,030,524	622,827,063	34.0	6.8

Note: (1) Metropolitan Statistical Area - see Appendix A for areas included
Source: U.S. Department of Commerce, International Trade Association, Metropolitan Area Exports: An Export Performance Report on Over 250 U.S. Cities, October 1997

Imports/Exports by Port

Type	Cargo Value			Share of U.S. Total	
	1995 (US$mil.)	1996 (US$mil.)	% Change 1995-1996	1995 (%)	1996 (%)
Imports	0	0	0	0	0
Exports	0	0	0	0	0

Source: Global Trade Information Services, WaterBorne Trade Atlas 1997

CITY FINANCES

City Government Finances

Component	FY94 ($000)	FY94 (per capita $)
Revenue	1,561,799	1,495.75
Expenditure	1,537,863	1,472.82
Debt Outstanding	3,875,959	3,712.03
Cash & Securities	3,018,488	2,890.83

Source: U.S. Bureau of the Census, City Government Finances: 1993-94

City Government Revenue by Source

Source	FY94 ($000)	FY94 (per capita $)	FY94 (%)
From Federal Government	56,274	53.89	3.6
From State Governments	12,419	11.89	0.8
From Local Governments	4,526	4.33	0.3
Property Taxes	284,809	272.76	18.2
General Sales Taxes	120,027	114.95	7.7
Selective Sales Taxes	86,724	83.06	5.6
Income Taxes	0	0.00	0.0
Current Charges	440,806	422.16	28.2
Utility/Liquor Store	139,559	133.66	8.9
Employee Retirement[1]	277,619	265.88	17.8
Other	139,036	133.16	8.9

Note: (1) Excludes "city contributions," classified as "nonrevenue," intragovernmental transfers.
Source: U.S. Bureau of the Census, City Government Finances: 1993-94

City Government Expenditures by Function

Function	FY94 ($000)	FY94 (per capita $)	FY94 (%)
Educational Services	14,896	14.27	1.0
Employee Retirement[1]	106,174	101.68	6.9
Environment/Housing	269,766	258.36	17.5
Government Administration	68,854	65.94	4.5
Interest on General Debt	210,004	201.12	13.7
Public Safety	260,647	249.62	16.9
Social Services	18,397	17.62	1.2
Transportation	382,748	366.56	24.9
Utility/Liquor Store	171,390	164.14	11.1
Other	34,987	33.51	2.3

Note: (1) Payments to beneficiaries including withdrawal of contributions.
Source: U.S. Bureau of the Census, City Government Finances: 1993-94

Municipal Bond Ratings

Area	Moody's	S & P
Dallas	Aaa	AAA

Note: n/a not available; n/r not rated
Source: Moody's Bond Record, 2/98; Statistical Abstract of the U.S., 1997; Governing Magazine, 9/97, 3/98

POPULATION

Population Growth

Area	1980	1990	% Chg. 1980-90	July 1996 Estimate	% Chg. 1990-96
City	904,074	1,006,831	11.4	1,053,292	4.6
MSA[1]	1,957,378	2,553,362	30.4	3,047,983	19.4
U.S.	226,545,805	248,765,170	9.8	265,179,411	6.6

Note: (1) Metropolitan Statistical Area - see Appendix A for areas included
Source: 1980/1990 Census of Housing and Population, Summary Tape File 3C; Census Bureau Population Estimates

Population Characteristics

Race	City 1980 Population	%	City 1990 Population	%	% Chg. 1980-90	MSA[1] 1990 Population	%
White	558,443	61.8	557,957	55.4	-0.1	1,856,119	72.7
Black	265,105	29.3	297,018	29.5	12.0	410,458	16.1
Amer Indian/Esk/Aleut	3,878	0.4	4,646	0.5	19.8	13,378	0.5
Asian/Pacific Islander	9,163	1.0	21,543	2.1	135.1	66,097	2.6
Other	67,485	7.5	125,667	12.5	86.2	207,310	8.1
Hispanic Origin[2]	111,083	12.3	204,712	20.3	84.3	359,484	14.1

Note: (1) Metropolitan Statistical Area - see Appendix A for areas included;
(2) people of Hispanic origin can be of any race
Source: 1980/1990 Census of Housing and Population, Summary Tape File 3C

Ancestry

Area	German	Irish	English	Italian	U.S.	French	Polish	Dutch
City	12.4	10.4	11.1	1.7	3.7	2.7	1.3	1.4
MSA[1]	18.4	15.5	14.4	2.3	5.7	3.5	1.5	2.2
U.S.	23.3	15.6	13.1	5.9	5.3	4.2	3.8	2.5

Note: Figures are percentages and include persons that reported multiple ancestry (eg. if a person reported being Irish and Italian, they were included in both columns); (1) Metropolitan Statistical Area - see Appendix A for areas included
Source: 1990 Census of Population and Housing, Summary Tape File 3C

Age

Area	Median Age (Years)	Under 5	Under 18	18-24	25-44	45-64	65+	80+
City	30.5	8.0	25.0	11.4	37.6	16.4	9.7	2.2
MSA[1]	30.4	8.4	27.2	10.7	37.7	16.7	7.7	1.7
U.S.	32.9	7.3	25.6	10.5	32.6	18.7	12.5	2.8

Note: (1) Metropolitan Statistical Area - see Appendix A for areas included
Source: 1990 Census of Population and Housing, Summary Tape File 3C

Male/Female Ratio

Area	Number of males per 100 females (all ages)	Number of males per 100 females (18 years old+)
City	97.0	94.5
MSA[1]	97.2	94.5
U.S.	95.0	91.9

Note: (1) Metropolitan Statistical Area - see Appendix A for areas included
Source: 1990 Census of Population, General Population Characteristics

INCOME

Per Capita/Median/Average Income

Area	Per Capita ($)	Median Household ($)	Average Household ($)
City	16,300	27,489	40,299
MSA[1]	16,455	33,277	43,582
U.S.	14,420	30,056	38,453

Note: all figures are for 1989; (1) Metropolitan Statistical Area - see Appendix A for areas included
Source: 1990 Census of Population and Housing, Summary Tape File 3C

Household Income Distribution by Race

Income ($)	City (%)					U.S. (%)				
	Total	White	Black	Other	Hisp.[1]	Total	White	Black	Other	Hisp.[1]
Less than 5,000	7.3	4.1	14.8	8.4	7.4	6.2	4.8	15.2	8.6	8.8
5,000 - 9,999	8.2	6.5	12.5	8.7	9.2	9.3	8.6	14.2	9.9	11.1
10,000 - 14,999	9.2	7.6	12.1	12.2	12.4	8.8	8.5	11.0	9.8	11.0
15,000 - 24,999	20.2	18.4	22.7	25.8	27.1	17.5	17.3	18.9	18.5	20.5
25,000 - 34,999	16.7	16.9	15.4	18.3	18.2	15.8	16.1	14.2	15.4	16.4
35,000 - 49,999	15.7	16.9	12.8	15.8	15.4	17.9	18.6	13.3	16.1	16.0
50,000 - 74,999	11.8	14.2	7.4	7.5	7.7	15.0	15.8	9.3	13.4	11.1
75,000 - 99,999	4.6	6.3	1.6	1.9	1.6	5.1	5.5	2.6	4.7	3.1
100,000+	6.2	9.1	0.7	1.4	1.0	4.4	4.8	1.3	3.7	1.9

Note: all figures are for 1989; (1) people of Hispanic origin can be of any race
Source: 1990 Census of Population and Housing, Summary Tape File 3C

Effective Buying Income

Area	Per Capita ($)	Median Household ($)	Average Household ($)
City	18,644	32,897	47,180
MSA[1]	19,075	40,337	51,436
U.S.	15,444	33,201	41,849

Note: data as of 1/1/97; (1) Metropolitan Statistical Area - see Appendix A for areas included
Source: Standard Rate & Data Service, Newspaper Advertising Source, 2/98

Effective Household Buying Income Distribution

Area	% of Households Earning						
	$10,000 -$19,999	$20,000 -$34,999	$35,000 -$49,999	$50,000 -$74,999	$75,000 -$99,000	$100,000 -$124,999	$125,000 and up
City	15.9	24.7	17.0	15.4	6.5	2.9	5.0
MSA[1]	12.5	21.4	18.1	20.9	9.6	3.7	4.6
U.S.	16.5	23.4	18.3	18.2	6.4	2.1	2.4

Note: data as of 1/1/97; (1) Metropolitan Statistical Area - see Appendix A for areas included
Source: Standard Rate & Data Service, Newspaper Advertising Source, 2/98

Poverty Rates by Race and Age

Area	Total (%)	By Race (%)				By Age (%)		
		White	Black	Other	Hisp.[2]	Under 5 years old	Under 18 years old	65 years and over
City	18.0	9.5	29.1	27.2	27.8	27.8	27.3	14.6
MSA[1]	12.0	7.2	26.7	22.7	24.0	17.2	16.2	13.1
U.S.	13.1	9.8	29.5	23.1	25.3	20.1	18.3	12.8

Note: figures show the percent of people living below the poverty line in 1989. The average poverty threshold was $12,674 for a family of four in 1989; (1) Metropolitan Statistical Area - see Appendix A for areas included; (2) people of Hispanic origin can be of any race
Source: 1990 Census of Population and Housing, Summary Tape File 3C

EMPLOYMENT

Labor Force and Employment

Area	Civilian Labor Force			Workers Employed		
	Dec. '95	Dec. '96	% Chg.	Dec. '95	Dec. '96	% Chg.
City	642,910	659,571	2.6	614,681	633,958	3.1
MSA[1]	1,787,077	1,836,829	2.8	1,727,171	1,781,340	3.1
U.S.	134,583,000	136,742,000	1.6	127,903,000	130,785,000	2.3

Note: Data is not seasonally adjusted and covers workers 16 years of age and older;
(1) Metropolitan Statistical Area - see Appendix A for areas included
Source: Bureau of Labor Statistics, http://stats.bls.gov

Unemployment Rate

Area	1997											
	Jan.	Feb.	Mar.	Apr.	May	Jun.	Jul.	Aug.	Sep.	Oct.	Nov.	Dec.
City	5.1	5.3	5.1	4.6	4.7	5.5	5.2	5.0	4.8	4.5	4.4	3.9
MSA[1]	3.9	4.0	3.9	3.6	3.6	4.3	4.0	3.8	3.7	3.5	3.4	3.0
U.S.	5.9	5.7	5.5	4.8	4.7	5.2	5.0	4.8	4.7	4.4	4.3	4.4

Note: Data is not seasonally adjusted and covers workers 16 years of age and older; All figures are percentages; (1) Metropolitan Statistical Area - see Appendix A for areas included
Source: Bureau of Labor Statistics, http://stats.bls.gov

Employment by Industry

Sector	MSA[1]		U.S.
	Number of Employees	Percent of Total	Percent of Total
Services	558,700	30.7	29.0
Retail Trade	307,000	16.9	18.5
Government	202,900	11.1	16.1
Manufacturing	249,000	13.7	15.0
Finance/Insurance/Real Estate	142,400	7.8	5.7
Wholesale Trade	138,200	7.6	5.4
Transportation/Public Utilities	124,900	6.9	5.3
Construction	85,200	4.7	4.5
Mining	11,600	0.6	0.5

Note: Figures cover non-farm employment as of 12/97 and are not seasonally adjusted;
(1) Metropolitan Statistical Area - see Appendix A for areas included
Source: Bureau of Labor Statistics, http://stats.bls.gov

Employment by Occupation

Occupation Category	City (%)	MSA[1] (%)	U.S. (%)
White Collar	62.3	65.3	58.1
Executive/Admin./Management	14.4	15.3	12.3
Professional	13.9	13.9	14.1
Technical & Related Support	3.5	4.2	3.7
Sales	13.1	13.6	11.8
Administrative Support/Clerical	17.3	18.3	16.3
Blue Collar	22.0	21.7	26.2
Precision Production/Craft/Repair	8.4	9.7	11.3
Machine Operators/Assem./Insp.	6.0	5.3	6.8
Transportation/Material Movers	3.4	3.3	4.1
Cleaners/Helpers/Laborers	4.3	3.5	3.9
Services	14.5	11.8	13.2
Farming/Forestry/Fishing	1.2	1.2	2.5

Note: figures cover employed persons 16 years old and over;
(1) Metropolitan Statistical Area - see Appendix A for areas included
Source: 1990 Census of Population and Housing, Summary Tape File 3C

Occupational Employment Projections: 1993 - 2000

Occupations Expected to have the Largest Job Growth (ranked by numerical growth)	Fast-Growing Occupations[1] (ranked by percent growth)
1. General office clerks	1. Physical therapy assistants and aides
2. Child care workers, private household	2. Physical therapists
3. Guards	3. Occupational therapists
4. Cashiers	4. Demonstrators/promoters/models
5. General managers & top executives	5. Air hammer operators
6. Salespersons, retail	6. Housekeepers and butlers
7. Food preparation workers	7. Computer scientists
8. Waiters & waitresses	8. Cleaners/servants, private home
9. Registered nurses	9. Occupational therapy assistants
10. Secretaries, except legal & medical	10. Therapists

Projections cover Collin, Dallas, Denton, Erath, Hood, Hunt, Johnson, Kaufman, Navarro, Palo, Parker, Pinto, Rockwall, Somervell and Wise Counties.
Note: (1) Includes occupations with absolute job growth of 200 or more
Source: Texas Employment Commission, Texas Employment Projections Reporting System, Statewide and Regional Projections 1993-2000, Ver. 1.0

Average Wages

Occupation	Wage	Occupation	Wage
Professional/Technical/Clerical	$/Week	**Health/Protective Services**	$/Week
Accountants III	831	Corrections Officers	417
Attorneys III	1,183	Firefighters	616
Budget Analysts III	813	Nurses, Licensed Practical II	-
Buyers/Contracting Specialists II	652	Nurses, Registered II	-
Clerks, Accounting III	442	Nursing Assistants II	-
Clerks, General III	401	Police Officers I	647
Computer Operators II	459	**Hourly Workers**	$/Hour
Computer Programmers II	637	Forklift Operators	9.95
Drafters II	466	General Maintenance Workers	8.74
Engineering Technicians III	590	Guards I	6.79
Engineering Technicians, Civil III	508	Janitors	-
Engineers III	939	Maintenance Electricians	15.49
Key Entry Operators I	305	Maintenance Electronics Techs II	18.62
Personnel Assistants III	477	Maintenance Machinists	-
Personnel Specialists III	783	Maintenance Mechanics, Machinery	14.06
Secretaries III	529	Material Handling Laborers	7.65
Switchboard Operator-Receptionist	337	Motor Vehicle Mechanics	15.66
Systems Analysts II	909	Shipping/Receiving Clerks	10.02
Systems Analysts Supervisor/Mgr II	1,350	Tool and Die Makers	17.27
Tax Collectors II	437	Truckdrivers, Tractor Trailer	-
Word Processors II	486	Warehouse Specialists	-

Note: Wage data includes full-time workers only for 3/96 and cover the Metropolitan Statistical Area (see Appendix A for areas included). Dashes indicate that data was not available.
Source: Bureau of Labor Statistics, Occupational Compensation Survey, 8/96

TAXES

Major State and Local Tax Rates

State Corp. Income (%)	State Personal Income (%)	Residential Property (effective rate per $100)	Sales & Use		State Gasoline (cents/ gallon)	State Cigarette (cents/ 20-pack)
			State (%)	Local (%)		
None[a]	None	n/a	6.25	2.0	20	41

Note: Personal/corporate income tax rates as of 1/97. Sales, gasoline and cigarette tax rates as of 1/98; (a) Texas imposes a franchise tax of 4.5% of earned surplus
Source: Federation of Tax Administrators, www.taxadmin.org; Washington D.C. Department of Finance and Revenue, Tax Rates and Tax Burdens in the District of Columbia: A Nationwide Comparison, June 1997; Chamber of Commerce

Total Taxes Per Capita and as a Percent of Income

Area	Per Capita Income ($)	Per Capita Taxes ($)			Taxes as Pct. of Income (%)		
		Total	Federal	State/Local	Total	Federal	State/Local
Texas	24,145	8,118	5,538	2,580	33.6	22.9	10.7
U.S.	26,187	9,205	6,127	3,078	35.2	23.4	11.8

Note: Figures are for 1997
Source: Tax Foundation, Web Site, www.taxfoundation.org

Estimated Tax Burden

Area	State Income	Local Income	Property	Sales	Total
Dallas	0	0	4,500	701	5,201

Note: The numbers are estimates of taxes paid by a married couple with two kids and annual earnings of $65,000. Sales tax estimates assume they spend average amounts on food, clothing, household goods and gasoline. Property tax estimates assume they live in a $225,000 home.
Source: Kiplinger's Personal Finance Magazine, June 1997

COMMERCIAL REAL ESTATE

Office Market

Class/Location	Total Space (sq. ft.)	Vacant Space (sq. ft.)	Vac. Rate (%)	Under Constr. (sq. ft.)	Net Absorp. (sq. ft.)	Rental Rates ($/sq.ft./yr.)
Class A						
CBD	13,440,499	3,104,755	23.1	0	172,152	15.00-25.00
Outside CBD	44,848,721	2,819,552	6.3	3,077,684	-1,021,259	15.50-33.00
Class B						
CBD	14,911,239	5,921,853	39.7	0	52,123	12.00-19.00
Outside CBD	43,808,146	5,674,854	13.0	2,178,994	3,780,287	11.00-21.25

Note: Data as of 10/97 and covers Dallas; CBD = Central Business District; n/a not available;
Source: Society of Industrial and Office Realtors, 1998 Comparative Statistics of Industrial and Office Real Estate Markets

"Rental rates increased sharply last year and increases in assessed values will lead to higher real estate taxes being passed on to the tenants. This could lead to some unpleasant surprises for tenants whose leases roll over during 1998. Our SIOR reporter expects both absorption and construction activity to accelerate during 1998. The increase in absorption will push vacancy rates down slightly in the near term. However, the strength in the suburban office markets has led to several proposals for additional construction which could total more than 13 million sq. ft. of space. If a significant proportion of these projects are built, the suburban vacancy rate could climb sharply in 18 to 24 months." *Society of Industrial and Office Realtors, 1998 Comparative Statistics of Industrial and Office Real Estate Markets*

Industrial Market

Location	Total Space (sq. ft.)	Vacant Space (sq. ft.)	Vac. Rate (%)	Under Constr. (sq. ft.)	Net Absorp. (sq. ft.)	Net Lease ($/sq.ft./yr.)
Central City	n/a	n/a	n/a	n/a	n/a	n/a
Suburban	276,000,000	17,900,000	6.5	15,000,000	18,100,000	3.25-4.50

Note: Data as of 10/97 and covers Dallas; n/a not available
Source: Society of Industrial and Office Realtors, 1998 Comparative Statistics of Industrial and Office Real Estate Markets

"As long as strong absorption holds up in the speculative projects, institutional investors are expected to be waiting with their check books. During 1997, the warehouse/distribution segment of the market accounted for the lion's share of the absorption. This is also expected to be the case during 1998. Our SIOR reporters anticipate that absorption in the warehouse/distribution segment of the market will reach 14.5 million sq. ft. during 1998. The migration of traditional office tenants into High Tech/R&D space will likely support an increase in absorption during 1998. During 1997 High Tech/R&D absorption was 1.8 million sq. ft. During 1998, absorption in this segment of the market could increase by another 100,000 sq. ft." *Society of Industrial and Office Realtors, 1998 Comparative Statistics of Industrial and Office Real Estate Markets*

Retail Market

Shopping Center Inventory (sq. ft.)	Shopping Center Construction (sq. ft.)	Construction as a Percent of Inventory (%)	Torto Wheaton Rent Index[1] ($/sq. ft.)
57,368,000	1,180,000	2.1	14.41

Note: Data as of 1997 and covers the Metropolitan Statistical Area - see Appendix A for areas included; (1) Index is based on a model that predicts what the average rent should be for leases with certain characteristics, in certain locations during certain years.
Source: National Association of Realtors, 1997-1998 Market Conditions Report

"The Dallas retail market has improved since 1994, with the retail rent index climbing 39%. The area's economy expanded at a 3.8% pace last year, pouring nearly 60,000 jobs into the MSA. Much of this strong growth is centered in areas north of Dallas. Two new shopping malls are proposed for North Dallas including the 1.2 million square foot Stonebriar Mall at the intersection of the Dallas North Tollway and State Highway 121 (opening spring 1999), and a high-end fashion mall by Taubman Centers Inc. Competition is fierce among the area's malls, and the additions may doom any struggling retail centers in North Dallas." *National Association of Realtors, 1997-1998 Market Conditions Report*

COMMERCIAL UTILITIES

Typical Monthly Electric Bills

Area	Commercial Service ($/month)		Industrial Service ($/month)	
	12 kW demand 1,500 kWh	100 kW demand 30,000 kWh	1,000 kW demand 400,000 kWh	20,000 kW demand 10,000,000 kWh
City	152	2,161	23,072	478,215
U.S.	162	2,360	25,590	545,677

Note: Based on rates in effect July 1, 1997
Source: Edison Electric Institute, Typical Residential, Commercial and Industrial Bills, Summer 1997

TRANSPORTATION

Transportation Statistics

Avg. travel time to work (min.)	24.0
Interstate highways	I-20; I-30; I-35E; I-45
Bus lines	
In-city	Dallas Area Rapid Transit, 1,066 vehicles
Inter-city	4
Passenger air service	
Airport	Dallas/Ft. Worth International; Love Field
Airlines	23
Aircraft departures	429,509 (1995)
Enplaned passengers	29,375,972 (1995)
Rail service	Amtrak; Dallas Area Rapid Transit (Light Rail)
Motor freight carriers	120
Major waterways/ports	None

Source: OAG, Business Travel Planner, Summer 1997; Editor & Publisher Market Guide, 1998; FAA Airport Activity Statistics, 1996; Amtrak National Time Table, Northeast Timetable, Fall/Winter 1997-98; 1990 Census of Population and Housing, STF 3C; Chamber of Commerce/Economic Development 1997; Jane's Urban Transport Systems 1997-98; Transit Fact Book 1997

A survey of 90,000 airline passengers during the first half of 1997 ranked most of the largest airports in the U.S. Dallas-Ft. Worth International ranked number 26 out of 36. Criteria: cleanliness, quality of restaurants, attractiveness, speed of baggage delivery, ease of reaching gates, available ground transportation, ease of following signs and closeness of parking. *Plog Research Inc., First Half 1997*

Means of Transportation to Work

| Area | Car/Truck/Van | | Public Transportation | | | Bicycle | Walked | Other Means | Worked at Home |
	Drove Alone	Car-pooled	Bus	Subway	Railroad				
City	72.5	15.2	6.4	0.0	0.0	0.2	2.4	1.2	2.2
MSA[1]	77.6	14.0	3.1	0.0	0.0	0.1	1.9	1.0	2.3
U.S.	73.2	13.4	3.0	1.5	0.5	0.4	3.9	1.2	3.0

Note: figures shown are percentages and only include workers 16 years old and over;
(1) Metropolitan Statistical Area - see Appendix A for areas included
Source: 1990 Census of Population and Housing, Summary Tape File 3C

BUSINESSES

Major Business Headquarters

| Company Name | 1997 Rankings | |
	Fortune 500	Forbes 500
Austin Industries	-	284
Avatex	260	-
Ben E Keith	-	332
Centex	435	-
Central & South West	259	-
Chief Auto Parts	-	458
Club Corporation International	-	275
CompUSA	357	-
County Seat Stores	-	359
Dresser Industries	219	-
Glazer's Wholesale Distributors	-	318
Halliburton	193	-
Home Interiors & Gifts	-	500
Hunt Consolidated/Hunt Oil	-	331
Lennox International	-	80
Lincoln Property	-	156
Marcus Cable	-	499
Mary Kay Cosmetics	-	190
Perot Systems	-	358
Sammons Enterprises	-	107
Southern Foods Group	-	383
Southwest Airlines	399	-
Texas Instruments	117	-
Texas Utilities	220	-

Note: Companies listed are located in the city; Dashes indicate no ranking
Fortune 500: companies that produce a 10-K are ranked 1 - 500 based on 1996 revenue
Forbes 500: private companies are ranked 1 - 500 based on 1996 revenue
Source: Forbes 12/1/97; Fortune 4/28/97

Fast-Growing Businesses

According to *Inc.*, Dallas is home to two of America's 100 fastest-growing private companies: Natural Gas Transmission Services and Hartex Property Group. Criteria for inclusion: must be an independent, privately-held, U.S. corporation, proprietorship or partnership; sales of at least $200,000 in 1993; five-year operating/sales history; increase in 1997 sales over 1996 sales; holding companies, regulated banks, and utilities were excluded. *Inc. 500, 1997*

Dallas is home to three of *Business Week's* "hot growth" companies: Benchmarq Microelectronics, Gadzooks and Arrow-Magnolia International. Criteria: sales and earnings, return on capital and stock price. *Business Week, 5/26/97*

According to *Fortune*, Dallas is home to three of America's 100 fastest-growing companies: ATC Communications Group, CompUSA and Whitehall. Companies were ranked based on three years' earnings-per-share growth using least squares analysis to smooth out distortions.

Criteria for inclusion: public companies with sales of least $50 million. Companies that lost money in the most recent quarter, or ended in the red for the past four quarters as a whole, were not eligible. Limited partnerships and REITs were also not considered. *Fortune, 9/29/97*

According to Deloitte & Touche LLP, Dallas is home to one of America's 100 fastest-growing high-technology companies: Excel Communications Inc. Companies are ranked by percentage growth in revenue over a five-year period. Criteria for inclusion: must be a U.S. company developing and/or providing technology products or services; company must have been in business for five years with 1992 revenues of at least $50,000. *Deloitte & Touche LLP, January 7, 1998*

Dallas was ranked #18 out of 24 (#1 is best) in terms of the best-performing local stocks in 1996 according to the Money/Norby Cities Index. The index measures stocks of companies that have headquarters in 24 metro areas. *Money, 2/7/97*

Women-Owned Businesses: Number, Employment, Sales and Share

Area	Women-Owned Businesses in 1996				Share of Women-Owned Businesses in 1996	
	Number	Employment	Sales ($000)	Rank[2]	Percent (%)	Rank[3]
MSA[1]	108,500	236,300	33,384,500	10	35.7	35

Note: (1) Metropolitan Statistical Area - see Appendix A for areas included; (2) Calculated on an averaging of number of businesses, employment and sales and ranges from 1 to 50 where 1 is best; (3) Ranges from 1 to 50 where 1 is best
Source: The National Foundation for Women Business Owners, 1996 Facts on Women-Owned Businesses: Trends in the Top 50 Metropolitan Areas, March 26, 1997

Women-Owned Businesses: Growth

Area	Growth in Women-Owned Businesses (% change from 1987 to 1996)				Relative Growth in the Number of Women-Owned and All Businesses (% change from 1987 to 1996)			
	Num.	Empl.	Sales	Rank[2]	Women-Owned	All Firms	Absolute Difference	Relative Difference
MSA[1]	74.3	356.0	391.1	8	74.3	51.3	23.0	1.4:1

Note: (1) Metropolitan Statistical Area - see Appendix A for areas included; (2) Calculated on an averaging of the percent growth of number of businesses, employment and sales and ranges from 1 to 50 where 1 is best
Source: The National Foundation for Women Business Owners, 1996 Facts on Women-Owned Businesses: Trends in the Top 50 Metropolitan Areas, March 26, 1997

Minority Business Opportunity

Dallas is home to one company which is on the Black Enterprise Industrial/Service 100 list (largest based on gross sales): Pro-Line Corp. (hair care products mfg. and distrib.). Criteria: 1) operational in previous calendar year; 2) at least 51% black-owned; 3) manufactures/owns the product it sells or provides industrial or consumer services. Brokerages, real estate firms and firms that provide professional services are not eligible. *Black Enterprise, July 1997*

Dallas is home to one company which is on the Black Enterprise Auto Dealer 100 list (largest based on gross sales): Davis Automotive Inc. (GM/Honda/Hyundai). Criteria: 1) operational in previous calendar year; 2) at least 51% black-owned. *Black Enterprise, June 1997*

Five of the 500 largest Hispanic-owned companies in the U.S. are located in Dallas. *Hispanic Business, June 1997*

Dallas is home to three companies which are on the Hispanic Business Fastest-Growing 100 list (greatest sales growth from 1992 to 1996): Wendy Lopez & Associates Inc. (engr. consulting svcs.), M.A.P.A. Inc. (healthcare reimbursement svcs.), and Yoko Trucking Co. Inc. (general construction) *Hispanic Business, July/August 1997*

Dallas was listed among the top 25 metropolitan areas in terms of the number of Hispanic-owned companies. The city was ranked number 14 with 21,892 companies. *Hispanic Business, May 1997*

Small Business Opportunity

According to *Forbes*, Dallas is home to four of America's 200 best small companies: Dallas Semiconductor, Fresh America, Source Services, Sterling Commerce. Criteria: companies must be publicly traded, U.S.-based corporations with latest 12-month sales of between $5 and $350 million. Earnings must be at least $1 million for the 12-month period. Limited partnerships, REITs and closed-end mutual funds were not considered. Banks, S&Ls and electric utilities were not included. *Forbes, November 3, 1997*

HOTELS & MOTELS

Hotels/Motels

Area	Hotels/ Motels	Rooms	Luxury-Level Hotels/Motels		Average Minimum Rates ($)		
			♦♦♦♦	♦♦♦♦♦	♦♦	♦♦♦	♦♦♦♦
City	82	19,850	4	3	71	129	168
Airport	44	10,192	2	0	n/a	n/a	n/a
Suburbs	57	6,771	0	0	n/a	n/a	n/a
Total	183	36,813	6	3	n/a	n/a	n/a

Note: n/a not available; Classifications range from one diamond (budget properties with basic amenities) to five diamond (luxury properties with the finest service, rooms and facilities).
Source: OAG, Business Travel Planner, Summer 1997

Dallas is home to one of the top 100 hotels in the world according to *Travel & Leisure*: Mansion on Turtle Creek. Criteria: value, rooms/ambience, location, facilities/activities and service. *Travel & Leisure, September 1997*

CONVENTION CENTERS

Major Convention Centers

Center Name	Meeting Rooms	Exhibit Space (sf)
Dallas Apparel Mart	3	1,000,000
Dallas Convention Center	105	807,000
Dallas Market Center	318	313,000
Fairmont Hotel of Dallas	24	n/a
Infomart	30	300,000
Fair Park	n/a	747,180

Note: n/a not available
Source: Trade Shows Worldwide 1997

Living Environment

COST OF LIVING

Cost of Living Index

Composite Index	Housing	Utilities	Groceries	Health Care	Trans-portation	Misc. Goods/ Services
98.2	94.2	95.9	97.6	106.4	105.2	98.9

Note: U.S. = 100; Figures are for the Metropolitan Statistical Area - see Appendix A for areas included
Source: ACCRA, Cost of Living Index, 3rd Quarter 1997

HOUSING

Median Home Prices and Housing Affordability

Area	Median Price[2] 3rd Qtr. 1997 ($)	HOI[3] 3rd Qtr. 1997	Afford-ability Rank[4]
MSA[1]	130,000	59.6	151
U.S.	127,000	63.7	–

Note: (1) Metropolitan Statistical Area - see Appendix A for areas included; (2) U.S. figures calculated from the sales of 625,000 new and existing homes in 195 markets; (3) Housing Opportunity Index - percent of homes sold that were within the reach of the median income household at the prevailing mortgage interest rate; (4) Rank is from 1-195 with 1 being most affordable
Source: National Association of Home Builders, Housing Opportunity Index, 3rd Quarter 1997

It is projected that the median price of existing single-family homes in the metro area will increase by 11.5% in 1998. Nationwide, home prices are projected to increase 6.6%.
Kiplinger's Personal Finance Magazine, January 1998

Average New Home Price

Area	Price ($)
MSA[1]	117,498
U.S.	135,710

Note: Figures are based on a new home with 1,800 sq. ft. of living area on an 8,000 sq. ft. lot;
(1) Metropolitan Statistical Area - see Appendix A for areas included
Source: ACCRA, Cost of Living Index, 3rd Quarter 1997

Average Apartment Rent

Area	Rent ($/mth)
MSA[1]	745
U.S.	569

Note: Figures are based on an unfurnished two bedroom, 1-1/2 or 2 bath apartment, approximately 950 sq. ft. in size, excluding all utilities except water; (1) Metropolitan Statistical Area - see Appendix A for areas included
Source: ACCRA, Cost of Living Index, 3rd Quarter 1997

RESIDENTIAL UTILITIES

Average Residential Utility Costs

Area	All Electric ($/mth)	Part Electric ($/mth)	Other Energy ($/mth)	Phone ($/mth)
MSA[1]	–	76.65	23.53	16.33
U.S.	109.40	55.25	43.64	19.48

Note: (1) (1) Metropolitan Statistical Area - see Appendix A for areas included
Source: ACCRA, Cost of Living Index, 3rd Quarter 1997

HEALTH CARE

Average Health Care Costs

Area	Hospital ($/day)	Doctor ($/visit)	Dentist ($/visit)
MSA[1]	457.50	51.10	63.40
U.S.	392.91	48.76	60.84

Note: Hospital - based on a semi-private room. Doctor - based on a general practitioner's routine exam of an established patient. Dentist - based on adult teeth cleaning and periodic oral exam; (1) Metropolitan Statistical Area - see Appendix A for areas included
Source: ACCRA, Cost of Living Index, 3rd Quarter 1997

Distribution of Office-Based Physicians

Area	Family/Gen. Practitioners	Specialists		
		Medical	Surgical	Other
MSA[1]	516	1,453	1,339	1,408

Note: Data as of 12/31/96; (1) Metropolitan Statistical Area - see Appendix A for areas included
Source: American Medical Assn., Physician Characteristics & Distribution in the U.S., 1997-1998

Hospitals

Dallas has 18 general medical and surgical hospitals, 3 rehabilitation, 1 chronic disease, 2 children's general, 1 children's other specialty. *AHA Guide to the Healthcare Field 1997-98*

According to *U.S. News and World Report,* Dallas has 2 of the best hospitals in the U.S.: **Baylor University Medical Center,** noted for AIDS, cancer, cardiology, endocrinology, gastroenterology, gynecology, neurology, orthopedics, otolaryngology, pulmonology, rehabilitation, urology; **Parkland Memorial Hospital,** noted for AIDS, endocrinology, gynecology, pulmonology, rheumatology, urology; *U.S. News and World Report, "America's Best Hospitals", 7/28/97*

EDUCATION

Public School District Statistics

District Name	Num. Sch.	Enroll.	Classroom Teachers[1]	Pupils per Teacher	Minority Pupils (%)	Current Exp.[2] ($/pupil)
Dallas ISD	203	148,839	8,881	16.8	88.1	4,941
Highland Park ISD	7	5,222	355	14.7	n/a	n/a
Wilmer-Hutchins ISD	8	3,837	260	14.8	n/a	n/a

Note: Data covers the 1995-1996 school year unless otherwise noted; (1) Excludes teachers reported as working in school district offices rather than in schools; (2) Based on 1993-94 enrollment collected by the Census Bureau, not the enrollment figure shown in column 3; SD = School District; ISD = Independent School District; n/a not available
Source: National Center for Education Statistics, Common Core of Data Survey; Bureau of the Census

Educational Quality

School District	Education Quotient[1]	Graduate Outcome[2]	Community Index[3]	Resource Index[4]
Dallas	79.0	57.0	111.0	68.0

Note: Nearly 1,000 secondary school districts were rated in terms of educational quality. The scores range from a low of 50 to a high of 150; (1) Average of the Graduate Outcome, Community and Resource indexes; (2) Based on graduation rates and college board scores (SAT/ACT); (3) Based on the surrounding community's average level of education and the area's average income level; (4) Based on teacher salaries, per-pupil expenditures and student-teacher ratios.
Source: Expansion Management, Ratings Issue 1997

Educational Attainment by Race

Area	High School Graduate (%)					Bachelor's Degree (%)				
	Total	White	Black	Other	Hisp.[2]	Total	White	Black	Other	Hisp.[2]
City	73.5	82.5	67.2	38.6	33.9	27.1	36.9	10.9	10.9	7.0
MSA[1]	79.0	84.1	70.1	50.0	41.7	27.6	31.5	13.5	16.5	8.9
U.S.	75.2	77.9	63.1	60.4	49.8	20.3	21.5	11.4	19.4	9.2

Note: figures shown cover persons 25 years old and over; (1) Metropolitan Statistical Area - see Appendix A for areas included; (2) people of Hispanic origin can be of any race
Source: 1990 Census of Population and Housing, Summary Tape File 3C

School Enrollment by Type

Area	Preprimary				Elementary/High School			
	Public		Private		Public		Private	
	Enrollment	%	Enrollment	%	Enrollment	%	Enrollment	%
City	8,029	52.2	7,349	47.8	147,967	90.2	16,105	9.8
MSA[1]	24,235	49.1	25,151	50.9	413,238	92.3	34,313	7.7
U.S.	2,679,029	59.5	1,824,256	40.5	38,379,689	90.2	4,187,099	9.8

Note: figures shown cover persons 3 years old and over;
(1) Metropolitan Statistical Area - see Appendix A for areas included
Source: 1990 Census of Population and Housing, Summary Tape File 3C

School Enrollment by Race

Area	Preprimary (%)				Elementary/High School (%)			
	White	Black	Other	Hisp.[1]	White	Black	Other	Hisp.[1]
City	56.1	31.5	12.4	16.8	38.2	39.7	22.2	30.3
MSA[2]	76.1	15.8	8.2	10.6	64.7	20.3	15.0	19.3
U.S.	80.4	12.5	7.1	7.8	74.1	15.6	10.3	12.5

Note: figures shown cover persons 3 years old and over; (1) people of Hispanic origin can be of any race; (2) Metropolitan Statistical Area - see Appendix A for areas included
Source: 1990 Census of Population and Housing, Summary Tape File 3C

SAT/ACT Scores

Area/District	1995 SAT				1995 ACT	
	Percent of Graduates Tested (%)	Average Math Score	Average Verbal Score	Average Combined Score	Percent of Graduates Tested (%)	Average Composite Score
Dallas SD	49	359	409	768	20	17.8
State	47	474	419	893	33	20.1
U.S.	41	482	428	910	37	20.8

Note: Math and verbal SAT scores are out of a possible 800; ACT scores are out of a possible 36
Caution: Comparing or ranking states/cities on the basis of SAT/ACT scores alone is invalid and strongly discouraged by the The College Board and The American College Testing Program as students who take the tests are self-selected and do not represent the entire student population.
Source: Texas Education Agency, 1995; American College Testing Program, 1995; College Board, 1995

Classroom Teacher Salaries in Public Schools

District	B.A. Degree		M.A. Degree		Ph.D. Degree	
	Min. ($)	Max. ($)	Min. ($)	Max. ($)	Min. ($)	Max. ($)
Dallas	25,250	40,402	26,250	45,608	27,250	46,720
Average[1]	26,120	39,270	28,175	44,667	31,643	49,825

Note: Salaries are for 1996-1997; (1) Based on all school districts covered
Source: American Federation of Teachers (unpublished data)

Higher Education

Two-Year Colleges		Four-Year Colleges		Medical Schools	Law Schools	Voc/ Tech
Public	Private	Public	Private			
3	4	1	6	1	1	23

Source: College Blue Book, Occupational Education 1997; Medical School Admission Requirements, 1998-99; Peterson's Guide to Two-Year Colleges, 1997; Peterson's Guide to Four-Year Colleges, 1997; Barron's Guide to Law Schools 1997

MAJOR EMPLOYERS

Major Employers

Army & Air Force Exchange Service	BancOne Texas Corp.
Baylor University Medical Center	Dallas County Hospital District
Dallas Morning News	GTE Directories Corp.
International Brotherhood of Electrical Workers	Mary Kay Corp.
Nationsbank of Texas	Presbyterian Hospital
Southwest Airlines	St. Paul Medical Center
Anatole Hotel Investors	Vought Aircraft
Texas Instruments	Centex Homes Partnership (real estate)
Children's Medical Center of Dallas	

Note: companies listed are located in the city
Source: Dun's Business Rankings 1997; Ward's Business Directory, 1997

PUBLIC SAFETY

Crime Rate

Area	All Crimes	Violent Crimes				Property Crimes		
		Murder	Forcible Rape	Robbery	Aggrav. Assault	Burglary	Larceny -Theft	Motor Vehicle Theft
City	9,466.6	20.5	69.8	577.2	867.5	1,693.4	4,621.8	1,616.4
Suburbs[1]	4,564.3	3.7	29.2	72.2	249.1	818.8	3,072.3	319.0
MSA[2]	6,350.2	9.8	44.0	256.2	474.4	1,137.4	3,636.8	791.6
U.S.	5,078.9	7.4	36.1	202.4	388.2	943.0	2,975.9	525.9

Note: Crime rate is the number of crimes per 100,000 pop.; (1) defined as all areas within the MSA but located outside the central city; (2) Metropolitan Statistical Area - see Appendix A for areas incl.
Source: FBI Uniform Crime Reports 1996

RECREATION

Culture and Recreation

Museums	Symphony Orchestras	Opera Companies	Dance Companies	Professional Theatres	Zoos	Pro Sports Teams
12	3	1	3	6	1	3

Source: International Directory of the Performing Arts, 1996; Official Museum Directory, 1998; Chamber of Commerce/Economic Development 1997

Library System

The Dallas Public Library has 22 branches, holdings of 2,490,486 volumes and a budget of $16,827,753 (1994-1995). *American Library Directory, 1997-1998*

MEDIA

Newspapers

Name	Type	Freq.	Distribution	Circulation
The Dallas Morning News	General	7x/wk	Area	536,153
Dallas Observer	General	1x/wk	Local	105,000
The Dallas Weekly	Black	1x/wk	Local	25,000
El Extra	Hispanic	1x/wk	Area	28,334
El Hispano	Hispanic	1x/wk	Area	35,000
El Sol de Texas	Hispanic	1x/wk	Area	26,000
La Fuente	Hispanic	1x/wk	Area	105,000
La Prensa	Hispanic	1x/wk	Local	40,000
Novedades News	Hispanic	1x/wk	Local	32,000
Texas Catholic	n/a	2x/mo	Local	45,200
United Methodist Reporter	Religious	1x/wk	National	405,000

Note: Includes newspapers with circulations of 25,000 or more located in the city; n/a not available
Source: Burrelle's Media Directory, 1998 Edition

AM Radio Stations

Call Letters	Freq. (kHz)	Target Audience	Station Format	Music Format
KDFT	540	n/a	M/N/S	Christian
KLIF	570	General	N/S	n/a
KSKY	660	General	M/N/S	Christian
KKDA	730	Black	M	Urban Contemporary
KPBC	770	Religious	M/T	Christian
WBAP	820	General	N/T	n/a
KHVN	970	Black	M	Christian
KGGR	1040	Black/Relig	M/N/S	Christian
KRLD	1080	General	N/T	n/a
KDMM	1150	n/a	N	n/a
KOOO	1190	General	T	n/a
KESS	1270	Hispanic	M/N/S	n/a
KTCK	1310	n/a	S/T	n/a
KINF	1440	Hispanic	M/N/S	Spanish
KMRT	1480	Hispanic	M/N	Spanish
KEGG	1560	Religious	E/M/N/S/T	Christian
KRVA	1600	Hispanic	M/N/S	Adult Contemporary

Note: Stations included broadcast in the Dallas metro area; n/a not available
Station Format: E = Educational; M = Music; N = News; S = Sports; T = Talk
Source: Burrelle's Media Directory, 1998 Edition

FM Radio Stations

Call Letters	Freq. (mHz)	Target Audience	Station Format	Music Format
KEOM	88.5	General	M/N/S	Contemporary Top 40
KNON	89.3	General	M/T	n/a
KERA	90.1	Black	E/M/N/T	Alternative
KCBI	90.9	General	M/N/S	Christian
KVTT	91.7	General	M	Christian
KZPS	92.5	General	M	Classic Rock
KKZN	93.3	n/a	M/N	Alternative
KLTY	94.1	General	M	Christian
KDGE	94.5	General	M	Alternative
KEGL	97.1	General	M/T	AOR
KBFB	97.9	General	M	Adult Contemporary
KLUV	98.7	General	M	Oldies
KHCK	99.1	n/a	M	Spanish
KPLX	99.5	General	M	Country
KRBV	100.3	Black	M	Urban Contemporary
WRR	101.1	General	M	Classical
KTXQ	102.1	General	M	AOR
KDMX	102.9	n/a	M	Adult Contemporary
KVIL	103.7	General	M	Adult Contemporary
KKDA	104.5	General	M	Urban Contemporary
KYNG	105.3	General	M	Country
KRNB	105.7	General	M/N/S	R&B
KHKS	106.1	General	M	Contemporary Top 40
KMRT	106.7	n/a	n/a	n/a
KRVA	106.9	Hispanic	M/N/S	Spanish
KOAI	107.5	General	M	Adult Contemporary/Contemporary Top 40/Jazz/R&B
KICI	107.9	Hispanic	N/S/T	n/a

Note: Stations included broadcast in the Dallas metro area; n/a not available
Station Format: E = Educational; M = Music; N = News; S = Sports; T = Talk
Music Format: AOR = Album Oriented Rock; MOR = Middle-of-the-Road
Source: Burrelle's Media Directory, 1998 Edition

Television Stations

Name	Ch.	Affiliation	Type	Owner
KDTN	2	PBS	Public	North Texas Public Broadcasting Inc.
KDFW	4	Fox	Commercial	New World Communications of Texas
WFAA	8	ABC	Commercial	A.H. Belo Corporation
KERA	13	PBS	Public	North Texas Public Broadcasting Inc.
KTXA	21	UPN	Commercial	Paramount Communications
KUVN	23	Univision	Commercial	Perenchio Television Inc.
KDFI	27	n/a	Commercial	Dallas Media Investors
KDAF	33	WB	Commercial	Renaissance Communications Corp.
KXTX	39	n/a	Commercial	Lin Television
KHSX	49	HSN	Commercial	Silver King Communications Inc.
KFWD	52	Telemundo	Commercial	Interspan Communications Ltd.
KDTX	58	n/a	Non-Commercial	Trinity Broadcasting

Note: Stations included broadcast in the Dallas metro area
Source: Burrelle's Media Directory, 1998 Edition

CLIMATE

Average and Extreme Temperatures

Temperature	Jan	Feb	Mar	Apr	May	Jun	Jul	Aug	Sep	Oct	Nov	Dec	Ann
Extreme High (°F)	85	90	100	100	101	112	111	109	107	101	91	87	112
Average High (°F)	55	60	68	76	84	92	96	96	89	79	67	58	77
Average Temp. (°F)	45	50	57	66	74	82	86	86	79	68	56	48	67
Average Low (°F)	35	39	47	56	64	72	76	75	68	57	46	38	56
Extreme Low (°F)	-2	9	12	30	39	53	58	58	42	24	16	0	-2

Note: Figures cover the years 1945-1993
Source: National Climatic Data Center, International Station Meteorological Climate Summary, 3/95

Average Precipitation/Snowfall/Humidity

Precip./Humidity	Jan	Feb	Mar	Apr	May	Jun	Jul	Aug	Sep	Oct	Nov	Dec	Ann
Avg. Precip. (in.)	1.9	2.3	2.6	3.8	4.9	3.4	2.1	2.3	2.9	3.3	2.3	2.1	33.9
Avg. Snowfall (in.)	1	1	Tr	Tr	0	0	0	0	0	Tr	Tr	Tr	3
Avg. Rel. Hum. 6am (%)	78	77	75	77	82	81	77	76	80	79	78	77	78
Avg. Rel. Hum. 3pm (%)	53	51	47	49	51	48	43	41	46	46	48	51	48

Note: Figures cover the years 1945-1993; Tr = Trace amounts (<0.05 in. of rain; <0.5 in. of snow)
Source: National Climatic Data Center, International Station Meteorological Climate Summary, 3/95

Weather Conditions

Temperature			Daytime Sky			Precipitation		
10°F & below	32°F & below	90°F & above	Clear	Partly cloudy	Cloudy	0.01 inch or more precip.	0.1 inch or more snow/ice	Thunder-storms
1	34	102	108	160	97	78	2	49

Note: Figures are average number of days per year and covers the years 1945-1993
Source: National Climatic Data Center, International Station Meteorological Climate Summary, 3/95

AIR & WATER QUALITY

Maximum Pollutant Concentrations

	Particulate Matter (ug/m³)	Carbon Monoxide (ppm)	Sulfur Dioxide (ppm)	Nitrogen Dioxide (ppm)	Ozone (ppm)	Lead (ug/m³)
MSA[1] Level	102	6	0.046	0.019	0.14	0.17
NAAQS[2]	150	9	0.140	0.053	0.12	1.50
Met NAAQS?	Yes	Yes	Yes	Yes	No	Yes

Note: (1) Metropolitan Statistical Area - see Appendix A for areas included; (2) National Ambient Air Quality Standards; ppm = parts per million; ug/m³ = micrograms per cubic meter; n/a not available
Source: EPA, National Air Quality and Emissions Trends Report, 1996

Pollutant Standards Index

In the Dallas MSA (see Appendix A for areas included), the Pollutant Standards Index (PSI) exceeded 100 on 6 days in 1996. A PSI value greater than 100 indicates that air quality would be in the unhealthful range on that day. *EPA, National Air Quality and Emissions Trends Report, 1996*

Drinking Water

Water System Name	Pop. Served	Primary Water Source Type	Number of Violations in Fiscal Year 1997	Type of Violation/ Contaminants
Dallas Water Utility	1,003,150	Surface	None	None

Note: Data as of January 16, 1998
Source: EPA, Office of Ground Water and Drinking Water, Safe Drinking Water Information System

Dallas tap water is moderately hard and fluoridated.
Editor & Publisher Market Guide, 1998

Fort Lauderdale, Florida

Background

To those unfamiliar with Fort Lauderdale, the city can rightfully boast of its title, the "Venice of America". Located on the Atlantic Ocean in southeast Florida, Fort Lauderdale is a city of tiny residential islands, canals, and yacht basins.

Originally built as a fortification in 1837 for the Seminole War, Fort Lauderdale eased into more peaceful times as a top tourist spot. Photo's of Spring Break; cars cruising "The Strip", the main thoroughfare bordering the beach; and cute tan young men and women stimulated the imagination of people around the world.

Today Fort Lauderdale prefers to focus on its other assets. Fashionable Las Olas Boulevard is the main artery of downtown. Full of shops and restaurants, it is a quaint and easily accessible street on which to stroll. The Museum of Art is a handsome modern edifice that showcases 19th and 20th century paintings, and Japanese objects d'art. It is especially noted has having the largest collection of artwork from Copenhagen, Brussels and Amsterdam, in the United States. The Museum of Discovery and Science, which includes the Blockbuster IMAX Theater compliments of the multi-corporation mogul Wayne Huizenga, is fascinating to children of all ages. The Broward Center for Performing Arts hosts Broadway plays and other major cultural events.

As home to one of the biggest yacht basins in the country, the main industry outside of tourism, is in boating products. However, because of its largely residential character, the home improvement industry, such as concrete, air-conditioning, and roofing, lays a large claim to the economy as well.

Fort Lauderdale's climate is primarily subtropical marine which produces a long, warm summer with abundant rainfall, followed by a mild, dry winter. Hurricanes occasionally affect the area. The months of greatest frequency are September and October. Funnel clouds and waterspouts are occasionally sighted during the summer months but neither cause significant damage. Strong and sometimes spectacular lightening events occur most often during June, July and August.

General Rankings and Evaluative Comments

■ Fort Lauderdale was ranked #15 out of 300 cities by *Money's* 1997 "Survey of the Best Places to Live." Criteria used: health services, crime, economy, housing, education, transportation, weather, leisure and the arts. The city was ranked #4 in 1996 and #6 in 1995. *Money, July 1997; Money, September 1996; Money, September 1995*

■ *Ladies Home Journal* ranked America's 200 largest cities based on the qualities women care about most. Fort Lauderdale ranked 83 out of 200. Criteria: low crime rate, good public schools, well-paying jobs, quality health and child care, the presence of women in government, proportion of women-owned businesses, size of the wage gap with men, local economy, divorce rates, the ratio of single men to single women, whether there are laws that require at least the same number of public toilets for women as men, and the probability of good hair days. *Ladies Home Journal, November 1997*

■ Fort Lauderdale was ranked #197 out of 219 cities in terms of children's health, safety, and economic well-being. Criteria: total population, percent population change, birth rate, child immunization rate, infant mortality rate, percent low birth weight infants, percent of births to teens, physician-to-population ratio, student-to-teacher ratio, dropout rate, unemployment rate, median family income, percent of children in poverty, violent and property crime rates, number of juvenile arrests for violent crimes as a percent of the total crime index, number of days with pollution standard index (PSI) over 100, pounds toxic releases per 1,000 people and number of superfund sites. *Zero Population Growth, Children's Environmental Index 1997*

■ Century Village at Pembroke Pines, located 20 miles southwest of Fort Lauderdale, is among America's best retirement communities. Criteria: communities must have state-of-the-art facilities, newly built homes for sale, and give you the most value for your money in every price range. Communities must also welcome newcomers of all races and religions. *New Choices, July/August 1997*

■ According to *Working Mother,* "Florida stands out among the Southern states for its aggressive action to improve and expand child care. As we went to press, the governor had asked state lawmakers for a significant increase in state funds to create new child care slots. Some $49 million would be earmarked for a very important group—16,000 children of low-wage workers.

In the past year the state also boosted funding for its prekindergarten program by $4 million, bringing its pre-K spending to $102 million. This translates into free pre-K for 27,000 kids, about 2,000 more than last year. This program is funded with state lottery money and is available in all of Florida's 67 school districts.

The state has also improved its requirements for playground surfaces in child care setting. As of March 1997, all centers were required to have soft surfaces under playground equipment. This is a vital change, given that injuries from falls are the most common in child care.

Finally, lawmakers approved a new program to recognize quality child care programs. Any facility that attains state or NAEYC accreditation can now post a 'good seal' certificate and will be listed in a state database as a 'Gold Seal' program—to show it meets high standards of care. So far, about 370 centers have received certificates, and about 800 more are in the pipeline." *Working Mother, July/August 1997*

Business Environment

STATE ECONOMY

State Economic Profile

''Florida's economy continues to expand strongly....

Florida is becoming increasingly dependent on the service industry for job growth. Currently, one in three Florida jobs is service-related. In the past year, however, nearly half of all jobs created were in the service industry. One in four jobs created was in business services, compared to one in seven for the U.S....

Florida's tourist industry continues to rebound and will be an important source of growth for this year. Household income growth and savings rates are high, and the values of individual stock portfolios has been booming, leaving households across the U.S. in good financial shape to take a vacation.

A risk to Florida's economy is a sharp slowing in population growth. In 1996, Florida experienced a population gain of only 1.5%, the slowest rate of growth since World War II. Contributing to the slower population growth is weaker retiree migration due to a slowing national retiree population growth.

Supporting growth are Florida's moderate climate, favorable quality of life, affordable housing, and low cost of doing business, which will continue to attract businesses and households. Population growth will continue to slow for the next decade as the number of people reaching retirement age nationwide is falling. Population growth will begin to accelerate once the baby boom generation hits retirement age beginning around 2005. One downside risk for Florida is its dependence on tourism and interest and property income that makes it vulnerable to national and international business cycles. Florida will remain one of the nation's fastest-growing economies through the remainder of this century.'' *National Association of Realtors, Economic Profiles: The Fifty States, July 1997*

IMPORTS/EXPORTS

Total Export Sales

Area	1993 ($000)	1994 ($000)	1995 ($000)	1996 ($000)	% Chg. 1993-96	% Chg. 1995-96
MSA[1]	1,321,448	1,506,662	1,774,654	1,864,518	41.1	5.1
U.S.	464,858,354	512,415,609	583,030,524	622,827,063	34.0	6.8

Note: (1) Metropolitan Statistical Area - see Appendix A for areas included
Source: U.S. Department of Commerce, International Trade Association, Metropolitan Area Exports: An Export Performance Report on Over 250 U.S. Cities, October 1997

Imports/Exports by Port

Type	Cargo Value			Share of U.S. Total	
	1995 (US$mil.)	1996 (US$mil.)	% Change 1995-1996	1995 (%)	1996 (%)
Imports	5,670	6,003	5.87	1.45	1.56
Exports	4,389	4,520	2.99	1.92	1.91

Source: Global Trade Information Services, WaterBorne Trade Atlas 1997

CITY FINANCES

City Government Finances

Component	FY92 ($000)	FY92 (per capita $)
Revenue	271,657	1,805.02
Expenditure	247,353	1,643.53
Debt Outstanding	110,999	737.53
Cash & Securities	381,498	2,534.85

Source: U.S. Bureau of the Census, City Government Finances: 1991-92

City Government Revenue by Source

Source	FY92 ($000)	FY92 (per capita $)	FY92 (%)
From Federal Government	9,475	62.96	3.5
From State Governments	22,201	147.51	8.2
From Local Governments	5,701	37.88	2.1
Property Taxes	44,418	295.13	16.4
General Sales Taxes	0	0.00	0.0
Selective Sales Taxes	32,808	217.99	12.1
Income Taxes	0	0.00	0.0
Current Charges	28,945	192.32	10.7
Utility/Liquor Store	39,592	263.07	14.6
Employee Retirement[1]	53,282	354.03	19.6
Other	35,235	234.12	13.0

Note: (1) Excludes "city contributions," classified as "nonrevenue," intragovernmental transfers.
Source: U.S. Bureau of the Census, City Government Finances: 1991-92

City Government Expenditures by Function

Function	FY92 ($000)	FY92 (per capita $)	FY92 (%)
Educational Services	0	0.00	0.0
Employee Retirement[1]	12,945	86.01	5.2
Environment/Housing	77,621	515.75	31.4
Government Administration	11,453	76.10	4.6
Interest on General Debt	5,915	39.30	2.4
Public Safety	62,686	416.52	25.3
Social Services	0	0.00	0.0
Transportation	22,076	146.68	8.9
Utility/Liquor Store	41,059	272.82	16.6
Other	13,598	90.35	5.5

Note: (1) Payments to beneficiaries including withdrawal of contributions.
Source: U.S. Bureau of the Census, City Government Finances: 1991-92

Municipal Bond Ratings

Area	Moody's	S & P
Fort Lauderdale	Aa3	n/a

Note: n/a not available; n/r not rated
Source: Moody's Bond Record, 2/98; Statistical Abstract of the U.S., 1997;
Governing Magazine, 9/97, 3/98

POPULATION

Population Growth

Area	1980	1990	% Chg. 1980-90	July 1996 Estimate	% Chg. 1990-96
City	153,279	149,377	-2.5	151,805	1.6
MSA[1]	1,018,200	1,255,488	23.3	1,438,228	14.6
U.S.	226,545,805	248,765,170	9.8	265,179,411	6.6

Note: (1) Metropolitan Statistical Area - see Appendix A for areas included
Source: 1980/1990 Census of Housing and Population, Summary Tape File 3C;
Census Bureau Population Estimates

Population Characteristics

Race	City 1980 Population	%	City 1990 Population	%	% Chg. 1980-90	MSA[1] 1990 Population	%
White	119,327	77.8	104,015	69.6	-12.8	1,027,465	81.8
Black	32,222	21.0	41,997	28.1	30.3	193,360	15.4
Amer Indian/Esk/Aleut	246	0.2	383	0.3	55.7	2,907	0.2
Asian/Pacific Islander	685	0.4	1,125	0.8	64.2	16,499	1.3
Other	799	0.5	1,857	1.2	132.4	15,257	1.2
Hispanic Origin[2]	6,402	4.2	10,574	7.1	65.2	105,668	8.4

Note: (1) Metropolitan Statistical Area - see Appendix A for areas included;
(2) people of Hispanic origin can be of any race
Source: 1980/1990 Census of Housing and Population, Summary Tape File 3C

Ancestry

Area	German	Irish	English	Italian	U.S.	French	Polish	Dutch
City	16.5	13.1	12.8	7.6	3.3	3.9	3.3	1.7
MSA[1]	16.3	13.4	10.1	11.2	4.1	3.4	5.8	1.4
U.S.	23.3	15.6	13.1	5.9	5.3	4.2	3.8	2.5

Note: Figures are percentages and include persons that reported multiple ancestry (eg. if a person reported being Irish and Italian, they were included in both columns); (1) Metropolitan Statistical Area - see Appendix A for areas included
Source: 1990 Census of Population and Housing, Summary Tape File 3C

Age

Area	Median Age (Years)	Age Distribution (%) Under 5	Under 18	18-24	25-44	45-64	65+	80+
City	37.1	6.0	18.8	8.1	34.8	20.4	17.9	5.0
MSA[1]	37.6	6.2	20.4	8.0	32.0	18.9	20.7	5.1
U.S.	32.9	7.3	25.6	10.5	32.6	18.7	12.5	2.8

Note: (1) Metropolitan Statistical Area - see Appendix A for areas included
Source: 1990 Census of Population and Housing, Summary Tape File 3C

Male/Female Ratio

Area	Number of males per 100 females (all ages)	Number of males per 100 females (18 years old+)
City	100.9	101.6
MSA[1]	91.7	88.8
U.S.	95.0	91.9

Note: (1) Metropolitan Statistical Area - see Appendix A for areas included
Source: 1990 Census of Population, General Population Characteristics

INCOME

Per Capita/Median/Average Income

Area	Per Capita ($)	Median Household ($)	Average Household ($)
City	19,814	27,239	43,756
MSA[1]	16,883	30,571	39,823
U.S.	14,420	30,056	38,453

Note: all figures are for 1989; (1) Metropolitan Statistical Area - see Appendix A for areas included
Source: 1990 Census of Population and Housing, Summary Tape File 3C

Household Income Distribution by Race

Income ($)	City (%)					U.S. (%)				
	Total	White	Black	Other	Hisp.[1]	Total	White	Black	Other	Hisp.[1]
Less than 5,000	7.5	5.1	17.7	10.6	10.2	6.2	4.8	15.2	8.6	8.8
5,000 - 9,999	8.9	7.3	15.4	9.2	8.3	9.3	8.6	14.2	9.9	11.1
10,000 - 14,999	9.7	8.8	13.1	12.5	11.2	8.8	8.5	11.0	9.8	11.0
15,000 - 24,999	19.9	18.6	25.2	22.4	22.3	17.5	17.3	18.9	18.5	20.5
25,000 - 34,999	14.9	15.4	13.0	11.2	16.2	15.8	16.1	14.2	15.4	16.4
35,000 - 49,999	14.7	15.8	10.1	18.5	17.1	17.9	18.6	13.3	16.1	16.0
50,000 - 74,999	12.7	14.8	4.0	7.3	7.8	15.0	15.8	9.3	13.4	11.1
75,000 - 99,999	4.6	5.5	1.1	4.0	2.5	5.1	5.5	2.6	4.7	3.1
100,000+	7.1	8.7	0.4	4.2	4.5	4.4	4.8	1.3	3.7	1.9

Note: all figures are for 1989; (1) people of Hispanic origin can be of any race
Source: 1990 Census of Population and Housing, Summary Tape File 3C

Effective Buying Income

Area	Per Capita ($)	Median Household ($)	Average Household ($)
City	20,401	29,292	46,104
MSA[1]	18,145	33,566	43,263
U.S.	15,444	33,201	41,849

Note: data as of 1/1/97; (1) Metropolitan Statistical Area - see Appendix A for areas included
Source: Standard Rate & Data Service, Newspaper Advertising Source, 2/98

Effective Household Buying Income Distribution

Area	% of Households Earning						
	$10,000 -$19,999	$20,000 -$34,999	$35,000 -$49,999	$50,000 -$74,999	$75,000 -$99,000	$100,000 -$124,999	$125,000 and up
City	18.6	24.5	15.1	14.4	5.3	2.5	4.7
MSA[1]	16.6	23.9	17.9	18.1	6.7	2.4	2.9
U.S.	16.5	23.4	18.3	18.2	6.4	2.1	2.4

Note: data as of 1/1/97; (1) Metropolitan Statistical Area - see Appendix A for areas included
Source: Standard Rate & Data Service, Newspaper Advertising Source, 2/98

Poverty Rates by Race and Age

Area	Total (%)	By Race (%)				By Age (%)		
		White	Black	Other	Hisp.[2]	Under 5 years old	Under 18 years old	65 years and over
City	17.1	8.8	38.1	17.3	21.0	33.2	31.0	10.8
MSA[1]	10.2	7.0	26.8	13.2	13.7	15.5	15.0	9.0
U.S.	13.1	9.8	29.5	23.1	25.3	20.1	18.3	12.8

Note: figures show the percent of people living below the poverty line in 1989. The average poverty threshold was $12,674 for a family of four in 1989; (1) Metropolitan Statistical Area - see Appendix A for areas included; (2) people of Hispanic origin can be of any race
Source: 1990 Census of Population and Housing, Summary Tape File 3C

EMPLOYMENT

Labor Force and Employment

Area	Civilian Labor Force			Workers Employed		
	Dec. '95	Dec. '96	% Chg.	Dec. '95	Dec. '96	% Chg.
City	90,552	93,681	3.5	85,383	88,451	3.6
MSA[1]	737,842	763,545	3.5	704,192	729,497	3.6
U.S.	134,583,000	136,742,000	1.6	127,903,000	130,785,000	2.3

Note: Data is not seasonally adjusted and covers workers 16 years of age and older;
(1) Metropolitan Statistical Area - see Appendix A for areas included
Source: Bureau of Labor Statistics, http://stats.bls.gov

Fort Lauderdale was listed among the top 20 metro areas (out of 114 major areas) in terms of projected job growth from 1997 to 2002 with an annual percent change of 2.1%.
Standard & Poor's DRI, July 23, 1997

Unemployment Rate

Area	1997											
	Jan.	Feb.	Mar.	Apr.	May	Jun.	Jul.	Aug.	Sep.	Oct.	Nov.	Dec.
City	6.6	5.9	5.9	6.2	6.3	6.5	5.9	6.0	6.4	6.0	6.1	5.6
MSA[1]	5.3	4.7	4.7	4.9	5.1	5.2	4.7	4.8	5.1	4.8	4.9	4.5
U.S.	5.9	5.7	5.5	4.8	4.7	5.2	5.0	4.8	4.7	4.4	4.3	4.4

Note: Data is not seasonally adjusted and covers workers 16 years of age and older; All figures are percentages; (1) Metropolitan Statistical Area - see Appendix A for areas included
Source: Bureau of Labor Statistics, http://stats.bls.gov

Employment by Industry

Sector	MSA[1]		U.S.
	Number of Employees	Percent of Total	Percent of Total
Services	224,500	34.6	29.0
Retail Trade	145,100	22.4	18.5
Government	85,800	13.2	16.1
Manufacturing	40,500	6.2	15.0
Finance/Insurance/Real Estate	46,200	7.1	5.7
Wholesale Trade	41,200	6.3	5.4
Transportation/Public Utilities	32,000	4.9	5.3
Construction	33,800	5.2	4.5
Mining	100	0.0	0.5

Note: Figures cover non-farm employment as of 12/97 and are not seasonally adjusted;
(1) Metropolitan Statistical Area - see Appendix A for areas included
Source: Bureau of Labor Statistics, http://stats.bls.gov

Employment by Occupation

Occupation Category	City (%)	MSA[1] (%)	U.S. (%)
White Collar	57.8	62.4	58.1
Executive/Admin./Management	13.5	14.0	12.3
Professional	12.3	12.2	14.1
Technical & Related Support	2.9	3.7	3.7
Sales	14.9	15.5	11.8
Administrative Support/Clerical	14.1	17.0	16.3
Blue Collar	21.3	21.2	26.2
Precision Production/Craft/Repair	10.1	11.7	11.3
Machine Operators/Assem./Insp.	3.6	3.1	6.8
Transportation/Material Movers	3.9	3.1	4.1
Cleaners/Helpers/Laborers	3.7	3.2	3.9
Services	19.2	14.8	13.2
Farming/Forestry/Fishing	1.7	1.6	2.5

Note: figures cover employed persons 16 years old and over;
(1) Metropolitan Statistical Area - see Appendix A for areas included
Source: 1990 Census of Population and Housing, Summary Tape File 3C

Occupational Employment Projections: 1995 - 2005

Occupations Expected to have the Largest Job Growth (ranked by numerical growth)	Fast-Growing Occupations[1] (ranked by percent growth)
1. Waiters & waitresses	1. Systems analysts
2. Salespersons, retail	2. Computer engineers
3. Cashiers	3. Corrections officers & jailers
4. General managers & top executives	4. Personal and home care aides
5. First line supervisor, sales & related	5. Home health aides
6. Registered nurses	6. Human services workers
7. Home health aides	7. Residential counselors
8. Guards	8. Physical therapy assistants and aides
9. Food preparation workers	9. Occupational therapy assistants
10. Child care workers, private household	10. Physical therapists

Projections cover Broward County.
Note: (1) Excludes occupations with total growth of less than 100 jobs
Source: Florida Department of Labor and Employment Security, Florida Industry and Occupational Employment Projections 1995-2005

Average Wages

Occupation	Wage	Occupation	Wage
Professional/Technical/Clerical	$/Week	**Health/Protective Services**	$/Week
Accountants III	-	Corrections Officers	-
Attorneys III	-	Firefighters	-
Budget Analysts III	-	Nurses, Licensed Practical II	-
Buyers/Contracting Specialists II	-	Nurses, Registered II	-
Clerks, Accounting III	412	Nursing Assistants II	-
Clerks, General III	465	Police Officers I	-
Computer Operators II	464	**Hourly Workers**	$/Hour
Computer Programmers II	676	Forklift Operators	11.76
Drafters II	-	General Maintenance Workers	8.69
Engineering Technicians III	-	Guards I	5.56
Engineering Technicians, Civil III	-	Janitors	-
Engineers III	-	Maintenance Electricians	16.03
Key Entry Operators I	337	Maintenance Electronics Techs II	17.09
Personnel Assistants III	-	Maintenance Machinists	16.30
Personnel Specialists III	-	Maintenance Mechanics, Machinery	13.89
Secretaries III	495	Material Handling Laborers	7.99
Switchboard Operator-Receptionist	334	Motor Vehicle Mechanics	15.20
Systems Analysts II	923	Shipping/Receiving Clerks	9.76
Systems Analysts Supervisor/Mgr II	-	Tool and Die Makers	-
Tax Collectors II	-	Truckdrivers, Tractor Trailer	15.86
Word Processors II	-	Warehouse Specialists	-

Note: Wage data includes full-time workers only for 5/95 and cover the Metropolitan Statistical Area (see Appendix A for areas included). Dashes indicate that data was not available.
Source: Bureau of Labor Statistics, Occupational Compensation Survey, 10/95

TAXES

Major State and Local Tax Rates

State Corp. Income (%)	State Personal Income (%)	Residential Property (effective rate per $100)	Sales & Use		State Gasoline (cents/ gallon)	State Cigarette (cents/ 20-pack)
			State (%)	Local (%)		
5.5[a]	None	n/a	6.0	None	12.8[b]	33.9

Note: Personal/corporate income tax rates as of 1/97. Sales, gasoline and cigarette tax rates as of 1/98; (a) 3.3% Alternative Minimum Tax. An exemption of $5,000 is allowed; (b) Rate is comprised of 4 cents excise and 8.8 cents motor carrier tax
Source: Federation of Tax Administrators, www.taxadmin.org; Washington D.C. Department of Finance and Revenue, Tax Rates and Tax Burdens in the District of Columbia: A Nationwide Comparison, June 1997; Chamber of Commerce

Total Taxes Per Capita and as a Percent of Income

Area	Per Capita Income ($)	Per Capita Taxes ($)			Taxes as Pct. of Income (%)		
		Total	Federal	State/Local	Total	Federal	State/Local
Florida	26,438	9,172	6,286	2,886	34.7	23.8	10.9
U.S.	26,187	9,205	6,127	3,078	35.2	23.4	11.8

Note: Figures are for 1997
Source: Tax Foundation, Web Site, www.taxfoundation.org

COMMERCIAL REAL ESTATE

Office Market

Class/Location	Total Space (sq. ft.)	Vacant Space (sq. ft.)	Vac. Rate (%)	Under Constr. (sq. ft.)	Net Absorp. (sq. ft.)	Rental Rates ($/sq.ft./yr.)
Class A						
CBD	2,391,186	87,480	3.7	0	279,534	21.00-28.50
Outside CBD	2,919,274	250,744	8.6	171,000	378,702	17.00-27.25
Class B						
CBD	1,191,048	143,314	12.0	16,000	12,756	12.00-24.00
Outside CBD	8,167,566	825,420	10.1	38,793	241,265	12.00-38.22

Note: Data as of 10/97 and covers Fort Lauderdale-Broward County; CBD = Central Business District;
n/a not available;
Source: Society of Industrial and Office Realtors, 1998 Comparative Statistics of Industrial and Office Real Estate Markets

"A strong economy, tight leasing conditions, modest amounts of new construction to date, and rising rental rates all provide incentives for new construction. As of mid-1997, some 25 new projects were in active stages of planning. Of these, about 700,000 sq. ft. of new construction are underway and should be finished in 1998. One building will be constructed in the downtown. The remaining space is scheduled for the suburbs. West Broward is the most active new building location. Throughout the market renovations of older buildings also are underway. Even with a robust economy, tenants requiring expansion space, notably health care and high-tech firms, are rethinking their space needs. Our SIOR reporter expects to see a movement away from Class 'A' space and into Class 'B' or build-to-suit space for tenants who do not require the Class 'A' image." *Society of Industrial and Office Realtors, 1998 Comparative Statistics of Industrial and Office Real Estate Markets*

Industrial Market

Location	Total Space (sq. ft.)	Vacant Space (sq. ft.)	Vac. Rate (%)	Under Constr. (sq. ft.)	Net Absorp. (sq. ft.)	Net Lease ($/sq.ft./yr.)
Central City	n/a	n/a	n/a	500,000	1,000,000	3.75-5.00
Suburban	n/a	n/a	n/a	500,000	1,000,000	4.50-5.50

Note: Data as of 10/97 and covers Ft. Lauderdale-Broward County; n/a not available
Source: Society of Industrial and Office Realtors, 1998 Comparative Statistics of Industrial and Office Real Estate Markets

"Existing rents have not reached levels to justify new higher-cost buildings. Consequently, few speculative projects are underway. New structural codes, high impact fees, and other government-related costs have also restricted new development. International trade will continue to grow in importance for the area's economic expansion. Both the port and airport are expanding rapidly. Financing for quality development is affordable and readily available for build-to-suits, but speculative construction will still require pre-leasing. About one million sq. ft. are under construction. Several build-to-suits are being developed for large distribution and shipping companies. The area's affordable housing and business relocations will work to further market growth." *Society of Industrial and Office Realtors, 1998 Comparative Statistics of Industrial and Office Real Estate Markets*

Retail Market

Shopping Center Inventory (sq. ft.)	Shopping Center Construction (sq. ft.)	Construction as a Percent of Inventory (%)	Torto Wheaton Rent Index[1] ($/sq. ft.)
42,661,000	862,000	2.0	13.88

Note: Data as of 1997 and covers the Metropolitan Statistical Area - see Appendix A for areas included; (1) Index is based on a model that predicts what the average rent should be for leases with certain characteristics, in certain locations during certain years.
Source: National Association of Realtors, 1997-1998 Market Conditions Report

"Fort Lauderdale's retail market is on the rise, as higher rates of absorption from a year ago helped the retail rent index jump 12.7% in 1997. The opening of the 290,000 square foot Pembroke Crossing shopping center contributed to the increase in demand. Considerable shopping center space was filled with entertainment-oriented and nontraditional tenants. Seven new shopping centers are currently under construction in Broward County, which should add an estimated 900,000 square feet of retail space by the spring of next year. The retail rent index is expected to increase another 9.0% in 1998." *National Association of Realtors, 1997-1998 Market Conditions Report*

COMMERCIAL UTILITIES

Typical Monthly Electric Bills

Area	Commercial Service ($/month)		Industrial Service ($/month)	
	12 kW demand 1,500 kWh	100 kW demand 30,000 kWh	1,000 kW demand 400,000 kWh	20,000 kW demand 10,000,000 kWh
City	137	2,333	27,081	554,864
U.S.	162	2,360	25,590	545,677

Note: Based on rates in effect July 1, 1997
Source: Edison Electric Institute, Typical Residential, Commercial and Industrial Bills, Summer 1997

TRANSPORTATION

Transportation Statistics

Avg. travel time to work (min.)	20.6
Interstate highways	I-95
Bus lines	
In-city	Broward County TS
Inter-city	4
Passenger air service	
Airport	Ft. Lauderdale-Hollywood International Airport
Airlines	25
Aircraft departures	46,791 (1995)
Enplaned passengers	4,187,844 (1995)
Rail service	Amtrak; Tri-Rail
Motor freight carriers	33
Major waterways/ports	Intracoastal Waterway; Port Everglades

Source: OAG, Business Travel Planner, Summer 1997; Editor & Publisher Market Guide, 1998; FAA Airport Activity Statistics, 1996; Amtrak National Time Table, Northeast Timetable, Fall/Winter 1997-98; 1990 Census of Population and Housing, STF 3C; Chamber of Commerce/Economic Development 1997; Jane's Urban Transport Systems 1997-98; Transit Fact Book 1997

Means of Transportation to Work

Area	Car/Truck/Van		Public Transportation			Bicycle	Walked	Other Means	Worked at Home
	Drove Alone	Car-pooled	Bus	Subway	Railroad				
City	73.6	13.3	4.4	0.0	0.2	1.1	3.3	1.6	2.6
MSA[1]	79.7	12.8	1.8	0.0	0.1	0.7	1.8	1.2	1.9
U.S.	73.2	13.4	3.0	1.5	0.5	0.4	3.9	1.2	3.0

Note: figures shown are percentages and only include workers 16 years old and over; (1) Metropolitan Statistical Area - see Appendix A for areas included
Source: 1990 Census of Population and Housing, Summary Tape File 3C

BUSINESSES

Major Business Headquarters

Company Name	1997 Rankings	
	Fortune 500	Forbes 500
Ed Morse Automotive Group	-	72

Note: Companies listed are located in the city; Dashes indicate no ranking
Fortune 500: companies that produce a 10-K are ranked 1 - 500 based on 1996 revenue
Forbes 500: private companies are ranked 1 - 500 based on 1996 revenue
Source: Forbes 12/1/97; Fortune 4/28/97

Women-Owned Businesses: Number, Employment, Sales and Share

Area	Women-Owned Businesses in 1996				Share of Women-Owned Businesses in 1996	
	Number	Employment	Sales ($000)	Rank[2]	Percent (%)	Rank[3]
MSA[1]	57,300	127,700	18,033,800	29	38.2	13

Note: (1) Metropolitan Statistical Area - see Appendix A for areas included; (2) Calculated on an averaging of number of businesses, employment and sales and ranges from 1 to 50 where 1 is best; (3) Ranges from 1 to 50 where 1 is best
Source: The National Foundation for Women Business Owners, 1996 Facts on Women-Owned Businesses: Trends in the Top 50 Metropolitan Areas, March 26, 1997

Women-Owned Businesses: Growth

Area	Growth in Women-Owned Businesses (% change from 1987 to 1996)				Relative Growth in the Number of Women-Owned and All Businesses (% change from 1987 to 1996)			
	Num.	Empl.	Sales	Rank[2]	Women-Owned	All Firms	Absolute Difference	Relative Difference
MSA[1]	109.1	181.1	317.0	14	109.1	69.1	40.0	1.6:1

Note: (1) Metropolitan Statistical Area - see Appendix A for areas included; (2) Calculated on an averaging of the percent growth of number of businesses, employment and sales and ranges from 1 to 50 where 1 is best
Source: The National Foundation for Women Business Owners, 1996 Facts on Women-Owned Businesses: Trends in the Top 50 Metropolitan Areas, March 26, 1997

Minority Business Opportunity

Two of the 500 largest Hispanic-owned companies in the U.S. are located in Fort Lauderdale.
Hispanic Business, June 1997

Fort Lauderdale is home to one company which is on the Hispanic Business Fastest-Growing 100 list (greatest sales growth from 1992 to 1996): UCS Inc. (software products mfg.)
Hispanic Business, July/August 1997

Fort Lauderdale was listed among the top 25 metropolitan areas in terms of the number of Hispanic-owned companies. The city was ranked number 12 with 23,211 companies.
Hispanic Business, May 1997

Small Business Opportunity

According to *Forbes*, Fort Lauderdale is home to one of America's 200 best small companies: Pediatrix Medical Group. Criteria: companies must be publicly traded, U.S.-based corporations with latest 12-month sales of between $5 and $350 million. Earnings must be at least $1 million for the 12-month period. Limited partnerships, REITs and closed-end mutual funds were not considered. Banks, S&Ls and electric utilities were not included. *Forbes, November 3, 1997*

HOTELS & MOTELS

Hotels/Motels

Area	Hotels/Motels	Rooms	Luxury-Level Hotels/Motels		Average Minimum Rates ($)		
			♦♦♦♦	♦♦♦♦♦	♦♦	♦♦♦	♦♦♦♦
City	49	9,408	2	0	73	118	219
Airport	16	2,972	0	0	n/a	n/a	n/a
Suburbs	56	5,908	1	0	n/a	n/a	n/a
Total	121	18,288	3	0	n/a	n/a	n/a

Note: n/a not available; Classifications range from one diamond (budget properties with basic amenities) to five diamond (luxury properties with the finest service, rooms and facilities).
Source: OAG, Business Travel Planner, Summer 1997

CONVENTION CENTERS

Major Convention Centers

Center Name	Meeting Rooms	Exhibit Space (sf)
The Inverrary Golf Resort & Conference Center	15	14,000
War Memorial Auditorium (Fort Lauderdale)	1	20,000

Source: Trade Shows Worldwide 1997

Living Environment

COST OF LIVING

Cost of Living Index

Composite Index	Housing	Utilities	Groceries	Health Care	Trans-portation	Misc. Goods/ Services
n/a	n/a	n/a	n/a	n/a	n/a	n/a

Note: U.S. = 100; n/a not available
Source: ACCRA, Cost of Living Index, 3rd Quarter 1997

HOUSING

Median Home Prices and Housing Affordability

Area	Median Price[2] 3rd Qtr. 1997 ($)	HOI[3] 3rd Qtr. 1997	Afford-ability Rank[4]
MSA[1]	112,000	71.9	80
U.S.	127,000	63.7	–

Note: (1) Metropolitan Statistical Area - see Appendix A for areas included; (2) U.S. figures calculated from the sales of 625,000 new and existing homes in 195 markets; (3) Housing Opportunity Index - percent of homes sold that were within the reach of the median income household at the prevailing mortgage interest rate; (4) Rank is from 1-195 with 1 being most affordable
Source: National Association of Home Builders, Housing Opportunity Index, 3rd Quarter 1997

It is projected that the median price of existing single-family homes in the metro area will increase by 0.2% in 1998. Nationwide, home prices are projected to increase 6.6%.
Kiplinger's Personal Finance Magazine, January 1998

Average New Home Price

Area	Price ($)
City	n/a
U.S.	135,710

Note: n/a not available
Source: ACCRA, Cost of Living Index, 3rd Quarter 1997

Average Apartment Rent

Area	Rent ($/mth)
City	n/a
U.S.	569

Note: n/a not available
Source: ACCRA, Cost of Living Index, 3rd Quarter 1997

RESIDENTIAL UTILITIES

Average Residential Utility Costs

Area	All Electric ($/mth)	Part Electric ($/mth)	Other Energy ($/mth)	Phone ($/mth)
City	n/a	n/a	n/a	n/a
U.S.	109.40	55.25	43.64	19.48

Note: n/a not available
Source: ACCRA, Cost of Living Index, 3rd Quarter 1997

HEALTH CARE

Average Health Care Costs

Area	Hospital ($/day)	Doctor ($/visit)	Dentist ($/visit)
City	n/a	n/a	n/a
U.S.	392.91	48.76	60.84

Note: n/a not available
Source: ACCRA, Cost of Living Index, 3rd Quarter 1997

Distribution of Office-Based Physicians

Area	Family/Gen. Practitioners	Specialists		
		Medical	Surgical	Other
MSA[1]	239	1,062	684	616

Note: Data as of 12/31/96; (1) Metropolitan Statistical Area - see Appendix A for areas included
Source: American Medical Assn., Physician Characteristics & Distribution in the U.S., 1997-1998

Hospitals

Fort Lauderdale has 7 general medical and surgical hospitals, 2 psychiatric, 1 rehabilitation.
AHA Guide to the Healthcare Field 1997-98

EDUCATION

Public School District Statistics

District Name	Num. Sch.	Enroll.	Classroom Teachers[1]	Pupils per Teacher	Minority Pupils (%)	Current Exp.[2] ($/pupil)
Broward County School District	192	208,359	9,870	21.1	51.0	5,097

Note: Data covers the 1995-1996 school year unless otherwise noted; (1) Excludes teachers reported as working in school district offices rather than in schools; (2) Based on 1993-94 enrollment collected by the Census Bureau, not the enrollment figure shown in column 3; SD = School District; ISD = Independent School District; n/a not available
Source: National Center for Education Statistics, Common Core of Data Survey; Bureau of the Census

Educational Quality

School District	Education Quotient[1]	Graduate Outcome[2]	Community Index[3]	Resource Index[4]
Fort Lauderdale	70.0	68.0	92.0	51.0

Note: Nearly 1,000 secondary school districts were rated in terms of educational quality. The scores range from a low of 50 to a high of 150; (1) Average of the Graduate Outcome, Community and Resource indexes; (2) Based on graduation rates and college board scores (SAT/ACT); (3) Based on the surrounding community's average level of education and the area's average income level; (4) Based on teacher salaries, per-pupil expenditures and student-teacher ratios.
Source: Expansion Management, Ratings Issue 1997

Educational Attainment by Race

Area	High School Graduate (%)					Bachelor's Degree (%)				
	Total	White	Black	Other	Hisp.[2]	Total	White	Black	Other	Hisp.[2]
City	74.2	83.1	41.6	68.0	61.3	21.9	26.5	4.7	21.2	14.6
MSA[1]	76.8	79.9	55.5	71.5	68.2	18.8	19.9	10.1	21.4	15.7
U.S.	75.2	77.9	63.1	60.4	49.8	20.3	21.5	11.4	19.4	9.2

Note: figures shown cover persons 25 years old and over; (1) Metropolitan Statistical Area - see Appendix A for areas included; (2) people of Hispanic origin can be of any race
Source: 1990 Census of Population and Housing, Summary Tape File 3C

School Enrollment by Type

Area	Preprimary				Elementary/High School			
	Public		Private		Public		Private	
	Enrollment	%	Enrollment	%	Enrollment	%	Enrollment	%
City	946	46.1	1,108	53.9	15,660	84.4	2,903	15.6
MSA[1]	9,740	43.6	12,606	56.4	146,453	87.1	21,625	12.9
U.S.	2,679,029	59.5	1,824,256	40.5	38,379,689	90.2	4,187,099	9.8

Note: figures shown cover persons 3 years old and over;
(1) Metropolitan Statistical Area - see Appendix A for areas included
Source: 1990 Census of Population and Housing, Summary Tape File 3C

School Enrollment by Race

Area	Preprimary (%)				Elementary/High School (%)			
	White	Black	Other	Hisp.[1]	White	Black	Other	Hisp.[1]
City	59.2	39.5	1.3	3.0	41.2	55.4	3.4	8.8
MSA[2]	77.7	19.9	2.4	7.8	67.7	28.3	4.0	11.4
U.S.	80.4	12.5	7.1	7.8	74.1	15.6	10.3	12.5

Note: figures shown cover persons 3 years old and over; (1) people of Hispanic origin can be of any race; (2) Metropolitan Statistical Area - see Appendix A for areas included
Source: 1990 Census of Population and Housing, Summary Tape File 3C

SAT/ACT Scores

Area/District	1997 SAT				1997 ACT	
	Percent of Graduates Tested (%)	Average Math Score	Average Verbal Score	Average Combined Score	Percent of Graduates Tested (%)	Average Composite Score
Broward County SD	n/a	496	485	981	n/a	20.4
State	50	499	499	998	36	20.7
U.S.	42	511	505	1,016	36	21.0

Note: Math and verbal SAT scores are out of a possible 800; ACT scores are out of a possible 36
Caution: Comparing or ranking states/cities on the basis of SAT/ACT scores alone is invalid and strongly discouraged by the The College Board and The American College Testing Program as students who take the tests are self-selected and do not represent the entire student population.
Source: Broward County School Board, Testing & Assessment, 1997; American College Testing Program, 1997; College Board, 1997

Classroom Teacher Salaries in Public Schools

District	B.A. Degree		M.A. Degree		Ph.D. Degree	
	Min. ($)	Max. ($)	Min. ($)	Max. ($)	Min. ($)	Max. ($)
Fort Lauderdale	28,245	48,400	30,385	50,540	33,280	53,435
Average[1]	26,120	39,270	28,175	44,667	31,643	49,825

Note: Salaries are for 1996-1997; (1) Based on all school districts covered
Source: American Federation of Teachers (unpublished data)

Higher Education

Two-Year Colleges		Four-Year Colleges		Medical Schools	Law Schools	Voc/ Tech
Public	Private	Public	Private			
1	2	0	3	0	1	10

Source: College Blue Book, Occupational Education 1997; Medical School Admission Requirements, 1998-99; Peterson's Guide to Two-Year Colleges, 1997; Peterson's Guide to Four-Year Colleges, 1997; Barron's Guide to Law Schools 1997

MAJOR EMPLOYERS

Major Employers

Beneficial Payroll Services
Columbia Hospital Corp.
Sun Energy Products
Holy Cross Hospital
Racal Corp. (telephone apparatus)
University Hospital

Certified Tours
Encore Computer Corp.
Florida Medical Center
Interim Healthcare of Hollywood
Sunshine Cleaning Systems
Kemper National Services (health services)

Note: companies listed are located in the city
Source: Dun's Business Rankings 1997; Ward's Business Directory, 1997

PUBLIC SAFETY

Crime Rate

Area	All Crimes	Violent Crimes				Property Crimes		
		Murder	Forcible Rape	Robbery	Aggrav. Assault	Burglary	Larceny -Theft	Motor Vehicle Theft
City	15,165.5	20.2	57.1	705.7	754.5	2,822.8	8,999.8	1,805.3
Suburbs[1]	n/a	n/a	n/a	n/a	n/a	n/a	n/a	n/a
MSA[2]	n/a	n/a	n/a	n/a	n/a	n/a	n/a	n/a
U.S.	5,078.9	7.4	36.1	202.4	388.2	943.0	2,975.9	525.9

Note: Crime rate is the number of crimes per 100,000 pop.; (1) defined as all areas within the MSA but located outside the central city; (2) Metropolitan Statistical Area - see Appendix A for areas incl.
Source: FBI Uniform Crime Reports 1996

RECREATION

Culture and Recreation

Museums	Symphony Orchestras	Opera Companies	Dance Companies	Professional Theatres	Zoos	Pro Sports Teams
5	1	0	0	1	0	0

Source: International Directory of the Performing Arts, 1996; Official Museum Directory, 1998; Chamber of Commerce/Economic Development 1997

Library System

The Broward County Library has 29 branches, holdings of 1,788,603 volumes and a budget of $31,268,272 (1995-1996). *American Library Directory, 1997-1998*

MEDIA

Newspapers

Name	Type	Freq.	Distribution	Circulation
El Heraldo de Broward	n/a	1x/wk	Area	15,000
Jewish Journal Palm Beach South	n/a	1x/wk	Area	151,000
Sun-Sentinel	General	7x/wk	Area	272,258
Westside Gazette	Black	1x/wk	Area	35,000
XS	General	1x/wk	Area	56,000

Note: Includes newspapers with circulations of 500 or more located in the city; Source: Burrelle's Media Directory, 1998 Edition

AM Radio Stations

Call Letters	Freq. (kHz)	Target Audience	Station Format	Music Format
WQAM	560	General	S/T	n/a
WIOD	610	General	N/T	n/a
WQBA	1140	Hispanic	N/S/T	n/a
WAVS	1170	Black	E/M/N/S/T	Christian/R&B/Urban Contemporary
WJNA	1230	General	M	Urban Contemporary
WSUA	1260	Hispanic	M/N/S/T	Adult Contemporary
WFTL	1400	n/a	T	n/a
WRBD	1470	General	M/N/S	R&B
WEXY	1520	General	M	Christian
WSRF	1580	n/a	M/N/S	n/a

Note: Stations included broadcast in the Fort Lauderdale metro area; n/a not available
Station Format: E = Educational; M = Music; N = News; S = Sports; T = Talk
Source: Burrelle's Media Directory, 1998 Edition

FM Radio Stations

Call Letters	Freq. (mHz)	Target Audience	Station Format	Music Format
WKPX	88.5	General	E/M/N/S	Alternative
WAFG	90.3	General	E/M/T	Christian
WKIS	99.9	General	M/N/S	Country
WHYI	100.7	General	M/N	Adult Contemporary
WPLL	103.5	General	M	Adult Contemporary
WBGG	105.9	General	M/N/S	Oldies

Note: Stations included broadcast in the Fort Lauderdale metro area
Station Format: E = Educational; M = Music; N = News; S = Sports; T = Talk
Source: Burrelle's Media Directory, 1998 Edition

Television Stations

Name	Ch.	Affiliation	Type	Owner
WDZL	39	WB	Commercial	Tribune Broadcasting
WHFT	45	n/a	Non-Commercial	Trinity Broadcasting Network
WYHS	69	HSN	Commercial	Silver King Broadcasting Inc.

Note: Stations included broadcast in the Fort Lauderdale metro area
Source: Burrelle's Media Directory, 1998 Edition

CLIMATE

Average and Extreme Temperatures

Temperature	Jan	Feb	Mar	Apr	May	Jun	Jul	Aug	Sep	Oct	Nov	Dec	Ann
Extreme High (°F)	88	89	92	96	95	98	98	98	97	95	89	87	98
Average High (°F)	75	77	79	82	85	88	89	90	88	85	80	77	83
Average Temp. (°F)	68	69	72	75	79	82	83	83	82	78	73	69	76
Average Low (°F)	59	60	64	68	72	75	76	76	76	72	66	61	69
Extreme Low (°F)	30	35	32	42	55	60	69	68	68	53	39	30	30

Note: Figures cover the years 1948-1990
Source: National Climatic Data Center, International Station Meteorological Climate Summary, 3/95

Average Precipitation/Snowfall/Humidity

Precip./Humidity	Jan	Feb	Mar	Apr	May	Jun	Jul	Aug	Sep	Oct	Nov	Dec	Ann
Avg. Precip. (in.)	1.9	2.0	2.3	3.0	6.2	8.7	6.1	7.5	8.2	6.6	2.7	1.8	57.1
Avg. Snowfall (in.)	0	0	0	0	0	0	0	0	0	0	0	0	0
Avg. Rel. Hum. 7am (%)	84	84	82	80	81	84	84	86	88	87	85	84	84
Avg. Rel. Hum. 4pm (%)	59	57	57	57	62	68	66	67	69	65	63	60	63

Note: Figures cover the years 1948-1990; Tr = Trace amounts (<0.05 in. of rain; <0.5 in. of snow)
Source: National Climatic Data Center, International Station Meteorological Climate Summary, 3/95

Weather Conditions

Temperature			Daytime Sky			Precipitation		
32°F & below	45°F & below	90°F & above	Clear	Partly cloudy	Cloudy	0.01 inch or more precip.	0.1 inch or more snow/ice	Thunder-storms
< 1	7	55	48	263	54	128	0	74

Note: Figures are average number of days per year and covers the years 1948-1990
Source: National Climatic Data Center, International Station Meteorological Climate Summary, 3/95

AIR & WATER QUALITY

Maximum Pollutant Concentrations

	Particulate Matter (ug/m³)	Carbon Monoxide (ppm)	Sulfur Dioxide (ppm)	Nitrogen Dioxide (ppm)	Ozone (ppm)	Lead (ug/m³)
MSA[1] Level	48	4	0.008	0.010	0.10	0.05
NAAQS[2]	150	9	0.140	0.053	0.12	1.50
Met NAAQS?	Yes	Yes	Yes	Yes	Yes	Yes

Note: (1) Metropolitan Statistical Area - see Appendix A for areas included; (2) National Ambient Air Quality Standards; ppm = parts per million; ug/m³ = micrograms per cubic meter; n/a not available
Source: EPA, National Air Quality and Emissions Trends Report, 1996

Pollutant Standards Index

In the Fort Lauderdale MSA (see Appendix A for areas included), the Pollutant Standards Index (PSI) exceeded 100 on 0 days in 1996. A PSI value greater than 100 indicates that air quality would be in the unhealthful range on that day. *EPA, National Air Quality and Emissions Trends Report, 1996*

Drinking Water

Water System Name	Pop. Served	Primary Water Source Type	Number of Violations in Fiscal Year 1997	Type of Violation/ Contaminants
City of Ft. Lauderdale	172,680	Ground	2	(1), (2)

Note: Data as of January 16, 1998; (1) System failed to collect samples for a period under the total coliform rule; (2) System failed to conduct initial or repeat sampling, or to accurately report an analytical result for a specific contaminant (nitrate).
Source: EPA, Office of Ground Water and Drinking Water, Safe Drinking Water Information System

Fort Lauderdale tap water is alkaline, very soft and fluoridated.
Editor & Publisher Market Guide, 1998

Fort Worth, Texas

Background

Despite its modern skyscrapers, multiple freeways, shopping malls and extensive industry, Ft. Worth maintains its easy-going western atmosphere.

The area has seen many travelers. Nomadic Native Americans of the Plains rode through on horses bred from those brought by Spanish explorers. The 1840s saw American-Anglos settle in the region. On June 6, 1849 Major Ripley A. Arnold and his U.S. Cavalry troop established an outpost on the Trinity River to protect settlers moving westward. The fort was named for General William J. Worth, Commander of the U.S. Army's Texas department. When the fort was abandoned in 1853, settlers moved in and converted the vacant barracks into trading establishments and homes and stole the county seat from Birdville (an act made legal in the 1860 election).

In the 1860's Ft. Worth, close to the Chisholm Trail, became an oasis for cowboys leaving to, and returning from, Kansas.

Although the town's growth stopped during the Civil War, Ft. Worth was incorporated as a city in 1873. In a race against time the final 26 miles of the Texas & Pacific Line were completed and Ft. Worth survived to be a part of the West Texas oil boom in 1917.

Real prosperity followed at the end of World War II, when the city became a center for a number of military installations. Aviation has been the city's principal source of economic growth. Among the city's leading industries are the manufacture of aircraft, automobiles, machinery, containers, food processing, and brewing. The city will be home to Intel's new $1.3 billion advanced logic wafer fabrication plant which will be located in the Alliance industrial transportation center near Alliance Airport. *World Trade 4/97*

Ft. Worth lies in north central Texas near the headwaters of the Trinity River.

Winter temperatures and rainfall are both modified by the northeast-northwest mountain barrier which prevents shallow cold air masses from crossing over into the area from the west. The summer temperatures vary with the cloudiness and shower activity, but are generally mild. Summer precipitation is largely from local thunderstorms and varies from year to year. Damaging rains are infrequent. Hurricanes have produced heavy rainfall here, but not winds of destructive force.

General Rankings and Evaluative Comments

- Fort Worth was ranked #57 out of 300 cities by *Money's* 1997 "Survey of the Best Places to Live." Criteria used: health services, crime, economy, housing, education, transportation, weather, leisure and the arts. The city was ranked #55 in 1996 and #39 in 1995.
  Money, July 1997; Money, September 1996; Money, September 1995

- *Ladies Home Journal* ranked America's 200 largest cities based on the qualities women care about most. Fort Worth ranked 61 out of 200. Criteria: low crime rate, good public schools, well-paying jobs, quality health and child care, the presence of women in government, proportion of women-owned businesses, size of the wage gap with men, local economy, divorce rates, the ratio of single men to single women, whether there are laws that require at least the same number of public toilets for women as men, and the probability of good hair days. *Ladies Home Journal, November 1997*

- Fort Worth was ranked #138 out of 219 cities in terms of children's health, safety, and economic well-being. Criteria: total population, percent population change, birth rate, child immunization rate, infant mortality rate, percent low birth weight infants, percent of births to teens, physician-to-population ratio, student-to-teacher ratio, dropout rate, unemployment rate, median family income, percent of children in poverty, violent and property crime rates, number of juvenile arrests for violent crimes as a percent of the total crime index, number of days with pollution standard index (PSI) over 100, pounds toxic releases per 1,000 people and number of superfund sites. *Zero Population Growth, Children's Environmental Index 1997*

- *Reader's Digest* non-scientifically ranked the 12 largest U.S. metropolitan areas in terms of having the worst drivers. The Dallas-Fort Worth metro area ranked number 9. The areas were selected by asking approximately 1,200 readers on the *Reader's Digest* Web site and 200 interstate bus drivers and long-haul truckers which metro areas have the worst drivers. Their responses were factored in with fatality, insurance and rental-car rates to create the rankings. *Reader's Digest, March 1998*

- According to *Working Mother,* "This year, the Texas Licensed Child Care Association lobbied heavily against proposed standards that would have improved the adult-to-child ratios in many programs. Unfortunately, it prevailed. Lawmakers delayed adoption of the new rules.

  Texas may finally get statewide resource and referral services, however, with new federal funds coming into the state. In addition to helping parents find care, R&Rs may handle both caregiver training and consumer education—a positive development.

  Providers across the state may also get low-interest loans to buy new equipment, upgrade their facilities and do other things to improve the quality of care, under a bill pending in the state legislature that looked likely to pass as we went to press." *Working Mother, July/August 1997*

Business Environment

STATE ECONOMY

State Economic Profile

"The Texas economy remains among the strongest in the nation....

Overall, Texas gained over 141,000 people last year through in-migration. While this is down from the three-year average of over 170,000, it still represents 43% of the Texas population increase. By far, throughout this decade, California has been the largest domestic source of in-migrants into Texas. With the California economy rebounding, in-migration to Texas is slowing.

The slowdown in household growth, coupled with solid residential construction, is creating a slight oversupply throughout the state. As a result, house price growth is decelerating. New residential permits have yet to slow, with new permits up by 14% last year—nearly twice the national increase. The slowdown in population and household growth cannot sustain such robust growth in permits, and as a result, new permits will slow this year.

The Texas economy shows no major imbalances. Although the important computer-chip industry remains moribund, the economy continues to expand solidly. The turnaround in computer memory prices will help the state continue to expand. Texas' growth is becoming increasingly supported by in-migrants. With an increasing presence in high-tech, an attractive business environment, and close proximity to Mexico, Texas will continue to expand faster than the nation and lure workers from other locales. In addition, as an attractive destination for retirees, Texas will continue to experience solid population and household growth as the population ages. Texas is ranked above average for short-and long-term growth." *National Association of Realtors, Economic Profiles: The Fifty States, July 1997*

IMPORTS/EXPORTS

Total Export Sales

Area	1993 ($000)	1994 ($000)	1995 ($000)	1996 ($000)	% Chg. 1993-96	% Chg. 1995-96
MSA[1]	1,600,206	2,052,001	1,915,014	2,372,703	48.3	23.9
U.S.	464,858,354	512,415,609	583,030,524	622,827,063	34.0	6.8

Note: (1) Metropolitan Statistical Area - see Appendix A for areas included
Source: U.S. Department of Commerce, International Trade Association, Metropolitan Area Exports: An Export Performance Report on Over 250 U.S. Cities, October 1997

Imports/Exports by Port

Type	Cargo Value			Share of U.S. Total	
	1995 (US$mil.)	1996 (US$mil.)	% Change 1995-1996	1995 (%)	1996 (%)
Imports	0	0	0	0	0
Exports	0	0	0	0	0

Source: Global Trade Information Services, WaterBorne Trade Atlas 1997

CITY FINANCES

City Government Finances

Component	FY92 ($000)	FY92 (per capita $)
Revenue	500,619	1,085.38
Expenditure	522,690	1,133.23
Debt Outstanding	934,606	2,026.29
Cash & Securities	1,028,431	2,229.71

Source: U.S. Bureau of the Census, City Government Finances: 1991-92

City Government Revenue by Source

Source	FY92 ($000)	FY92 (per capita $)	FY92 (%)
From Federal Government	19,343	41.94	3.9
From State Governments	19,018	41.23	3.8
From Local Governments	3,652	7.92	0.7
Property Taxes	130,086	282.04	26.0
General Sales Taxes	39,809	86.31	8.0
Selective Sales Taxes	21,651	46.94	4.3
Income Taxes	0	0.00	0.0
Current Charges	69,168	149.96	13.8
Utility/Liquor Store	64,998	140.92	13.0
Employee Retirement[1]	54,901	119.03	11.0
Other	77,993	169.09	15.6

Note: (1) Excludes "city contributions," classified as "nonrevenue," intragovernmental transfers.
Source: U.S. Bureau of the Census, City Government Finances: 1991-92

City Government Expenditures by Function

Function	FY92 ($000)	FY92 (per capita $)	FY92 (%)
Educational Services	7,530	16.33	1.4
Employee Retirement[1]	21,869	47.41	4.2
Environment/Housing	144,587	313.48	27.7
Government Administration	23,988	52.01	4.6
Interest on General Debt	54,655	118.50	10.5
Public Safety	87,841	190.45	16.8
Social Services	10,583	22.94	2.0
Transportation	81,269	176.20	15.5
Utility/Liquor Store	64,559	139.97	12.4
Other	25,809	55.96	4.9

Note: (1) Payments to beneficiaries including withdrawal of contributions.
Source: U.S. Bureau of the Census, City Government Finances: 1991-92

Municipal Bond Ratings

Area	Moody's	S & P
Fort Worth	Aa2	AA

Note: n/a not available; n/r not rated
Source: Moody's Bond Record, 2/98; Statistical Abstract of the U.S., 1997;
Governing Magazine, 9/97, 3/98

POPULATION

Population Growth

Area	1980	1990	% Chg. 1980-90	July 1996 Estimate	% Chg. 1990-96
City	385,166	447,619	16.2	479,716	7.2
MSA[1]	n/a	1,332,053	n/a	1,526,578	14.6
U.S.	226,545,805	248,765,170	9.8	265,179,411	6.6

Note: (1) Metropolitan Statistical Area - see Appendix A for areas included
Source: 1980/1990 Census of Housing and Population, Summary Tape File 3C;
Census Bureau Population Estimates

Population Characteristics

Race	City 1980 Population	%	City 1990 Population	%	% Chg. 1980-90	MSA[1] 1990 Population	%
White	266,638	69.2	286,072	63.9	7.3	1,070,993	80.4
Black	87,635	22.8	98,679	22.0	12.6	143,824	10.8
Amer Indian/Esk/Aleut	1,841	0.5	1,990	0.4	8.1	6,554	0.5
Asian/Pacific Islander	2,954	0.8	8,465	1.9	186.6	29,728	2.2
Other	26,098	6.8	52,413	11.7	100.8	80,954	6.1
Hispanic Origin[2]	48,568	12.6	85,835	19.2	76.7	146,143	11.0

Note: (1) Metropolitan Statistical Area - see Appendix A for areas included;
(2) people of Hispanic origin can be of any race
Source: 1980/1990 Census of Housing and Population, Summary Tape File 3C

Ancestry

Area	German	Irish	English	Italian	U.S.	French	Polish	Dutch
City	14.8	13.2	12.3	1.5	4.9	3.0	1.1	1.9
MSA[1]	20.9	18.2	15.5	2.2	6.8	3.9	1.5	2.7
U.S.	23.3	15.6	13.1	5.9	5.3	4.2	3.8	2.5

Note: Figures are percentages and include persons that reported multiple ancestry (eg. if a person reported being Irish and Italian, they were included in both columns); (1) Metropolitan Statistical Area - see Appendix A for areas included
Source: 1990 Census of Population and Housing, Summary Tape File 3C

Age

Area	Median Age (Years)	Age Distribution (%) Under 5	Under 18	18-24	25-44	45-64	65+	80+
City	30.3	8.6	26.6	11.7	34.7	15.9	11.2	2.6
MSA[1]	30.6	8.4	27.3	10.7	36.3	17.1	8.6	1.8
U.S.	32.9	7.3	25.6	10.5	32.6	18.7	12.5	2.8

Note: (1) Metropolitan Statistical Area - see Appendix A for areas included
Source: 1990 Census of Population and Housing, Summary Tape File 3C

Male/Female Ratio

Area	Number of males per 100 females (all ages)	Number of males per 100 females (18 years old+)
City	96.3	94.3
MSA[1]	97.8	95.4
U.S.	95.0	91.9

Note: (1) Metropolitan Statistical Area - see Appendix A for areas included
Source: 1990 Census of Population, General Population Characteristics

INCOME

Per Capita/Median/Average Income

Area	Per Capita ($)	Median Household ($)	Average Household ($)
City	13,162	26,547	34,359
MSA[1]	14,842	32,121	39,560
U.S.	14,420	30,056	38,453

Note: all figures are for 1989; (1) Metropolitan Statistical Area - see Appendix A for areas included
Source: 1990 Census of Population and Housing, Summary Tape File 3C

Household Income Distribution by Race

Income ($)	City (%)					U.S. (%)				
	Total	White	Black	Other	Hisp.[1]	Total	White	Black	Other	Hisp.[1]
Less than 5,000	7.7	5.0	17.1	7.9	7.9	6.2	4.8	15.2	8.6	8.8
5,000 - 9,999	9.4	8.1	14.0	10.0	10.0	9.3	8.6	14.2	9.9	11.1
10,000 - 14,999	10.1	9.1	13.2	11.2	11.7	8.8	8.5	11.0	9.8	11.0
15,000 - 24,999	19.7	18.8	20.9	24.1	24.3	17.5	17.3	18.9	18.5	20.5
25,000 - 34,999	17.1	17.5	14.1	20.2	20.3	15.8	16.1	14.2	15.4	16.4
35,000 - 49,999	16.7	18.2	11.7	15.5	15.0	17.9	18.6	13.3	16.1	16.0
50,000 - 74,999	12.5	14.6	7.1	8.5	8.3	15.0	15.8	9.3	13.4	11.1
75,000 - 99,999	3.6	4.5	1.3	1.6	2.1	5.1	5.5	2.6	4.7	3.1
100,000+	3.2	4.3	0.5	0.9	0.3	4.4	4.8	1.3	3.7	1.9

Note: all figures are for 1989; (1) people of Hispanic origin can be of any race
Source: 1990 Census of Population and Housing, Summary Tape File 3C

Effective Buying Income

Area	Per Capita ($)	Median Household ($)	Average Household ($)
City	15,063	30,943	40,209
MSA[1]	17,405	38,608	46,856
U.S.	15,444	33,201	41,849

Note: data as of 1/1/97; (1) Metropolitan Statistical Area - see Appendix A for areas included
Source: Standard Rate & Data Service, Newspaper Advertising Source, 2/98

Effective Household Buying Income Distribution

Area	% of Households Earning						
	$10,000 -$19,999	$20,000 -$34,999	$35,000 -$49,999	$50,000 -$74,999	$75,000 -$99,000	$100,000 -$124,999	$125,000 and up
City	17.6	24.5	17.6	16.3	5.7	1.9	2.3
MSA[1]	13.6	22.2	18.7	21.0	9.1	3.1	3.0
U.S.	16.5	23.4	18.3	18.2	6.4	2.1	2.4

Note: data as of 1/1/97; (1) Metropolitan Statistical Area - see Appendix A for areas included
Source: Standard Rate & Data Service, Newspaper Advertising Source, 2/98

Poverty Rates by Race and Age

Area	Total (%)	By Race (%)				By Age (%)		
		White	Black	Other	Hisp.[2]	Under 5 years old	Under 18 years old	65 years and over
City	17.4	10.8	31.3	25.4	25.9	26.0	24.9	14.4
MSA[1]	11.0	7.7	27.0	21.8	22.2	16.5	14.7	12.2
U.S.	13.1	9.8	29.5	23.1	25.3	20.1	18.3	12.8

Note: figures show the percent of people living below the poverty line in 1989. The average poverty threshold was $12,674 for a family of four in 1989; (1) Metropolitan Statistical Area - see Appendix A for areas included; (2) people of Hispanic origin can be of any race
Source: 1990 Census of Population and Housing, Summary Tape File 3C

EMPLOYMENT

Labor Force and Employment

Area	Civilian Labor Force			Workers Employed		
	Dec. '95	Dec. '96	% Chg.	Dec. '95	Dec. '96	% Chg.
City	256,691	263,985	2.8	246,141	253,873	3.1
MSA[1]	843,922	868,132	2.9	817,088	842,756	3.1
U.S.	134,583,000	136,742,000	1.6	127,903,000	130,785,000	2.3

Note: Data is not seasonally adjusted and covers workers 16 years of age and older; (1) Metropolitan Statistical Area - see Appendix A for areas included
Source: Bureau of Labor Statistics, http://stats.bls.gov

Fort Worth was listed among the top 20 metro areas (out of 114 major areas) in terms of projected job growth from 1997 to 2002 with an annual percent change of 1.9%.
Standard & Poor's DRI, July 23, 1997

Unemployment Rate

Area	1997											
	Jan.	Feb.	Mar.	Apr.	May	Jun.	Jul.	Aug.	Sep.	Oct.	Nov.	Dec.
City	5.2	5.4	5.0	4.5	4.6	5.4	5.1	4.8	4.7	4.3	4.3	3.8
MSA[1]	4.0	4.1	3.8	3.5	3.5	4.2	3.9	3.7	3.5	3.3	3.3	2.9
U.S.	5.9	5.7	5.5	4.8	4.7	5.2	5.0	4.8	4.7	4.4	4.3	4.4

Note: Data is not seasonally adjusted and covers workers 16 years of age and older; All figures are percentages; (1) Metropolitan Statistical Area - see Appendix A for areas included
Source: Bureau of Labor Statistics, http://stats.bls.gov

Employment by Industry

Sector	MSA[1]		U.S.
	Number of Employees	Percent of Total	Percent of Total
Services	193,700	26.7	29.0
Retail Trade	149,900	20.7	18.5
Government	92,800	12.8	16.1
Manufacturing	110,300	15.2	15.0
Finance/Insurance/Real Estate	32,300	4.5	5.7
Wholesale Trade	39,300	5.4	5.4
Transportation/Public Utilities	67,800	9.4	5.3
Construction	34,700	4.8	4.5
Mining	4,300	0.6	0.5

Note: Figures cover non-farm employment as of 12/97 and are not seasonally adjusted;
(1) Metropolitan Statistical Area - see Appendix A for areas included
Source: Bureau of Labor Statistics, http://stats.bls.gov

Employment by Occupation

Occupation Category	City (%)	MSA[1] (%)	U.S. (%)
White Collar	57.0	62.0	58.1
Executive/Admin./Management	11.0	13.4	12.3
Professional	14.6	13.8	14.1
Technical & Related Support	3.6	4.3	3.7
Sales	11.5	13.0	11.8
Administrative Support/Clerical	16.2	17.6	16.3
Blue Collar	27.9	25.1	26.2
Precision Production/Craft/Repair	11.5	11.8	11.3
Machine Operators/Assem./Insp.	8.5	6.3	6.8
Transportation/Material Movers	3.4	3.5	4.1
Cleaners/Helpers/Laborers	4.6	3.6	3.9
Services	13.9	11.7	13.2
Farming/Forestry/Fishing	1.3	1.1	2.5

Note: figures cover employed persons 16 years old and over;
(1) Metropolitan Statistical Area - see Appendix A for areas included
Source: 1990 Census of Population and Housing, Summary Tape File 3C

Occupational Employment Projections: 1993 - 2000

Occupations Expected to have the Largest Job Growth (ranked by numerical growth)	Fast-Growing Occupations[1] (ranked by percent growth)
1. General office clerks	1. Physical therapy assistants and aides
2. Child care workers, private household	2. Physical therapists
3. Guards	3. Occupational therapists
4. Cashiers	4. Demonstrators/promoters/models
5. General managers & top executives	5. Air hammer operators
6. Salespersons, retail	6. Housekeepers and butlers
7. Food preparation workers	7. Computer scientists
8. Waiters & waitresses	8. Cleaners/servants, private home
9. Registered nurses	9. Occupational therapy assistants
10. Secretaries, except legal & medical	10. Therapists

Projections cover Collin, Dallas, Denton, Erath, Hood, Hunt, Johnson, Kaufman, Navarro, Palo, Parker, Pinto, Rockwall, Somervell and Wise Counties.
Note: (1) Includes occupations with absolute job growth of 200 or more
Source: Texas Employment Commission, Texas Employment Projections Reporting System, Statewide and Regional Projections 1993-2000, Ver. 1.0

Average Wages

Occupation	Wage	Occupation	Wage
Professional/Technical/Clerical	$/Week	**Health/Protective Services**	$/Week
Accountants III	-	Corrections Officers	-
Attorneys III	-	Firefighters	-
Budget Analysts III	-	Nurses, Licensed Practical II	-
Buyers/Contracting Specialists II	-	Nurses, Registered II	-
Clerks, Accounting III	442	Nursing Assistants II	-
Clerks, General III	469	Police Officers I	-
Computer Operators II	388	**Hourly Workers**	$/Hour
Computer Programmers II	633	Forklift Operators	8.90
Drafters II	493	General Maintenance Workers	7.91
Engineering Technicians III	-	Guards I	5.33
Engineering Technicians, Civil III	-	Janitors	5.85
Engineers III	-	Maintenance Electricians	-
Key Entry Operators I	305	Maintenance Electronics Techs II	-
Personnel Assistants III	-	Maintenance Machinists	-
Personnel Specialists III	-	Maintenance Mechanics, Machinery	14.58
Secretaries III	498	Material Handling Laborers	8.74
Switchboard Operator-Receptionist	316	Motor Vehicle Mechanics	16.92
Systems Analysts II	827	Shipping/Receiving Clerks	8.24
Systems Analysts Supervisor/Mgr II	-	Tool and Die Makers	18.05
Tax Collectors II	-	Truckdrivers, Tractor Trailer	12.61
Word Processors II	412	Warehouse Specialists	9.89

Note: Wage data includes full-time workers only for 10/93 and cover the Metropolitan Statistical Area (see Appendix A for areas included). Dashes indicate that data was not available.
Source: Bureau of Labor Statistics, Occupational Compensation Survey

TAXES

Major State and Local Tax Rates

State Corp. Income (%)	State Personal Income (%)	Residential Property (effective rate per $100)	Sales & Use		State Gasoline (cents/ gallon)	State Cigarette (cents/ 20-pack)
			State (%)	Local (%)		
None[a]	None	n/a	6.25	2.0	20	41

Note: Personal/corporate income tax rates as of 1/97. Sales, gasoline and cigarette tax rates as of 1/98; (a) Texas imposes a franchise tax of 4.5% of earned surplus
Source: Federation of Tax Administrators, www.taxadmin.org; Washington D.C. Department of Finance and Revenue, Tax Rates and Tax Burdens in the District of Columbia: A Nationwide Comparison, June 1997; Chamber of Commerce

Total Taxes Per Capita and as a Percent of Income

Area	Per Capita Income ($)	Per Capita Taxes ($)			Taxes as Pct. of Income (%)		
		Total	Federal	State/Local	Total	Federal	State/Local
Texas	24,145	8,118	5,538	2,580	33.6	22.9	10.7
U.S.	26,187	9,205	6,127	3,078	35.2	23.4	11.8

Note: Figures are for 1997
Source: Tax Foundation, Web Site, www.taxfoundation.org

COMMERCIAL REAL ESTATE

Office Market

Class/ Location	Total Space (sq. ft.)	Vacant Space (sq. ft.)	Vac. Rate (%)	Under Constr. (sq. ft.)	Net Absorp. (sq. ft.)	Rental Rates ($/sq.ft./yr.)
Class A						
CBD	4,935,115	768,815	15.6	0	-40,883	13.00-16.50
Outside CBD	6,837,611	249,303	3.6	75,000	257,053	11.00-22.00
Class B						
CBD	1,993,481	564,589	28.3	n/a	-145,672	9.50-14.00
Outside CBD	4,545,616	531,698	11.7	n/a	244,351	7.00-17.75

Note: Data as of 10/97 and covers Fort Worth-Tarrant County; CBD = Central Business District; n/a not available;
Source: Society of Industrial and Office Realtors, 1998 Comparative Statistics of Industrial and Office Real Estate Markets

"During the fourth quarter of 1997, 75,000 sq. ft. of suburban Class 'A' space was under construction. In addition, several smaller developments have been proposed primarily in northeast Tarrant County, Alliance, and North Alliance. The industrial real estate market in suburban Fort Worth is very strong. Intel is building a new $1.3 billion manufacturing facility in Alliance. Some of the proposals for new office space have been floated to see if firms in the business services sector will make a commitment to pre-lease in order to locate near Intel. Net absorption is expected to remain steady during 1998, leading to additional declines in vacancies outside of the CBD. This will place upward pressure on rental rates and sales prices." *Society of Industrial and Office Realtors, 1998 Comparative Statistics of Industrial and Office Real Estate Markets*

Industrial Market

Location	Total Space (sq. ft.)	Vacant Space (sq. ft.)	Vac. Rate (%)	Under Constr. (sq. ft.)	Net Absorp. (sq. ft.)	Net Lease ($/sq.ft./yr.)
Central City	n/a	n/a	n/a	n/a	n/a	n/a
Suburban	144,736,796	12,910,522	8.9	4,096,745	7,154,185	3.25-4.50

Note: Data as of 10/97 and covers Fort Worth-Tarrant County; n/a not available
Source: Society of Industrial and Office Realtors, 1998 Comparative Statistics of Industrial and Office Real Estate Markets

"Speculative development will be one of the major forces shaping the market during 1998. There has been an ample supply of financing from insurance companies, commercial banks, and pension funds. The areas which are likely to be the center of the development are north and northeast of the city. The Alliance Airport development and the Dallas-Fort Worth Airport area could see a total of five to eight million sq. ft. of new space during 1998. During the later part of 1997 there were substantial shortages of space smaller than 60,000 sq. ft. Some of the speculative development during 1998 will likely be targeted at this market segment. Overall construction of warehouse/distribution space is expected to increase substantially from 1997 levels with more modest increases in High Tech/R&D space and manufacturing. Absorption and construction should be balanced leaving vacancy at or near 97 levels." *Society of Industrial and Office Realtors, 1998 Comparative Statistics of Industrial and Office Real Estate Markets*

Retail Market

Shopping Center Inventory (sq. ft.)	Shopping Center Construction (sq. ft.)	Construction as a Percent of Inventory (%)	Torto Wheaton Rent Index[1] ($/sq. ft.)
38,755,000	904,000	2.3	13.33

Note: Data as of 1997 and covers the Metropolitan Statistical Area - see Appendix A for areas included; (1) Index is based on a model that predicts what the average rent should be for leases with certain characteristics, in certain locations during certain years.
Source: National Association of Realtors, 1997-1998 Market Conditions Report

"Fort Worth has come a long way since Dallasites called it the 'Panther City', claiming that the city was so sedate that a large panther could sleep peacefully in its downtown streets. Indeed, healthy population growth has buoyed the retail sector, which has added jobs at a staggering rate. Robust growth has caused the area's unemployment rate to fall to 3.9%, the lowest rate in more than a decade. Fort Worth's retail rent index has jumped 53% since 1995, and should continue to rise over the next few years amid the area's burgeoning economy."
National Association of Realtors, 1997-1998 Market Conditions Report

COMMERCIAL UTILITIES

Typical Monthly Electric Bills

Area	Commercial Service ($/month)		Industrial Service ($/month)	
	12 kW demand 1,500 kWh	100 kW demand 30,000 kWh	1,000 kW demand 400,000 kWh	20,000 kW demand 10,000,000 kWh
City	152	2,161	23,072	478,215
U.S.	162	2,360	25,590	545,677

Note: Based on rates in effect July 1, 1997
Source: Edison Electric Institute, Typical Residential, Commercial and Industrial Bills, Summer 1997

TRANSPORTATION

Transportation Statistics

Avg. travel time to work (min.)	21.0
Interstate highways	I-20; I-35W; I-30
Bus lines	
In-city	The T (The Ft. Worth TA), 184 vehicles
Inter-city	2
Passenger air service	
Airport	Dallas/Ft. Worth International Airport; Love Field
Airlines	14
Aircraft departures	382,224 (1995)
Enplaned passengers	25,963,950 (1995)
Rail service	Amtrak; Light Rail
Motor freight carriers	45
Major waterways/ports	None

Source: OAG, Business Travel Planner, Summer 1997; Editor & Publisher Market Guide, 1998; FAA Airport Activity Statistics, 1996; Amtrak National Time Table, Northeast Timetable, Fall/Winter 1997-98; 1990 Census of Population and Housing, STF 3C; Chamber of Commerce/Economic Development 1997; Jane's Urban Transport Systems 1997-98; Transit Fact Book 1997

A survey of 90,000 airline passengers during the first half of 1997 ranked most of the largest airports in the U.S. Dallas-Ft. Worth International ranked number 26 out of 36. Criteria: cleanliness, quality of restaurants, attractiveness, speed of baggage delivery, ease of reaching gates, available ground transportation, ease of following signs and closeness of parking. *Plog Research Inc., First Half 1997*

Means of Transportation to Work

Area	Car/Truck/Van		Public Transportation			Bicycle	Walked	Other Means	Worked at Home
	Drove Alone	Car-pooled	Bus	Subway	Railroad				
City	76.7	16.3	1.6	0.0	0.0	0.2	2.3	1.2	1.8
MSA[1]	80.9	13.5	0.6	0.0	0.0	0.1	1.7	0.9	2.2
U.S.	73.2	13.4	3.0	1.5	0.5	0.4	3.9	1.2	3.0

Note: figures shown are percentages and only include workers 16 years old and over;
(1) Metropolitan Statistical Area - see Appendix A for areas included
Source: 1990 Census of Population and Housing, Summary Tape File 3C

BUSINESSES

Major Business Headquarters

Company Name	1997 Rankings	
	Fortune 500	Forbes 500
AMR	61	-
Burlington Northern Santa Fe	182	-
Tandy	229	-
Williamson-Dickie Manufacturing	-	439

Note: Companies listed are located in the city; Dashes indicate no ranking
Fortune 500: companies that produce a 10-K are ranked 1 - 500 based on 1996 revenue
Forbes 500: private companies are ranked 1 - 500 based on 1996 revenue
Source: Forbes 12/1/97; Fortune 4/28/97

Fast-Growing Businesses

According to *Fortune*, Fort Worth is home to two of America's 100 fastest-growing companies: Americredit and Lomak Petroleum. Companies were ranked based on three years' earnings-per-share growth using least squares analysis to smooth out distortions. Criteria for inclusion: public companies with sales of least $50 million. Companies that lost money in the most recent quarter, or ended in the red for the past four quarters as a whole, were not eligible. Limited partnerships and REITs were also not considered. *Fortune, 9/29/97*

Women-Owned Businesses: Number, Employment, Sales and Share

Area	Women-Owned Businesses in 1996				Share of Women-Owned Businesses in 1996	
	Number	Employment	Sales ($000)	Rank[2]	Percent (%)	Rank[3]
MSA[1]	47,400	55,500	8,753,800	44	36.2	31

Note: (1) Metropolitan Statistical Area - see Appendix A for areas included; (2) Calculated on an averaging of number of businesses, employment and sales and ranges from 1 to 50 where 1 is best; (3) Ranges from 1 to 50 where 1 is best
Source: The National Foundation for Women Business Owners, 1996 Facts on Women-Owned Businesses: Trends in the Top 50 Metropolitan Areas, March 26, 1997

Women-Owned Businesses: Growth

Area	Growth in Women-Owned Businesses (% change from 1987 to 1996)				Relative Growth in the Number of Women-Owned and All Businesses (% change from 1987 to 1996)			
	Num.	Empl.	Sales	Rank[2]	Women-Owned	All Firms	Absolute Difference	Relative Difference
MSA[1]	74.6	125.1	247.5	39	74.6	47.1	27.5	1.6:1

Note: (1) Metropolitan Statistical Area - see Appendix A for areas included; (2) Calculated on an averaging of the percent growth of number of businesses, employment and sales and ranges from 1 to 50 where 1 is best
Source: The National Foundation for Women Business Owners, 1996 Facts on Women-Owned Businesses: Trends in the Top 50 Metropolitan Areas, March 26, 1997

Minority Business Opportunity

Fort Worth is home to one company which is on the Black Enterprise Auto Dealer 100 list (largest based on gross sales): Alan Young Buick-GMC Truck Inc. (GM). Criteria: 1) operational in previous calendar year; 2) at least 51% black-owned. *Black Enterprise, June 1997*

Two of the 500 largest Hispanic-owned companies in the U.S. are located in Fort Worth. *Hispanic Business, June 1997*

Small Business Opportunity

Fort Worth was included among *Entrepreneur* magazines listing of the ''20 Best Cities for Small Business.'' It was ranked #14 among large metro areas. Criteria: risk of failure, business performance, economic growth, affordability and state attitude towards business. *Entrepreneur, 10/97*

According to *Forbes*, Fort Worth is home to one of America's 200 best small companies: Tecnol Medical Products. Criteria: companies must be publicly traded, U.S.-based corporations with latest 12-month sales of between $5 and $350 million. Earnings must be at least $1 million for the 12-month period. Limited partnerships, REITs and closed-end mutual funds were not considered. Banks, S&Ls and electric utilities were not included. *Forbes, November 3, 1997*

HOTELS & MOTELS

Hotels/Motels

Area	Hotels/ Motels	Rooms	Luxury-Level Hotels/Motels		Average Minimum Rates ($)		
			♦♦♦♦	♦♦♦♦♦	♦♦	♦♦♦	♦♦♦♦
City	26	4,216	0	0	63	100	n/a
Suburbs	35	4,949	0	0	n/a	n/a	n/a
Total	61	9,165	0	0	n/a	n/a	n/a

Note: n/a not available; Classifications range from one diamond (budget properties with basic amenities) to five diamond (luxury properties with the finest service, rooms and facilities). Source: OAG, Business Travel Planner, Summer 1997

CONVENTION CENTERS

Major Convention Centers

Center Name	Meeting Rooms	Exhibit Space (sf)
American Airlines Training & Conference Center	8	n/a
Tarrant County Convention Center	25	170,000
Will Rogers Memorial Center	6	124,000

Note: n/a not available
Source: Trade Shows Worldwide 1997

Living Environment

COST OF LIVING

Cost of Living Index

Composite Index	Housing	Utilities	Groceries	Health Care	Trans- portation	Misc. Goods/ Services
95.9	82.9	99.9	106.1	97.8	95.7	100.6

Note: U.S. = 100
Source: ACCRA, Cost of Living Index, 3rd Quarter 1997

HOUSING

Median Home Prices and Housing Affordability

Area	Median Price[2] 3rd Qtr. 1997 ($)	HOI[3] 3rd Qtr. 1997	Afford- ability Rank[4]
MSA[1]	100,000	71.1	87
U.S.	127,000	63.7	–

Note: (1) Metropolitan Statistical Area - see Appendix A for areas included; (2) U.S. figures calculated from the sales of 625,000 new and existing homes in 195 markets; (3) Housing Opportunity Index - percent of homes sold that were within the reach of the median income household at the prevailing mortgage interest rate; (4) Rank is from 1-195 with 1 being most affordable
Source: National Association of Home Builders, Housing Opportunity Index, 3rd Quarter 1997

Average New Home Price

Area	Price ($)
City	105,550
U.S.	135,710

Note: Figures are based on a new home with 1,800 sq. ft. of living area on an 8,000 sq. ft. lot.
Source: ACCRA, Cost of Living Index, 3rd Quarter 1997

Average Apartment Rent

Area	Rent ($/mth)
City	617
U.S.	569

Note: Figures are based on an unfurnished two bedroom, 1-1/2 or 2 bath apartment, approximately 950 sq. ft. in size, excluding all utilities except water
Source: ACCRA, Cost of Living Index, 3rd Quarter 1997

RESIDENTIAL UTILITIES

Average Residential Utility Costs

Area	All Electric ($/mth)	Part Electric ($/mth)	Other Energy ($/mth)	Phone ($/mth)
City	–	73.85	30.27	17.33
U.S.	109.40	55.25	43.64	19.48

Source: ACCRA, Cost of Living Index, 3rd Quarter 1997

HEALTH CARE

Average Health Care Costs

Area	Hospital ($/day)	Doctor ($/visit)	Dentist ($/visit)
City	342.60	44.40	64.80
U.S.	392.91	48.76	60.84

Note: Hospital - based on a semi-private room. Doctor - based on a general practitioner's routine exam of an established patient. Dentist - based on adult teeth cleaning and periodic oral exam.
Source: ACCRA, Cost of Living Index, 3rd Quarter 1997

Distribution of Office-Based Physicians

Area	Family/Gen. Practitioners	Specialists		
		Medical	Surgical	Other
MSA[1]	299	513	518	470

Note: Data as of 12/31/96; (1) Metropolitan Statistical Area - see Appendix A for areas included
Source: American Medical Assn., Physician Characteristics & Distribution in the U.S., 1997-1998

Hospitals

Fort Worth has 9 general medical and surgical hospitals, 2 rehabilitation, 1 other specialty, 1 children's general, 1 children's psychiatric, 1 children's chronic disease. *AHA Guide to the Healthcare Field 1997-98*

Harris Methodist is among the 100 best-run hospitals in the U.S.
Modern Healthcare, January 5, 1998

EDUCATION

Public School District Statistics

District Name	Num. Sch.	Enroll.	Classroom Teachers[1]	Pupils per Teacher	Minority Pupils (%)	Current Exp.[2] ($/pupil)
Birdville ISD	34	20,129	1,223	16.5	18.1	4,274
Castleberry ISD	7	3,138	210	14.9	n/a	n/a
Eagle Mt-Saginaw ISD	8	5,468	304	18.0	n/a	n/a
Fort Worth ISD	129	74,021	4,150	17.8	73.0	4,686
Masonic Home ISD	1	109	15	7.3	n/a	n/a

Note: Data covers the 1995-1996 school year unless otherwise noted; (1) Excludes teachers reported as working in school district offices rather than in schools; (2) Based on 1993-94 enrollment collected by the Census Bureau, not the enrollment figure shown in column 3; SD = School District; ISD = Independent School District; n/a not available
Source: National Center for Education Statistics, Common Core of Data Survey; Bureau of the Census

Educational Quality

School District	Education Quotient[1]	Graduate Outcome[2]	Community Index[3]	Resource Index[4]
Fort Worth	85.0	66.0	121.0	69.0

Note: Nearly 1,000 secondary school districts were rated in terms of educational quality. The scores range from a low of 50 to a high of 150; (1) Average of the Graduate Outcome, Community and Resource indexes; (2) Based on graduation rates and college board scores (SAT/ACT); (3) Based on the surrounding community's average level of education and the area's average income level; (4) Based on teacher salaries, per-pupil expenditures and student-teacher ratios.
Source: Expansion Management, Ratings Issue 1997

Educational Attainment by Race

Area	High School Graduate (%)					Bachelor's Degree (%)				
	Total	White	Black	Other	Hisp.[2]	Total	White	Black	Other	Hisp.[2]
City	71.6	79.2	62.6	39.6	37.4	21.5	27.0	8.8	9.7	6.3
MSA[1]	79.1	82.4	69.4	52.9	47.9	22.6	24.2	12.8	16.1	9.3
U.S.	75.2	77.9	63.1	60.4	49.8	20.3	21.5	11.4	19.4	9.2

Note: figures shown cover persons 25 years old and over; (1) Metropolitan Statistical Area - see Appendix A for areas included; (2) people of Hispanic origin can be of any race
Source: 1990 Census of Population and Housing, Summary Tape File 3C

School Enrollment by Type

Area	Preprimary				Elementary/High School			
	Public		Private		Public		Private	
	Enrollment	%	Enrollment	%	Enrollment	%	Enrollment	%
City	4,297	60.0	2,866	40.0	69,185	90.9	6,935	9.1
MSA[1]	13,513	55.4	10,874	44.6	216,997	92.6	17,279	7.4
U.S.	2,679,029	59.5	1,824,256	40.5	38,379,689	90.2	4,187,099	9.8

Note: figures shown cover persons 3 years old and over;
(1) Metropolitan Statistical Area - see Appendix A for areas included
Source: 1990 Census of Population and Housing, Summary Tape File 3C

School Enrollment by Race

Area	Preprimary (%)				Elementary/High School (%)			
	White	Black	Other	Hisp.[1]	White	Black	Other	Hisp.[1]
City	66.5	23.3	10.3	14.9	50.6	28.9	20.5	27.9
MSA[2]	83.3	10.5	6.2	8.1	74.3	14.0	11.6	14.9
U.S.	80.4	12.5	7.1	7.8	74.1	15.6	10.3	12.5

Note: figures shown cover persons 3 years old and over; (1) people of Hispanic origin can be of any race; (2) Metropolitan Statistical Area - see Appendix A for areas included
Source: 1990 Census of Population and Housing, Summary Tape File 3C

SAT/ACT Scores

Area/District	1996 SAT				1996 ACT	
	Percent of Graduates Tested (%)	Average Math Score	Average Verbal Score	Average Combined Score	Percent of Graduates Tested (%)	Average Composite Score
Ft. Worth ISD	46	473	473	946	16	19.4
State	48	500	495	995	30	20.2
U.S.	41	508	505	1,013	35	20.9

Note: Math and verbal SAT scores are out of a possible 800; ACT scores are out of a possible 36
Caution: Comparing or ranking states/cities on the basis of SAT/ACT scores alone is invalid and strongly discouraged by the The College Board and The American College Testing Program as students who take the tests are self-selected and do not represent the entire student population. 1996 SAT scores cannot be compared to previous years due to recentering.
Source: Ft. Worth Independent School District, 1996; American College Testing Program, 1996; College Board, 1996

Classroom Teacher Salaries in Public Schools

District	B.A. Degree		M.A. Degree		Ph.D. Degree	
	Min. ($)	Max. ($)	Min. ($)	Max. ($)	Min. ($)	Max. ($)
Fort Worth	27,100	44,680	27,707	46,000	28,718	48,224
Average[1]	26,120	39,270	28,175	44,667	31,643	49,825

Note: Salaries are for 1996-1997; (1) Based on all school districts covered; n/a not available
Source: American Federation of Teachers (unpublished data)

Higher Education

Two-Year Colleges		Four-Year Colleges		Medical Schools	Law Schools	Voc/ Tech
Public	Private	Public	Private			
1	1	0	1	0	1	13

Source: College Blue Book, Occupational Education 1997; Medical School Admission Requirements, 1998-99; Peterson's Guide to Two-Year Colleges, 1997; Peterson's Guide to Four-Year Colleges, 1997; Barron's Guide to Law Schools 1997

MAJOR EMPLOYERS

Major Employers

AMR Corp. (air transportation)
All Saints Health System
Burlington Northern
Tarrant County Hospital District
Tandy Corp.
Nokia Mobile Phones America
Ft. Worth Medical Plaza

Alcon Laboratories
American Airlines
Cook Children's Medical Center
Sabre Group (business services)
Teleservice Resources
Union Pacific Resources (oil & gas)

Note: companies listed are located in the city
Source: Dun's Business Rankings 1997; Ward's Business Directory, 1997

PUBLIC SAFETY

Crime Rate

Area	All Crimes	Violent Crimes				Property Crimes		
		Murder	Forcible Rape	Robbery	Aggrav. Assault	Burglary	Larceny -Theft	Motor Vehicle Theft
City	8,272.6	14.5	67.8	359.8	617.8	1,683.6	4,568.0	961.2
Suburbs[1]	4,881.7	3.5	40.5	96.4	358.9	852.9	3,113.7	415.8
MSA[2]	5,865.3	6.7	48.4	172.8	434.0	1,093.8	3,535.6	574.0
U.S.	5,078.9	7.4	36.1	202.4	388.2	943.0	2,975.9	525.9

Note: Crime rate is the number of crimes per 100,000 pop.; (1) defined as all areas within the MSA but located outside the central city; (2) Metropolitan Statistical Area - see Appendix A for areas incl.
Source: FBI Uniform Crime Reports 1996

RECREATION

Culture and Recreation

Museums	Symphony Orchestras	Opera Companies	Dance Companies	Professional Theatres	Zoos	Pro Sports Teams
6	1	1	1	1	1	0

Source: International Directory of the Performing Arts, 1996; Official Museum Directory, 1998; Chamber of Commerce/Economic Development 1997

Library System

The Ft. Worth Public Library has nine branches, holdings of 1,157,390 volumes and a budget of $8,014,275 (1995-1996). The North Texas Regional Library System has no branches, holdings of n/a volumes and a budget of $855,400 (1994-1995). Note: n/a means not available. *American Library Directory, 1997-1998*

MEDIA

Newspapers

Name	Type	Freq.	Distribution	Circulation
Benbrook News	General	1x/wk	Local	6,000
El Informador Hispano	Hispanic	1x/wk	Local	30,000
Fort Worth Star Telegram	General	7x/wk	Area	263,470
Fort Worth Texas Times	General	1x/wk	Local	50,000
La Vida News	Black	1x/wk	Local	35,000
North Texas Catholic	Religious	1x/wk	Local	26,500
River Oaks News	General	1x/wk	Local	4,500
TCU Daily Skiff	n/a	4x/wk	Campus	4,600
White Settlement Bomber News	General	1x/wk	Local	7,060

Note: Includes newspapers with circulations of 1,000 or more located in the city; Source: Burrelle's Media Directory, 1998 Edition

AM Radio Stations

Call Letters	Freq. (kHz)	Target Audience	Station Format	Music Format
WBAP	820	General	N/T	n/a
KFJZ	870	Hispanic	M	n/a
KRLD	1080	General	N/T	n/a
KAHZ	1360	General	E/M/N/S/T	n/a
KIWF	1540	Hispanic	M/N/T	n/a

Note: Stations included broadcast in the Fort Worth metro area; n/a not available
Station Format: E = Educational; M = Music; N = News; S = Sports; T = Talk
Source: Burrelle's Media Directory, 1998 Edition

FM Radio Stations

Call Letters	Freq. (mHz)	Target Audience	Station Format	Music Format
KTCU	88.7	General	M/N/S	Adult Standards
KCBI	90.9	General	M/N/S	Christian
KSYE	91.5	General	M/N/S	Christian/MOR
KSCS	96.3	General	M	Country

Note: Stations included broadcast in the Fort Worth metro area
Station Format: E = Educational; M = Music; N = News; S = Sports; T = Talk
Music Format: AOR = Album Oriented Rock; MOR = Middle-of-the-Road
Source: Burrelle's Media Directory, 1998 Edition

Television Stations

Name	Ch.	Affiliation	Type	Owner
KXAS	5	NBC	Commercial	LIN Television
KTVT	11	CBS	Commercial	Gaylord Broadcasting
KTXA	21	UPN	Commercial	Paramount Communications
KFWD	52	Telemundo	Commercial	Interspan Communications Ltd.

Note: Stations included broadcast in the Fort Worth metro area
Source: Burrelle's Media Directory, 1998 Edition

CLIMATE

Average and Extreme Temperatures

Temperature	Jan	Feb	Mar	Apr	May	Jun	Jul	Aug	Sep	Oct	Nov	Dec	Ann
Extreme High (°F)	88	88	96	98	103	113	110	108	107	106	89	90	113
Average High (°F)	54	59	67	76	83	92	96	96	88	79	67	58	76
Average Temp. (°F)	44	49	57	66	73	81	85	85	78	68	56	47	66
Average Low (°F)	33	38	45	54	63	71	75	74	67	56	45	37	55
Extreme Low (°F)	4	6	11	29	41	51	59	56	43	29	19	-1	-1

Note: Figures cover the years 1953-1990
Source: National Climatic Data Center, International Station Meteorological Climate Summary, 3/95

Average Precipitation/Snowfall/Humidity

Precip./Humidity	Jan	Feb	Mar	Apr	May	Jun	Jul	Aug	Sep	Oct	Nov	Dec	Ann
Avg. Precip. (in.)	1.8	2.2	2.6	3.7	4.9	2.8	2.1	1.9	3.0	3.3	2.1	1.7	32.3
Avg. Snowfall (in.)	1	1	Tr	0	0	0	0	0	0	0	Tr	Tr	3
Avg. Rel. Hum. 6am (%)	79	79	79	81	86	85	80	79	83	82	80	79	81
Avg. Rel. Hum. 3pm (%)	52	51	48	50	53	47	42	41	46	47	49	51	48

Note: Figures cover the years 1953-1990; Tr = Trace amounts (<0.05 in. of rain; <0.5 in. of snow)
Sourcc: National Climatic Data Center, International Station Meteorological Climate Summary, 3/95

Weather Conditions

Temperature			Daytime Sky			Precipitation		
10°F & below	32°F & below	90°F & above	Clear	Partly cloudy	Cloudy	0.01 inch or more precip.	0.1 inch or more snow/ice	Thunderstorms
1	40	100	123	136	106	79	3	47

Note: Figures are average number of days per year and covers the years 1953-1990
Source: National Climatic Data Center, International Station Meteorological Climate Summary, 3/95

AIR & WATER QUALITY

Maximum Pollutant Concentrations

	Particulate Matter (ug/m^3)	Carbon Monoxide (ppm)	Sulfur Dioxide (ppm)	Nitrogen Dioxide (ppm)	Ozone (ppm)	Lead (ug/m^3)
MSA[1] Level	56	3	0.011	0.021	0.13	0.02
NAAQS[2]	150	9	0.140	0.053	0.12	1.50
Met NAAQS?	Yes	Yes	Yes	Yes	No	Yes

Note: (1) Metropolitan Statistical Area - see Appendix A for areas included; (2) National Ambient Air Quality Standards; ppm = parts per million; ug/m^3 = micrograms per cubic meter; n/a not available
Source: EPA, National Air Quality and Emissions Trends Report, 1996

Pollutant Standards Index

In the Fort Worth MSA (see Appendix A for areas included), the Pollutant Standards Index (PSI) exceeded 100 on 3 days in 1996. A PSI value greater than 100 indicates that air quality would be in the unhealthful range on that day. *EPA, National Air Quality and Emissions Trends Report, 1996*

Drinking Water

Water System Name	Pop. Served	Primary Water Source Type	Number of Violations in Fiscal Year 1997	Type of Violation/ Contaminants
City of Fort Worth	900,000	Surface	None	None

Note: Data as of January 16, 1998
Source: EPA, Office of Ground Water and Drinking Water, Safe Drinking Water Information System

Fort Worth tap water is alkaline, hard and fluoridated.
Editor & Publisher Market Guide, 1998

Houston, Texas

Background

Two brothers back in 1836, John K. and Augustus C. Allen, bought a 6,642 acre tract of marshy, mosquito-infested land 56 miles north of the Gulf of Mexico and named it Houston, after the hero of San Jacinto. From that moment on, Houston has experienced nothing but impressive economic and population growth.

By the end of its first year in the Republic of Texas, Houston claimed 1,500 residents, one theater, and interestingly, no churches. The first churches came three years later. By the end of its second year, Houston saw its first steamship, and its position as one of the top ranking ports in the country had been defined.

Certainly, Houston owes much to the Houston ship channel, the "golden strip" on which oil refineries, chemical plants, cement factories, and grain elevators conduct their bustling economic activity. The diversity of the above-mentioned industries is a testament to Houston's economy in general.

Houston, like Miami and Los Angeles has been transformed by a trade economy that now accounts for about 10% of regional employment. Since 1986 tonnage through the Port of Houston has grown by one-third, helping the city recover the jobs lost during the "oil bust" of the early 1980s. *World Trade, 6/96*

As Texas' biggest city, Houston is also enjoying new manufacturing expansion in its diversified economy. A revitalized downtown will soon become Continental Airlines' relocated worldwide headquarters, bringing in over 3,000 jobs from the suburbs.

Not limited to manufacturing, Houston boasts of being one of the finest centers for scientific research in the world. The presence of the Lyndon B. Johnson Space Center has spawned a number of related industries in medical and technological research. The Texas Medical Center oversees a network of medical institutions, including St. Luke's Episcopal Hospital, the Texas Children's Hospital, and the Methodist Hospital.

A city whose reputation lies upon top, advanced research will certainly be devoted to education and to the arts. Rice University, for example, whose admission standards rank as one of the highest in the nation, is located in Houston, as are Dominican College and the University of St. Thomas..

Houston also plays patron to the Museum of Fine Arts, the Contemporary Arts Museum, and the Houston Ballet and Grand Opera. A host of smaller cultural institutions, such as the Gilbert and Sullivan Society, the Virtuoso Quartet, and the Houston Harpsichord Society enliven the scene. Two new privately funded museums, The Holocaust Museum Houston and the Museum of Health & Medical Science, opened last year. A downtown baseball stadium is also being planned.

Located in the flat Coastal Plains, Houston's climate is predominantly marine. The terrain includes many small streams and bayous which, together with the nearness to Galveston Bay, favor the development of fog. Temperatures are moderated by the influence of winds from the Gulf of Mexico, which is 50 miles away. Mild winters are the norm, as is abundant rainfall. Polar air penetrates the area frequently enough to provide variability in the weather.

General Rankings and Evaluative Comments

- Houston was ranked #50 out of 300 cities by *Money's* 1997 "Survey of the Best Places to Live." Criteria used: health services, crime, economy, housing, education, transportation, weather, leisure and the arts. The city was ranked #35 in 1996 and #162 in 1995. *Money, July 1997; Money, September 1996; Money, September 1995*

- *Ladies Home Journal* ranked America's 200 largest cities based on the qualities women care about most. Houston ranked 114 out of 200. Criteria: low crime rate, good public schools, well-paying jobs, quality health and child care, the presence of women in government, proportion of women-owned businesses, size of the wage gap with men, local economy, divorce rates, the ratio of single men to single women, whether there are laws that require at least the same number of public toilets for women as men, and the probability of good hair days. *Ladies Home Journal, November 1997*

- Houston was ranked #187 out of 219 cities in terms of children's health, safety, and economic well-being. Criteria: total population, percent population change, birth rate, child immunization rate, infant mortality rate, percent low birth weight infants, percent of births to teens, physician-to-population ratio, student-to-teacher ratio, dropout rate, unemployment rate, median family income, percent of children in poverty, violent and property crime rates, number of juvenile arrests for violent crimes as a percent of the total crime index, number of days with pollution standard index (PSI) over 100, pounds toxic releases per 1,000 people and number of superfund sites. *Zero Population Growth, Children's Environmental Index 1997*

- *Yahoo! Internet Life* selected "America's 100 Most Wired Cities & Towns". 50 cities were large and 50 cities were small. Houston ranked 17 out of 50 large cities. Criteria: Internet users per capita, number of networked computers, number of registered domain names, Internet backbone traffic, and the per-capita number of Web sites devoted to each city. *Yahoo! Internet Life, March 1998*

- *Reader's Digest* non-scientifically ranked the 12 largest U.S. metropolitan areas in terms of having the worst drivers. The Houston metro area ranked number 10. The areas were selected by asking approximately 1,200 readers on the *Reader's Digest* Web site and 200 interstate bus drivers and long-haul truckers which metro areas have the worst drivers. Their responses were factored in with fatality, insurance and rental-car rates to create the rankings. *Reader's Digest, March 1998*

- Houston was among "The 10 Hotbeds of Entrepreneurial Activity" in 1996 with 1.60 start-ups per 100 people. Rank: 4 out of 200 metro areas. *Inc., The State of Small Business 1997*

- Compaq Computer and Shell Oil, headquartered in Houston, are among the "100 Best Companies to Work for in America." Criteria: trust in management, pride in work/company, camaraderie, company responses to the Hewitt People Practices Inventory, and employee responses to their Great Place to Work survey. The companies also had to be at least 10 years old and have a minimum of 500 employees. *Fortune, January 12, 1998*

- According to *Working Mother,* "This year, the Texas Licensed Child Care Association lobbied heavily against proposed standards that would have improved the adult-to-child ratios in many programs. Unfortunately, it prevailed. Lawmakers delayed adoption of the new rules.

  Texas may finally get statewide resource and referral services, however, with new federal funds coming into the state. In addition to helping parents find care, R&Rs may handle both caregiver training and consumer education—a positive development.

  Providers across the state may also get low-interest loans to buy new equipment, upgrade their facilities and do other things to improve the quality of care, under a bill pending in the state legislature that looked likely to pass as we went to press." *Working Mother, July/August 1997*

Business Environment

STATE ECONOMY

State Economic Profile

"The Texas economy remains among the strongest in the nation....

Overall, Texas gained over 141,000 people last year through in-migration. While this is down from the three-year average of over 170,000, it still represents 43% of the Texas population increase. By far, throughout this decade, California has been the largest domestic source of in-migrants into Texas. With the California economy rebounding, in-migration to Texas is slowing.

The slowdown in household growth, coupled with solid residential construction, is creating a slight oversupply throughout the state. As a result, house price growth is decelerating. New residential permits have yet to slow, with new permits up by 14% last year—nearly twice the national increase. The slowdown in population and household growth cannot sustain such robust growth in permits, and as a result, new permits will slow this year.

The Texas economy shows no major imbalances. Although the important computer-chip industry remains moribund, the economy continues to expand solidly. The turnaround in computer memory prices will help the state continue to expand. Texas' growth is becoming increasingly supported by in-migrants. With an increasing presence in high-tech, an attractive business environment, and close proximity to Mexico, Texas will continue to expand faster than the nation and lure workers from other locales. In addition, as an attractive destination for retirees, Texas will continue to experience solid population and household growth as the population ages. Texas is ranked above average for short-and long-term growth." *National Association of Realtors, Economic Profiles: The Fifty States, July 1997*

IMPORTS/EXPORTS

Total Export Sales

Area	1993 ($000)	1994 ($000)	1995 ($000)	1996 ($000)	% Chg. 1993-96	% Chg. 1995-96
MSA[1]	12,284,566	13,388,170	16,247,880	16,541,463	34.7	1.8
U.S.	464,858,354	512,415,609	583,030,524	622,827,063	34.0	6.8

Note: (1) Metropolitan Statistical Area - see Appendix A for areas included
Source: U.S. Department of Commerce, International Trade Association, Metropolitan Area Exports: An Export Performance Report on Over 250 U.S. Cities, October 1997

Imports/Exports by Port

Type	Cargo Value			Share of U.S. Total	
	1995 (US$mil.)	1996 (US$mil.)	% Change 1995-1996	1995 (%)	1996 (%)
Imports	11,966	13,790	15.25	3.06	3.59
Exports	19,884	19,386	-2.50	8.69	8.18

Source: Global Trade Information Services, WaterBorne Trade Atlas 1997

CITY FINANCES

City Government Finances

Component	FY94 ($000)	FY94 (per capita $)
Revenue	2,022,210	1,174.84
Expenditure	2,055,402	1,194.12
Debt Outstanding	3,822,263	2,220.61
Cash & Securities	3,929,559	2,282.95

Source: U.S. Bureau of the Census, City Government Finances: 1993-94

City Government Revenue by Source

Source	FY94 ($000)	FY94 (per capita $)	FY94 (%)
From Federal Government	66,040	38.37	3.3
From State Governments	19,702	11.45	1.0
From Local Governments	10,152	5.90	0.5
Property Taxes	407,904	236.98	20.2
General Sales Taxes	226,361	131.51	11.2
Selective Sales Taxes	140,584	81.67	7.0
Income Taxes	0	0.00	0.0
Current Charges	434,987	252.71	21.5
Utility/Liquor Store	252,502	146.70	12.5
Employee Retirement[1]	283,521	164.72	14.0
Other	180,457	104.84	8.9

Note: (1) Excludes "city contributions," classified as "nonrevenue," intragovernmental transfers.
Source: U.S. Bureau of the Census, City Government Finances: 1993-94

City Government Expenditures by Function

Function	FY94 ($000)	FY94 (per capita $)	FY94 (%)
Educational Services	27,739	16.12	1.3
Employee Retirement[1]	83,418	48.46	4.1
Environment/Housing	404,820	235.19	19.7
Government Administration	84,816	49.28	4.1
Interest on General Debt	154,720	89.89	7.5
Public Safety	513,730	298.46	25.0
Social Services	68,504	39.80	3.3
Transportation	347,943	202.14	16.9
Utility/Liquor Store	274,054	159.22	13.3
Other	95,658	55.57	4.7

Note: (1) Payments to beneficiaries including withdrawal of contributions.
Source: U.S. Bureau of the Census, City Government Finances: 1993-94

Municipal Bond Ratings

Area	Moody's	S & P
Houston	Aa3	AA-

Note: n/a not available; n/r not rated
Source: Moody's Bond Record, 2/98; Statistical Abstract of the U.S., 1997;
Governing Magazine, 9/97, 3/98

POPULATION

Population Growth

Area	1980	1990	% Chg. 1980-90	July 1996 Estimate	% Chg. 1990-96
City	1,595,167	1,630,672	2.2	1,744,058	7.0
MSA[1]	2,735,766	3,301,937	20.7	3,791,921	14.8
U.S.	226,545,805	248,765,170	9.8	265,179,411	6.6

Note: (1) Metropolitan Statistical Area - see Appendix A for areas included
Source: 1980/1990 Census of Housing and Population, Summary Tape File 3C;
Census Bureau Population Estimates

Population Characteristics

Race	City 1980 Population	%	City 1990 Population	%	% Chg. 1980-90	MSA[1] 1990 Population	%
White	981,563	61.5	860,323	52.8	-12.4	2,191,107	66.4
Black	439,604	27.6	457,574	28.1	4.1	610,377	18.5
Amer Indian/Esk/Aleut	3,945	0.2	4,376	0.3	10.9	9,912	0.3
Asian/Pacific Islander	35,448	2.2	66,008	4.0	86.2	124,723	3.8
Other	134,607	8.4	242,391	14.9	80.1	365,818	11.1
Hispanic Origin[2]	281,331	17.6	442,943	27.2	57.4	696,208	21.1

Note: (1) Metropolitan Statistical Area - see Appendix A for areas included;
(2) people of Hispanic origin can be of any race
Source: 1980/1990 Census of Housing and Population, Summary Tape File 3C

Ancestry

Area	German	Irish	English	Italian	U.S.	French	Polish	Dutch
City	11.7	8.4	8.8	2.1	2.9	3.0	1.5	1.0
MSA[1]	17.0	12.5	11.4	2.6	4.1	3.9	2.0	1.5
U.S.	23.3	15.6	13.1	5.9	5.3	4.2	3.8	2.5

Note: Figures are percentages and include persons that reported multiple ancestry (eg. if a person reported being Irish and Italian, they were included in both columns); (1) Metropolitan Statistical Area - see Appendix A for areas included
Source: 1990 Census of Population and Housing, Summary Tape File 3C

Age

Area	Median Age (Years)	Under 5	Under 18	18-24	25-44	45-64	65+	80+
City	30.3	8.3	26.7	11.6	36.4	17.1	8.2	1.6
MSA[1]	30.4	8.5	28.9	10.4	36.9	16.7	7.0	1.4
U.S.	32.9	7.3	25.6	10.5	32.6	18.7	12.5	2.8

Note: (1) Metropolitan Statistical Area - see Appendix A for areas included
Source: 1990 Census of Population and Housing, Summary Tape File 3C

Male/Female Ratio

Area	Number of males per 100 females (all ages)	Number of males per 100 females (18 years old+)
City	98.4	96.3
MSA[1]	98.8	96.6
U.S.	95.0	91.9

Note: (1) Metropolitan Statistical Area - see Appendix A for areas included
Source: 1990 Census of Population, General Population Characteristics

INCOME

Per Capita/Median/Average Income

Area	Per Capita ($)	Median Household ($)	Average Household ($)
City	14,261	26,261	37,296
MSA[1]	15,091	31,473	41,650
U.S.	14,420	30,056	38,453

Note: all figures are for 1989; (1) Metropolitan Statistical Area - see Appendix A for areas included
Source: 1990 Census of Population and Housing, Summary Tape File 3C

Household Income Distribution by Race

Income ($)	City (%)					U.S. (%)				
	Total	White	Black	Other	Hisp.[1]	Total	White	Black	Other	Hisp.[1]
Less than 5,000	8.9	5.2	16.4	10.6	9.7	6.2	4.8	15.2	8.6	8.8
5,000 - 9,999	9.1	6.9	13.2	10.7	11.1	9.3	8.6	14.2	9.9	11.1
10,000 - 14,999	9.9	8.1	12.2	13.3	14.5	8.8	8.5	11.0	9.8	11.0
15,000 - 24,999	19.7	17.9	21.5	24.0	25.4	17.5	17.3	18.9	18.5	20.5
25,000 - 34,999	15.8	16.2	14.9	15.8	16.8	15.8	16.1	14.2	15.4	16.4
35,000 - 49,999	15.2	16.9	12.3	13.4	12.8	17.9	18.6	13.3	16.1	16.0
50,000 - 74,999	12.1	15.2	7.1	8.1	6.7	15.0	15.8	9.3	13.4	11.1
75,000 - 99,999	4.5	6.3	1.6	2.3	1.7	5.1	5.5	2.6	4.7	3.1
100,000+	4.8	7.3	0.7	1.8	1.2	4.4	4.8	1.3	3.7	1.9

Note: all figures are for 1989; (1) people of Hispanic origin can be of any race
Source: 1990 Census of Population and Housing, Summary Tape File 3C

Effective Buying Income

Area	Per Capita ($)	Median Household ($)	Average Household ($)
City	16,632	31,794	44,389
MSA[1]	18,065	39,455	50,894
U.S.	15,444	33,201	41,849

Note: data as of 1/1/97; (1) Metropolitan Statistical Area - see Appendix A for areas included
Source: Standard Rate & Data Service, Newspaper Advertising Source, 2/98

Effective Household Buying Income Distribution

Area	% of Households Earning						
	$10,000 -$19,999	$20,000 -$34,999	$35,000 -$49,999	$50,000 -$74,999	$75,000 -$99,000	$100,000 -$124,999	$125,000 and up
City	16.6	23.5	16.4	15.5	6.9	2.8	3.9
MSA[1]	13.1	20.8	17.1	19.9	9.8	3.9	4.6
U.S.	16.5	23.4	18.3	18.2	6.4	2.1	2.4

Note: data as of 1/1/97; (1) Metropolitan Statistical Area - see Appendix A for areas included
Source: Standard Rate & Data Service, Newspaper Advertising Source, 2/98

Poverty Rates by Race and Age

Area	Total (%)	By Race (%)				By Age (%)		
		White	Black	Other	Hisp.[2]	Under 5 years old	Under 18 years old	65 years and over
City	20.7	12.4	30.7	29.3	30.7	31.4	30.0	17.8
MSA[1]	15.1	9.4	27.9	24.8	26.6	21.6	20.2	16.0
U.S.	13.1	9.8	29.5	23.1	25.3	20.1	18.3	12.8

Note: figures show the percent of people living below the poverty line in 1989. The average poverty threshold was $12,674 for a family of four in 1989; (1) Metropolitan Statistical Area - see Appendix A for areas included; (2) people of Hispanic origin can be of any race
Source: 1990 Census of Population and Housing, Summary Tape File 3C

EMPLOYMENT

Labor Force and Employment

Area	Civilian Labor Force			Workers Employed		
	Dec. '95	Dec. '96	% Chg.	Dec. '95	Dec. '96	% Chg.
City	986,035	998,579	1.3	929,435	950,619	2.3
MSA[1]	2,034,311	2,064,833	1.5	1,939,278	1,983,477	2.3
U.S.	134,583,000	136,742,000	1.6	127,903,000	130,785,000	2.3

Note: Data is not seasonally adjusted and covers workers 16 years of age and older;
(1) Metropolitan Statistical Area - see Appendix A for areas included
Source: Bureau of Labor Statistics, http://stats.bls.gov

Unemployment Rate

Area	1997											
	Jan.	Feb.	Mar.	Apr.	May	Jun.	Jul.	Aug.	Sep.	Oct.	Nov.	Dec.
City	6.8	6.6	6.7	6.2	6.1	7.3	6.6	6.1	5.9	5.5	5.4	4.8
MSA[1]	5.5	5.5	5.4	5.1	5.0	6.0	5.4	5.0	4.8	4.5	4.4	3.9
U.S.	5.9	5.7	5.5	4.8	4.7	5.2	5.0	4.8	4.7	4.4	4.3	4.4

Note: Data is not seasonally adjusted and covers workers 16 years of age and older; All figures are percentages; (1) Metropolitan Statistical Area - see Appendix A for areas included
Source: Bureau of Labor Statistics, http://stats.bls.gov

Employment by Industry

Sector	MSA[1]		U.S.
	Number of Employees	Percent of Total	Percent of Total
Services	584,300	30.0	29.0
Retail Trade	329,400	16.9	18.5
Government	253,500	13.0	16.1
Manufacturing	214,600	11.0	15.0
Finance/Insurance/Real Estate	102,300	5.3	5.7
Wholesale Trade	124,700	6.4	5.4
Transportation/Public Utilities	137,200	7.0	5.3
Construction	132,100	6.8	4.5
Mining	70,100	3.6	0.5

Note: Figures cover non-farm employment as of 12/97 and are not seasonally adjusted;
(1) Metropolitan Statistical Area - see Appendix A for areas included
Source: Bureau of Labor Statistics, http://stats.bls.gov

Employment by Occupation

Occupation Category	City (%)	MSA[1] (%)	U.S. (%)
White Collar	60.6	62.6	58.1
Executive/Admin./Management	13.0	14.0	12.3
Professional	14.8	14.8	14.1
Technical & Related Support	4.3	4.4	3.7
Sales	12.6	13.0	11.8
Administrative Support/Clerical	16.0	16.4	16.3
Blue Collar	23.5	23.8	26.2
Precision Production/Craft/Repair	10.4	11.6	11.3
Machine Operators/Assem./Insp.	4.6	4.3	6.8
Transportation/Material Movers	4.0	3.9	4.1
Cleaners/Helpers/Laborers	4.5	4.0	3.9
Services	14.8	12.5	13.2
Farming/Forestry/Fishing	1.1	1.1	2.5

Note: figures cover employed persons 16 years old and over;
(1) Metropolitan Statistical Area - see Appendix A for areas included
Source: 1990 Census of Population and Housing, Summary Tape File 3C

Occupational Employment Projections: 1993 - 2000

Occupations Expected to have the Largest Job Growth (ranked by numerical growth)	Fast-Growing Occupations[1] (ranked by percent growth)
1. General office clerks	1. Housekeepers and butlers
2. Cashiers	2. Demonstrators/promoters/models
3. Child care workers, private household	3. Computer engineers
4. Janitors/cleaners/maids, ex. priv. hshld.	4. Physical therapists
5. Salespersons, retail	5. Physical scientists
6. Home health aides	6. Transportation inspectors
7. Guards	7. Human services workers
8. Food preparation workers	8. Cleaners/servants, private home
9. General managers & top executives	9. Computer systems analysts
10. Waiters & waitresses	10. Home health aides

Projections cover Austin, Brazoria, Chambers, Colorado, Fort Bend, Galveston, Harris, Liberty, Matagorda, Montgomery, Walker, Waller and Wharton Counties.
Note: (1) Includes occupations with absolute job growth of 100 or more
Source: Texas Employment Commission, Texas Employment Projections Reporting System, Statewide and Regional Projections 1993-2000, Ver. 1.0

Average Wages

Occupation	Wage	Occupation	Wage
Professional/Technical/Clerical	$/Week	**Health/Protective Services**	$/Week
Accountants III	881	Corrections Officers	441
Attorneys III	1,430	Firefighters	617
Budget Analysts III	862	Nurses, Licensed Practical II	-
Buyers/Contracting Specialists II	722	Nurses, Registered II	-
Clerks, Accounting III	493	Nursing Assistants II	-
Clerks, General III	479	Police Officers I	603
Computer Operators II	453	**Hourly Workers**	$/Hour
Computer Programmers II	703	Forklift Operators	-
Drafters II	-	General Maintenance Workers	9.22
Engineering Technicians III	689	Guards I	6.55
Engineering Technicians, Civil III	532	Janitors	5.34
Engineers III	985	Maintenance Electricians	18.67
Key Entry Operators I	341	Maintenance Electronics Techs II	18.51
Personnel Assistants III	-	Maintenance Machinists	-
Personnel Specialists III	877	Maintenance Mechanics, Machinery	18.46
Secretaries III	573	Material Handling Laborers	-
Switchboard Operator-Receptionist	363	Motor Vehicle Mechanics	14.63
Systems Analysts II	1,021	Shipping/Receiving Clerks	10.94
Systems Analysts Supervisor/Mgr II	1,455	Tool and Die Makers	17.22
Tax Collectors II	446	Truckdrivers, Tractor Trailer	13.30
Word Processors II	477	Warehouse Specialists	-

Note: Wage data includes full-time workers only for 3/96 and cover the Metropolitan Statistical Area (see Appendix A for areas included). Dashes indicate that data was not available.
Source: Bureau of Labor Statistics, Occupational Compensation Survey, 9/96

TAXES

Major State and Local Tax Rates

State Corp. Income (%)	State Personal Income (%)	Residential Property (effective rate per $100)	Sales & Use		State Gasoline (cents/ gallon)	State Cigarette (cents/ 20-pack)
			State (%)	Local (%)		
None[a]	None	2.61	6.25	2.0	20	41

Note: Personal/corporate income tax rates as of 1/97. Sales, gasoline and cigarette tax rates as of 1/98; (a) Texas imposes a franchise tax of 4.5% of earned surplus
Source: Federation of Tax Administrators, www.taxadmin.org; Washington D.C. Department of Finance and Revenue, Tax Rates and Tax Burdens in the District of Columbia: A Nationwide Comparison, June 1997; Chamber of Commerce

Total Taxes Per Capita and as a Percent of Income

Area	Per Capita Income ($)	Per Capita Taxes ($)			Taxes as Pct. of Income (%)		
		Total	Federal	State/Local	Total	Federal	State/Local
Texas	24,145	8,118	5,538	2,580	33.6	22.9	10.7
U.S.	26,187	9,205	6,127	3,078	35.2	23.4	11.8

Note: Figures are for 1997
Source: Tax Foundation, Web Site, www.taxfoundation.org

Estimated Tax Burden

Area	State Income	Local Income	Property	Sales	Total
Houston	0	0	5,175	701	5,876

Note: The numbers are estimates of taxes paid by a married couple with two kids and annual earnings of $65,000. Sales tax estimates assume they spend average amounts on food, clothing, household goods and gasoline. Property tax estimates assume they live in a $225,000 home.
Source: Kiplinger's Personal Finance Magazine, June 1997

COMMERCIAL REAL ESTATE

Office Market

Class/Location	Total Space (sq. ft.)	Vacant Space (sq. ft.)	Vac. Rate (%)	Under Constr. (sq. ft.)	Net Absorp. (sq. ft.)	Rental Rates ($/sq.ft./yr.)
Class A						
CBD	19,540,792	1,519,329	7.8	0	697,571	11.28-21.58
Outside CBD	25,189,987	1,352,158	5.4	289,663	507,676	13.00-24.00
Class B						
CBD	9,744,786	1,690,659	17.3	0	763,508	10.01-20.00
Outside CBD	53,593,657	5,809,844	10.8	0	4,531,697	7.00-19.00

Note: Data as of 10/97 and covers Houston; CBD = Central Business District; n/a not available;
Source: Society of Industrial and Office Realtors, 1998 Comparative Statistics of Industrial and Office Real Estate Markets

"Our SIOR reporter foresees a modest increase in absorption during 1998 and this could lead to some very low vacancy rates during the later part of the year. During late 1997 there was less than 300,000 sq. ft. of Class 'A' office space under construction outside the central business district and no new construction in the CBD. If absorption of Class 'A' space increases a very modest two and a half percent from the 1997 level during 1998 the Class 'A' vacancy rate for the market as whole would fall to less than four percent. One possible constraint to this outlook would be a shortage of space. New construction might not be completed in time to allow absorption to increase. " *Society of Industrial and Office Realtors, 1998 Comparative Statistics of Industrial and Office Real Estate Markets*

Industrial Market

Location	Total Space (sq. ft.)	Vacant Space (sq. ft.)	Vac. Rate (%)	Under Constr. (sq. ft.)	Net Absorp. (sq. ft.)	Gross Lease ($/sq.ft./yr.)
Central City	105,172,599	9,529,095	9.1	0	3,326,890	1.90-4.80
Suburban	123,128,121	11,765,654	9.6	1,610,251	9,492,669	2.00-4.80

Note: Data as of 10/97 and covers Houston; n/a not available
Source: Society of Industrial and Office Realtors, 1998 Comparative Statistics of Industrial and Office Real Estate Markets

"Development activity increased more than 10 percent during 1997. The coming year will bring an additional increase in the six to 10 percent range. Although new construction has increased, developers are still cautious. During 1998, the majority of speculative development will be concentrated in the northwest and southwest quadrants of Houston. One example of activity in this submarket is Vantage Houston, Inc., which broke ground on its first speculative building in almost a decade with the start of a 620,000 sq. ft. industrial park in northwest Houston. The first phase of Northwest Point will consist of three buildings totaling more than

390,000 sq. ft. The outlook for absorption in 1998 is very strong. Absorption of warehousing/distribution space is expected to increase 11 to 15 percent. Demand for warehouse/distribution space should push up lease prices and sale prices during the year."
Society of Industrial and Office Realtors, 1998 Comparative Statistics of Industrial and Office Real Estate Markets

Retail Market

Shopping Center Inventory (sq. ft.)	Shopping Center Construction (sq. ft.)	Construction as a Percent of Inventory (%)	Torto Wheaton Rent Index[1] ($/sq. ft.)
67,233,000	1,250,000	1.9	14.04

Note: Data as of 1997 and covers the Metropolitan Statistical Area - see Appendix A for areas included; (1) Index is based on a model that predicts what the average rent should be for leases with certain characteristics, in certain locations during certain years.
Source: National Association of Realtors, 1997-1998 Market Conditions Report

"Houston's rebounding economy has aided its retail sector. With the exception of 1995, the area's retail rent index has risen every year since 1991. Houston residents command relatively high per capita incomes. In 1996, the MSA's per-capita income was $25,700 compared to $22,200 for Texas and $24,200 nationally. The return of the oil industry is expected to further boost the economy. 1996 and 1997 were strong years for retail development; however, the market seems to have settled into a sustainable pace. Most developers are expected to concentrate on grocery store-anchored centers and niche market centers. Shopping center completions are expected to average 1.4 million square feet over the next two years."
National Association of Realtors, 1997-1998 Market Conditions Report

COMMERCIAL UTILITIES

Typical Monthly Electric Bills

Area	Commercial Service ($/month)		Industrial Service ($/month)	
	12 kW demand 1,500 kWh	100 kW demand 30,000 kWh	1,000 kW demand 400,000 kWh	20,000 kW demand 10,000,000 kWh
City	131	2,152	23,330	404,391
U.S.	162	2,360	25,590	545,677

Note: Based on rates in effect July 1, 1997
Source: Edison Electric Institute, Typical Residential, Commercial and Industrial Bills, Summer 1997

TRANSPORTATION

Transportation Statistics

Avg. travel time to work (min.)	24.7
Interstate highways	I-10; I-45
Bus lines	
In-city	Metropolitan Transit Authority of Harris County, 1,365 vehicles
Inter-city	9
Passenger air service	
Airport	Ellington Field; Bush Inter-Continental; William P. Hobby
Airlines	36
Aircraft departures	234,806 (1995)
Enplaned passengers	14,899,044 (1995)
Rail service	Amtrak
Motor freight carriers	170 local; 634 non-local truck lines
Major waterways/ports	Gulf of Mexico; Port of Houston

Source: OAG, Business Travel Planner, Summer 1997; Editor & Publisher Market Guide, 1998; FAA Airport Activity Statistics, 1996; Amtrak National Time Table, Northeast Timetable, Fall/Winter 1997-98; 1990 Census of Population and Housing, STF 3C; Chamber of Commerce/Economic Development 1997; Jane's Urban Transport Systems 1997-98; Transit Fact Book 1997

A survey of 90,000 airline passengers during the first half of 1997 ranked most of the largest airports in the U.S. George W. Bush International ranked number 17 out of 36. Criteria: cleanliness, quality of restaurants, attractiveness, speed of baggage delivery, ease of reaching gates, available ground transportation, ease of following signs and closeness of parking. *Plog Research Inc., First Half 1997*

Means of Transportation to Work

| Area | Car/Truck/Van | | Public Transportation | | | Bicycle | Walked | Other Means | Worked at Home |
	Drove Alone	Car-pooled	Bus	Subway	Railroad				
City	71.7	15.5	6.3	0.0	0.0	0.4	3.0	1.2	2.0
MSA[1]	75.7	14.6	4.0	0.0	0.0	0.3	2.2	1.1	2.1
U.S.	73.2	13.4	3.0	1.5	0.5	0.4	3.9	1.2	3.0

Note: figures shown are percentages and only include workers 16 years old and over;
(1) Metropolitan Statistical Area - see Appendix A for areas included
Source: 1990 Census of Population and Housing, Summary Tape File 3C

BUSINESSES

Major Business Headquarters

| Company Name | 1997 Rankings | |
	Fortune 500	Forbes 500
American General	206	-
Baker Hughes	448	-
Browning-Ferris	246	-
Charlie Thomas Dealerships	-	223
Coastal	115	-
Compaq Computer	60	-
Continental Airlines	227	-
Cooper Industries	270	-
David Weekley Homes	-	465
El Paso Natural Gas	450	-
Enron	94	-
Enterprise Products	-	122
Fiesta Mart	-	291
Goodman Manufacturing	-	84
Grocers Supply Co	-	139
Gulf States Toyota	-	60
Houston Industries	333	-
Lyondell Petrochemical	281	-
NGC	197	-
Noram Energy	296	-
Panenergy	192	-
Randall's Food Markets	-	50
Sysco	92	-
Texas Petrochemicals	-	446

Note: Companies listed are located in the city; Dashes indicate no ranking
Fortune 500: companies that produce a 10-K are ranked 1 - 500 based on 1996 revenue
Forbes 500: private companies are ranked 1 - 500 based on 1996 revenue
Source: Forbes 12/1/97; Fortune 4/28/97

Fast-Growing Businesses

According to *Inc.*, Houston is home to one of America's 100 fastest-growing private companies: Rigid Structures. Criteria for inclusion: must be an independent, privately-held, U.S. corporation, proprietorship or partnership; sales of at least $200,000 in 1993; five-year operating/sales history; increase in 1997 sales over 1996 sales; holding companies, regulated banks, and utilities were excluded. *Inc. 500, 1997*

Houston is home to one of *Business Week's* "hot growth" companies: Metro Networks. Criteria: sales and earnings, return on capital and stock price. *Business Week, 5/26/97*

According to *Fortune*, Houston is home to of America's 100 fastest-growing companies: BJ Services, Cliffs Drilling, EVI, Global Marine, Nuevo Energy, Plains Resources, Pride International, Seacor Smit, Smith International, Swift Energy, and Transocean Offshore. Companies were ranked based on three years' earnings-per-share growth using least squares analysis to smooth out distortions. Criteria for inclusion: public companies with sales of least

$50 million. Companies that lost money in the most recent quarter, or ended in the red for the past four quarters as a whole, were not eligible. Limited partnerships and REITs were also not considered. *Fortune, 9/29/97*

Houston was ranked #17 out of 24 (#1 is best) in terms of the best-performing local stocks in 1996 according to the Money/Norby Cities Index. The index measures stocks of companies that have headquarters in 24 metro areas. *Money, 2/7/97*

Women-Owned Businesses: Number, Employment, Sales and Share

Area	Women-Owned Businesses in 1996				Share of Women-Owned Businesses in 1996	
	Number	Employment	Sales ($000)	Rank[2]	Percent (%)	Rank[3]
MSA[1]	118,600	284,200	38,176,600	6	35.0	39

Note: (1) Metropolitan Statistical Area - see Appendix A for areas included; (2) Calculated on an averaging of number of businesses, employment and sales and ranges from 1 to 50 where 1 is best; (3) Ranges from 1 to 50 where 1 is best
Source: The National Foundation for Women Business Owners, 1996 Facts on Women-Owned Businesses: Trends in the Top 50 Metropolitan Areas, March 26, 1997

Women-Owned Businesses: Growth

Area	Growth in Women-Owned Businesses (% change from 1987 to 1996)				Relative Growth in the Number of Women-Owned and All Businesses (% change from 1987 to 1996)			
	Num.	Empl.	Sales	Rank[2]	Women-Owned	All Firms	Absolute Difference	Relative Difference
MSA[1]	81.3	437.9	484.9	4	81.3	56.8	24.5	1.4:1

Note: (1) Metropolitan Statistical Area - see Appendix A for areas included; (2) Calculated on an averaging of the percent growth of number of businesses, employment and sales and ranges from 1 to 50 where 1 is best
Source: The National Foundation for Women Business Owners, 1996 Facts on Women-Owned Businesses: Trends in the Top 50 Metropolitan Areas, March 26, 1997

Minority Business Opportunity

Houston is home to three companies which are on the Black Enterprise Industrial/Service 100 list (largest based on gross sales): Sykes Communications Inc. (advertising, marketing, PR and promotions); Wilson Financial Group Inc. (death care industry); GB Tech Inc. (information systems support, systems engineering and integration). Criteria: 1) operational in previous calendar year; 2) at least 51% black-owned; 3) manufactures/owns the product it sells or provides industrial or consumer services. Brokerages, real estate firms and firms that provide professional services are not eligible. *Black Enterprise, July 1997*

Houston is home to one company which is on the Black Enterprise Auto Dealer 100 list (largest based on gross sales): Barnett Automotive Group (GM). Criteria: 1) operational in previous calendar year; 2) at least 51% black-owned. *Black Enterprise, June 1997*

19 of the 500 largest Hispanic-owned companies in the U.S. are located in Houston. *Hispanic Business, June 1997*

Houston is home to two companies which are on the Hispanic Business Fastest-Growing 100 list (greatest sales growth from 1992 to 1996): Rho Industries Inc. (raw materials whsl.) and Marimon Business Machines Inc. (office machine whsl. and svcs.) *Hispanic Business, July/August 1997*

Houston was listed among the top 25 metropolitan areas in terms of the number of Hispanic-owned companies. The city was ranked number 4 with 64,420 companies. *Hispanic Business, May 1997*

Small Business Opportunity

According to *Forbes*, Houston is home to three of America's 200 best small companies: Consolidated Graphics, Eagle USA Airfreight, HCC Insurance. Criteria: companies must be publicly traded, U.S.-based corporations with latest 12-month sales of between $5 and $350 million. Earnings must be at least $1 million for the 12-month period. Limited partnerships, REITs and closed-end mutual funds were not considered. Banks, S&Ls and electric utilities were not included. *Forbes, November 3, 1997*

HOTELS & MOTELS

Hotels/Motels

Area	Hotels/ Motels	Rooms	Luxury-Level Hotels/Motels		Average Minimum Rates ($)		
			♦♦♦♦	♦♦♦♦♦	♦♦	♦♦♦	♦♦♦♦
City	105	22,701	5	0	59	111	172
Airport	22	6,357	0	0	n/a	n/a	n/a
Suburbs	21	1,467	0	0	n/a	n/a	n/a
Total	148	30,525	5	0	n/a	n/a	n/a

Note: n/a not available; Classifications range from one diamond (budget properties with basic amenities) to five diamond (luxury properties with the finest service, rooms and facilities).
Source: OAG, Business Travel Planner, Summer 1997

CONVENTION CENTERS

Major Convention Centers

Center Name	Meeting Rooms	Exhibit Space (sf)
Astrodome USA	28	1,150,000
George R. Brown Convention Center	41	451,500
INNOVA	5	19,138
Krystal Vallarta	5	13,000
The Summit	n/a	n/a
Westin Galleria	16	28,000

Note: n/a not available
Source: Trade Shows Worldwide 1997

Living Environment

COST OF LIVING

Cost of Living Index

Composite Index	Housing	Utilities	Groceries	Health Care	Trans-portation	Misc. Goods/ Services
94.3	82.5	101.0	93.6	102.4	106.1	98.2

Note: U.S. = 100; Figures are for the Metropolitan Statistical Area - see Appendix A for areas included
Source: ACCRA, Cost of Living Index, 3rd Quarter 1997

HOUSING

Median Home Prices and Housing Affordability

Area	Median Price[2] 3rd Qtr. 1997 ($)	HOI[3] 3rd Qtr. 1997	Afford-ability Rank[4]
MSA[1]	107,000	63.4	130
U.S.	127,000	63.7	--

Note: (1) Metropolitan Statistical Area - see Appendix A for areas included; (2) U.S. figures calculated from the sales of 625,000 new and existing homes in 195 markets; (3) Housing Opportunity Index - percent of homes sold that were within the reach of the median income household at the prevailing mortgage interest rate; (4) Rank is from 1-195 with 1 being most affordable
Source: National Association of Home Builders, Housing Opportunity Index, 3rd Quarter 1997

It is projected that the median price of existing single-family homes in the metro area will increase by 10.3% in 1998. Nationwide, home prices are projected to increase 6.6%.
Kiplinger's Personal Finance Magazine, January 1998

Average New Home Price

Area	Price ($)
MSA[1]	105,031
U.S.	135,710

Note: Figures are based on a new home with 1,800 sq. ft. of living area on an 8,000 sq. ft. lot; (1) Metropolitan Statistical Area - see Appendix A for areas included
Source: ACCRA, Cost of Living Index, 3rd Quarter 1997

Average Apartment Rent

Area	Rent ($/mth)
MSA[1]	646
U.S.	569

Note: Figures are based on an unfurnished two bedroom, 1-1/2 or 2 bath apartment, approximately 950 sq. ft. in size, excluding all utilities except water; (1) Metropolitan Statistical Area - see Appendix A for areas included
Source: ACCRA, Cost of Living Index, 3rd Quarter 1997

RESIDENTIAL UTILITIES

Average Residential Utility Costs

Area	All Electric ($/mth)	Part Electric ($/mth)	Other Energy ($/mth)	Phone ($/mth)
MSA[1]	--	77.69	27.58	17.50
U.S.	109.40	55.25	43.64	19.48

Note: (1) (1) Metropolitan Statistical Area - see Appendix A for areas included
Source: ACCRA, Cost of Living Index, 3rd Quarter 1997

HEALTH CARE

Average Health Care Costs

Area	Hospital ($/day)	Doctor ($/visit)	Dentist ($/visit)
MSA[1]	414.11	48.20	62.50
U.S.	392.91	48.76	60.84

Note: Hospital - based on a semi-private room. Doctor - based on a general practitioner's routine exam of an established patient. Dentist - based on adult teeth cleaning and periodic oral exam; (1) Metropolitan Statistical Area - see Appendix A for areas included
Source: ACCRA, Cost of Living Index, 3rd Quarter 1997

Distribution of Office-Based Physicians

Area	Family/Gen. Practitioners	Specialists		
		Medical	Surgical	Other
MSA[1]	851	2,066	1,747	1,883

Note: Data as of 12/31/96; (1) Metropolitan Statistical Area - see Appendix A for areas included
Source: American Medical Assn., Physician Characteristics & Distribution in the U.S., 1997-1998

Hospitals

Houston has 27 general medical and surgical hospitals, 7 psychiatric, 1 obstetrics and gynecology, 4 rehabilitation, 2 orthopedic, 3 other specialty, 1 children's general. *AHA Guide to the Healthcare Field 1997-98*

According to *U.S. News and World Report,* Houston has 4 of the best hospitals in the U.S.: **University of Texas M.D. Anderson Cancer Center**, noted for cancer, endocrinology, gastroenterology, gynecology, otolaryngology, urology; **Texas Heart Institute-St. Luke's Episcopal**, noted for cardiology; **Hermann Hospital**, noted for endocrinology; **TIRR (The Institute for Rehabilitation and Research)**, noted for rehabilitation; *U.S. News and World Report, "America's Best Hospitals", 7/28/97*

EDUCATION

Public School District Statistics

District Name	Num. Sch.	Enroll.	Classroom Teachers[1]	Pupils per Teacher	Minority Pupils (%)	Current Exp.[2] ($/pupil)
Aldine ISD	48	45,139	2,950	15.3	79.8	4,393
Cypress-Fairbanks ISD	49	50,817	3,102	16.4	32.8	5,126
Houston ISD	272	206,704	11,922	17.3	88.5	4,558
North Forest ISD	16	13,450	843	16.0	n/a	n/a
Sheldon ISD	6	3,917	245	16.0	n/a	n/a
Spring Branch ISD	36	29,543	1,883	15.7	58.7	5,545
Spring ISD	22	20,246	1,249	16.2	43.9	5,047

Note: Data covers the 1995-1996 school year unless otherwise noted; (1) Excludes teachers reported as working in school district offices rather than in schools; (2) Based on 1993-94 enrollment collected by the Census Bureau, not the enrollment figure shown in column 3; SD = School District; ISD = Independent School District; n/a not available
Source: National Center for Education Statistics, Common Core of Data Survey; Bureau of the Census

Educational Quality

School District	Education Quotient[1]	Graduate Outcome[2]	Community Index[3]	Resource Index[4]
Houston	89.0	62.0	109.0	95.0

Note: Nearly 1,000 secondary school districts were rated in terms of educational quality. The scores range from a low of 50 to a high of 150; (1) Average of the Graduate Outcome, Community and Resource indexes; (2) Based on graduation rates and college board scores (SAT/ACT); (3) Based on the surrounding community's average level of education and the area's average income level; (4) Based on teacher salaries, per-pupil expenditures and student-teacher ratios.
Source: Expansion Management, Ratings Issue 1997

Educational Attainment by Race

Area	High School Graduate (%)					Bachelor's Degree (%)				
	Total	White	Black	Other	Hisp.[2]	Total	White	Black	Other	Hisp.[2]
City	70.5	79.1	66.3	45.0	36.6	25.1	33.0	13.4	14.8	7.3
MSA[1]	75.1	81.1	68.9	50.2	41.6	25.1	29.0	15.1	16.3	7.9
U.S.	75.2	77.9	63.1	60.4	49.8	20.3	21.5	11.4	19.4	9.2

Note: figures shown cover persons 25 years old and over; (1) Metropolitan Statistical Area - see Appendix A for areas included; (2) people of Hispanic origin can be of any race
Source: 1990 Census of Population and Housing, Summary Tape File 3C

School Enrollment by Type

Area	Preprimary				Elementary/High School			
	Public		Private		Public		Private	
	Enrollment	%	Enrollment	%	Enrollment	%	Enrollment	%
City	14,485	54.0	12,343	46.0	274,727	92.3	22,938	7.7
MSA[1]	34,923	52.8	31,273	47.2	607,238	93.9	39,303	6.1
U.S.	2,679,029	59.5	1,824,256	40.5	38,379,689	90.2	4,187,099	9.8

Note: figures shown cover persons 3 years old and over;
(1) Metropolitan Statistical Area - see Appendix A for areas included
Source: 1990 Census of Population and Housing, Summary Tape File 3C

School Enrollment by Race

Area	Preprimary (%)				Elementary/High School (%)			
	White	Black	Other	Hisp.[1]	White	Black	Other	Hisp.[1]
City	54.6	29.7	15.6	22.8	40.2	33.3	26.5	38.1
MSA[2]	71.3	17.7	11.0	16.0	58.6	21.4	20.1	28.5
U.S.	80.4	12.5	7.1	7.8	74.1	15.6	10.3	12.5

Note: figures shown cover persons 3 years old and over; (1) people of Hispanic origin can be of any race; (2) Metropolitan Statistical Area - see Appendix A for areas included
Source: 1990 Census of Population and Housing, Summary Tape File 3C

SAT/ACT Scores

Area/District	1997 SAT				1997 ACT	
	Percent of Graduates Tested (%)	Average Math Score	Average Verbal Score	Average Combined Score	Percent of Graduates Tested (%)	Average Composite Score
Houston ISD	60	466	472	938	16	18.6
State	49	501	494	995	30	20.2
U.S.	42	511	505	1,016	36	21.0

Note: Math and verbal SAT scores are out of a possible 800; ACT scores are out of a possible 36
Caution: Comparing or ranking states/cities on the basis of SAT/ACT scores alone is invalid and strongly discouraged by the The College Board and The American College Testing Program as students who take the tests are self-selected and do not represent the entire student population.
Source: Houston Independent School District, Department of Research & Evaluation, 1997; College Board, 1997; American College Testing Program, 1997

Classroom Teacher Salaries in Public Schools

District	B.A. Degree		M.A. Degree		Ph.D. Degree	
	Min. ($)	Max ($)	Min. ($)	Max. ($)	Min. ($)	Max. ($)
Houston	26,290	41,402	27,322	43,777	28,353	46,153
Average[1]	26,120	39,270	28,175	44,667	31,643	49,825

Note: Salaries are for 1996-1997; (1) Based on all school districts covered
Source: American Federation of Teachers (unpublished data)

Higher Education

Two-Year Colleges		Four-Year Colleges		Medical Schools	Law Schools	Voc/ Tech
Public	Private	Public	Private			
4	4	5	3	2	3	40

Source: College Blue Book, Occupational Education 1997; Medical School Admission Requirements, 1998-99; Peterson's Guide to Two-Year Colleges, 1997; Peterson's Guide to Four-Year Colleges, 1997; Barron's Guide to Law Schools 1997

MAJOR EMPLOYERS

Major Employers

Brown & Root Holdings (engineering services)
Conoco (petroleum)
KCI Constructors
Memorial Hospital
Shell Oil
Tennessee Gas Pipeline
Texas Commerce Bank
El Paso Natural Gas
Compaq Computer Corp.
Hermann Hospital
MW Kellogg Co. (construction)
Goodman Manufacturing (air conditioning)
St. Luke's Episcopal Hospital
Texas Children's Hospital
U. of Texas MD Anderson Cancer Center
Tenneco Energy

Note: companies listed are located in the city
Source: Dun's Business Rankings 1997; Ward's Business Directory, 1997

PUBLIC SAFETY

Crime Rate

Area	All Crimes	Violent Crimes				Property Crimes		
		Murder	Forcible Rape	Robbery	Aggrav. Assault	Burglary	Larceny -Theft	Motor Vehicle Theft
City	7,636.5	14.7	56.5	467.0	728.9	1,433.4	3,672.4	1,263.5
Suburbs[1]	4,123.8	5.5	34.8	110.0	352.3	883.4	2,306.5	431.3
MSA[2]	5,761.0	9.8	44.9	276.4	527.8	1,139.8	2,943.1	819.2
U.S.	5,078.9	7.4	36.1	202.4	388.2	943.0	2,975.9	525.9

Note: Crime rate is the number of crimes per 100,000 pop.; (1) defined as all areas within the MSA but located outside the central city; (2) Metropolitan Statistical Area - see Appendix A for areas incl.
Source: FBI Uniform Crime Reports 1996

RECREATION

Culture and Recreation

Museums	Symphony Orchestras	Opera Companies	Dance Companies	Professional Theatres	Zoos	Pro Sports Teams
13	2	1	8	9	1	3

Source: International Directory of the Performing Arts, 1996; Official Museum Directory, 1998; Chamber of Commerce/Economic Development 1997

Library System

The Harris County Public Library has 25 branches, holdings of 1,108,863 volumes and a budget of $9,197,515 (1994-1995). The Houston Area Library System has no branches, holdings of n/a volumes and a budget of $1,775,037 (1995-1996). Note: n/a means not available. *American Library Directory, 1997-1998*

MEDIA

Newspapers

Name	Type	Freq.	Distribution	Circulation
The Bay Area Sun	n/a	1x/wk	Area	35,000
The Citizen	General	1x/wk	Local	26,450
El Mexica	Hispanic	1x/wk	Local	57,500
Houston Chronicle	General	7x/wk	Local	549,856
Houston Defender	Black	1x/wk	Local	27,000
Houston Forward Times	Black	1x/wk	Local	60,000
Houston Newspages	Black	1x/wk	Local	61,571
The Houston Press	n/a	1x/wk	Local	97,000
Houston Sun	Black	1x/wk	Local	80,000
The Informer and Texas Freeman	Black	1x/wk	Local	30,000
La Buena Suerte	Hispanic	1x/wk	Area	100,000
La Informacion	Hispanic	1x/wk	Local	78,000
La Subasta	Hispanic	3x/wk	State	185,000
La Voz de Houston Newspaper	Hispanic	1x/wk	Local	61,000
The Leader	General	1x/wk	Local	77,160
Metro Weekender	Black	1x/wk	Local	75,000
The 1960 Sun	General	1x/wk	Area	80,000
Northeast News	General	1x/wk	Local	30,000
Semana	Hispanic	1x/wk	Area	125,000
Southern Chinese News	Asian	7x/wk	Local	25,000
Spring Branch and Memorial Sun	General	1x/wk	Local	75,000

Note: Includes newspapers with circulations of 25,000 or more located in the city; n/a not available
Source: Burrelle's Media Directory, 1998 Edition

AM Radio Stations

Call Letters	Freq. (kHz)	Target Audience	Station Format	Music Format
KILT	610	General	S	n/a
KIKK	650	General	M/N/S	Country
KSEV	700	n/a	T	n/a
KTRH	740	General	N/S	n/a
KKBQ	790	n/a	M	Country
KEYH	850	Hispanic	M	Spanish
KJOJ	880	Religious	M/N/S/T	Christian
KYST	920	Hispanic	M	n/a
KPRC	950	General	M/N/S	n/a
KLAT	1010	Hispanic	M	Spanish
KENR	1070	General	M/T	Adult Contemporary
KTEK	1110	Religious	M/N/S	Christian
KGOL	1180	Asian	E/M/N/S/T	Jazz/R&B
KQUE	1230	General	N/T	n/a
KXYZ	1320	Hispanic	M	Spanish
KHCB	1400	Hispanic	M/N/S	Christian/Spanish
KCUL	1410	n/a	M/N/S/T	Oldies
KCOH	1430	Black	E/M/N/S/T	Adult Contemporary/R&B/Urban Contemporary
KMHT	1450	n/a	M	Oldies
KLVL	1480	Hispanic	M	Spanish

Note: Stations included broadcast in the Houston metro area; n/a not available
Station Format: E = Educational; M = Music; N = News; S = Sports; T = Talk
Source: Burrelle's Media Directory, 1998 Edition

FM Radio Stations

Call Letters	Freq. (mHz)	Target Audience	Station Format	Music Format
KUHF	88.7	General	M/N	Classical
KSBJ	89.3	General	E/M/N/S	Christian
KPFT	90.1	General	M	n/a
KTSU	90.9	General	M	n/a
KBWC	91.1	General	E/M	Christian/Jazz/R&B
KPVU	91.3	General	M/N/S/T	n/a
KTRU	91.7	n/a	M	n/a
KRTS	92.1	General	M	Classical
KCUL	92.3	General	M/N/S	Oldies
KKBQ	92.9	General	M	Country
KLTN	93.3	General	M	Spanish
KKRW	93.7	General	M	Classic Rock
KLDE	94.5	General	M	Oldies
KIKK	95.7	General	M	Country
KHMX	96.5	General	M/N/S	Adult Contemporary/Contemporary Top 40
KBXX	97.9	Black/Hisp	M	Urban Contemporary
KODA	99.1	General	M	Adult Contemporary/Jazz
KILT	100.3	General	M/N/S	Country
KLOL	101.1	General	M/N/S	AOR
KMJQ	102.1	General	M	Urban Contemporary
KQUE	102.9	General	M	Adult Contemporary
KJOJ	103.3	General	M	Urban Contemporary
KZEY	103.9	n/a	M	Adult Contemporary/Christian/Contemporary Top 40/Gospel/Jazz/Oldies/R&B/Urban Contemporary
KRBE	104.1	General	M	Contemporary Top 40
KHCB	105.7	Religious	M/N/S	Christian
KQQK	106.5	Hispanic	M	Spanish
KTBZ	107.5	General	M	Alternative

Note: Stations included broadcast in the Houston metro area; n/a not available
Station Format: E = Educational; M = Music; N = News; S = Sports; T = Talk
Music Format: AOR = Album Oriented Rock; MOR = Middle-of-the-Road
Source: Burrelle's Media Directory, 1998 Edition

Television Stations

Name	Ch.	Affiliation	Type	Owner
KPRC	2	NBC	Commercial	Post-Newsweek
KUHT	8	PBS	Public	University of Houston System
KHOU	11	CBS	Commercial	A.H. Belo Corporation
KTRK	13	ABC	Commercial	ABC Inc.
KTXH	20	UPN	Commercial	Paramount Communications Inc.
KLTJ	22	n/a	Public	GO Inc.
KRIV	26	Fox	Commercial	Fox Television Stations Inc.
KHTV	39	WB	Commercial	Gaylord Entertainment
KXLN	45	Univision	Commercial	Univision Television Group
KTMD	48	Telemundo	Commercial	Telemundo Group Inc.
KTFH	49	Paxson Communications Corporation	Commercial	San Jacinto Corp
KVVV	57	n/a	Commercial	ValueVision International Inc.

Note: Stations included broadcast in the Houston metro area
Source: Burrelle's Media Directory, 1998 Edition

CLIMATE

Average and Extreme Temperatures

Temperature	Jan	Feb	Mar	Apr	May	Jun	Jul	Aug	Sep	Oct	Nov	Dec	Ann
Extreme High (°F)	84	91	91	95	97	103	104	107	102	94	89	83	107
Average High (°F)	61	65	73	79	85	91	93	93	89	81	72	65	79
Average Temp. (°F)	51	54	62	69	75	81	83	83	79	70	61	54	69
Average Low (°F)	41	43	51	58	65	71	73	73	68	58	50	43	58
Extreme Low (°F)	12	20	22	31	44	52	62	62	48	32	19	7	7

Note: Figures cover the years 1969-1990
Source: National Climatic Data Center, International Station Meteorological Climate Summary, 3/95

Average Precipitation/Snowfall/Humidity

Precip./Humidity	Jan	Feb	Mar	Apr	May	Jun	Jul	Aug	Sep	Oct	Nov	Dec	Ann
Avg. Precip. (in.)	3.3	2.7	3.3	3.3	5.6	4.9	3.7	3.7	4.8	4.7	3.7	3.3	46.9
Avg. Snowfall (in.)	Tr	Tr	0	0	0	0	0	0	0	0	Tr	Tr	Tr
Avg. Rel. Hum. 6am (%)	85	86	87	89	91	92	93	93	93	91	89	86	90
Avg. Rel. Hum. 3pm (%)	58	55	54	54	57	56	55	55	57	53	55	57	55

Note: Figures cover the years 1969-1990; Tr = Trace amounts (<0.05 in. of rain; <0.5 in. of snow)
Source: National Climatic Data Center, International Station Meteorological Climate Summary, 3/95

Weather Conditions

Temperature			Daytime Sky			Precipitation		
32°F & below	45°F & below	90°F & above	Clear	Partly cloudy	Cloudy	0.01 inch or more precip.	0.1 inch or more snow/ice	Thunder-storms
21	87	96	83	168	114	101	1	62

Note: Figures are average number of days per year and covers the years 1969-1990
Source: National Climatic Data Center, International Station Meteorological Climate Summary, 3/95

AIR & WATER QUALITY

Maximum Pollutant Concentrations

	Particulate Matter (ug/m^3)	Carbon Monoxide (ppm)	Sulfur Dioxide (ppm)	Nitrogen Dioxide (ppm)	Ozone (ppm)	Lead (ug/m^3)
MSA[1] Level	68	7	0.046	0.023	0.18	0.02
NAAQS[2]	150	9	0.140	0.053	0.12	1.50
Met NAAQS?	Yes	Yes	Yes	Yes	No	Yes

Note: (1) Metropolitan Statistical Area - see Appendix A for areas included; (2) National Ambient Air Quality Standards; ppm = parts per million; ug/m^3 = micrograms per cubic meter; n/a not available
Source: EPA, National Air Quality and Emissions Trends Report, 1996

Pollutant Standards Index

In the Houston MSA (see Appendix A for areas included), the Pollutant Standards Index (PSI) exceeded 100 on 32 days in 1996. A PSI value greater than 100 indicates that air quality would be in the unhealthful range on that day. *EPA, National Air Quality and Emissions Trends Report, 1996*

Drinking Water

Water System Name	Pop. Served	Primary Water Source Type	Number of Violations in Fiscal Year 1997	Type of Violation/ Contaminants
Houston Public Works Dept.	1,608,000	Surface	1	(1)

Note: Data as of January 16, 1998; (1) System failed to report violation of the Surface Water Treatment Rule.
Source: EPA, Office of Ground Water and Drinking Water, Safe Drinking Water Information System

Houston tap water is alkaline, hard.
Editor & Publisher Market Guide, 1998

Jacksonville, Florida

Background

The Jacksonville we see today is largely a product of the reconstruction that occurred during the 1940's, after a fire had razed 147 city blocks a few decades earlier. Lying under the modern structures, however, is a history that dates back earlier than the settlement of Plymouth Rock by the Pilgrims.

The temperate city of Jacksonville, located in the northeast part of Florida and on the St. John's River, was explored and settled by English, Spanish, and French explorers from the Sixteenth through Eighteenth centuries. Sites commemorating their presence include the Fort Caroline National Monument, which marks the French settlement led by Rene de Laudonniere in 1564; Spanish Pond, the site one quarter miles east of Fort Caroline, where Spanish forces led by Pedro Menendez, captured Fort Caroline; and Fort George Island, from which General James Oglethorpe led English attacks against the Spanish during the Eighteenth century.

Jacksonville was attractive to these early settlers because of its easy access to the Atlantic Ocean, which meant a favorable port.

Today, Jacksonville is still a favorable port. In addition, it is the financial hub of Florida, with a branch of the Federal Reserve Bank located there. However, most of its busy activities revolve around transportation, machinery, paper, beer, and pulpwood.

Jacksonville has the Children's Museum, the Jacksonville Symphony Orchestra, the Gator Bowl and its beach facilities.

Summers are long, warm and relatively humid. Winters are generally mild, although periodic invasions of cold northern air bring the temperature down. Temperatures along the beaches rarely rise above 90 degrees. Summer thunderstorms usually occur before noon along the beaches, and inland in the afternoons. The greatest rainfall, mostly in the form of local thundershowers occurs during the summer months. Although the area is in the Hurricane Belt, this section of the coast has been very fortunate in escaping hurricane-force winds.

General Rankings and Evaluative Comments

- Jacksonville was ranked #9 out of 300 cities by *Money's* 1997 "Survey of the Best Places to Live." Criteria used: health services, crime, economy, housing, education, transportation, weather, leisure and the arts. The city was ranked #20 in 1996 and #3 in 1995.
  Money, July 1997; Money, September 1996; Money, September 1995

  "...this booming northeast Florida metropolis has much to offer: great jobs, fun along the St. Johns River, nearly 100 golf courses, 40 miles of Atlantic beaches and four mild seasons....Many would credit the young, motivated work force197for attracting some of the biggest names in regional and national business. In mid-1995, for instance, America Online began hiring 1,200 people for its technical support center. Merrill Lynch is planning to expand from 1,700 locally to 2,200 in the next two years, mostly for its back-office operations....The community is eager to celebrate the opening of the 400-acre World Golf Village, including the International Golf Hall of Fame, in 1998....The job market is really perking....Jacksonville's location at the intersection of I-95 and I-10, as well as its busy seaport, bodes well for future job growth too....

  Jacksonville is one of the most affordable places in the Southeast, especially for home buyers.

  Jacksonville is among the most racially diverse of our top 10 places. More than 20% of the population is African American, for example. And although Jax—like many U.S. communities—confesses to its share of racial disharmony over the years, residents give the city credit for facing its problems.... *Money, July 1997*

- *Ladies Home Journal* ranked America's 200 largest cities based on the qualities women care about most. Jacksonville ranked 141 out of 200. Criteria: low crime rate, good public schools, well-paying jobs, quality health and child care, the presence of women in government, proportion of women-owned businesses, size of the wage gap with men, local economy, divorce rates, the ratio of single men to single women, whether there are laws that require at least the same number of public toilets for women as men, and the probability of good hair days. *Ladies Home Journal, November 1997*

- Jacksonville was ranked #121 out of 219 cities in terms of children's health, safety, and economic well-being. Criteria: total population, percent population change, birth rate, child immunization rate, infant mortality rate, percent low birth weight infants, percent of births to teens, physician-to-population ratio, student-to-teacher ratio, dropout rate, unemployment rate, median family income, percent of children in poverty, violent and property crime rates, number of juvenile arrests for violent crimes as a percent of the total crime index, number of days with pollution standard index (PSI) over 100, pounds toxic releases per 1,000 people and number of superfund sites. *Zero Population Growth, Children's Environmental Index 1997*

- *Yahoo! Internet Life* selected "America's 100 Most Wired Cities & Towns". 50 cities were large and 50 cities were small. Jacksonville ranked 29 out of 50 large cities. Criteria: Internet users per capita, number of networked computers, number of registered domain names, Internet backbone traffic, and the per-capita number of Web sites devoted to each city. *Yahoo! Internet Life, March 1998*

- Barnett Banks, Inc., headquartered in Jacksonville, is among the "100 Best Companies for Working Mothers." Criteria: pay compared with competition, opportunities for women to advance, support for child care, flexible work schedules and family-friendly benefits. *Working Mother, October 1997*

- According to *Working Mother*, "Florida stands out among the Southern states for its aggressive action to improve and expand child care. As we went to press, the governor had asked state lawmakers for a significant increase in state funds to create new child care slots. Some $49 million would be earmarked for a very important group—16,000 children of low-wage workers.

  In the past year the state also boosted funding for its prekindergarten program by $4 million, bringing its pre-K spending to $102 million. This translates into free pre-K for 27,000 kids, about 2,000 more than last year. This program is funded with state lottery money and is available in all of Florida's 67 school districts.

The state has also improved its requirements for playground surfaces in child care setting. As of March 1997, all centers were required to have soft surfaces under playground equipment. This is a vital change, given that injuries from falls are the most common in child care.

Finally, lawmakers approved a new program to recognize quality child care programs. Any facility that attains state or NAEYC accreditation can now post a 'good seal' certificate and will be listed in a state database as a 'Gold Seal' program—to show it meets high standards of care. So far, about 370 centers have received certificates, and about 800 more are in the pipeline.'' *Working Mother, July/August 1997*

Business Environment

STATE ECONOMY

State Economic Profile

"Florida's economy continues to expand strongly....

Florida is becoming increasingly dependent on the service industry for job growth. Currently, one in three Florida jobs is service-related. In the past year, however, nearly half of all jobs created were in the service industry. One in four jobs created was in business services, compared to one in seven for the U.S....

Florida's tourist industry continues to rebound and will be an important source of growth for this year. Household income growth and savings rates are high, and the values of individual stock portfolios has been booming, leaving households across the U.S. in good financial shape to take a vacation.

A risk to Florida's economy is a sharp slowing in population growth. In 1996, Florida experienced a population gain of only 1.5%, the slowest rate of growth since World War II. Contributing to the slower population growth is weaker retiree migration due to a slowing national retiree population growth.

Supporting growth are Florida's moderate climate, favorable quality of life, affordable housing, and low cost of doing business, which will continue to attract businesses and households. Population growth will continue to slow for the next decade as the number of people reaching retirement age nationwide is falling. Population growth will begin to accelerate once the baby boom generation hits retirement age beginning around 2005. One downside risk for Florida is its dependence on tourism and interest and property income that makes it vulnerable to national and international business cycles. Florida will remain one of the nation's fastest-growing economies through the remainder of this century." *National Association of Realtors, Economic Profiles: The Fifty States, July 1997*

IMPORTS/EXPORTS

Total Export Sales

Area	1993 ($000)	1994 ($000)	1995 ($000)	1996 ($000)	% Chg. 1993-96	% Chg. 1995-96
MSA[1]	404,853	500,396	604,066	676,985	67.2	12.1
U.S.	464,858,354	512,415,609	583,030,524	622,827,063	34.0	6.8

Note: (1) Metropolitan Statistical Area - see Appendix A for areas included
Source: U.S. Department of Commerce, International Trade Association, Metropolitan Area Exports: An Export Performance Report on Over 250 U.S. Cities, October 1997

Imports/Exports by Port

Type	Cargo Value			Share of U.S. Total	
	1995 (US$mil.)	1996 (US$mil.)	% Change 1995-1996	1995 (%)	1996 (%)
Imports	6,699	6,270	-6.41	1.71	1.63
Exports	3,204	3,334	4.05	1.40	1.41

Source: Global Trade Information Services, WaterBorne Trade Atlas 1997

CITY FINANCES

City Government Finances

Component	FY94 ($000)	FY94 (per capita $)
Revenue	1,690,773	2,549.34
Expenditure	1,597,821	2,409.18
Debt Outstanding	4,797,598	7,233.78
Cash & Securities	3,766,545	5,679.17

Source: U.S. Bureau of the Census, City Government Finances: 1993-94

City Government Revenue by Source

Source	FY94 ($000)	FY94 (per capita $)	FY94 (%)
From Federal Government	69,842	105.31	4.1
From State Governments	63,624	95.93	3.8
From Local Governments	230	0.35	0.0
Property Taxes	207,022	312.15	12.2
General Sales Taxes	41,513	62.59	2.5
Selective Sales Taxes	66,418	100.14	3.9
Income Taxes	0	0.00	0.0
Current Charges	152,855	230.47	9.0
Utility/Liquor Store	752,009	1,133.87	44.5
Employee Retirement[1]	133,037	200.59	7.9
Other	204,223	307.93	12.1

Note: (1) Excludes "city contributions," classified as "nonrevenue," intragovernmental transfers.
Source: U.S. Bureau of the Census, City Government Finances: 1993-94

City Government Expenditures by Function

Function	FY94 ($000)	FY94 (per capita $)	FY94 (%)
Educational Services	10,588	15.96	0.7
Employee Retirement[1]	47,320	71.35	3.0
Environment/Housing	190,257	286.87	11.9
Government Administration	61,596	92.87	3.9
Interest on General Debt	185,035	278.99	11.6
Public Safety	194,520	293.30	12.2
Social Services	49,281	74.31	3.1
Transportation	88,850	133.97	5.6
Utility/Liquor Store	686,108	1,034.51	42.9
Other	84,266	127.06	5.3

Note: (1) Payments to beneficiaries including withdrawal of contributions.
Source: U.S. Bureau of the Census, City Government Finances: 1993-94

Municipal Bond Ratings

Area	Moody's	S & P
Jacksonville	Aa2	AA

Note: n/a not available; n/r not rated
Source: Moody's Bond Record, 2/98; Statistical Abstract of the U.S., 1997;
Governing Magazine, 9/97, 3/98

POPULATION

Population Growth

Area	1980	1990	% Chg. 1980-90	July 1996 Estimate	% Chg. 1990-96
City	540,920	635,230	17.4	679,792	7.0
MSA[1]	722,252	906,727	25.5	1,008,633	11.2
U.S.	226,545,805	248,765,170	9.8	265,179,411	6.6

Note: (1) Metropolitan Statistical Area - see Appendix A for areas included
Source: 1980/1990 Census of Housing and Population, Summary Tape File 3C;
Census Bureau Population Estimates

Population Characteristics

Race	City					MSA[1]	
	1980		1990		% Chg. 1980-90	1990	
	Population	%	Population	%		Population	%
White	394,661	73.0	456,358	71.8	15.6	701,960	77.4
Black	137,150	25.4	160,421	25.3	17.0	181,026	20.0
Amer Indian/Esk/Aleut	1,950	0.4	2,270	0.4	16.4	3,182	0.4
Asian/Pacific Islander	5,485	1.0	11,791	1.9	115.0	14,873	1.6
Other	1,674	0.3	4,390	0.7	162.2	5,686	0.6
Hispanic Origin[2]	9,775	1.8	15,572	2.5	59.3	22,206	2.4

Note: (1) Metropolitan Statistical Area - see Appendix A for areas included;
(2) people of Hispanic origin can be of any race
Source: 1980/1990 Census of Housing and Population, Summary Tape File 3C

Ancestry

Area	German	Irish	English	Italian	U.S.	French	Polish	Dutch
City	16.7	15.4	14.1	3.3	6.4	3.6	1.7	1.9
MSA[1]	18.1	16.8	15.7	3.7	7.0	4.0	1.9	2.1
U.S.	23.3	15.6	13.1	5.9	5.3	4.2	3.8	2.5

Note: Figures are percentages and include persons that reported multiple ancestry (eg. if a person reported being Irish and Italian, they were included in both columns); (1) Metropolitan Statistical Area - see Appendix A for areas included
Source: 1990 Census of Population and Housing, Summary Tape File 3C

Age

Area	Median Age (Years)	Age Distribution (%)						
		Under 5	Under 18	18-24	25-44	45-64	65+	80+
City	31.2	8.1	26.1	11.1	34.6	17.5	10.6	2.1
MSA[1]	32.0	7.8	26.0	10.6	34.2	18.3	10.9	2.2
U.S.	32.9	7.3	25.6	10.5	32.6	18.7	12.5	2.8

Note: (1) Metropolitan Statistical Area - see Appendix A for areas included
Source: 1990 Census of Population and Housing, Summary Tape File 3C

Male/Female Ratio

Area	Number of males per 100 females (all ages)	Number of males per 100 females (18 years old+)
City	95.4	92.9
MSA[1]	95.5	93.1
U.S.	95.0	91.9

Note: (1) Metropolitan Statistical Area - see Appendix A for areas included
Source: 1990 Census of Population, General Population Characteristics

INCOME

Per Capita/Median/Average Income

Area	Per Capita ($)	Median Household ($)	Average Household ($)
City	13,661	28,305	35,281
MSA[1]	14,141	29,514	36,739
U.S.	14,420	30,056	38,453

Note: all figures are for 1989; (1) Metropolitan Statistical Area - see Appendix A for areas included
Source: 1990 Census of Population and Housing, Summary Tape File 3C

Household Income Distribution by Race

Income ($)	City (%)					U.S. (%)				
	Total	White	Black	Other	Hisp.[1]	Total	White	Black	Other	Hisp.[1]
Less than 5,000	6.9	4.2	16.1	5.2	9.0	6.2	4.8	15.2	8.6	8.8
5,000 - 9,999	8.3	6.7	14.0	5.9	6.3	9.3	8.6	14.2	9.9	11.1
10,000 - 14,999	9.1	7.8	13.4	10.6	12.1	8.8	8.5	11.0	9.8	11.0
15,000 - 24,999	19.3	19.1	20.0	19.8	19.7	17.5	17.3	18.9	18.5	20.5
25,000 - 34,999	17.3	18.2	14.3	17.6	19.0	15.8	16.1	14.2	15.4	16.4
35,000 - 49,999	18.9	20.7	12.9	18.7	16.9	17.9	18.6	13.3	16.1	16.0
50,000 - 74,999	13.4	15.2	7.2	16.0	12.1	15.0	15.8	9.3	13.4	11.1
75,000 - 99,999	4.0	4.7	1.7	2.8	3.1	5.1	5.5	2.6	4.7	3.1
100,000+	2.7	3.4	0.5	3.4	1.7	4.4	4.8	1.3	3.7	1.9

Note: all figures are for 1989; (1) people of Hispanic origin can be of any race
Source: 1990 Census of Population and Housing, Summary Tape File 3C

Effective Buying Income

Area	Per Capita ($)	Median Household ($)	Average Household ($)
City	15,500	32,781	41,119
MSA[1]	16,757	35,504	44,623
U.S.	15,444	33,201	41,849

Note: data as of 1/1/97; (1) Metropolitan Statistical Area - see Appendix A for areas included
Source: Standard Rate & Data Service, Newspaper Advertising Source, 2/98

Effective Household Buying Income Distribution

Area	% of Households Earning						
	$10,000 -$19,999	$20,000 -$34,999	$35,000 -$49,999	$50,000 -$74,999	$75,000 -$99,000	$100,000 -$124,999	$125,000 and up
City	16.2	24.6	19.3	17.7	6.0	1.8	1.9
MSA[1]	14.8	23.6	19.4	19.2	7.2	2.3	2.6
U.S.	16.5	23.4	18.3	18.2	6.4	2.1	2.4

Note: data as of 1/1/97; (1) Metropolitan Statistical Area - see Appendix A for areas included
Source: Standard Rate & Data Service, Newspaper Advertising Source, 2/98

Poverty Rates by Race and Age

Area	Total (%)	By Race (%)				By Age (%)		
		White	Black	Other	Hisp.[2]	Under 5 years old	Under 18 years old	65 years and over
City	13.0	7.5	28.6	12.3	15.0	19.9	18.6	16.1
MSA[1]	11.8	7.4	29.2	12.0	13.9	18.6	16.8	14.5
U.S.	13.1	9.8	29.5	23.1	25.3	20.1	18.3	12.8

Note: figures show the percent of people living below the poverty line in 1989. The average poverty threshold was $12,674 for a family of four in 1989; (1) Metropolitan Statistical Area - see Appendix A for areas included; (2) people of Hispanic origin can be of any race
Source: 1990 Census of Population and Housing, Summary Tape File 3C

EMPLOYMENT

Labor Force and Employment

Area	Civilian Labor Force			Workers Employed		
	Dec. '95	Dec. '96	% Chg.	Dec. '95	Dec. '96	% Chg.
City	347,615	359,408	3.4	335,607	347,361	3.5
MSA[1]	515,041	532,507	3.4	498,165	515,612	3.5
U.S.	134,583,000	136,742,000	1.6	127,903,000	130,785,000	2.3

Note: Data is not seasonally adjusted and covers workers 16 years of age and older; (1) Metropolitan Statistical Area - see Appendix A for areas included
Source: Bureau of Labor Statistics, http://stats.bls.gov

Unemployment Rate

Area	1997											
	Jan.	Feb.	Mar.	Apr.	May	Jun.	Jul.	Aug.	Sep.	Oct.	Nov.	Dec.
City	4.3	3.8	3.8	3.8	4.0	4.3	3.9	3.8	3.9	3.6	3.7	3.4
MSA[1]	4.1	3.6	3.6	3.6	3.7	4.0	3.7	3.5	3.6	3.4	3.5	3.2
U.S.	5.9	5.7	5.5	4.8	4.7	5.2	5.0	4.8	4.7	4.4	4.3	4.4

Note: Data is not seasonally adjusted and covers workers 16 years of age and older; All figures are percentages; (1) Metropolitan Statistical Area - see Appendix A for areas included
Source: Bureau of Labor Statistics, http://stats.bls.gov

Employment by Industry

Sector	MSA[1]		U.S.
	Number of Employees	Percent of Total	Percent of Total
Services	173,200	32.5	29.0
Retail Trade	103,300	19.4	18.5
Government	69,400	13.0	16.1
Manufacturing	38,200	7.2	15.0
Finance/Insurance/Real Estate	53,100	10.0	5.7
Wholesale Trade	29,900	5.6	5.4
Transportation/Public Utilities	37,300	7.0	5.3
Construction/Mining	400	0.1	5.0

Note: Figures cover non-farm employment as of 12/97 and are not seasonally adjusted;
(1) Metropolitan Statistical Area - see Appendix A for areas included
Source: Bureau of Labor Statistics, http://stats.bls.gov

Employment by Occupation

Occupation Category	City (%)	MSA[1] (%)	U.S. (%)
White Collar	62.4	61.7	58.1
Executive/Admin./Management	13.1	13.2	12.3
Professional	11.7	12.0	14.1
Technical & Related Support	3.7	3.8	3.7
Sales	13.2	13.7	11.8
Administrative Support/Clerical	20.6	19.1	16.3
Blue Collar	23.9	24.0	26.2
Precision Production/Craft/Repair	11.2	11.5	11.3
Machine Operators/Assem./Insp.	4.1	4.0	6.8
Transportation/Material Movers	4.4	4.4	4.1
Cleaners/Helpers/Laborers	4.2	4.1	3.9
Services	12.6	12.8	13.2
Farming/Forestry/Fishing	1.1	1.5	2.5

Note: figures cover employed persons 16 years old and over;
(1) Metropolitan Statistical Area - see Appendix A for areas included
Source: 1990 Census of Population and Housing, Summary Tape File 3C

Occupational Employment Projections: 1995 - 2005

Occupations Expected to have the Largest Job Growth (ranked by numerical growth)	Fast-Growing Occupations[1] (ranked by percent growth)
1. Waiters & waitresses	1. Computer engineers
2. General managers & top executives	2. Systems analysts
3. Cashiers	3. Physical therapy assistants and aides
4. Salespersons, retail	4. Aircraft pilots/flight engineers
5. Systems analysts	5. Corrections officers & jailers
6. First line supervisor, sales & related	6. Physical therapists
7. First line supervisors, clerical	7. Manicurists
8. Guards	8. Operations research analysts
9. Registered nurses	9. Medical assistants
10. Secretaries, except legal & medical	10. Computer support specialists

Projections cover Duval County.
Note: (1) Excludes occupations with total growth of less than 100 jobs
Source: Florida Department of Labor and Employment Security, Florida Industry and Occupational Employment Projections 1995-2005

Average Wages

Occupation	Wage	Occupation	Wage
Professional/Technical/Clerical	$/Week	**Health/Protective Services**	$/Week
Accountants III	-	Corrections Officers	-
Attorneys III	-	Firefighters	-
Budget Analysts III	-	Nurses, Licensed Practical II	-
Buyers/Contracting Specialists II	-	Nurses, Registered II	-
Clerks, Accounting III	389	Nursing Assistants II	-
Clerks, General III	369	Police Officers I	-
Computer Operators II	391	**Hourly Workers**	$/Hour
Computer Programmers II	596	Forklift Operators	10.20
Drafters II	-	General Maintenance Workers	9.83
Engineering Technicians III	-	Guards I	5.45
Engineering Technicians, Civil III	-	Janitors	5.33
Engineers III	-	Maintenance Electricians	17.77
Key Entry Operators I	317	Maintenance Electronics Techs II	17.59
Personnel Assistants III	-	Maintenance Machinists	19.12
Personnel Specialists III	-	Maintenance Mechanics, Machinery	15.12
Secretaries III	517	Material Handling Laborers	6.68
Switchboard Operator-Receptionist	327	Motor Vehicle Mechanics	14.20
Systems Analysts II	829	Shipping/Receiving Clerks	8.45
Systems Analysts Supervisor/Mgr II	-	Tool and Die Makers	-
Tax Collectors II	-	Truckdrivers, Tractor Trailer	14.35
Word Processors II	404	Warehouse Specialists	11.96

Note: Wage data includes full-time workers only for 3/95 and cover the Metropolitan Statistical Area (see Appendix A for areas included). Dashes indicate that data was not available.
Source: Bureau of Labor Statistics, Occupational Compensation Survey

TAXES

Major State and Local Tax Rates

State Corp. Income (%)	State Personal Income (%)	Residential Property (effective rate per $100)	Sales & Use		State Gasoline (cents/ gallon)	State Cigarette (cents/ 20-pack)
			State (%)	Local (%)		
5.5[a]	None	1.11	6.0	0.5	12.8[b]	33.9

Note: Personal/corporate income tax rates as of 1/97. Sales, gasoline and cigarette tax rates as of 1/98; (a) 3.3% Alternative Minimum Tax. An exemption of $5,000 is allowed; (b) Rate is comprised of 4 cents excise and 8.8 cents motor carrier tax
Source: Federation of Tax Administrators, www.taxadmin.org; Washington D.C. Department of Finance and Revenue, Tax Rates and Tax Burdens in the District of Columbia: A Nationwide Comparison, June 1997; Chamber of Commerce

Total Taxes Per Capita and as a Percent of Income

Area	Per Capita Income ($)	Per Capita Taxes ($)			Taxes as Pct. of Income (%)		
		Total	Federal	State/Local	Total	Federal	State/Local
Florida	26,438	9,172	6,286	2,886	34.7	23.8	10.9
U.S.	26,187	9,205	6,127	3,078	35.2	23.4	11.8

Note: Figures are for 1997
Source: Tax Foundation, Web Site, www.taxfoundation.org

COMMERCIAL REAL ESTATE

Office Market

Class/Location	Total Space (sq. ft.)	Vacant Space (sq. ft.)	Vac. Rate (%)	Under Constr. (sq. ft.)	Net Absorp. (sq. ft.)	Rental Rates ($/sq.ft./yr.)
Class A						
CBD	5,796,277	405,000	7.0	0	10,000	14.00-16.50
Outside CBD	6,204,549	136,500	2.2	874,540	163,990	17.00-20.00
Class B						
CBD	4,448,501	398,200	9.0	0	18,000	13.00-15.00
Outside CBD	3,613,781	440,000	12.2	0	30,000	12.00-14.50

Note: Data as of 10/97 and covers Jacksonville; CBD = Central Business District; n/a not available;
Source: Society of Industrial and Office Realtors, 1998 Comparative Statistics of Industrial and Office Real Estate Markets

"Employment is expected to grow more than one percent per year into the next century, even with the loss of Barnett Bank's 5,500 employes. But, when compared to the three to six percent annual gains experienced in the first half of this decade, growth has slowed considerably. Build-to-suit and expansions will drive new construction. The Butler Corridor, Jacksonville's strongest submarket, will be home to most speculative construction in 1998, An overall rise in building of 11-15 percent is anticipated marketwide. Sales prices are projected to advance, particularly in the suburbs. Competition spurred by the arrival of REITs investment may upwardly influence prices." *Society of Industrial and Office Realtors, 1998 Comparative Statistics of Industrial and Office Real Estate Markets*

Industrial Market

Location	Total Space (sq. ft.)	Vacant Space (sq. ft.)	Vac. Rate (%)	Under Constr. (sq. ft.)	Net Absorp. (sq. ft.)	Gross Lease ($/sq.ft./yr.)
Central City	n/a	n/a	n/a	n/a	n/a	n/a
Suburban	73,860,000	3,950,000	5.3	1,540,000	4,377,170	2.00-7.00

Note: Data as of 10/97 and covers Jacksonville; n/a not available
Source: Society of Industrial and Office Realtors, 1998 Comparative Statistics of Industrial and Office Real Estate Markets

"The planned expansion of Jaxport is an important development, and will help moderate the impact of any further defense cutbacks. Additionally, Jacksonville's low business cost structure should continue to prompt business expansions and relocations. SIOR's reporters expect growth across all industrial indicators during 1998. Sales, lease, and site prices should increase more than six percent. Construction levels will climb, particularly in terms of build-to-suit activity. This transportation and shipping hub is also poised for an increase in demand due to a growing international trade sector. Look for increased dollar volume for both sales and leases." *Society of Industrial and Office Realtors, 1998 Comparative Statistics of Industrial and Office Real Estate Markets*

Retail Market

Shopping Center Inventory (sq. ft.)	Shopping Center Construction (sq. ft.)	Construction as a Percent of Inventory (%)	Torto Wheaton Rent Index[1] ($/sq. ft.)
24,723,000	989,000	4.0	11.99

Note: Data as of 1997 and covers the Metropolitan Statistical Area - see Appendix A for areas included; (1) Index is based on a model that predicts what the average rent should be for leases with certain characteristics, in certain locations during certain years.
Source: National Association of Realtors, 1997-1998 Market Conditions Report

"Jacksonville's retail market has been a virtual roller coaster in recent years. The area's retail rent index dropped over 20% in 1995, rebounded 36% in 1996, and fell 2% last year. The area has both positive and negative forces affecting the retail sector. Unlike Orlando and Fort Lauderdale, employment growth has been below the state average of 3.1%, and Jacksonville's per-capita income is among the lowest in the nation. Positively, the area has a diverse economic base and low business costs. New retail projects include: Sleiman Enterprises Timberlin Parc project (150,000 square feet) and a Publix-anchored Kernan Square on Beach Boulevard (80,000 square feet)." *National Association of Realtors, 1997-1998 Market Conditions Report*

COMMERCIAL UTILITIES

Typical Monthly Electric Bills

Area	Commercial Service ($/month)		Industrial Service ($/month)	
	12 kW demand 1,500 kWh	120 kW demand 30,000 kWh	1,000 kW demand 400,000 kWh	20,000 kW demand 10,000,000 kWh
City[1]	96	1,823	20,450	450,200
U.S.[2]	162	2,360[a]	25,590	545,677

Note: (1) Based on rates in effect January 1, 1997; (2) Based on rates in effect July 1, 1997; (a) Based on 100 kW demand and 30,000 kWh usage.
Source: Memphis Light, Gas and Water, 1997 Utility Bill Comparisons for Selected U.S. Cities; Edison Electric Institute, Typical Residential, Commercial and Industrial Bills, Summer 1997

TRANSPORTATION

Transportation Statistics

Avg. travel time to work (min.)	21.6
Interstate highways	I-10; I-95
Bus lines	
In-city	Jacksonville TA, 184 vehicles
Inter-city	2
Passenger air service	
Airport	Jacksonville International
Airlines	8
Aircraft departures	29,043 (1995)
Enplaned passengers	1,617,047 (1995)
Rail service	Amtrak
Motor freight carriers	10
Major waterways/ports	St. Johns River

Source: OAG, Business Travel Planner, Summer 1997; Editor & Publisher Market Guide, 1998; FAA Airport Activity Statistics, 1996; Amtrak National Time Table, Northeast Timetable, Fall/Winter 1997-98; 1990 Census of Population and Housing, STF 3C; Chamber of Commerce/Economic Development 1997; Jane's Urban Transport Systems 1997-98; Transit Fact Book 1997

Means of Transportation to Work

Area	Car/Truck/Van		Public Transportation			Bicycle	Walked	Other Means	Worked at Home
	Drove Alone	Car-pooled	Bus	Subway	Railroad				
City	75.5	14.2	2.5	0.0	0.0	0.6	2.7	1.7	2.7
MSA[1]	76.2	14.3	1.9	0.0	0.0	0.7	2.6	1.7	2.6
U.S.	73.2	13.4	3.0	1.5	0.5	0.4	3.9	1.2	3.0

Note: figures shown are percentages and only include workers 16 years old and over; (1) Metropolitan Statistical Area - see Appendix A for areas included
Source: 1990 Census of Population and Housing, Summary Tape File 3C

BUSINESSES

Major Business Headquarters

Company Name	1997 Rankings	
	Fortune 500	Forbes 500
Barnett Banks	358	-
Coggin Automotive Group	-	468
Winn-Dixie Stores	101	-

Note: Companies listed are located in the city; Dashes indicate no ranking
Fortune 500: companies that produce a 10-K are ranked 1 - 500 based on 1996 revenue
Forbes 500: private companies are ranked 1 - 500 based on 1996 revenue
Source: Forbes 12/1/97; Fortune 4/28/97

Fast-Growing Businesses

Jacksonville is home to one of *Business Week's* "hot growth" companies: Computer Management Sciences. Criteria: sales and earnings, return on capital and stock price. *Business Week, 5/26/97*

Small Business Opportunity

According to *Forbes*, Jacksonville is home to two of America's 200 best small companies: Barnett Bank, Computer Management Sciences. Criteria: companies must be publicly traded, U.S.-based corporations with latest 12-month sales of between $5 and $350 million. Earnings must be at least $1 million for the 12-month period. Limited partnerships, REITs and closed-end mutual funds were not considered. Banks, S&Ls and electric utilities were not included. *Forbes, November 3, 1997*

HOTELS & MOTELS

Hotels/Motels

Area	Hotels/ Motels	Rooms	Luxury-Level Hotels/Motels		Average Minimum Rates ($)		
			♦♦♦♦	♦♦♦♦♦	♦♦	♦♦♦	♦♦♦♦
City	39	5,445	0	0	64	110	n/a
Airport	6	694	0	0	n/a	n/a	n/a
Suburbs	16	2,576	3	0	n/a	n/a	n/a
Total	61	8,715	3	0	n/a	n/a	n/a

Note: n/a not available; Classifications range from one diamond (budget properties with basic amenities) to five diamond (luxury properties with the finest service, rooms and facilities). Source: OAG, Business Travel Planner, Summer 1997

CONVENTION CENTERS

Major Convention Centers

Center Name	Meeting Rooms	Exhibit Space (sf)
Civic Auditorium and Exposition Center	8	21,500
Prime F. Osborn III Convention Center	22	100,000
Veterans Memorial Coliseum (Jacksonville)	1	23,575
Greater Jacksonville Fairgrounds	1	91,458
Morroco Shrine Auditorium	12	32,000

Source: Trade Shows Worldwide 1997

Living Environment

COST OF LIVING

Cost of Living Index

Composite Index	Housing	Utilities	Groceries	Health Care	Trans-portation	Misc. Goods/ Services
94.4	85.6	97.1	101.6	88.7	106.3	95.5

Note: U.S. = 100
Source: ACCRA, Cost of Living Index, 2nd Quarter 1997

HOUSING

Median Home Prices and Housing Affordability

Area	Median Price[2] 3rd Qtr. 1997 ($)	HOI[3] 3rd Qtr. 1997	Afford-ability Rank[4]
MSA[1]	97,000	73.5	63
U.S.	127,000	63.7	–

Note: (1) Metropolitan Statistical Area - see Appendix A for areas included; (2) U.S. figures calculated from the sales of 625,000 new and existing homes in 195 markets; (3) Housing Opportunity Index - percent of homes sold that were within the reach of the median income household at the prevailing mortgage interest rate; (4) Rank is from 1-195 with 1 being most affordable
Source: National Association of Home Builders, Housing Opportunity Index, 3rd Quarter 1997

It is projected that the median price of existing single-family homes in the metro area will increase by 7.3% in 1998. Nationwide, home prices are projected to increase 6.6%.
Kiplinger's Personal Finance Magazine, January 1998

Average New Home Price

Area	Price ($)
City	107,180
U.S.	135,150

Note: Figures are based on a new home with 1,800 sq. ft. of living area on an 8,000 sq. ft. lot.
Source: ACCRA, Cost of Living Index, 2nd Quarter 1997

Average Apartment Rent

Area	Rent ($/mth)
City	654
U.S.	575

Note: Figures are based on an unfurnished two bedroom, 1-1/2 or 2 bath apartment, approximately 950 sq. ft. in size, excluding all utilities except water
Source: ACCRA, Cost of Living Index, 2nd Quarter 1997

RESIDENTIAL UTILITIES

Average Residential Utility Costs

Area	All Electric ($/mth)	Part Electric ($/mth)	Other Energy ($/mth)	Phone ($/mth)
City	102.47	–	–	16.22
U.S.	108.38	56.32	44.12	19.66

Source: ACCRA, Cost of Living Index, 2nd Quarter 1997

HEALTH CARE

Average Health Care Costs

Area	Hospital ($/day)	Doctor ($/visit)	Dentist ($/visit)
City	327.60	45.40	50.40
U.S.	390.32	48.32	60.14

Note: Hospital - based on a semi-private room. Doctor - based on a general practitioner's routine exam of an established patient. Dentist - based on adult teeth cleaning and periodic oral exam.
Source: ACCRA, Cost of Living Index, 2nd Quarter 1997

Distribution of Office-Based Physicians

Area	Family/Gen. Practitioners	Specialists		
		Medical	Surgical	Other
MSA[1]	263	576	455	454

Note: Data as of 12/31/96; (1) Metropolitan Statistical Area - see Appendix A for areas included
Source: American Medical Assn., Physician Characteristics & Distribution in the U.S., 1997-1998

Hospitals

Jacksonville has 7 general medical and surgical hospitals, 2 psychiatric, 1 rehabilitation, 1 alcoholism and other chemical dependency, 1 other specialty. *AHA Guide to the Healthcare Field 1997-98*

Baptist Medical Center; Memorial Hospital are among the 100 best-run hospitals in the U.S. *Modern Healthcare, January 5, 1998*

EDUCATION

Public School District Statistics

District Name	Num. Sch.	Enroll.	Classroom Teachers[1]	Pupils per Teacher	Minority Pupils (%)	Current Exp.[2] ($/pupil)
Duval County School District	155	123,910	6,096	20.3	45.2	4,419

Note: Data covers the 1995-1996 school year unless otherwise noted; (1) Excludes teachers reported as working in school district offices rather than in schools; (2) Based on 1993-94 enrollment collected by the Census Bureau, not the enrollment figure shown in column 3; SD = School District; ISD = Independent School District; n/a not available
Source: National Center for Education Statistics, Common Core of Data Survey; Bureau of the Census

Educational Quality

School District	Education Quotient[1]	Graduate Outcome[2]	Community Index[3]	Resource Index[4]
Jacksonville	97.0	69.0	94.0	129.0

Note: Nearly 1,000 secondary school districts were rated in terms of educational quality. The scores range from a low of 50 to a high of 150; (1) Average of the Graduate Outcome, Community and Resource indexes; (2) Based on graduation rates and college board scores (SAT/ACT); (3) Based on the surrounding community's average level of education and the area's average income level; (4) Based on teacher salaries, per-pupil expenditures and student-teacher ratios.
Source: Expansion Management, Ratings Issue 1997

Educational Attainment by Race

Area	High School Graduate (%)					Bachelor's Degree (%)				
	Total	White	Black	Other	Hisp.[2]	Total	White	Black	Other	Hisp.[2]
City	76.4	80.2	63.6	77.1	78.9	17.9	19.6	10.9	25.3	20.2
MSA[1]	77.4	80.6	62.5	76.6	78.5	18.6	20.1	10.8	25.0	20.3
U.S.	75.2	77.9	63.1	60.4	49.8	20.3	21.5	11.4	19.4	9.2

Note: figures shown cover persons 25 years old and over; (1) Metropolitan Statistical Area - see Appendix A for areas included; (2) people of Hispanic origin can be of any race
Source: 1990 Census of Population and Housing, Summary Tape File 3C

School Enrollment by Type

Area	Preprimary				Elementary/High School			
	Public		Private		Public		Private	
	Enrollment	%	Enrollment	%	Enrollment	%	Enrollment	%
City	6,877	55.5	5,519	44.5	92,698	87.5	13,236	12.5
MSA[1]	9,288	54.2	7,843	45.8	135,736	88.8	17,193	11.2
U.S.	2,679,029	59.5	1,824,256	40.5	38,379,689	90.2	4,187,099	9.8

Note: figures shown cover persons 3 years old and over;
(1) Metropolitan Statistical Area - see Appendix A for areas included
Source: 1990 Census of Population and Housing, Summary Tape File 3C

School Enrollment by Race

Area	Preprimary (%)				Elementary/High School (%)			
	White	Black	Other	Hisp.[1]	White	Black	Other	Hisp.[1]
City	71.3	26.7	2.0	2.1	62.4	33.6	4.0	2.8
MSA[2]	76.9	21.2	1.9	2.1	69.8	26.6	3.5	2.9
U.S.	80.4	12.5	7.1	7.8	74.1	15.6	10.3	12.5

Note: figures shown cover persons 3 years old and over; (1) people of Hispanic origin can be of any race; (2) Metropolitan Statistical Area - see Appendix A for areas included
Source: 1990 Census of Population and Housing, Summary Tape File 3C

SAT/ACT Scores

Area/District	1997 SAT				1997 ACT	
	Percent of Graduates Tested (%)	Average Math Score	Average Verbal Score	Average Combined Score	Percent of Graduates Tested (%)	Average Composite Score
Duval County PS	52	487	500	987	38	20.7
State	50	499	499	998	36	20.7
U.S.	42	511	505	1,016	36	21.0

Note: Math and verbal SAT scores are out of a possible 800; ACT scores are out of a possible 36
Caution: Comparing or ranking states/cities on the basis of SAT/ACT scores alone is invalid and strongly discouraged by the The College Board and The American College Testing Program as students who take the tests are self-selected and do not represent the entire student population.
Source: Duval County School Board, Instructional Information Services, 1997; American College Testing Program, 1997; College Board, 1997

Classroom Teacher Salaries in Public Schools

District	B.A. Degree		M.A. Degree		Ph.D. Degree	
	Min. ($)	Max. ($)	Min. ($)	Max. ($)	Min. ($)	Max. ($)
Jacksonville	24,000	40,841	25,080	43,252	27,395	45,976
Average[1]	26,120	39,270	28,175	44,667	31,643	49,825

Note: Salaries are for 1996-1997; (1) Based on all school districts covered
Source: American Federation of Teachers (unpublished data)

Higher Education

Two-Year Colleges		Four-Year Colleges		Medical Schools	Law Schools	Voc/ Tech
Public	Private	Public	Private			
0	1	1	4	0	1	15

Source: College Blue Book, Occupational Education 1997; Medical School Admission Requirements, 1998-99; Peterson's Guide to Two-Year Colleges, 1997; Peterson's Guide to Four-Year Colleges, 1997; Barron's Guide to Law Schools 1997

MAJOR EMPLOYERS

Major Employers

Vistakon Vision Products
Barnett Banks
CSX Transportation
Memorial Healthcare Group
St. Vincent's Medical Center
Mayo Clinic Jacksonville
Southeastern Resources (help supply services)

American Transtech (business services)
Blue Cross & Blue Shield of Florida
First Union National Bank of Florida
Southern Baptist Hospital of Florida
University Medical Center
Alltel Mortgage Information Services

Note: companies listed are located in the city
Source: Dun's Business Rankings 1997; Ward's Business Directory, 1997

PUBLIC SAFETY

Crime Rate

Area	All Crimes	Violent Crimes				Property Crimes		
		Murder	Forcible Rape	Robbery	Aggrav. Assault	Burglary	Larceny -Theft	Motor Vehicle Theft
City	8,623.5	12.3	98.6	404.4	899.1	1,907.8	4,613.8	687.5
Suburbs[1]	n/a	n/a	n/a	n/a	n/a	n/a	n/a	n/a
MSA[2]	n/a	n/a	n/a	n/a	n/a	n/a	n/a	n/a
U.S.	5,078.9	7.4	36.1	202.4	388.2	943.0	2,975.9	525.9

Note: Crime rate is the number of crimes per 100,000 pop.; (1) defined as all areas within the MSA but located outside the central city; (2) Metropolitan Statistical Area - see Appendix A for areas incl.
Source: FBI Uniform Crime Reports 1996

RECREATION

Culture and Recreation

Museums	Symphony Orchestras	Opera Companies	Dance Companies	Professional Theatres	Zoos	Pro Sports Teams
7	1	0	2	1	1	1

Source: International Directory of the Performing Arts, 1996; Official Museum Directory, 1998; Chamber of Commerce/Economic Development 1997

Library System

The Jacksonville Public Library has 16 branches, holdings of 1,826,432 volumes and a budget of $13,746,814 (1995-1996). *American Library Directory, 1997-1998*

MEDIA

Newspapers

Name	Type	Freq.	Distribution	Circulation
The Beaches Leader	General	2x/wk	Area	22,500
The Florida Times-Union	General	7x/wk	Area	197,706
Jacksonville Advocate	Black	1x/wk	Area	31,624
Jacksonville Free Press	Black	1x/wk	Area	33,055
Jacksonville Shopping Guide	n/a	1x/wk	Local	100,000
The Mirror	n/a	1x/wk	Local	10,500
Northeast Florida Advocate	Black	1x/wk	National	35,308
Sun Times Weekly	n/a	1x/wk	Local	11,000
The Veteran Voice	n/a	1x/mo	Regional	10,000

Note: Includes newspapers with circulations of 10,000 or more located in the city; n/a not available
Source: Burrelle's Media Directory, 1998 Edition

AM Radio Stations

Call Letters	Freq. (kHz)	Target Audience	Station Format	Music Format
WOKV	600	General	N/S/T	n/a
WNZS	930	General	S	n/a
WXTL	1010	General	M/N/S	Christian
WROS	1050	General	E/M/T	Christian
WJAX	1220	General	M	Easy Listening
WJGR	1320	General	N/S/T	n/a
WCGL	1360	General	M/N	Christian
WZAZ	1400	Religious	M	Christian
WZNZ	1460	General	n/a	n/a

Note: Stations included broadcast in the Jacksonville metro area; n/a not available
Station Format: E = Educational; M = Music; N = News; S = Sports; T = Talk
Source: Burrelle's Media Directory, 1998 Edition

FM Radio Stations

Call Letters	Freq. (mHz)	Target Audience	Station Format	Music Format
WJFR	88.7	General	E/M/N	Christian
WJCT	89.9	General	M/N	Classical/Jazz
WKTZ	90.9	General	M	Easy Listening
WJXR	92.1	General	M/T	Country
WJBT	92.7	General	M	Contemporary Top 40
WPLA	93.3	General	M/N	Alternative
WAPE	95.1	General	M/N/S	Contemporary Top 40
WEJZ	96.1	General	M	Adult Contemporary
WKQL	96.9	General	M	Oldies
WFSJ	97.9	General	M/N/S	Jazz
WQIK	99.1	General	M	Country
WSOL	101.5	Black	M/N/S	Urban Contemporary
WIVY	102.9	General	M/N/S	Adult Contemporary
WFYV	104.5	General	M/N/S	AOR
WROO	107.3	General	E/M/N/S	Country

Note: Stations included broadcast in the Jacksonville metro area
Station Format: E = Educational; M = Music; N = News; S = Sports; T = Talk
Music Format: AOR = Album Oriented Rock; MOR = Middle-of-the-Road
Source: Burrelle's Media Directory, 1998 Edition

Television Stations

Name	Ch.	Affiliation	Type	Owner
WJXT	4	CBS	Commercial	Post-Newsweek Stations Inc.
WJCT	7	PBS	Public	WJCT Inc.
WTLV	12	NBC	Commercial	Gannett Company Inc.
WJWB	17	ABC/WB	Commercial	Media General Inc.
WAWS	30	Fox/UPN	Commercial	Clear Channel Communications
WTEV	47	UPN	Commercial	RDS Communications
WJEB	59	TBN	n/a	TBN

Note: Stations included broadcast in the Jacksonville metro area
Source: Burrelle's Media Directory, 1998 Edition

CLIMATE

Average and Extreme Temperatures

Temperature	Jan	Feb	Mar	Apr	May	Jun	Jul	Aug	Sep	Oct	Nov	Dec	Ann
Extreme High (°F)	84	88	91	95	100	103	103	102	98	96	88	84	103
Average High (°F)	65	68	74	80	86	90	92	91	87	80	73	67	79
Average Temp. (°F)	54	57	62	69	75	80	83	82	79	71	62	56	69
Average Low (°F)	43	45	51	57	64	70	73	73	70	61	51	44	58
Extreme Low (°F)	7	22	23	34	45	47	61	63	48	36	21	11	7

Note: Figures cover the years 1948-1990
Source: National Climatic Data Center, International Station Meteorological Climate Summary, 3/95

Average Precipitation/Snowfall/Humidity

Precip./Humidity	Jan	Feb	Mar	Apr	May	Jun	Jul	Aug	Sep	Oct	Nov	Dec	Ann
Avg. Precip. (in.)	3.0	3.7	3.8	3.0	3.6	5.3	6.2	7.4	7.8	3.7	2.0	2.6	52.0
Avg. Snowfall (in.)	Tr	Tr	Tr	0	0	0	0	0	0	0	0	Tr	0
Avg. Rel. Hum. 7am (%)	86	86	87	86	86	88	89	91	92	91	89	88	88
Avg. Rel. Hum. 4pm (%)	56	53	50	49	54	61	64	65	66	62	58	58	58

Note: Figures cover the years 1948-1990; Tr = Trace amounts (<0.05 in. of rain; <0.5 in. of snow)
Source: National Climatic Data Center, International Station Meteorological Climate Summary, 3/95

Weather Conditions

Temperature			Daytime Sky			Precipitation		
10°F & below	32°F & below	90°F & above	Clear	Partly cloudy	Cloudy	0.01 inch or more precip.	0.1 inch or more snow/ice	Thunder-storms
< 1	16	83	86	181	98	114	1	65

Note: Figures are average number of days per year and covers the years 1948-1990
Source: National Climatic Data Center, International Station Meteorological Climate Summary, 3/95

AIR & WATER QUALITY

Maximum Pollutant Concentrations

	Particulate Matter (ug/m³)	Carbon Monoxide (ppm)	Sulfur Dioxide (ppm)	Nitrogen Dioxide (ppm)	Ozone (ppm)	Lead (ug/m³)
MSA[1] Level	61	4	0.030	0.015	0.10	0.02
NAAQS[2]	150	9	0.140	0.053	0.12	1.50
Met NAAQS?	Yes	Yes	Yes	Yes	Yes	Yes

Note: (1) Metropolitan Statistical Area - see Appendix A for areas included; (2) National Ambient Air Quality Standards; ppm = parts per million; ug/m³ = micrograms per cubic meter; n/a not available
Source: EPA, National Air Quality and Emissions Trends Report, 1996

Pollutant Standards Index

In the Jacksonville MSA (see Appendix A for areas included), the Pollutant Standards Index (PSI) exceeded 100 on 0 days in 1996. A PSI value greater than 100 indicates that air quality would be in the unhealthful range on that day. *EPA, National Air Quality and Emissions Trends Report, 1996*

Drinking Water

Water System Name	Pop. Served	Primary Water Source Type	Number of Violations in Fiscal Year 1997	Type of Violation/ Contaminants
City of Jacksonville-North Grid	430,000	Ground	None	None
City of Jacksonville-South Grid	303,564	Ground	None	None

Note: Data as of January 16, 1998
Source: EPA, Office of Ground Water and Drinking Water, Safe Drinking Water Information System

Jacksonville tap water is alkaline, very hard and naturally fluoridated.
Editor & Publisher Market Guide, 1998

Knoxville, Tennessee

Background

Home of the Tennessee Valley Authority, "Bleak House" (Confederate Memorial Hall), and the 1982 World's Fair, Knoxville's central business district reflects every period of its history.

Knoxville was settled at the end of the 18th century when a flood of pioneers migrated to Tennessee. It soon established itself as the gateway to the west. In 1791, William Blount, its first territorial governor, chose James White's Fort as the capital of the territory, subsequently renaming it for Secretary of War, James Knox.

The city played an important part in the Civil War and was occupied by both the Confederate and Union Armies. Knoxville rapidly recovered during Reconstruction and became the business center of the east Tennessee Valley.

The city is located where the Holston and French Broad rivers meet to create the Tennessee River, about 110 miles northeast of Chattanooga. It lies in a broad valley between the Cumberland Mountains to the northwest and the Great Smoky Mountains to the southeast. The Cumberland Mountains serve to weaken the force of cold winter air which frequently moves south of the Knoxville latitude and to modify the hot summer winds common to the plains to the west. The topography also affects the wind direction. As a result the winds are generally light and tornadoes are extremely rare.

Metropolitan Knoxville is home to a large number of widely diversified industries. Aluminum and clothing constitute the primary manufactured products. Chemicals, plastics, textiles, electronic components, electrical machinery, paper, railroad equipment, rubber goods, tobacco, and fertilizer are some of its other products.

Oak Ridge which is close by, was built during World War II in order to develop the atomic bomb. Nuclear research is still carried on.

Through the years Knoxville has played host to numerous sports championships from the 1988 National Chess Championship for elementary school children, the 1993 A.A.U. Junior Olympic Games, the 1996 National Gymnastics Championship to the 1997 Super National Scholastic Chess Championships.The Chess Tournament was the largest ever held in the United States and possibly the world. *New York Times April 27, 1997*

Pulitzer Prize-winner James Agee, is Knoxville's native son. The author fondly depicts his background in a number of his works.

General Rankings and Evaluative Comments

- Knoxville was ranked #96 out of 300 cities by *Money's* 1997 "Survey of the Best Places to Live." Criteria used: health services, crime, economy, housing, education, transportation, weather, leisure and the arts. The city was ranked #160 in 1996 and #103 in 1995. *Money, July 1997; Money, September 1996; Money, September 1995*

- *Ladies Home Journal* ranked America's 200 largest cities based on the qualities women care about most. Knoxville ranked 104 out of 200. Criteria: low crime rate, good public schools, well-paying jobs, quality health and child care, the presence of women in government, proportion of women-owned businesses, size of the wage gap with men, local economy, divorce rates, the ratio of single men to single women, whether there are laws that require at least the same number of public toilets for women as men, and the probability of good hair days. *Ladies Home Journal, November 1997*

- Knoxville is among "The Best Places to Raise a Family". Rank: 14 out of 301 metro areas. Criteria: low crime rate, low drug and alcohol abuse, good public schools, high-quality health care, a clean environment, affordable cost of living and strong economic growth. *Reader's Digest, April 1997*

- Knoxville was ranked #113 out of 219 cities in terms of children's health, safety, and economic well-being. Criteria: total population, percent population change, birth rate, child immunization rate, infant mortality rate, percent low birth weight infants, percent of births to teens, physician-to-population ratio, student-to-teacher ratio, dropout rate, unemployment rate, median family income, percent of children in poverty, violent and property crime rates, number of juvenile arrests for violent crimes as a percent of the total crime index, number of days with pollution standard index (PSI) over 100, pounds toxic releases per 1,000 people and number of superfund sites. *Zero Population Growth, Children's Environmental Index 1997*

- According to *Working Mother,* "Like so many other states, Tennessee has boosted its funding for child care in the face of welfare reform. In his budget for the next fiscal year, Governor Don Sundquist has pledged $10 million in new funds. Much of that money will go to boost payments to caregivers—which may in turn lower parents' bills. At the same time, state officials are still dragging their feet over new rules that were proposed three years ago to improve the quality of care for Tennessee's kids. The rules would upgrade caregiver training and lower adult-to-child ratios—important changes that studies show make programs better for kids. It looks af if the rules will soon be approved, but they'll then be phased in over nearly four years—an unfortunate delay. 'A lot of us are really distressed that the state has not implemented these standards yet,' says Phil Acord of the Children's Home and Shelter, a 24-hour child care center in Chattanooga." *Working Mother, July/August 1997*

Business Environment

STATE ECONOMY

State Economic Profile

''Tennessee's economic growth is becoming more moderate. Apparel-related layoffs and sizable consolidations at major employers such as Knoxville's Oak Ridge National Laboratory are impeding growth. Spurred by ongoing commercial and hotel projects as well as still-high homebuilding demand, construction companies are the most active job creator, hiring workers at more than a 5% clip over the past twelve months.

Tennessee is experiencing fiscal problems due to the combination of an extensive state-sponsored Medicaid program and an absence of personal income taxes. The projected budget shortfalls are necessitating cuts in public spending and infrastructure projects, exerting a drag on the construction industry.

Tennessee's homeownership rate is at an historic high. Firm housing affordability and extensive efforts to extend financing to lower-income buyers have been the principal factors in the rise in homeownership to date. However, the rate of growth in homeownership will cool this year due to lenders being less aggressive in expanding their affordable housing programs, and tighter monetary policy.

Tennessee possesses one of the South's highest rates of population growth attributable to domestic migration. Current population growth outpaces the 1% national annual rate by nearly 50 basis points. Tennessee's positive in-flows of migration are an essential source of labor, enabling the economy to expand. Over the longer run, the attractiveness of Tennessee's labor market conditions and housing affordability vis-a-vis northern economies remains a fundamental impetus for continued net positive in-migration.

As expected, Tennessee's economy has slowed moderately, while enduring structural changes in its manufacturing industry. Modest gains in local support industries will be offset by defense-related cutbacks and aggressive restructuring of Tennessee's largest employers. Tennessee's smaller metropolitan areas and surrounding rural communities will thus exhibit the slowest economic growth. Longer term, the most prominent risks to Tennessee's economy remain concentrated on the upside-enhanced industrial diversification, low business costs, solid housing affordability, strong demographic trends, and inherent geographic advantages for distribution and trade. As the decade ends, Tennessee will return as one of the strongest southern economies....'' *National Association of Realtors, Economic Profiles: The Fifty States, July 1997*

IMPORTS/EXPORTS

Total Export Sales

Area	1993 ($000)	1994 ($000)	1995 ($000)	1996 ($000)	% Chg. 1993-96	% Chg. 1995-96
MSA[1]	580,408	689,179	633,188	764,137	31.7	20.7
U.S.	464,858,354	512,415,609	583,030,524	622,827,063	34.0	6.8

Note: (1) Metropolitan Statistical Area - see Appendix A for areas included
Source: U.S. Department of Commerce, International Trade Association, Metropolitan Area Exports: An Export Performance Report on Over 250 U.S. Cities, October 1997

Imports/Exports by Port

Type	Cargo Value			Share of U.S. Total	
	1995 (US$mil.)	1996 (US$mil.)	% Change 1995-1996	1995 (%)	1996 (%)
Imports	0	0	0	0	0
Exports	0	0	0	0	0

Source: Global Trade Information Services, WaterBorne Trade Atlas 1997

CITY FINANCES

City Government Finances

Component	FY92 ($000)	FY92 (per capita $)
Revenue	513,661	3,021.71
Expenditure	470,518	2,767.92
Debt Outstanding	297,959	1,752.80
Cash & Securities	444,569	2,615.27

Source: U.S. Bureau of the Census, City Government Finances: 1991-92

City Government Revenue by Source

Source	FY92 ($000)	FY92 (per capita $)	FY92 (%)
From Federal Government	5,981	35.18	1.2
From State Governments	17,132	100.78	3.3
From Local Governments	23,047	135.58	4.5
Property Taxes	46,846	275.58	9.1
General Sales Taxes	0	0.00	0.0
Selective Sales Taxes	9,236	54.33	1.8
Income Taxes	0	0.00	0.0
Current Charges	25,868	152.17	5.0
Utility/Liquor Store	323,431	1,902.65	63.0
Employee Retirement[1]	47,856	281.52	9.3
Other	14,264	83.91	2.8

Note: (1) Excludes "city contributions," classified as "nonrevenue," intragovernmental transfers.
Source: U.S. Bureau of the Census, City Government Finances: 1991-92

City Government Expenditures by Function

Function	FY92 ($000)	FY92 (per capita $)	FY92 (%)
Educational Services	4,464	26.26	0.9
Employee Retirement[1]	16,128	94.88	3.4
Environment/Housing	33,381	196.37	7.1
Government Administration	4,905	28.85	1.0
Interest on General Debt	11,240	66.12	2.4
Public Safety	36,905	217.10	7.8
Social Services	3,910	23.00	0.8
Transportation	4,606	27.10	1.0
Utility/Liquor Store	343,754	2,022.20	73.1
Other	11,225	66.03	2.4

Note: (1) Payments to beneficiaries including withdrawal of contributions.
Source: U.S. Bureau of the Census, City Government Finances: 1991-92

Municipal Bond Ratings

Area	Moody's	S & P
Knoxville	Aa3	AA

Note: n/a not available; n/r not rated
Source: Moody's Bond Record, 2/98; Statistical Abstract of the U.S., 1997;
Governing Magazine, 9/97, 3/98

POPULATION

Population Growth

Area	1980	1990	% Chg. 1980-90	July 1996 Estimate	% Chg. 1990-96
City	175,030	165,121	-5.7	167,535	1.5
MSA[1]	565,970	604,816	6.9	649,277	7.4
U.S.	226,545,805	248,765,170	9.8	265,179,411	6.6

Note: (1) Metropolitan Statistical Area - see Appendix A for areas included
Source: 1980/1990 Census of Housing and Population, Summary Tape File 3C;
Census Bureau Population Estimates

Population Characteristics

Race	City 1980 Population	%	City 1990 Population	%	% Chg. 1980-90	MSA[1] 1990 Population	%
White	147,892	84.5	136,789	82.8	-7.5	562,156	92.9
Black	25,438	14.5	25,770	15.6	1.3	35,881	5.9
Amer Indian/Esk/Aleut	475	0.3	592	0.4	24.6	1,716	0.3
Asian/Pacific Islander	907	0.5	1,653	1.0	82.2	4,275	0.7
Other	318	0.2	317	0.2	-0.3	788	0.1
Hispanic Origin[2]	1,317	0.8	986	0.6	-25.1	3,444	0.6

Note: (1) Metropolitan Statistical Area - see Appendix A for areas included;
(2) people of Hispanic origin can be of any race
Source: 1980/1990 Census of Housing and Population, Summary Tape File 3C

Ancestry

Area	German	Irish	English	Italian	U.S.	French	Polish	Dutch
City	17.8	18.1	15.4	1.7	9.8	2.5	0.8	3.6
MSA[1]	19.6	19.7	16.9	1.5	12.3	2.5	0.8	4.1
U.S.	23.3	15.6	13.1	5.9	5.3	4.2	3.8	2.5

Note: Figures are percentages and include persons that reported multiple ancestry (eg. if a person reported being Irish and Italian, they were included in both columns); (1) Metropolitan Statistical Area - see Appendix A for areas included
Source: 1990 Census of Population and Housing, Summary Tape File 3C

Age

Area	Median Age (Years)	Age Distribution (%) Under 5	Under 18	18-24	25-44	45-64	65+	80+
City	32.4	5.9	19.8	16.5	31.1	17.2	15.4	3.8
MSA[1]	34.5	6.2	22.9	11.4	32.0	20.5	13.3	2.8
U.S.	32.9	7.3	25.6	10.5	32.6	18.7	12.5	2.8

Note: (1) Metropolitan Statistical Area - see Appendix A for areas included
Source: 1990 Census of Population and Housing, Summary Tape File 3C

Male/Female Ratio

Area	Number of males per 100 females (all ages)	Number of males per 100 females (18 years old+)
City	86.7	83.7
MSA[1]	92.2	88.9
U.S.	95.0	91.9

Note: (1) Metropolitan Statistical Area - see Appendix A for areas included
Source: 1990 Census of Population, General Population Characteristics

INCOME

Per Capita/Median/Average Income

Area	Per Capita ($)	Median Household ($)	Average Household ($)
City	12,108	19,923	27,960
MSA[1]	12,984	25,134	32,693
U.S.	14,420	30,056	38,453

Note: all figures are for 1989; (1) Metropolitan Statistical Area - see Appendix A for areas included
Source: 1990 Census of Population and Housing, Summary Tape File 3C

Household Income Distribution by Race

Income ($)	City (%)					U.S. (%)				
	Total	White	Black	Other	Hisp.[1]	Total	White	Black	Other	Hisp.[1]
Less than 5,000	11.7	9.5	25.6	12.8	10.0	6.2	4.8	15.2	8.6	8.8
5,000 - 9,999	14.7	14.0	17.9	21.3	16.4	9.3	8.6	14.2	9.9	11.1
10,000 - 14,999	12.8	12.7	13.8	13.9	10.6	8.8	8.5	11.0	9.8	11.0
15,000 - 24,999	20.4	20.7	17.9	21.4	29.4	17.5	17.3	18.9	18.5	20.5
25,000 - 34,999	15.0	15.7	10.5	17.3	12.1	15.8	16.1	14.2	15.4	16.4
35,000 - 49,999	13.1	13.8	9.1	6.5	8.2	17.9	18.6	13.3	16.1	16.0
50,000 - 74,999	8.0	8.7	3.7	4.5	10.9	15.0	15.8	9.3	13.4	11.1
75,000 - 99,999	2.0	2.1	1.2	1.0	0.0	5.1	5.5	2.6	4.7	3.1
100,000+	2.3	2.6	0.3	1.4	2.4	4.4	4.8	1.3	3.7	1.9

Note: all figures are for 1989; (1) people of Hispanic origin can be of any race
Source: 1990 Census of Population and Housing, Summary Tape File 3C

Effective Buying Income

Area	Per Capita ($)	Median Household ($)	Average Household ($)
City	15,019	24,643	35,092
MSA[1]	16,583	31,837	41,476
U.S.	15,444	33,201	41,849

Note: data as of 1/1/97; (1) Metropolitan Statistical Area - see Appendix A for areas included
Source: Standard Rate & Data Service, Newspaper Advertising Source, 2/98

Effective Household Buying Income Distribution

Area	% of Households Earning						
	$10,000 -$19,999	$20,000 -$34,999	$35,000 -$49,999	$50,000 -$74,999	$75,000 -$99,000	$100,000 -$124,999	$125,000 and up
City	21.9	23.4	15.2	12.2	4.1	1.2	2.0
MSA[1]	17.6	23.0	17.2	16.9	6.8	2.2	2.4
U.S.	16.5	23.4	18.3	18.2	6.4	2.1	2.4

Note: data as of 1/1/97; (1) Metropolitan Statistical Area - see Appendix A for areas included
Source: Standard Rate & Data Service, Newspaper Advertising Source, 2/98

Poverty Rates by Race and Age

Area	Total (%)	By Race (%)				By Age (%)		
		White	Black	Other	Hisp.[2]	Under 5 years old	Under 18 years old	65 years and over
City	20.8	17.4	38.6	25.3	34.4	32.0	29.8	16.2
MSA[1]	14.2	12.9	33.6	19.7	18.7	21.8	18.7	16.1
U.S.	13.1	9.8	29.5	23.1	25.3	20.1	18.3	12.8

Note: figures show the percent of people living below the poverty line in 1989. The average poverty threshold was $12,674 for a family of four in 1989; (1) Metropolitan Statistical Area - see Appendix A for areas included; (2) people of Hispanic origin can be of any race
Source: 1990 Census of Population and Housing, Summary Tape File 3C

EMPLOYMENT

Labor Force and Employment

Area	Civilian Labor Force			Workers Employed		
	Dec. '95	Dec. '96	% Chg.	Dec. '95	Dec. '96	% Chg.
City	92,712	91,615	-1.2	89,425	88,537	-1.0
MSA[1]	347,731	343,762	-1.1	335,309	331,979	-1.0
U.S.	134,583,000	136,742,000	1.6	127,903,000	130,785,000	2.3

Note: Data is not seasonally adjusted and covers workers 16 years of age and older;
(1) Metropolitan Statistical Area - see Appendix A for areas included
Source: Bureau of Labor Statistics, http://stats.bls.gov

Unemployment Rate

Area	1997											
	Jan.	Feb.	Mar.	Apr.	May	Jun.	Jul.	Aug.	Sep.	Oct.	Nov.	Dec.
City	4.6	4.5	4.6	4.3	4.0	5.0	4.9	4.5	4.1	4.2	4.3	3.4
MSA[1]	5.5	5.4	5.1	4.3	3.7	4.5	4.1	3.8	3.4	3.5	3.9	3.4
U.S.	5.9	5.7	5.5	4.8	4.7	5.2	5.0	4.8	4.7	4.4	4.3	4.4

Note: Data is not seasonally adjusted and covers workers 16 years of age and older; All figures are percentages; (1) Metropolitan Statistical Area - see Appendix A for areas included
Source: Bureau of Labor Statistics, http://stats.bls.gov

Employment by Industry

Sector	MSA[1]		U.S.
	Number of Employees	Percent of Total	Percent of Total
Services	86,900	27.1	29.0
Retail Trade	69,200	21.6	18.5
Government	54,900	17.1	16.1
Manufacturing	49,200	15.3	15.0
Finance/Insurance/Real Estate	13,900	4.3	5.7
Wholesale Trade	16,300	5.1	5.4
Transportation/Public Utilities	14,100	4.4	5.3
Construction	15,500	4.8	4.5
Mining	600	0.2	0.5

Note: Figures cover non-farm employment as of 12/97 and are not seasonally adjusted;
(1) Metropolitan Statistical Area - see Appendix A for areas included
Source: Bureau of Labor Statistics, http://stats.bls.gov

Employment by Occupation

Occupation Category	City (%)	MSA[1] (%)	U.S. (%)
White Collar	60.1	57.2	58.1
Executive/Admin./Management	11.0	11.4	12.3
Professional	16.6	14.5	14.1
Technical & Related Support	3.7	3.9	3.7
Sales	13.7	13.2	11.8
Administrative Support/Clerical	15.2	14.4	16.3
Blue Collar	22.7	28.4	26.2
Precision Production/Craft/Repair	8.4	12.1	11.3
Machine Operators/Assem./Insp.	6.1	7.9	6.8
Transportation/Material Movers	4.2	4.3	4.1
Cleaners/Helpers/Laborers	3.9	4.1	3.9
Services	16.2	12.8	13.2
Farming/Forestry/Fishing	1.0	1.6	2.5

Note: figures cover employed persons 16 years old and over;
(1) Metropolitan Statistical Area - see Appendix A for areas included
Source: 1990 Census of Population and Housing, Summary Tape File 3C

Occupational Employment Projections: 1994 - 2005

Occupations Expected to have the Largest Job Growth (ranked by numerical growth)	Fast-Growing Occupations (ranked by percent growth)
1. Salespersons, retail	1. Personal and home care aides
2. Truck drivers, heavy & light	2. Home health aides
3. Cashiers	3. Residential counselors
4. Waiters & waitresses	4. Computer engineers
5. Janitors/cleaners/maids, ex. priv. hshld.	5. Occupational therapy assistants
6. General managers & top executives	6. Physical therapy assistants and aides
7. Registered nurses	7. Physical therapists
8. Marketing & sales, supervisors	8. Systems analysts
9. Nursing aides/orderlies/attendants	9. Occupational therapists
10. Teachers aides, clerical & paraprofess.	10. Computer scientists

Projections cover Tennessee.
Source: U.S. Department of Labor, Employment and Training Administration, America's Labor Market Information System (ALMIS)

Average Wages

Occupation	Wage	Occupation	Wage
Professional/Technical/Clerical	**$/Week**	**Health/Protective Services**	**$/Week**
Accountants III	-	Corrections Officers	-
Attorneys III	-	Firefighters	-
Budget Analysts III	-	Nurses, Licensed Practical II	-
Buyers/Contracting Specialists II	-	Nurses, Registered II	-
Clerks, Accounting III	336	Nursing Assistants II	-
Clerks, General III	344	Police Officers I	-
Computer Operators II	369	**Hourly Workers**	**$/Hour**
Computer Programmers II	603	Forklift Operators	8.53
Drafters II	439	General Maintenance Workers	9.81
Engineering Technicians III	544	Guards I	-
Engineering Technicians, Civil III	-	Janitors	6.81
Engineers III	-	Maintenance Electricians	16.60
Key Entry Operators I	295	Maintenance Electronics Techs II	14.05
Personnel Assistants III	-	Maintenance Machinists	16.69
Personnel Specialists III	-	Maintenance Mechanics, Machinery	14.74
Secretaries III	460	Material Handling Laborers	6.80
Switchboard Operator-Receptionist	305	Motor Vehicle Mechanics	13.32
Systems Analysts II	802	Shipping/Receiving Clerks	8.31
Systems Analysts Supervisor/Mgr II	-	Tool and Die Makers	13.42
Tax Collectors II	-	Truckdrivers, Tractor Trailer	9.72
Word Processors II	396	Warehouse Specialists	9.65

Note: Wage data includes full-time workers only for 11/93 and cover the Metropolitan Statistical Area (see Appendix A for areas included). Dashes indicate that data was not available.
Source: Bureau of Labor Statistics, Occupational Compensation Survey

TAXES

Major State and Local Tax Rates

State Corp. Income (%)	State Personal Income (%)	Residential Property (effective rate per $100)	Sales & Use		State Gasoline (cents/ gallon)	State Cigarette (cents/ 20-pack)
			State (%)	Local (%)		
6.0	6.0[a]	n/a	6.0	2.25	21[b]	13[c]

Note: Personal/corporate income tax rates as of 1/97. Sales, gasoline and cigarette tax rates as of 1/98; (a) Applies to interest and dividend income only; (b) Rate is comprised of 20 cents excise and 1 cent motor carrier tax. Does not include a 1 cent local option tax; (c) Counties and cities may impose an additional tax of 1 cent per pack
Source: Federation of Tax Administrators, www.taxadmin.org; Washington D.C. Department of Finance and Revenue, Tax Rates and Tax Burdens in the District of Columbia: A Nationwide Comparison, June 1997; Chamber of Commerce

Total Taxes Per Capita and as a Percent of Income

Area	Per Capita Income ($)	Per Capita Taxes ($)			Taxes as Pct. of Income (%)		
		Total	Federal	State/Local	Total	Federal	State/Local
Tennessee	23,748	7,574	5,460	2,114	31.9	23.0	8.9
U.S.	26,187	9,205	6,127	3,078	35.2	23.4	11.8

Note: Figures are for 1997
Source: Tax Foundation, Web Site, www.taxfoundation.org

COMMERCIAL REAL ESTATE

Office Market

Class/Location	Total Space (sq. ft.)	Vacant Space (sq. ft.)	Vac. Rate (%)	Under Constr. (sq. ft.)	Net Absorp. (sq. ft.)	Rental Rates ($/sq.ft./yr.)
Class A						
CBD	1,240,000	111,600	9.0	0	28,400	14.00-15.50
Outside CBD	475,000	23,750	5.0	0	11,250	15.00-17.00
Class B						
CBD	3,500,000	500,000	14.3	0	10,000	10.00-12.00
Outside CBD	4,500,000	315,000	7.0	0	85,000	12.00-14.00

Note: Data as of 10/97 and covers Knoxville; CBD = Central Business District; n/a not available;
Source: Society of Industrial and Office Realtors, 1998 Comparative Statistics of Industrial and Office Real Estate Markets

"The anticipated growth is moderate compared to 1997's performance. West Knoxville is expected to have the most construction. A new 80,000 sq. ft. multi-tenant building is planned for West Knoxville at Pellissippi Parkway. ABB Environmental is moving into the new building, with 30,000 sq. ft. of space left to lease. Tourism, business services, and financial services industries are expected to grow. Restructuring at the DOE Oak Ridge complex will send workers looking for private sector jobs and could hobble 1998 activity." *Society of Industrial and Office Realtors, 1998 Comparative Statistics of Industrial and Office Real Estate Markets*

Industrial Market

Location	Total Space (sq. ft.)	Vacant Space (sq. ft.)	Vac. Rate (%)	Under Constr. (sq. ft.)	Net Absorp. (sq. ft.)	Net Lease ($/sq.ft./yr.)
Central City	19,722,267	904,934	4.6	n/a	237,333	2.50-5.00
Suburban	12,840,017	364,893	2.8	n/a	225,124	3.00-5.50

Note: Data as of 10/97 and covers Knoxville; n/a not available
Source: Society of Industrial and Office Realtors, 1998 Comparative Statistics of Industrial and Office Real Estate Markets

"Market conditions are solid as 1998 begins. Growth in the automotive, transportation, and forest product manufacturing industries will aid Knoxville's industrial sector. Sales and lease prices are expected to rise in 1998. The U.S. Department of Energy has begun to reindustrialize the Oak Ridge complex making available thousands of acres and hundreds of thousands of sq. ft. of industrial buildings with infrastructure. They also put a well-trained, high-technology work force into the private market. Due to excellent interstate roadways including a secondary road infrastructure that is helpful to tractor-trailers, Knoxville will continue to be enticing as a regional and south-central U.S. distribution center." *Society of Industrial and Office Realtors, 1998 Comparative Statistics of Industrial and Office Real Estate Markets*

COMMERCIAL UTILITIES

Typical Monthly Electric Bills

Area	Commercial Service ($/month)		Industrial Service ($/month)	
	12 kW demand 1,500 kWh	100 kW demand 30,000 kWh	1,000 kW demand 400,000 kWh	20,000 kW demand 10,000,000 kWh
City	n/a	n/a	n/a	n/a
U.S.	162	2,360	25,590	545,677

Note: Based on rates in effect July 1, 1997; n/a not available
Source: Edison Electric Institute, Typical Residential, Commercial and Industrial Bills, Summer 1997

TRANSPORTATION

Transportation Statistics

Avg. travel time to work (min.)	18.1
Interstate highways	I-40; I-75
Bus lines	
In-city	Knoxville Area Transit
Inter-city	1
Passenger air service	
Airport	McGhee-Tyson
Airlines	9
Aircraft departures	11,514 (1995)
Enplaned passengers	565,266 (1995)
Rail service	No Amtrak service
Motor freight carriers	39
Major waterways/ports	Tennessee River; Port of Knoxville

Source: OAG, Business Travel Planner, Summer 1997; Editor & Publisher Market Guide, 1998; FAA Airport Activity Statistics, 1996; Amtrak National Time Table, Northeast Timetable, Fall/Winter 1997-98; 1990 Census of Population and Housing, STF 3C; Chamber of Commerce/Economic Development 1997; Jane's Urban Transport Systems 1997-98; Transit Fact Book 1997

Means of Transportation to Work

Area	Car/Truck/Van		Public Transportation			Bicycle	Walked	Other Means	Worked at Home
	Drove Alone	Car-pooled	Bus	Subway	Railroad				
City	77.1	13.1	1.8	0.0	0.0	0.2	4.8	1.0	1.9
MSA[1]	80.5	13.2	0.6	0.0	0.0	0.1	2.3	0.8	2.5
U.S.	73.2	13.4	3.0	1.5	0.5	0.4	3.9	1.2	3.0

Note: figures shown are percentages and only include workers 16 years old and over;
(1) Metropolitan Statistical Area - see Appendix A for areas included
Source: 1990 Census of Population and Housing, Summary Tape File 3C

BUSINESSES

Major Business Headquarters

Company Name	1997 Rankings	
	Fortune 500	Forbes 500
HT Hackney	-	88
Pilot	-	99

Note: Companies listed are located in the city; Dashes indicate no ranking
Fortune 500: companies that produce a 10-K are ranked 1 - 500 based on 1996 revenue
Forbes 500: private companies are ranked 1 - 500 based on 1996 revenue
Source: Forbes 12/1/97; Fortune 4/28/97

Fast-Growing Businesses

According to *Fortune*, Knoxville is home to one of America's 100 fastest-growing companies: Regal Cinemas. Companies were ranked based on three years' earnings-per-share growth using least squares analysis to smooth out distortions. Criteria for inclusion: public companies with sales of least $50 million. Companies that lost money in the most recent quarter, or ended in the red for the past four quarters as a whole, were not eligible. Limited partnerships and REITs were also not considered. *Fortune, 9/29/97*

Small Business Opportunity

According to *Forbes*, Knoxville is home to one of America's 200 best small companies: Regal Cinemas. Criteria: companies must be publicly traded, U.S.-based corporations with latest 12-month sales of between $5 and $350 million. Earnings must be at least $1 million for the 12-month period. Limited partnerships, REITs and closed-end mutual funds were not considered. Banks, S&Ls and electric utilities were not included. *Forbes, November 3, 1997*

HOTELS & MOTELS

Hotels/Motels

Area	Hotels/ Motels	Rooms	Luxury-Level Hotels/Motels		Average Minimum Rates ($)		
			♦♦♦♦	♦♦♦♦♦	♦♦	♦♦♦	♦♦♦♦
City	41	4,818	0	0	n/a	n/a	n/a
Airport	6	668	0	0	n/a	n/a	n/a
Total	47	5,486	0	0	n/a	n/a	n/a

Note: n/a not available; Classifications range from one diamond (budget properties with basic amenities) to five diamond (luxury properties with the finest service, rooms and facilities).
Source: OAG, Business Travel Planner, Summer 1997

CONVENTION CENTERS

Major Convention Centers

Center Name	Meeting Rooms	Exhibit Space (sf)
Civic Auditorium/Coliseum/Convention Center	15	67,000
Hyatt Regency Knoxville	13	15,378
Tennessee Valley Fairgrounds	n/a	60,000
Thompson-Boling Assembly Center and Arena	n/a	22,000
Knoxville Convention/Exhibition Center	16	66,396

Note: n/a not available
Source: Trade Shows Worldwide 1997

Living Environment

COST OF LIVING

Cost of Living Index

Composite Index	Housing	Utilities	Groceries	Health Care	Trans-portation	Misc. Goods/Services
95.5	91.4	90.5	95.1	95.2	91.6	101.4

Note: U.S. = 100
Source: ACCRA, Cost of Living Index, 3rd Quarter 1997

HOUSING

Median Home Prices and Housing Affordability

Area	Median Price[2] 3rd Qtr. 1997 ($)	HOI[3] 3rd Qtr. 1997	Afford-ability Rank[4]
MSA[1]	85,000	76.8	40
U.S.	127,000	63.7	–

Note: (1) Metropolitan Statistical Area - see Appendix A for areas included; (2) U.S. figures calculated from the sales of 625,000 new and existing homes in 195 markets; (3) Housing Opportunity Index - percent of homes sold that were within the reach of the median income household at the prevailing mortgage interest rate; (4) Rank is from 1-195 with 1 being most affordable
Source: National Association of Home Builders, Housing Opportunity Index, 3rd Quarter 1997

It is projected that the median price of existing single-family homes in the metro area will increase by 5.1% in 1998. Nationwide, home prices are projected to increase 6.6%.
Kiplinger's Personal Finance Magazine, January 1998

Average New Home Price

Area	Price ($)
City	120,740
U.S.	135,710

Note: Figures are based on a new home with 1,800 sq. ft. of living area on an 8,000 sq. ft. lot.
Source: ACCRA, Cost of Living Index, 3rd Quarter 1997

Average Apartment Rent

Area	Rent ($/mth)
City	572
U.S.	569

Note: Figures are based on an unfurnished two bedroom, 1-1/2 or 2 bath apartment, approximately 950 sq. ft. in size, excluding all utilities except water
Source: ACCRA, Cost of Living Index, 3rd Quarter 1997

RESIDENTIAL UTILITIES

Average Residential Utility Costs

Area	All Electric ($/mth)	Part Electric ($/mth)	Other Energy ($/mth)	Phone ($/mth)
City	–	44.16	47.05	19.47
U.S.	109.40	55.25	43.64	19.48

Source: ACCRA, Cost of Living Index, 3rd Quarter 1997

HEALTH CARE

Average Health Care Costs

Area	Hospital ($/day)	Doctor ($/visit)	Dentist ($/visit)
City	368.80	51.20	53.00
U.S.	392.91	48.76	60.84

Note: Hospital - based on a semi-private room. Doctor - based on a general practitioner's routine exam of an established patient. Dentist - based on adult teeth cleaning and periodic oral exam.
Source: ACCRA, Cost of Living Index, 3rd Quarter 1997

Distribution of Office-Based Physicians

| Area | Family/Gen. Practitioners | Specialists | | |
		Medical	Surgical	Other
MSA[1]	220	447	366	357

Note: Data as of 12/31/96; (1) Metropolitan Statistical Area - see Appendix A for areas included
Source: American Medical Assn., Physician Characteristics & Distribution in the U.S., 1997-1998

Hospitals

Knoxville has 5 general medical and surgical hospitals, 2 psychiatric, 1 children's general.
AHA Guide to the Healthcare Field 1997-98

Baptist Hospital of East Tennessee is among the 100 best-run hospitals in the U.S.
Modern Healthcare, January 5, 1998

EDUCATION

Public School District Statistics

District Name	Num. Sch.	Enroll.	Classroom Teachers[1]	Pupils per Teacher	Minority Pupils (%)	Current Exp.[2] ($/pupil)
Knox County School District	86	52,627	n/a	n/a	15.4	4,125

Note: Data covers the 1995-1996 school year unless otherwise noted; (1) Excludes teachers reported as working in school district offices rather than in schools; (2) Based on 1993-94 enrollment collected by the Census Bureau, not the enrollment figure shown in column 3; SD = School District; ISD = Independent School District; n/a not available
Source: National Center for Education Statistics, Common Core of Data Survey; Bureau of the Census

Educational Quality

School District	Education Quotient[1]	Graduate Outcome[2]	Community Index[3]	Resource Index[4]
Knox County	96.0	100.0	97.0	92.0

Note: Nearly 1,000 secondary school districts were rated in terms of educational quality. The scores range from a low of 50 to a high of 150; (1) Average of the Graduate Outcome, Community and Resource indexes; (2) Based on graduation rates and college board scores (SAT/ACT); (3) Based on the surrounding community's average level of education and the area's average income level; (4) Based on teacher salaries, per-pupil expenditures and student-teacher ratios.
Source: Expansion Management, Ratings Issue 1997

Educational Attainment by Race

| Area | High School Graduate (%) | | | | | Bachelor's Degree (%) | | | | |
	Total	White	Black	Other	Hisp.[2]	Total	White	Black	Other	Hisp.[2]
City	70.8	71.5	64.9	82.7	89.6	21.7	22.9	11.0	48.2	49.3
MSA[1]	70.3	70.3	66.8	80.1	80.8	19.2	19.2	13.5	42.5	33.7
U.S.	75.2	77.9	63.1	60.4	49.8	20.3	21.5	11.4	19.4	9.2

Note: figures shown cover persons 25 years old and over; (1) Metropolitan Statistical Area - see Appendix A for areas included; (2) people of Hispanic origin can be of any race
Source: 1990 Census of Population and Housing, Summary Tape File 3C

School Enrollment by Type

| Area | Preprimary | | | | Elementary/High School | | | |
| | Public | | Private | | Public | | Private | |
	Enrollment	%	Enrollment	%	Enrollment	%	Enrollment	%
City	1,461	68.5	673	31.5	19,991	94.3	1,216	5.7
MSA[1]	5,577	65.8	2,903	34.2	89,754	95.4	4,299	4.6
U.S.	2,679,029	59.5	1,824,256	40.5	38,379,689	90.2	4,187,099	9.8

Note: figures shown cover persons 3 years old and over;
(1) Metropolitan Statistical Area - see Appendix A for areas included
Source: 1990 Census of Population and Housing, Summary Tape File 3C

School Enrollment by Race

Area	Preprimary (%)				Elementary/High School (%)			
	White	Black	Other	Hisp.[1]	White	Black	Other	Hisp.[1]
City	78.3	19.2	2.5	0.4	71.8	26.4	1.8	0.9
MSA[2]	91.3	6.5	2.2	0.8	90.4	8.2	1.4	0.8
U.S.	80.4	12.5	7.1	7.8	74.1	15.6	10.3	12.5

Note: figures shown cover persons 3 years old and over; (1) people of Hispanic origin can be of any race; (2) Metropolitan Statistical Area - see Appendix A for areas included
Source: 1990 Census of Population and Housing, Summary Tape File 3C

SAT/ACT Scores

Area/District	1997 SAT				1997 ACT	
	Percent of Graduates Tested (%)	Average Math Score	Average Verbal Score	Average Combined Score	Percent of Graduates Tested (%)	Average Composite Score
Knox County SD	16	558	563	1,121	76	20.3
State	13	556	564	1,120	83	19.7
U.S.	42	511	505	1,016	36	21.0

Note: Math and verbal SAT scores are out of a possible 800; ACT scores are out of a possible 36
Caution: Comparing or ranking states/cities on the basis of SAT/ACT scores alone is invalid and strongly discouraged by the The College Board and The American College Testing Program as students who take the tests are self-selected and do not represent the entire student population.
Source: Knox County School District, 1997; American College Testing Program, 1997; College Board, 1997

Classroom Teacher Salaries in Public Schools

District	B.A. Degree		M.A. Degree		Ph.D. Degree	
	Min. ($)	Max ($)	Min. ($)	Max. ($)	Min. ($)	Max. ($)
Knoxville	24,571	34,976	26,247	37,102	29,781	40,641
Average[1]	26,120	39,270	28,175	44,667	31,643	49,825

Note: Salaries are for 1996-1997; (1) Based on all school districts covered
Source: American Federation of Teachers (unpublished data)

Higher Education

Two-Year Colleges		Four-Year Colleges		Medical Schools	Law Schools	Voc/ Tech
Public	Private	Public	Private			
1	3	1	3	0	1	7

Source: College Blue Book, Occupational Education 1997; Medical School Admission Requirements, 1998-99; Peterson's Guide to Two-Year Colleges, 1997; Peterson's Guide to Four-Year Colleges, 1997; Barron's Guide to Law Schools 1997

MAJOR EMPLOYERS

Major Employers

Baptist Hospital of East Tennessee	Matsushita Electronic Components
East Tennessee Children's Hospital Assn.	Employers Security
Fort Sanders Regional Medical Center	Goody's Family Clothing
Knoxville News-Sentinel	St. Mary's Health System
Tennessee Valley Authority	KTPJ Inc. (eating places)

Note: companies listed are located in the city
Source: Dun's Business Rankings 1997; Ward's Business Directory, 1997

PUBLIC SAFETY

Crime Rate

Area	All Crimes	Violent Crimes				Property Crimes		
		Murder	Forcible Rape	Robbery	Aggrav. Assault	Burglary	Larceny -Theft	Motor Vehicle Theft
City	6,186.0	13.2	38.5	340.7	484.9	1,345.0	3,047.3	916.4
Suburbs[1]	n/a	n/a	n/a	n/a	n/a	n/a	n/a	n/a
MSA[2]	n/a	n/a	n/a	n/a	n/a	n/a	n/a	n/a
U.S.	5,078.9	7.4	36.1	202.4	388.2	943.0	2,975.9	525.9

Note: Crime rate is the number of crimes per 100,000 pop.; (1) defined as all areas within the MSA but located outside the central city; (2) Metropolitan Statistical Area - see Appendix A for areas incl.
Source: FBI Uniform Crime Reports 1996

RECREATION

Culture and Recreation

Museums	Symphony Orchestras	Opera Companies	Dance Companies	Professional Theatres	Zoos	Pro Sports Teams
10	1	1	6	1	1	0

Source: International Directory of the Performing Arts, 1996; Official Museum Directory, 1998; Chamber of Commerce/Economic Development 1997

Library System

The Knox County Public Library System has 16 branches, holdings of 696,796 volumes and a budget of $6,080,951 (1995-1996). *American Library Directory, 1997-1998*

MEDIA

Newspapers

Name	Type	Freq.	Distribution	Circulation
The Daily Beacon	n/a	5x/wk	Campus & community	16,000
The East Tennessee Catholic	Religious	2x/mo	Area	15,000
The Knoxville News-Sentinel	General	7x/wk	Area	119,529
Press Enterprise	General	1x/wk	Local	15,000

Note: Includes newspapers with circulations of 1,000 or more located in the city; n/a not available
Source: Burrelle's Media Directory, 1998 Edition

AM Radio Stations

Call Letters	Freq. (kHz)	Target Audience	Station Format	Music Format
WRJZ	620	Religious	E/M/N/T	Christian
WKXV	900	General	M/T	n/a
WIVK	990	General	N/T	n/a
WQBB	1040	General	N/S/T	n/a
WHJM	1180	Religious	M	Christian
WIMZ	1240	General	S	n/a
WITA	1490	General	M/N/S	Christian

Note: Stations included broadcast in the Knoxville metro area; n/a not available
Station Format: E = Educational; M = Music; N = News; S = Sports; T = Talk
Source: Burrelle's Media Directory, 1998 Edition

FM Radio Stations

Call Letters	Freq. (mHz)	Target Audience	Station Format	Music Format
WUTK	90.3	General	M	Alternative/Christian/Country/Jazz/Oldies/R&B/Urban Contemporary
WKCS	91.1	General	M	Adult Contemporary/Country
WUOT	91.9	General	M	Classical/Jazz
WNFZ	94.3	General	M	Alternative
WJXB	97.5	General	M	Adult Contemporary
WNOX	99.1	General	M	Adult Contemporary/Urban Contemporary
WOKI	100.3	General	M	Country
WMYU	102.1	General	M	Oldies
WIMZ	103.5	General	M/N/S	Classic Rock
WQBB	104.5	General	M/N	Adult Standards/Big Band/Christian/Easy Listening
WXST	105.3	General	M/N/S	Oldies
WIVK	107.7	General	M/N/S	Country

Note: Stations included broadcast in the Knoxville metro area
Station Format: E = Educational; M = Music; N = News; S = Sports; T = Talk
Source: Burrelle's Media Directory, 1998 Edition

Television Stations

Name	Ch.	Affiliation	Type	Owner
WSJK	2	PBS	Public	East Tennessee Public Communications Corp.
WATE	6	ABC	Commercial	Young Broadcasting Inc.
WVLT	8	CBS	Commercial	Gray Communications Systems Inc.
WBIR	10	NBC	Commercial	Gannett Company Inc.
WKOP	15	PBS	Public	East Tennessee Public Communications Corp.
WTNZ	43	Fox	Commercial	Raycom Media Inc.

Note: Stations included broadcast in the Knoxville metro area
Source: Burrelle's Media Directory, 1998 Edition

CLIMATE

Average and Extreme Temperatures

Temperature	Jan	Feb	Mar	Apr	May	Jun	Jul	Aug	Sep	Oct	Nov	Dec	Ann
Extreme High (°F)	77	83	86	91	94	102	103	102	103	91	84	80	103
Average High (°F)	47	52	61	71	78	85	88	87	82	71	59	50	69
Average Temp. (°F)	38	42	50	59	67	75	78	77	71	60	49	41	59
Average Low (°F)	29	32	39	47	56	64	68	67	61	48	38	32	48
Extreme Low (°F)	-24	-2	1	22	32	43	49	53	36	25	5	-6	-24

Note: Figures cover the years 1948-1990
Source: National Climatic Data Center, International Station Meteorological Climate Summary, 3/95

Average Precipitation/Snowfall/Humidity

Precip./Humidity	Jan	Feb	Mar	Apr	May	Jun	Jul	Aug	Sep	Oct	Nov	Dec	Ann
Avg. Precip. (in.)	4.5	4.3	5.0	3.6	3.9	3.8	4.5	3.1	2.9	2.8	3.8	4.5	46.7
Avg. Snowfall (in.)	5	4	2	1	0	0	0	0	0	Tr	1	2	13
Avg. Rel. Hum. 7am (%)	81	80	79	80	85	86	89	91	91	89	84	82	85
Avg. Rel. Hum. 4pm (%)	60	54	50	46	52	54	56	55	54	51	54	59	54

Note: Figures cover the years 1948-1990; Tr = Trace amounts (<0.05 in. of rain; <0.5 in. of snow)
Source: National Climatic Data Center, International Station Meteorological Climate Summary, 3/95

Weather Conditions

Temperature			Daytime Sky			Precipitation		
10°F & below	32°F & below	90°F & above	Clear	Partly cloudy	Cloudy	0.01 inch or more precip.	0.1 inch or more snow/ice	Thunder-storms
3	73	33	85	142	138	125	8	47

Note: Figures are average number of days per year and covers the years 1948-1990
Source: National Climatic Data Center, International Station Meteorological Climate Summary, 3/95

AIR & WATER QUALITY

Maximum Pollutant Concentrations

	Particulate Matter (ug/m³)	Carbon Monoxide (ppm)	Sulfur Dioxide (ppm)	Nitrogen Dioxide (ppm)	Ozone (ppm)	Lead (ug/m³)
MSA[1] Level	78	3	0.058	0.014	0.11	n/a
NAAQS[2]	150	9	0.140	0.053	0.12	1.50
Met NAAQS?	Yes	Yes	Yes	Yes	Yes	n/a

Note: (1) Metropolitan Statistical Area - see Appendix A for areas included; (2) National Ambient Air Quality Standards; ppm = parts per million; ug/m³ = micrograms per cubic meter; n/a not available
Source: EPA, National Air Quality and Emissions Trends Report, 1996

Pollutant Standards Index

In the Knoxville MSA (see Appendix A for areas included), the Pollutant Standards Index (PSI) exceeded 100 on 1 day in 1996. A PSI value greater than 100 indicates that air quality would be in the unhealthful range on that day. *EPA, National Air Quality and Emissions Trends Report, 1996*

Drinking Water

Water System Name	Pop. Served	Primary Water Source Type	Number of Violations in Fiscal Year 1997	Type of Violation/ Contaminants
Knoxville UB#1 Whitaker Plant	161,709	Surface	None	None

Note: Data as of January 16, 1998
Source: EPA, Office of Ground Water and Drinking Water, Safe Drinking Water Information System

Knoxville tap water is alkaline, hard and fluoridated.
Editor & Publisher Market Guide, 1998

Miami, Florida

Background

Miami is the United States in a whole different way. While the majority of its residents are Caucasian of European descent, a growing number of its residents are of Cuban, Puerto Rican, and Haitian descent. Given this flavorful mix, Miami may be the city for those who like a hot international setting, with a decidedly Latin American accent.

Thanks to early pioneer Julia Tuttle, railroad magnate Henry Flagler extended the East Coast Railroad beyond Palm Beach. Within 15 years of that decision, Miami became known as the "Gold Coast". The land boom of the 1920's brought wealthy socialites, as well as African-Americans in search of work. Pink and aquamarine hued Art Deco hotels were squeezed onto a tiny tract of land called Miami Beach and the population of the Miami metro area swelled from 1,681 in 1900 to 1,934,014 in 1990.

Given Miami's origins in a tourist-oriented economy, many of the activities in which residents engage are "leisurely" including swimming, scuba diving, golf, tennis, and boating. Due to the increasing number of senior citizens retiring to the Miami area, shuffle board is popular as well.

For those who enjoy professional sports, one may attend games by the Miami Dolphin football team, the Florida Marlins baseball team, the Miami Heat basketball team, or the Florida Panther hockey team. Cultural activities range from the Miami City Ballet and the Coconut Grove Playhouse to numerous art galleries and museums, including the Bass Museum of Art. Visit the Villa Vizcaya, a gorgeous palazzo in the Italian Renaissance style built by industrialist James Deering, or spend a day at the Miami MetroZoo.

Miami's prime location on Biscayne Bay and in the southeastern United States makes it a perfect nexus for travel and trade. The Port of Miami is a bustling center for many cruise and cargo ships. The Port is also a base of the National Oceanic and Atmospheric Administration. The Miami International Airport is a busy destination point to and from many Latin American and Caribbean countries.

Even with Miami's corruption scandal and financial problems, local economists viewing the situation from an economic development standpoint, do not see the problem as an indicator of market weakness. Miami is still at the trading crossroads of the Western Hemisphere as the chief shipment point for exports and imports with Latin America and the Caribbean. Merchandise trade through the Miami Customs District exceeded $36 billion in 1995. The Port of Miami alone handles 42% of all U.S. Caribbean nations and 36 percent of all U.S. trade with Central and South America. In 1996, the port handled nearly 6 million tons of cargo valued at $15 billion. In 1997, the port is expecting a 6 to 8 percent increase in cargo tonnage. *Site Selection Feb/March 1997*

The sultry, sub-tropical climate against a backdrop of Spanish, Art Deco, and modern architecture makes Miami a uniquely cosmopolitan city. The Art Deco Historic District, also known as South Beach and located on the tip of Miami Beach, has in recent years developed an international reputation in the fashion, film and music industries. Greater Miami and the Beaches is now the third-largest center for film, television and print production in the country.

Long, warm summers are typical of this subtropical area, as are mild, dry winters. The marine influence is evidenced by the narrow daily range of temperature and the rapid warming of cold air masses. During the summer months, if you live closer to the ocean you will probably experience early morning rainfall rather than the afternoon showers which occur inland.

Hurricanes occasionally affect the Miami area. The months of greatest frequency are September and October. Destructive tornadoes are quite rare. Funnel clouds are occasionally sighted and a few touch the ground briefly, but significant destruction is unusual. Waterspouts are visible from the beaches during the summer months but seldom cause any damage. During June, July and August, there are numerous beautiful, but dangerous, lightning events.

General Rankings and Evaluative Comments

- Miami was ranked #56 out of 300 cities by *Money's* 1997 "Survey of the Best Places to Live." Criteria used: health services, crime, economy, housing, education, transportation, weather, leisure and the arts. The city was ranked #22 in 1996 and #67 in 1995. *Money, July 1997; Money, September 1996; Money, September 1995*

- *Ladies Home Journal* ranked America's 200 largest cities based on the qualities women care about most. Miami ranked 126 out of 200. Criteria: low crime rate, good public schools, well-paying jobs, quality health and child care, the presence of women in government, proportion of women-owned businesses, size of the wage gap with men, local economy, divorce rates, the ratio of single men to single women, whether there are laws that require at least the same number of public toilets for women as men, and the probability of good hair days. *Ladies Home Journal, November 1997*

- Miami was ranked #202 out of 219 cities in terms of children's health, safety, and economic well-being. Criteria: total population, percent population change, birth rate, child immunization rate, infant mortality rate, percent low birth weight infants, percent of births to teens, physician-to-population ratio, student-to-teacher ratio, dropout rate, unemployment rate, median family income, percent of children in poverty, violent and property crime rates, number of juvenile arrests for violent crimes as a percent of the total crime index, number of days with pollution standard index (PSI) over 100, pounds toxic releases per 1,000 people and number of superfund sites. *Zero Population Growth, Children's Environmental Index 1997*

- *Yahoo! Internet Life* selected "America's 100 Most Wired Cities & Towns". 50 cities were large and 50 cities were small. Miami ranked 10 out of 50 large cities. Criteria: Internet users per capita, number of networked computers, number of registered domain names, Internet backbone traffic, and the per-capita number of Web sites devoted to each city. *Yahoo! Internet Life, March 1998*

- *Reader's Digest* non-scientifically ranked the 12 largest U.S. metropolitan areas in terms of having the worst drivers. The Miami metro area ranked number 11. The areas were selected by asking approximately 1,200 readers on the *Reader's Digest* Web site and 200 interstate bus drivers and long-haul truckers which metro areas have the worst drivers. Their responses were factored in with fatality, insurance and rental-car rates to create the rankings. *Reader's Digest, March 1998*

- Baptist Health Systems, headquartered in Miami, is among the "100 Best Companies to Work for in America." Criteria: trust in management, pride in work/company, camaraderie, company responses to the Hewitt People Practices Inventory, and employee responses to their Great Place to Work survey. The companies also had to be at least 10 years old and have a minimum of 500 employees. *Fortune, January 12, 1998*

- According to *Working Mother,* "Florida stands out among the Southern states for its aggressive action to improve and expand child care. As we went to press, the governor had asked state lawmakers for a significant increase in state funds to create new child care slots. Some $49 million would be earmarked for a very important group—16,000 children of low-wage workers.

  In the past year the state also boosted funding for its prekindergarten program by $4 million, bringing its pre-K spending to $102 million. This translates into free pre-K for 27,000 kids, about 2,000 more than last year. This program is funded with state lottery money and is available in all of Florida's 67 school districts.

  The state has also improved its requirements for playground surfaces in child care setting. As of March 1997, all centers were required to have soft surfaces under playground equipment. This is a vital change, given that injuries from falls are the most common in child care.

  Finally, lawmakers approved a new program to recognize quality child care programs. Any facility that attains state or NAEYC accreditation can now post a 'good seal' certificate and will be listed in a state database as a 'Gold Seal' program—to show it meets high standards of care. So far, about 370 centers have received certificates, and about 800 more are in the pipeline." *Working Mother, July/August 1997*

Business Environment

STATE ECONOMY

State Economic Profile

"Florida's economy continues to expand strongly....

Florida is becoming increasingly dependent on the service industry for job growth. Currently, one in three Florida jobs is service-related. In the past year, however, nearly half of all jobs created were in the service industry. One in four jobs created was in business services, compared to one in seven for the U.S....

Florida's tourist industry continues to rebound and will be an important source of growth for this year. Household income growth and savings rates are high, and the values of individual stock portfolios has been booming, leaving households across the U.S. in good financial shape to take a vacation.

A risk to Florida's economy is a sharp slowing in population growth. In 1996, Florida experienced a population gain of only 1.5%, the slowest rate of growth since World War II. Contributing to the slower population growth is weaker retiree migration due to a slowing national retiree population growth.

Supporting growth are Florida's moderate climate, favorable quality of life, affordable housing, and low cost of doing business, which will continue to attract businesses and households. Population growth will continue to slow for the next decade as the number of people reaching retirement age nationwide is falling. Population growth will begin to accelerate once the baby boom generation hits retirement age beginning around 2005. One downside risk for Florida is its dependence on tourism and interest and property income that makes it vulnerable to national and international business cycles. Florida will remain one of the nation's fastest-growing economies through the remainder of this century." *National Association of Realtors, Economic Profiles: The Fifty States, July 1997*

IMPORTS/EXPORTS

Total Export Sales

Area	1993 ($000)	1994 ($000)	1995 ($000)	1996 ($000)	% Chg. 1993-96	% Chg. 1995-96
MSA[1]	8,264,304	9,266,746	10,200,815	10,681,236	29.2	4.7
U.S.	464,858,354	512,415,609	583,030,524	622,827,063	34.0	6.8

Note: (1) Metropolitan Statistical Area - see Appendix A for areas included
Source: U.S. Department of Commerce, International Trade Association, Metropolitan Area Exports: An Export Performance Report on Over 250 U.S. Cities, October 1997

Imports/Exports by Port

Type	Cargo Value			Share of U.S. Total	
	1995 (US$mil.)	1996 (US$mil.)	% Change 1995-1996	1995 (%)	1996 (%)
Imports	11,246	6,157	-45.25	2.87	1.60
Exports	7,806	8,963	14.82	3.41	3.78

Source: Global Trade Information Services, WaterBorne Trade Atlas 1997

CITY FINANCES

City Government Finances

Component	FY92 ($000)	FY92 (per capita $)
Revenue	380,926	1,051.68
Expenditure	358,865	990.77
Debt Outstanding	564,770	1,559.25
Cash & Securities	888,982	2,454.35

Source: U.S. Bureau of the Census, City Government Finances: 1991-92

City Government Revenue by Source

Source	FY92 ($000)	FY92 (per capita $)	FY92 (%)
From Federal Government	13,931	38.46	3.7
From State Governments	27,921	77.09	7.3
From Local Governments	6,608	18.24	1.7
Property Taxes	126,851	350.22	33.3
General Sales Taxes	0	0.00	0.0
Selective Sales Taxes	34,681	95.75	9.1
Income Taxes	0	0.00	0.0
Current Charges	56,342	155.55	14.8
Utility/Liquor Store	0	0.00	0.0
Employee Retirement[1]	74,743	206.35	19.6
Other	39,849	110.02	10.5

Note: (1) Excludes "city contributions," classified as "nonrevenue," intragovernmental transfers.
Source: U.S. Bureau of the Census, City Government Finances: 1991-92

City Government Expenditures by Function

Function	FY92 ($000)	FY92 (per capita $)	FY92 (%)
Educational Services	0	0.00	0.0
Employee Retirement[1]	35,004	96.64	9.8
Environment/Housing	95,188	262.80	26.5
Government Administration	24,610	67.94	6.9
Interest on General Debt	33,189	91.63	9.2
Public Safety	136,733	377.50	38.1
Social Services	1,125	3.11	0.3
Transportation	16,117	44.50	4.5
Utility/Liquor Store	0	0.00	0.0
Other	16,899	46.66	4.7

Note: (1) Payments to beneficiaries including withdrawal of contributions.
Source: U.S. Bureau of the Census, City Government Finances: 1991-92

Municipal Bond Ratings

Area	Moody's	S & P
Miami	Ba1	BB

Note: n/a not available; n/r not rated
Source: Moody's Bond Record, 2/98; Statistical Abstract of the U.S., 1997; Governing Magazine, 9/97, 3/98

POPULATION

Population Growth

Area	1980	1990	% Chg. 1980-90	July 1996 Estimate	% Chg. 1990-96
City	346,865	358,548	3.4	365,127	1.8
MSA[1]	1,625,781	1,937,094	19.1	2,076,175	7.2
U.S.	226,545,805	248,765,170	9.8	265,179,411	6.6

Note: (1) Metropolitan Statistical Area - see Appendix A for areas included
Source: 1980/1990 Census of Housing and Population, Summary Tape File 3C; Census Bureau Population Estimates

Population Characteristics

Race	City 1980 Population	%	City 1990 Population	%	% Chg. 1980-90	MSA[1] 1990 Population	%
White	225,200	64.9	236,040	65.8	4.8	1,415,346	73.1
Black	87,018	25.1	97,822	27.3	12.4	398,424	20.6
Amer Indian/Esk/Aleut	334	0.1	526	0.1	57.5	2,889	0.1
Asian/Pacific Islander	2,050	0.6	2,151	0.6	4.9	24,773	1.3
Other	32,263	9.3	22,009	6.1	-31.8	95,662	4.9
Hispanic Origin[2]	194,037	55.9	223,438	62.3	15.2	949,700	49.0

Note: (1) Metropolitan Statistical Area - see Appendix A for areas included;
(2) people of Hispanic origin can be of any race
Source: 1980/1990 Census of Housing and Population, Summary Tape File 3C

Ancestry

Area	German	Irish	English	Italian	U.S.	French	Polish	Dutch
City	1.9	1.6	1.9	1.0	2.2	0.9	0.7	0.2
MSA[1]	5.9	4.5	4.6	2.9	3.1	1.5	2.1	0.6
U.S.	23.3	15.6	13.1	5.9	5.3	4.2	3.8	2.5

Note: Figures are percentages and include persons that reported multiple ancestry (eg. if a person
reported being Irish and Italian, they were included in both columns); (1) Metropolitan Statistical Area -
see Appendix A for areas included
Source: 1990 Census of Population and Housing, Summary Tape File 3C

Age

Area	Median Age (Years)	Under 5	Under 18	18-24	25-44	45-64	65+	80+
City	35.9	7.1	23.0	9.1	29.6	21.6	16.7	4.1
MSA[1]	34.2	7.1	24.2	9.7	31.6	20.5	14.0	3.5
U.S.	32.9	7.3	25.6	10.5	32.6	18.7	12.5	2.8

Note: (1) Metropolitan Statistical Area - see Appendix A for areas included
Source: 1990 Census of Population and Housing, Summary Tape File 3C

Male/Female Ratio

Area	Number of males per 100 females (all ages)	Number of males per 100 females (18 years old+)
City	92.6	90.1
MSA[1]	91.6	88.1
U.S.	95.0	91.9

Note: (1) Metropolitan Statistical Area - see Appendix A for areas included
Source: 1990 Census of Population, General Population Characteristics

INCOME

Per Capita/Median/Average Income

Area	Per Capita ($)	Median Household ($)	Average Household ($)
City	9,799	16,925	26,507
MSA[1]	13,686	26,909	37,903
U.S.	14,420	30,056	38,453

Note: all figures are for 1989; (1) Metropolitan Statistical Area - see Appendix A for areas included
Source: 1990 Census of Population and Housing, Summary Tape File 3C

Household Income Distribution by Race

Income ($)	City (%)					U.S. (%)				
	Total	White	Black	Other	Hisp.[1]	Total	White	Black	Other	Hisp.[1]
Less than 5,000	17.1	15.2	22.6	16.1	17.5	6.2	4.8	15.2	8.6	8.8
5,000 - 9,999	15.0	14.1	18.3	13.5	15.4	9.3	8.6	14.2	9.9	11.1
10,000 - 14,999	13.3	12.5	15.3	13.8	13.7	8.8	8.5	11.0	9.8	11.0
15,000 - 24,999	19.5	19.3	19.5	22.2	20.9	17.5	17.3	18.9	18.5	20.5
25,000 - 34,999	12.7	12.6	11.6	17.4	12.8	15.8	16.1	14.2	15.4	16.4
35,000 - 49,999	10.6	11.6	7.9	9.2	10.2	17.9	18.6	13.3	16.1	16.0
50,000 - 74,999	6.9	8.3	3.4	5.2	6.3	15.0	15.8	9.3	13.4	11.1
75,000 - 99,999	2.4	2.9	0.9	2.2	1.8	5.1	5.5	2.6	4.7	3.1
100,000+	2.6	3.4	0.6	0.4	1.5	4.4	4.8	1.3	3.7	1.9

Note: all figures are for 1989; (1) people of Hispanic origin can be of any race
Source: 1990 Census of Population and Housing, Summary Tape File 3C

Effective Buying Income

Area	Per Capita ($)	Median Household ($)	Average Household ($)
City	10,351	18,910	29,009
MSA[1]	14,582	29,945	41,546
U.S.	15,444	33,201	41,849

Note: data as of 1/1/97; (1) Metropolitan Statistical Area - see Appendix A for areas included
Source: Standard Rate & Data Service, Newspaper Advertising Source, 2/98

Effective Household Buying Income Distribution

Area	% of Households Earning						
	$10,000 -$19,999	$20,000 -$34,999	$35,000 -$49,999	$50,000 -$74,999	$75,000 -$99,000	$100,000 -$124,999	$125,000 and up
City	23.7	21.9	11.4	8.5	3.0	1.1	1.7
MSA[1]	17.6	22.5	15.9	15.7	6.0	2.3	3.3
U.S.	16.5	23.4	18.3	18.2	6.4	2.1	2.4

Note: data as of 1/1/97; (1) Metropolitan Statistical Area - see Appendix A for areas included
Source: Standard Rate & Data Service, Newspaper Advertising Source, 2/98

Poverty Rates by Race and Age

Area	Total (%)	By Race (%)				By Age (%)		
		White	Black	Other	Hisp.[2]	Under 5 years old	Under 18 years old	65 years and over
City	31.2	25.0	46.0	32.0	28.5	46.9	44.1	32.2
MSA[1]	17.9	14.2	30.3	21.5	19.5	24.9	24.3	20.0
U.S.	13.1	9.8	29.5	23.1	25.3	20.1	18.3	12.8

Note: figures show the percent of people living below the poverty line in 1989. The average poverty threshold was $12,674 for a family of four in 1989; (1) Metropolitan Statistical Area - see Appendix A for areas included; (2) people of Hispanic origin can be of any race
Source: 1990 Census of Population and Housing, Summary Tape File 3C

EMPLOYMENT

Labor Force and Employment

Area	Civilian Labor Force			Workers Employed		
	Dec. '95	Dec. '96	% Chg.	Dec. '95	Dec. '96	% Chg.
City	179,578	181,432	1.0	161,848	164,547	1.7
MSA[1]	1,034,502	1,047,201	1.2	963,771	979,842	1.7
U.S.	134,583,000	136,742,000	1.6	127,903,000	130,785,000	2.3

Note: Data is not seasonally adjusted and covers workers 16 years of age and older;
(1) Metropolitan Statistical Area - see Appendix A for areas included
Source: Bureau of Labor Statistics, http://stats.bls.gov

Unemployment Rate

Area	1997											
	Jan.	Feb.	Mar.	Apr.	May	Jun.	Jul.	Aug.	Sep.	Oct.	Nov.	Dec.
City	11.2	10.0	10.1	10.5	10.8	11.4	10.3	10.0	10.5	10.0	10.1	9.3
MSA[1]	7.8	6.9	7.0	7.3	7.5	7.9	7.2	6.9	7.3	6.9	7.0	6.4
U.S.	5.9	5.7	5.5	4.8	4.7	5.2	5.0	4.8	4.7	4.4	4.3	4.4

Note: Data is not seasonally adjusted and covers workers 16 years of age and older; All figures are percentages; (1) Metropolitan Statistical Area - see Appendix A for areas included
Source: Bureau of Labor Statistics, http://stats.bls.gov

Employment by Industry

Sector	MSA[1]		U.S.
	Number of Employees	Percent of Total	Percent of Total
Services	316,100	32.2	29.0
Retail Trade	183,500	18.7	18.5
Government	136,900	13.9	16.1
Manufacturing	74,300	7.6	15.0
Finance/Insurance/Real Estate	68,300	7.0	5.7
Wholesale Trade	83,000	8.5	5.4
Transportation/Public Utilities	84,900	8.7	5.3
Construction	34,200	3.5	4.5
Mining	300	0.0	0.5

Note: Figures cover non-farm employment as of 12/97 and are not seasonally adjusted;
(1) Metropolitan Statistical Area - see Appendix A for areas included
Source: Bureau of Labor Statistics, http://stats.bls.gov

Employment by Occupation

Occupation Category	City (%)	MSA[1] (%)	U.S. (%)
White Collar	46.1	59.3	58.1
Executive/Admin./Management	8.7	12.4	12.3
Professional	8.6	12.1	14.1
Technical & Related Support	2.4	3.3	3.7
Sales	11.5	13.5	11.8
Administrative Support/Clerical	14.9	17.9	16.3
Blue Collar	31.6	24.2	26.2
Precision Production/Craft/Repair	12.2	10.7	11.3
Machine Operators/Assem./Insp.	8.9	5.6	6.8
Transportation/Material Movers	4.6	4.0	4.1
Cleaners/Helpers/Laborers	6.0	4.0	3.9
Services	20.4	14.9	13.2
Farming/Forestry/Fishing	1.9	1.7	2.5

Note: figures cover employed persons 16 years old and over;
(1) Metropolitan Statistical Area - see Appendix A for areas included
Source: 1990 Census of Population and Housing, Summary Tape File 3C

Occupational Employment Projections: 1995 - 2005

Occupations Expected to have the Largest Job Growth (ranked by numerical growth)	Fast-Growing Occupations[1] (ranked by percent growth)
1. Waiters & waitresses	1. Computer engineers
2. General managers & top executives	2. Systems analysts
3. Salespersons, retail	3. Home health aides
4. Cashiers	4. Personal and home care aides
5. Registered nurses	5. Operations research analysts
6. First line supervisor, sales & related	6. Human services workers
7. Guards	7. Residential counselors
8. Sales reps, non-technical, exc retail	8. Corrections officers & jailers
9. General office clerks	9. Database administrators
10. First line supervisors, clerical	10. Physical therapy assistants and aides

Projections cover Dade County.
Note: (1) Excludes occupations with total growth of less than 100 jobs
Source: Florida Department of Labor and Employment Security, Florida Industry and Occupational Employment Projections 1995-2005

Average Wages

Occupation	Wage	Occupation	Wage
Professional/Technical/Clerical	$/Week	**Health/Protective Services**	$/Week
Accountants III	811	Corrections Officers	614
Attorneys III	1,386	Firefighters	837
Budget Analysts III	-	Nurses, Licensed Practical II	-
Buyers/Contracting Specialists II	616	Nurses, Registered II	-
Clerks, Accounting III	435	Nursing Assistants II	-
Clerks, General III	486	Police Officers I	790
Computer Operators II	452	**Hourly Workers**	$/Hour
Computer Programmers II	599	Forklift Operators	10.35
Drafters II	547	General Maintenance Workers	8.93
Engineering Technicians III	624	Guards I	5.97
Engineering Technicians, Civil III	645	Janitors	6.22
Engineers III	1,049	Maintenance Electricians	15.61
Key Entry Operators I	304	Maintenance Electronics Techs II	18.57
Personnel Assistants III	546	Maintenance Machinists	16.68
Personnel Specialists III	770	Maintenance Mechanics, Machinery	13.49
Secretaries III	524	Material Handling Laborers	8.39
Switchboard Operator-Receptionist	343	Motor Vehicle Mechanics	14.49
Systems Analysts II	929	Shipping/Receiving Clerks	9.10
Systems Analysts Supervisor/Mgr II	-	Tool and Die Makers	15.21
Tax Collectors II	593	Truckdrivers, Tractor Trailer	16.94
Word Processors II	454	Warehouse Specialists	-

Note: Wage data includes full-time workers only for 11/96 and cover the Metropolitan Statistical Area (see Appendix A for areas included). Dashes indicate that data was not available.
Source: Bureau of Labor Statistics, Occupational Compensation Survey, 5/97

TAXES

Major State and Local Tax Rates

State Corp. Income (%)	State Personal Income (%)	Residential Property (effective rate per $100)	Sales & Use		State Gasoline (cents/ gallon)	State Cigarette (cents/ 20-pack)
			State (%)	Local (%)		
5.5[a]	None	n/a	6.0	0.5	12.8[b]	33.9

Note: Personal/corporate income tax rates as of 1/97. Sales, gasoline and cigarette tax rates as of 1/98; (a) 3.3% Alternative Minimum Tax. An exemption of $5,000 is allowed; (b) Rate is comprised of 4 cents excise and 8.8 cents motor carrier tax
Source: Federation of Tax Administrators, www.taxadmin.org; Washington D.C. Department of Finance and Revenue, Tax Rates and Tax Burdens in the District of Columbia: A Nationwide Comparison, June 1997; Chamber of Commerce

Total Taxes Per Capita and as a Percent of Income

Area	Per Capita Income ($)	Per Capita Taxes ($)			Taxes as Pct. of Income (%)		
		Total	Federal	State/Local	Total	Federal	State/Local
Florida	26,438	9,172	6,286	2,886	34.7	23.8	10.9
U.S.	26,187	9,205	6,127	3,078	35.2	23.4	11.8

Note: Figures are for 1997
Source: Tax Foundation, Web Site, www.taxfoundation.org

Estimated Tax Burden

Area	State Income	Local Income	Property	Sales	Total
Miami	0	0	4,050	553	4,603

Note: The numbers are estimates of taxes paid by a married couple with two kids and annual earnings of $65,000. Sales tax estimates assume they spend average amounts on food, clothing, household goods and gasoline. Property tax estimates assume they live in a $225,000 home.
Source: Kiplinger's Personal Finance Magazine, June 1997

COMMERCIAL REAL ESTATE

Office Market

Class/Location	Total Space (sq. ft.)	Vacant Space (sq. ft.)	Vac. Rate (%)	Under Constr. (sq. ft.)	Net Absorp. (sq. ft.)	Rental Rates ($/sq.ft./yr.)
Class A						
CBD	5,154,797	477,676	9.3	0	117,342	20.00-30.00
Outside CBD	4,324,438	358,801	8.3	630,000	406,454	19.00-30.00
Class B						
CBD	4,277,147	926,107	21.7	0	257,348	14.50-27.00
Outside CBD	13,969,954	1,092,438	7.8	0	277,083	10.00-30.00

Note: Data as of 10/97 and covers Miami-Dade County; CBD = Central Business District; n/a not available;
Source: Society of Industrial and Office Realtors, 1998 Comparative Statistics of Industrial and Office Real Estate Markets

"Miami is seeing robust tourist trade, continued foreign immigration, and strong trade and financial ties to Latin America. The economy should continue to register solid economic gains even though its growth may lag Florida as a whole. Coral Gables will continue to be the location of choice for Latin American firms seeking a new United States outpost. The increased availability of financing will play an important role in the stabilization of values and the acceptance of lower returns by investors in the marketplace. Heightened sales activity and sales prices, both growing by more than 6 percent, are anticipated by SIOR's reporter. Rental rates, new construction, and absorption will increase by more modest amounts between 1 and 5 percent. Vacancies also should continue to tighten accordingly." *Society of Industrial and Office Realtors, 1998 Comparative Statistics of Industrial and Office Real Estate Markets*

Industrial Market

Location	Total Space (sq. ft.)	Vacant Space (sq. ft.)	Vac. Rate (%)	Under Constr. (sq. ft.)	Net Absorp. (sq. ft.)	Gross Lease ($/sq.ft./yr.)
Central City	62,480,000	3,750,000	6.0	10,000	150,000	2.35-3.35
Suburban	92,500,000	4,400,000	4.8	750,000	2,420,000	5.35-7.25

Note: Data as of 10/97 and covers Miami; n/a not available
Source: Society of Industrial and Office Realtors, 1998 Comparative Statistics of Industrial and Office Real Estate Markets

"Most new development will be concentrated in the Airport/West Dade submarket. About 1.2 million sq. ft. west of the airport is scheduled to come on line during 1998, piggy-backing on the two million sq. ft. completed last year. Construction and sales prices continue to rise, but suburban sales prices still surpass replacement costs. User appetite for space should be strong through the remainder of the century. Over the next few years, industrial employment is projected to increase by 11 percent in the Airport/West submarket. International trade and tourism will remain the market's stimuli for growth making it sensitive to global economic trends. Industrial condominiums have taken hold in the area and small businesses are thinking positively about such properties for the first time." *Society of Industrial and Office Realtors, 1998 Comparative Statistics of Industrial and Office Real Estate Markets*

Retail Market

Shopping Center Inventory (sq. ft.)	Shopping Center Construction (sq. ft.)	Construction as a Percent of Inventory (%)	Torto Wheaton Rent Index[1] ($/sq. ft.)
32,943,000	853,000	2.6	14.37

Note: Data as of 1997 and covers the Metropolitan Statistical Area - see Appendix A for areas included; (1) Index is based on a model that predicts what the average rent should be for leases with certain characteristics, in certain locations during certain years.
Source: National Association of Realtors, 1997-1998 Market Conditions Report

"Retail trade is indeed one of Miami's most important sectors. Retail accounts for 27% of the area's jobs, buoyed by the strength of the tourism industry. The economic impact of tourism is estimated to be $13.5 billion. The demographics of Miami's millions of visitors have been changing. In 1989, 61% of the area's tourists were Americans; in 1996, and estimated 61% were foreign. Miami's retail vacancy rate has stabilized, while the rent index rose 4% last year. Shopping center completions remained robust at 850,000 square feet, with that rate expected to continue through 2000." *National Association of Realtors, 1997-1998 Market Conditions Report*

COMMERCIAL UTILITIES

Typical Monthly Electric Bills

Area	Commercial Service ($/month)		Industrial Service ($/month)	
	12 kW demand 1,500 kWh	100 kW demand 30,000 kWh	1,000 kW demand 400,000 kWh	20,000 kW demand 10,000,000 kWh
City	137	2,333	27,081	554,864
U.S.	162	2,360	25,590	545,677

Note: Based on rates in effect July 1, 1997
Source: Edison Electric Institute, Typical Residential, Commercial and Industrial Bills, Summer 1997

TRANSPORTATION

Transportation Statistics

Avg. travel time to work (min.)	23.8
Interstate highways	I-95
Bus lines	
In-city	Metro Dade Transit Agency, 743 vehicles
Inter-city	1
Passenger air service	
Airport	Miami International
Airlines	85 scheduled airlines
Aircraft departures	140,100 (1995)
Enplaned passengers	12,030,812 (1995)
Rail service	Amtrak; Tri-Rail; Metro Rail
Motor freight carriers	57
Major waterways/ports	Port of Miami; Atlantic Intracoastal

Source: OAG, Business Travel Planner, Summer 1997; Editor & Publisher Market Guide, 1998; FAA Airport Activity Statistics, 1996; Amtrak National Time Table, Northeast Timetable, Fall/Winter 1997-98; 1990 Census of Population and Housing, STF 3C; Chamber of Commerce/Economic Development 1997; Jane's Urban Transport Systems 1997-98; Transit Fact Book 1997

A survey of 90,000 airline passengers during the first half of 1997 ranked most of the largest airports in the U.S. Miami International ranked number 28 out of 36. Criteria: cleanliness, quality of restaurants, attractiveness, speed of baggage delivery, ease of reaching gates, available ground transportation, ease of following signs and closeness of parking. *Plog Research Inc., First Half 1997*

Means of Transportation to Work

Area	Car/Truck/Van		Public Transportation			Bicycle	Walked	Other Means	Worked at Home
	Drove Alone	Car-pooled	Bus	Subway	Railroad				
City	60.9	18.0	11.8	0.6	0.2	0.6	4.2	1.8	1.9
MSA[1]	72.4	15.6	4.8	0.7	0.1	0.5	2.5	1.3	2.0
U.S.	73.2	13.4	3.0	1.5	0.5	0.4	3.9	1.2	3.0

Note: figures shown are percentages and only include workers 16 years old and over;
(1) Metropolitan Statistical Area - see Appendix A for areas included
Source: 1990 Census of Population and Housing, Summary Tape File 3C

BUSINESSES

Major Business Headquarters

Company Name	1997 Rankings	
	Fortune 500	Forbes 500
Braman Enterprises	-	455
Coulter	-	301
Knight-Ridder	474	-
Potamkin Cos	-	145
Ryder System	258	-
Southern Wine & Spirits	-	68

Note: Companies listed are located in the city; Dashes indicate no ranking
Fortune 500: companies that produce a 10-K are ranked 1 - 500 based on 1996 revenue
Forbes 500: private companies are ranked 1 - 500 based on 1996 revenue
Source: Forbes 12/1/97; Fortune 4/28/97

Fast-Growing Businesses

Miami is home to one of *Business Week's* "hot growth" companies: Vitech America. Criteria: sales and earnings, return on capital and stock price. *Business Week, 5/26/97*

According to *Fortune*, Miami is home to one of America's 100 fastest-growing companies: MasTec. Companies were ranked based on three years' earnings-per-share growth using least squares analysis to smooth out distortions. Criteria for inclusion: public companies with sales of at least $50 million. Companies that lost money in the most recent quarter, or ended in the red for the past four quarters as a whole, were not eligible. Limited partnerships and REITs were also not considered. *Fortune, 9/29/97*

Miami was ranked #15 out of 24 (#1 is best) in terms of the best-performing local stocks in 1996 according to the Money/Norby Cities Index. The index measures stocks of companies that have headquarters in 24 metro areas. *Money, 2/7/97*

Women-Owned Businesses: Number, Employment, Sales and Share

Area	Women-Owned Businesses in 1996				Share of Women-Owned Businesses in 1996	
	Number	Employment	Sales ($000)	Rank[2]	Percent (%)	Rank[3]
MSA[1]	77,900	242,200	29,385,800	16	35.7	35

Note: (1) Metropolitan Statistical Area - see Appendix A for areas included; (2) Calculated on an averaging of number of businesses, employment and sales and ranges from 1 to 50 where 1 is best; (3) Ranges from 1 to 50 where 1 is best
Source: The National Foundation for Women Business Owners, 1996 Facts on Women-Owned Businesses: Trends in the Top 50 Metropolitan Areas, March 26, 1997

Women-Owned Businesses: Growth

Area	Growth in Women-Owned Businesses (% change from 1987 to 1996)				Relative Growth in the Number of Women-Owned and All Businesses (% change from 1987 to 1996)			
	Num.	Empl.	Sales	Rank[2]	Women-Owned	All Firms	Absolute Difference	Relative Difference
MSA[1]	117.3	258.2	306.1	6	117.3	76.4	40.9	1.5:1

Note: (1) Metropolitan Statistical Area - see Appendix A for areas included; (2) Calculated on an averaging of the percent growth of number of businesses, employment and sales and ranges from 1 to 50 where 1 is best
Source: The National Foundation for Women Business Owners, 1996 Facts on Women-Owned Businesses: Trends in the Top 50 Metropolitan Areas, March 26, 1997

Minority Business Opportunity

Miami is home to one company which is on the Black Enterprise Industrial/Service 100 list (largest based on gross sales): Urban Organization Inc. (general contracting, engineering and construction mgmt.). Criteria: 1) operational in previous calendar year; 2) at least 51% black-owned; 3) manufactures/owns the product it sells or provides industrial or consumer services. Brokerages, real estate firms and firms that provide professional services are not eligible. *Black Enterprise, July 1997*

78 of the 500 largest Hispanic-owned companies in the U.S. are located in Miami. *Hispanic Business, June 1997*

Miami is home to companies which are on the Hispanic Business Fastest-Growing 100 list (greatest sales growth from 1992 to 1996): Edwards Paper Co. (toilet paper & paper towel mfg.), MasTec (telecom. infrastructure const.), Generic Chemical (water treatment chem. mfg.), Rovel Construction (general contracting), Eagle Cos. (intl. logistics/transport. svcs.), Bermello, Ajamil & Partners (arch. & engr. svcs.), India Beverages of Florida (beverage & food distr.), International Shipping Bureau (marine consulting svcs.), Magnum Construction Management Corp. (general contracting), Microretailing (microcomputer whsl. & svcs.), Caremed Health Systems (healthcare mgmt. svcs.), Supreme International Corp. (men's apparel design & whsl.), Ibiley School Uniforms (school uniform sales), Metro USA (law enforcement equip. whsl.), and R.C. Aluminum Industries (window mfg.) *Hispanic Business, July/August 1997*

Miami was listed among the top 25 metropolitan areas in terms of the number of Hispanic-owned companies. The city was ranked number 2 with 136,204 companies. *Hispanic Business, May 1997*

Small Business Opportunity

According to *Forbes*, Miami is home to two of America's 200 best small companies: Benihana, Supreme International. Criteria: companies must be publicly traded, U.S.-based corporations with latest 12-month sales of between $5 and $350 million. Earnings must be at least $1 million for the 12-month period. Limited partnerships, REITs and closed-end mutual funds were not considered. Banks, S&Ls and electric utilities were not included. *Forbes, November 3, 1997*

HOTELS & MOTELS

Hotels/Motels

Area	Hotels/Motels	Rooms	Luxury-Level Hotels/Motels		Average Minimum Rates ($)		
			♦♦♦♦	♦♦♦♦♦	♦♦	♦♦♦	♦♦♦♦
City	31	7,695	1	0	83	143	235
Airport	20	6,097	0	0	n/a	n/a	n/a
Suburbs	99	15,650	3	0	n/a	n/a	n/a
Total	150	29,442	4	0	n/a	n/a	n/a

Note: n/a not available; Classifications range from one diamond (budget properties with basic amenities) to five diamond (luxury properties with the finest service, rooms and facilities).
Source: OAG, Business Travel Planner, Summer 1997

CONVENTION CENTERS

Major Convention Centers

Center Name	Meeting Rooms	Exhibit Space (sf)
Coconut Grove Convention Center	10	150,000
Miami Convention Center	37	28,000
Radisson Centre/Radisson Mart Plaza Hotel	32	137,600
Dade County Youth Fair & Exposition Center	12	110,000
Mahi Shrine Auditorium	1	18,000

Source: Trade Shows Worldwide 1997

Living Environment

COST OF LIVING

Cost of Living Index

Composite Index	Housing	Utilities	Groceries	Health Care	Trans-portation	Misc. Goods/Services
106.4	108.1	108.8	101.1	111.9	117.6	103.0

Note: U.S. = 100; Figures are for the Metropolitan Statistical Area - see Appendix A for areas included
Source: ACCRA, Cost of Living Index, 3rd Quarter 1997

HOUSING

Median Home Prices and Housing Affordability

Area	Median Price[2] 3rd Qtr. 1997 ($)	HOI[3] 3rd Qtr. 1997	Afford-ability Rank[4]
MSA[1]	102,000	59.7	150
U.S.	127,000	63.7	–

Note: (1) Metropolitan Statistical Area - see Appendix A for areas included; (2) U.S. figures calculated from the sales of 625,000 new and existing homes in 195 markets; (3) Housing Opportunity Index - percent of homes sold that were within the reach of the median income household at the prevailing mortgage interest rate; (4) Rank is from 1-195 with 1 being most affordable
Source: National Association of Home Builders, Housing Opportunity Index, 3rd Quarter 1997

It is projected that the median price of existing single-family homes in the metro area will decrease by -5.2% in 1998. Nationwide, home prices are projected to increase 6.6%.
Kiplinger's Personal Finance Magazine, January 1998

Average New Home Price

Area	Price ($)
MSA[1]	139,900
U.S.	135,710

Note: Figures are based on a new home with 1,800 sq. ft. of living area on an 8,000 sq. ft. lot; (1) Metropolitan Statistical Area - see Appendix A for areas included
Source: ACCRA, Cost of Living Index, 3rd Quarter 1997

Average Apartment Rent

Area	Rent ($/mth)
MSA[1]	725
U.S.	569

Note: Figures are based on an unfurnished two bedroom, 1-1/2 or 2 bath apartment, approximately 950 sq. ft. in size, excluding all utilities except water; (1) Metropolitan Statistical Area - see Appendix A for areas included
Source: ACCRA, Cost of Living Index, 3rd Quarter 1997

RESIDENTIAL UTILITIES

Average Residential Utility Costs

Area	All Electric ($/mth)	Part Electric ($/mth)	Other Energy ($/mth)	Phone ($/mth)
MSA[1]	115.52	–	–	16.27
U.S.	109.40	55.25	43.64	19.48

Note: (1) (1) Metropolitan Statistical Area - see Appendix A for areas included
Source: ACCRA, Cost of Living Index, 3rd Quarter 1997

HEALTH CARE

Average Health Care Costs

Area	Hospital ($/day)	Doctor ($/visit)	Dentist ($/visit)
MSA[1]	466.00	68.00	53.00
U.S.	392.91	48.76	60.84

Note: Hospital - based on a semi-private room. Doctor - based on a general practitioner's routine exam of an established patient. Dentist - based on adult teeth cleaning and periodic oral exam; (1) Metropolitan Statistical Area - see Appendix A for areas included
Source: ACCRA, Cost of Living Index, 3rd Quarter 1997

Distribution of Office-Based Physicians

Area	Family/Gen. Practitioners	Specialists		
		Medical	Surgical	Other
MSA[1]	747	1,769	1,220	1,228

Note: Data as of 12/31/96; (1) Metropolitan Statistical Area - see Appendix A for areas included
Source: American Medical Assn., Physician Characteristics & Distribution in the U.S., 1997-1998

Hospitals

Miami has 14 general medical and surgical hospitals, 3 psychiatric, 1 eye, ear, nose and throat, 1 other specialty, 1 children's general. *AHA Guide to the Healthcare Field 1997-98*

According to *U.S. News and World Report,* Miami has 2 of the best hospitals in the U.S.: **University of Miami (Jackson Memorial Hospital)**, noted for AIDS, gastroenterology, pediatrics; **University of Miami (Bascom Palmer Eye Institute)**, noted for ophthalmology; *U.S. News and World Report, "America's Best Hospitals", 7/28/97*

Columbia Cedars Medical Center; Columbia Kendall Medical Center; Columbia Aventura Hospital and Medical Center are among the 100 best-run hospitals in the U.S.
Modern Healthcare, January 5, 1998

EDUCATION

Public School District Statistics

District Name	Num. Sch.	Enroll.	Classroom Teachers[1]	Pupils per Teacher	Minority Pupils (%)	Current Exp.[2] ($/pupil)
Dade County School District	322	333,817	16,692	20.0	85.8	5,550

Note: Data covers the 1995-1996 school year unless otherwise noted; (1) Excludes teachers reported as working in school district offices rather than in schools; (2) Based on 1993-94 enrollment collected by the Census Bureau, not the enrollment figure shown in column 3; SD = School District; ISD = Independent School District; n/a not available
Source: National Center for Education Statistics, Common Core of Data Survey; Bureau of the Census

Educational Quality

School District	Education Quotient[1]	Graduate Outcome[2]	Community Index[3]	Resource Index[4]
Miami	79.0	61.0	56.0	120.0

Note: Nearly 1,000 secondary school districts were rated in terms of educational quality. The scores range from a low of 50 to a high of 150; (1) Average of the Graduate Outcome, Community and Resource indexes; (2) Based on graduation rates and college board scores (SAT/ACT); (3) Based on the surrounding community's average level of education and the area's average income level; (4) Based on teacher salaries, per-pupil expenditures and student-teacher ratios.
Source: Expansion Management, Ratings Issue 1997

Educational Attainment by Race

Area	High School Graduate (%)					Bachelor's Degree (%)				
	Total	White	Black	Other	Hisp.[2]	Total	White	Black	Other	Hisp.[2]
City	47.6	50.6	39.7	42.6	43.0	12.8	15.5	4.9	10.7	10.5
MSA[1]	65.0	67.6	56.0	57.0	55.1	18.8	20.8	9.9	17.1	14.1
U.S.	75.2	77.9	63.1	60.4	49.8	20.3	21.5	11.4	19.4	9.2

Note: figures shown cover persons 25 years old and over; (1) Metropolitan Statistical Area - see Appendix A for areas included; (2) people of Hispanic origin can be of any race
Source: 1990 Census of Population and Housing, Summary Tape File 3C

School Enrollment by Type

Area	Preprimary				Elementary/High School			
	Public		Private		Public		Private	
	Enrollment	%	Enrollment	%	Enrollment	%	Enrollment	%
City	2,688	61.0	1,720	39.0	53,740	90.3	5,750	9.7
MSA[1]	14,892	43.9	19,029	56.1	281,730	86.5	44,139	13.5
U.S.	2,679,029	59.5	1,824,256	40.5	38,379,689	90.2	4,187,099	9.8

Note: figures shown cover persons 3 years old and over;
(1) Metropolitan Statistical Area - see Appendix A for areas included
Source: 1990 Census of Population and Housing, Summary Tape File 3C

School Enrollment by Race

Area	Preprimary (%)				Elementary/High School (%)			
	White	Black	Other	Hisp.[1]	White	Black	Other	Hisp.[1]
City	48.8	46.8	4.4	40.9	51.7	40.5	7.8	53.5
MSA[2]	66.7	28.6	4.6	35.5	62.4	30.2	7.4	47.6
U.S.	80.4	12.5	7.1	7.8	74.1	15.6	10.3	12.5

Note: figures shown cover persons 3 years old and over; (1) people of Hispanic origin can be of any race; (2) Metropolitan Statistical Area - see Appendix A for areas included
Source: 1990 Census of Population and Housing, Summary Tape File 3C

SAT/ACT Scores

Area/District	1997 SAT				1997 ACT	
	Percent of Graduates Tested (%)	Average Math Score	Average Verbal Score	Average Combined Score	Percent of Graduates Tested (%)	Average Composite Score
Dade County SD	39	466	463	929	26	19.0
State	50	499	499	998	36	20.7
U.S.	42	511	505	1,016	36	21.0

Note: Math and verbal SAT scores are out of a possible 800; ACT scores are out of a possible 36
Caution: Comparing or ranking states/cities on the basis of SAT/ACT scores alone is invalid and strongly discouraged by the The College Board and The American College Testing Program as students who take the tests are self-selected and do not represent the entire student population.
Source: Dade County Public Schools, Office of Educational Accountability, 1997; American College Testing Program, 1997; College Board, 1997

Classroom Teacher Salaries in Public Schools

District	B.A. Degree		M.A. Degree		Ph.D. Degree	
	Min. ($)	Max. ($)	Min. ($)	Max. ($)	Min. ($)	Max. ($)
Miami	28,150	50,500	31,150	53,500	35,150	57,500
Average[1]	26,120	39,270	28,175	44,667	31,643	49,825

Note: Salaries are for 1996-1997; (1) Based on all school districts covered; n/a not available
Source: American Federation of Teachers (unpublished data)

Higher Education

Two-Year Colleges		Four-Year Colleges		Medical Schools	Law Schools	Voc/ Tech
Public	Private	Public	Private			
1	3	1	7	1	2	26

Source: College Blue Book, Occupational Education 1997; Medical School Admission Requirements, 1998-99; Peterson's Guide to Two-Year Colleges, 1997; Peterson's Guide to Four-Year Colleges, 1997; Barron's Guide to Law Schools 1997

MAJOR EMPLOYERS

Major Employers

American Bankers Insurance	Baptist Hospital of Miami
Carnival Corp.	Cedars Medical Center
Hotelerama Associates	John Alden Life Insurance
Mercy Hospital	Miami Jewish Home & Hospital for the Aged
Mount Sinai Medical Center of Greater Miami	North Shore Medical Center
Royal Caribbean Cruises Ltd.	Ryder Truck Rental
South Miami Hospital	Kenbourne (groceries)
Variety Children's Hospital	Worldex Travel Center
Diatomite Corp. (nonmetallic mineral services)	Coulter Corp. (laboratory apparatus)

Note: companies listed are located in the city
Source: Dun's Business Rankings 1997; Ward's Business Directory, 1997

PUBLIC SAFETY

Crime Rate

Area	All Crimes	Violent Crimes				Property Crimes		
		Murder	Forcible Rape	Robbery	Aggrav. Assault	Burglary	Larceny -Theft	Motor Vehicle Theft
City	13,745.8	32.2	52.2	1,334.9	1,695.2	2,546.7	6,086.4	1,998.3
Suburbs[1]	n/a	n/a	n/a	n/a	n/a	n/a	n/a	n/a
MSA[2]	n/a	n/a	n/a	n/a	n/a	n/a	n/a	n/a
U.S.	5,078.9	7.4	36.1	202.4	388.2	943.0	2,975.9	525.9

Note: Crime rate is the number of crimes per 100,000 pop.; (1) defined as all areas within the MSA but located outside the central city; (2) Metropolitan Statistical Area - see Appendix A for areas incl.
Source: FBI Uniform Crime Reports 1996

RECREATION

Culture and Recreation

Museums	Symphony Orchestras	Opera Companies	Dance Companies	Professional Theatres	Zoos	Pro Sports Teams
16	3	1	4	4	1	4

Source: International Directory of the Performing Arts, 1996; Official Museum Directory, 1998; Chamber of Commerce/Economic Development 1997

Library System

The Miami-Dade Public Library System has 31 branches, holdings of 3,983,968 volumes and a budget of $34,815,998 (1995-1996). *American Library Directory, 1997-1998*

MEDIA

Newspapers

Name	Type	Freq.	Distribution	Circulation
Aventura News	n/a	1x/wk	Local	30,000
Coral Gables News	General	2x/wk	Local	15,000
Daily Business Review	n/a	5x/wk	Area	10,979
Diario las Americas	Hispanic	6x/wk	Local	68,374
El Nuevo Herald	Hispanic	7x/wk	Area	101,389
El Nuevo Patria	Hispanic	1x/wk	Local	28,000
EXITO	Hispanic	1x/wk	National	80,000
The Flyer	n/a	1x/wk	Area	1,030,000
Hialeah/Opa-Locka News	General	2x/wk	Local	15,000
Kendall Gazette	General	2x/wk	Local	30,000
Kendall News	n/a	2x/wk	Local	18,000
Libre Weekly	Hispanic	1x/wk	Area	27,000
Miami Beach News	n/a	2x/wk	Local	4,000
Miami Herald	n/a	7x/wk	Area	419,187
Miami Laker	General	1x/mo	Local	27,000
The Miami Times	Black	1x/wk	Area	28,170
North Bay Village News	General	2x/wk	Local	6,000
North Miami Beach News	General	2x/wk	Local	90,000
North Miami News	n/a	2x/wk	Local	15,000
Prensa Grafica	Hispanic	1x/wk	Local	28,000
River Cities Gazette	n/a	1x/wk	Local	12,000
South Dade News	General	2x/wk	Local	15,500
South Miami News	General	2x/wk	Local	7,500
South West News	General	2x/wk	Local	13,000
The Sun Post	General	1x/wk	Local	45,000
TWN	Alternative	1x/wk	Area	32,000
The Wire	Alternative	1x/wk	Local	13,000

Note: Includes newspapers with circulations of 1,000 or more located in the city; n/a not available
Source: Burrelle's Media Directory, 1998 Edition

AM Radio Stations

Call Letters	Freq. (kHz)	Target Audience	Station Format	Music Format
WIOD	610	General	N/T	n/a
WWFE	670	General	M/N/S	Spanish
WAQI	710	n/a	N/T	n/a
WAXY	790	General	E/M/N/S/T	n/a
WINZ	940	General	N/T	n/a
WQBA	1140	Hispanic	N/S/T	n/a
WCMQ	1210	Hispanic	N/S/T	n/a
WJNA	1230	General	M	Urban Contemporary
WSUA	1260	Hispanic	M/N/S/T	Adult Contemporary
WDCF	1350	Hispanic	M/S	Spanish
WKAT	1360	Hispanic	M/N/S/T	Spanish
WFTL	1400	n/a	T	n/a
WOCN	1450	General	N/S/T	n/a
WMBM	1490	n/a	E/M/N/S/T	Christian
WRHC	1550	General	T	n/a

Note: Stations included broadcast in the Miami metro area; n/a not available
Station Format: E = Educational; M = Music; N = News; S = Sports; T = Talk
Source: Burrelle's Media Directory, 1998 Edition

FM Radio Stations

Call Letters	Freq. (mHz)	Target Audience	Station Format	Music Format
WDNA	88.9	General	M	Jazz
WMCU	89.7	Religious	M/N/S	Adult Contemporary/Christian
WVUM	90.5	Religious	M/N/S	n/a
WLRN	91.3	General	M	Alternative/Big Band/Classical/Jazz
WCMQ	92.3	Hispanic	M	Oldies/Spanish
WTMI	93.1	General	M	Classical
WLVE	93.9	General	M	Jazz
WZTA	94.9	General	M/N/S	AOR/Alternative
WPOW	96.5	General	M	Contemporary Top 40
WFLC	97.3	General	M/N	Adult Contemporary
WRTO	98.3	n/a	M	Adult Contemporary
WEDR	99.1	Black	M	Urban Contemporary
WLYF	101.5	General	M/N/S	Adult Contemporary
WMXJ	102.7	General	M	Oldies
WPLL	103.5	General	M	Adult Contemporary
WHQT	105.1	n/a	M	n/a
WRMA	106.7	Hispanic	M	Adult Contemporary
WAMR	107.5	Hispanic	M	Adult Contemporary

Note: Stations included broadcast in the Miami metro area; n/a not available
Station Format: E = Educational; M = Music; N = News; S = Sports; T = Talk
Music Format: AOR = Album Oriented Rock; MOR = Middle-of-the-Road
Source: Burrelle's Media Directory, 1998 Edition

Television Stations

Name	Ch.	Affiliation	Type	Owner
WPBT	2	PBS	Public	Community TV Foundation of South Florida Inc.
WFOR	4	CBS	Commercial	Westinghouse Broadcasting Company
WTVJ	6	NBC	Commercial	General Electric Company
WSVN	7	Fox/CNN	Commercial	Edmund N. Ansin
WPLG	10	ABC	Commercial	Post Newsweek
WLRN	17	PBS	Public	School Board of Dade County
WLTV	23	Univision	Commercial	Univision Communications Inc.
WBFS	33	n/a	Commercial	United Paramount Network
WCTD	35	n/a	Commercial	Paxson Communications Corporation
WSCV	51	Telemundo	Commercial	Telemundo Group Inc.

Note: Stations included broadcast in the Miami metro area
Source: Burrelle's Media Directory, 1998 Edition

CLIMATE

Average and Extreme Temperatures

Temperature	Jan	Feb	Mar	Apr	May	Jun	Jul	Aug	Sep	Oct	Nov	Dec	Ann
Extreme High (°F)	88	89	92	96	95	98	98	98	97	95	89	87	98
Average High (°F)	75	77	79	82	85	88	89	90	88	85	80	77	83
Average Temp. (°F)	68	69	72	75	79	82	83	83	82	78	73	69	76
Average Low (°F)	59	60	64	68	72	75	76	76	76	72	66	61	69
Extreme Low (°F)	30	35	32	42	55	60	69	68	68	53	39	30	30

Note: Figures cover the years 1948-1990
Source: National Climatic Data Center, International Station Meteorological Climate Summary, 3/95

Average Precipitation/Snowfall/Humidity

Precip./Humidity	Jan	Feb	Mar	Apr	May	Jun	Jul	Aug	Sep	Oct	Nov	Dec	Ann
Avg. Precip. (in.)	1.9	2.0	2.3	3.0	6.2	8.7	6.1	7.5	8.2	6.6	2.7	1.8	57.1
Avg. Snowfall (in.)	0	0	0	0	0	0	0	0	0	0	0	0	0
Avg. Rel. Hum. 7am (%)	84	84	82	80	81	84	84	86	88	87	85	84	84
Avg. Rel. Hum. 4pm (%)	59	57	57	57	62	68	66	67	69	65	63	60	63

Note: Figures cover the years 1948-1990; Tr = Trace amounts (<0.05 in. of rain; <0.5 in. of snow)
Source: National Climatic Data Center, International Station Meteorological Climate Summary, 3/95

Weather Conditions

Temperature			Daytime Sky			Precipitation		
32°F & below	45°F & below	90°F & above	Clear	Partly cloudy	Cloudy	0.01 inch or more precip.	0.1 inch or more snow/ice	Thunder-storms
< 1	7	55	48	263	54	128	0	74

Note: Figures are average number of days per year and covers the years 1948-1990
Source: National Climatic Data Center, International Station Meteorological Climate Summary, 3/95

AIR & WATER QUALITY

Maximum Pollutant Concentrations

	Particulate Matter (ug/m³)	Carbon Monoxide (ppm)	Sulfur Dioxide (ppm)	Nitrogen Dioxide (ppm)	Ozone (ppm)	Lead (ug/m³)
MSA[1] Level	62	5	0.005	0.016	0.10	0.01
NAAQS[2]	150	9	0.140	0.053	0.12	1.50
Met NAAQS?	Yes	Yes	Yes	Yes	Yes	Yes

Note: (1) Metropolitan Statistical Area - see Appendix A for areas included; (2) National Ambient Air Quality Standards; ppm = parts per million; ug/m³ = micrograms per cubic meter; n/a not available
Source: EPA, National Air Quality and Emissions Trends Report, 1996

Pollutant Standards Index

In the Miami MSA (see Appendix A for areas included), the Pollutant Standards Index (PSI) exceeded 100 on 1 day in 1996. A PSI value greater than 100 indicates that air quality would be in the unhealthful range on that day. *EPA, National Air Quality and Emissions Trends Report, 1996*

Drinking Water

Water System Name	Pop. Served	Primary Water Source Type	Number of Violations in Fiscal Year 1997	Type of Violation/ Contaminants
MDWASA-Main System	1,705,156	Ground	None	None

Note: Data as of January 16, 1998
Source: EPA, Office of Ground Water and Drinking Water, Safe Drinking Water Information System

Miami tap water is alkaline, soft and fluoridated.
Editor & Publisher Market Guide, 1998

Mobile, Alabama

Background

Mobile is located on the shores of Mobile Bay and the west bank of the Mobile River. It is Alabama's only seaport.

As early as 1519 the Spaniards had explored the site. In 1702 Fort Louis de la Mobile was established as a trading post by French colonists under Jean-Baptiste Le Moyne de Bienville. The fort was moved to the present site in 1711 due to floods and famine. It served as the capital of French Louisiana and later the Louisiana Territory until 1720. Mobile was an adaptation of the name of a local Native American tribe, Maubilian, meaning "canoe paddler".

Control over Mobile changed hands several times during its early history. France ceded it to Britain in 1763, Spain took it in 1780, the United States seized it in 1813, and then purchased it from Spain in 1819.

During this time the city grew into an important seaport handling the flourishing cotton trade. It became one of the Confederacy's most important ports during the Civil War. It functioned until August of 1864, when the Battle of Mobile Bay was won by the Federal Admiral David G. Farragut. The city itself did not fall until April 12, 1865, three days after the surrender at Appomattox.

In 1879 the municipality went bankrupt, but the economy eventually improved and in 1887 Mobile was again chartered as a city. By the start of World War II Mobile had become a shipbuilding center. It now ranks as one of the major transportation hubs in the Southeast.

Manufacturing, government services and shipping comprise the foundation of Mobile's economy. The city's varied manufactures include pulp, paper, chemical and petroleum products, and textiles. Other products include aircraft engines, cement, aluminum, rayon fibers, clothing, naval stores, bakery goods, pumps, batteries, and paint.

The summers are consistently warm, with the day beginning in the low 70s and the temperature rising rapidly before noon to the high 80s or low 90s when it is checked by the onset of sea breezes.

Winter weather is generally mild except for occasional invasions of cold air that last for about three days.

The yearly rainfall is among the highest in the country. It generally consists of showers with long periods of continuous rain rarely occurring. The area is subject to hurricanes from the West Indies, the western Caribbean, and the Gulf of Mexico.

During the spring of each year Mobile celebrates Mardi Gras ("fat Tuesday") with carnival activities, dances, parties and parades.

General Rankings and Evaluative Comments

■ Mobile was ranked #74 out of 300 cities by *Money's* 1997 "Survey of the Best Places to Live." Criteria used: health services, crime, economy, housing, education, transportation, weather, leisure and the arts. The city was ranked #79 in 1996 and #130 in 1995.
Money, July 1997; Money, September 1996; Money, September 1995

■ *Ladies Home Journal* ranked America's 200 largest cities based on the qualities women care about most. Mobile ranked 197 out of 200. Criteria: low crime rate, good public schools, well-paying jobs, quality health and child care, the presence of women in government, proportion of women-owned businesses, size of the wage gap with men, local economy, divorce rates, the ratio of single men to single women, whether there are laws that require at least the same number of public toilets for women as men, and the probability of good hair days. *Ladies Home Journal, November 1997*

■ Mobile was ranked #163 out of 219 cities in terms of children's health, safety, and economic well-being. Criteria: total population, percent population change, birth rate, child immunization rate, infant mortality rate, percent low birth weight infants, percent of births to teens, physician-to-population ratio, student-to-teacher ratio, dropout rate, unemployment rate, median family income, percent of children in poverty, violent and property crime rates, number of juvenile arrests for violent crimes as a percent of the total crime index, number of days with pollution standard index (PSI) over 100, pounds toxic releases per 1,000 people and number of superfund sites. *Zero Population Growth, Children's Environmental Index 1997*

■ According to *Working Mother*, "As we went to press, state lawmakers were considering a proposal to improve the state's very low standards. If it passes, it will improve adult-to-child ratios in child care centers and boost training requirements for family child care providers.

Meanwhile, there was good news in the private sector. Seventeen companies in Lee County banded together to help expand the supply of child care in their community. And the city of Birmingham collaborated with 18 employers there to build and run a new child care center." *Working Mother, July/August 1997*

Business Environment

STATE ECONOMY

State Economic Profile

"Alabama's economy remains soft. Employment growth is one-half the national rate. As the state's manufacturing industry struggles with structural changes, retailers and support services industries remain hesitant to step up hiring. Lagging income gains relative to the southern region are not helping to relieve still-high consumer debt service burdens; consumer delinquency rates are more than 25 basis points above the national rate.

Alabama's mortgage delinquency rate exceeds the national rate. Mortgage delinquencies on conventional loans are approaching 3% according to the Mortgage Bankers Association. Although sub-par job and income growth are applying upward pressure on delinquencies, aggressive affordable housing programs are also playing a significant role in higher delinquency rates.

Mounting credit problems will induce some lenders to pare back on their affordable housing originations this year. Combined with expectations of tighter monetary policy, diminished housing affordability will thus cool expansion in the homeownership rate. After two years of strong house price appreciation, further restraints on housing affordability will bolster a greater share of apartment building in Alabama's residential construction activity.

Alabama's economy will significantly lag the national pace during the next several quarters, as manufacturing setbacks continue to reverberate through the remaining industries, especially at construction firms and retailers. Further along the forecast horizon, the shortage of highly-skilled workers in Alabama's labor market will inhibit the relocation of higher value-added, high-tech firms, partially offsetting the region's inherent cost structure advantage. On the upside, expansion in the transportation, health care, and financial services industries offers the potential for greater per capita income parity with the U.S. Overall, Alabama's economy will be a slightly better-than-average performer in the long term."
National Association of Realtors, Economic Profiles: The Fifty States, July 1997

IMPORTS/EXPORTS

Total Export Sales

Area	1993 ($000)	1994 ($000)	1995 ($000)	1996 ($000)	% Chg. 1993-96	% Chg. 1995-96
MSA[1]	356,695	395,276	415,827	459,850	28.9	10.6
U.S.	464,858,354	512,415,609	583,030,524	622,827,063	34.0	6.8

Note: (1) Metropolitan Statistical Area - see Appendix A for areas included
Source: U.S. Department of Commerce, International Trade Association, Metropolitan Area Exports: An Export Performance Report on Over 250 U.S. Cities, October 1997

Imports/Exports by Port

Type	Cargo Value			Share of U.S. Total	
	1995 (US$mil.)	1996 (US$mil.)	% Change 1995-1996	1995 (%)	1996 (%)
Imports	1,394	1,434	2.86	0.36	0.37
Exports	2,189	2,008	-8.25	0.96	0.85

Source: Global Trade Information Services, WaterBorne Trade Atlas 1997

CITY FINANCES

City Government Finances

Component	FY92 ($000)	FY92 (per capita $)
Revenue	193,865	958.80
Expenditure	178,626	883.43
Debt Outstanding	628,132	3,106.55
Cash & Securities	450,186	2,226.48

Source: U.S. Bureau of the Census, City Government Finances: 1991-92

City Government Revenue by Source

Source	FY92 ($000)	FY92 (per capita $)	FY92 (%)
From Federal Government	0	0.00	0.0
From State Governments	7,260	35.91	3.7
From Local Governments	2,478	12.26	1.3
Property Taxes	6,699	33.13	3.5
General Sales Taxes	71,707	354.64	37.0
Selective Sales Taxes	10,440	51.63	5.4
Income Taxes	0	0.00	0.0
Current Charges	27,944	138.20	14.4
Utility/Liquor Store	16,074	79.50	8.3
Employee Retirement[1]	0	0.00	0.0
Other	51,263	253.53	26.4

Note: (1) Excludes "city contributions," classified as "nonrevenue," intragovernmental transfers.
Source: U.S. Bureau of the Census, City Government Finances: 1991-92

City Government Expenditures by Function

Function	FY92 ($000)	FY92 (per capita $)	FY92 (%)
Educational Services	2,518	12.45	1.4
Employee Retirement[1]	0	0.00	0.0
Environment/Housing	42,046	207.95	23.5
Government Administration	10,761	53.22	6.0
Interest on General Debt	29,495	145.87	16.5
Public Safety	39,160	193.67	21.9
Social Services	2,255	11.15	1.3
Transportation	11,564	57.19	6.5
Utility/Liquor Store	23,369	115.58	13.1
Other	17,458	86.34	9.8

Note: (1) Payments to beneficiaries including withdrawal of contributions.
Source: U.S. Bureau of the Census, City Government Finances: 1991-92

Municipal Bond Ratings

Area	Moody's	S & P
Mobile	A	n/r

Note: n/a not available; n/r not rated
Source: Moody's Bond Record, 2/98; Statistical Abstract of the U.S., 1997; Governing Magazine, 9/97, 3/98

POPULATION

Population Growth

Area	1980	1990	% Chg. 1980-90	July 1996 Estimate	% Chg. 1990-96
City	200,396	196,278	-2.1	202,581	3.2
MSA[1]	443,536	476,923	7.5	518,975	8.8
U.S.	226,545,805	248,765,170	9.8	265,179,411	6.6

Note: (1) Metropolitan Statistical Area - see Appendix A for areas included
Source: 1980/1990 Census of Housing and Population, Summary Tape File 3C; Census Bureau Population Estimates

Population Characteristics

Race	City 1980 Population	%	City 1990 Population	%	% Chg. 1980-90	MSA[1] 1990 Population	%
White	125,466	62.6	116,872	59.5	-6.8	339,297	71.1
Black	72,697	36.3	76,510	39.0	5.2	130,390	27.3
Amer Indian/Esk/Aleut	539	0.3	651	0.3	20.8	3,115	0.7
Asian/Pacific Islander	1,289	0.6	1,878	1.0	45.7	3,405	0.7
Other	405	0.2	367	0.2	-9.4	716	0.2
Hispanic Origin[2]	2,418	1.2	2,152	1.1	-11.0	4,353	0.9

Note: (1) Metropolitan Statistical Area - see Appendix A for areas included;
(2) people of Hispanic origin can be of any race
Source: 1980/1990 Census of Housing and Population, Summary Tape File 3C

Ancestry

Area	German	Irish	English	Italian	U.S.	French	Polish	Dutch
City	12.3	13.1	12.1	1.9	8.5	4.7	0.6	1.2
MSA[1]	13.0	15.2	12.2	1.7	12.5	4.6	0.7	1.8
U.S.	23.3	15.6	13.1	5.9	5.3	4.2	3.8	2.5

Note: Figures are percentages and include persons that reported multiple ancestry (eg. if a person reported being Irish and Italian, they were included in both columns); (1) Metropolitan Statistical Area - see Appendix A for areas included
Source: 1990 Census of Population and Housing, Summary Tape File 3C

Age

Area	Median Age (Years)	Age Distribution (%) Under 5	Under 18	18-24	25-44	45-64	65+	80+
City	32.5	7.5	26.3	10.9	31.1	17.9	13.7	3.1
MSA[1]	32.6	7.5	27.9	9.8	31.0	18.8	12.5	2.5
U.S.	32.9	7.3	25.6	10.5	32.6	18.7	12.5	2.8

Note: (1) Metropolitan Statistical Area - see Appendix A for areas included
Source: 1990 Census of Population and Housing, Summary Tape File 3C

Male/Female Ratio

Area	Number of males per 100 females (all ages)	Number of males per 100 females (18 years old+)
City	86.3	81.2
MSA[1]	91.3	86.2
U.S.	95.0	91.9

Note: (1) Metropolitan Statistical Area - see Appendix A for areas included
Source: 1990 Census of Population, General Population Characteristics

INCOME

Per Capita/Median/Average Income

Area	Per Capita ($)	Median Household ($)	Average Household ($)
City	12,509	22,446	31,715
MSA[1]	11,388	23,645	30,703
U.S.	14,420	30,056	38,453

Note: all figures are for 1989; (1) Metropolitan Statistical Area - see Appendix A for areas included
Source: 1990 Census of Population and Housing, Summary Tape File 3C

Household Income Distribution by Race

Income ($)	City (%)					U.S. (%)				
	Total	White	Black	Other	Hisp.[1]	Total	White	Black	Other	Hisp.[1]
Less than 5,000	12.6	6.3	24.3	16.8	6.8	6.2	4.8	15.2	8.6	8.8
5,000 - 9,999	11.7	8.7	17.3	11.6	8.3	9.3	8.6	14.2	9.9	11.1
10,000 - 14,999	10.6	9.5	12.7	12.3	16.7	8.8	8.5	11.0	9.8	11.0
15,000 - 24,999	19.3	19.5	18.9	20.1	23.8	17.5	17.3	18.9	18.5	20.5
25,000 - 34,999	15.0	16.9	11.6	14.2	17.8	15.8	16.1	14.2	15.4	16.4
35,000 - 49,999	13.9	16.4	9.2	12.7	8.8	17.9	18.6	13.3	16.1	16.0
50,000 - 74,999	10.8	14.0	4.9	8.4	16.3	15.0	15.8	9.3	13.4	11.1
75,000 - 99,999	3.1	4.2	1.0	2.7	0.7	5.1	5.5	2.6	4.7	3.1
100,000+	3.1	4.6	0.3	1.1	0.9	4.4	4.8	1.3	3.7	1.9

Note: all figures are for 1989; (1) people of Hispanic origin can be of any race
Source: 1990 Census of Population and Housing, Summary Tape File 3C

Effective Buying Income

Area	Per Capita ($)	Median Household ($)	Average Household ($)
City	15,296	28,292	39,295
MSA[1]	14,734	30,936	39,739
U.S.	15,444	33,201	41,849

Note: data as of 1/1/97; (1) Metropolitan Statistical Area - see Appendix A for areas included
Source: Standard Rate & Data Service, Newspaper Advertising Source, 2/98

Effective Household Buying Income Distribution

Area	% of Households Earning						
	$10,000 -$19,999	$20,000 -$34,999	$35,000 -$49,999	$50,000 -$74,999	$75,000 -$99,000	$100,000 -$124,999	$125,000 and up
City	17.9	22.9	15.6	14.9	5.5	1.8	2.6
MSA[1]	17.0	23.3	16.9	17.1	6.1	1.9	2.1
U.S.	16.5	23.4	18.3	18.2	6.4	2.1	2.4

Note: data as of 1/1/97; (1) Metropolitan Statistical Area - see Appendix A for areas included
Source: Standard Rate & Data Service, Newspaper Advertising Source, 2/98

Poverty Rates by Race and Age

Area	Total (%)	By Race (%)				By Age (%)		
		White	Black	Other	Hisp.[2]	Under 5 years old	Under 18 years old	65 years and over
City	22.4	9.3	41.9	30.1	19.3	35.4	33.4	17.8
MSA[1]	19.9	10.8	42.9	31.1	17.4	30.4	28.6	17.9
U.S.	13.1	9.8	29.5	23.1	25.3	20.1	18.3	12.8

Note: figures show the percent of people living below the poverty line in 1989. The average poverty threshold was $12,674 for a family of four in 1989; (1) Metropolitan Statistical Area - see Appendix A for areas included; (2) people of Hispanic origin can be of any race
Source: 1990 Census of Population and Housing, Summary Tape File 3C

EMPLOYMENT

Labor Force and Employment

Area	Civilian Labor Force			Workers Employed		
	Dec. '95	Dec. '96	% Chg.	Dec. '95	Dec. '96	% Chg.
City	103,442	107,809	4.2	99,120	103,271	4.2
MSA[1]	259,203	269,529	4.0	249,797	260,259	4.2
U.S.	134,583,000	136,742,000	1.6	127,903,000	130,785,000	2.3

Note: Data is not seasonally adjusted and covers workers 16 years of age and older;
(1) Metropolitan Statistical Area - see Appendix A for areas included
Source: Bureau of Labor Statistics, http://stats.bls.gov

Unemployment Rate

Area	1997											
	Jan.	Feb.	Mar.	Apr.	May	Jun.	Jul.	Aug.	Sep.	Oct.	Nov.	Dec.
City	4.7	5.0	4.6	4.5	4.6	6.1	5.5	6.0	5.6	5.4	4.8	4.2
MSA[1]	4.5	4.8	4.2	4.2	4.1	5.3	4.8	5.0	4.7	4.6	4.0	3.4
U.S.	5.9	5.7	5.5	4.8	4.7	5.2	5.0	4.8	4.7	4.4	4.3	4.4

Note: Data is not seasonally adjusted and covers workers 16 years of age and older; All figures are percentages; (1) Metropolitan Statistical Area - see Appendix A for areas included
Source: Bureau of Labor Statistics, http://stats.bls.gov

Employment by Industry

Sector	MSA[1]		U.S.
	Number of Employees	Percent of Total	Percent of Total
Services	60,300	27.2	29.0
Retail Trade	47,400	21.4	18.5
Government	34,800	15.7	16.1
Manufacturing	27,800	12.5	15.0
Finance/Insurance/Real Estate	10,000	4.5	5.7
Wholesale Trade	11,900	5.4	5.4
Transportation/Public Utilities	13,400	6.0	5.3
Construction/Mining	16,300	7.3	5.0

Note: Figures cover non-farm employment as of 12/97 and are not seasonally adjusted;
(1) Metropolitan Statistical Area - see Appendix A for areas included
Source: Bureau of Labor Statistics, http://stats.bls.gov

Employment by Occupation

Occupation Category	City (%)	MSA[1] (%)	U.S. (%)
White Collar	63.9	55.5	58.1
Executive/Admin./Management	11.5	10.2	12.3
Professional	17.3	13.2	14.1
Technical & Related Support	4.2	3.7	3.7
Sales	15.1	13.4	11.8
Administrative Support/Clerical	15.7	14.9	16.3
Blue Collar	21.8	29.3	26.2
Precision Production/Craft/Repair	9.1	13.0	11.3
Machine Operators/Assem./Insp.	4.5	6.7	6.8
Transportation/Material Movers	4.2	5.2	4.1
Cleaners/Helpers/Laborers	3.9	4.5	3.9
Services	13.6	13.2	13.2
Farming/Forestry/Fishing	0.8	2.0	2.5

Note: figures cover employed persons 16 years old and over;
(1) Metropolitan Statistical Area - see Appendix A for areas included
Source: 1990 Census of Population and Housing, Summary Tape File 3C

Occupational Employment Projections: 1994 - 2005

Occupations Expected to have the Largest Job Growth (ranked by numerical growth)	Fast-Growing Occupations (ranked by percent growth)
1. Cashiers	1. Personal and home care aides
2. Salespersons, retail	2. Occupational therapists
3. General managers & top executives	3. Systems analysts
4. Teachers, secondary school	4. Home health aides
5. Registered nurses	5. Computer support specialists
6. Child care workers, private household	6. Computer engineers
7. Nursing aides/orderlies/attendants	7. Physical therapists
8. Marketing & sales, supervisors	8. Medical records technicians
9. Home health aides	9. Human services workers
10. Waiters & waitresses	10. Paralegals

Projections cover Mobile and Baldwin Counties.
Source: Alabama Dept. of Industrial Relations, Occupational Trends for 2005, Employment by Occupation 1994-2005, June 1997

Average Wages

Occupation	Wage	Occupation	Wage
Professional/Technical/Clerical	$/Week	**Health/Protective Services**	$/Week
Accountants III	-	Corrections Officers	-
Attorneys III	-	Firefighters	-
Budget Analysts III	-	Nurses, Licensed Practical II	-
Buyers/Contracting Specialists II	-	Nurses, Registered II	-
Clerks, Accounting III	423	Nursing Assistants II	-
Clerks, General III	338	Police Officers I	-
Computer Operators II	-	**Hourly Workers**	$/Hour
Computer Programmers II	-	Forklift Operators	9.71
Drafters II	-	General Maintenance Workers	6.91
Engineering Technicians III	-	Guards I	4.88
Engineering Technicians, Civil III	-	Janitors	4.94
Engineers III	-	Maintenance Electricians	15.93
Key Entry Operators I	-	Maintenance Electronics Techs II	18.41
Personnel Assistants III	-	Maintenance Machinists	-
Personnel Specialists III	-	Maintenance Mechanics, Machinery	14.11
Secretaries III	541	Material Handling Laborers	-
Switchboard Operator-Receptionist	290	Motor Vehicle Mechanics	13.37
Systems Analysts II	807	Shipping/Receiving Clerks	9.83
Systems Analysts Supervisor/Mgr II	-	Tool and Die Makers	-
Tax Collectors II	-	Truckdrivers, Tractor Trailer	9.64
Word Processors II	-	Warehouse Specialists	-

Note: Wage data includes full-time workers only for 6/96 and cover the Metropolitan Statistical Area (see Appendix A for areas included). Dashes indicate that data was not available.
Source: Bureau of Labor Statistics, Occupational Compensation Survey, 9/96

TAXES

Major State and Local Tax Rates

State Corp. Income (%)	State Personal Income (%)	Residential Property (effective rate per $100)	Sales & Use		State Gasoline (cents/gallon)	State Cigarette (cents/20-pack)
			State (%)	Local (%)		
5.0	2.0 - 5.0	n/a	4.0	5.0	18[a]	16.5[b]

Note: Personal/corporate income tax rates as of 1/97. Sales, gasoline and cigarette tax rates as of 1/98; (a) Rate is comprised of 16 cents excise plus 2 cents motor carrier tax. Rate does not include 1 - 3 cents local option tax; (b) Counties and cities may impose an additional tax of 1 - 6 cents per pack
Source: Federation of Tax Administrators, www.taxadmin.org; Washington D.C. Department of Finance and Revenue, Tax Rates and Tax Burdens in the District of Columbia: A Nationwide Comparison, June 1997; Chamber of Commerce

Total Taxes Per Capita and as a Percent of Income

Area	Per Capita Income ($)	Per Capita Taxes ($)			Taxes as Pct. of Income (%)		
		Total	Federal	State/Local	Total	Federal	State/Local
Alabama	21,732	6,982	4,923	2,060	32.1	22.7	9.5
U.S.	26,187	9,205	6,127	3,078	35.2	23.4	11.8

Note: Figures are for 1997
Source: Tax Foundation, Web Site, www.taxfoundation.org

COMMERCIAL REAL ESTATE

Office Market

Class/Location	Total Space (sq. ft.)	Vacant Space (sq. ft.)	Vac. Rate (%)	Under Constr. (sq. ft.)	Net Absorp. (sq. ft.)	Rental Rates ($/sq.ft./yr.)
Class A						
CBD	1,000,000	100,000	10.0	0	0	11.00-16.50
Outside CBD	750,000	37,000	4.9	0	161,000	12.00-22.00
Class B						
CBD	500,000	100,000	20.0	0	0	8.80-11.00
Outside CBD	900,000	180,000	20.0	0	0	5.50-8.80

Note: Data as of 10/97 and covers Mobile; CBD = Central Business District; n/a not available;
Source: Society of Industrial and Office Realtors, 1998 Comparative Statistics of Industrial and Office Real Estate Markets

"SIOR's local correspondent expects that demand will be strong in both leasing and sales of major office space in 1998. Construction activity is anticipated to increase to up to 10 percent in 1998. Most new space will be pre-committed and no speculative development is assumed. Rental rates should rise to 10 percent after increasing in all submarkets this past year. Landlord concessions will grow from 1 - 5 percent and will include a 3 percent discount rate, parking, moving allowances, and interior improvements. Population growth should support growth in the service industries. The area's low business costs will remain one of its strengths." *Society of Industrial and Office Realtors, 1998 Comparative Statistics of Industrial and Office Real Estate Markets*

Industrial Market

Location	Total Space (sq. ft.)	Vacant Space (sq. ft.)	Vac. Rate (%)	Under Constr. (sq. ft.)	Net Absorp. (sq. ft.)	Lease ($/sq.ft./yr.)
Central City	3,500,000	50,000	1.4	0	0	2.50-4.00
Suburban	8,910,000	0	0.0	900,000	1,210,000	2.50-4.00

Note: Data as of 10/97 and covers Mobile; n/a not available
Source: Society of Industrial and Office Realtors, 1998 Comparative Statistics of Industrial and Office Real Estate Markets

"The Theodore/Rangeline Road area is particularly active. But even with occupancy near 100 percent, very little speculative construction is anticipated for 1998. High Tech/R&D activity in this sector is expected to influence the MSA in 1998. According to SIOR's reporter, Mobile's diverse manufacturing and services sectors will insulate it from individual industry trends. The market will remain attractive due to its below average business costs. But a deterrent could still be the quality of available labor." *Society of Industrial and Office Realtors, 1998 Comparative Statistics of Industrial and Office Real Estate Markets*

COMMERCIAL UTILITIES

Typical Monthly Electric Bills

Area	Commercial Service ($/month)		Industrial Service ($/month)	
	12 kW demand 1,500 kWh	100 kW demand 30,000 kWh	1,000 kW demand 400,000 kWh	20,000 kW demand 10,000,000 kWh
City	146	2,167	18,733	394,725
U.S.	162	2,360	25,590	545,677

Note: Based on rates in effect July 1, 1997
Source: Edison Electric Institute, Typical Residential, Commercial and Industrial Bills, Summer 1997

TRANSPORTATION

Transportation Statistics

Avg. travel time to work (min.)	19.1
Interstate highways	I-10; I-65
Bus lines	
In-city	MTA
Inter-city	1
Passenger air service	
Airport	Bates Field
Airlines	5
Aircraft departures	8,090 (1995)
Enplaned passengers	266,706 (1995)
Rail service	Amtrak
Motor freight carriers	65
Major waterways/ports	Mobile Bay

Source: OAG, Business Travel Planner, Summer 1997; Editor & Publisher Market Guide, 1998; FAA Airport Activity Statistics, 1996; Amtrak National Time Table, Northeast Timetable, Fall/Winter 1997-98; 1990 Census of Population and Housing, STF 3C; Chamber of Commerce/Economic Development 1997; Jane's Urban Transport Systems 1997-98; Transit Fact Book 1997

Means of Transportation to Work

Area	Car/Truck/Van		Public Transportation			Bicycle	Walked	Other Means	Worked at Home
	Drove Alone	Car-pooled	Bus	Subway	Railroad				
City	81.8	12.2	1.5	0.0	0.0	0.2	1.8	1.0	1.4
MSA[1]	80.6	13.8	0.9	0.0	0.0	0.2	1.7	1.2	1.7
U.S.	73.2	13.4	3.0	1.5	0.5	0.4	3.9	1.2	3.0

Note: figures shown are percentages and only include workers 16 years old and over;
(1) Metropolitan Statistical Area - see Appendix A for areas included
Source: 1990 Census of Population and Housing, Summary Tape File 3C

BUSINESSES

Major Business Headquarters

Company Name	1997 Rankings	
	Fortune 500	Forbes 500

No companies listed.

Note: Companies listed are located in the city; Dashes indicate no ranking
Fortune 500: companies that produce a 10-K are ranked 1 - 500 based on 1996 revenue
Forbes 500: private companies are ranked 1 - 500 based on 1996 revenue
Source: Forbes 12/1/97; Fortune 4/28/97

Minority Business Opportunity

Mobile is home to one company which is on the Black Enterprise Auto Dealer 100 list (largest based on gross sales): Coastal Ford Inc. (Ford). Criteria: 1) operational in previous calendar year; 2) at least 51% black-owned. *Black Enterprise, June 1997*

HOTELS & MOTELS

Hotels/Motels

| Area | Hotels/ Motels | Rooms | Luxury-Level Hotels/Motels | | Average Minimum Rates ($) | | |
			♦♦♦♦	♦♦♦♦♦	♦♦	♦♦♦	♦♦♦♦
City	24	2,631	0	0	52	79	n/a
Airport	3	219	0	0	n/a	n/a	n/a
Suburbs	3	570	0	0	n/a	n/a	n/a
Total	30	3,420	0	0	n/a	n/a	n/a

Note: n/a not available; Classifications range from one diamond (budget properties with basic amenities) to five diamond (luxury properties with the finest service, rooms and facilities).
Source: OAG, Business Travel Planner, Summer 1997

CONVENTION CENTERS

Major Convention Centers

Center Name	Meeting Rooms	Exhibit Space (sf)
Mobile Convention Center	17	115,000
Mobile Civic Center	15	108,000

Source: Trade Shows Worldwide 1997

Living Environment

COST OF LIVING

Cost of Living Index

Composite Index	Housing	Utilities	Groceries	Health Care	Trans-portation	Misc. Goods/ Services
96.0	82.0	105.2	100.5	91.1	102.6	102.6

Note: U.S. = 100
Source: ACCRA, Cost of Living Index, 3rd Quarter 1997

HOUSING

Median Home Prices and Housing Affordability

Area	Median Price[2] 3rd Qtr. 1997 ($)	HOI[3] 3rd Qtr. 1997	Afford-ability Rank[4]
MSA[1]	n/a	n/a	n/a
U.S.	127,000	63.7	--

Note: (1) Metropolitan Statistical Area - see Appendix A for areas included; (2) U.S. figures calculated from the sales of 625,000 new and existing homes in 195 markets; (3) Housing Opportunity Index - percent of homes sold that were within the reach of the median income household at the prevailing mortgage interest rate; (4) Rank is from 1-195 with 1 being most affordable; n/a not available
Source: National Association of Home Builders, Housing Opportunity Index, 3rd Quarter 1997

It is projected that the median price of existing single-family homes in the metro area will increase by 5.8% in 1998. Nationwide, home prices are projected to increase 6.6%.
Kiplinger's Personal Finance Magazine, January 1998

Average New Home Price

Area	Price ($)
City	113,500
U.S.	135,710

Note: Figures are based on a new home with 1,800 sq. ft. of living area on an 8,000 sq. ft. lot.
Source: ACCRA, Cost of Living Index, 3rd Quarter 1997

Average Apartment Rent

Area	Rent ($/mth)
City	445
U.S.	569

Note: Figures are based on an unfurnished two bedroom, 1-1/2 or 2 bath apartment, approximately 950 sq. ft. in size, excluding all utilities except water
Source: ACCRA, Cost of Living Index, 3rd Quarter 1997

RESIDENTIAL UTILITIES

Average Residential Utility Costs

Area	All Electric ($/mth)	Part Electric ($/mth)	Other Energy ($/mth)	Phone ($/mth)
City	--	68.71	37.12	22.85
U.S.	109.40	55.25	43.64	19.48

Source: ACCRA, Cost of Living Index, 3rd Quarter 1997

HEALTH CARE

Average Health Care Costs

Area	Hospital ($/day)	Doctor ($/visit)	Dentist ($/visit)
City	211.40	47.60	60.00
U.S.	392.91	48.76	60.84

Note: Hospital - based on a semi-private room. Doctor - based on a general practitioner's routine exam of an established patient. Dentist - based on adult teeth cleaning and periodic oral exam.
Source: ACCRA, Cost of Living Index, 3rd Quarter 1997

Distribution of Office-Based Physicians

Area	Family/Gen. Practitioners	Specialists		
		Medical	Surgical	Other
MSA[1]	109	279	269	209

Note: Data as of 12/31/96; (1) Metropolitan Statistical Area - see Appendix A for areas included
Source: American Medical Assn., Physician Characteristics & Distribution in the U.S., 1997-1998

Hospitals

Mobile has 6 general medical and surgical hospitals, 1 psychiatric. *AHA Guide to the Healthcare Field 1997-98*

EDUCATION

Public School District Statistics

District Name	Num. Sch.	Enroll.	Classroom Teachers[1]	Pupils per Teacher	Minority Pupils (%)	Current Exp.[2] ($/pupil)
Mobile County Sch Dist	88	65,602	3,560	18.4	50.8	3,321

Note: Data covers the 1995-1996 school year unless otherwise noted; (1) Excludes teachers reported as working in school district offices rather than in schools; (2) Based on 1993-94 enrollment collected by the Census Bureau, not the enrollment figure shown in column 3; SD = School District; ISD = Independent School District; n/a not available
Source: National Center for Education Statistics, Common Core of Data Survey; Bureau of the Census

Educational Quality

School District	Education Quotient[1]	Graduate Outcome[2]	Community Index[3]	Resource Index[4]
Mobile County	81.0	63.0	60.0	119.0

Note: Nearly 1,000 secondary school districts were rated in terms of educational quality. The scores range from a low of 50 to a high of 150; (1) Average of the Graduate Outcome, Community and Resource indexes; (2) Based on graduation rates and college board scores (SAT/ACT); (3) Based on the surrounding community's average level of education and the area's average income level; (4) Based on teacher salaries, per-pupil expenditures and student-teacher ratios.
Source: Expansion Management, Ratings Issue 1997

Educational Attainment by Race

Area	High School Graduate (%)					Bachelor's Degree (%)				
	Total	White	Black	Other	Hisp.[2]	Total	White	Black	Other	Hisp.[2]
City	74.8	82.2	61.1	69.9	71.2	21.4	27.0	10.7	25.5	17.2
MSA[1]	70.8	75.2	57.5	59.5	69.3	15.8	18.1	8.6	15.7	15.1
U.S.	75.2	77.9	63.1	60.4	49.8	20.3	21.5	11.4	19.4	9.2

Note: figures shown cover persons 25 years old and over; (1) Metropolitan Statistical Area - see Appendix A for areas included; (2) people of Hispanic origin can be of any race
Source: 1990 Census of Population and Housing, Summary Tape File 3C

School Enrollment by Type

Area	Preprimary				Elementary/High School			
	Public		Private		Public		Private	
	Enrollment	%	Enrollment	%	Enrollment	%	Enrollment	%
City	1,602	44.3	2,015	55.7	28,538	81.1	6,641	18.9
MSA[1]	4,123	50.8	3,999	49.2	79,476	86.1	12,784	13.9
U.S.	2,679,029	59.5	1,824,256	40.5	38,379,689	90.2	4,187,099	9.8

Note: figures shown cover persons 3 years old and over;
(1) Metropolitan Statistical Area - see Appendix A for areas included
Source: 1990 Census of Population and Housing, Summary Tape File 3C

School Enrollment by Race

Area	Preprimary (%)				Elementary/High School (%)			
	White	Black	Other	Hisp.[1]	White	Black	Other	Hisp.[1]
City	64.4	33.9	1.7	1.0	45.8	52.5	1.6	1.1
MSA[2]	71.2	27.6	1.2	1.2	62.2	35.8	2.1	1.0
U.S.	80.4	12.5	7.1	7.8	74.1	15.6	10.3	12.5

Note: figures shown cover persons 3 years old and over; (1) people of Hispanic origin can be of any race; (2) Metropolitan Statistical Area - see Appendix A for areas included
Source: 1990 Census of Population and Housing, Summary Tape File 3C

SAT/ACT Scores

Area/District	1996 SAT				1997 ACT	
	Percent of Graduates Tested (%)	Average Math Score	Average Verbal Score	Average Combined Score	Percent of Graduates Tested (%)	Average Composite Score
Mobile County SD	10	540	566	1,106	50	19.4
State	8	558	565	1,123	61	20.2
U.S.	41	508	505	1,013	36	21.0

Note: Math and verbal SAT scores are out of a possible 800; ACT scores are out of a possible 36
Caution: Comparing or ranking states/cities on the basis of SAT/ACT scores alone is invalid and strongly discouraged by the The College Board and The American College Testing Program as students who take the tests are self-selected and do not represent the entire student population. 1996 SAT scores cannot be compared to previous years due to recentering.
Source: Mobile County SD, 1997; American College Testing Program, 1997; College Board, 1996

Classroom Teacher Salaries in Public Schools

District	B.A. Degree		M.A. Degree		Ph.D. Degree	
	Min. ($)	Max ($)	Min. ($)	Max. ($)	Min. ($)	Max. ($)
Mobile	25,410	30,297	28,915	34,170	32,702	38,763
Average[1]	26,120	39,270	28,175	44,667	31,643	49,825

Note: Salaries are for 1996-1997; (1) Based on all school districts covered; n/a not available
Source: American Federation of Teachers (unpublished data)

Higher Education

Two-Year Colleges		Four-Year Colleges		Medical Schools	Law Schools	Voc/ Tech
Public	Private	Public	Private			
1	0	1	2	1	0	5

Source: College Blue Book, Occupational Education 1997; Medical School Admission Requirements, 1998-99; Peterson's Guide to Two-Year Colleges, 1997; Peterson's Guide to Four-Year Colleges, 1997; Barron's Guide to Law Schools 1997

MAJOR EMPLOYERS

Major Employers

Atlantic Marine (shipbuilding)
Home Nursing Services
Mobile Press Register
Providence Hospital
Springhill Medical Complex
Alabama State Docks Dept.

C.J. Gayfer (department stores)
Mobile Infirmary Association
Pilot Catastrophe Services
QMS Inc. (Metals Service Centers)
University of South Alabama Medical Center

Note: companies listed are located in the city
Source: Dun's Business Rankings 1997; Ward's Business Directory, 1997

PUBLIC SAFETY

Crime Rate

Area	All Crimes	Violent Crimes				Property Crimes		
		Murder	Forcible Rape	Robbery	Aggrav. Assault	Burglary	Larceny -Theft	Motor Vehicle Theft
City	9,421.3	24.6	57.5	619.5	353.4	2,126.4	5,306.5	933.3
Suburbs[1]	4,077.6	9.3	37.6	126.1	365.9	977.0	2,281.3	280.5
MSA[2]	6,211.3	15.4	45.5	323.1	360.9	1,435.9	3,489.2	541.2
U.S.	5,078.9	7.4	36.1	202.4	388.2	943.0	2,975.9	525.9

Note: Crime rate is the number of crimes per 100,000 pop.; (1) defined as all areas within the MSA but located outside the central city; (2) Metropolitan Statistical Area - see Appendix A for areas incl. Source: FBI Uniform Crime Reports 1996

RECREATION

Culture and Recreation

Museums	Symphony Orchestras	Opera Companies	Dance Companies	Professional Theatres	Zoos	Pro Sports Teams
8	0	1	0	1	0	0

Source: International Directory of the Performing Arts, 1996; Official Museum Directory, 1998; Chamber of Commerce/Economic Development 1997

Library System

The Mobile Public Library has six branches, holdings of 439,908 volumes and a budget of $n/a (1995-1996). Note: n/a means not available. *American Library Directory, 1997-1998*

MEDIA

Newspapers

Name	Type	Freq.	Distribution	Circulation
Catholic Week	Religious	1x/wk	Area	15,400
Mobile Beacon and Alabama Citizen	Black	1x/wk	Local	7,000
The Mobile Register	n/a	7x/wk	Local	107,000
National Inner City	Black	1x/mo	Local	8,000

Note: Includes newspapers with circulations of 1,000 or more located in the city; n/a not available Source: Burrelle's Media Directory, 1998 Edition

AM Radio Stations

Call Letters	Freq. (kHz)	Target Audience	Station Format	Music Format
WBLX	660	n/a	M	n/a
WNTM	710	n/a	N/T	n/a
WBHY	840	General	M/T	Christian
WGOK	900	Black	M	Christian
WKSJ	1270	n/a	M	Country
WMOB	1360	n/a	M/T	Christian
WABB	1480	General	N/S/T	n/a

Note: Stations included broadcast in the Mobile metro area; n/a not available Station Format: E = Educational; M = Music; N = News; S = Sports; T = Talk Source: Burrelle's Media Directory, 1998 Edition

FM Radio Stations

Call Letters	Freq. (mHz)	Target Audience	Station Format	Music Format
WBHY	88.5	n/a	M	Christian
WHIL	91.3	General	E/M/N	Classical
WBLX	92.9	Black	M	R&B/Urban Contemporary
WKSJ	94.9	n/a	M/N/S	Country
WABB	97.5	General	M	Adult Contemporary
WDLT	98.3	n/a	M	Adult Contemporary
WMXC	99.9	n/a	M	Adult Contemporary
WDWG	104.1	n/a	M	Country
WYOK	104.9	General	M	Urban Contemporary
WAVH	106.5	General	M/N/S	Adult Contemporary/Oldies

Note: Stations included broadcast in the Mobile metro area; n/a not available
Station Format: E = Educational; M = Music; N = News; S = Sports; T = Talk
Source: Burrelle's Media Directory, 1998 Edition

Television Stations

Name	Ch.	Affiliation	Type	Owner
WKRG	5	CBS	Commercial	WKRG TV Inc.
WALA	10	Fox	Commercial	S.F. Broadcasting
WPMI	15	NBC	Commercial	Clear Channel Communications
WMPV	21	TBN	Non-Commercial	All American Network

Note: Stations included broadcast in the Mobile metro area
Source: Burrelle's Media Directory, 1998 Edition

CLIMATE

Average and Extreme Temperatures

Temperature	Jan	Feb	Mar	Apr	May	Jun	Jul	Aug	Sep	Oct	Nov	Dec	Ann
Extreme High (°F)	84	84	89	94	100	102	104	102	99	93	87	81	104
Average High (°F)	61	64	70	78	85	90	91	91	87	79	70	63	77
Average Temp. (°F)	51	54	60	68	75	81	82	82	78	69	59	53	68
Average Low (°F)	41	44	50	57	64	71	73	73	69	57	48	43	57
Extreme Low (°F)	3	11	23	32	43	49	62	59	42	32	22	8	3

Note: Figures cover the years 1949-1990
Source: National Climatic Data Center, International Station Meteorological Climate Summary, 3/95

Average Precipitation/Snowfall/Humidity

Precip./Humidity	Jan	Feb	Mar	Apr	May	Jun	Jul	Aug	Sep	Oct	Nov	Dec	Ann
Avg. Precip. (in.)	4.5	5.3	6.7	5.2	5.4	5.4	7.7	7.0	6.4	2.8	3.9	5.4	65.6
Avg. Snowfall (in.)	Tr	Tr	Tr	Tr	0	0	0	0	0	0	Tr	Tr	Tr
Avg. Rel. Hum. 6am (%)	83	83	84	87	87	87	90	91	89	86	84	84	86
Avg. Rel. Hum. 3pm (%)	58	55	53	52	53	57	63	63	59	51	54	58	56

Note: Figures cover the years 1949-1990; Tr = Trace amounts (<0.05 in. of rain; <0.5 in. of snow)
Source: National Climatic Data Center, International Station Meteorological Climate Summary, 3/95

Weather Conditions

Temperature			Daytime Sky			Precipitation		
32°F & below	45°F & below	90°F & above	Clear	Partly cloudy	Cloudy	0.01 inch or more precip.	0.1 inch or more snow/ice	Thunder-storms
21	86	76	92	166	107	121	1	79

Note: Figures are average number of days per year and covers the years 1949-1990
Source: National Climatic Data Center, International Station Meteorological Climate Summary, 3/95

AIR & WATER QUALITY

Maximum Pollutant Concentrations

	Particulate Matter (ug/m^3)	Carbon Monoxide (ppm)	Sulfur Dioxide (ppm)	Nitrogen Dioxide (ppm)	Ozone (ppm)	Lead (ug/m^3)
MSA[1] Level	91	n/a	0.070	n/a	0.10	n/a
NAAQS[2]	150	9	0.140	0.053	0.12	1.50
Met NAAQS?	Yes	n/a	Yes	n/a	Yes	n/a

Note: (1) Metropolitan Statistical Area - see Appendix A for areas included; (2) National Ambient Air Quality Standards; ppm = parts per million; ug/m^3 = micrograms per cubic meter; n/a not available
Source: EPA, National Air Quality and Emissions Trends Report, 1996

Pollutant Standards Index

Data not available. *EPA, National Air Quality and Emissions Trends Report, 1996*

Drinking Water

Water System Name	Pop. Served	Primary Water Source Type	Number of Violations in Fiscal Year 1997	Type of Violation/ Contaminants
Mobile Area Water Svc Sys	279,000	Surface	None	None

Note: Data as of January 16, 1998
Source: EPA, Office of Ground Water and Drinking Water, Safe Drinking Water Information System

Mobile tap water is alkaline, very soft and fluoridated.
Editor & Publisher Market Guide, 1998

Nashville, Tennessee

Background

Nashville, the capital of Tennessee, founded on Christmas Day in 1779 by James Robertson and John Donelson, sits in the minds of millions as the country music capital of the world. After all, this is the place to record, if you want to make it into the country music industry. This is also where the Grand Ole Opry—the longest running radio show in the country—still captures the hearts of millions of devoted listeners. It is no wonder, given how profoundly this industry has touched people, names like Dolly, Chet, Loretta, Hank, and Johnny are more familiar than the city's true native sons: Andrew, James, and Sam...Jackson, Polk, and Houston, that is.

According to the Country Music Association, over half of the single records produced in the United States come from Nashville. This puts the city on a par with Los Angeles and New York in music recording, publishing, distribution, and production. Luckily for Nashville, its recording industry has spawned opportunities in the related fields of the television and motion picture industries as well.

The magnitude of Nashville's recording industry is impressive. But music ranks second to the printing and publishing of Bibles in the city's economy. Known as the "Protestant Vatican" and "Buckle on The Bible Belt", Fundamentalism is strong in Nashville. However, Nashville is also a devoted patron of the arts and education. The Davidson Academy, forerunner of the George Peabody College for Teachers, was founded in Nashville, as were Vanderbilt and Fisk Universities. Fisk was the first private black university in the United States. In addition, the citizens take pride in their numerous art galleries, prize-winning national parks, historical mansions, and specialty-interest museums.

Located on the Cumberland River in central Tennessee, Nashville's weather is moderate with great extremes of either heat or cold rarely occurring. The average relative humidity is moderate.

The city is not in the most common path of the storms that cross the country, but it is in a zone of moderate frequency for thunderstorms.

General Rankings and Evaluative Comments

- Nashville was ranked #116 out of 300 cities by *Money's* 1997 "Survey of the Best Places to Live." Criteria used: health services, crime, economy, housing, education, transportation, weather, leisure and the arts. The city was ranked #101 in 1996 and #223 in 1995. *Money, July 1997; Money, September 1996; Money, September 1995*

- *Ladies Home Journal* ranked America's 200 largest cities based on the qualities women care about most. Nashville ranked 73 out of 200. Criteria: low crime rate, good public schools, well-paying jobs, quality health and child care, the presence of women in government, proportion of women-owned businesses, size of the wage gap with men, local economy, divorce rates, the ratio of single men to single women, whether there are laws that require at least the same number of public toilets for women as men, and the probability of good hair days. *Ladies Home Journal, November 1997*

- Nashville was ranked #120 out of 219 cities in terms of children's health, safety, and economic well-being. Criteria: total population, percent population change, birth rate, child immunization rate, infant mortality rate, percent low birth weight infants, percent of births to teens, physician-to-population ratio, student-to-teacher ratio, dropout rate, unemployment rate, median family income, percent of children in poverty, violent and property crime rates, number of juvenile arrests for violent crimes as a percent of the total crime index, number of days with pollution standard index (PSI) over 100, pounds toxic releases per 1,000 people and number of superfund sites. *Zero Population Growth, Children's Environmental Index 1997*

- *Conde Nast Traveler* polled 37,000 readers in terms of travel satisfaction. Cities were ranked based on the following criteria: people/friendliness, environment/ambiance, cultural enrichment, restaurants and fun/energy. Nashville appeared in the top thirty, ranking number 8, with an overall rating of 69.2 out of 100 based on all the criteria. The cities were also ranked in each category separately. Nashville appeared in the top 10 based on people/friendliness, ranking number 2 with a rating of 84.8 out of 100. Nashville appeared in the top 10 based on fun/energy, ranking number 6 with a rating of 78.3 out of 100. *Conde Nast Traveler, Readers' Choice Poll 1997*

- *Yahoo! Internet Life* selected "America's 100 Most Wired Cities & Towns". 50 cities were large and 50 cities were small. Nashville ranked 38 out of 50 large cities. Criteria: Internet users per capita, number of networked computers, number of registered domain names, Internet backbone traffic, and the per-capita number of Web sites devoted to each city. *Yahoo! Internet Life, March 1998*

- Nashville appeared on *Sales & Marketing Management's* list of the 20 hottest domestic markets to do business in. Rank: 20 out of 20. America's 320 Metropolitan Statistical Areas were ranked based on the market's potential to buy products in certain industries like high-tech, manufacturing, office equipment and business services, as well as population and household income growth. The study had nine criteria in all.

  "Thanks to an increasingly wealthy population and a low unemployment rate, Music City, USA is thriving. As a major entertainment attraction. Opryland brings thousands of tourists to the market every year. Companies selling office equipment of consumer retail goods should consider Nashville." *Sales & Marketing Management, January 1998*

- According to *Working Mother*, "Like so many other states, Tennessee has boosted its funding for child care in the face of welfare reform. In his budget for the next fiscal year, Governor Don Sundquist has pledged $10 million in new funds. Much of that money will go to boost payments to caregivers—which may in turn lower parents' bills. At the same time, state officials are still dragging their feet over new rules that were proposed three years ago to improve the quality of care for Tennessee's kids. The rules would upgrade caregiver training and lower adult-to-child ratios—important changes that studies show make programs better for kids. It looks af if the rules will soon be approved, but they'll then be phased in over nearly four years—an unfortunate delay. 'A lot of us are really distressed that the state has not implemented these standards yet,' says Phil Acord of the Children's Home and Shelter, a 24-hour child care center in Chattanooga." *Working Mother, July/August 1997*

Business Environment

STATE ECONOMY

State Economic Profile

"Tennessee's economic growth is becoming more moderate. Apparel-related layoffs and sizable consolidations at major employers such as Knoxville's Oak Ridge National Laboratory are impeding growth. Spurred by ongoing commercial and hotel projects as well as still-high homebuilding demand, construction companies are the most active job creator, hiring workers at more than a 5% clip over the past twelve months.

Tennessee is experiencing fiscal problems due to the combination of an extensive state-sponsored Medicaid program and an absence of personal income taxes. The projected budget shortfalls are necessitating cuts in public spending and infrastructure projects, exerting a drag on the construction industry.

Tennessee's homeownership rate is at an historic high. Firm housing affordability and extensive efforts to extend financing to lower-income buyers have been the principal factors in the rise in homeownership to date. However, the rate of growth in homeownership will cool this year due to lenders being less aggressive in expanding their affordable housing programs, and tighter monetary policy.

Tennessee possesses one of the South's highest rates of population growth attributable to domestic migration. Current population growth outpaces the 1% national annual rate by nearly 50 basis points. Tennessee's positive in-flows of migration are an essential source of labor, enabling the economy to expand. Over the longer run, the attractiveness of Tennessee's labor market conditions and housing affordability vis-a-vis northern economies remains a fundamental impetus for continued net positive in-migration.

As expected, Tennessee's economy has slowed moderately, while enduring structural changes in its manufacturing industry. Modest gains in local support industries will be offset by defense-related cutbacks and aggressive restructuring of Tennessee's largest employers. Tennessee's smaller metropolitan areas and surrounding rural communities will thus exhibit the slowest economic growth. Longer term, the most prominent risks to Tennessee's economy remain concentrated on the upside-enhanced industrial diversification, low business costs, solid housing affordability, strong demographic trends, and inherent geographic advantages for distribution and trade. As the decade ends, Tennessee will return as one of the strongest southern economies...." *National Association of Realtors, Economic Profiles: The Fifty States, July 1997*

IMPORTS/EXPORTS

Total Export Sales

Area	1993 ($000)	1994 ($000)	1995 ($000)	1996 ($000)	% Chg. 1993-96	% Chg. 1995-96
MSA[1]	1,104,101	1,310,492	1,412,348	1,445,492	30.9	2.3
U.S.	464,858,354	512,415,609	583,030,524	622,827,063	34.0	6.8

Note: (1) Metropolitan Statistical Area - see Appendix A for areas included
Source: U.S. Department of Commerce, International Trade Association, Metropolitan Area Exports: An Export Performance Report on Over 250 U.S. Cities, October 1997

Imports/Exports by Port

Type	Cargo Value			Share of U.S. Total	
	1995 (US$mil.)	1996 (US$mil.)	% Change 1995-1996	1995 (%)	1996 (%)
Imports	0	0	0	0	0
Exports	0	0	0	0	0

Source: Global Trade Information Services, WaterBorne Trade Atlas 1997

CITY FINANCES

City Government Finances

Component	FY92 ($000)	FY92 (per capita $)
Revenue	1,636,251	3,309.15
Expenditure	1,525,110	3,084.38
Debt Outstanding	2,215,909	4,481.45
Cash & Securities	2,084,832	4,216.36

Source: U.S. Bureau of the Census, City Government Finances: 1991-92

City Government Revenue by Source

Source	FY92 ($000)	FY92 (per capita $)	FY92 (%)
From Federal Government	12,614	25.51	0.8
From State Governments	244,750	494.98	15.0
From Local Governments	779	1.58	0.0
Property Taxes	263,324	532.55	16.1
General Sales Taxes	145,263	293.78	8.9
Selective Sales Taxes	27,793	56.21	1.7
Income Taxes	0	0.00	0.0
Current Charges	135,850	274.74	8.3
Utility/Liquor Store	604,657	1,222.86	37.0
Employee Retirement[1]	42,154	85.25	2.6
Other	159,067	321.70	9.7

Note: (1) Excludes "city contributions," classified as "nonrevenue," intragovernmental transfers.
Source: U.S. Bureau of the Census, City Government Finances: 1991-92

City Government Expenditures by Function

Function	FY92 ($000)	FY92 (per capita $)	FY92 (%)
Educational Services	280,035	566.34	18.4
Employee Retirement[1]	39,648	80.18	2.6
Environment/Housing	114,342	231.25	7.5
Government Administration	44,535	90.07	2.9
Interest on General Debt	115,288	233.16	7.6
Public Safety	137,297	277.67	9.0
Social Services	91,165	184.37	6.0
Transportation	35,672	72.14	2.3
Utility/Liquor Store	628,504	1,271.09	41.2
Other	38,624	78.11	2.5

Note: (1) Payments to beneficiaries including withdrawal of contributions.
Source: U.S. Bureau of the Census, City Government Finances: 1991-92

Municipal Bond Ratings

Area	Moody's	S & P
Nashville	Aa	AA

Note: n/a not available; n/r not rated
Source: Moody's Bond Record, 2/98; Statistical Abstract of the U.S., 1997; Governing Magazine, 9/97, 3/98

POPULATION

Population Growth

Area	1980	1990	% Chg. 1980-90	July 1996 Estimate	% Chg. 1990-96
City	455,663	488,518	7.2	511,263	4.7
MSA[1]	850,505	985,026	15.8	1,117,178	13.4
U.S.	226,545,805	248,765,170	9.8	265,179,411	6.6

Note: (1) Metropolitan Statistical Area - see Appendix A for areas included
Source: 1980/1990 Census of Housing and Population, Summary Tape File 3C; Census Bureau Population Estimates

Population Characteristics

Race	City 1980 Population	%	City 1990 Population	%	% Chg. 1980-90	MSA[1] 1990 Population	%
White	345,766	75.9	360,795	73.9	4.3	818,848	83.1
Black	105,869	23.2	118,802	24.3	12.2	152,302	15.5
Amer Indian/Esk/Aleut	743	0.2	1,439	0.3	93.7	2,663	0.3
Asian/Pacific Islander	2,418	0.5	6,220	1.3	157.2	9,349	0.9
Other	867	0.2	1,262	0.3	45.6	1,864	0.2
Hispanic Origin[2]	3,627	0.8	4,131	0.8	13.9	7,250	0.7

Note: (1) Metropolitan Statistical Area - see Appendix A for areas included;
(2) people of Hispanic origin can be of any race
Source: 1980/1990 Census of Housing and Population, Summary Tape File 3C

Ancestry

Area	German	Irish	English	Italian	U.S.	French	Polish	Dutch
City	14.9	16.5	15.2	1.9	9.3	3.0	0.9	1.9
MSA[1]	16.2	18.3	16.5	1.9	11.9	3.0	0.9	2.2
U.S.	23.3	15.6	13.1	5.9	5.3	4.2	3.8	2.5

Note: Figures are percentages and include persons that reported multiple ancestry (eg. if a person reported being Irish and Italian, they were included in both columns); (1) Metropolitan Statistical Area - see Appendix A for areas included
Source: 1990 Census of Population and Housing, Summary Tape File 3C

Age

Area	Median Age (Years)	Under 5	Under 18	18-24	25-44	45-64	65+	80+
City	32.2	7.0	22.9	11.6	36.2	17.9	11.4	2.6
MSA[1]	32.4	7.1	25.1	10.7	35.0	18.5	10.6	2.3
U.S.	32.9	7.3	25.6	10.5	32.6	18.7	12.5	2.8

Note: (1) Metropolitan Statistical Area - see Appendix A for areas included
Source: 1990 Census of Population and Housing, Summary Tape File 3C

Male/Female Ratio

Area	Number of males per 100 females (all ages)	Number of males per 100 females (18 years old+)
City	90.2	86.5
MSA[1]	93.2	89.5
U.S.	95.0	91.9

Note: (1) Metropolitan Statistical Area - see Appendix A for areas included
Source: 1990 Census of Population, General Population Characteristics

INCOME

Per Capita/Median/Average Income

Area	Per Capita ($)	Median Household ($)	Average Household ($)
City	14,490	27,821	35,188
MSA[1]	14,567	30,223	37,811
U.S.	14,420	30,056	38,453

Note: all figures are for 1989; (1) Metropolitan Statistical Area - see Appendix A for areas included
Source: 1990 Census of Population and Housing, Summary Tape File 3C

Household Income Distribution by Race

Income ($)	City (%)					U.S. (%)				
	Total	White	Black	Other	Hisp.[1]	Total	White	Black	Other	Hisp.[1]
Less than 5,000	7.6	4.8	17.9	8.2	3.2	6.2	4.8	15.2	8.6	8.8
5,000 - 9,999	8.3	7.2	12.1	8.9	7.1	9.3	8.6	14.2	9.9	11.1
10,000 - 14,999	9.0	8.2	11.7	9.2	8.6	8.8	8.5	11.0	9.8	11.0
15,000 - 24,999	19.6	19.4	20.4	18.7	23.3	17.5	17.3	18.9	18.5	20.5
25,000 - 34,999	17.3	18.1	14.3	21.9	21.6	15.8	16.1	14.2	15.4	16.4
35,000 - 49,999	17.9	19.5	12.3	17.0	17.6	17.9	18.6	13.3	16.1	16.0
50,000 - 74,999	13.5	14.9	8.6	11.2	14.3	15.0	15.8	9.3	13.4	11.1
75,000 - 99,999	3.7	4.2	2.0	2.7	2.5	5.1	5.5	2.6	4.7	3.1
100,000+	3.1	3.8	0.7	2.1	1.8	4.4	4.8	1.3	3.7	1.9

Note: all figures are for 1989; (1) people of Hispanic origin can be of any race
Source: 1990 Census of Population and Housing, Summary Tape File 3C

Effective Buying Income

Area	Per Capita ($)	Median Household ($)	Average Household ($)
City	18,826	36,179	45,647
MSA[1]	19,141	39,910	49,810
U.S.	15,444	33,201	41,849

Note: data as of 1/1/97; (1) Metropolitan Statistical Area - see Appendix A for areas included
Source: Standard Rate & Data Service, Newspaper Advertising Source, 2/98

Effective Household Buying Income Distribution

Area	% of Households Earning						
	$10,000 -$19,999	$20,000 -$34,999	$35,000 -$49,999	$50,000 -$74,999	$75,000 -$99,000	$100,000 -$124,999	$125,000 and up
City	13.9	22.9	18.3	19.6	8.0	2.7	2.9
MSA[1]	12.6	20.7	18.5	21.3	9.4	3.4	3.9
U.S.	16.5	23.4	18.3	18.2	6.4	2.1	2.4

Note: data as of 1/1/97; (1) Metropolitan Statistical Area - see Appendix A for areas included
Source: Standard Rate & Data Service, Newspaper Advertising Source, 2/98

Poverty Rates by Race and Age

Area	Total (%)	By Race (%)				By Age (%)		
		White	Black	Other	Hisp.[2]	Under 5 years old	Under 18 years old	65 years and over
City	13.4	8.6	27.9	18.1	14.3	22.5	20.4	15.1
MSA[1]	11.3	8.4	27.2	16.1	12.1	17.1	15.0	16.6
U.S.	13.1	9.8	29.5	23.1	25.3	20.1	18.3	12.8

Note: figures show the percent of people living below the poverty line in 1989. The average poverty threshold was $12,674 for a family of four in 1989; (1) Metropolitan Statistical Area - see Appendix A for areas included; (2) people of Hispanic origin can be of any race
Source: 1990 Census of Population and Housing, Summary Tape File 3C

EMPLOYMENT

Labor Force and Employment

Area	Civilian Labor Force			Workers Employed		
	Dec. '95	Dec. '96	% Chg.	Dec. '95	Dec. '96	% Chg.
City	294,593	297,900	1.1	286,962	290,338	1.2
MSA[1]	624,666	631,251	1.1	607,199	614,344	1.2
U.S.	134,583,000	136,742,000	1.6	127,903,000	130,785,000	2.3

Note: Data is not seasonally adjusted and covers workers 16 years of age and older;
(1) Metropolitan Statistical Area - see Appendix A for areas included
Source: Bureau of Labor Statistics, http://stats.bls.gov

Unemployment Rate

Area	1997											
	Jan.	Feb.	Mar.	Apr.	May	Jun.	Jul.	Aug.	Sep.	Oct.	Nov.	Dec.
City	3.2	3.0	3.1	3.1	3.0	4.0	3.7	3.7	3.5	3.4	3.1	2.5
MSA[1]	3.5	3.2	3.3	3.2	3.0	3.9	3.7	3.8	3.7	3.4	3.2	2.7
U.S.	5.9	5.7	5.5	4.8	4.7	5.2	5.0	4.8	4.7	4.4	4.3	4.4

Note: Data is not seasonally adjusted and covers workers 16 years of age and older; All figures are percentages; (1) Metropolitan Statistical Area - see Appendix A for areas included
Source: Bureau of Labor Statistics, http://stats.bls.gov

Employment by Industry

Sector	MSA[1]		U.S.
	Number of Employees	Percent of Total	Percent of Total
Services	197,700	30.9	29.0
Retail Trade	120,000	18.7	18.5
Government	84,100	13.1	16.1
Manufacturing	96,900	15.1	15.0
Finance/Insurance/Real Estate	39,400	6.2	5.7
Wholesale Trade	38,300	6.0	5.4
Transportation/Public Utilities	32,100	5.0	5.3
Construction/Mining	31,600	4.9	5.0

Note: Figures cover non-farm employment as of 12/97 and are not seasonally adjusted;
(1) Metropolitan Statistical Area - see Appendix A for areas included
Source: Bureau of Labor Statistics, http://stats.bls.gov

Employment by Occupation

Occupation Category	City (%)	MSA[1] (%)	U.S. (%)
White Collar	64.7	60.9	58.1
Executive/Admin./Management	13.5	13.1	12.3
Professional	15.4	13.7	14.1
Technical & Related Support	4.0	3.6	3.7
Sales	13.3	13.3	11.8
Administrative Support/Clerical	18.5	17.1	16.3
Blue Collar	20.8	25.5	26.2
Precision Production/Craft/Repair	8.7	10.8	11.3
Machine Operators/Assem./Insp.	5.0	6.7	6.8
Transportation/Material Movers	3.7	4.1	4.1
Cleaners/Helpers/Laborers	3.5	3.9	3.9
Services	13.6	12.1	13.2
Farming/Forestry/Fishing	0.8	1.5	2.5

Note: figures cover employed persons 16 years old and over;
(1) Metropolitan Statistical Area - see Appendix A for areas included
Source: 1990 Census of Population and Housing, Summary Tape File 3C

Occupational Employment Projections: 1994 - 2005

Occupations Expected to have the Largest Job Growth (ranked by numerical growth)	Fast-Growing Occupations (ranked by percent growth)
1. Salespersons, retail	1. Personal and home care aides
2. Truck drivers, heavy & light	2. Home health aides
3. Cashiers	3. Residential counselors
4. Waiters & waitresses	4. Computer engineers
5. Janitors/cleaners/maids, ex. priv. hshld.	5. Occupational therapy assistants
6. General managers & top executives	6. Physical therapy assistants and aides
7. Registered nurses	7. Physical therapists
8. Marketing & sales, supervisors	8. Systems analysts
9. Nursing aides/orderlies/attendants	9. Occupational therapists
10. Teachers aides, clerical & paraprofess.	10. Computer scientists

Projections cover Tennessee.
Source: U.S. Department of Labor, Employment and Training Administration, America's Labor Market Information System (ALMIS)

Average Wages

Occupation	Wage	Occupation	Wage
Professional/Technical/Clerical	$/Week	**Health/Protective Services**	$/Week
Accountants III	746	Corrections Officers	-
Attorneys III	1,072	Firefighters	537
Budget Analysts III	-	Nurses, Licensed Practical II	-
Buyers/Contracting Specialists II	607	Nurses, Registered II	-
Clerks, Accounting III	418	Nursing Assistants II	-
Clerks, General III	341	Police Officers I	556
Computer Operators II	427	**Hourly Workers**	$/Hour
Computer Programmers II	539	Forklift Operators	10.12
Drafters II	474	General Maintenance Workers	9.50
Engineering Technicians III	639	Guards I	6.60
Engineering Technicians, Civil III	580	Janitors	6.66
Engineers III	876	Maintenance Electricians	15.48
Key Entry Operators I	314	Maintenance Electronics Techs II	-
Personnel Assistants III	451	Maintenance Machinists	-
Personnel Specialists III	769	Maintenance Mechanics, Machinery	13.95
Secretaries III	495	Material Handling Laborers	-
Switchboard Operator-Receptionist	354	Motor Vehicle Mechanics	14.34
Systems Analysts II	838	Shipping/Receiving Clerks	10.73
Systems Analysts Supervisor/Mgr II	-	Tool and Die Makers	16.04
Tax Collectors II	501	Truckdrivers, Tractor Trailer	17.97
Word Processors II	473	Warehouse Specialists	-

Note: Wage data includes full-time workers only for 5/96 and cover the Metropolitan Statistical Area (see Appendix A for areas included). Dashes indicate that data was not available.
Source: Bureau of Labor Statistics, Occupational Compensation Survey, 8/96

TAXES

Major State and Local Tax Rates

State Corp. Income (%)	State Personal Income (%)	Residential Property (effective rate per $100)	Sales & Use		State Gasoline (cents/ gallon)	State Cigarette (cents/ 20-pack)
			State (%)	Local (%)		
6.0	6.0[a]	n/a	6.0	2.25	21[b]	13[c]

Note: Personal/corporate income tax rates as of 1/97. Sales, gasoline and cigarette tax rates as of 1/98; (a) Applies to interest and dividend income only; (b) Rate is comprised of 20 cents excise and 1 cent motor carrier tax. Does not include a 1 cent local option tax; (c) Counties and cities may impose an additional tax of 1 cent per pack
Source: Federation of Tax Administrators, www.taxadmin.org; Washington D.C. Department of Finance and Revenue, Tax Rates and Tax Burdens in the District of Columbia: A Nationwide Comparison, June 1997; Chamber of Commerce

Total Taxes Per Capita and as a Percent of Income

Area	Per Capita Income ($)	Per Capita Taxes ($)			Taxes as Pct. of Income (%)		
		Total	Federal	State/Local	Total	Federal	State/Local
Tennessee	23,748	7,574	5,460	2,114	31.9	23.0	8.9
U.S.	26,187	9,205	6,127	3,078	35.2	23.4	11.8

Note: Figures are for 1997
Source: Tax Foundation, Web Site, www.taxfoundation.org

Estimated Tax Burden

Area	State Income	Local Income	Property	Sales	Total
Nashville	0	0	2,025	1,130	3,155

Note: The numbers are estimates of taxes paid by a married couple with two kids and annual earnings of $65,000. Sales tax estimates assume they spend average amounts on food, clothing, household goods and gasoline. Property tax estimates assume they live in a $225,000 home.
Source: Kiplinger's Personal Finance Magazine, June 1997

COMMERCIAL REAL ESTATE

Office Market

Class/Location	Total Space (sq. ft.)	Vacant Space (sq. ft.)	Vac. Rate (%)	Under Constr. (sq. ft.)	Net Absorp. (sq. ft.)	Rental Rates ($/sq.ft./yr.)
Class A						
CBD	2,820,646	180,673	6.4	0	199,369	15.00-24.00
Outside CBD	6,741,958	274,783	4.1	1,157,353	512,486	12.50-23.00
Class B						
CBD	1,506,026	122,797	8.2	0	47,549	12.00-16.00
Outside CBD	3,559,345	187,564	5.3	0	-82,102	12.00-22.00

Note: Data as of 10/97 and covers Nashville; CBD = Central Business District; n/a not available;
Source: Society of Industrial and Office Realtors, 1998 Comparative Statistics of Industrial and Office Real Estate Markets

"Speculative development will be fueled mostly by REITs and will take place in suburban markets. Seventy percent of new spec space will be located in the Brentwood sub-market. The balance will be in the West End submarket with the development of Archon Group's Phase II development of the American Center, adding 220,000 sq. ft. These buildings should be fully leased upon completion. Absorption is expected to increase by at least six percent, but with more than one million sq. ft. of space under construction, vacancy will remain the same. As available Class 'B' CBD space reduces, sales prices will continue to rise." *Society of Industrial and Office Realtors, 1998 Comparative Statistics of Industrial and Office Real Estate Markets*

Industrial Market

Location	Total Space (sq. ft.)	Vacant Space (sq. ft.)	Vac. Rate (%)	Under Constr. (sq. ft.)	Net Absorp. (sq. ft.)	Gross Lease ($/sq.ft./yr.)
Central City	9,000,000	100,000	1.1	100,000	-156,000	3.20-4.75
Suburban	160,225,000	5,624,750	3.5	3,500,000	2,577,000	3.00-4.25

Note: Data as of 10/97 and covers Nashville; n/a not available
Source: Society of Industrial and Office Realtors, 1998 Comparative Statistics of Industrial and Office Real Estate Markets

"1998 looks to be one of the biggest speculative development years, yet. There is a concentration of development in the I-24 South/Interchange City area. LaVergne will have the strongest demand for speculative space. Our SIOR reporter expects all sectors to participate in speculative building. The diversity of the local and regional economy will keep Nashville solid. Previously Nashville drew labor from low growth areas and now it will have to compete with healthier markets. User relocations from rental space to owner occupied will continue at a steady pace, thus freeing up older warehouse space. Lease prices on older space will continue to rise, buoyed by the rate of four dollars per sq. ft. on new space. As Nashville matures, it should enhance its reputation as the bellwether for the Mid-South region." *Society of Industrial and Office Realtors, 1998 Comparative Statistics of Industrial and Office Real Estate Markets*

Retail Market

Shopping Center Inventory (sq. ft.)	Shopping Center Construction (sq. ft.)	Construction as a Percent of Inventory (%)	Torto Wheaton Rent Index[1] ($/sq. ft.)
23,502,000	2,000	0.0	12.56

Note: Data as of 1997 and covers the Metropolitan Statistical Area - see Appendix A for areas included; (1) Index is based on a model that predicts what the average rent should be for leases with certain characteristics, in certain locations during certain years.
Source: National Association of Realtors, 1997-1998 Market Conditions Report

"After experiencing vigorous growth in 1994, 1995 and 1996, Nashville's economy has slowed somewhat to a more sustainable pace. However, the area's retail market continues to surge behind a burgeoning tourism industry that contributes an estimated $8 billion to the state's economy and strong personal income growth. The number of shopping center completions slowed in 1997, which allowed the retail rent index to increase 8.1%. Big-box retailers have accounted for a large portion of demand, which is expected to continue at a robust pace in the near future. Nashville's retail rent index is expected to climb to near $15.00 per square foot by 2000." *National Association of Realtors, 1997-1998 Market Conditions Report*

COMMERCIAL UTILITIES

Typical Monthly Electric Bills

Area	Commercial Service ($/month)		Industrial Service ($/month)	
	12 kW demand 1,500 kWh	100 kW demand 30,000 kWh	1,000 kW demand 400,000 kWh	20,000 kW demand 10,000,000 kWh
City	n/a	n/a	n/a	n/a
U.S.	162	2,360	25,590	545,677

Note: Based on rates in effect July 1, 1997; n/a not available
Source: Edison Electric Institute, Typical Residential, Commercial and Industrial Bills, Summer 1997

TRANSPORTATION

Transportation Statistics

Avg. travel time to work (min.)	20.3
Interstate highways	I-24; I-40; I-65
Bus lines	
In-city	Metropolitan TA, 160 vehicles
Inter-city	2
Passenger air service	
Airport	Nashville International
Airlines	9
Aircraft departures	48,968 (1995)
Enplaned passengers	3,134,042 (1995)
Rail service	Amtrak Thruway Motorcoach Connections
Motor freight carriers	140
Major waterways/ports	Cumberland River; Port of Nashville

Source: OAG, Business Travel Planner, Summer 1997; Editor & Publisher Market Guide, 1998; FAA Airport Activity Statistics, 1996; Amtrak National Time Table, Northeast Timetable, Fall/Winter 1997-98; 1990 Census of Population and Housing, STF 3C; Chamber of Commerce/Economic Development 1997; Jane's Urban Transport Systems 1997-98; Transit Fact Book 1997

A survey of 90,000 airline passengers during the first half of 1997 ranked most of the largest airports in the U.S. Nashville International ranked number 4 out of 36. Criteria: cleanliness, quality of restaurants, attractiveness, speed of baggage delivery, ease of reaching gates, available ground transportation, ease of following signs and closeness of parking. *Plog Research Inc., First Half 1997*

Means of Transportation to Work

Area	Car/Truck/Van		Public Transportation			Bicycle	Walked	Other Means	Worked at Home
	Drove Alone	Car-pooled	Bus	Subway	Railroad				
City	78.1	13.4	2.8	0.0	0.0	0.1	2.6	0.8	2.2
MSA[1]	79.1	13.8	1.6	0.0	0.0	0.1	1.9	0.9	2.6
U.S.	73.2	13.4	3.0	1.5	0.5	0.4	3.9	1.2	3.0

Note: figures shown are percentages and only include workers 16 years old and over;
(1) Metropolitan Statistical Area - see Appendix A for areas included
Source: 1990 Census of Population and Housing, Summary Tape File 3C

BUSINESSES

Major Business Headquarters

Company Name	1997 Rankings	
	Fortune 500	Forbes 500
Columbia/HCA Healthcare	47	-
Ingram Industries	-	113

Note: Companies listed are located in the city; Dashes indicate no ranking
Fortune 500: companies that produce a 10-K are ranked 1 - 500 based on 1996 revenue
Forbes 500: private companies are ranked 1 - 500 based on 1996 revenue
Source: Forbes 12/1/97; Fortune 4/28/97

Fast-Growing Businesses

According to *Inc.*, Nashville is home to one of America's 100 fastest-growing private companies: AMICUS Legal Staffing. Criteria for inclusion: must be an independent, privately-held, U.S. corporation, proprietorship or partnership; sales of at least $200,000 in 1993; five-year operating/sales history; increase in 1997 sales over 1996 sales; holding companies, regulated banks, and utilities were excluded. *Inc. 500, 1997*

Nashville is home to one of *Business Week's* "hot growth" companies: Logan's Roadhouse. Criteria: sales and earnings, return on capital and stock price. *Business Week, 5/26/97*

According to *Fortune*, Nashville is home to one of America's 100 fastest-growing companies: Corrections Corp. of America. Companies were ranked based on three years' earnings-per-share growth using least squares analysis to smooth out distortions. Criteria for inclusion: public companies with sales of least $50 million. Companies that lost money in the most recent quarter, or ended in the red for the past four quarters as a whole, were not eligible. Limited partnerships and REITs were also not considered. *Fortune, 9/29/97*

Women-Owned Businesses: Number, Employment, Sales and Share

Area	Women-Owned Businesses in 1996				Share of Women-Owned Businesses in 1996	
	Number	Employment	Sales ($000)	Rank[2]	Percent (%)	Rank[3]
MSA[1]	36,800	81,600	9,755,600	46	34.4	43

Note: (1) Metropolitan Statistical Area - see Appendix A for areas included; (2) Calculated on an averaging of number of businesses, employment and sales and ranges from 1 to 50 where 1 is best; (3) Ranges from 1 to 50 where 1 is best
Source: The National Foundation for Women Business Owners, 1996 Facts on Women-Owned Businesses: Trends in the Top 50 Metropolitan Areas, March 26, 1997

Women-Owned Businesses: Growth

Area	Growth in Women-Owned Businesses (% change from 1987 to 1996)				Relative Growth in the Number of Women-Owned and All Businesses (% change from 1987 to 1996)			
	Num.	Empl.	Sales	Rank[2]	Women-Owned	All Firms	Absolute Difference	Relative Difference
MSA[1]	94.0	291.4	327.2	5	94.0	59.5	34.5	1.6:1

Note: (1) Metropolitan Statistical Area - see Appendix A for areas included; (2) Calculated on an averaging of the percent growth of number of businesses, employment and sales and ranges from 1 to 50 where 1 is best
Source: The National Foundation for Women Business Owners, 1996 Facts on Women-Owned Businesses: Trends in the Top 50 Metropolitan Areas, March 26, 1997

Small Business Opportunity

Nashville was included among *Entrepreneur* magazines listing of the "20 Best Cities for Small Business." It was ranked #15 among large metro areas. Criteria: risk of failure, business performance, economic growth, affordability and state attitude towards business. *Entrepreneur, 10/97*

According to *Forbes*, Nashville is home to three of America's 200 best small companies: Central Parking, Logan's Roadhouse, Renal Care Group. Criteria: companies must be publicly traded, U.S.-based corporations with latest 12-month sales of between $5 and $350 million. Earnings must be at least $1 million for the 12-month period. Limited partnerships, REITs and closed-end mutual funds were not considered. Banks, S&Ls and electric utilities were not included. *Forbes, November 3, 1997*

HOTELS & MOTELS

Hotels/Motels

Area	Hotels/Motels	Rooms	Luxury-Level Hotels/Motels		Average Minimum Rates ($)		
			♦♦♦♦	♦♦♦♦♦	♦♦	♦♦♦	♦♦♦♦
City	57	11,245	0	0	65	110	159
Airport	28	5,108	0	0	n/a	n/a	n/a
Suburbs	23	2,643	0	0	n/a	n/a	n/a
Total	108	18,996	0	0	n/a	n/a	n/a

Note: n/a not available; Classifications range from one diamond (budget properties with basic amenities) to five diamond (luxury properties with the finest service, rooms and facilities).
Source: OAG, Business Travel Planner, Summer 1997

CONVENTION CENTERS

Major Convention Centers

Center Name	Meeting Rooms	Exhibit Space (sf)
Holiday Inn Crowne Plaza	15	15,748
Nashville Convention Center	36	118,675
Nashville Municipal Auditorium	4	63,000
Opryland Hotel Convention Center	74	500,000
Stouffer Nashville Hotel	14	25,054
Tennessee State Fairgrounds	n/a	243,014
Willis Corroon Conference Center	17	n/a

Note: n/a not available
Source: Trade Shows Worldwide 1997

Living Environment

COST OF LIVING

Cost of Living Index

Composite Index	Housing	Utilities	Groceries	Health Care	Trans- portation	Misc. Goods/ Services
95.6	94.9	91.2	99.2	94.5	97.4	95.3

Note: U.S. = 100; Figures are for Nashville-Davidson
Source: ACCRA, Cost of Living Index, 3rd Quarter 1997

HOUSING

Median Home Prices and Housing Affordability

Area	Median Price[2] 3rd Qtr. 1997 ($)	HOI[3] 3rd Qtr. 1997	Afford- ability Rank[4]
MSA[1]	118,000	69.1	99
U.S.	127,000	63.7	–

Note: (1) Metropolitan Statistical Area - see Appendix A for areas included; (2) U.S. figures calculated from the sales of 625,000 new and existing homes in 195 markets; (3) Housing Opportunity Index - percent of homes sold that were within the reach of the median income household at the prevailing mortgage interest rate; (4) Rank is from 1-195 with 1 being most affordable
Source: National Association of Home Builders, Housing Opportunity Index, 3rd Quarter 1997

It is projected that the median price of existing single-family homes in the metro area will increase by 8.2% in 1998. Nationwide, home prices are projected to increase 6.6%.
Kiplinger's Personal Finance Magazine, January 1998

Average New Home Price

Area	Price ($)
City[1]	126,000
U.S.	135,710

Note: Figures are based on a new home with 1,800 sq. ft. of living area on an 8,000 sq. ft. lot; (1) Nashville-Davidson
Source: ACCRA, Cost of Living Index, 3rd Quarter 1997

Average Apartment Rent

Area	Rent ($/mth)
City[1]	624
U.S.	569

Note: Figures are based on an unfurnished two bedroom, 1-1/2 or 2 bath apartment, approximately 950 sq. ft. in size, excluding all utilities except water; (1) Nashville-Davidson
Source: ACCRA, Cost of Living Index, 3rd Quarter 1997

RESIDENTIAL UTILITIES

Average Residential Utility Costs

Area	All Electric ($/mth)	Part Electric ($/mth)	Other Energy ($/mth)	Phone ($/mth)
City[1]	92.53	–	–	18.85
U.S.	109.40	55.25	43.64	19.48

Note: (1) Nashville-Davidson
Source: ACCRA, Cost of Living Index, 3rd Quarter 1997

HEALTH CARE

Average Health Care Costs

Area	Hospital ($/day)	Doctor ($/visit)	Dentist ($/visit)
City[1]	275.60	53.14	56.20
U.S.	392.91	48.76	60.84

Note: Hospital - based on a semi-private room. Doctor - based on a general practitioner's routine exam of an established patient. Dentist - based on adult teeth cleaning and periodic oral exam; (1) (1) Nashville-Davidson
Source: ACCRA, Cost of Living Index, 3rd Quarter 1997

Distribution of Office-Based Physicians

Area	Family/Gen. Practitioners	Specialists		
		Medical	Surgical	Other
MSA[1]	207	857	711	719

Note: Data as of 12/31/96; (1) Metropolitan Statistical Area - see Appendix A for areas included
Source: American Medical Assn., Physician Characteristics & Distribution in the U.S., 1997-1998

Hospitals

Nashville has 7 general medical and surgical hospitals, 2 psychiatric, 1 rehabilitation, 1 chronic disease. *AHA Guide to the Healthcare Field 1997-98*

According to *U.S. News and World Report,* Nashville has 1 of the best hospitals in the U.S.: **Vanderbilt University Hospital and Clinic**, noted for cancer, endocrinology, gynecology, otolaryngology, pulmonology, rehabilitation; *U.S. News and World Report, "America's Best Hospitals", 7/28/97*

Centennial Medical Center is among the 100 best-run hospitals in the U.S.
Modern Healthcare, January 5, 1998

EDUCATION

Public School District Statistics

District Name	Num. Sch.	Enroll.	Classroom Teachers[1]	Pupils per Teacher	Minority Pupils (%)	Current Exp.[2] ($/pupil)
Nashville-Davidson County SD	122	70,913	n/a	n/a	47.1	4,520

Note: Data covers the 1995-1996 school year unless otherwise noted; (1) Excludes teachers reported as working in school district offices rather than in schools; (2) Based on 1993-94 enrollment collected by the Census Bureau, not the enrollment figure shown in column 3; SD = School District; ISD = Independent School District; n/a not available
Source: National Center for Education Statistics, Common Core of Data Survey; Bureau of the Census

Educational Quality

School District	Education Quotient[1]	Graduate Outcome[2]	Community Index[3]	Resource Index[4]
Nashville-Davidson Co.	96.0	63.0	108.0	116.0

Note: Nearly 1,000 secondary school districts were rated in terms of educational quality. The scores range from a low of 50 to a high of 150; (1) Average of the Graduate Outcome, Community and Resource indexes; (2) Based on graduation rates and college board scores (SAT/ACT); (3) Based on the surrounding community's average level of education and the area's average income level; (4) Based on teacher salaries, per-pupil expenditures and student-teacher ratios.
Source: Expansion Management, Ratings Issue 1997

Educational Attainment by Race

Area	High School Graduate (%)					Bachelor's Degree (%)				
	Total	White	Black	Other	Hisp.[2]	Total	White	Black	Other	Hisp.[2]
City	75.4	77.7	66.7	73.8	73.5	23.6	25.4	16.6	32.3	24.7
MSA[1]	74.0	75.6	64.4	75.2	74.2	21.4	22.3	15.1	31.2	23.4
U.S.	75.2	77.9	63.1	60.4	49.8	20.3	21.5	11.4	19.4	9.2

Note: figures shown cover persons 25 years old and over; (1) Metropolitan Statistical Area - see Appendix A for areas included; (2) people of Hispanic origin can be of any race
Source: 1990 Census of Population and Housing, Summary Tape File 3C

School Enrollment by Type

Area	Preprimary				Elementary/High School			
	Public		Private		Public		Private	
	Enrollment	%	Enrollment	%	Enrollment	%	Enrollment	%
City	3,671	51.4	3,472	48.6	61,254	84.7	11,083	15.3
MSA[1]	9,119	56.1	7,129	43.9	143,901	88.2	19,299	11.8
U.S.	2,679,029	59.5	1,824,256	40.5	38,379,689	90.2	4,187,099	9.8

Note: figures shown cover persons 3 years old and over;
(1) Metropolitan Statistical Area - see Appendix A for areas included
Source: 1990 Census of Population and Housing, Summary Tape File 3C

School Enrollment by Race

Area	Preprimary (%)				Elementary/High School (%)			
	White	Black	Other	Hisp.[1]	White	Black	Other	Hisp.[1]
City	73.3	24.3	2.4	0.8	63.8	34.0	2.2	1.1
MSA[2]	83.9	14.4	1.7	1.0	79.0	19.3	1.7	1.0
U.S.	80.4	12.5	7.1	7.8	74.1	15.6	10.3	12.5

Note: figures shown cover persons 3 years old and over; (1) people of Hispanic origin can be of any
race; (2) Metropolitan Statistical Area - see Appendix A for areas included
Source: 1990 Census of Population and Housing, Summary Tape File 3C

SAT/ACT Scores

Area/District	1997 SAT				1997 ACT	
	Percent of Graduates Tested (%)	Average Math Score	Average Verbal Score	Average Combined Score	Percent of Graduates Tested (%)	Average Composite Score
Metro Nashville PS	15	552	561	1,113	85	19.1
State	13	556	564	1,120	83	19.7
U.S.	42	511	505	1,016	36	21.0

Note: Math and verbal SAT scores are out of a possible 800; ACT scores are out of a possible 36
Caution: Comparing or ranking states/cities on the basis of SAT/ACT scores alone is invalid and
strongly discouraged by the The College Board and The American College Testing Program as
students who take the tests are self-selected and do not represent the entire student population.
Source: Metropolitan Public Schools, Guidance, 1997; American College Testing Program, 1997;
College Board, 1997

Classroom Teacher Salaries in Public Schools

District	B.A. Degree		M.A. Degree		Ph.D. Degree	
	Min. ($)	Max ($)	Min. ($)	Max. ($)	Min. ($)	Max. ($)
Nashville	23,884	37,617	26,750	41,140	32,482	48,723
Average[1]	26,120	39,270	28,175	44,667	31,643	49,825

Note: Salaries are for 1996-1997; (1) Based on all school districts covered
Source: American Federation of Teachers (unpublished data)

Higher Education

Two-Year Colleges		Four-Year Colleges		Medical Schools	Law Schools	Voc/ Tech
Public	Private	Public	Private			
1	5	1	9	2	2	13

Source: College Blue Book, Occupational Education 1997; Medical School Admission Requirements,
1998-99; Peterson's Guide to Two-Year Colleges, 1997; Peterson's Guide to Four-Year Colleges,
1997; Barron's Guide to Law Schools 1997

MAJOR EMPLOYERS

Major Employers

AGC Life Insurance	Aladdin Manufacturing
Baptist Hospital	Columbia/HCA Information Services
Direct General Corp. (insurance)	Flagship Airlines
Gaylord Entertainment	Genesco (men's footwear)
Intermedia Management (electrical work)	Metro Water Department
Opryland USA	Robert Orr\Sysco Food Services
SunTrust Bank of Tennessee	Sunday School Board of the Southern Baptist Convention
United Methodist Publishing House	Willis Corroon Corp. (insurance)

Note: companies listed are located in the city
Source: Dun's Business Rankings 1997; Ward's Business Directory, 1997

PUBLIC SAFETY

Crime Rate

Area	All Crimes	Violent Crimes				Property Crimes		
		Murder	Forcible Rape	Robbery	Aggrav. Assault	Burglary	Larceny -Theft	Motor Vehicle Theft
City	11,218.9	16.8	91.9	549.0	1,232.9	1,514.0	6,262.5	1,551.9
Suburbs[1]	4,222.1	4.4	27.9	55.6	372.2	833.7	2,666.7	261.6
MSA[2]	7,593.9	10.4	58.7	293.4	787.0	1,161.5	4,399.5	883.4
U.S.	5,078.9	7.4	36.1	202.4	388.2	943.0	2,975.9	525.9

Note: Crime rate is the number of crimes per 100,000 pop.; (1) defined as all areas within the MSA but located outside the central city; (2) Metropolitan Statistical Area - see Appendix A for areas incl.
Source: FBI Uniform Crime Reports 1996

RECREATION

Culture and Recreation

Museums	Symphony Orchestras	Opera Companies	Dance Companies	Professional Theatres	Zoos	Pro Sports Teams
13	1	1	3	4	1	0

Source: International Directory of the Performing Arts, 1996; Official Museum Directory, 1998; Chamber of Commerce/Economic Development 1997

Library System

The Public Library of Nashville & Davidson County has 19 branches, holdings of 704,160 volumes and a budget of $11,283,940 (1994-1995). *American Library Directory, 1997-1998*

MEDIA

Newspapers

Name	Type	Freq.	Distribution	Circulation
Belle Meade News	General	1x/wk	Local	23,487
Green Hills News	General	1x/wk	Local	23,487
Nashville Banner	General	5x/wk	Area	46,000
The Nashville Pride	General	1x/wk	Area	30,000
Nashville Scene	General	1x/wk	Area	153,000
Nashville Today	General	1x/wk	Local	23,487
National Baptist Union Review	Black	1x/mo	National	15,000
Observer	Religious	23x/yr	Area	3,200
The Tennessean	n/a	7x/wk	Area	148,000
West Meade News	General	1x/wk	Local	20,000
West Side News	General	1x/wk	Local	23,487
Westview	n/a	1x/wk	Area	5,000

Note: Includes newspapers with circulations of 1,000 or more located in the city; n/a not available
Source: Burrelle's Media Directory, 1998 Edition

AM Radio Stations

Call Letters	Freq. (kHz)	Target Audience	Station Format	Music Format
WSM	650	General	M/N/S	Country
WENO	760	Religious	M/T	Christian
WMDB	880	General	M/N	Adult Contemporary/Christian/Jazz/R&B/Urban Contemporary
WMRB	910	Religious	M	Christian
WYFN	980	General	M	Christian
WAMB	1160	General	M/N/S	Big Band/Easy Listening/Jazz/MOR
WKDA	1240	General	N/T	n/a
WNQM	1300	Gen/Relig	M	Christian/Spanish
WNAH	1360	General	M	Christian
WVOL	1470	General	M	Classic Rock/Oldies
WLAC	1510	General	N/T	n/a

Note: Stations included broadcast in the Nashville metro area; n/a not available
Station Format: E = Educational; M = Music; N = News; S = Sports; T = Talk
Music Format: AOR = Album Oriented Rock; MOR = Middle-of-the-Road
Source: Burrelle's Media Directory, 1998 Edition

FM Radio Stations

Call Letters	Freq. (mHz)	Target Audience	Station Format	Music Format
WFSK	88.1	General	M	Christian/Jazz/R&B
WNAZ	89.1	Religious	M	Christian
WPLN	90.3	General	M/N	Classical
WRVU	91.1	General	M/N/S	n/a
WQQK	92.1	General	M	Urban Contemporary
WJXA	92.9	General	M/N	Adult Contemporary
WYYB	93.7	General	M/N/S	Alternative
WRLG	94.1	General	M	Alternative
WSM	95.5	General	M/N/S	Country
WRMX	96.3	General	M/N	Oldies
WSIX	97.9	General	M	Country
WWTN	99.7	n/a	T	n/a
WRLT	100.1	General	M	Alternative/Jazz
WJZC	101.1	General	M	Urban Contemporary
WZPC	102.9	General	M	Country
WKDF	103.3	Alternative	M/N/S	AOR
WVRY	105.1	General	M/N/S	Christian
WLAC	105.9	General	M	Adult Contemporary
WAMB	106.7	General	M/N/S	n/a
WRVW	107.5	General	M	Contemporary Top 40

Note: Stations included broadcast in the Nashville metro area; n/a not available
Station Format: E = Educational; M = Music; N = News; S = Sports; T = Talk
Music Format: AOR = Album Oriented Rock; MOR = Middle-of-the-Road
Source: Burrelle's Media Directory, 1998 Edition

Television Stations

Name	Ch.	Affiliation	Type	Owner
WKRN	2	ABC	Commercial	Young Broadcasting Inc.
WSMV	4	NBC	Commercial	Meredith Corporation
WTVF	5	CBS	Commercial	Landmark Television of Tennessee Inc.
WDCN	8	PBS	Public	Metro Board of Public Education
WZTV	17	Fox	Commercial	Sullivan Broadcasting
WUXP	30	UPN	n/a	n/a
WHTN	39	n/a	Commercial	Christian Television Network
WNAB	58	WB	n/a	Speer Communications Holding Company

Note: Stations included broadcast in the Nashville metro area
Source: Burrelle's Media Directory, 1998 Edition

CLIMATE

Average and Extreme Temperatures

Temperature	Jan	Feb	Mar	Apr	May	Jun	Jul	Aug	Sep	Oct	Nov	Dec	Ann
Extreme High (°F)	78	84	86	91	95	106	107	104	105	94	84	79	107
Average High (°F)	47	51	60	71	79	87	90	89	83	72	60	50	70
Average Temp. (°F)	38	41	50	60	68	76	80	79	72	61	49	41	60
Average Low (°F)	28	31	39	48	57	65	69	68	61	48	39	31	49
Extreme Low (°F)	-17	-13	2	23	34	42	54	49	36	26	-1	-10	-17

Note: Figures cover the years 1948-1990
Source: National Climatic Data Center, International Station Meteorological Climate Summary, 3/95

Average Precipitation/Snowfall/Humidity

Precip./Humidity	Jan	Feb	Mar	Apr	May	Jun	Jul	Aug	Sep	Oct	Nov	Dec	Ann
Avg. Precip. (in.)	4.4	4.2	5.0	4.1	4.6	3.7	3.8	3.3	3.2	2.6	3.9	4.6	47.4
Avg. Snowfall (in.)	4	3	1	Tr	0	0	0	0	0	Tr	1	1	11
Avg. Rel. Hum. 6am (%)	81	81	80	81	86	86	88	90	90	87	83	82	85
Avg. Rel. Hum. 3pm (%)	61	57	51	48	52	52	54	53	52	49	55	59	54

Note: Figures cover the years 1948-1990; Tr = Trace amounts (<0.05 in. of rain; <0.5 in. of snow)
Source: National Climatic Data Center, International Station Meteorological Climate Summary, 3/95

Weather Conditions

Temperature			Daytime Sky			Precipitation		
10°F & below	32°F & below	90°F & above	Clear	Partly cloudy	Cloudy	0.01 inch or more precip.	0.1 inch or more snow/ice	Thunder-storms
5	76	51	98	135	132	119	8	54

Note: Figures are average number of days per year and covers the years 1948-1990
Source: National Climatic Data Center, International Station Meteorological Climate Summary, 3/95

AIR & WATER QUALITY

Maximum Pollutant Concentrations

	Particulate Matter (ug/m³)	Carbon Monoxide (ppm)	Sulfur Dioxide (ppm)	Nitrogen Dioxide (ppm)	Ozone (ppm)	Lead (ug/m³)
MSA[1] Level	66	5	0.076	0.012	0.12	0.07
NAAQS[2]	150	9	0.140	0.053	0.12	1.50
Met NAAQS?	Yes	Yes	Yes	Yes	Yes	Yes

Note: (1) Metropolitan Statistical Area - see Appendix A for areas included; (2) National Ambient Air Quality Standards; ppm = parts per million; ug/m³ = micrograms per cubic meter; n/a not available
Source: EPA, National Air Quality and Emissions Trends Report, 1996

Pollutant Standards Index

In the Nashville MSA (see Appendix A for areas included), the Pollutant Standards Index (PSI) exceeded 100 on 2 days in 1996. A PSI value greater than 100 indicates that air quality would be in the unhealthful range on that day. *EPA, National Air Quality and Emissions Trends Report, 1996*

Drinking Water

Water System Name	Pop. Served	Primary Water Source Type	Number of Violations in Fiscal Year 1997	Type of Violation/ Contaminants
Nashville Water Dept. #1	414,209	Surface	None	None

Note: Data as of January 16, 1998
Source: EPA, Office of Ground Water and Drinking Water, Safe Drinking Water Information System

Nashville tap water is alkaline, soft.
Editor & Publisher Market Guide, 1998

New Orleans, Louisiana

Background

Many people agree that New Orleans, the largest city in Louisiana, sits atop a pedestal with San Francisco and New York City, as one of the most colorful cities in the United States. Indeed, like her cosmopolitan sisters to the East and West, New Orleans is rich with a unique local history, colorful "debauched" areas, and most importantly, an individual character that separates her from any city in the world.

New Orleans was founded by the brothers Le Moyne, Sieurs d'Iberville and de Bienville, in 1718. Despite early obstacles such as disease, starvation, and an unwilling working class, New Orleans nevertheless emerged as a genteel antebellum, slave society, fashioning itself after the rigid social hierarchy of Versailles. Even after New Orleans fell under Spanish hands, this perhaps gracious, but unequal lifestyle, continued.

The transfer of control from Spain to the United States in the Louisiana Purchase changed New Orleans's Old World isolation. The newly arrived American settlers introduced aggressive business acumen to the area, as well as the idea of respect for the self-made man. As trade opened up with countries around the world, this made for a very happy union. New Orleans became "Queen City of the South", growing prosperous from adventurous riverboat traders and speculators.

New Orleans was also an active slave market. It is not surprising therefore, that many residents of New Orleans are black. Arising from this significant portion of the population is the highly popular musical form, Dixieland Jazz. When one thinks of New Orleans, especially during Mardi Gras, one thinks of Dixieland musicians parading through the streets in joyous rhythm.

Today, despite a changing skyline, much of New Orlean's Old World charm still remains. It is a city resulting from a polyglot of Southern, Cajun, African-American, and European cultures.

Greater New Orleans is one of the 10 U.S. winners of the 1996 National Civic League's All-America City and Community Award. The programs recognized 10 communities for addressing problems such as racial and ethnic discord, crime, neighborhood blight, and joblessness. Greater New Orleans was singled out for its "forward-thinking" Career Academies which have helped prepare students to move from school into the workplace.

The New Orleans metro area is virtually surrounded by water which influences its climate. Although quite humid, the adjacent lakes and Gulf of Mexico help to modify the temperatures. Between mid-June and September the temperatures do not rise above 90 degrees due to the near-daily sporadic thunderstorms. Cold spells which sometimes reach the area in the winter, seldom last for more than three or four days.

The nearby lakes and marshes contribute to the formation of fogs which do not seriously affect automobile traffic, but can suspend air travel between New Orleans and the Gulf for several days at a time.

Frequent and sometimes very heavy rains are typical, but thunderstorms with damaging winds are infrequent. Tornadoes are extremely rare, although waterspouts are more common. Hurricanes have affected the area.

General Rankings and Evaluative Comments

- New Orleans was ranked #111 out of 300 cities by *Money's* 1997 "Survey of the Best Places to Live." Criteria used: health services, crime, economy, housing, education, transportation, weather, leisure and the arts. The city was ranked #105 in 1996 and #87 in 1995.
  Money, July 1997; Money, September 1996; Money, September 1995

- *Ladies Home Journal* ranked America's 200 largest cities based on the qualities women care about most. New Orleans ranked 187 out of 200. Criteria: low crime rate, good public schools, well-paying jobs, quality health and child care, the presence of women in government, proportion of women-owned businesses, size of the wage gap with men, local economy, divorce rates, the ratio of single men to single women, whether there are laws that require at least the same number of public toilets for women as men, and the probability of good hair days. *Ladies Home Journal, November 1997*

- New Orleans was ranked #209 out of 219 cities in terms of children's health, safety, and economic well-being. Criteria: total population, percent population change, birth rate, child immunization rate, infant mortality rate, percent low birth weight infants, percent of births to teens, physician-to-population ratio, student-to-teacher ratio, dropout rate, unemployment rate, median family income, percent of children in poverty, violent and property crime rates, number of juvenile arrests for violent crimes as a percent of the total crime index, number of days with pollution standard index (PSI) over 100, pounds toxic releases per 1,000 people and number of superfund sites. *Zero Population Growth, Children's Environmental Index 1997*

- New Orleans is among the 20 most livable cities for gay men and lesbians. The list was divided between 10 cities you might expect and 10 surprises. New Orleans was on the cities you wouldn't expect list. Rank: 2 out of 10. Criteria: legal protection from antigay discrimination, an annual gay pride celebration, a community center, gay bookstores and publications, and an array of organizations, religious groups, and health care facilities that cater to the needs of the local gay community. *The Advocate, June 1997*

- New Orleans appeared on *Travel & Leisure's* list of the world's best cities.
  Rank: 12 out of 25. Criteria: activities/attractions, culture/arts, people, restaurants/food, and value. *Travel & Leisure, September 1997*

- *Conde Nast Traveler* polled 37,000 readers in terms of travel satisfaction. Cities were ranked based on the following criteria: people/friendliness, environment/ambiance, cultural enrichment, restaurants and fun/energy. New Orleans appeared in the top thirty, ranking number 3, with an overall rating of 74.5 out of 100 based on all the criteria. The cities were also ranked in each category separately. New Orleans appeared in the top 10 based on restaurants, ranking number 2 with a rating of 88.6 out of 100. New Orleans appeared in the top 10 based on fun/energy, ranking number 4 with a rating of 85.1 out of 100. *Conde Nast Traveler, Readers' Choice Poll 1997*

- *Yahoo! Internet Life* selected "America's 100 Most Wired Cities & Towns". 50 cities were large and 50 cities were small. New Orleans ranked 33 out of 50 large cities. Criteria: Internet users per capita, number of networked computers, number of registered domain names, Internet backbone traffic, and the per-capita number of Web sites devoted to each city. *Yahoo! Internet Life, March 1998*

- According to *Working Mother*, "Officials at the state's department of social services have proposed the following: lowering the child/staff ratios, requiring TB tests and mandating more training for caregivers, especially for family child care workers who presently have no training requirements. 'We're finally on the verge of having some good things happen this year', says Steve Philips, director of the bureau of licensing in Louisiana's Department of Social Services.

  State officials and activists have also been working to create a career-development program for child care workers. A special advisory council, made up of a group of child care professionals, advocates, state education officials and others will run focus groups and workshops in an effort to design new caregiver training programs. The state's resource and referral agency as well as local universities and community colleges, will then offer the courses to interested caregivers." *Working Mother, July/August 1997*

Business Environment

STATE ECONOMY

State Economic Profile

"Louisiana's economy is re-accelerating due to the approval of state-wide gambling....

The state had a net loss of nearly 13,000 residents in 1996, due to the strength of the Texas economy and the resurgence of California's economy. These two states are Louisiana's largest source of in-migrants. Net out-migration has been a persistent phenomenon throughout the decade. While the resurgence of gambling will stem the tide somewhat, most of the new jobs are lower paying and will not attract workers from outside the state.

Louisiana's fiscal situation is one of the worst in the nation, with a 3.2% budget deficit in 1996. Moreover, the state's reserves, measured as a percentage of spending, are a low 0.1%, well below the national average of 5.7%.

Oil prices plunged during February, due to the extremely mild winter, which weakened the need for both distillate and residual fuels. The drop in energy prices will cause a drop in state revenues, putting further strain on state finances.

Louisiana is poised for continued growth as the gaming industry revives. Other advantages include an extremely low cost of doing business, driven particularly by low wages, and a strategic location between Central America and the U.S. Counterbalancing the low cost structure is the high crime rate and low education rates throughout much of the state. Louisiana will be an average performer over the forecast horizon." *National Association of Realtors, Economic Profiles: The Fifty States, July 1997*

IMPORTS/EXPORTS

Total Export Sales

Area	1993 ($000)	1994 ($000)	1995 ($000)	1996 ($000)	% Chg. 1993-96	% Chg. 1995-96
MSA[1]	2,034,209	2,326,231	3,037,819	3,316,761	63.0	9.2
U.S.	464,858,354	512,415,609	583,030,524	622,827,063	34.0	6.8

Note: (1) Metropolitan Statistical Area - see Appendix A for areas included
Source: U.S. Department of Commerce, International Trade Association, Metropolitan Area Exports: An Export Performance Report on Over 250 U.S. Cities, October 1997

Imports/Exports by Port

Type	Cargo Value			Share of U.S. Total	
	1995 (US$mil.)	1996 (US$mil.)	% Change 1995-1996	1995 (%)	1996 (%)
Imports	8,132	8,116	-0.20	2.08	2.12
Exports	10,930	9,223	-15.62	4.78	3.89

Source: Global Trade Information Services, WaterBorne Trade Atlas 1997

CITY FINANCES

City Government Finances

Component	FY92 ($000)	FY92 (per capita $)
Revenue	746,656	1,523.19
Expenditure	772,877	1,576.68
Debt Outstanding	1,125,844	2,296.74
Cash & Securities	1,107,565	2,259.45

Source: U.S. Bureau of the Census, City Government Finances: 1991-92

City Government Revenue by Source

Source	FY92 ($000)	FY92 (per capita $)	FY92 (%)
From Federal Government	77,804	158.72	10.4
From State Governments	44,968	91.74	6.0
From Local Governments	10	0.02	0.0
Property Taxes	137,619	280.74	18.4
General Sales Taxes	88,445	180.43	11.8
Selective Sales Taxes	48,641	99.23	6.5
Income Taxes	0	0.00	0.0
Current Charges	147,538	300.98	19.8
Utility/Liquor Store	55,727	113.68	7.5
Employee Retirement[1]	33,255	67.84	4.5
Other	112,649	229.81	15.1

Note: (1) Excludes "city contributions," classified as "nonrevenue," intragovernmental transfers.
Source: U.S. Bureau of the Census, City Government Finances: 1991-92

City Government Expenditures by Function

Function	FY92 ($000)	FY92 (per capita $)	FY92 (%)
Educational Services	7,520	15.34	1.0
Employee Retirement[1]	34,782	70.96	4.5
Environment/Housing	198,822	405.60	25.7
Government Administration	80,607	164.44	10.4
Interest on General Debt	93,950	191.66	12.2
Public Safety	167,735	342.18	21.7
Social Services	19,923	40.64	2.6
Transportation	90,392	184.40	11.7
Utility/Liquor Store	54,473	111.13	7.0
Other	24,673	50.33	3.2

Note: (1) Payments to beneficiaries including withdrawal of contributions.
Source: U.S. Bureau of the Census, City Government Finances: 1991-92

Municipal Bond Ratings

Area	Moody's	S & P
New Orleans	Baa2	BBB+

Note: n/a not available; n/r not rated
Source: Moody's Bond Record, 2/98; Statistical Abstract of the U.S., 1997;
Governing Magazine, 9/97, 3/98

POPULATION

Population Growth

Area	1980	1990	% Chg. 1980-90	July 1996 Estimate	% Chg. 1990-96
City	557,515	496,938	-10.9	476,625	-4.1
MSA[1]	1,256,256	1,238,816	-1.4	1,312,890	6.0
U.S.	226,545,805	248,765,170	9.8	265,179,411	6.6

Note: (1) Metropolitan Statistical Area - see Appendix A for areas included
Source: 1980/1990 Census of Housing and Population, Summary Tape File 3C;
Census Bureau Population Estimates

Population Characteristics

Race	City 1980 Population	%	City 1990 Population	%	% Chg. 1980-90	MSA[1] 1990 Population	%
White	238,192	42.7	173,305	34.9	-27.2	770,363	62.2
Black	308,039	55.3	308,364	62.1	0.1	430,894	34.8
Amer Indian/Esk/Aleut	623	0.1	815	0.2	30.8	3,838	0.3
Asian/Pacific Islander	7,458	1.3	9,295	1.9	24.6	20,976	1.7
Other	3,203	0.6	5,159	1.0	61.1	12,745	1.0
Hispanic Origin[2]	19,226	3.4	15,900	3.2	-17.3	51,574	4.2

Note: (1) Metropolitan Statistical Area - see Appendix A for areas included;
(2) people of Hispanic origin can be of any race
Source: 1980/1990 Census of Housing and Population, Summary Tape File 3C

Ancestry

Area	German	Irish	English	Italian	U.S.	French	Polish	Dutch
City	9.8	6.8	5.3	4.3	2.5	8.4	0.6	0.5
MSA[1]	17.0	11.9	7.2	9.0	3.5	17.3	0.8	0.8
U.S.	23.3	15.6	13.1	5.9	5.3	4.2	3.8	2.5

Note: Figures are percentages and include persons that reported multiple ancestry (eg. if a person reported being Irish and Italian, they were included in both columns); (1) Metropolitan Statistical Area - see Appendix A for areas included
Source: 1990 Census of Population and Housing, Summary Tape File 3C

Age

Area	Median Age (Years)	Age Distribution (%) Under 5	Under 18	18-24	25-44	45-64	65+	80+
City	31.5	7.7	27.6	11.1	31.4	16.9	13.0	3.0
MSA[1]	31.8	7.7	27.9	10.1	32.8	18.1	11.0	2.2
U.S.	32.9	7.3	25.6	10.5	32.6	18.7	12.5	2.8

Note: (1) Metropolitan Statistical Area - see Appendix A for areas included
Source: 1990 Census of Population and Housing, Summary Tape File 3C

Male/Female Ratio

Area	Number of males per 100 females (all ages)	Number of males per 100 females (18 years old+)
City	86.6	81.6
MSA[1]	90.5	86.3
U.S.	95.0	91.9

Note: (1) Metropolitan Statistical Area - see Appendix A for areas included
Source: 1990 Census of Population, General Population Characteristics

INCOME

Per Capita/Median/Average Income

Area	Per Capita ($)	Median Household ($)	Average Household ($)
City	11,372	18,477	29,283
MSA[1]	12,108	24,442	32,569
U.S.	14,420	30,056	38,453

Note: all figures are for 1989; (1) Metropolitan Statistical Area - see Appendix A for areas included
Source: 1990 Census of Population and Housing, Summary Tape File 3C

Household Income Distribution by Race

Income ($)	City (%)					U.S. (%)				
	Total	White	Black	Other	Hisp.[1]	Total	White	Black	Other	Hisp.[1]
Less than 5,000	18.0	8.4	25.4	17.5	13.3	6.2	4.8	15.2	8.6	8.8
5,000 - 9,999	13.4	10.2	15.9	12.4	14.0	9.3	8.6	14.2	9.9	11.1
10,000 - 14,999	11.9	10.1	13.2	13.5	14.1	8.8	8.5	11.0	9.8	11.0
15,000 - 24,999	17.9	17.6	17.9	22.9	20.8	17.5	17.3	18.9	18.5	20.5
25,000 - 34,999	12.6	13.8	11.6	12.2	13.1	15.8	16.1	14.2	15.4	16.4
35,000 - 49,999	11.4	14.3	9.2	9.3	12.7	17.9	18.6	13.3	16.1	16.0
50,000 - 74,999	8.6	13.0	5.2	8.4	7.8	15.0	15.8	9.3	13.4	11.1
75,000 - 99,999	2.8	5.2	1.0	1.9	2.5	5.1	5.5	2.6	4.7	3.1
100,000+	3.6	7.5	0.6	1.9	1.7	4.4	4.8	1.3	3.7	1.9

Note: all figures are for 1989; (1) people of Hispanic origin can be of any race
Source: 1990 Census of Population and Housing, Summary Tape File 3C

Effective Buying Income

Area	Per Capita ($)	Median Household ($)	Average Household ($)
City	13,684	22,908	36,135
MSA[1]	14,569	30,096	39,531
U.S.	15,444	33,201	41,849

Note: data as of 1/1/97; (1) Metropolitan Statistical Area - see Appendix A for areas included
Source: Standard Rate & Data Service, Newspaper Advertising Source, 2/98

Effective Household Buying Income Distribution

Area	% of Households Earning						
	$10,000 -$19,999	$20,000 -$34,999	$35,000 -$49,999	$50,000 -$74,999	$75,000 -$99,000	$100,000 -$124,999	$125,000 and up
City	19.7	20.6	12.7	11.7	4.7	1.8	2.9
MSA[1]	17.1	22.3	16.4	16.4	6.0	2.0	2.5
U.S.	16.5	23.4	18.3	18.2	6.4	2.1	2.4

Note: data as of 1/1/97; (1) Metropolitan Statistical Area - see Appendix A for areas included
Source: Standard Rate & Data Service, Newspaper Advertising Source, 2/98

Poverty Rates by Race and Age

Area	Total (%)	By Race (%)				By Age (%)		
		White	Black	Other	Hisp.[2]	Under 5 years old	Under 18 years old	65 years and over
City	31.6	11.8	42.2	37.4	26.1	48.8	46.3	24.6
MSA[1]	21.2	10.1	40.8	25.9	18.7	31.5	30.3	19.2
U.S.	13.1	9.8	29.5	23.1	25.3	20.1	18.3	12.8

Note: figures show the percent of people living below the poverty line in 1989. The average poverty threshold was $12,674 for a family of four in 1989; (1) Metropolitan Statistical Area - see Appendix A for areas included; (2) people of Hispanic origin can be of any race
Source: 1990 Census of Population and Housing, Summary Tape File 3C

EMPLOYMENT

Labor Force and Employment

Area	Civilian Labor Force			Workers Employed		
	Dec. '95	Dec. '96	% Chg.	Dec. '95	Dec. '96	% Chg.
City	203,096	203,502	0.2	190,033	191,841	1.0
MSA[1]	610,785	610,508	-0.0	576,686	582,172	1.0
U.S.	134,583,000	136,742,000	1.6	127,903,000	130,785,000	2.3

Note: Data is not seasonally adjusted and covers workers 16 years of age and older;
(1) Metropolitan Statistical Area - see Appendix A for areas included
Source: Bureau of Labor Statistics, http://stats.bls.gov

Unemployment Rate

Area	1997											
	Jan.	Feb.	Mar.	Apr.	May	Jun.	Jul.	Aug.	Sep.	Oct.	Nov.	Dec.
City	6.8	5.3	5.6	5.2	5.9	7.6	7.4	6.9	6.6	6.5	6.3	5.7
MSA[1]	5.8	4.6	4.8	4.4	4.9	6.5	6.3	5.6	5.4	5.4	5.1	4.6
U.S.	5.9	5.7	5.5	4.8	4.7	5.2	5.0	4.8	4.7	4.4	4.3	4.4

Note: Data is not seasonally adjusted and covers workers 16 years of age and older; All figures are percentages; (1) Metropolitan Statistical Area - see Appendix A for areas included
Source: Bureau of Labor Statistics, http://stats.bls.gov

Employment by Industry

Sector	MSA[1]		U.S.
	Number of Employees	Percent of Total	Percent of Total
Services	192,100	30.8	29.0
Retail Trade	118,500	19.0	18.5
Government	107,600	17.2	16.1
Manufacturing	49,200	7.9	15.0
Finance/Insurance/Real Estate	31,600	5.1	5.7
Wholesale Trade	35,900	5.8	5.4
Transportation/Public Utilities	42,700	6.8	5.3
Construction	31,100	5.0	4.5
Mining	15,200	2.4	0.5

Note: Figures cover non-farm employment as of 12/97 and are not seasonally adjusted;
(1) Metropolitan Statistical Area - see Appendix A for areas included
Source: Bureau of Labor Statistics, http://stats.bls.gov

Employment by Occupation

Occupation Category	City (%)	MSA[1] (%)	U.S. (%)
White Collar	61.6	62.5	58.1
Executive/Admin./Management	11.2	11.9	12.3
Professional	19.4	15.8	14.1
Technical & Related Support	3.5	3.9	3.7
Sales	10.7	13.2	11.8
Administrative Support/Clerical	16.8	17.7	16.3
Blue Collar	18.2	21.8	26.2
Precision Production/Craft/Repair	7.0	10.3	11.3
Machine Operators/Assem./Insp.	3.2	3.6	6.8
Transportation/Material Movers	4.5	4.6	4.1
Cleaners/Helpers/Laborers	3.5	3.4	3.9
Services	19.2	14.6	13.2
Farming/Forestry/Fishing	1.0	1.1	2.5

Note: figures cover employed persons 16 years old and over;
(1) Metropolitan Statistical Area - see Appendix A for areas included
Source: 1990 Census of Population and Housing, Summary Tape File 3C

Occupational Employment Projections: 1994 - 2005

Occupations Expected to have the Largest Job Growth (ranked by numerical growth)	Fast-Growing Occupations (ranked by percent growth)
1. Salespersons, retail	1. Home health aides
2. Cashiers	2. Musicians
3. Nursing aides/orderlies/attendants	3. Physical therapy assistants and aides
4. Registered nurses	4. Physical therapists
5. General managers & top executives	5. Occupational therapy assistants
6. Blue collar worker supervisors	6. Manicurists
7. Marketing & sales, supervisors	7. Occupational therapists
8. Waiters & waitresses	8. Amusement and recreation attendants
9. Home health aides	9. Electronic pagination systems workers
10. Truck drivers, heavy & light	10. Personal and home care aides

Projections cover Louisiana.
Source: U.S. Department of Labor, Employment and Training Administration, America's Labor Market Information System (ALMIS)

Average Wages

Occupation	Wage	Occupation	Wage
Professional/Technical/Clerical	$/Week	**Health/Protective Services**	$/Week
Accountants III	751	Corrections Officers	-
Attorneys III	1,129	Firefighters	423
Budget Analysts III	-	Nurses, Licensed Practical II	463
Buyers/Contracting Specialists II	580	Nurses, Registered II	756
Clerks, Accounting III	407	Nursing Assistants II	218
Clerks, General III	362	Police Officers I	413
Computer Operators II	403	**Hourly Workers**	$/Hour
Computer Programmers II	573	Forklift Operators	9.80
Drafters II	506	General Maintenance Workers	8.58
Engineering Technicians III	644	Guards I	5.66
Engineering Technicians, Civil III	430	Janitors	5.24
Engineers III	954	Maintenance Electricians	15.74
Key Entry Operators I	282	Maintenance Electronics Techs II	-
Personnel Assistants III	-	Maintenance Machinists	17.83
Personnel Specialists III	777	Maintenance Mechanics, Machinery	15.73
Secretaries III	500	Material Handling Laborers	-
Switchboard Operator-Receptionist	302	Motor Vehicle Mechanics	13.05
Systems Analysts II	905	Shipping/Receiving Clerks	8.68
Systems Analysts Supervisor/Mgr II	-	Tool and Die Makers	-
Tax Collectors II	337	Truckdrivers, Tractor Trailer	12.21
Word Processors II	366	Warehouse Specialists	10.13

Note: Wage data includes full-time workers only for 1/96 and cover the Metropolitan Statistical Area (see Appendix A for areas included). Dashes indicate that data was not available.
Source: Bureau of Labor Statistics, Occupational Compensation Survey

TAXES

Major State and Local Tax Rates

State Corp. Income (%)	State Personal Income (%)	Residential Property (effective rate per $100)	Sales & Use		State Gasoline (cents/ gallon)	State Cigarette (cents/ 20-pack)
			State (%)	Local (%)		
4.0 - 8.0	2.0 - 6.0	1.61	4.0	5.0	20	20

Note: Personal/corporate income tax rates as of 1/97. Sales, gasoline and cigarette tax rates as of 1/98.
Source: Federation of Tax Administrators, www.taxadmin.org; Washington D.C. Department of Finance and Revenue, Tax Rates and Tax Burdens in the District of Columbia: A Nationwide Comparison, June 1997; Chamber of Commerce

Total Taxes Per Capita and as a Percent of Income

Area	Per Capita Income ($)	Per Capita Taxes ($)			Taxes as Pct. of Income (%)		
		Total	Federal	State/Local	Total	Federal	State/Local
Louisiana	21,321	6,750	4,660	2,090	31.7	21.9	9.8
U.S.	26,187	9,205	6,127	3,078	35.2	23.4	11.8

Note: Figures are for 1997
Source: Tax Foundation, Web Site, www.taxfoundation.org

Estimated Tax Burden

Area	State Income	Local Income	Property	Sales	Total
New Orleans	1,211	0	2,025	1,233	4,469

Note: The numbers are estimates of taxes paid by a married couple with two kids and annual earnings of $65,000. Sales tax estimates assume they spend average amounts on food, clothing, household goods and gasoline. Property tax estimates assume they live in a $225,000 home.
Source: Kiplinger's Personal Finance Magazine, June 1997

COMMERCIAL REAL ESTATE

Office Market

Class/Location	Total Space (sq. ft.)	Vacant Space (sq. ft.)	Vac. Rate (%)	Under Constr. (sq. ft.)	Net Absorp. (sq. ft.)	Rental Rates ($/sq.ft./yr.)
Class A						
CBD	7,511,682	1,290,097	17.2	n/a	174,157	11.75-19.50
Outside CBD	2,178,349	67,145	3.1	n/a	24,207	15.50-19.50
Class B						
CBD	5,507,260	1,677,254	30.5	n/a	-53,368	8.00-12.00
Outside CBD	2,785,151	79,235	2.8	n/a	43,548	12.00-14.00

Note: Data as of 10/97 and covers New Orleans; CBD = Central Business District; n/a not available;
Source: Society of Industrial and Office Realtors, 1998 Comparative Statistics of Industrial and Office Real Estate Markets

"REITs and other investors have been attracted to several Class 'A' buildings in the marketplace and have influenced sales prices. Weighted average sales per sq. ft. rose by $45 per sq. ft. to $105 for Class 'A' space in the CBD. Sales prices here and in all other submarkets are expected to increase by 11 to 15 percent in 1998 but will still remain competitive. With few big blocks of space available, especially in suburban areas, developers have proposed several; however, buildings more than 100,000 sq. ft. none have come to fruition yet. The government plans to build at least two 100,000 sq. ft. properties next year. Continued consolidation of the oil industry in centers like Houston could constrain this market. The outlook is positive, but cautious for 1998. Absorption should expand by one to five percent and vacancy should drop by the same amount." *Society of Industrial and Office Realtors, 1998 Comparative Statistics of Industrial and Office Real Estate Markets*

Industrial Market

Location	Total Space (sq. ft.)	Vacant Space (sq. ft.)	Vac. Rate (%)	Under Constr. (sq. ft.)	Net Absorp. (sq. ft.)	Lease ($/sq.ft./yr.)
Central City	17,164,311	1,220,072	7.1	10,000	-226,839	1.20-2.75
Suburban	34,657,659	4,221,750	12.2	70,000	118,814	2.50-4.75

Note: Data as of 10/97 and covers New Orleans and Metairie; n/a not available
Source: Society of Industrial and Office Realtors, 1998 Comparative Statistics of Industrial and Office Real Estate Markets

"About 80,000 sq. ft. are being built in the market, 70,000 in the suburban area. Speculative development is possible for smaller facilities in 1998, but no large spec buildings are anticipated. Commercial banks will still be the prime source of financing, and the supply of funding has been upgraded in this market to ample. The major constraint to new development, is the lack of large developed industrial sites in the suburban market. This limited supply will put pressure on site prices, projected to increase by six to ten percent. Shortages will persist in all product categories, except for high-tech service center space. Turnover in this property type is caused by factors such as downsizing and relocation to larger facilities." *Society of Industrial and Office Realtors, 1998 Comparative Statistics of Industrial and Office Real Estate Markets*

COMMERCIAL UTILITIES

Typical Monthly Electric Bills

Area	Commercial Service ($/month)		Industrial Service ($/month)	
	12 kW demand 1,500 kWh	100 kW demand 30,000 kWh	1,000 kW demand 400,000 kWh	20,000 kW demand 10,000,000 kWh
City	194	2,233	23,179	n/a
U.S.	162	2,360	25,590	545,677

Note: Based on rates in effect July 1, 1997; n/a not available
Source: Edison Electric Institute, Typical Residential, Commercial and Industrial Bills, Summer 1997

TRANSPORTATION

Transportation Statistics

Avg. travel time to work (min.)	23.7
Interstate highways	I-10; I-59
Bus lines	
In-city	New Orleans Regional TA, 553 vehicles
Inter-city	3
Passenger air service	
Airport	New Orleans International
Airlines	12
Aircraft departures	60,512 (1995)
Enplaned passengers	3,982,632 (1995)
Rail service	Amtrak; Light Rail
Motor freight carriers	85
Major waterways/ports	Port of New Orleans; Mississippi River; Gulf of Mexico

Source: OAG, Business Travel Planner, Summer 1997; Editor & Publisher Market Guide, 1998; FAA Airport Activity Statistics, 1996; Amtrak National Time Table, Northeast Timetable, Fall/Winter 1997-98; 1990 Census of Population and Housing, STF 3C; Chamber of Commerce/Economic Development 1997; Jane's Urban Transport Systems 1997-98; Transit Fact Book 1997

Means of Transportation to Work

Area	Car/Truck/Van		Public Transportation			Bicycle	Walked	Other Means	Worked at Home
	Drove Alone	Car-pooled	Bus	Subway	Railroad				
City	58.6	15.4	15.6	0.0	0.0	0.9	5.2	2.3	1.9
MSA[1]	70.9	15.3	6.6	0.0	0.0	0.5	3.1	1.8	1.7
U.S.	73.2	13.4	3.0	1.5	0.5	0.4	3.9	1.2	3.0

Note: figures shown are percentages and only include workers 16 years old and over;
(1) Metropolitan Statistical Area - see Appendix A for areas included
Source: 1990 Census of Population and Housing, Summary Tape File 3C

BUSINESSES

Major Business Headquarters

Company Name	1997 Rankings	
	Fortune 500	Forbes 500
Entergy	201	-

Note: Companies listed are located in the city; Dashes indicate no ranking
Fortune 500: companies that produce a 10-K are ranked 1 - 500 based on 1996 revenue
Forbes 500: private companies are ranked 1 - 500 based on 1996 revenue
Source: Forbes 12/1/97; Fortune 4/28/97

Women-Owned Businesses: Number, Employment, Sales and Share

Area	Women-Owned Businesses in 1996				Share of Women-Owned Businesses in 1996	
	Number	Employment	Sales ($000)	Rank[2]	Percent (%)	Rank[3]
MSA[1]	34,900	124,000	12,665,500	39	37.1	23

Note: (1) Metropolitan Statistical Area - see Appendix A for areas included; (2) Calculated on an averaging of number of businesses, employment and sales and ranges from 1 to 50 where 1 is best; (3) Ranges from 1 to 50 where 1 is best
Source: The National Foundation for Women Business Owners, 1996 Facts on Women-Owned Businesses: Trends in the Top 50 Metropolitan Areas, March 26, 1997

Women-Owned Businesses: Growth

Area	Growth in Women-Owned Businesses (% change from 1987 to 1996)				Relative Growth in the Number of Women-Owned and All Businesses (% change from 1987 to 1996)			
	Num.	Empl.	Sales	Rank[2]	Women-Owned	All Firms	Absolute Difference	Relative Difference
MSA[1]	73.4	318.6	382.2	13	73.4	34.5	38.9	2.2:1

Note: (1) Metropolitan Statistical Area - see Appendix A for areas included; (2) Calculated on an averaging of the percent growth of number of businesses, employment and sales and ranges from 1 to 50 where 1 is best
Source: The National Foundation for Women Business Owners, 1996 Facts on Women-Owned Businesses: Trends in the Top 50 Metropolitan Areas, March 26, 1997

Minority Business Opportunity

New Orleans is home to one company which is on the Black Enterprise Industrial/Service 100 list (largest based on gross sales): Lundy Enterprises, Inc. (Pizza Hut restaurants). Criteria: 1) operational in previous calendar year; 2) at least 51% black-owned; 3) manufactures/owns the product it sells or provides industrial or consumer services. Brokerages, real estate firms and firms that provide professional services are not eligible. *Black Enterprise, July 1997*

HOTELS & MOTELS

Hotels/Motels

Area	Hotels/Motels	Rooms	Luxury-Level Hotels/Motels		Average Minimum Rates ($)		
			♦♦♦♦	♦♦♦♦♦	♦♦	♦♦♦	♦♦♦♦
City	86	18,475	4	1	76	144	183
Airport	18	3,348	0	0	n/a	n/a	n/a
Suburbs	10	1,513	0	0	n/a	n/a	n/a
Total	114	23,336	4	1	n/a	n/a	n/a

Note: n/a not available; Classifications range from one diamond (budget properties with basic amenities) to five diamond (luxury properties with the finest service, rooms and facilities).
Source: OAG, Business Travel Planner, Summer 1997

New Orleans is home to one of the top 100 hotels in the world according to *Travel & Leisure*: Windsor Court. Criteria: value, rooms/ambience, location, facilities/activities and service. *Travel & Leisure, September 1997*

CONVENTION CENTERS

Major Convention Centers

Center Name	Meeting Rooms	Exhibit Space (sf)
Fairmont Hotel of New Orleans	21	n/a
Louisiana Superdome	22	168,000
New Orleans Cultural Center	6	242,250
Waterbury Conference Center	n/a	n/a
Morial Convention Center	83	700,000
Pontchartraim Center	6	34,704

Note: n/a not available
Source: Trade Shows Worldwide 1997

Living Environment

COST OF LIVING

Cost of Living Index

Composite Index	Housing	Utilities	Groceries	Health Care	Trans-portation	Misc. Goods/ Services
95.3	84.1	141.6	99.0	76.1	98.8	94.4

Note: U.S. = 100
Source: ACCRA, Cost of Living Index, 3rd Quarter 1997

HOUSING

Median Home Prices and Housing Affordability

Area	Median Price[2] 3rd Qtr. 1997 ($)	HOI[3] 3rd Qtr. 1997	Afford-ability Rank[4]
MSA[1]	92,000	67.8	107
U.S.	127,000	63.7	–

Note: (1) Metropolitan Statistical Area - see Appendix A for areas included; (2) U.S. figures calculated from the sales of 625,000 new and existing homes in 195 markets; (3) Housing Opportunity Index - percent of homes sold that were within the reach of the median income household at the prevailing mortgage interest rate; (4) Rank is from 1-195 with 1 being most affordable
Source: National Association of Home Builders, Housing Opportunity Index, 3rd Quarter 1997

It is projected that the median price of existing single-family homes in the metro area will increase by 5.2% in 1998. Nationwide, home prices are projected to increase 6.6%.
Kiplinger's Personal Finance Magazine, January 1998

Average New Home Price

Area	Price ($)
City	109,160
U.S.	135,710

Note: Figures are based on a new home with 1,800 sq. ft. of living area on an 8,000 sq. ft. lot.
Source: ACCRA, Cost of Living Index, 3rd Quarter 1997

Average Apartment Rent

Area	Rent ($/mth)
City	578
U.S.	569

Note: Figures are based on an unfurnished two bedroom, 1-1/2 or 2 bath apartment, approximately 950 sq. ft. in size, excluding all utilities except water
Source: ACCRA, Cost of Living Index, 3rd Quarter 1997

RESIDENTIAL UTILITIES

Average Residential Utility Costs

Area	All Electric ($/mth)	Part Electric ($/mth)	Other Energy ($/mth)	Phone ($/mth)
City	148.64	–	–	23.23
U.S.	109.40	55.25	43.64	19.48

Source: ACCRA, Cost of Living Index, 3rd Quarter 1997

HEALTH CARE

Average Health Care Costs

Area	Hospital ($/day)	Doctor ($/visit)	Dentist ($/visit)
City	366.00	36.00	41.20
U.S.	392.91	48.76	60.84

Note: Hospital - based on a semi-private room. Doctor - based on a general practitioner's routine exam of an established patient. Dentist - based on adult teeth cleaning and periodic oral exam.
Source: ACCRA, Cost of Living Index, 3rd Quarter 1997

Distribution of Office-Based Physicians

Area	Family/Gen. Practitioners	Specialists		
		Medical	Surgical	Other
MSA[1]	206	1,060	905	893

Note: Data as of 12/31/96; (1) Metropolitan Statistical Area - see Appendix A for areas included
Source: American Medical Assn., Physician Characteristics & Distribution in the U.S., 1997-1998

Hospitals

New Orleans has 14 general medical and surgical hospitals, 5 psychiatric, 1 eye, ear, nose and throat, 1 rehabilitation, 1 children's general. *AHA Guide to the Healthcare Field 1997-98*

According to *U.S. News and World Report,* New Orleans has 1 of the best hospitals in the U.S.: **Ocshner Foundation Hospital**, noted for cancer, cardiology, gastroenterology, pulmonology; *U.S. News and World Report, "America's Best Hospitals", 7/28/97*

EDUCATION

Public School District Statistics

District Name	Num. Sch.	Enroll.	Classroom Teachers[1]	Pupils per Teacher	Minority Pupils (%)	Current Exp.[2] ($/pupil)
Orleans Parish School Board	121	85,596	3,855	22.2	94.4	4,242

Note: Data covers the 1995-1996 school year unless otherwise noted; (1) Excludes teachers reported as working in school district offices rather than in schools; (2) Based on 1993-94 enrollment collected by the Census Bureau, not the enrollment figure shown in column 3; SD = School District; ISD = Independent School District; n/a not available
Source: National Center for Education Statistics, Common Core of Data Survey; Bureau of the Census

Educational Quality

School District	Education Quotient[1]	Graduate Outcome[2]	Community Index[3]	Resource Index[4]
Orleans Parish	66.0	56.0	54.0	87.0

Note: Nearly 1,000 secondary school districts were rated in terms of educational quality. The scores range from a low of 50 to a high of 150; (1) Average of the Graduate Outcome, Community and Resource indexes; (2) Based on graduation rates and college board scores (SAT/ACT); (3) Based on the surrounding community's average level of education and the area's average income level; (4) Based on teacher salaries, per-pupil expenditures and student-teacher ratios.
Source: Expansion Management, Ratings Issue 1997

Educational Attainment by Race

Area	High School Graduate (%)					Bachelor's Degree (%)				
	Total	White	Black	Other	Hisp.[2]	Total	White	Black	Other	Hisp.[2]
City	68.1	81.4	58.4	57.6	60.3	22.4	36.6	11.6	20.4	18.7
MSA[1]	72.3	78.8	58.4	64.5	68.3	19.7	23.6	10.8	21.3	17.5
U.S.	75.2	77.9	63.1	60.4	49.8	20.3	21.5	11.4	19.4	9.2

Note: figures shown cover persons 25 years old and over; (1) Metropolitan Statistical Area - see Appendix A for areas included; (2) people of Hispanic origin can be of any race
Source: 1990 Census of Population and Housing, Summary Tape File 3C

School Enrollment by Type

Area	Preprimary				Elementary/High School			
	Public		Private		Public		Private	
	Enrollment	%	Enrollment	%	Enrollment	%	Enrollment	%
City	4,980	53.7	4,290	46.3	75,984	79.7	19,309	20.3
MSA[1]	10,527	42.0	14,557	58.0	178,094	75.0	59,271	25.0
U.S.	2,679,029	59.5	1,824,256	40.5	38,379,689	90.2	4,187,099	9.8

Note: figures shown cover persons 3 years old and over;
(1) Metropolitan Statistical Area - see Appendix A for areas included
Source: 1990 Census of Population and Housing, Summary Tape File 3C

School Enrollment by Race

Area	Preprimary (%)				Elementary/High School (%)			
	White	Black	Other	Hisp.[1]	White	Black	Other	Hisp.[1]
City	30.5	67.4	2.1	2.2	17.6	78.5	3.8	3.0
MSA[2]	63.6	34.1	2.3	3.1	51.1	45.3	3.6	4.2
U.S.	80.4	12.5	7.1	7.8	74.1	15.6	10.3	12.5

Note: figures shown cover persons 3 years old and over; (1) people of Hispanic origin can be of any race; (2) Metropolitan Statistical Area - see Appendix A for areas included
Source: 1990 Census of Population and Housing, Summary Tape File 3C

SAT/ACT Scores

Area/District	1997 SAT				1997 ACT	
	Percent of Graduates Tested (%)	Average Math Score	Average Verbal Score	Average Combined Score	Percent of Graduates Tested (%)	Average Composite Score
Orleans Parish SD	7	565	535	1,100	67	17.1
State	10	553	560	1,113	80	19.4
U.S.	42	511	505	1,016	36	21.0

Note: Math and verbal SAT scores are out of a possible 800; ACT scores are out of a possible 36
Caution: Comparing or ranking states/cities on the basis of SAT/ACT scores alone is invalid and strongly discouraged by the The College Board and The American College Testing Program as students who take the tests are self-selected and do not represent the entire student population.
Source: Orleans Parish Public Schools, 1997; American College Testing Program, 1997; College Board, 1997

Classroom Teacher Salaries in Public Schools

District	B.A. Degree		M.A. Degree		Ph.D. Degree	
	Min. ($)	Max ($)	Min. ($)	Max. ($)	Min. ($)	Max. ($)
New Orleans	22,605	36,859	23,210	38,579	24,734	39,955
Average[1]	26,120	39,270	28,175	44,667	31,643	49,825

Note: Salaries are for 1996-1997; (1) Based on all school districts covered
Source: American Federation of Teachers (unpublished data)

Higher Education

Two-Year Colleges		Four-Year Colleges		Medical Schools	Law Schools	Voc/ Tech
Public	Private	Public	Private			
1	1	3	7	2	2	13

Source: College Blue Book, Occupational Education 1997; Medical School Admission Requirements, 1998-99; Peterson's Guide to Two-Year Colleges, 1997; Peterson's Guide to Four-Year Colleges, 1997; Barron's Guide to Law Schools 1997

MAJOR EMPLOYERS

Major Employers

CS&M Associates (hotels)
Entergy Services (management services)
Shell Offshore
New Orleans Roosevelt Venture (hotels)
Pendleton Memorial Methodist Hospital
Audubon Institute (amusement services)
Touro Infirmary
Flamingo Casino New Orleans

Children's Hospital
First Commerce Service Corp.
Hibernia Corp. (bank holding)
Pan American Life Insurance
Great River Transportation Co.
Tidewater Marine
University Health Care System

Note: companies listed are located in the city
Source: Dun's Business Rankings 1997; Ward's Business Directory, 1997

PUBLIC SAFETY

Crime Rate

Area	All Crimes	Violent Crimes				Property Crimes		
		Murder	Forcible Rape	Robbery	Aggrav. Assault	Burglary	Larceny -Theft	Motor Vehicle Theft
City	11,042.2	71.9	79.9	1,167.3	937.9	2,038.5	4,663.9	2,082.7
Suburbs[1]	6,638.6	8.4	32.3	215.1	523.4	1,086.8	4,116.8	655.7
MSA[2]	8,267.7	31.9	49.9	567.4	676.8	1,438.9	4,319.2	1,183.6
U.S.	5,078.9	7.4	36.1	202.4	388.2	943.0	2,975.9	525.9

Note: Crime rate is the number of crimes per 100,000 pop.; (1) defined as all areas within the MSA but located outside the central city; (2) Metropolitan Statistical Area - see Appendix A for areas incl.
Source: FBI Uniform Crime Reports 1996

RECREATION

Culture and Recreation

Museums	Symphony Orchestras	Opera Companies	Dance Companies	Professional Theatres	Zoos	Pro Sports Teams
9	1	1	2	2	1	1

Source: International Directory of the Performing Arts, 1996; Official Museum Directory, 1998; Chamber of Commerce/Economic Development 1997

Library System

The New Orleans Public Library has 14 branches, holdings of 957,472 volumes and a budget of $5,666,492 (1995). *American Library Directory, 1997-1998*

MEDIA

Newspapers

Name	Type	Freq.	Distribution	Circulation
Clarion Herald	Religious	26x/yr	Area	60,000
Gambit	General	1x/wk	Local	40,000
Jewish Civic Press	Religious	1x/mo	Regional	16,240
Louisiana Weekly	Black	1x/wk	Local	8,000
New Orleans Data Newsweekly	Black	1x/wk	Local	20,000
New Orleans Tribune	n/a	1x/mo	Local	25,000
The Times-Picayune	General	7x/wk	Area	265,820

Note: Includes newspapers with circulations of 1,000 or more located in the city; n/a not available
Source: Burrelle's Media Directory, 1998 Edition

AM Radio Stations

Call Letters	Freq. (kHz)	Target Audience	Station Format	Music Format
WVOG	600	Religious	M/T	Christian
WASO	730	General	N/T	n/a
WSHO	800	General	M/N/S/T	Christian
WWL	870	General	N/S/T	n/a
WYLD	940	n/a	M/N/S	Christian
WBOK	1230	General	M	n/a
WODT	1280	General	M/N	n/a
WSMB	1350	General	T	n/a
WBYU	1450	General	M	Adult Standards

Note: Stations included broadcast in the New Orleans metro area; n/a not available
Station Format: E = Educational; M = Music; N = News; S = Sports; T = Talk
Source: Burrelle's Media Directory, 1998 Edition

FM Radio Stations

Call Letters	Freq. (mHz)	Target Audience	Station Format	Music Format
WBSN	89.1	Religious	M	Adult Contemporary/Christian
WWNO	89.9	General	E/M/N	Classical/Jazz
WWOZ	90.7	General	E/M/N	Big Band/Jazz/Oldies/R&B
WTUL	91.5	General	M/N/S	Alternative
WCKW	92.3	General	M	AOR/Classic Rock
WQUE	93.3	General	M/N	Urban Contemporary
WTIX	94.3	General	M	Oldies
WTKL	95.7	General	M	Oldies
WEZB	97.1	General	M	Alternative/Contemporary Top 40
WYLD	98.5	n/a	M/N/T	Urban Contemporary
WRNO	99.5	General	M	Adult Contemporary
WNOE	101.1	General	M	Country
WLMG	101.9	General	M/N	Adult Contemporary
KMEZ	102.9	n/a	M	R&B
KHOM	104.1	General	M	Contemporary Top 40
KKND	106.7	General	M	Alternative

Note: Stations included broadcast in the New Orleans metro area; n/a not available
Station Format: E = Educational; M = Music; N = News; S = Sports; T = Talk
Music Format: AOR = Album Oriented Rock; MOR = Middle-of-the-Road
Source: Burrelle's Media Directory, 1998 Edition

Television Stations

Name	Ch.	Affiliation	Type	Owner
WWL	4	CBS	Commercial	A.H. Belo Corporation
WDSU	6	NBC	Commercial	Pulitzer Broadcasting Company
WVUE	8	Fox	Commercial	SF Broadcasting of New Orleans
WYES	12	PBS	Public	Greater New Orleans Educational TV Foundation
WHNO	20	n/a	Commercial	LeSea Broadcasting
WGNO	26	ABC	Commercial	Tribune Broadcasting Co.
WLAE	32	PBS	Public	Educational Broadcasting Foundation
WNOL	38	WB	Commercial	Qwest Broadcasting

Note: Stations included broadcast in the New Orleans metro area
Source: Burrelle's Media Directory, 1998 Edition

CLIMATE

Average and Extreme Temperatures

Temperature	Jan	Feb	Mar	Apr	May	Jun	Jul	Aug	Sep	Oct	Nov	Dec	Ann
Extreme High (°F)	83	85	89	92	96	100	101	102	101	92	87	84	102
Average High (°F)	62	65	71	78	85	89	91	90	87	80	71	64	78
Average Temp. (°F)	53	56	62	69	75	81	82	82	79	70	61	55	69
Average Low (°F)	43	46	52	59	66	71	73	73	70	59	51	45	59
Extreme Low (°F)	14	19	25	32	41	50	60	60	42	35	24	11	11

Note: Figures cover the years 1948-1990
Source: National Climatic Data Center, International Station Meteorological Climate Summary, 3/95

Average Precipitation/Snowfall/Humidity

Precip./Humidity	Jan	Feb	Mar	Apr	May	Jun	Jul	Aug	Sep	Oct	Nov	Dec	Ann
Avg. Precip. (in.)	4.7	5.6	5.2	4.7	4.4	5.4	6.4	5.9	5.5	2.8	4.4	5.5	60.6
Avg. Snowfall (in.)	Tr	Tr	Tr	0	0	0	0	0	0	0	0	Tr	Tr
Avg. Rel. Hum. 6am (%)	85	84	84	88	89	89	91	91	89	87	86	85	88
Avg. Rel. Hum. 3pm (%)	62	59	57	57	58	61	66	65	63	56	59	62	60

Note: Figures cover the years 1948-1990; Tr = Trace amounts (<0.05 in. of rain; <0.5 in. of snow)
Source: National Climatic Data Center, International Station Meteorological Climate Summary, 3/95

Weather Conditions

Temperature			Daytime Sky			Precipitation		
10°F & below	32°F & below	90°F & above	Clear	Partly cloudy	Cloudy	0.01 inch or more precip.	0.1 inch or more snow/ice	Thunder-storms
0	13	70	90	169	106	114	1	69

Note: Figures are average number of days per year and covers the years 1948-1990
Source: National Climatic Data Center, International Station Meteorological Climate Summary, 3/95

AIR & WATER QUALITY

Maximum Pollutant Concentrations

	Particulate Matter (ug/m³)	Carbon Monoxide (ppm)	Sulfur Dioxide (ppm)	Nitrogen Dioxide (ppm)	Ozone (ppm)	Lead (ug/m³)
MSA[1] Level	64	4	0.035	0.018	0.11	0.09
NAAQS[2]	150	9	0.140	0.053	0.12	1.50
Met NAAQS?	Yes	Yes	Yes	Yes	Yes	Yes

Note: (1) Metropolitan Statistical Area - see Appendix A for areas included; (2) National Ambient Air Quality Standards; ppm = parts per million; ug/m³ = micrograms per cubic meter; n/a not available
Source: EPA, National Air Quality and Emissions Trends Report, 1996

Pollutant Standards Index

In the New Orleans MSA (see Appendix A for areas included), the Pollutant Standards Index (PSI) exceeded 100 on 1 day in 1996. A PSI value greater than 100 indicates that air quality would be in the unhealthful range on that day. *EPA, National Air Quality and Emissions Trends Report, 1996*

Drinking Water

Water System Name	Pop. Served	Primary Water Source Type	Number of Violations in Fiscal Year 1997	Type of Violation/ Contaminants
New Orleans-Carrolton WW	440,229	Surface	None	None

Note: Data as of January 16, 1998
Source: EPA, Office of Ground Water and Drinking Water, Safe Drinking Water Information System

New Orleans tap water is alkaline, soft and fluoridated.
Editor & Publisher Market Guide, 1998

Orlando, Florida

Background

The city of Orlando can hold the viewer aghast with its rampant tourism. Not only is it home to the "tame" tourist attractions of Disney World, Epcot Center, and Sea World, but Orlando and its surrounding area, is also home to institutions such as the Medieval Times Dinner Tournament, the Tupperware Exhibit and Museum, Wet-N-Wild, Watermania, the Sleuth's Mystery Dinner Theatre, and a host of T-shirt, citrus, and shell vendor shacks. The pundits may throw their hands up in exasperation, and complain about the meaninglessness and transience of a tourist-oriented society.

Orlando has its own high-tech corridor called "Laser Lane" because of the University of Central Florida Center for Research and Education in Optics and Lasers. The research facility has attracted 70 companies and is ranked #8 out of the top 10 research parks in the U.S. *World Trade, 11/97*

Aside from the glitz that pumps most of the money into Orlando's economy, Orlando is also called "The City Beautiful". The warm climate and abundant rains produce a variety of lush flora and fauna. This provides an attractive setting for the young people who settle in the area, and spend their nights in any number of the jazz clubs, restaurants, and pubs along Orange Avenue, and Church Street.

This genteel setting is a far cry from Orlando's rough and tumble origins. The city started out as a makeshift campsite in the middle of a cotton plantation. The Civil War and devastating rains brought an end to the cotton trade. Its settlers turned to raising livestock.

The transition to a new livelihood did not insure any peace and serenity. Rustling, chaotic brawls, and senseless shootings were an everyday occurrence. Martial law had to be imposed by a few large ranch families.

The greatest impetus toward modernity came from the installation of Cape Canaveral, 50 miles away, which brought missile assembly and electronic component production to the area; and Walt Disney World, created out of 27,000 acres of unexplored swampland, which set the tone for Orlando as a tourist- oriented economy. Recently it has become a major film production site, outside of New York and Los Angeles.

Stereotypically the land of orange juice and sunshine, Orlando may be the up and coming city for young job seekers and professionals.

Orlando is surrounded by many lakes. Its relative humidity remains high year round. In winter the humidity may drop. June through September is the rainy season. During this time, scattered afternoon thunderstorms are an almost daily occurrence. During the winter months rainfall is light and the afternoons are most pleasant. Hurricanes are not usually considered a threat to the area.

General Rankings and Evaluative Comments

■ Orlando was ranked #18 out of 300 cities by *Money's* 1997 "Survey of the Best Places to Live." Criteria used: health services, crime, economy, housing, education, transportation, weather, leisure and the arts. The city was ranked #12 in 1996 and #17 in 1995.
Money, July 1997; Money, September 1996; Money, September 1995

■ *Ladies Home Journal* ranked America's 200 largest cities based on the qualities women care about most. Orlando ranked 8 out of 200. Criteria: low crime rate, good public schools, well-paying jobs, quality health and child care, the presence of women in government, proportion of women-owned businesses, size of the wage gap with men, local economy, divorce rates, the ratio of single men to single women, whether there are laws that require at least the same number of public toilets for women as men, and the probability of good hair days. *Ladies Home Journal, November 1997*

■ Orlando was ranked #145 out of 219 cities in terms of children's health, safety, and economic well-being. Criteria: total population, percent population change, birth rate, child immunization rate, infant mortality rate, percent low birth weight infants, percent of births to teens, physician-to-population ratio, student-to-teacher ratio, dropout rate, unemployment rate, median family income, percent of children in poverty, violent and property crime rates, number of juvenile arrests for violent crimes as a percent of the total crime index, number of days with pollution standard index (PSI) over 100, pounds toxic releases per 1,000 people and number of superfund sites. *Zero Population Growth, Children's Environmental Index 1997*

■ *Conde Nast Traveler* polled 37,000 readers in terms of travel satisfaction. Cities were ranked based on the following criteria: people/friendliness, environment/ambiance, cultural enrichment, restaurants and fun/energy. Orlando appeared in the top thirty, ranking number 13, with an overall rating of 67.0 out of 100 based on all the criteria. The cities were also ranked in each category separately. Orlando appeared in the top 10 based on people/friendliness, ranking number 9 with a rating of 73.1 out of 100. Orlando appeared in the top 10 based on fun/energy, ranking number 2 with a rating of 91.0 out of 100. *Conde Nast Traveler, Readers' Choice Poll 1997*

■ According to *Working Mother,* "Florida stands out among the Southern states for its aggressive action to improve and expand child care. As we went to press, the governor had asked state lawmakers for a significant increase in state funds to create new child care slots. Some $49 million would be earmarked for a very important group—16,000 children of low-wage workers.

In the past year the state also boosted funding for its prekindergarten program by $4 million, bringing its pre-K spending to $102 million. This translates into free pre-K for 27,000 kids, about 2,000 more than last year. This program is funded with state lottery money and is available in all of Florida's 67 school districts.

The state has also improved its requirements for playground surfaces in child care setting. As of March 1997, all centers were required to have soft surfaces under playground equipment. This is a vital change, given that injuries from falls are the most common in child care.

Finally, lawmakers approved a new program to recognize quality child care programs. Any facility that attains state or NAEYC accreditation can now post a 'good seal' certificate and will be listed in a state database as a 'Gold Seal' program—to show it meets high standards of care. So far, about 370 centers have received certificates, and about 800 more are in the pipeline." *Working Mother, July/August 1997*

Business Environment

STATE ECONOMY

State Economic Profile

"Florida's economy continues to expand strongly....

Florida is becoming increasingly dependent on the service industry for job growth. Currently, one in three Florida jobs is service-related. In the past year, however, nearly half of all jobs created were in the service industry. One in four jobs created was in business services, compared to one in seven for the U.S....

Florida's tourist industry continues to rebound and will be an important source of growth for this year. Household income growth and savings rates are high, and the values of individual stock portfolios has been booming, leaving households across the U.S. in good financial shape to take a vacation.

A risk to Florida's economy is a sharp slowing in population growth. In 1996, Florida experienced a population gain of only 1.5%, the slowest rate of growth since World War II. Contributing to the slower population growth is weaker retiree migration due to a slowing national retiree population growth.

Supporting growth are Florida's moderate climate, favorable quality of life, affordable housing, and low cost of doing business, which will continue to attract businesses and households. Population growth will continue to slow for the next decade as the number of people reaching retirement age nationwide is falling. Population growth will begin to accelerate once the baby boom generation hits retirement age beginning around 2005. One downside risk for Florida is its dependence on tourism and interest and property income that makes it vulnerable to national and international business cycles. Florida will remain one of the nation's fastest-growing economies through the remainder of this century." *National Association of Realtors, Economic Profiles: The Fifty States, July 1997*

IMPORTS/EXPORTS

Total Export Sales

Area	1993 ($000)	1994 ($000)	1995 ($000)	1996 ($000)	% Chg. 1993-96	% Chg. 1995-96
MSA[1]	930,364	848,512	968,816	1,218,957	31.0	25.8
U.S.	464,858,354	512,415,609	583,030,524	622,827,063	34.0	6.8

Note: (1) Metropolitan Statistical Area - see Appendix A for areas included
Source: U.S. Department of Commerce, International Trade Association, Metropolitan Area Exports: An Export Performance Report on Over 250 U.S. Cities, October 1997

Imports/Exports by Port

Type	Cargo Value			Share of U.S. Total	
	1995 (US$mil.)	1996 (US$mil.)	% Change 1995-1996	1995 (%)	1996 (%)
Imports	0	0	0	0	0
Exports	0	0	0	0	0

Source: Global Trade Information Services, WaterBorne Trade Atlas 1997

CITY FINANCES

City Government Finances

Component	FY92 ($000)	FY92 (per capita $)
Revenue	344,245	2,002.34
Expenditure	294,755	1,714.48
Debt Outstanding	513,908	2,989.21
Cash & Securities	556,615	3,237.62

Source: U.S. Bureau of the Census, City Government Finances: 1991-92

City Government Revenue by Source

Source	FY92 ($000)	FY92 (per capita $)	FY92 (%)
From Federal Government	36,530	212.48	10.6
From State Governments	25,510	148.38	7.4
From Local Governments	26,005	151.26	7.6
Property Taxes	41,157	239.39	12.0
General Sales Taxes	0	0.00	0.0
Selective Sales Taxes	37,622	218.83	10.9
Income Taxes	0	0.00	0.0
Current Charges	98,752	574.40	28.7
Utility/Liquor Store	0	0.00	0.0
Employee Retirement[1]	14,716	85.60	4.3
Other	63,953	371.99	18.6

Note: (1) Excludes "city contributions," classified as "nonrevenue," intragovernmental transfers.
Source: U.S. Bureau of the Census, City Government Finances: 1991-92

City Government Expenditures by Function

Function	FY92 ($000)	FY92 (per capita $)	FY92 (%)
Educational Services	80	0.47	0.0
Employee Retirement[1]	5,258	30.58	1.8
Environment/Housing	92,816	539.88	31.5
Government Administration	20,138	117.14	6.8
Interest on General Debt	24,168	140.58	8.2
Public Safety	58,487	340.20	19.8
Social Services	0	0.00	0.0
Transportation	37,676	219.15	12.8
Utility/Liquor Store	800	4.65	0.3
Other	55,332	321.85	18.8

Note: (1) Payments to beneficiaries including withdrawal of contributions.
Source: U.S. Bureau of the Census, City Government Finances: 1991-92

Municipal Bond Ratings

Area	Moody's	S & P
Orlando	n/r	n/a

Note: n/a not available; n/r not rated
Source: Moody's Bond Record, 2/98; Statistical Abstract of the U.S., 1997;
Governing Magazine, 9/97, 3/98

POPULATION

Population Growth

Area	1980	1990	% Chg. 1980-90	July 1996 Estimate	% Chg. 1990-96
City	128,291	164,693	28.4	173,902	5.6
MSA[1]	700,055	1,072,748	53.2	1,417,291	32.1
U.S.	226,545,805	248,765,170	9.8	265,179,411	6.6

Note: (1) Metropolitan Statistical Area - see Appendix A for areas included
Source: 1980/1990 Census of Housing and Population, Summary Tape File 3C;
Census Bureau Population Estimates

Population Characteristics

Race	City 1980 Population	%	City 1990 Population	%	% Chg. 1980-90	MSA[1] 1990 Population	%
White	87,751	68.4	112,933	68.6	28.7	888,648	82.8
Black	38,380	29.9	44,342	26.9	15.5	132,796	12.4
Amer Indian/Esk/Aleut	300	0.2	510	0.3	70.0	3,704	0.3
Asian/Pacific Islander	782	0.6	2,516	1.5	221.7	20,332	1.9
Other	1,078	0.8	4,392	2.7	307.4	27,268	2.5
Hispanic Origin[2]	5,024	3.9	14,121	8.6	181.1	94,658	8.8

Note: (1) Metropolitan Statistical Area - see Appendix A for areas included;
(2) people of Hispanic origin can be of any race
Source: 1980/1990 Census of Housing and Population, Summary Tape File 3C

Ancestry

Area	German	Irish	English	Italian	U.S.	French	Polish	Dutch
City	18.2	13.3	13.1	4.8	4.3	3.7	2.2	1.9
MSA[1]	22.0	16.4	15.9	6.1	5.4	4.4	3.0	2.5
U.S.	23.3	15.6	13.1	5.9	5.3	4.2	3.8	2.5

Note: Figures are percentages and include persons that reported multiple ancestry (eg. if a person reported being Irish and Italian, they were included in both columns); (1) Metropolitan Statistical Area - see Appendix A for areas included
Source: 1990 Census of Population and Housing, Summary Tape File 3C

Age

Area	Median Age (Years)	Age Distribution (%) Under 5	Under 18	18-24	25-44	45-64	65+	80+
City	30.2	6.8	21.0	16.1	36.4	15.2	11.4	2.9
MSA[1]	32.1	7.2	24.3	11.3	35.2	18.3	10.9	2.2
U.S.	32.9	7.3	25.6	10.5	32.6	18.7	12.5	2.8

Note: (1) Metropolitan Statistical Area - see Appendix A for areas included
Source: 1990 Census of Population and Housing, Summary Tape File 3C

Male/Female Ratio

Area	Number of males per 100 females (all ages)	Number of males per 100 females (18 years old+)
City	101.0	101.0
MSA[1]	97.3	95.3
U.S.	95.0	91.9

Note: (1) Metropolitan Statistical Area - see Appendix A for areas included
Source: 1990 Census of Population, General Population Characteristics

INCOME

Per Capita/Median/Average Income

Area	Per Capita ($)	Median Household ($)	Average Household ($)
City	13,879	26,119	33,136
MSA[1]	14,895	31,230	39,069
U.S.	14,420	30,056	38,453

Note: all figures are for 1989; (1) Metropolitan Statistical Area - see Appendix A for areas included
Source: 1990 Census of Population and Housing, Summary Tape File 3C

Household Income Distribution by Race

Income ($)	City (%)					U.S. (%)				
	Total	White	Black	Other	Hisp.[1]	Total	White	Black	Other	Hisp.[1]
Less than 5,000	6.8	4.3	15.7	8.4	9.1	6.2	4.8	15.2	8.6	8.8
5,000 - 9,999	8.5	7.1	13.1	11.4	11.8	9.3	8.6	14.2	9.9	11.1
10,000 - 14,999	10.2	9.0	13.6	15.1	14.0	8.8	8.5	11.0	9.8	11.0
15,000 - 24,999	21.9	21.2	24.5	23.1	23.9	17.5	17.3	18.9	18.5	20.5
25,000 - 34,999	17.6	18.7	12.9	22.5	16.6	15.8	16.1	14.2	15.4	16.4
35,000 - 49,999	17.1	18.9	12.2	8.8	13.2	17.9	18.6	13.3	16.1	16.0
50,000 - 74,999	11.9	13.6	6.7	7.6	7.3	15.0	15.8	9.3	13.4	11.1
75,000 - 99,999	3.1	3.8	0.9	2.0	2.3	5.1	5.5	2.6	4.7	3.1
100,000+	2.7	3.4	0.5	1.2	1.9	4.4	4.8	1.3	3.7	1.9

Note: all figures are for 1989; (1) people of Hispanic origin can be of any race
Source: 1990 Census of Population and Housing, Summary Tape File 3C

Effective Buying Income

Area	Per Capita ($)	Median Household ($)	Average Household ($)
City	15,798	29,982	39,662
MSA[1]	16,817	35,073	44,469
U.S.	15,444	33,201	41,849

Note: data as of 1/1/97; (1) Metropolitan Statistical Area - see Appendix A for areas included
Source: Standard Rate & Data Service, Newspaper Advertising Source, 2/98

Effective Household Buying Income Distribution

Area	% of Households Earning						
	$10,000 -$19,999	$20,000 -$34,999	$35,000 -$49,999	$50,000 -$74,999	$75,000 -$99,000	$100,000 -$124,999	$125,000 and up
City	17.9	27.2	18.4	15.5	4.8	1.6	1.8
MSA[1]	15.6	25.0	19.2	18.6	7.2	2.4	2.7
U.S.	16.5	23.4	18.3	18.2	6.4	2.1	2.4

Note: data as of 1/1/97; (1) Metropolitan Statistical Area - see Appendix A for areas included
Source: Standard Rate & Data Service, Newspaper Advertising Source, 2/98

Poverty Rates by Race and Age

Area	Total (%)	By Race (%)				By Age (%)		
		White	Black	Other	Hisp.[2]	Under 5 years old	Under 18 years old	65 years and over
City	15.8	8.2	33.9	20.6	21.6	29.0	27.1	16.1
MSA[1]	10.0	7.3	26.4	15.0	15.9	14.8	14.0	10.7
U.S.	13.1	9.8	29.5	23.1	25.3	20.1	18.3	12.8

Note: figures show the percent of people living below the poverty line in 1989. The average poverty threshold was $12,674 for a family of four in 1989; (1) Metropolitan Statistical Area - see Appendix A for areas included; (2) people of Hispanic origin can be of any race
Source: 1990 Census of Population and Housing, Summary Tape File 3C

EMPLOYMENT

Labor Force and Employment

Area	Civilian Labor Force			Workers Employed		
	Dec. '95	Dec. '96	% Chg.	Dec. '95	Dec. '96	% Chg.
City	103,146	108,383	5.1	99,616	104,867	5.3
MSA[1]	786,133	825,864	5.1	760,769	800,868	5.3
U.S.	134,583,000	136,742,000	1.6	127,903,000	130,785,000	2.3

Note: Data is not seasonally adjusted and covers workers 16 years of age and older;
(1) Metropolitan Statistical Area - see Appendix A for areas included
Source: Bureau of Labor Statistics, http://stats.bls.gov

Orlando was listed among the top 20 metro areas (out of 114 major areas) in terms of projected job growth from 1997 to 2002 with an annual percent change of 2.5%.
Standard & Poor's DRI, July 23, 1997

Unemployment Rate

Area	1997											
	Jan.	Feb.	Mar.	Apr.	May	Jun.	Jul.	Aug.	Sep.	Oct.	Nov.	Dec.
City	4.1	3.5	3.5	3.5	3.6	3.8	3.7	3.7	3.8	3.4	3.5	3.2
MSA[1]	3.9	3.4	3.4	3.4	3.4	3.7	3.6	3.6	3.6	3.3	3.3	3.0
U.S.	5.9	5.7	5.5	4.8	4.7	5.2	5.0	4.8	4.7	4.4	4.3	4.4

Note: Data is not seasonally adjusted and covers workers 16 years of age and older; All figures are percentages; (1) Metropolitan Statistical Area - see Appendix A for areas included
Source: Bureau of Labor Statistics, http://stats.bls.gov

Employment by Industry

Sector	MSA[1]		U.S.
	Number of Employees	Percent of Total	Percent of Total
Services	339,300	41.2	29.0
Retail Trade	163,600	19.9	18.5
Government	86,800	10.5	16.1
Manufacturing	53,500	6.5	15.0
Finance/Insurance/Real Estate	47,600	5.8	5.7
Wholesale Trade	44,900	5.5	5.4
Transportation/Public Utilities	42,500	5.2	5.3
Construction/Mining	400	0.0	5.0

Note: Figures cover non-farm employment as of 12/97 and are not seasonally adjusted;
(1) Metropolitan Statistical Area - see Appendix A for areas included
Source: Bureau of Labor Statistics, http://stats.bls.gov

Employment by Occupation

Occupation Category	City (%)	MSA[1] (%)	U.S. (%)
White Collar	60.3	61.0	58.1
Executive/Admin./Management	13.4	13.7	12.3
Professional	13.9	12.9	14.1
Technical & Related Support	3.6	3.4	3.7
Sales	12.8	14.4	11.8
Administrative Support/Clerical	16.5	16.6	16.3
Blue Collar	19.5	21.4	26.2
Precision Production/Craft/Repair	8.9	10.6	11.3
Machine Operators/Assem./Insp.	3.1	3.4	6.8
Transportation/Material Movers	3.6	3.9	4.1
Cleaners/Helpers/Laborers	3.9	3.5	3.9
Services	18.7	15.6	13.2
Farming/Forestry/Fishing	1.6	1.9	2.5

Note: figures cover employed persons 16 years old and over;
(1) Metropolitan Statistical Area - see Appendix A for areas included
Source: 1990 Census of Population and Housing, Summary Tape File 3C

Occupational Employment Projections: 1995 - 2005

Occupations Expected to have the Largest Job Growth (ranked by numerical growth)	Fast-Growing Occupations[1] (ranked by percent growth)
1. Waiters & waitresses	1. Systems analysts
2. Cashiers	2. Physical therapy assistants and aides
3. General managers & top executives	3. Electronic pagination systems workers
4. Salespersons, retail	4. Computer engineers
5. Maids/housekeepers	5. Physical therapists
6. Amusement and recreation attendants	6. Manicurists
7. Maintenance repairers, general utility	7. Occupational therapists
8. First line supervisor, sales & related	8. Corrections officers & jailers
9. Guards	9. Human services workers
10. Janitors/cleaners/maids, ex. priv. hshld.	10. Amusement and recreation attendants

Projections cover Orange County.
Note: (1) Excludes occupations with total growth of less than 100 jobs
Source: Florida Department of Labor and Employment Security, Florida Industry and Occupational Employment Projections 1995-2005

Average Wages

Occupation	Wage	Occupation	Wage
Professional/Technical/Clerical	$/Week	**Health/Protective Services**	$/Week
Accountants III	763	Corrections Officers	518
Attorneys III	-	Firefighters	-
Budget Analysts III	747	Nurses, Licensed Practical II	-
Buyers/Contracting Specialists II	637	Nurses, Registered II	-
Clerks, Accounting III	428	Nursing Assistants II	-
Clerks, General III	331	Police Officers I	-
Computer Operators II	402	**Hourly Workers**	$/Hour
Computer Programmers II	551	Forklift Operators	10.10
Drafters II	498	General Maintenance Workers	8.40
Engineering Technicians III	547	Guards I	7.61
Engineering Technicians, Civil III	-	Janitors	7.45
Engineers III	963	Maintenance Electricians	14.74
Key Entry Operators I	317	Maintenance Electronics Techs II	14.97
Personnel Assistants III	440	Maintenance Machinists	-
Personnel Specialists III	720	Maintenance Mechanics, Machinery	-
Secretaries III	519	Material Handling Laborers	7.65
Switchboard Operator-Receptionist	340	Motor Vehicle Mechanics	13.40
Systems Analysts II	828	Shipping/Receiving Clerks	8.94
Systems Analysts Supervisor/Mgr II	-	Tool and Die Makers	-
Tax Collectors II	-	Truckdrivers, Tractor Trailer	12.20
Word Processors II	421	Warehouse Specialists	-

Note: Wage data includes full-time workers only for 4/96 and cover the Metropolitan Statistical Area (see Appendix A for areas included). Dashes indicate that data was not available.
Source: Bureau of Labor Statistics, Occupational Compensation Survey, 9/96

TAXES

Major State and Local Tax Rates

State Corp. Income (%)	State Personal Income (%)	Residential Property (effective rate per $100)	Sales & Use		State Gasoline (cents/ gallon)	State Cigarette (cents/ 20-pack)
			State (%)	Local (%)		
5.5[a]	None	n/a	6.0	None	12.8[b]	33.9

Note: Personal/corporate income tax rates as of 1/97. Sales, gasoline and cigarette tax rates as of 1/98; (a) 3.3% Alternative Minimum Tax. An exemption of $5,000 is allowed; (b) Rate is comprised of 4 cents excise and 8.8 cents motor carrier tax
Source: Federation of Tax Administrators, www.taxadmin.org; Washington D.C. Department of Finance and Revenue, Tax Rates and Tax Burdens in the District of Columbia: A Nationwide Comparison, June 1997; Chamber of Commerce

Total Taxes Per Capita and as a Percent of Income

Area	Per Capita Income ($)	Per Capita Taxes ($)			Taxes as Pct. of Income (%)		
		Total	Federal	State/Local	Total	Federal	State/Local
Florida	26,438	9,172	6,286	2,886	34.7	23.8	10.9
U.S.	26,187	9,205	6,127	3,078	35.2	23.4	11.8

Note: Figures are for 1997
Source: Tax Foundation, Web Site, www.taxfoundation.org

COMMERCIAL REAL ESTATE

Office Market

Class/Location	Total Space (sq. ft.)	Vacant Space (sq. ft.)	Vac. Rate (%)	Under Constr. (sq. ft.)	Net Absorp. (sq. ft.)	Rental Rates ($/sq.ft./yr.)
Class A						
CBD	4,195,790	207,162	4.9	0	80,166	19.00-28.00
Outside CBD	8,205,713	253,504	3.1	635,000	745,657	15.00-22.00
Class B						
CBD	1,190,494	69,251	5.8	0	51,722	12.00-20.00
Outside CBD	10,052,672	771,572	7.7	0	278,991	10.00-18.50

Note: Data as of 10/97 and covers Orlando; CBD = Central Business District; n/a not available;
Source: Society of Industrial and Office Realtors, 1998 Comparative Statistics of Industrial and Office Real Estate Markets

"More than 4,000,000 sq. ft. of speculative development is currently planned or under construction. Most new building is concentrated in the suburbs. However, another 3,000,000 sq. ft. of office tower space is planned in the CBD in the next six to thirty-six months. Landlord concessions remain nonexistent and rental rates are expected to rise by 11-15%. Tourism obviously drives Orlando's economy and several entertainment facility expansions are underway. In addition, demand will be generated by high-tech industries originating, expanding, and relocating to the area. Relatively low costs of doing business and high quality of life will continue to attract and retain industry. The only market constraint could be limited supply of labor. Unemployment is forecasted to remain below 4% through the remainder of the decade even with continuous population growth." *Society of Industrial and Office Realtors, 1998 Comparative Statistics of Industrial and Office Real Estate Markets*

Industrial Market

Location	Total Space (sq. ft.)	Vacant Space (sq. ft.)	Vac. Rate (%)	Under Constr. (sq. ft.)	Net Absorp. (sq. ft.)	Net Lease ($/sq.ft./yr.)
Central City	n/a	n/a	n/a	n/a	n/a	n/a
Suburban	71,754,000	5,468,168	7.6	1,713,130	1,410,987	3.50-6.00

Note: Data as of 10/97 and covers Orlando; n/a not available
Source: Society of Industrial and Office Realtors, 1998 Comparative Statistics of Industrial and Office Real Estate Markets

"Orlando will continue to attract an array of developers, including both foreign and domestic, public and private, as well as Reits. The government is poised to help accommodate growth with a proposed one-cent tax increase to improve and/or commence road projects. New speculative development, as proposed, will range between 500,000 to 700,000 sq. ft. Ninety percent of these facilities will be built in Southwest Orlando where land for this type of development is available. High-tech facilities will remain concentrated in such northeast Orlando locales as Lake Mary. SIOR's correspondent expects lease price increases for this next wave of development. Orlando's low business cost structure and desirable quality of life will continue to support a solid core of high-tech and manufacturing firms." *Society of Industrial and Office Realtors, 1998 Comparative Statistics of Industrial and Office Real Estate Markets*

Retail Market

Shopping Center Inventory (sq. ft.)	Shopping Center Construction (sq. ft.)	Construction as a Percent of Inventory (%)	Torto Wheaton Rent Index[1] ($/sq. ft.)
35,281,000	872,000	2.5	14.17

Note: Data as of 1997 and covers the Metropolitan Statistical Area - see Appendix A for areas included; (1) Index is based on a model that predicts what the average rent should be for leases with certain characteristics, in certain locations during certain years.
Source: National Association of Realtors, 1997-1998 Market Conditions Report

"Orlando's economy revolves around tourism. The most recent tourism numbers are up, which has bolstered the retail trade sector. Indeed, retail trade is Orlando's second-largest employer and its largest source of tax revenue. Shopping, especially at outlet malls has been brisk. Orlando's Belz Factory hosted an estimated 12 million visitors in 1996. The area's retail market has been robust, with strong demand outpacing new construction. The retail rent index jumped 20% in 1997 after an 18% increase the year before. Several community-sized shopping centers were constructed last year, anchored by Publix and Winn-Dixie, Orlando's rent index should continue to climb over the next two years." *National Association of Realtors, 1997-1998 Market Conditions Report*

COMMERCIAL UTILITIES

Typical Monthly Electric Bills

Area	Commercial Service ($/month)		Industrial Service ($/month)	
	12 kW demand 1,500 kWh	100 kW demand 30,000 kWh	1,000 kW demand 400,000 kWh	20,000 kW demand 10,000,000 kWh
City	137	2,333	27,081	554,864
U.S.	162	2,360	25,590	545,677

Note: Based on rates in effect July 1, 1997
Source: Edison Electric Institute, Typical Residential, Commercial and Industrial Bills, Summer 1997

TRANSPORTATION

Transportation Statistics

Avg. travel time to work (min.)	20.1
Interstate highways	I-4
Bus lines	
In-city	LYNX, 250 vehicles
Inter-city	5
Passenger air service	
Airport	Orlando International
Airlines	17
Aircraft departures	95,136 (1995)
Enplaned passengers	9,034,799 (1995)
Rail service	Amtrak
Motor freight carriers	34
Major waterways/ports	None

Source: OAG, Business Travel Planner, Summer 1997; Editor & Publisher Market Guide, 1998; FAA Airport Activity Statistics, 1996; Amtrak National Time Table, Northeast Timetable, Fall/Winter 1997-98; 1990 Census of Population and Housing, STF 3C; Chamber of Commerce/Economic Development 1997; Jane's Urban Transport Systems 1997-98; Transit Fact Book 1997

Means of Transportation to Work

Area	Car/Truck/Van		Public Transportation			Bicycle	Walked	Other Means	Worked at Home
	Drove Alone	Car-pooled	Bus	Subway	Railroad				
City	68.3	12.6	3.5	0.0	0.0	0.8	11.9	1.5	1.3
MSA[1]	78.1	13.3	1.4	0.0	0.0	0.6	3.5	1.2	2.0
U.S.	73.2	13.4	3.0	0.0	1.5	0.5	0.4	3.9	1.2	3.0

Note: figures shown are percentages and only include workers 16 years old and over;
(1) Metropolitan Statistical Area - see Appendix A for areas included
Source: 1990 Census of Population and Housing, Summary Tape File 3C

BUSINESSES

Major Business Headquarters

Company Name	1997 Rankings	
	Fortune 500	Forbes 500
Darden Restaurants	424	-

Note: Companies listed are located in the city; Dashes indicate no ranking
Fortune 500: companies that produce a 10-K are ranked 1 - 500 based on 1996 revenue
Forbes 500: private companies are ranked 1 - 500 based on 1996 revenue
Source: Forbes 12/1/97; Fortune 4/28/97

Women-Owned Businesses: Number, Employment, Sales and Share

Area	Women-Owned Businesses in 1996				Share of Women-Owned Businesses in 1996	
	Number	Employment	Sales ($000)	Rank[2]	Percent (%)	Rank[3]
MSA[1]	49,600	115,400	13,981,400	33	38.0	15

Note: (1) Metropolitan Statistical Area - see Appendix A for areas included; (2) Calculated on an averaging of number of businesses, employment and sales and ranges from 1 to 50 where 1 is best; (3) Ranges from 1 to 50 where 1 is best
Source: The National Foundation for Women Business Owners, 1996 Facts on Women-Owned Businesses: Trends in the Top 50 Metropolitan Areas, March 26, 1997

Women-Owned Businesses: Growth

Area	Growth in Women-Owned Businesses (% change from 1987 to 1996)				Relative Growth in the Number of Women-Owned and All Businesses (% change from 1987 to 1996)			
	Num.	Empl.	Sales	Rank[2]	Women-Owned	All Firms	Absolute Difference	Relative Difference
MSA[1]	131.1	229.5	292.0	9	131.1	82.0	49.1	1.6:1

Note: (1) Metropolitan Statistical Area - see Appendix A for areas included; (2) Calculated on an averaging of the percent growth of number of businesses, employment and sales and ranges from 1 to 50 where 1 is best
Source: The National Foundation for Women Business Owners, 1996 Facts on Women-Owned Businesses: Trends in the Top 50 Metropolitan Areas, March 26, 1997

Minority Business Opportunity

Orlando is home to one company which is on the Black Enterprise Auto Dealer 100 list (largest based on gross sales): Tropical Ford Inc. (Ford). Criteria: 1) operational in previous calendar year; 2) at least 51% black-owned. *Black Enterprise, June 1997*

Orlando is home to one company which is on the Hispanic Business Fastest-Growing 100 list (greatest sales growth from 1992 to 1996): American Paving Contractors Inc. (asphalt repair svcs.) *Hispanic Business, July/August 1997*

Small Business Opportunity

Orlando was ranked #2 out of 219 in terms of the best cities to start and grow a home-based business by *Home Office Computing*. Criteria: economic growth, population growth, industrial diversity, business climate, market access systems, work flexibility, lifestyle, education level, intellectual capital, age, and home-based business score (zoning flexibility, community support, regulatory streamlining). "In addition to hosting Mickey and Minnie, this Sunshine State city is a place where the traditional chamber of commerce and the home-based chamber of commerce battle to provide the best service to the small-business community. Each year, the traditional chamber gives awards to the 25 best Orlando small businesses. And membership in the home-based chamber has climbed to the point where chapters have begun opening in other states. A National HomeBased Chamber of Commerce umbrella organization is in the process of being launched...." *Home Office Computing, December 1997*

According to *Forbes*, Orlando is home to one of America's 200 best small companies: Elxsi. Criteria: companies must be publicly traded, U.S.-based corporations with latest 12-month sales of between $5 and $350 million. Earnings must be at least $1 million for the 12-month period. Limited partnerships, REITs and closed-end mutual funds were not considered. Banks, S&Ls and electric utilities were not included. *Forbes, November 3, 1997*

HOTELS & MOTELS

Hotels/Motels

Area	Hotels/ Motels	Rooms	Luxury-Level Hotels/Motels		Average Minimum Rates ($)		
			♦♦♦♦	♦♦♦♦♦	♦♦	♦♦♦	♦♦♦♦
City	94	29,349	5	5	59	91	173
Airport	15	3,975	0	0	n/a	n/a	n/a
Suburbs	141	51,013	5	0	n/a	n/a	n/a
Total	250	84,337	10	5	n/a	n/a	n/a

Note: n/a not available; Classifications range from one diamond (budget properties with basic amenities) to five diamond (luxury properties with the finest service, rooms and facilities).
Source: OAG, Business Travel Planner, Summer 1997

Orlando is home to two of the top 100 hotels in the world according to *Travel & Leisure*: Disney's Grand Floridian and Disney's Yacht Club Resort. Criteria: value, rooms/ambience, location, facilities/activities and service. *Travel & Leisure, September 1997*

CONVENTION CENTERS

Major Convention Centers

Center Name	Meeting Rooms	Exhibit Space (sf)
Centroplex Expo Centre	7	65,000
Orange County Convention Center	41	35,000
The Peabody Orlando	32	54,000
Stouffer Orlando Resort	45	180,000
Tupperware Convention Center	3	23,600
Twin Towers Hotel and Convention Center	n/a	n/a
Central Florida Fairgrounds	7	63,000

Note: n/a not available
Source: Trade Shows Worldwide 1997

Living Environment

COST OF LIVING

Cost of Living Index

Composite Index	Housing	Utilities	Groceries	Health Care	Trans-portation	Misc. Goods/ Services
99.6	94.1	103.7	102.9	106.4	99.9	100.5

Note: U.S. = 100
Source: ACCRA, Cost of Living Index, 3rd Quarter 1997

HOUSING

Median Home Prices and Housing Affordability

Area	Median Price[2] 3rd Qtr. 1997 ($)	HOI[3] 3rd Qtr. 1997	Afford-ability Rank[4]
MSA[1]	100,000	73.1	65
U.S.	127,000	63.7	–

Note: (1) Metropolitan Statistical Area - see Appendix A for areas included; (2) U.S. figures calculated from the sales of 625,000 new and existing homes in 195 markets; (3) Housing Opportunity Index - percent of homes sold that were within the reach of the median income household at the prevailing mortgage interest rate; (4) Rank is from 1-195 with 1 being most affordable
Source: National Association of Home Builders, Housing Opportunity Index, 3rd Quarter 1997

It is projected that the median price of existing single-family homes in the metro area will increase by 3.3% in 1998. Nationwide, home prices are projected to increase 6.6%.
Kiplinger's Personal Finance Magazine, January 1998

Average New Home Price

Area	Price ($)
City	126,729
U.S.	135,710

Note: Figures are based on a new home with 1,800 sq. ft. of living area on an 8,000 sq. ft. lot.
Source: ACCRA, Cost of Living Index, 3rd Quarter 1997

Average Apartment Rent

Area	Rent ($/mth)
City	591
U.S.	569

Note: Figures are based on an unfurnished two bedroom, 1-1/2 or 2 bath apartment, approximately 950 sq. ft. in size, excluding all utilities except water
Source: ACCRA, Cost of Living Index, 3rd Quarter 1997

RESIDENTIAL UTILITIES

Average Residential Utility Costs

Area	All Electric ($/mth)	Part Electric ($/mth)	Other Energy ($/mth)	Phone ($/mth)
City	106.15	–	–	20.29
U.S.	109.40	55.25	43.64	19.48

Source: ACCRA, Cost of Living Index, 3rd Quarter 1997

HEALTH CARE

Average Health Care Costs

Area	Hospital ($/day)	Doctor ($/visit)	Dentist ($/visit)
City	497.70	53.00	59.60
U.S.	392.91	48.76	60.84

Note: Hospital - based on a semi-private room. Doctor - based on a general practitioner's routine exam of an established patient. Dentist - based on adult teeth cleaning and periodic oral exam.
Source: ACCRA, Cost of Living Index, 3rd Quarter 1997

Distribution of Office-Based Physicians

Area	Family/Gen. Practitioners	Specialists		
		Medical	Surgical	Other
MSA[1]	332	699	617	523

Note: Data as of 12/31/96; (1) Metropolitan Statistical Area - see Appendix A for areas included
Source: American Medical Assn., Physician Characteristics & Distribution in the U.S., 1997-1998

Hospitals

Orlando has 4 general medical and surgical hospitals, 1 psychiatric, 1 children's psychiatric.
AHA Guide to the Healthcare Field 1997-98

EDUCATION

Public School District Statistics

District Name	Num. Sch.	Enroll.	Classroom Teachers[1]	Pupils per Teacher	Minority Pupils (%)	Current Exp.[2] ($/pupil)
Orange County School District	157	123,165	6,647	18.5	47.7	4,821

Note: Data covers the 1995-1996 school year unless otherwise noted; (1) Excludes teachers reported as working in school district offices rather than in schools; (2) Based on 1993-94 enrollment collected by the Census Bureau, not the enrollment figure shown in column 3; SD = School District; ISD = Independent School District; n/a not available
Source: National Center for Education Statistics, Common Core of Data Survey; Bureau of the Census

Educational Quality

School District	Education Quotient[1]	Graduate Outcome[2]	Community Index[3]	Resource Index[4]
Orlando	92.0	73.0	101.0	102.0

Note: Nearly 1,000 secondary school districts were rated in terms of educational quality. The scores range from a low of 50 to a high of 150; (1) Average of the Graduate Outcome, Community and Resource indexes; (2) Based on graduation rates and college board scores (SAT/ACT); (3) Based on the surrounding community's average level of education and the area's average income level; (4) Based on teacher salaries, per-pupil expenditures and student-teacher ratios.
Source: Expansion Management, Ratings Issue 1997

Educational Attainment by Race

Area	High School Graduate (%)					Bachelor's Degree (%)				
	Total	White	Black	Other	Hisp.[2]	Total	White	Black	Other	Hisp.[2]
City	78.1	85.2	56.5	69.3	67.0	22.6	26.6	9.8	21.2	17.0
MSA[1]	79.9	82.6	60.3	72.0	68.9	21.6	22.8	11.5	21.4	16.0
U.S.	75.2	77.9	63.1	60.4	49.8	20.3	21.5	11.4	19.4	9.2

Note: figures shown cover persons 25 years old and over; (1) Metropolitan Statistical Area - see Appendix A for areas included; (2) people of Hispanic origin can be of any race
Source: 1990 Census of Population and Housing, Summary Tape File 3C

School Enrollment by Type

Area	Preprimary				Elementary/High School			
	Public		Private		Public		Private	
	Enrollment	%	Enrollment	%	Enrollment	%	Enrollment	%
City	1,419	60.7	918	39.3	19,932	92.8	1,549	7.2
MSA[1]	9,698	49.2	9,997	50.8	154,434	91.4	14,467	8.6
U.S.	2,679,029	59.5	1,824,256	40.5	38,379,689	90.2	4,187,099	9.8

Note: figures shown cover persons 3 years old and over;
(1) Metropolitan Statistical Area - see Appendix A for areas included
Source: 1990 Census of Population and Housing, Summary Tape File 3C

School Enrollment by Race

Area	Preprimary (%)				Elementary/High School (%)			
	White	Black	Other	Hisp.[1]	White	Black	Other	Hisp.[1]
City	60.2	37.5	2.3	10.9	49.0	44.6	6.4	11.9
MSA[2]	82.3	14.2	3.5	7.5	74.8	18.7	6.5	11.8
U.S.	80.4	12.5	7.1	7.8	74.1	15.6	10.3	12.5

Note: figures shown cover persons 3 years old and over; (1) people of Hispanic origin can be of any race; (2) Metropolitan Statistical Area - see Appendix A for areas included
Source: 1990 Census of Population and Housing, Summary Tape File 3C

SAT/ACT Scores

Area/District	1997 SAT				1997 ACT	
	Percent of Graduates Tested (%)	Average Math Score	Average Verbal Score	Average Combined Score	Percent of Graduates Tested (%)	Average Composite Score
Orange County SD	43	501	495	996	28	20.9
State	50	499	499	998	36	20.7
U.S.	42	511	505	1,016	36	21.0

Note: Math and verbal SAT scores are out of a possible 800; ACT scores are out of a possible 36
Caution: Comparing or ranking states/cities on the basis of SAT/ACT scores alone is invalid and strongly discouraged by the The College Board and The American College Testing Program as students who take the tests are self-selected and do not represent the entire student population.
Source: Orange County Public Schools, Educational Improvement Services, 1997; American College Testing Program, 1997; College Board, 1997

Classroom Teacher Salaries in Public Schools

District	B.A. Degree		M.A. Degree		Ph.D. Degree	
	Min. ($)	Max ($)	Min. ($)	Max. ($)	Min. ($)	Max. ($)
Orlando	24,400	39,040	26,650	41,290	28,950	43,590
Average[1]	26,120	39,270	28,175	44,667	31,643	49,825

Note: Salaries are for 1996-1997; (1) Based on all school districts covered
Source: American Federation of Teachers (unpublished data)

Higher Education

Two-Year Colleges		Four-Year Colleges		Medical Schools	Law Schools	Voc/ Tech
Public	Private	Public	Private			
0	2	1	1	0	0	15

Source: College Blue Book, Occupational Education 1997; Medical School Admission Requirements, 1998-99; Peterson's Guide to Two-Year Colleges, 1997; Peterson's Guide to Four-Year Colleges, 1997; Barron's Guide to Law Schools 1997

MAJOR EMPLOYERS

Major Employers

Airport Limousine Service
Columbia Park Medical Center
Harcourt Brace & Co.
Sea World of Orlando
Service America
Tamar Convention Hotel

Transpo Electronics
GMRI Inc. (restaurants)
Orlando Regional Healthcare System
Sentinel Communications
SunTrust Bank-Central Florida
Walt Disney World

Note: companies listed are located in the city
Source: Dun's Business Rankings 1997; Ward's Business Directory, 1997

PUBLIC SAFETY

Crime Rate

Area	All Crimes	Violent Crimes				Property Crimes		
		Murder	Forcible Rape	Robbery	Aggrav. Assault	Burglary	Larceny -Theft	Motor Vehicle Theft
City	13,172.4	7.1	90.4	591.4	1,502.6	2,419.3	7,361.9	1,199.8
Suburbs[1]	n/a	n/a	n/a	n/a	n/a	n/a	n/a	n/a
MSA[2]	n/a	n/a	n/a	n/a	n/a	n/a	n/a	n/a
U.S.	5,078.9	7.4	36.1	202.4	388.2	943.0	2,975.9	525.9

Note: Crime rate is the number of crimes per 100,000 pop.; (1) defined as all areas within the MSA but located outside the central city; (2) Metropolitan Statistical Area - see Appendix A for areas incl.
Source: FBI Uniform Crime Reports 1996

RECREATION

Culture and Recreation

Museums	Symphony Orchestras	Opera Companies	Dance Companies	Professional Theatres	Zoos	Pro Sports Teams
3	1	1	1	2	1	1

Source: International Directory of the Performing Arts, 1996; Official Museum Directory, 1998; Chamber of Commerce/Economic Development 1997

Library System

The Orange County Library System has 11 branches, holdings of 1,739,300 volumes and a budget of $16,846,314 (1995-1996). *American Library Directory, 1997-1998*

MEDIA

Newspapers

Name	Type	Freq.	Distribution	Circulation
Central Florida Advocate	n/a	1x/wk	Local	10,000
The Orlando Sentinel	General	7x/wk	Regional	281,104
Orlando Sun Review	General	1x/wk	Area	16,000
Orlando Times	Black	1x/wk	Area	10,000

Note: Includes newspapers with circulations of 1,000 or more located in the city; n/a not available
Source: Burrelle's Media Directory, 1998 Edition

AM Radio Stations

Call Letters	Freq. (kHz)	Target Audience	Station Format	Music Format
WQTM	540	General	S	n/a
WDBO	580	General	M/N/S	Adult Contemporary
WWNZ	740	n/a	N/T	n/a
WZKD	950	General	M/S	n/a
WHOO	990	General	M/N/S	Adult Standards/Big Band/MOR
WONQ	1030	Hispanic	M/N/S	Adult Contemporary/Spanish
WAJL	1190	Religious	E/M/N/T	Christian
WPRD	1440	General	M/N/S/T	Spanish
WUNA	1480	Hispanic	M	n/a
WOKB	1600	General	M/T	Christian

Note: Stations included broadcast in the Orlando metro area; n/a not available
Station Format: E = Educational; M = Music; N = News; S = Sports; T = Talk
Music Format: AOR = Album Oriented Rock; MOR = Middle-of-the-Road
Source: Burrelle's Media Directory, 1998 Edition

FM Radio Stations

Call Letters	Freq. (mHz)	Target Audience	Station Format	Music Format
WUCF	89.9	Men	E/M/N/S	Jazz
WMFE	90.7	General	E/M/N	Classical
WPRK	91.5	General	E/M	Alternative/Classical
WWKA	92.3	General	M/N/S	Country
WCFB	94.5	General	M/N/S	Urban Contemporary
WHTQ	96.5	General	M/N/S	Classic Rock
WMMO	98.9	General	M	Adult Contemporary
WSHE	100.3	General	M/N/S	AOR/Alternative/Classic Rock
WJRR	101.1	General	M	AOR
WJHM	101.9	General	M	Urban Contemporary
WLOQ	103.1	General	M	Jazz
WOMX	105.1	General	M	Adult Contemporary
WOCL	105.9	n/a	M	Oldies
WXXL	106.7	n/a	M	Adult Contemporary/Contemporary Top 40
WMGF	107.7	General	M/N	Adult Contemporary

Note: Stations included broadcast in the Orlando metro area; n/a not available
Station Format: E = Educational; M = Music; N = News; S = Sports; T = Talk
Music Format: AOR = Album Oriented Rock; MOR = Middle-of-the-Road
Source: Burrelle's Media Directory, 1998 Edition

Television Stations

Name	Ch.	Affiliation	Type	Owner
WESH	2	NBC	Commercial	Pulitzer Broadcasting Company
WCPX	6	CBS	Commercial	First Media L.P.
WFTV	9	ABC	Commercial	Cox Enterprises Inc.
WKCF	18	WB	Commercial	Asbury Park Press Broadcasting, Inc.
WMFE	24	PBS	Public	Community Communications, Inc.
WACX	55	TBN	Commercial	Associated Christian Television System, Inc.
WRBW	65	UPN	Commercial	Rainbow Broadcasting Ltd.

Note: Stations included broadcast in the Orlando metro area
Source: Burrelle's Media Directory, 1998 Edition

CLIMATE

Average and Extreme Temperatures

Temperature	Jan	Feb	Mar	Apr	May	Jun	Jul	Aug	Sep	Oct	Nov	Dec	Ann
Extreme High (°F)	86	89	90	95	100	100	99	100	98	95	89	90	100
Average High (°F)	70	72	77	82	87	90	91	91	89	83	78	72	82
Average Temp. (°F)	59	62	67	72	77	81	82	82	81	75	68	62	72
Average Low (°F)	48	51	56	60	66	71	73	74	72	66	58	51	62
Extreme Low (°F)	19	29	25	38	51	53	64	65	57	44	32	20	19

Note: Figures cover the years 1952-1990
Source: National Climatic Data Center, International Station Meteorological Climate Summary, 3/95

Average Precipitation/Snowfall/Humidity

Precip./Humidity	Jan	Feb	Mar	Apr	May	Jun	Jul	Aug	Sep	Oct	Nov	Dec	Ann
Avg. Precip. (in.)	2.3	2.8	3.4	2.0	3.2	7.0	7.2	5.8	5.8	2.7	3.5	2.0	47.7
Avg. Snowfall (in.)	Tr	0	0	0	0	0	0	0	0	0	0	0	Tr
Avg. Rel. Hum. 7am (%)	87	87	88	87	88	89	90	92	92	89	89	87	89
Avg. Rel. Hum. 4pm (%)	53	51	49	47	51	61	65	66	66	59	56	55	57

Note: Figures cover the years 1952-1990; Tr = Trace amounts (<0.05 in. of rain; <0.5 in. of snow)
Source: National Climatic Data Center, International Station Meteorological Climate Summary, 3/95

Weather Conditions

Temperature			Daytime Sky			Precipitation		
32°F & below	45°F & below	90°F & above	Clear	Partly cloudy	Cloudy	0.01 inch or more precip.	0.1 inch or more snow/ice	Thunder-storms
3	35	90	76	208	81	115	0	80

Note: Figures are average number of days per year and covers the years 1952-1990
Source: National Climatic Data Center, International Station Meteorological Climate Summary, 3/95

AIR & WATER QUALITY

Maximum Pollutant Concentrations

	Particulate Matter (ug/m³)	Carbon Monoxide (ppm)	Sulfur Dioxide (ppm)	Nitrogen Dioxide (ppm)	Ozone (ppm)	Lead (ug/m³)
MSA[1] Level	67	4	0.008	0.013	0.10	0.00
NAAQS[2]	150	9	0.140	0.053	0.12	1.50
Met NAAQS?	Yes	Yes	Yes	Yes	Yes	Yes

Note: (1) Metropolitan Statistical Area - see Appendix A for areas included; (2) National Ambient Air Quality Standards; ppm = parts per million; ug/m³ = micrograms per cubic meter; n/a not available
Source: EPA, National Air Quality and Emissions Trends Report, 1996

Pollutant Standards Index

In the Orlando MSA (see Appendix A for areas included), the Pollutant Standards Index (PSI) exceeded 100 on 0 days in 1996. A PSI value greater than 100 indicates that air quality would be in the unhealthful range on that day. *EPA, National Air Quality and Emissions Trends Report, 1996*

Drinking Water

Water System Name	Pop. Served	Primary Water Source Type	Number of Violations in Fiscal Year 1997	Type of Violation/ Contaminants
Orlando Utilities Commission	356,041	Ground	None	None

Note: Data as of January 16, 1998
Source: EPA, Office of Ground Water and Drinking Water, Safe Drinking Water Information System

Orlando tap water is alkaline, hard and fluoridated.
Editor & Publisher Market Guide, 1998

San Antonio, Texas

Background

San Antonio, Texas is a charming preservation of its Mexican-Spanish heritage. Walking along its famous Paseo Del Rio at night is enough to make one cry. Who cannot be touched by the cream colored stucco structures with its seashell ornamented facades, gently illuminated by tiny lights?

Emotional intensity is nothing new to San Antonio. The city began in the early 18th century as a cohesion of different Spanish missions, whose zealous aim was to convert the Coahuiltecan natives to Christianity and European ways of farming. A debilitating epidemic, however, killed most of the natives, as well as the missions' goal. Thus, the area became abandoned for awhile.

In 1836, San Antonio became the site of interest again, when a small band of American soldiers were unable to successfully defend themselves against an army of 4,000 Mexican soldiers, led by General Antonio de Lopez Santa Anna. Fighting desperately from within the walls of the Mission San Antonio de Valero, or The Alamo, all 183 men were killed. This commendable act of courage inspired the cry "Remember the Alamo", from the throats of every American soldier led by General Sam Houston, who were determined to wrest Texas territory and independence from Mexico.

Despite the Anglo victory over the Mexicans more than 150 years ago, the Mexican culture and its influence remains strong. We see the evidence of this in the architecture; the Franciscan educational system; the variety of Spanish-speaking newspapers, television stations and radio stations; and the racial composition of the population, in which over half the city's residents are Latino.

This picturesque and practical blend of old and new makes San Antonio unique among American cities. One will see this not only in the lifestyle, but in the types of jobs available as well—particularly in the military sector.

The city also has diversified growth sectors which continue to build on its core tourism and trade strengths. The city's Kelly Air Force Base is becoming a city-run industrial and warehouse complex and much of the nearly 5,000 acre base will be available for economic development. The city is also investing $12 million in a new downtown International Center that will be home to the North American Development Bank. Other projects include a $22 million plant expansion by Frito Lay and a new San Antonio call center by Southwestern Bell which will employ 1,000 by the year 2000. *Site Selection Dec 1977/Jan1988*

San Antonio's location on the edge of the Gulf Coastal Plains exposes it to a modified subtropical climate. Summers are hot with temperatures above 90 degrees 80% of the time, although extremely high temperatures are rare. Winters are mild.

Since the city is only 140 miles from the Gulf of Mexico, tropical storms occasionally occur. These can bring strong winds and heavy rains. Relative humidity is above 80% during the early morning hours, dropping to near 50% in the late afternoon.

General Rankings and Evaluative Comments

- San Antonio was ranked #53 out of 300 cities by *Money's* 1997 "Survey of the Best Places to Live." Criteria used: health services, crime, economy, housing, education, transportation, weather, leisure and the arts. The city was ranked #17 in 1996 and #129 in 1995. *Money, July 1997; Money, September 1996; Money, September 1995*

- *Ladies Home Journal* ranked America's 200 largest cities based on the qualities women care about most. San Antonio ranked 88 out of 200. Criteria: low crime rate, good public schools, well-paying jobs, quality health and child care, the presence of women in government, proportion of women-owned businesses, size of the wage gap with men, local economy, divorce rates, the ratio of single men to single women, whether there are laws that require at least the same number of public toilets for women as men, and the probability of good hair days. *Ladies Home Journal, November 1997*

- San Antonio was ranked #83 out of 219 cities in terms of children's health, safety, and economic well-being. Criteria: total population, percent population change, birth rate, child immunization rate, infant mortality rate, percent low birth weight infants, percent of births to teens, physician-to-population ratio, student-to-teacher ratio, dropout rate, unemployment rate, median family income, percent of children in poverty, violent and property crime rates, number of juvenile arrests for violent crimes as a percent of the total crime index, number of days with pollution standard index (PSI) over 100, pounds toxic releases per 1,000 people and number of superfund sites. *Zero Population Growth, Children's Environmental Index 1997*

- *Conde Nast Traveler* polled 37,000 readers in terms of travel satisfaction. Cities were ranked based on the following criteria: people/friendliness, environment/ambiance, cultural enrichment, restaurants and fun/energy. San Antonio appeared in the top thirty, ranking number 11, with an overall rating of 68.1 out of 100 based on all the criteria. The cities were also ranked in each category separately. San Antonio appeared in the top 10 based on people/friendliness, ranking number 7 with a rating of 75.0 out of 100. *Conde Nast Traveler, Readers' Choice Poll 1997*

- *Yahoo! Internet Life* selected "America's 100 Most Wired Cities & Towns". 50 cities were large and 50 cities were small. San Antonio ranked 27 out of 50 large cities. Criteria: Internet users per capita, number of networked computers, number of registered domain names, Internet backbone traffic, and the per-capita number of Web sites devoted to each city. *Yahoo! Internet Life, March 1998*

- USAA (auto & life insurance), headquartered in San Antonio, is among the "100 Best Companies to Work for in America." Criteria: trust in management, pride in work/company, camaraderie, company responses to the Hewitt People Practices Inventory, and employee responses to their Great Place to Work survey. The companies also had to be at least 10 years old and have a minimum of 500 employees. *Fortune, January 12, 1998*

- United Services Automobile Association, headquartered in San Antonio, is among the "100 Best Companies for Working Mothers." Criteria: pay compared with competition, opportunities for women to advance, support for child care, flexible work schedules and family-friendly benefits. *Working Mother, October 1997*

- According to *Working Mother,* "This year, the Texas Licensed Child Care Association lobbied heavily against proposed standards that would have improved the adult-to-child ratios in many programs. Unfortunately, it prevailed. Lawmakers delayed adoption of the new rules.

  Texas may finally get statewide resource and referral services, however, with new federal funds coming into the state. In addition to helping parents find care, R&Rs may handle both caregiver training and consumer education—a positive development.

  Providers across the state may also get low-interest loans to buy new equipment, upgrade their facilities and do other things to improve the quality of care, under a bill pending in the state legislature that looked likely to pass as we went to press." *Working Mother, July/August 1997*

Business Environment

STATE ECONOMY

State Economic Profile

"The Texas economy remains among the strongest in the nation....

Overall, Texas gained over 141,000 people last year through in-migration. While this is down from the three-year average of over 170,000, it still represents 43% of the Texas population increase. By far, throughout this decade, California has been the largest domestic source of in-migrants into Texas. With the California economy rebounding, in-migration to Texas is slowing.

The slowdown in household growth, coupled with solid residential construction, is creating a slight oversupply throughout the state. As a result, house price growth is decelerating. New residential permits have yet to slow, with new permits up by 14% last year—nearly twice the national increase. The slowdown in population and household growth cannot sustain such robust growth in permits, and as a result, new permits will slow this year.

The Texas economy shows no major imbalances. Although the important computer-chip industry remains moribund, the economy continues to expand solidly. The turnaround in computer memory prices will help the state continue to expand. Texas' growth is becoming increasingly supported by in-migrants. With an increasing presence in high-tech, an attractive business environment, and close proximity to Mexico, Texas will continue to expand faster than the nation and lure workers from other locales. In addition, as an attractive destination for retirees, Texas will continue to experience solid population and household growth as the population ages. Texas is ranked above average for short-and long-term growth." *National Association of Realtors, Economic Profiles: The Fifty States, July 1997*

IMPORTS/EXPORTS

Total Export Sales

Area	1993 ($000)	1994 ($000)	1995 ($000)	1996 ($000)	% Chg. 1993-96	% Chg. 1995-96
MSA[1]	563,928	656,276	771,089	1,049,965	86.2	36.2
U.S.	464,858,354	512,415,609	583,030,524	622,827,063	34.0	6.8

Note: (1) Metropolitan Statistical Area - see Appendix A for areas included
Source: U.S. Department of Commerce, International Trade Association, Metropolitan Area Exports: An Export Performance Report on Over 250 U.S. Cities, October 1997

Imports/Exports by Port

Type	Cargo Value 1995 (US$mil.)	1996 (US$mil.)	% Change 1995-1996	Share of U.S. Total 1995 (%)	1996 (%)
Imports	0	0	0	0	0
Exports	0	0	0	0	0

Source: Global Trade Information Services, WaterBorne Trade Atlas 1997

CITY FINANCES

City Government Finances

Component	FY94 ($000)	FY94 (per capita $)
Revenue	1,677,193	1,622.08
Expenditure	1,685,100	1,629.72
Debt Outstanding	4,274,074	4,133.62
Cash & Securities	1,257,491	1,216.17

Source: U.S. Bureau of the Census, City Government Finances: 1993-94

City Government Revenue by Source

Source	FY94 ($000)	FY94 (per capita $)	FY94 (%)
From Federal Government	24,556	23.75	1.5
From State Governments	74,339	71.90	4.4
From Local Governments	52,142	50.43	3.1
Property Taxes	131,262	126.95	7.8
General Sales Taxes	80,683	78.03	4.8
Selective Sales Taxes	33,386	32.29	2.0
Income Taxes	0	0.00	0.0
Current Charges	192,260	185.94	11.5
Utility/Liquor Store	975,098	943.05	58.1
Employee Retirement[1]	33,295	32.20	2.0
Other	80,172	77.54	4.8

Note: (1) Excludes "city contributions," classified as "nonrevenue," intragovernmental transfers.
Source: U.S. Bureau of the Census, City Government Finances: 1993-94

City Government Expenditures by Function

Function	FY94 ($000)	FY94 (per capita $)	FY94 (%)
Educational Services	27,126	26.23	1.6
Employee Retirement[1]	13,918	13.46	0.8
Environment/Housing	249,846	241.64	14.8
Government Administration	31,553	30.52	1.9
Interest on General Debt	56,321	54.47	3.3
Public Safety	194,829	188.43	11.6
Social Services	46,703	45.17	2.8
Transportation	99,377	96.11	5.9
Utility/Liquor Store	908,336	878.49	53.9
Other	57,091	55.21	3.4

Note: (1) Payments to beneficiaries including withdrawal of contributions.
Source: U.S. Bureau of the Census, City Government Finances: 1993-94

Municipal Bond Ratings

Area	Moody's	S & P
San Antonio	Aa	AA

Note: n/a not available; n/r not rated
Source: Moody's Bond Record, 2/98; Statistical Abstract of the U.S., 1997;
Governing Magazine, 9/97, 3/98

POPULATION

Population Growth

Area	1980	1990	% Chg. 1980-90	July 1996 Estimate	% Chg. 1990-96
City	785,809	935,927	19.1	1,067,816	14.1
MSA[1]	1,072,125	1,302,099	21.5	1,490,111	14.4
U.S.	226,545,805	248,765,170	9.8	265,179,411	6.6

Note: (1) Metropolitan Statistical Area - see Appendix A for areas included
Source: 1980/1990 Census of Housing and Population, Summary Tape File 3C;
Census Bureau Population Estimates

Population Characteristics

Race	City				% Chg. 1980-90	MSA[1]	
	1980		1990			1990	
	Population	%	Population	%		Population	%
White	621,679	79.1	676,464	72.3	8.8	979,319	75.2
Black	57,566	7.3	65,852	7.0	14.4	88,709	6.8
Amer Indian/Esk/Aleut	2,375	0.3	3,447	0.4	45.1	4,673	0.4
Asian/Pacific Islander	5,821	0.7	10,625	1.1	82.5	16,020	1.2
Other	98,368	12.5	179,539	19.2	82.5	213,378	16.4
Hispanic Origin[2]	421,954	53.7	517,974	55.3	22.8	616,878	47.4

Note: (1) Metropolitan Statistical Area - see Appendix A for areas included;
(2) people of Hispanic origin can be of any race
Source: 1980/1990 Census of Housing and Population, Summary Tape File 3C

Ancestry

Area	German	Irish	English	Italian	U.S.	French	Polish	Dutch
City	14.0	8.2	7.7	1.7	2.1	2.4	1.6	0.9
MSA[1]	17.9	9.8	9.2	1.9	2.4	2.8	2.0	1.1
U.S.	23.3	15.6	13.1	5.9	5.3	4.2	3.8	2.5

Note: Figures are percentages and include persons that reported multiple ancestry (eg. if a person reported being Irish and Italian, they were included in both columns); (1) Metropolitan Statistical Area - see Appendix A for areas included
Source: 1990 Census of Population and Housing, Summary Tape File 3C

Age

Area	Median Age (Years)	Age Distribution (%)						
		Under 5	Under 18	18-24	25-44	45-64	65+	80+
City	29.8	8.4	29.1	11.5	32.4	16.7	10.4	2.2
MSA[1]	30.3	8.3	29.0	11.0	32.7	17.2	10.2	2.1
U.S.	32.9	7.3	25.6	10.5	32.6	18.7	12.5	2.8

Note: (1) Metropolitan Statistical Area - see Appendix A for areas included
Source: 1990 Census of Population and Housing, Summary Tape File 3C

Male/Female Ratio

Area	Number of males per 100 females (all ages)	Number of males per 100 females (18 years old+)
City	93.0	88.7
MSA[1]	94.6	90.7
U.S.	95.0	91.9

Note: (1) Metropolitan Statistical Area - see Appendix A for areas included
Source: 1990 Census of Population, General Population Characteristics

INCOME

Per Capita/Median/Average Income

Area	Per Capita ($)	Median Household ($)	Average Household ($)
City	10,884	23,584	30,622
MSA[1]	11,865	26,092	33,646
U.S.	14,420	30,056	38,453

Note: all figures are for 1989; (1) Metropolitan Statistical Area - see Appendix A for areas included
Source: 1990 Census of Population and Housing, Summary Tape File 3C

Household Income Distribution by Race

Income ($)	City (%)					U.S. (%)				
	Total	White	Black	Other	Hisp.[1]	Total	White	Black	Other	Hisp.[1]
Less than 5,000	9.8	8.2	17.9	13.7	13.2	6.2	4.8	15.2	8.6	8.8
5,000 - 9,999	10.1	9.3	12.9	12.5	12.6	9.3	8.6	14.2	9.9	11.1
10,000 - 14,999	11.2	10.5	13.0	13.8	13.2	8.8	8.5	11.0	9.8	11.0
15,000 - 24,999	21.3	20.7	22.0	23.8	23.1	17.5	17.3	18.9	18.5	20.5
25,000 - 34,999	16.3	16.3	14.4	16.9	15.9	15.8	16.1	14.2	15.4	16.4
35,000 - 49,999	15.1	16.1	11.2	12.4	13.2	17.9	18.6	13.3	16.1	16.0
50,000 - 74,999	10.5	12.1	6.5	5.4	6.6	15.0	15.8	9.3	13.4	11.1
75,000 - 99,999	3.1	3.8	1.4	1.0	1.3	5.1	5.5	2.6	4.7	3.1
100,000+	2.4	2.9	0.8	0.6	0.8	4.4	4.8	1.3	3.7	1.9

Note: all figures are for 1989; (1) people of Hispanic origin can be of any race
Source: 1990 Census of Population and Housing, Summary Tape File 3C

Effective Buying Income

Area	Per Capita ($)	Median Household ($)	Average Household ($)
City	12,566	27,690	36,061
MSA[1]	13,995	31,298	40,458
U.S.	15,444	33,201	41,849

Note: data as of 1/1/97; (1) Metropolitan Statistical Area - see Appendix A for areas included
Source: Standard Rate & Data Service, Newspaper Advertising Source, 2/98

Effective Household Buying Income Distribution

Area	% of Households Earning						
	$10,000 -$19,999	$20,000 -$34,999	$35,000 -$49,999	$50,000 -$74,999	$75,000 -$99,000	$100,000 -$124,999	$125,000 and up
City	19.2	25.4	16.6	14.0	4.9	1.6	1.7
MSA[1]	17.0	24.3	17.5	16.7	6.1	2.0	2.2
U.S.	16.5	23.4	18.3	18.2	6.4	2.1	2.4

Note: data as of 1/1/97; (1) Metropolitan Statistical Area - see Appendix A for areas included
Source: Standard Rate & Data Service, Newspaper Advertising Source, 2/98

Poverty Rates by Race and Age

Area	Total (%)	By Race (%)				By Age (%)		
		White	Black	Other	Hisp.[2]	Under 5 years old	Under 18 years old	65 years and over
City	22.6	19.1	30.3	32.3	30.8	35.4	32.5	19.1
MSA[1]	19.5	16.2	26.4	30.5	29.3	30.3	27.7	17.2
U.S.	13.1	9.8	29.5	23.1	25.3	20.1	18.3	12.8

Note: figures show the percent of people living below the poverty line in 1989. The average poverty threshold was $12,674 for a family of four in 1989; (1) Metropolitan Statistical Area - see Appendix A for areas included; (2) people of Hispanic origin can be of any race
Source: 1990 Census of Population and Housing, Summary Tape File 3C

EMPLOYMENT

Labor Force and Employment

Area	Civilian Labor Force			Workers Employed		
	Dec. '95	Dec. '96	% Chg.	Dec. '95	Dec. '96	% Chg.
City	509,509	519,826	2.0	489,275	500,305	2.3
MSA[1]	733,657	748,785	2.1	707,779	723,734	2.3
U.S.	134,583,000	136,742,000	1.6	127,903,000	130,785,000	2.3

Note: Data is not seasonally adjusted and covers workers 16 years of age and older;
(1) Metropolitan Statistical Area - see Appendix A for areas included
Source: Bureau of Labor Statistics, http://stats.bls.gov

Unemployment Rate

Area	1997											
	Jan.	Feb.	Mar.	Apr.	May	Jun.	Jul.	Aug.	Sep.	Oct.	Nov.	Dec.
City	4.7	4.7	4.6	4.1	4.3	5.6	5.1	4.9	4.6	4.3	4.3	3.8
MSA[1]	4.2	4.2	4.1	3.7	3.8	5.0	4.6	4.4	4.1	3.8	3.8	3.3
U.S.	5.9	5.7	5.5	4.8	4.7	5.2	5.0	4.8	4.7	4.4	4.3	4.4

Note: Data is not seasonally adjusted and covers workers 16 years of age and older; All figures are percentages; (1) Metropolitan Statistical Area - see Appendix A for areas included
Source: Bureau of Labor Statistics, http://stats.bls.gov

Employment by Industry

Sector	MSA[1]		U.S.
	Number of Employees	Percent of Total	Percent of Total
Services	213,900	31.5	29.0
Retail Trade	137,200	20.2	18.5
Government	135,000	19.9	16.1
Manufacturing	50,400	7.4	15.0
Finance/Insurance/Real Estate	45,200	6.6	5.7
Wholesale Trade	29,900	4.4	5.4
Transportation/Public Utilities	31,300	4.6	5.3
Construction	35,100	5.2	4.5
Mining	2,000	0.3	0.5

Note: Figures cover non-farm employment as of 12/97 and are not seasonally adjusted; (1) Metropolitan Statistical Area - see Appendix A for areas included
Source: Bureau of Labor Statistics, http://stats.bls.gov

Employment by Occupation

Occupation Category	City (%)	MSA[1] (%)	U.S. (%)
White Collar	59.7	60.9	58.1
Executive/Admin./Management	11.7	12.3	12.3
Professional	13.3	14.0	14.1
Technical & Related Support	4.0	4.1	3.7
Sales	13.0	13.1	11.8
Administrative Support/Clerical	17.7	17.4	16.3
Blue Collar	23.1	22.8	26.2
Precision Production/Craft/Repair	10.7	10.9	11.3
Machine Operators/Assem./Insp.	4.4	4.3	6.8
Transportation/Material Movers	3.9	3.9	4.1
Cleaners/Helpers/Laborers	4.0	3.7	3.9
Services	16.2	15.0	13.2
Farming/Forestry/Fishing	1.0	1.3	2.5

Note: figures cover employed persons 16 years old and over; (1) Metropolitan Statistical Area - see Appendix A for areas included
Source: 1990 Census of Population and Housing, Summary Tape File 3C

Occupational Employment Projections: 1993 - 2000

Occupations Expected to have the Largest Job Growth (ranked by numerical growth)	Fast-Growing Occupations[1] (ranked by percent growth)
1. Home health aides	1. Home health aides
2. Salespersons, retail	2. Personal and home care aides
3. General office clerks	3. Engineers, chemical
4. Cashiers	4. Human services workers
5. Registered nurses	5. Demonstrators/promoters/models
6. Child care workers, private household	6. Physical therapists
7. Food preparation workers	7. Health service workers
8. Waiters & waitresses	8. Flight attendants
9. Guards	9. Customer service representatives
10. General managers & top executives	10. Emergency medical technicians

Projections cover Atascosa, Bandera, Bexar, Comal, Frio, Gillespie, Guadalupe, Karnes, Kendall, Kerr, Medina and Wilson Counties.
Note: (1) Includes occupations with absolute job growth of 100 or more
Source: Texas Employment Commission, Texas Employment Projections Reporting System, Statewide and Regional Projections 1993-2000, Ver. 1.0

Average Wages

Occupation	Wage	Occupation	Wage
Professional/Technical/Clerical	$/Week	**Health/Protective Services**	$/Week
Accountants III	-	Corrections Officers	-
Attorneys III	-	Firefighters	-
Budget Analysts III	-	Nurses, Licensed Practical II	-
Buyers/Contracting Specialists II	-	Nurses, Registered II	-
Clerks, Accounting III	404	Nursing Assistants II	-
Clerks, General III	395	Police Officers I	-
Computer Operators II	-	**Hourly Workers**	$/Hour
Computer Programmers II	645	Forklift Operators	8.22
Drafters II	452	General Maintenance Workers	8.03
Engineering Technicians III	-	Guards I	5.68
Engineering Technicians, Civil III	-	Janitors	5.36
Engineers III	-	Maintenance Electricians	14.31
Key Entry Operators I	-	Maintenance Electronics Techs II	19.00
Personnel Assistants III	-	Maintenance Machinists	-
Personnel Specialists III	-	Maintenance Mechanics, Machinery	-
Secretaries III	500	Material Handling Laborers	-
Switchboard Operator-Receptionist	301	Motor Vehicle Mechanics	12.98
Systems Analysts II	946	Shipping/Receiving Clerks	7.44
Systems Analysts Supervisor/Mgr II	-	Tool and Die Makers	-
Tax Collectors II	-	Truckdrivers, Tractor Trailer	11.12
Word Processors II	-	Warehouse Specialists	-

Note: Wage data includes full-time workers only for 8/96 and cover the Metropolitan Statistical Area (see Appendix A for areas included). Dashes indicate that data was not available.
Source: Bureau of Labor Statistics, Occupational Compensation Survey, 12/96

TAXES

Major State and Local Tax Rates

State Corp. Income (%)	State Personal Income (%)	Residential Property (effective rate per $100)	Sales & Use		State Gasoline (cents/ gallon)	State Cigarette (cents/ 20-pack)
			State (%)	Local (%)		
None[a]	None	n/a	6.25	1.5	20	41

Note: Personal/corporate income tax rates as of 1/97. Sales, gasoline and cigarette tax rates as of 1/98; (a) Texas imposes a franchise tax of 4.5% of earned surplus
Source: Federation of Tax Administrators, www.taxadmin.org; Washington D.C. Department of Finance and Revenue, Tax Rates and Tax Burdens in the District of Columbia: A Nationwide Comparison, June 1997; Chamber of Commerce

Total Taxes Per Capita and as a Percent of Income

Area	Per Capita Income ($)	Per Capita Taxes ($)			Taxes as Pct. of Income (%)		
		Total	Federal	State/ Local	Total	Federal	State/ Local
Texas	24,145	8,118	5,538	2,580	33.6	22.9	10.7
U.S.	26,187	9,205	6,127	3,078	35.2	23.4	11.8

Note: Figures are for 1997
Source: Tax Foundation, Web Site, www.taxfoundation.org

COMMERCIAL REAL ESTATE

Office Market

Class/ Location	Total Space (sq. ft.)	Vacant Space (sq. ft.)	Vac. Rate (%)	Under Constr. (sq. ft.)	Net Absorp. (sq. ft.)	Rental Rates ($/sq.ft./yr.)
Class A						
CBD	1,983,233	125,131	6.3	0	31,444	14.00-19.00
Outside CBD	4,994,191	201,047	4.0	0	156,087	14.00-22.50
Class B						
CBD	2,677,036	513,005	19.2	0	383,845	10.20-14.50
Outside CBD	6,657,099	642,236	9.6	0	211,015	9.60-18.00

Note: Data as of 10/97 and covers San Antonio; CBD = Central Business District; n/a not available;
Source: Society of Industrial and Office Realtors, 1998 Comparative Statistics of Industrial and Office Real Estate Markets

"Although existing vacant space was on a steady decline during 1997 and rental rates increased, only one new speculative Class 'A' building was proposed for 1998. During 1998 our SIOR reporters expect absorptions to accelerate modestly placing more downward pressure on vacancy rates. Falling vacancy rates wil lead to additional increases in rental rates of six to 10 percent during 1998. Strong absorption in the Class 'B' market will lift sales prices by a similar amount. With vacancy rates in the single digit range for both Class 'A' and 'B' space outside of the central business district at the beginning of 1998, the estimates for increases in rental rates and sales prices may be conservative." *Society of Industrial and Office Realtors, 1998 Comparative Statistics of Industrial and Office Real Estate Markets*

Industrial Market

Location	Total Space (sq. ft.)	Vacant Space (sq. ft.)	Vac. Rate (%)	Under Constr. (sq. ft.)	Net Absorp. (sq. ft.)	Net Lease ($/sq.ft./yr.)
Central City	12,500,000	461,343	3.7	0	128,000	2.64-3.60
Suburban	46,242,970	3,503,665	7.6	106,000	344,689	3.12-7.44

Note: Data as of 10/97 and covers San Antonio; n/a not available
Source: Society of Industrial and Office Realtors, 1998 Comparative Statistics of Industrial and Office Real Estate Markets

"At the end of 1997 nearly 500,000 sq. ft. of speculative space was planned in the north central corridor and northeast quadrant. Development in the north central corridor will be largely flex space while development in the northeast quadrant will be warehouse/distribution. Warehousing and distribution construction fell to almost nothing during 1997 but is it expected to come back strongly during 1998. High-Tech/R&D construction dropped off during 1997 as well but it is anticipated that this sector will also recover during 1998. Strong industrial sales prices encourage new development, though lenders are still quite disciplined. While sales prices are expected to move up six to 10 percent during 1998 the additional supply of space from new construction should help keep lease prices stable." *Society of Industrial and Office Realtors, 1998 Comparative Statistics of Industrial and Office Real Estate Markets*

COMMERCIAL UTILITIES

Typical Monthly Electric Bills

Area	Commercial Service ($/month)		Industrial Service ($/month)	
	12 kW demand 1,500 kWh	120 kW demand 30,000 kWh	1,000 kW demand 400,000 kWh	20,000 kW demand 10,000,000 kWh
City[1]	98	1,808	18,512	324,300
U.S.[2]	162	2,360[a]	25,590	545,677

Note: (1) Based on rates in effect January 1, 1997; (2) Based on rates in effect July 1, 1997;
(a) Based on 100 kW demand and 30,000 kWh usage.
Source: Memphis Light, Gas and Water, 1997 Utility Bill Comparisons for Selected U.S. Cities;
Edison Electric Institute, Typical Residential, Commercial and Industrial Bills, Summer 1997

TRANSPORTATION

Transportation Statistics

Avg. travel time to work (min.)	21.7
Interstate highways	I-10; I-35; I-37
Bus lines	
In-city	VIA Metro Transit, 522 vehicles
Inter-city	3
Passenger air service	
Airport	San Antonio International
Airlines	18
Aircraft departures	42,210 (1995)
Enplaned passengers	2,965,785 (1995)
Rail service	Amtrak
Motor freight carriers	40
Major waterways/ports	None

Source: OAG, Business Travel Planner, Summer 1997; Editor & Publisher Market Guide, 1998; FAA
Airport Activity Statistics, 1996; Amtrak National Time Table, Northeast Timetable, Fall/Winter
1997-98; 1990 Census of Population and Housing, STF 3C; Chamber of Commerce/Economic
Development 1997; Jane's Urban Transport Systems 1997-98; Transit Fact Book 1997

Means of Transportation to Work

Area	Car/Truck/Van		Public Transportation			Bicycle	Walked	Other Means	Worked at Home
	Drove Alone	Car-pooled	Bus	Subway	Railroad				
City	73.4	15.5	4.8	0.0	0.0	0.1	3.1	1.1	1.9
MSA[1]	74.6	14.8	3.6	0.0	0.0	0.2	3.6	1.0	2.3
U.S.	73.2	13.4	3.0	1.5	0.5	0.4	3.9	1.2	3.0

Note: figures shown are percentages and only include workers 16 years old and over;
(1) Metropolitan Statistical Area - see Appendix A for areas included
Source: 1990 Census of Population and Housing, Summary Tape File 3C

BUSINESSES

Major Business Headquarters

Company Name	1997 Rankings	
	Fortune 500	Forbes 500
HB Zachry	-	273
HE Butt Grocery	-	18
McCombs Automotive	-	137
SBC Communications	85	-
Ultramar Diamond Shamrock	181	-
United Services Automobile Assn.	212	-
Valero Energy	287	-

Note: Companies listed are located in the city; Dashes indicate no ranking
Fortune 500: companies that produce a 10-K are ranked 1 - 500 based on 1996 revenue
Forbes 500: private companies are ranked 1 - 500 based on 1996 revenue
Source: Forbes 12/1/97; Fortune 4/28/97

Fast-Growing Businesses

San Antonio is home to one of *Business Week's* "hot growth" companies: Billing Information Concepts. Criteria: sales and earnings, return on capital and stock price. *Business Week, 5/26/97*

Women-Owned Businesses: Number, Employment, Sales and Share

Area	Women-Owned Businesses in 1996				Share of Women-Owned Businesses in 1996	
	Number	Employment	Sales ($000)	Rank[2]	Percent (%)	Rank[3]
MSA[1]	37,100	88,400	7,386,700	42	35.3	38

Note: (1) Metropolitan Statistical Area - see Appendix A for areas included; (2) Calculated on an averaging of number of businesses, employment and sales and ranges from 1 to 50 where 1 is best; (3) Ranges from 1 to 50 where 1 is best
Source: The National Foundation for Women Business Owners, 1996 Facts on Women-Owned Businesses: Trends in the Top 50 Metropolitan Areas, March 26, 1997

Women-Owned Businesses: Growth

Area	Growth in Women-Owned Businesses (% change from 1987 to 1996)				Relative Growth in the Number of Women-Owned and All Businesses (% change from 1987 to 1996)			
	Num.	Empl.	Sales	Rank[2]	Women-Owned	All Firms	Absolute Difference	Relative Difference
MSA[1]	70.3	222.5	220.2	33	70.3	43.4	26.9	1.7:1

Note: (1) Metropolitan Statistical Area - see Appendix A for areas included; (2) Calculated on an averaging of the percent growth of number of businesses, employment and sales and ranges from 1 to 50 where 1 is best
Source: The National Foundation for Women Business Owners, 1996 Facts on Women-Owned Businesses: Trends in the Top 50 Metropolitan Areas, March 26, 1997

Minority Business Opportunity

12 of the 500 largest Hispanic-owned companies in the U.S. are located in San Antonio. *Hispanic Business, June 1997*

San Antonio is home to three companies which are on the Hispanic Business Fastest-Growing 100 list (greatest sales growth from 1992 to 1996): H.J. Group Ventures Inc. (construction mgmt. and general contracting), Q.I.V. Systems Inc. (computer consulting & devel. svcs.), and Operational Technologies Corp. (info. systems/environ. engr. svcs.) *Hispanic Business, July/August 1997*

San Antonio was listed among the top 25 metropolitan areas in terms of the number of Hispanic-owned companies. The city was ranked number 9 with 30,449 companies. *Hispanic Business, May 1997*

HOTELS & MOTELS

Hotels/Motels

Area	Hotels/ Motels	Rooms	Luxury-Level Hotels/Motels		Average Minimum Rates ($)		
			♦♦♦♦	♦♦♦♦♦	♦♦	♦♦♦	♦♦♦♦
City	103	16,364	5	0	64	105	178
Airport	15	2,703	0	0	n/a	n/a	n/a
Suburbs	2	160	0	0	n/a	n/a	n/a
Total	120	19,227	5	0	n/a	n/a	n/a

Note: n/a not available; Classifications range from one diamond (budget properties with basic amenities) to five diamond (luxury properties with the finest service, rooms and facilities).
Source: OAG, Business Travel Planner, Summer 1997

CONVENTION CENTERS   **Major Convention Centers**

Center Name	Meeting Rooms	Exhibit Space (sf)
Alamodome	16	160,000
Joe Freeman Coliseum	n/a	155,964
Henry B. Gonzalez Convention Center	46	240,000
San Antonio Convention	43	240,000
Villita Assembly Building	3	12,880
San Antonio Municipal Auditorium	8	23,000

Note: n/a not available
Source: Trade Shows Worldwide 1997

Living Environment

COST OF LIVING

Cost of Living Index

Composite Index	Housing	Utilities	Groceries	Health Care	Trans-portation	Misc. Goods/ Services
91.8	91.5	77.6	88.4	95.0	95.4	95.5

Note: U.S. = 100
Source: ACCRA, Cost of Living Index, 3rd Quarter 1997

HOUSING

Median Home Prices and Housing Affordability

Area	Median Price[2] 3rd Qtr. 1997 ($)	HOI[3] 3rd Qtr. 1997	Afford-ability Rank[4]
MSA[1]	92,000	63.5	128
U.S.	127,000	63.7	–

Note: (1) Metropolitan Statistical Area - see Appendix A for areas included; (2) U.S. figures calculated from the sales of 625,000 new and existing homes in 195 markets; (3) Housing Opportunity Index - percent of homes sold that were within the reach of the median income household at the prevailing mortgage interest rate; (4) Rank is from 1-195 with 1 being most affordable
Source: National Association of Home Builders, Housing Opportunity Index, 3rd Quarter 1997

It is projected that the median price of existing single-family homes in the metro area will increase by 7.6% in 1998. Nationwide, home prices are projected to increase 6.6%.
Kiplinger's Personal Finance Magazine, January 1998

Average New Home Price

Area	Price ($)
City	125,200
U.S.	135,710

Note: Figures are based on a new home with 1,800 sq. ft. of living area on an 8,000 sq. ft. lot.
Source: ACCRA, Cost of Living Index, 3rd Quarter 1997

Average Apartment Rent

Area	Rent ($/mth)
City	563
U.S.	569

Note: Figures are based on an unfurnished two bedroom, 1-1/2 or 2 bath apartment, approximately 950 sq. ft. in size, excluding all utilities except water
Source: ACCRA, Cost of Living Index, 3rd Quarter 1997

RESIDENTIAL UTILITIES

Average Residential Utility Costs

Area	All Electric ($/mth)	Part Electric ($/mth)	Other Energy ($/mth)	Phone ($/mth)
City	–	54.29	24.23	16.38
U.S.	109.40	55.25	43.64	19.48

Source: ACCRA, Cost of Living Index, 3rd Quarter 1997

HEALTH CARE

Average Health Care Costs

Area	Hospital ($/day)	Doctor ($/visit)	Dentist ($/visit)
City	365.60	48.20	54.00
U.S.	392.91	48.76	60.84

Note: Hospital - based on a semi-private room. Doctor - based on a general practitioner's routine exam of an established patient. Dentist - based on adult teeth cleaning and periodic oral exam.
Source: ACCRA, Cost of Living Index, 3rd Quarter 1997

Distribution of Office-Based Physicians

Area	Family/Gen. Practitioners	Specialists		
		Medical	Surgical	Other
MSA[1]	362	753	622	725

Note: Data as of 12/31/96; (1) Metropolitan Statistical Area - see Appendix A for areas included
Source: American Medical Assn., Physician Characteristics & Distribution in the U.S., 1997-1998

Hospitals

San Antonio has 14 general medical and surgical hospitals, 3 psychiatric, 1 tuberculosis and other respiratory disease, 1 obstetrics and gynecology, 2 rehabilitation, 1 chronic disease, 1 other specialty. *AHA Guide to the Healthcare Field 1997-98*

University Health System is among the 100 best-run hospitals in the U.S. *Modern Healthcare, January 5, 1998*

EDUCATION

Public School District Statistics

District Name	Num. Sch.	Enroll.	Classroom Teachers[1]	Pupils per Teacher	Minority Pupils (%)	Current Exp.[2] ($/pupil)
Alamo Heights ISD	5	4,054	266	15.2	n/a	n/a
East Central ISD	8	6,673	405	16.5	n/a	n/a
Edgewood ISD	26	14,587	979	14.9	n/a	n/a
Ft Sam Houston ISD	3	1,185	101	11.7	n/a	n/a
Harlandale ISD	26	14,847	941	15.8	n/a	n/a
Lackland ISD	2	887	71	12.5	n/a	n/a
North East ISD	53	44,447	2,844	15.6	44.2	4,198
Northside ISD	74	57,409	3,652	15.7	59.0	4,523
San Antonio ISD	111	60,794	3,667	16.6	94.4	5,275
South San Antonio ISD	17	10,314	690	14.9	n/a	n/a
Southside ISD	4	3,400	230	14.8	n/a	n/a
Southwest ISD	12	9,036	601	15.0	n/a	n/a

Note: Data covers the 1995-1996 school year unless otherwise noted; (1) Excludes teachers reported as working in school district offices rather than in schools; (2) Based on 1993-94 enrollment collected by the Census Bureau, not the enrollment figure shown in column 3; SD = School District; ISD = Independent School District; n/a not available
Source: National Center for Education Statistics, Common Core of Data Survey; Bureau of the Census

Educational Quality

School District	Education Quotient[1]	Graduate Outcome[2]	Community Index[3]	Resource Index[4]
San Antonio	86.0	52.0	72.0	134.0

Note: Nearly 1,000 secondary school districts were rated in terms of educational quality. The scores range from a low of 50 to a high of 150; (1) Average of the Graduate Outcome, Community and Resource indexes; (2) Based on graduation rates and college board scores (SAT/ACT); (3) Based on the surrounding community's average level of education and the area's average income level; (4) Based on teacher salaries, per-pupil expenditures and student-teacher ratios.
Source: Expansion Management, Ratings Issue 1997

Educational Attainment by Race

Area	High School Graduate (%)					Bachelor's Degree (%)				
	Total	White	Black	Other	Hisp.[2]	Total	White	Black	Other	Hisp.[2]
City	69.1	72.5	72.8	53.4	52.8	17.8	20.6	13.0	7.8	7.1
MSA[1]	72.7	75.8	75.9	55.4	54.4	19.4	22.0	14.4	8.2	7.7
U.S.	75.2	77.9	63.1	60.4	49.8	20.3	21.5	11.4	19.4	9.2

Note: figures shown cover persons 25 years old and over; (1) Metropolitan Statistical Area - see Appendix A for areas included; (2) people of Hispanic origin can be of any race
Source: 1990 Census of Population and Housing, Summary Tape File 3C

School Enrollment by Type

Area	Preprimary				Elementary/High School			
	Public		Private		Public		Private	
	Enrollment	%	Enrollment	%	Enrollment	%	Enrollment	%
City	9,035	61.2	5,735	38.8	173,354	92.5	14,116	7.5
MSA[1]	12,989	59.1	8,978	40.9	240,288	92.4	19,686	7.6
U.S.	2,679,029	59.5	1,824,256	40.5	38,379,689	90.2	4,187,099	9.8

Note: figures shown cover persons 3 years old and over;
(1) Metropolitan Statistical Area - see Appendix A for areas included
Source: 1990 Census of Population and Housing, Summary Tape File 3C

School Enrollment by Race

Area	Preprimary (%)				Elementary/High School (%)			
	White	Black	Other	Hisp.[1]	White	Black	Other	Hisp.[1]
City	71.9	7.5	20.6	51.9	67.0	6.8	26.2	68.2
MSA[2]	75.1	7.9	17.0	42.9	70.1	7.0	22.8	59.1
U.S.	80.4	12.5	7.1	7.8	74.1	15.6	10.3	12.5

Note: figures shown cover persons 3 years old and over; (1) people of Hispanic origin can be of any
race; (2) Metropolitan Statistical Area - see Appendix A for areas included
Source: 1990 Census of Population and Housing, Summary Tape File 3C

SAT/ACT Scores

Area/District	1997 SAT				1997 ACT	
	Percent of Graduates Tested (%)	Average Math Score	Average Verbal Score	Average Combined Score	Percent of Graduates Tested (%)	Average Composite Score
San Antonio ISD	44	411	415	826	34	17.3
State	49	501	494	995	30	20.2
U.S.	42	511	505	1,016	36	21.0

Note: Math and verbal SAT scores are out of a possible 800; ACT scores are out of a possible 36
Caution: Comparing or ranking states/cities on the basis of SAT/ACT scores alone is invalid and
strongly discouraged by the The College Board and The American College Testing Program as
students who take the tests are self-selected and do not represent the entire student population.
Source: San Antonio Independent School District, Office of Testing, 1997; American College Testing
Program, 1997; College Board, 1997

Classroom Teacher Salaries in Public Schools

District	B.A. Degree		M.A. Degree		Ph.D. Degree	
	Min. ($)	Max ($)	Min. ($)	Max. ($)	Min. ($)	Max. ($)
San Antonio	26,200	40,595	27,528	47,458	n/a	n/a
Average[1]	26,120	39,270	28,175	44,667	31,643	49,825

Note: Salaries are for 1996-1997; (1) Based on all school districts covered; n/a not available
Source: American Federation of Teachers (unpublished data)

Higher Education

Two-Year Colleges		Four-Year Colleges		Medical Schools	Law Schools	Voc/ Tech
Public	Private	Public	Private			
3	1	2	4	1	1	21

Source: College Blue Book, Occupational Education 1997; Medical School Admission Requirements,
1998-99; Peterson's Guide to Two-Year Colleges, 1997; Peterson's Guide to Four-Year Colleges,
1997; Barron's Guide to Law Schools 1997

MAJOR EMPLOYERS

Major Employers

Baptist Memorial Healthcare System	Bexar County Hospital District
Fiesta Texas Theme Park	Frost National Bank
Hawkins Associates (help supply)	Our Staff Inc. (help supply)
QVC San Antonio (mail order)	Staff Professionals (help supply)
United Services Automobile Assn.	Via Metropolitan Transit
Southwest Research Institute	H.E. Butt Grocery

Note: companies listed are located in the city
Source: Dun's Business Rankings 1997; Ward's Business Directory, 1997

PUBLIC SAFETY

Crime Rate

Area	All Crimes	Violent Crimes				Property Crimes		
		Murder	Forcible Rape	Robbery	Aggrav. Assault	Burglary	Larceny -Theft	Motor Vehicle Theft
City	8,586.6	11.5	62.4	230.1	160.3	1,339.7	5,921.6	861.1
Suburbs[1]	3,838.6	4.8	26.8	43.2	276.1	753.7	2,535.5	198.5
MSA[2]	7,080.7	9.4	51.1	170.8	197.0	1,153.9	4,847.7	651.0
U.S.	5,078.9	7.4	36.1	202.4	388.2	943.0	2,975.9	525.9

Note: Crime rate is the number of crimes per 100,000 pop.; (1) defined as all areas within the MSA but located outside the central city; (2) Metropolitan Statistical Area - see Appendix A for areas incl.
Source: FBI Uniform Crime Reports 1996

RECREATION

Culture and Recreation

Museums	Symphony Orchestras	Opera Companies	Dance Companies	Professional Theatres	Zoos	Pro Sports Teams
12	2	1	5	2	1	1

Source: International Directory of the Performing Arts, 1996; Official Museum Directory, 1998; Chamber of Commerce/Economic Development 1997

Library System

The San Antonio Public Library has 18 branches, holdings of 1,660,470 volumes and a budget of $17,649,900 (1995-1996). The Alamo Area Library System has no branches, holdings of n/a volumes and a budget of $744,437 (1995-1996). Note: n/a means not available. *American Library Directory, 1997-1998*

MEDIA

Newspapers

Name	Type	Freq.	Distribution	Circulation
La Prensa de San Antonio	Hispanic	2x/wk	Regional	162,000
North San Antonio Times	General	1x/wk	Local	10,000
The Recorder Times	General	1x/wk	Local	90,600
San Antonio Current	General	1x/wk	Local	32,000
San Antonio Express-News	n/a	7x/wk	Area	235,002
Southside Reporter	General	1x/wk	Local	68,000
Southside Sun	Hispanic	1x/wk	Local	31,000
Today's Catholic	Religious	26x/yr	Local	25,000
Visitante	Hispanic	1x/wk	National	16,500
Westside Sun	Hispanic	1x/wk	Local	50,000

Note: Includes newspapers with circulations of 10,000 or more located in the city; n/a not available
Source: Burrelle's Media Directory, 1998 Edition

AM Radio Stations

Call Letters	Freq. (kHz)	Target Audience	Station Format	Music Format
KTSA	550	General	N/T	n/a
KSLR	630	General	M/N/T	Christian
KKYX	680	n/a	M/N/S	Country
KSAH	720	Hispanic	M/N/S	Spanish
KTKR	760	General	S	n/a
KCHG	810	General	M/N/S/T	Adult Contemporary/Christian
KONO	860	General	M	Oldies
KLUP	930	General	M/N	Adult Standards
KDRY	1100	Religious	M	Christian
KENS	1160	General	N/T	n/a
WOAI	1200	n/a	S/T	n/a
KZDC	1250	General	M	AOR
KCOR	1350	Hispanic	M/N/S	Spanish
KEDA	1540	Hispanic	M/N/S	Spanish

Note: Stations included broadcast in the San Antonio metro area; n/a not available
Station Format: E = Educational; M = Music; N = News; S = Sports; T = Talk
Music Format: AOR = Album Oriented Rock; MOR = Middle-of-the-Road
Source: Burrelle's Media Directory, 1998 Edition

FM Radio Stations

Call Letters	Freq. (mHz)	Target Audience	Station Format	Music Format
KPAC	88.3	General	M	Classical
KSTX	89.1	General	E/M/N/T	Alternative/Jazz/R&B
KSYM	90.1	Alternative	M	Alternative/Jazz/Spanish
KRTU	91.7	n/a	M	Big Band/Classical/Jazz/R&B
KROM	92.9	Hispanic	M	Spanish
KRIO	94.1	Hispanic	M/N/S	Spanish
KSJL	96.1	General	M	Urban Contemporary
KAJA	97.3	General	M/N/S	Country
KBUC	98.3	n/a	M	Country
KISS	99.5	General	M/N/S	AOR/Alternative
KCYY	100.3	General	M	Country
KONO	101.1	n/a	M/N/S	Oldies
KQXT	101.9	General	M	Easy Listening
KTFM	102.7	General	M	Adult Contemporary
KZEP	104.5	General	M	Classic Rock
KSMG	105.3	General	M	Adult Contemporary
KCJZ	106.7	General	M	Jazz
KXTN	107.5	Hispanic	M	Spanish

Note: Stations included broadcast in the San Antonio metro area; n/a not available
Station Format: E = Educational; M = Music; N = News; S = Sports; T = Talk
Music Format: AOR = Album Oriented Rock; MOR = Middle-of-the-Road
Source: Burrelle's Media Directory, 1998 Edition

Television Stations

Name	Ch.	Affiliation	Type	Owner
KMOL	4	NBC	Commercial	Chris-Craft/United Television
KENS	5	CBS	Commercial	Harte-Hanks Communications Inc.
KLRN	9	PBS	Public	Alamo Public Telecommunications Council
KSAT	12	ABC	Commercial	Post-Newsweek Stations Inc.
KABB	29	Fox	Commercial	Sinclair Broadcast Group
KRRT	35	Fox/UPN	Commercial	Glen-Kairin Ltd.
KWEX	41	Univision	Commercial	Univision Television Group
KVDA	60	Telemundo	Commercial	Telemundo Group Inc.

Note: Stations included broadcast in the San Antonio metro area
Source: Burrelle's Media Directory, 1998 Edition

CLIMATE

Average and Extreme Temperatures

Temperature	Jan	Feb	Mar	Apr	May	Jun	Jul	Aug	Sep	Oct	Nov	Dec	Ann
Extreme High (°F)	89	97	100	100	103	105	106	108	103	98	94	90	108
Average High (°F)	62	66	74	80	86	92	95	95	90	82	71	64	80
Average Temp. (°F)	51	55	62	70	76	82	85	85	80	71	60	53	69
Average Low (°F)	39	43	50	58	66	72	74	74	69	59	49	41	58
Extreme Low (°F)	0	6	19	31	43	53	62	61	46	33	21	6	0

Note: Figures cover the years 1948-1990
Source: National Climatic Data Center, International Station Meteorological Climate Summary, 3/95

Average Precipitation/Snowfall/Humidity

Precip./Humidity	Jan	Feb	Mar	Apr	May	Jun	Jul	Aug	Sep	Oct	Nov	Dec	Ann
Avg. Precip. (in.)	1.5	1.8	1.5	2.6	3.8	3.6	2.0	2.5	3.3	3.2	2.3	1.4	29.6
Avg. Snowfall (in.)	1	Tr	Tr	0	0	0	0	0	0	0	Tr	Tr	1
Avg. Rel. Hum. 6am (%)	79	80	79	82	87	87	87	86	85	83	81	79	83
Avg. Rel. Hum. 3pm (%)	51	48	45	48	51	48	43	42	47	46	48	49	47

Note: Figures cover the years 1948-1990; Tr = Trace amounts (<0.05 in. of rain; <0.5 in. of snow)
Source: National Climatic Data Center, International Station Meteorological Climate Summary, 3/95

Weather Conditions

Temperature			Daytime Sky			Precipitation		
32°F & below	45°F & below	90°F & above	Clear	Partly cloudy	Cloudy	0.01 inch or more precip.	0.1 inch or more snow/ice	Thunder-storms
23	91	112	97	153	115	81	1	36

Note: Figures are average number of days per year and covers the years 1948-1990
Source: National Climatic Data Center, International Station Meteorological Climate Summary, 3/95

AIR & WATER QUALITY

Maximum Pollutant Concentrations

	Particulate Matter (ug/m³)	Carbon Monoxide (ppm)	Sulfur Dioxide (ppm)	Nitrogen Dioxide (ppm)	Ozone (ppm)	Lead (ug/m³)
MSA[1] Level	38	5	n/a	0.009	0.13	0.02
NAAQS[2]	150	9	0.140	0.053	0.12	1.50
Met NAAQS?	Yes	Yes	n/a	Yes	No	Yes

Note: (1) Metropolitan Statistical Area - see Appendix A for areas included; (2) National Ambient Air Quality Standards; ppm = parts per million; ug/m³ = micrograms per cubic meter; n/a not available
Source: EPA, National Air Quality and Emissions Trends Report, 1996

Pollutant Standards Index

In the San Antonio MSA (see Appendix A for areas included), the Pollutant Standards Index (PSI) exceeded 100 on 2 days in 1996. A PSI value greater than 100 indicates that air quality would be in the unhealthful range on that day. *EPA, National Air Quality and Emissions Trends Report, 1996*

Drinking Water

Water System Name	Pop. Served	Primary Water Source Type	Number of Violations in Fiscal Year 1997	Type of Violation/ Contaminants
San Antonio Water System	1,035,726	Ground	None	None

Note: Data as of January 16, 1998
Source: EPA, Office of Ground Water and Drinking Water, Safe Drinking Water Information System

San Antonio tap water is not fluoridated and has moderate mineral content, chiefly sodium bicarbonate.
Editor & Publisher Market Guide, 1998

Tallahassee, Florida

Background

Built on seven hills, the city is proud of its beautiful live oaks, gardens, and historic homes and plantations many of which were built before the Civil War.

Tallahassee, a Creek word meaning "Old Friend" or "Old Town", was originally inhabited by the Apalachee Native American tribe now extinct. The area was occupied by the Seminoles after the Apalachee towns were destroyed by Englishmen and Creek tribes. The Seminoles were still there when Florida became an American Territory. At that time St. Augustine and Pensacola were the two capitals of Florida. In 1823 Tallahassee was chosen as the territorial capital.

The first town lots were sold in 1825, the same year the city was incorporated. It developed rapidly drawing settlers from other southern states who opened plantations. The capital was soon to become the trade center of the area.

During the Civil War Tallahassee was the only Southern capital east of the Mississippi not captured by the Union forces.

Tallahassee is now the commercial, educational and administrative center of Florida.

Located about 20 miles from the Gulf of Mexico, Tallahassee has the mild moist climate of the Gulf states. Unlike the southern part of Florida, the area experiences the four seasons with considerable winter rainfall and quite a bit less winter sunshine. Summer is the least pleasant time of year. Thunderstorms occur every other day and rather high temperatures and humidity can cause considerable discomfort. High winds are infrequent and of short duration, usually associated with strong cold fronts in late winter and early spring. The likelihood of a hurricane is about once every 17 years.

General Rankings and Evaluative Comments

- Tallahassee was ranked #45 out of 300 cities by *Money's* 1997 "Survey of the Best Places to Live." Criteria used: health services, crime, economy, housing, education, transportation, weather, leisure and the arts. The city was ranked #53 in 1996 and #55 in 1995.
Money, July 1997; Money, September 1996; Money, September 1995

- *Ladies Home Journal* ranked America's 200 largest cities based on the qualities women care about most. Tallahassee ranked 64 out of 200. Criteria: low crime rate, good public schools, well-paying jobs, quality health and child care, the presence of women in government, proportion of women-owned businesses, size of the wage gap with men, local economy, divorce rates, the ratio of single men to single women, whether there are laws that require at least the same number of public toilets for women as men, and the probability of good hair days. *Ladies Home Journal, November 1997*

- Tallahassee was ranked #73 out of 219 cities in terms of children's health, safety, and economic well-being. Criteria: total population, percent population change, birth rate, child immunization rate, infant mortality rate, percent low birth weight infants, percent of births to teens, physician-to-population ratio, student-to-teacher ratio, dropout rate, unemployment rate, median family income, percent of children in poverty, violent and property crime rates, number of juvenile arrests for violent crimes as a percent of the total crime index, number of days with pollution standard index (PSI) over 100, pounds toxic releases per 1,000 people and number of superfund sites. *Zero Population Growth, Children's Environmental Index 1997*

- According to *Working Mother,* "Florida stands out among the Southern states for its aggressive action to improve and expand child care. As we went to press, the governor had asked state lawmakers for a significant increase in state funds to create new child care slots. Some $49 million would be earmarked for a very important group—16,000 children of low-wage workers.

  In the past year the state also boosted funding for its prekindergarten program by $4 million, bringing its pre-K spending to $102 million. This translates into free pre-K for 27,000 kids, about 2,000 more than last year. This program is funded with state lottery money and is available in all of Florida's 67 school districts.

  The state has also improved its requirements for playground surfaces in child care setting. As of March 1997, all centers were required to have soft surfaces under playground equipment. This is a vital change, given that injuries from falls are the most common in child care.

  Finally, lawmakers approved a new program to recognize quality child care programs. Any facility that attains state or NAEYC accreditation can now post a 'good seal' certificate and will be listed in a state database as a 'Gold Seal' program—to show it meets high standards of care. So far, about 370 centers have received certificates, and about 800 more are in the pipeline." *Working Mother, July/August 1997*

Business Environment

STATE ECONOMY

State Economic Profile

''Florida's economy continues to expand strongly....

Florida is becoming increasingly dependent on the service industry for job growth. Currently, one in three Florida jobs is service-related. In the past year, however, nearly half of all jobs created were in the service industry. One in four jobs created was in business services, compared to one in seven for the U.S....

Florida's tourist industry continues to rebound and will be an important source of growth for this year. Household income growth and savings rates are high, and the values of individual stock portfolios has been booming, leaving households across the U.S. in good financial shape to take a vacation.

A risk to Florida's economy is a sharp slowing in population growth. In 1996, Florida experienced a population gain of only 1.5%, the slowest rate of growth since World War II. Contributing to the slower population growth is weaker retiree migration due to a slowing national retiree population growth.

Supporting growth are Florida's moderate climate, favorable quality of life, affordable housing, and low cost of doing business, which will continue to attract businesses and households. Population growth will continue to slow for the next decade as the number of people reaching retirement age nationwide is falling. Population growth will begin to accelerate once the baby boom generation hits retirement age beginning around 2005. One downside risk for Florida is its dependence on tourism and interest and property income that makes it vulnerable to national and international business cycles. Florida will remain one of the nation's fastest-growing economies through the remainder of this century.'' *National Association of Realtors, Economic Profiles: The Fifty States, July 1997*

IMPORTS/EXPORTS

Total Export Sales

Area	1993 ($000)	1994 ($000)	1995 ($000)	1996 ($000)	% Chg. 1993-96	% Chg. 1995-96
MSA[1]	16,093	18,727	24,235	27,238	69.3	12.4
U.S.	464,858,354	512,415,609	583,030,524	622,827,063	34.0	6.8

Note: (1) Metropolitan Statistical Area - see Appendix A for areas included
Source: U.S. Department of Commerce, International Trade Association, Metropolitan Area Exports: An Export Performance Report on Over 250 U.S. Cities, October 1997

Imports/Exports by Port

Type	Cargo Value			Share of U.S. Total	
	1995 (US$mil.)	1996 (US$mil.)	% Change 1995-1996	1995 (%)	1996 (%)
Imports	0	0	0	0	0
Exports	0	0	0	0	0

Source: Global Trade Information Services, WaterBorne Trade Atlas 1997

CITY FINANCES

City Government Finances

Component	FY92 ($000)	FY92 (per capita $)
Revenue	331,022	2,550.99
Expenditure	304,121	2,343.68
Debt Outstanding	258,389	1,991.25
Cash & Securities	707,456	5,451.95

Source: U.S. Bureau of the Census, City Government Finances: 1991-92

City Government Revenue by Source

Source	FY92 ($000)	FY92 (per capita $)	FY92 (%)
From Federal Government	4,291	33.07	1.3
From State Governments	12,095	93.21	3.7
From Local Governments	1,451	11.18	0.4
Property Taxes	9,187	70.80	2.8
General Sales Taxes	7,767	59.86	2.3
Selective Sales Taxes	13,521	104.20	4.1
Income Taxes	0	0.00	0.0
Current Charges	52,895	407.63	16.0
Utility/Liquor Store	179,058	1,379.90	54.1
Employee Retirement[1]	19,261	148.43	5.8
Other	31,496	242.72	9.5

Note: (1) Excludes "city contributions," classified as "nonrevenue," intragovernmental transfers.
Source: U.S. Bureau of the Census, City Government Finances: 1991-92

City Government Expenditures by Function

Function	FY92 ($000)	FY92 (per capita $)	FY92 (%)
Educational Services	0	0.00	0.0
Employee Retirement[1]	7,276	56.07	2.4
Environment/Housing	50,882	392.12	16.7
Government Administration	7,686	59.23	2.5
Interest on General Debt	9,717	74.88	3.2
Public Safety	32,191	248.08	10.6
Social Services	504	3.88	0.2
Transportation	25,760	198.52	8.5
Utility/Liquor Store	158,670	1,222.78	52.2
Other	11,435	88.12	3.8

Note: (1) Payments to beneficiaries including withdrawal of contributions.
Source: U.S. Bureau of the Census, City Government Finances: 1991-92

Municipal Bond Ratings

Area	Moody's	S & P
Tallahassee	Aaa	n/a

Note: n/a not available; n/r not rated
Source: Moody's Bond Record, 2/98; Statistical Abstract of the U.S., 1997;
Governing Magazine, 9/97, 3/98

POPULATION

Population Growth

Area	1980	1990	% Chg. 1980-90	July 1996 Estimate	% Chg. 1990-96
City	81,548	124,773	53.0	136,812	9.6
MSA[1]	190,329	233,598	22.7	259,380	11.0
U.S.	226,545,805	248,765,170	9.8	265,179,411	6.6

Note: (1) Metropolitan Statistical Area - see Appendix A for areas included
Source: 1980/1990 Census of Housing and Population, Summary Tape File 3C;
Census Bureau Population Estimates

Population Characteristics

Race	City 1980 Population	%	City 1990 Population	%	% Chg. 1980-90	MSA[1] 1990 Population	%
White	54,110	66.4	85,116	68.2	57.3	158,396	67.8
Black	25,985	31.9	36,276	29.1	39.6	70,425	30.1
Amer Indian/Esk/Aleut	269	0.3	247	0.2	-8.2	564	0.2
Asian/Pacific Islander	594	0.7	2,208	1.8	271.7	2,736	1.2
Other	590	0.7	926	0.7	56.9	1,477	0.6
Hispanic Origin[2]	1,452	1.8	3,878	3.1	167.1	5,777	2.5

Note: (1) Metropolitan Statistical Area - see Appendix A for areas included;
(2) people of Hispanic origin can be of any race
Source: 1980/1990 Census of Housing and Population, Summary Tape File 3C

Ancestry

Area	German	Irish	English	Italian	U.S.	French	Polish	Dutch
City	16.9	13.7	15.1	3.7	5.3	3.8	1.6	1.7
MSA[1]	15.5	14.1	14.5	3.0	7.1	3.5	1.3	1.8
U.S.	23.3	15.6	13.1	5.9	5.3	4.2	3.8	2.5

Note: Figures are percentages and include persons that reported multiple ancestry (eg. if a person reported being Irish and Italian, they were included in both columns); (1) Metropolitan Statistical Area - see Appendix A for areas included
Source: 1990 Census of Population and Housing, Summary Tape File 3C

Age

Area	Median Age (Years)	Under 5	Under 18	18-24	25-44	45-64	65+	80+
City	26.9	5.5	19.3	26.4	31.9	13.6	8.8	1.9
MSA[1]	29.3	6.6	23.9	18.4	33.2	15.6	8.8	1.8
U.S.	32.9	7.3	25.6	10.5	32.6	18.7	12.5	2.8

Note: (1) Metropolitan Statistical Area - see Appendix A for areas included
Source: 1990 Census of Population and Housing, Summary Tape File 3C

Male/Female Ratio

Area	Number of males per 100 females (all ages)	Number of males per 100 females (18 years old+)
City	90.8	88.3
MSA[1]	91.5	88.9
U.S.	95.0	91.9

Note: (1) Metropolitan Statistical Area - see Appendix A for areas included
Source: 1990 Census of Population, General Population Characteristics

INCOME

Per Capita/Median/Average Income

Area	Per Capita ($)	Median Household ($)	Average Household ($)
City	13,247	23,453	32,019
MSA[1]	13,122	26,209	34,215
U.S.	14,420	30,056	38,453

Note: all figures are for 1989; (1) Metropolitan Statistical Area - see Appendix A for areas included
Source: 1990 Census of Population and Housing, Summary Tape File 3C

Household Income Distribution by Race

Income ($)	City (%)					U.S. (%)				
	Total	White	Black	Other	Hisp.[1]	Total	White	Black	Other	Hisp.[1]
Less than 5,000	11.3	8.5	18.7	16.5	17.1	6.2	4.8	15.2	8.6	8.8
5,000 - 9,999	11.8	9.7	17.5	16.0	16.1	9.3	8.6	14.2	9.9	11.1
10,000 - 14,999	10.1	8.5	14.4	12.2	9.2	8.8	8.5	11.0	9.8	11.0
15,000 - 24,999	19.5	19.2	20.2	23.3	21.7	17.5	17.3	18.9	18.5	20.5
25,000 - 34,999	14.5	15.8	11.6	6.3	10.8	15.8	16.1	14.2	15.4	16.4
35,000 - 49,999	13.3	14.8	9.7	7.0	9.6	17.9	18.6	13.3	16.1	16.0
50,000 - 74,999	12.5	14.9	6.0	12.0	7.8	15.0	15.8	9.3	13.4	11.1
75,000 - 99,999	4.2	5.3	1.1	4.4	6.2	5.1	5.5	2.6	4.7	3.1
100,000+	2.7	3.3	0.9	2.4	1.5	4.4	4.8	1.3	3.7	1.9

Note: all figures are for 1989; (1) people of Hispanic origin can be of any race
Source: 1990 Census of Population and Housing, Summary Tape File 3C

Effective Buying Income

Area	Per Capita ($)	Median Household ($)	Average Household ($)
City	15,643	28,173	38,942
MSA[1]	16,078	32,532	42,642
U.S.	15,444	33,201	41,849

Note: data as of 1/1/97; (1) Metropolitan Statistical Area - see Appendix A for areas included
Source: Standard Rate & Data Service, Newspaper Advertising Source, 2/98

Effective Household Buying Income Distribution

Area	% of Households Earning						
	$10,000 -$19,999	$20,000 -$34,999	$35,000 -$49,999	$50,000 -$74,999	$75,000 -$99,000	$100,000 -$124,999	$125,000 and up
City	18.0	22.6	14.9	14.6	7.2	2.2	2.0
MSA[1]	16.1	21.9	16.6	16.8	7.9	2.7	2.6
U.S.	16.5	23.4	18.3	18.2	6.4	2.1	2.4

Note: data as of 1/1/97; (1) Metropolitan Statistical Area - see Appendix A for areas included
Source: Standard Rate & Data Service, Newspaper Advertising Source, 2/98

Poverty Rates by Race and Age

Area	Total (%)	By Race (%)				By Age (%)		
		White	Black	Other	Hisp.[2]	Under 5 years old	Under 18 years old	65 years and over
City	22.3	16.7	34.8	31.5	38.3	24.8	21.6	13.5
MSA[1]	18.9	12.2	33.5	30.7	32.7	22.8	20.9	18.0
U.S.	13.1	9.8	29.5	23.1	25.3	20.1	18.3	12.8

Note: figures show the percent of people living below the poverty line in 1989. The average poverty threshold was $12,674 for a family of four in 1989; (1) Metropolitan Statistical Area - see Appendix A for areas included; (2) people of Hispanic origin can be of any race
Source: 1990 Census of Population and Housing, Summary Tape File 3C

EMPLOYMENT

Labor Force and Employment

Area	Civilian Labor Force			Workers Employed		
	Dec. '95	Dec. '96	% Chg.	Dec. '95	Dec. '96	% Chg.
City	78,855	80,669	2.3	76,420	78,121	2.2
MSA[1]	142,470	145,695	2.3	138,511	141,593	2.2
U.S.	134,583,000	136,742,000	1.6	127,903,000	130,785,000	2.3

Note: Data is not seasonally adjusted and covers workers 16 years of age and older; (1) Metropolitan Statistical Area - see Appendix A for areas included
Source: Bureau of Labor Statistics, http://stats.bls.gov

Unemployment Rate

Area	1997											
	Jan.	Feb.	Mar.	Apr.	May	Jun.	Jul.	Aug.	Sep.	Oct.	Nov.	Dec.
City	3.8	3.3	3.4	3.4	3.9	4.2	3.7	3.4	3.6	3.4	3.5	3.2
MSA[1]	3.4	3.0	3.0	3.0	3.3	3.6	3.1	3.0	3.2	2.9	3.0	2.8
U.S.	5.9	5.7	5.5	4.8	4.7	5.2	5.0	4.8	4.7	4.4	4.3	4.4

Note: Data is not seasonally adjusted and covers workers 16 years of age and older; All figures are percentages; (1) Metropolitan Statistical Area - see Appendix A for areas included
Source: Bureau of Labor Statistics, http://stats.bls.gov

Employment by Industry

Sector	MSA[1]		U.S.
	Number of Employees	Percent of Total	Percent of Total
Services	38,600	25.8	29.0
Retail Trade	26,700	17.8	18.5
Government	59,100	39.5	16.1
Manufacturing	5,100	3.4	15.0
Finance/Insurance/Real Estate	5,700	3.8	5.7
Wholesale Trade	4,200	2.8	5.4
Transportation/Public Utilities	4,300	2.9	5.3
Construction/Mining	200	0.1	5.0

Note: Figures cover non-farm employment as of 12/97 and are not seasonally adjusted;
(1) Metropolitan Statistical Area - see Appendix A for areas included
Source: Bureau of Labor Statistics, http://stats.bls.gov

Employment by Occupation

Occupation Category	City (%)	MSA[1] (%)	U.S. (%)
White Collar	75.3	70.2	58.1
Executive/Admin./Management	16.0	15.7	12.3
Professional	21.5	18.7	14.1
Technical & Related Support	4.9	4.3	3.7
Sales	12.0	11.3	11.8
Administrative Support/Clerical	20.9	20.2	16.3
Blue Collar	11.2	15.3	26.2
Precision Production/Craft/Repair	5.0	7.2	11.3
Machine Operators/Assem./Insp.	1.4	2.5	6.8
Transportation/Material Movers	2.1	2.6	4.1
Cleaners/Helpers/Laborers	2.7	2.9	3.9
Services	12.6	12.7	13.2
Farming/Forestry/Fishing	0.9	1.8	2.5

Note: figures cover employed persons 16 years old and over;
(1) Metropolitan Statistical Area - see Appendix A for areas included
Source: 1990 Census of Population and Housing, Summary Tape File 3C

Occupational Employment Projections: 1995 - 2005

Occupations Expected to have the Largest Job Growth (ranked by numerical growth)	Fast-Growing Occupations[1] (ranked by percent growth)
1. Systems analysts	1. Computer engineers
2. Management analyst	2. Systems analysts
3. Waiters & waitresses	3. Home health aides
4. General office clerks	4. Computer support specialists
5. Salespersons, retail	5. Medical assistants
6. Cashiers	6. Corrections officers & jailers
7. Secretaries, except legal & medical	7. Sheriffs/deputy sheriffs
8. General managers & top executives	8. Adjustment clerks
9. Lawyers	9. Police patrol officers
10. First line supervisor, sales & related	10. Engineers, electrical & electronic

Projections cover Leon County.
Note: (1) Excludes occupations with total growth of less than 100 jobs
Source: Florida Department of Labor and Employment Security, Florida Industry and Occupational Employment Projections 1995-2005

Average Wages

Occupation	Wage	Occupation	Wage
Professional/Technical/Clerical	**$/Week**	**Health/Protective Services**	**$/Week**
Accountants III	-	Corrections Officers	-
Attorneys III	-	Firefighters	-
Budget Analysts III	-	Nurses, Licensed Practical II	-
Buyers/Contracting Specialists II	-	Nurses, Registered II	-
Clerks, Accounting III	497	Nursing Assistants II	-
Clerks, General III	361	Police Officers I	-
Computer Operators II	-	**Hourly Workers**	**$/Hour**
Computer Programmers II	-	Forklift Operators	11.17
Drafters II	546	General Maintenance Workers	7.44
Engineering Technicians III	-	Guards I	5.05
Engineering Technicians, Civil III	-	Janitors	5.92
Engineers III	-	Maintenance Electricians	-
Key Entry Operators I	297	Maintenance Electronics Techs II	18.63
Personnel Assistants III	-	Maintenance Machinists	-
Personnel Specialists III	-	Maintenance Mechanics, Machinery	-
Secretaries III	521	Material Handling Laborers	-
Switchboard Operator-Receptionist	268	Motor Vehicle Mechanics	14.44
Systems Analysts II	-	Shipping/Receiving Clerks	10.80
Systems Analysts Supervisor/Mgr II	-	Tool and Die Makers	-
Tax Collectors II	-	Truckdrivers, Tractor Trailer	-
Word Processors II	-	Warehouse Specialists	11.43

Note: Wage data includes full-time workers only for 5/96 and cover northwest Florida. Dashes indicate that data was not available.
Source: Bureau of Labor Statistics, Occupational Compensation Survey, 8/96

TAXES

Major State and Local Tax Rates

State Corp. Income (%)	State Personal Income (%)	Residential Property (effective rate per $100)	Sales & Use		State Gasoline (cents/ gallon)	State Cigarette (cents/ 20-pack)
			State (%)	Local (%)		
5.5[a]	None	n/a	6.0	1.0	12.8[b]	33.9

Note: Personal/corporate income tax rates as of 1/97. Sales, gasoline and cigarette tax rates as of 1/98; (a) 3.3% Alternative Minimum Tax. An exemption of $5,000 is allowed; (b) Rate is comprised of 4 cents excise and 8.8 cents motor carrier tax
Source: Federation of Tax Administrators, www.taxadmin.org; Washington D.C. Department of Finance and Revenue, Tax Rates and Tax Burdens in the District of Columbia: A Nationwide Comparison, June 1997; Chamber of Commerce

Total Taxes Per Capita and as a Percent of Income

Area	Per Capita Income ($)	Per Capita Taxes ($)			Taxes as Pct. of Income (%)		
		Total	Federal	State/Local	Total	Federal	State/Local
Florida	26,438	9,172	6,286	2,886	34.7	23.8	10.9
U.S.	26,187	9,205	6,127	3,078	35.2	23.4	11.8

Note: Figures are for 1997
Source: Tax Foundation, Web Site, www.taxfoundation.org

Estimated Tax Burden

Area	State Income	Local Income	Property	Sales	Total
Tallahassee	0	0	2,700	595	3,295

Note: The numbers are estimates of taxes paid by a married couple with two kids and annual earnings of $65,000. Sales tax estimates assume they spend average amounts on food, clothing, household goods and gasoline. Property tax estimates assume they live in a $225,000 home.
Source: Kiplinger's Personal Finance Magazine, June 1997

COMMERCIAL REAL ESTATE

Data not available at time of publication.

COMMERCIAL UTILITIES

Typical Monthly Electric Bills

Area	Commercial Service ($/month)		Industrial Service ($/month)	
	12 kW demand 1,500 kWh	100 kW demand 30,000 kWh	1,000 kW demand 400,000 kWh	20,000 kW demand 10,000,000 kWh
City	137	2,333	27,081	554,864
U.S.	162	2,360	25,590	545,677

Note: Based on rates in effect July 1, 1997
Source: Edison Electric Institute, Typical Residential, Commercial and Industrial Bills, Summer 1997

TRANSPORTATION

Transportation Statistics

Avg. travel time to work (min.)	16.2
Interstate highways	I-10
Bus lines	
In-city	TALTRAN
Inter-city	2
Passenger air service	
Airport	Tallahassee Regional
Airlines	6
Aircraft departures	13,782 (1995)
Enplaned passengers	390,581 (1995)
Rail service	Amtrak
Motor freight carriers	13
Major waterways/ports	None

Source: OAG, Business Travel Planner, Summer 1997; Editor & Publisher Market Guide, 1998; FAA Airport Activity Statistics, 1996; Amtrak National Time Table, Northeast Timetable, Fall/Winter 1997-98; 1990 Census of Population and Housing, STF 3C; Chamber of Commerce/Economic Development 1997; Jane's Urban Transport Systems 1997-98; Transit Fact Book 1997

Means of Transportation to Work

Area	Car/Truck/Van		Public Transportation			Bicycle	Walked	Other Means	Worked at Home
	Drove Alone	Car-pooled	Bus	Subway	Railroad				
City	75.0	13.5	2.7	0.0	0.0	0.8	5.0	1.3	1.7
MSA[1]	75.2	16.4	1.8	0.0	0.0	0.5	3.2	1.1	1.9
U.S.	73.2	13.4	3.0	1.5	0.5	0.4	3.9	1.2	3.0

Note: figures shown are percentages and only include workers 16 years old and over;
(1) Metropolitan Statistical Area - see Appendix A for areas included
Source: 1990 Census of Population and Housing, Summary Tape File 3C

BUSINESSES

Major Business Headquarters

Company Name	1997 Rankings	
	Fortune 500	Forbes 500

No companies listed.

Note: Companies listed are located in the city; Dashes indicate no ranking
Fortune 500: companies that produce a 10-K are ranked 1 - 500 based on 1996 revenue
Forbes 500: private companies are ranked 1 - 500 based on 1996 revenue
Source: Forbes 12/1/97; Fortune 4/28/97

Fast-Growing Businesses

According to *Inc.*, Tallahassee is home to one of America's 100 fastest-growing private companies: Mainline Information Systems. Criteria for inclusion: must be an independent, privately-held, U.S. corporation, proprietorship or partnership; sales of at least $200,000 in 1993; five-year operating/sales history; increase in 1997 sales over 1996 sales; holding companies, regulated banks, and utilities were excluded. *Inc. 500, 1997*

HOTELS & MOTELS

Hotels/Motels

Area	Hotels/ Motels	Rooms	Luxury-Level Hotels/Motels		Average Minimum Rates ($)		
			♦♦♦♦	♦♦♦♦♦	♦♦	♦♦♦	♦♦♦♦
City	29	3,029	0	0	54	88	n/a
Airport	2	378	0	0	n/a	n/a	n/a
Suburbs	1	39	0	0	n/a	n/a	n/a
Total	32	3,446	0	0	n/a	n/a	n/a

Note: n/a not available; Classifications range from one diamond (budget properties with basic amenities) to five diamond (luxury properties with the finest service, rooms and facilities).
Source: OAG, Business Travel Planner, Summer 1997

CONVENTION CENTERS

Major Convention Centers

Center Name	Meeting Rooms	Exhibit Space (sf)
Florida State Conference Center	14	3,000
Tallahassee-Leon County Civic Center	7	67,000

Source: Trade Shows Worldwide 1997

Living Environment

COST OF LIVING

Cost of Living Index

Composite Index	Housing	Utilities	Groceries	Health Care	Trans-portation	Misc. Goods/ Services
104.1	101.8	97.9	106.5	110.0	105.7	105.0

Note: U.S. = 100
Source: ACCRA, Cost of Living Index, 3rd Quarter 1997

HOUSING

Median Home Prices and Housing Affordability

Area	Median Price[2] 3rd Qtr. 1997 ($)	HOI[3] 3rd Qtr. 1997	Afford-ability Rank[4]
MSA[1]	96,000	76.3	45
U.S.	127,000	63.7	–

Note: (1) Metropolitan Statistical Area - see Appendix A for areas included; (2) U.S. figures calculated from the sales of 625,000 new and existing homes in 195 markets; (3) Housing Opportunity Index - percent of homes sold that were within the reach of the median income household at the prevailing mortgage interest rate; (4) Rank is from 1-195 with 1 being most affordable
Source: National Association of Home Builders, Housing Opportunity Index, 3rd Quarter 1997

Average New Home Price

Area	Price ($)
City	132,592
U.S.	135,710

Note: Figures are based on a new home with 1,800 sq. ft. of living area on an 8,000 sq. ft. lot.
Source: ACCRA, Cost of Living Index, 3rd Quarter 1997

Average Apartment Rent

Area	Rent ($/mth)
City	644
U.S.	569

Note: Figures are based on an unfurnished two bedroom, 1-1/2 or 2 bath apartment, approximately 950 sq. ft. in size, excluding all utilities except water
Source: ACCRA, Cost of Living Index, 3rd Quarter 1997

RESIDENTIAL UTILITIES

Average Residential Utility Costs

Area	All Electric ($/mth)	Part Electric ($/mth)	Other Energy ($/mth)	Phone ($/mth)
City	101.33	–	–	17.77
U.S.	109.40	55.25	43.64	19.48

Source: ACCRA, Cost of Living Index, 3rd Quarter 1997

HEALTH CARE

Average Health Care Costs

Area	Hospital ($/day)	Doctor ($/visit)	Dentist ($/visit)
City	443.00	60.20	60.80
U.S.	392.91	48.76	60.84

Note: Hospital - based on a semi-private room. Doctor - based on a general practitioner's routine exam of an established patient. Dentist - based on adult teeth cleaning and periodic oral exam.
Source: ACCRA, Cost of Living Index, 3rd Quarter 1997

Distribution of Office-Based Physicians

Area	Family/Gen. Practitioners	Specialists		
		Medical	Surgical	Other
MSA[1]	92	117	112	106

Note: Data as of 12/31/96; (1) Metropolitan Statistical Area - see Appendix A for areas included
Source: American Medical Assn., Physician Characteristics & Distribution in the U.S., 1997-1998

Hospitals

Tallahassee has 2 general medical and surgical hospitals, 1 rehabilitation. *AHA Guide to the Healthcare Field 1997-98*

EDUCATION

Public School District Statistics

District Name	Num. Sch.	Enroll.	Classroom Teachers[1]	Pupils per Teacher	Minority Pupils (%)	Current Exp.[2] ($/pupil)
Florida A&M Univ Lab School	1	575	n/a	n/a	n/a	n/a
Florida State Univ Lab School	1	958	n/a	n/a	n/a	n/a
Leon County School District	47	31,335	1,771	17.7	41.0	4,745

Note: Data covers the 1995-1996 school year unless otherwise noted; (1) Excludes teachers reported as working in school district offices rather than in schools; (2) Based on 1993-94 enrollment collected by the Census Bureau, not the enrollment figure shown in column 3; SD = School District; ISD = Independent School District; n/a not available
Source: National Center for Education Statistics, Common Core of Data Survey; Bureau of the Census

Educational Quality

School District	Education Quotient[1]	Graduate Outcome[2]	Community Index[3]	Resource Index[4]
Tallahassee	n/a	n/a	n/a	n/a

Note: Nearly 1,000 secondary school districts were rated in terms of educational quality. The scores range from a low of 50 to a high of 150; (1) Average of the Graduate Outcome, Community and Resource indexes; (2) Based on graduation rates and college board scores (SAT/ACT); (3) Based on the surrounding community's average level of education and the area's average income level; (4) Based on teacher salaries, per-pupil expenditures and student-teacher ratios.
Source: Expansion Management, Ratings Issue 1997

Educational Attainment by Race

Area	High School Graduate (%)					Bachelor's Degree (%)				
	Total	White	Black	Other	Hisp.[2]	Total	White	Black	Other	Hisp.[2]
City	85.5	91.4	68.1	92.4	84.4	40.7	46.2	23.3	61.5	33.7
MSA[1]	80.3	87.7	59.8	84.8	79.4	32.4	37.6	16.6	53.4	31.3
U.S.	75.2	77.9	63.1	60.4	49.8	20.3	21.5	11.4	19.4	9.2

Note: figures shown cover persons 25 years old and over; (1) Metropolitan Statistical Area - see Appendix A for areas included; (2) people of Hispanic origin can be of any race
Source: 1990 Census of Population and Housing, Summary Tape File 3C

School Enrollment by Type

Area	Preprimary				Elementary/High School			
	Public		Private		Public		Private	
	Enrollment	%	Enrollment	%	Enrollment	%	Enrollment	%
City	1,297	53.2	1,141	46.8	14,252	91.1	1,393	8.9
MSA[1]	2,725	51.8	2,540	48.2	32,875	89.0	4,048	11.0
U.S.	2,679,029	59.5	1,824,256	40.5	38,379,689	90.2	4,187,099	9.8

Note: figures shown cover persons 3 years old and over;
(1) Metropolitan Statistical Area - see Appendix A for areas included
Source: 1990 Census of Population and Housing, Summary Tape File 3C

School Enrollment by Race

Area	Preprimary (%)				Elementary/High School (%)			
	White	Black	Other	Hisp.[1]	White	Black	Other	Hisp.[1]
City	61.2	37.0	1.8	2.8	55.6	42.1	2.3	1.9
MSA[2]	67.5	30.8	1.8	2.0	56.1	42.1	1.8	2.0
U.S.	80.4	12.5	7.1	7.8	74.1	15.6	10.3	12.5

Note: figures shown cover persons 3 years old and over; (1) people of Hispanic origin can be of any race; (2) Metropolitan Statistical Area - see Appendix A for areas included
Source: 1990 Census of Population and Housing, Summary Tape File 3C

SAT/ACT Scores

Area/District	1997 SAT				1997 ACT	
	Percent of Graduates Tested (%)	Average Math Score	Average Verbal Score	Average Combined Score	Percent of Graduates Tested (%)	Average Composite Score
Leon County SD	51	530	528	1,058	42	20.8
State	50	499	499	998	36	20.7
U.S.	42	511	505	1,016	36	21.0

Note: Math and verbal SAT scores are out of a possible 800; ACT scores are out of a possible 36
Caution: Comparing or ranking states/cities on the basis of SAT/ACT scores alone is invalid and strongly discouraged by the The College Board and The American College Testing Program as students who take the tests are self-selected and do not represent the entire student population.
Source: Leon County Schools, Program Monitoring & Evaluation, 1997; American College Testing Program, 1997; College Board, 1997

Classroom Teacher Salaries in Public Schools

District	B.A. Degree		M.A. Degree		Ph.D. Degree	
	Min. ($)	Max ($)	Min. ($)	Max. ($)	Min. ($)	Max. ($)
Tallahassee	23,316	39,000	23,842	40,675	26,022	42,833
Average[1]	26,120	39,270	28,175	44,667	31,643	49,825

Note: Salaries are for 1996-1997; (1) Based on all school districts covered
Source: American Federation of Teachers (unpublished data)

Higher Education

Two-Year Colleges		Four-Year Colleges		Medical Schools	Law Schools	Voc/ Tech
Public	Private	Public	Private			
1	1	2	0	0	1	2

Source: College Blue Book, Occupational Education 1997; Medical School Admission Requirements, 1998-99; Peterson's Guide to Two-Year Colleges, 1997; Peterson's Guide to Four-Year Colleges, 1997; Barron's Guide to Law Schools 1997

MAJOR EMPLOYERS

Major Employers

Ajax Construction Co. of Tallahassee
McKenzie Tank Lines
Tallahassee Democrat
Tallahassee Memorial Regional Medical Center
Barnett Bank of Tallahassee

CMS/Data Corp.
Ingram Enterprises (ready-mixed concrete)
Tallahassee Leon County Civic Center
Watkins Engineers & Constructors

Note: companies listed are located in the city
Source: Dun's Business Rankings 1997; Ward's Business Directory, 1997

PUBLIC SAFETY

Crime Rate

Area	All Crimes	Violent Crimes				Property Crimes		
		Murder	Forcible Rape	Robbery	Aggrav. Assault	Burglary	Larceny -Theft	Motor Vehicle Theft
City	10,157.9	7.2	68.8	263.0	792.7	1,563.0	6,887.6	575.4
Suburbs[1]	n/a	n/a	n/a	n/a	n/a	n/a	n/a	n/a
MSA[2]	n/a	n/a	n/a	n/a	n/a	n/a	n/a	n/a
U.S.	5,078.9	7.4	36.1	202.4	388.2	943.0	2,975.9	525.9

Note: Crime rate is the number of crimes per 100,000 pop.; (1) defined as all areas within the MSA but located outside the central city; (2) Metropolitan Statistical Area - see Appendix A for areas incl.
Source: FBI Uniform Crime Reports 1996

RECREATION

Culture and Recreation

Museums	Symphony Orchestras	Opera Companies	Dance Companies	Professional Theatres	Zoos	Pro Sports Teams
5	1	0	1	1	0	0

Source: International Directory of the Performing Arts, 1996; Official Museum Directory, 1998; Chamber of Commerce/Economic Development 1997

Library System

The Leroy Collins Leon County Public Library has four branches, holdings of 314,263 volumes and a budget of $3,250,693 (1995-1996). *American Library Directory, 1997-1998*

MEDIA

Newspapers

Name	Type	Freq.	Distribution	Circulation
Capital Outlook	Black	1x/wk	State	15,000
Florida Flambeau	n/a	5x/wk	Campus & community	21,000
Tallahassean	General	1x/wk	Local	15,000
Tallahassee Democrat	General	7x/wk	Area	57,151

Note: Includes newspapers with circulations of 500 or more located in the city; n/a not available
Source: Burrelle's Media Directory, 1998 Edition

AM Radio Stations

Call Letters	Freq. (kHz)	Target Audience	Station Format	Music Format
WANM	1070	General	N	n/a
WNLS	1270	General	S	n/a
WCVC	1330	General	M/S/T	Adult Contemporary/Country
WTAL	1450	General	N/T	n/a

Note: Stations included broadcast in the Tallahassee metro area; n/a not available
Station Format: E = Educational; M = Music; N = News; S = Sports; T = Talk
Source: Burrelle's Media Directory, 1998 Edition

FM Radio Stations

Call Letters	Freq. (mHz)	Target Audience	Station Format	Music Format
WFSU	88.9	General	M/N	Jazz
WAMF	90.5	General	M/N/S	Christian/R&B
WFSQ	91.5	General	M	Big Band/Classical
WTNT	94.9	General	M/N/S	Country
WHBX	96.1	n/a	M	Urban Contemporary
WBZE	98.9	General	M/N/S	Adult Contemporary
WJZT	100.7	General	M	Jazz
WXSR	101.5	Alternative	M/N/T	Alternative
WAIB	103.1	n/a	M	Country
WGLF	104.1	General	M	AOR
WMLO	104.9	General	M/N/S	Adult Contemporary
WSNI	107.1	General	M	Adult Contemporary/Contemporary Top 40

Note: Stations included broadcast in the Tallahassee metro area; n/a not available
Station Format: E = Educational; M = Music; N = News; S = Sports; T = Talk
Music Format: AOR = Album Oriented Rock; MOR = Middle-of-the-Road
Source: Burrelle's Media Directory, 1998 Edition

Television Stations

Name	Ch.	Affiliation	Type	Owner
WCTV	6	CBS	Commercial	Gray Communications, Inc.
WFSU	11	PBS	Public	Florida State University
WTXL	27	ABC	Commercial	Media Venture Partners
WTWC	40	NBC	Commercial	Guy Gannett Communications
WTLH	49	Fox	Commercial	Pegasus Media & Communications Inc.
WFSG	56	PBS	Public	Florida State University

Note: Stations included broadcast in the Tallahassee metro area
Source: Burrelle's Media Directory, 1998 Edition

CLIMATE

Average and Extreme Temperatures

Temperature	Jan	Feb	Mar	Apr	May	Jun	Jul	Aug	Sep	Oct	Nov	Dec	Ann
Extreme High (°F)	83	89	90	95	102	103	103	102	99	94	88	84	103
Average High (°F)	64	67	73	80	86	90	91	91	88	81	72	66	79
Average Temp. (°F)	52	55	61	67	74	80	81	81	78	69	60	54	68
Average Low (°F)	40	42	48	53	62	69	71	72	68	57	47	41	56
Extreme Low (°F)	6	14	20	29	34	46	57	61	40	30	13	10	6

Note: Figures cover the years 1948-1990
Source: National Climatic Data Center, International Station Meteorological Climate Summary, 3/95

Average Precipitation/Snowfall/Humidity

Precip./Humidity	Jan	Feb	Mar	Apr	May	Jun	Jul	Aug	Sep	Oct	Nov	Dec	Ann
Avg. Precip. (in.)	4.2	5.1	6.0	4.2	4.5	6.8	8.8	7.1	5.7	2.9	3.5	4.5	63.3
Avg. Snowfall (in.)	Tr	Tr	Tr	0	0	0	0	0	0	0	0	Tr	Tr
Avg. Rel. Hum. 7am (%)	86	87	88	89	89	91	93	94	93	90	89	87	90
Avg. Rel. Hum. 4pm (%)	54	51	49	46	50	58	66	64	60	51	52	55	55

Note: Figures cover the years 1948-1990; Tr = Trace amounts (<0.05 in. of rain; <0.5 in. of snow)
Source: National Climatic Data Center, International Station Meteorological Climate Summary, 3/95

Weather Conditions

Temperature			Daytime Sky			Precipitation		
10°F & below	32°F & below	90°F & above	Clear	Partly cloudy	Cloudy	0.01 inch or more precip.	0.1 inch or more snow/ice	Thunder-storms
< 1	31	86	93	175	97	114	1	83

Note: Figures are average number of days per year and covers the years 1948-1990
Source: National Climatic Data Center, International Station Meteorological Climate Summary, 3/95

AIR & WATER QUALITY

Maximum Pollutant Concentrations

	Particulate Matter (ug/m^3)	Carbon Monoxide (ppm)	Sulfur Dioxide (ppm)	Nitrogen Dioxide (ppm)	Ozone (ppm)	Lead (ug/m^3)
MSA[1] Level	33	n/a	n/a	n/a	n/a	n/a
NAAQS[2]	150	9	0.140	0.053	0.12	1.50
Met NAAQS?	Yes	n/a	n/a	n/a	n/a	n/a

Note: (1) Metropolitan Statistical Area - see Appendix A for areas included; (2) National Ambient Air Quality Standards; ppm = parts per million; ug/m^3 = micrograms per cubic meter; n/a not available
Source: EPA, National Air Quality and Emissions Trends Report, 1996

Pollutant Standards Index

Data not available. *EPA, National Air Quality and Emissions Trends Report, 1996*

Drinking Water

Water System Name	Pop. Served	Primary Water Source Type	Number of Violations in Fiscal Year 1997	Type of Violation/ Contaminants
City of Tallahassee	162,750	Ground	None	None

Note: Data as of January 16, 1998
Source: EPA, Office of Ground Water and Drinking Water, Safe Drinking Water Information System

Tallahassee tap water is alkaline, soft and fluoridated.
Editor & Publisher Market Guide, 1998

Tampa, Florida

Background

Although Tampa was explored by the Spanish, such as Ponce de Leon and Hernando De Soto as early as 1521, this city located on the mouth of the Hillsborough River on Tampa Bay, did not see significant growth until the mid-nineteenth century.

Like many cities of northern Florida such as Jacksonville, Tampa played a role as a fort during the Seminole War, and during the Civil War, was captured by Union Armies. Like many Florida cities, Tampa enjoyed prosperity and development when a railroad line transported tourists from up north, to partake in the warmth and sunshine of Florida.

Two historical events in the late nineteenth century set Tampa apart from other Florida cities. First, Tampa played a significant role during the Spanish-American War in 1898, as a chief port of embarkation for American troops to Cuba. During that time, Col. Theodore Roosevelt occupied a Tampa hotel as his military headquarters. Second, a cigar factory in nearby Ybor City, named after factory owner Vicente Martinez Ybor, was the site where Jose Marti—the George Washington of Cuba—exhorted workers to take up arms against the tyranny of Spanish rule in the late 1800's.

Today, Tampa enjoys its role as the 7th largest port in the United States. Industries as varied as phosphate export, shrimp fishing, and citrus canning to electronic equipment, cigar, beer, and paint manufacturing comprise the chief income-earning sectors. Although Tampa struggles with rapid growth, it remains a relaxed city of sunshine and people in bathing suits.

Winters are mild. Summers are long, quite warm and humid. Freezing temperatures occur on one or two mornings per year during December, January and February. An outstanding feature of the Tampa climate is the summer thunderstorm season. Most occur during the late afternoon and sometimes the temperature can drop 20 degrees as a result.

The area is vulnerable to tidal surges as the land has an elevation less than 15 feet above sea level.

General Rankings and Evaluative Comments

■ Tampa was ranked #31 out of 300 cities by *Money's* 1997 "Survey of the Best Places to Live." Criteria used: health services, crime, economy, housing, education, transportation, weather, leisure and the arts. The city was ranked #11 in 1996 and #11 in 1995.
Money, July 1997; Money, September 1996; Money, September 1995

■ *Ladies Home Journal* ranked America's 200 largest cities based on the qualities women care about most. Tampa ranked 46 out of 200. Criteria: low crime rate, good public schools, well-paying jobs, quality health and child care, the presence of women in government, proportion of women-owned businesses, size of the wage gap with men, local economy, divorce rates, the ratio of single men to single women, whether there are laws that require at least the same number of public toilets for women as men, and the probability of good hair days. *Ladies Home Journal, November 1997*

■ Tampa was ranked #210 out of 219 cities in terms of children's health, safety, and economic well-being. Criteria: total population, percent population change, birth rate, child immunization rate, infant mortality rate, percent low birth weight infants, percent of births to teens, physician-to-population ratio, student-to-teacher ratio, dropout rate, unemployment rate, median family income, percent of children in poverty, violent and property crime rates, number of juvenile arrests for violent crimes as a percent of the total crime index, number of days with pollution standard index (PSI) over 100, pounds toxic releases per 1,000 people and number of superfund sites. *Zero Population Growth, Children's Environmental Index 1997*

■ *Conde Nast Traveler* polled 37,000 readers in terms of travel satisfaction. Cities were ranked based on the following criteria: people/friendliness, environment/ambiance, cultural enrichment, restaurants and fun/energy. Tampa appeared in the top thirty, ranking number 27, with an overall rating of 55.0 out of 100 based on all the criteria. *Conde Nast Traveler, Readers' Choice Poll 1997*

■ *Yahoo! Internet Life* selected "America's 100 Most Wired Cities & Towns". 50 cities were large and 50 cities were small. Tampa ranked 23 out of 50 large cities. Criteria: Internet users per capita, number of networked computers, number of registered domain names, Internet backbone traffic, and the per-capita number of Web sites devoted to each city. *Yahoo! Internet Life, March 1998*

■ According to *Working Mother,* "Florida stands out among the Southern states for its aggressive action to improve and expand child care. As we went to press, the governor had asked state lawmakers for a significant increase in state funds to create new child care slots. Some $49 million would be earmarked for a very important group—16,000 children of low-wage workers.

In the past year the state also boosted funding for its prekindergarten program by $4 million, bringing its pre-K spending to $102 million. This translates into free pre-K for 27,000 kids, about 2,000 more than last year. This program is funded with state lottery money and is available in all of Florida's 67 school districts.

The state has also improved its requirements for playground surfaces in child care setting. As of March 1997, all centers were required to have soft surfaces under playground equipment. This is a vital change, given that injuries from falls are the most common in child care.

Finally, lawmakers approved a new program to recognize quality child care programs. Any facility that attains state or NAEYC accreditation can now post a 'good seal' certificate and will be listed in a state database as a 'Gold Seal' program—to show it meets high standards of care. So far, about 370 centers have received certificates, and about 800 more are in the pipeline." *Working Mother, July/August 1997*

Business Environment

STATE ECONOMY

State Economic Profile

"Florida's economy continues to expand strongly....

Florida is becoming increasingly dependent on the service industry for job growth. Currently, one in three Florida jobs is service-related. In the past year, however, nearly half of all jobs created were in the service industry. One in four jobs created was in business services, compared to one in seven for the U.S....

Florida's tourist industry continues to rebound and will be an important source of growth for this year. Household income growth and savings rates are high, and the values of individual stock portfolios has been booming, leaving households across the U.S. in good financial shape to take a vacation.

A risk to Florida's economy is a sharp slowing in population growth. In 1996, Florida experienced a population gain of only 1.5%, the slowest rate of growth since World War II. Contributing to the slower population growth is weaker retiree migration due to a slowing national retiree population growth.

Supporting growth are Florida's moderate climate, favorable quality of life, affordable housing, and low cost of doing business, which will continue to attract businesses and households. Population growth will continue to slow for the next decade as the number of people reaching retirement age nationwide is falling. Population growth will begin to accelerate once the baby boom generation hits retirement age beginning around 2005. One downside risk for Florida is its dependence on tourism and interest and property income that makes it vulnerable to national and international business cycles. Florida will remain one of the nation's fastest-growing economies through the remainder of this century." *National Association of Realtors, Economic Profiles: The Fifty States, July 1997*

IMPORTS/EXPORTS

Total Export Sales

Area	1993 ($000)	1994 ($000)	1995 ($000)	1996 ($000)	% Chg. 1993-96	% Chg. 1995-96
MSA[1]	1,295,739	1,835,814	2,116,050	1,921,833	48.3	-9.2
U.S.	464,858,354	512,415,609	583,030,524	622,827,063	34.0	6.8

Note: (1) Metropolitan Statistical Area - see Appendix A for areas included
Source: U.S. Department of Commerce, International Trade Association, Metropolitan Area Exports: An Export Performance Report on Over 250 U.S. Cities, October 1997

Imports/Exports by Port

Type	Cargo Value			Share of U.S. Total	
	1995 (US$mil.)	1996 (US$mil.)	% Change 1995-1996	1995 (%)	1996 (%)
Imports	781	776	-0.64	0.20	0.20
Exports	2,158	1,929	-10.61	0.94	0.81

Source: Global Trade Information Services, WaterBorne Trade Atlas 1997

CITY FINANCES

City Government Finances

Component	FY92 ($000)	FY92 (per capita $)
Revenue	382,821	1,358.02
Expenditure	407,824	1,446.72
Debt Outstanding	682,771	2,422.07
Cash & Securities	752,383	2,669.01

Source: U.S. Bureau of the Census, City Government Finances: 1991-92

City Government Revenue by Source

Source	FY92 ($000)	FY92 (per capita $)	FY92 (%)
From Federal Government	12,098	42.92	3.2
From State Governments	25,261	89.61	6.6
From Local Governments	12,446	44.15	3.3
Property Taxes	57,829	205.14	15.1
General Sales Taxes	0	0.00	0.0
Selective Sales Taxes	58,813	208.63	15.4
Income Taxes	0	0.00	0.0
Current Charges	96,723	343.12	25.3
Utility/Liquor Store	30,377	107.76	7.9
Employee Retirement[1]	46,069	163.43	12.0
Other	43,205	153.27	11.3

Note: (1) Excludes "city contributions," classified as "nonrevenue," intragovernmental transfers.
Source: U.S. Bureau of the Census, City Government Finances: 1991-92

City Government Expenditures by Function

Function	FY92 ($000)	FY92 (per capita $)	FY92 (%)
Educational Services	0	0.00	0.0
Employee Retirement[1]	26,792	95.04	6.6
Environment/Housing	153,717	545.30	37.7
Government Administration	10,622	37.68	2.6
Interest on General Debt	38,694	137.26	9.5
Public Safety	79,323	281.39	19.5
Social Services	3,873	13.74	0.9
Transportation	31,301	111.04	7.7
Utility/Liquor Store	53,634	190.26	13.2
Other	9,868	35.01	2.4

Note: (1) Payments to beneficiaries including withdrawal of contributions.
Source: U.S. Bureau of the Census, City Government Finances: 1991-92

Municipal Bond Ratings

Area	Moody's	S & P
Tampa	Aaa	n/r

Note: n/a not available; n/r not rated
Source: Moody's Bond Record, 2/98; Statistical Abstract of the U.S., 1997;
Governing Magazine, 9/97, 3/98

POPULATION

Population Growth

Area	1980	1990	% Chg. 1980-90	July 1996 Estimate	% Chg. 1990-96
City	271,523	280,015	3.1	285,206	1.9
MSA[1]	1,613,621	2,067,959	28.2	2,199,231	6.3
U.S.	226,545,805	248,765,170	9.8	265,179,411	6.6

Note: (1) Metropolitan Statistical Area - see Appendix A for areas included
Source: 1980/1990 Census of Housing and Population, Summary Tape File 3C;
Census Bureau Population Estimates

Population Characteristics

Race	City 1980 Population	%	City 1990 Population	%	% Chg. 1980-90	MSA[1] 1990 Population	%
White	202,507	74.6	198,756	71.0	-1.9	1,828,737	88.4
Black	63,578	23.4	69,871	25.0	9.9	184,087	8.9
Amer Indian/Esk/Aleut	607	0.2	997	0.4	64.3	6,752	0.3
Asian/Pacific Islander	1,894	0.7	3,948	1.4	108.4	22,860	1.1
Other	2,937	1.1	6,443	2.3	119.4	25,523	1.2
Hispanic Origin[2]	35,982	13.3	41,247	14.7	14.6	136,027	6.6

Note: (1) Metropolitan Statistical Area - see Appendix A for areas included;
(2) people of Hispanic origin can be of any race
Source: 1980/1990 Census of Housing and Population, Summary Tape File 3C

Ancestry

Area	German	Irish	English	Italian	U.S.	French	Polish	Dutch
City	15.2	12.3	12.5	6.2	4.7	3.2	1.8	1.8
MSA[1]	23.5	17.3	16.9	7.8	5.0	4.8	3.7	2.6
U.S.	23.3	15.6	13.1	5.9	5.3	4.2	3.8	2.5

Note: Figures are percentages and include persons that reported multiple ancestry (eg. if a person reported being Irish and Italian, they were included in both columns); (1) Metropolitan Statistical Area - see Appendix A for areas included
Source: 1990 Census of Population and Housing, Summary Tape File 3C

Age

Area	Median Age (Years)	Age Distribution (%) Under 5	Under 18	18-24	25-44	45-64	65+	80+
City	33.2	7.4	22.9	10.8	33.0	18.7	14.6	3.4
MSA[1]	38.5	6.0	20.4	8.4	29.7	20.0	21.5	4.9
U.S.	32.9	7.3	25.6	10.5	32.6	18.7	12.5	2.8

Note: (1) Metropolitan Statistical Area - see Appendix A for areas included
Source: 1990 Census of Population and Housing, Summary Tape File 3C

Male/Female Ratio

Area	Number of males per 100 females (all ages)	Number of males per 100 females (18 years old+)
City	92.8	88.7
MSA[1]	91.0	87.8
U.S.	95.0	91.9

Note: (1) Metropolitan Statistical Area - see Appendix A for areas included
Source: 1990 Census of Population, General Population Characteristics

INCOME

Per Capita/Median/Average Income

Area	Per Capita ($)	Median Household ($)	Average Household ($)
City	13,277	22,772	31,813
MSA[1]	14,374	26,036	33,685
U.S.	14,420	30,056	38,453

Note: all figures are for 1989; (1) Metropolitan Statistical Area - see Appendix A for areas included
Source: 1990 Census of Population and Housing, Summary Tape File 3C

Household Income Distribution by Race

Income ($)	City (%)					U.S. (%)				
	Total	White	Black	Other	Hisp.[1]	Total	White	Black	Other	Hisp.[1]
Less than 5,000	9.7	6.6	20.4	12.1	13.0	6.2	4.8	15.2	8.6	8.8
5,000 - 9,999	11.7	10.2	17.2	10.7	11.7	9.3	8.6	14.2	9.9	11.1
10,000 - 14,999	11.5	10.9	13.8	13.3	13.7	8.8	8.5	11.0	9.8	11.0
15,000 - 24,999	21.0	21.0	20.2	25.6	20.9	17.5	17.3	18.9	18.5	20.5
25,000 - 34,999	16.1	17.0	12.4	17.6	16.2	15.8	16.1	14.2	15.4	16.4
35,000 - 49,999	14.6	16.0	9.8	12.0	13.3	17.9	18.6	13.3	16.1	16.0
50,000 - 74,999	9.2	10.5	4.9	6.2	7.9	15.0	15.8	9.3	13.4	11.1
75,000 - 99,999	2.9	3.5	0.9	1.3	1.7	5.1	5.5	2.6	4.7	3.1
100,000+	3.4	4.3	0.5	1.3	1.7	4.4	4.8	1.3	3.7	1.9

Note: all figures are for 1989; (1) people of Hispanic origin can be of any race
Source: 1990 Census of Population and Housing, Summary Tape File 3C

Effective Buying Income

Area	Per Capita ($)	Median Household ($)	Average Household ($)
City	15,312	27,031	37,528
MSA[1]	16,754	30,996	40,199
U.S.	15,444	33,201	41,849

Note: data as of 1/1/97; (1) Metropolitan Statistical Area - see Appendix A for areas included
Source: Standard Rate & Data Service, Newspaper Advertising Source, 2/98

Effective Household Buying Income Distribution

Area	% of Households Earning						
	$10,000 -$19,999	$20,000 -$34,999	$35,000 -$49,999	$50,000 -$74,999	$75,000 -$99,000	$100,000 -$124,999	$125,000 and up
City	20.0	24.7	16.3	13.2	4.4	1.6	2.7
MSA[1]	18.5	26.1	17.9	15.9	5.7	2.0	2.3
U.S.	16.5	23.4	18.3	18.2	6.4	2.1	2.4

Note: data as of 1/1/97; (1) Metropolitan Statistical Area - see Appendix A for areas included
Source: Standard Rate & Data Service, Newspaper Advertising Source, 2/98

Poverty Rates by Race and Age

Area	Total (%)	By Race (%)				By Age (%)		
		White	Black	Other	Hisp.[2]	Under 5 years old	Under 18 years old	65 years and over
City	19.4	12.2	39.8	21.0	20.6	35.0	30.9	19.4
MSA[1]	11.4	9.0	33.1	20.4	19.4	20.2	17.6	9.4
U.S.	13.1	9.8	29.5	23.1	25.3	20.1	18.3	12.8

Note: figures show the percent of people living below the poverty line in 1989. The average poverty threshold was $12,674 for a family of four in 1989; (1) Metropolitan Statistical Area - see Appendix A for areas included; (2) people of Hispanic origin can be of any race
Source: 1990 Census of Population and Housing, Summary Tape File 3C

EMPLOYMENT

Labor Force and Employment

Area	Civilian Labor Force			Workers Employed		
	Dec. '95	Dec. '96	% Chg.	Dec. '95	Dec. '96	% Chg.
City	157,781	163,166	3.4	151,425	156,998	3.7
MSA[1]	1,105,649	1,144,836	3.5	1,068,275	1,107,594	3.7
U.S.	134,583,000	136,742,000	1.6	127,903,000	130,785,000	2.3

Note: Data is not seasonally adjusted and covers workers 16 years of age and older; (1) Metropolitan Statistical Area - see Appendix A for areas included
Source: Bureau of Labor Statistics, http://stats.bls.gov

Unemployment Rate

Area	1997											
	Jan.	Feb.	Mar.	Apr.	May	Jun.	Jul.	Aug.	Sep.	Oct.	Nov.	Dec.
City	4.8	4.3	4.2	4.3	4.4	4.6	4.3	4.2	4.4	4.0	4.0	3.8
MSA[1]	4.0	3.5	3.4	3.5	3.6	3.8	3.6	3.5	3.7	3.4	3.4	3.3
U.S.	5.9	5.7	5.5	4.8	4.7	5.2	5.0	4.8	4.7	4.4	4.3	4.4

Note: Data is not seasonally adjusted and covers workers 16 years of age and older; All figures are percentages; (1) Metropolitan Statistical Area - see Appendix A for areas included
Source: Bureau of Labor Statistics, http://stats.bls.gov

Employment by Industry

Sector	MSA[1]		U.S.
	Number of Employees	Percent of Total	Percent of Total
Services	429,200	38.9	29.0
Retail Trade	205,800	18.7	18.5
Government	135,500	12.3	16.1
Manufacturing	87,800	8.0	15.0
Finance/Insurance/Real Estate	78,100	7.1	5.7
Wholesale Trade	63,300	5.7	5.4
Transportation/Public Utilities	49,600	4.5	5.3
Construction	53,600	4.9	4.5
Mining	400	0.0	0.5

Note: Figures cover non-farm employment as of 12/97 and are not seasonally adjusted;
(1) Metropolitan Statistical Area - see Appendix A for areas included
Source: Bureau of Labor Statistics, http://stats.bls.gov

Employment by Occupation

Occupation Category	City (%)	MSA[1] (%)	U.S. (%)
White Collar	59.8	61.2	58.1
Executive/Admin./Management	12.3	12.9	12.3
Professional	13.4	12.6	14.1
Technical & Related Support	3.5	3.9	3.7
Sales	12.6	14.8	11.8
Administrative Support/Clerical	18.0	17.1	16.3
Blue Collar	23.2	22.6	26.2
Precision Production/Craft/Repair	9.8	11.0	11.3
Machine Operators/Assem./Insp.	4.8	4.2	6.8
Transportation/Material Movers	4.2	3.8	4.1
Cleaners/Helpers/Laborers	4.5	3.6	3.9
Services	15.3	13.9	13.2
Farming/Forestry/Fishing	1.7	2.4	2.5

Note: figures cover employed persons 16 years old and over;
(1) Metropolitan Statistical Area - see Appendix A for areas included
Source: 1990 Census of Population and Housing, Summary Tape File 3C

Occupational Employment Projections: 1995 - 2005

Occupations Expected to have the Largest Job Growth (ranked by numerical growth)	Fast-Growing Occupations[1] (ranked by percent growth)
1. Cashiers	1. Systems analysts
2. General managers & top executives	2. Computer engineers
3. Waiters & waitresses	3. Physical therapy assistants and aides
4. Systems analysts	4. Physical therapists
5. Hand packers & packagers	5. Electronic pagination systems workers
6. First line supervisor, sales & related	6. Occupational therapists
7. Salespersons, retail	7. Human services workers
8. Receptionists and information clerks	8. Residential counselors
9. Secretaries, except legal & medical	9. Corrections officers & jailers
10. First line supervisors, clerical	10. Medical assistants

Projections cover Hillsborough County.
Note: (1) Excludes occupations with total growth of less than 100 jobs
Source: Florida Department of Labor and Employment Security, Florida Industry and Occupational Employment Projections 1995-2005

Average Wages

Occupation	Wage	Occupation	Wage
Professional/Technical/Clerical	$/Week	**Health/Protective Services**	$/Week
Accountants III	759	Corrections Officers	-
Attorneys III	1,255	Firefighters	573
Budget Analysts III	-	Nurses, Licensed Practical II	-
Buyers/Contracting Specialists II	673	Nurses, Registered II	-
Clerks, Accounting III	407	Nursing Assistants II	-
Clerks, General III	354	Police Officers I	665
Computer Operators II	404	**Hourly Workers**	$/Hour
Computer Programmers II	-	Forklift Operators	8.94
Drafters II	478	General Maintenance Workers	9.06
Engineering Technicians III	593	Guards I	5.78
Engineering Technicians, Civil III	602	Janitors	6.26
Engineers III	983	Maintenance Electricians	-
Key Entry Operators I	284	Maintenance Electronics Techs II	14.09
Personnel Assistants III	514	Maintenance Machinists	13.93
Personnel Specialists III	757	Maintenance Mechanics, Machinery	13.92
Secretaries III	516	Material Handling Laborers	9.47
Switchboard Operator-Receptionist	320	Motor Vehicle Mechanics	14.02
Systems Analysts II	925	Shipping/Receiving Clerks	9.20
Systems Analysts Supervisor/Mgr II	-	Tool and Die Makers	16.04
Tax Collectors II	447	Truckdrivers, Tractor Trailer	12.06
Word Processors II	413	Warehouse Specialists	8.56

Note: Wage data includes full-time workers only for 7/96 and cover the Metropolitan Statistical Area (see Appendix A for areas included). Dashes indicate that data was not available.
Source: Bureau of Labor Statistics, Occupational Compensation Survey, 1/97

TAXES

Major State and Local Tax Rates

State Corp. Income (%)	State Personal Income (%)	Residential Property (effective rate per $100)	Sales & Use		State Gasoline (cents/ gallon)	State Cigarette (cents/ 20-pack)
			State (%)	Local (%)		
5.5[a]	None	n/a	6.0	1.0	12.8[b]	33.9

Note: Personal/corporate income tax rates as of 1/97. Sales, gasoline and cigarette tax rates as of 1/98; (a) 3.3% Alternative Minimum Tax. An exemption of $5,000 is allowed; (b) Rate is comprised of 4 cents excise and 8.8 cents motor carrier tax
Source: Federation of Tax Administrators, www.taxadmin.org; Washington D.C. Department of Finance and Revenue, Tax Rates and Tax Burdens in the District of Columbia: A Nationwide Comparison, June 1997; Chamber of Commerce

Total Taxes Per Capita and as a Percent of Income

Area	Per Capita Income ($)	Per Capita Taxes ($)			Taxes as Pct. of Income (%)		
		Total	Federal	State/Local	Total	Federal	State/Local
Florida	26,438	9,172	6,286	2,886	34.7	23.8	10.9
U.S.	26,187	9,205	6,127	3,078	35.2	23.4	11.8

Note: Figures are for 1997
Source: Tax Foundation, Web Site, www.taxfoundation.org

COMMERCIAL REAL ESTATE

Office Market

Class/ Location	Total Space (sq. ft.)	Vacant Space (sq. ft.)	Vac. Rate (%)	Under Constr. (sq. ft.)	Net Absorp. (sq. ft.)	Rental Rates ($/sq.ft./yr.)
Class A						
CBD	4,507,212	372,484	8.3	n/a	147,015	15.50-22.00
Outside CBD	7,476,432	402,119	5.4	n/a	337,563	14.00-24.00
Class B						
CBD	896,974	250,429	27.9	n/a	45,543	12.00-17.00
Outside CBD	8,256,168	809,070	9.8	n/a	198,636	13.00-19.00

Note: Data as of 10/97 and covers the Tampa Bay Area; CBD = Central Business District; n/a not available;
Source: Society of Industrial and Office Realtors, 1998 Comparative Statistics of Industrial and Office Real Estate Markets

"Several new buildings are underway with completion dates set for 1998. Build-to-suit projects involving Western/AEGON, Templeton, Raymond James, and Atlantic/Lucent will add 920,000 sq. ft. to the market. New speculative construction will increase inventory by 440,000 sq. ft. to the market. New speculative construction will increase inventory by 440,000 sq. ft. Only one of these buildings is situated downtown. The CBD will face an uphill battle, with the buyout of First of America Bank by Barnett putting First of America's substantial space back on the market. The merger of NationsBank and Barnett will further increase the amount of sublease space available. Nonetheless, SIOR's observer expects the market to generate enough growth to leave the overall vacancy level unchanged in 1998." *Society of Industrial and Office Realtors, 1998 Comparative Statistics of Industrial and Office Real Estate Markets*

Industrial Market

Location	Total Space (sq. ft.)	Vacant Space (sq. ft.)	Vac. Rate (%)	Under Constr. (sq. ft.)	Net Absorp. (sq. ft.)	Lease ($/sq.ft./yr.)
Central City	n/a	n/a	n/a	n/a	n/a	n/a
Suburban	62,937,319	3,946,087	6.3	1,163,931	1,699,709	3.25-4.00

Note: Data as of 10/97 and covers Tampa Bay; n/a not available
Source: Society of Industrial and Office Realtors, 1998 Comparative Statistics of Industrial and Office Real Estate Markets

"The quest to develop modern distribution centers in Tampa is fueling the ongoing construction cycle. During the latter part of 1997 1.2 million sq. ft. were under construction with another 800,000 sq. ft. expected to enter the development pipeline during 1998. The MSA's ability to sustain economic growth is the basis for the anticipated increase in absorption levels across all of the industrial property sectors. Strong absorption should fuel an increase in terms of dollar volume. Increased diversity in the industrial sector, particularly a long-term movement away from defense, bolsters the anticipation of future market improvement in the wake of the development of plans underway." *Society of Industrial and Office Realtors, 1998 Comparative Statistics of Industrial and Office Real Estate Markets*

Retail Market

Shopping Center Inventory (sq. ft.)	Shopping Center Construction (sq. ft.)	Construction as a Percent of Inventory (%)	Torto Wheaton Rent Index[1] ($/sq. ft.)
45,090,000	396,000	0.9	11.13

Note: Data as of 1997 and covers the Metropolitan Statistical Area - see Appendix A for areas included; (1) Index is based on a model that predicts what the average rent should be for leases with certain characteristics, in certain locations during certain years.
Source: National Association of Realtors, 1997-1998 Market Conditions Report

"Money magazine recently ranked Tampa as the nation's most solid economy out of more than 300 metro areas. The area's retail rent index has been rising since 1994, buoyed by strong demand. The 980,000 square foot Brandon TownCenter at the intersection of Interstate 75 and Route 60 currently has a 94% occupancy rate. Its success has prompted the construction of the 1.2 million square foot Citrus Park Mall, due to open in early 1999. The mall will be located in northwest Hillsborough County, with Dillards, Burdines, Sears and J.C. Penney as anchors. Strong economic and population growth in the Tampa area, particularly Hillsborough, will bolster the retail market over the next few years." *National Association of Realtors, 1997-1998 Market Conditions Report*

COMMERCIAL UTILITIES

Typical Monthly Electric Bills

Area	Commercial Service ($/month)		Industrial Service ($/month)	
	12 kW demand 1,500 kWh	100 kW demand 30,000 kWh	1,000 kW demand 400,000 kWh	20,000 kW demand 10,000,000 kWh
City	116	1,980	23,536	545,316
U.S.	162	2,360	25,590	545,677

Note: Based on rates in effect July 1, 1997
Source: Edison Electric Institute, Typical Residential, Commercial and Industrial Bills, Summer 1997

TRANSPORTATION

Transportation Statistics

Avg. travel time to work (min.)	19.2
Interstate highways	I-4; I-75
Bus lines	
In-city	Hillsborough Area RTA, 173 vehicles
Inter-city	3
Passenger air service	
Airport	Tampa International
Airlines	22
Aircraft departures	65,229 (1995)
Enplaned passengers	4,958,794 (1995)
Rail service	Amtrak
Motor freight carriers	46
Major waterways/ports	Port of Tampa

Source: OAG, Business Travel Planner, Summer 1997; Editor & Publisher Market Guide, 1998; FAA Airport Activity Statistics, 1996; Amtrak National Time Table, Northeast Timetable, Fall/Winter 1997-98; 1990 Census of Population and Housing, STF 3C; Chamber of Commerce/Economic Development 1997; Jane's Urban Transport Systems 1997-98; Transit Fact Book 1997

A survey of 90,000 airline passengers during the first half of 1997 ranked most of the largest airports in the U.S. Tampa International ranked number 1 out of 36. Criteria: cleanliness, quality of restaurants, attractiveness, speed of baggage delivery, ease of reaching gates, available ground transportation, ease of following signs and closeness of parking. *Plog Research Inc., First Half 1997*

Means of Transportation to Work

Area	Car/Truck/Van		Public Transportation			Bicycle	Walked	Other Means	Worked at Home
	Drove Alone	Car-pooled	Bus	Subway	Railroad				
City	74.8	14.3	3.2	0.0	0.0	0.9	3.4	1.5	1.9
MSA[1]	78.8	13.3	1.3	0.0	0.0	0.7	2.3	1.3	2.3
U.S.	73.2	13.4	3.0	1.5	0.5	0.4	3.9	1.2	3.0

Note: figures shown are percentages and only include workers 16 years old and over;
(1) Metropolitan Statistical Area - see Appendix A for areas included
Source: 1990 Census of Population and Housing, Summary Tape File 3C

BUSINESSES

Major Business Headquarters

Company Name	1997 Rankings	
	Fortune 500	Forbes 500
Evenflo & Spalding	-	289
Lykes Bros	-	189

Note: Companies listed are located in the city; Dashes indicate no ranking
Fortune 500: companies that produce a 10-K are ranked 1 - 500 based on 1996 revenue
Forbes 500: private companies are ranked 1 - 500 based on 1996 revenue
Source: Forbes 12/1/97; Fortune 4/28/97

Fast-Growing Businesses

According to *Inc.*, Tampa is home to one of America's 100 fastest-growing private companies: Microsystems Technology. Criteria for inclusion: must be an independent, privately-held, U.S. corporation, proprietorship or partnership; sales of at least $200,000 in 1993; five-year operating/sales history; increase in 1997 sales over 1996 sales; holding companies, regulated banks, and utilities were excluded. *Inc. 500, 1997*

According to Deloitte & Touche LLP, Tampa is home to three of America's 100 fastest-growing high-technology companies: PowerCerv, Reptron Electronics, and Technical Resource Connection Inc. Companies are ranked by percentage growth in revenue over a five-year period. Criteria for inclusion: must be a U.S. company developing and/or providing technology products or services; company must have been in business for five years with 1992 revenues of at least $50,000. *Deloitte & Touche LLP, January 7, 1998*

Tampa was ranked #22 out of 24 (#1 is best) in terms of the best-performing local stocks in 1996 according to the Money/Norby Cities Index. The index measures stocks of companies that have headquarters in 24 metro areas. *Money, 2/7/97*

Women-Owned Businesses: Number, Employment, Sales and Share

Area	Women-Owned Businesses in 1996				Share of Women-Owned Businesses in 1996	
	Number	Employment	Sales ($000)	Rank[2]	Percent (%)	Rank[3]
MSA[1]	72,400	225,400	17,769,300	21	39.4	7

Note: (1) Metropolitan Statistical Area - see Appendix A for areas included; (2) Calculated on an averaging of number of businesses, employment and sales and ranges from 1 to 50 where 1 is best; (3) Ranges from 1 to 50 where 1 is best
Source: The National Foundation for Women Business Owners, 1996 Facts on Women-Owned Businesses: Trends in the Top 50 Metropolitan Areas, March 26, 1997

Women-Owned Businesses: Growth

Area	Growth in Women-Owned Businesses (% change from 1987 to 1996)				Relative Growth in the Number of Women-Owned and All Businesses (% change from 1987 to 1996)			
	Num.	Empl.	Sales	Rank[2]	Women-Owned	All Firms	Absolute Difference	Relative Difference
MSA[1]	89.0	254.5	169.8	24	89.0	47.3	41.7	1.9:1

Note: (1) Metropolitan Statistical Area - see Appendix A for areas included; (2) Calculated on an averaging of the percent growth of number of businesses, employment and sales and ranges from 1 to 50 where 1 is best
Source: The National Foundation for Women Business Owners, 1996 Facts on Women-Owned Businesses: Trends in the Top 50 Metropolitan Areas, March 26, 1997

Minority Business Opportunity

Tampa is home to one company which is on the Black Enterprise Auto Dealer 100 list (largest based on gross sales): Brandon Dodge Inc. (Chrysler/Toyota). Criteria: 1) operational in previous calendar year; 2) at least 51% black-owned. *Black Enterprise, June 1997*

Six of the 500 largest Hispanic-owned companies in the U.S. are located in Tampa. *Hispanic Business, June 1997*

Tampa is home to one company which is on the Hispanic Business Fastest-Growing 100 list (greatest sales growth from 1992 to 1996): Aero Simulation Inc. (flight simulator mfg.) *Hispanic Business, July/August 1997*

Tampa was listed among the top 25 metropolitan areas in terms of the number of Hispanic-owned companies. The city was ranked number 20 with 15,577 companies. *Hispanic Business, May 1997*

Small Business Opportunity

According to *Forbes*, Tampa is home to one of America's 200 best small companies: Romac International. Criteria: companies must be publicly traded, U.S.-based corporations with latest 12-month sales of between $5 and $350 million. Earnings must be at least $1 million for the 12-month period. Limited partnerships, REITs and closed-end mutual funds were not considered. Banks, S&Ls and electric utilities were not included. *Forbes, November 3, 1997*

HOTELS & MOTELS

Hotels/Motels

Area	Hotels/ Motels	Rooms	Luxury-Level Hotels/Motels		Average Minimum Rates ($)		
			♦♦♦♦	♦♦♦♦♦	♦♦	♦♦♦	♦♦♦♦
City	40	6,054	0	0	57	113	n/a
Airport	19	4,896	1	0	n/a	n/a	n/a
Suburbs	6	1,137	0	0	n/a	n/a	n/a
Total	65	12,087	1	0	n/a	n/a	n/a

Note: n/a not available; Classifications range from one diamond (budget properties with basic amenities) to five diamond (luxury properties with the finest service, rooms and facilities).
Source: OAG, Business Travel Planner, Summer 1997

CONVENTION CENTERS

Major Convention Centers

Center Name	Meeting Rooms	Exhibit Space (sf)
Florida State Fair and Expo Park	n/a	168,000
Tampa Convention Center	18	200,000
Phyllis P. Marshall Center/Univ. of South Florida	13	65,794

Note: n/a not available
Source: Trade Shows Worldwide 1997

Living Environment

COST OF LIVING

Cost of Living Index

Composite Index	Housing	Utilities	Groceries	Health Care	Trans-portation	Misc. Goods/ Services
97.7	89.8	113.5	100.6	110.0	100.7	96.1

Note: U.S. = 100
Source: ACCRA, Cost of Living Index, 2nd Quarter 1997

HOUSING

Median Home Prices and Housing Affordability

Area	Median Price[2] 3rd Qtr. 1997 ($)	HOI[3] 3rd Qtr. 1997	Afford-ability Rank[4]
MSA[1]	88,000	72.4	75
U.S.	127,000	63.7	--

Note: (1) Metropolitan Statistical Area - see Appendix A for areas included; (2) U.S. figures calculated from the sales of 625,000 new and existing homes in 195 markets; (3) Housing Opportunity Index - percent of homes sold that were within the reach of the median income household at the prevailing mortgage interest rate; (4) Rank is from 1-195 with 1 being most affordable
Source: National Association of Home Builders, Housing Opportunity Index, 3rd Quarter 1997

It is projected that the median price of existing single-family homes in the metro area will increase by 5.1% in 1998. Nationwide, home prices are projected to increase 6.6%.
Kiplinger's Personal Finance Magazine, January 1998

Average New Home Price

Area	Price ($)
City	107,000
U.S.	135,150

Note: Figures are based on a new home with 1,800 sq. ft. of living area on an 8,000 sq. ft. lot.
Source: ACCRA, Cost of Living Index, 2nd Quarter 1997

Average Apartment Rent

Area	Rent ($/mth)
City	607
U.S.	575

Note: Figures are based on an unfurnished two bedroom, 1-1/2 or 2 bath apartment, approximately 950 sq. ft. in size, excluding all utilities except water
Source: ACCRA, Cost of Living Index, 2nd Quarter 1997

RESIDENTIAL UTILITIES

Average Residential Utility Costs

Area	All Electric ($/mth)	Part Electric ($/mth)	Other Energy ($/mth)	Phone ($/mth)
City	112.15	--	--	19.63
U.S.	108.38	56.32	44.12	19.66

Source: ACCRA, Cost of Living Index, 2nd Quarter 1997

HEALTH CARE

Average Health Care Costs

Area	Hospital ($/day)	Doctor ($/visit)	Dentist ($/visit)
City	374.60	46.40	55.20
U.S.	390.32	48.32	60.14

Note: Hospital - based on a semi-private room. Doctor - based on a general practitioner's routine exam of an established patient. Dentist - based on adult teeth cleaning and periodic oral exam.
Source: ACCRA, Cost of Living Index, 2nd Quarter 1997

Distribution of Office-Based Physicians

| Area | Family/Gen. Practitioners | Specialists | | |
		Medical	Surgical	Other
MSA[1]	466	1,436	1,019	1,067

Note: Data as of 12/31/96; (1) Metropolitan Statistical Area - see Appendix A for areas included
Source: American Medical Assn., Physician Characteristics & Distribution in the U.S., 1997-1998

Hospitals

Tampa has 7 general medical and surgical hospitals, 1 psychiatric, 1 orthopedic, 1 chronic disease, 2 other specialty. *AHA Guide to the Healthcare Field 1997-98*

EDUCATION

Public School District Statistics

District Name	Num. Sch.	Enroll.	Classroom Teachers[1]	Pupils per Teacher	Minority Pupils (%)	Current Exp.[2] ($/pupil)
Hillsborough County Sch Dist	172	143,192	8,652	16.6	43.0	5,163

Note: Data covers the 1995-1996 school year unless otherwise noted; (1) Excludes teachers reported as working in school district offices rather than in schools; (2) Based on 1993-94 enrollment collected by the Census Bureau, not the enrollment figure shown in column 3; SD = School District; ISD = Independent School District; n/a not available
Source: National Center for Education Statistics, Common Core of Data Survey; Bureau of the Census

Educational Quality

School District	Education Quotient[1]	Graduate Outcome[2]	Community Index[3]	Resource Index[4]
Tampa	107.0	96.0	92.0	132.0

Note: Nearly 1,000 secondary school districts were rated in terms of educational quality. The scores range from a low of 50 to a high of 150; (1) Average of the Graduate Outcome, Community and Resource indexes; (2) Based on graduation rates and college board scores (SAT/ACT); (3) Based on the surrounding community's average level of education and the area's average income level; (4) Based on teacher salaries, per-pupil expenditures and student-teacher ratios.
Source: Expansion Management, Ratings Issue 1997

Educational Attainment by Race

| Area | High School Graduate (%) | | | | | Bachelor's Degree (%) | | | | |
	Total	White	Black	Other	Hisp.[2]	Total	White	Black	Other	Hisp.[2]
City	70.6	74.7	57.1	61.5	54.4	18.7	21.7	8.0	15.1	11.3
MSA[1]	75.1	76.5	60.4	64.4	59.9	17.3	17.7	10.8	18.4	14.2
U.S.	75.2	77.9	63.1	60.4	49.8	20.3	21.5	11.4	19.4	9.2

Note: figures shown cover persons 25 years old and over; (1) Metropolitan Statistical Area - see Appendix A for areas included; (2) people of Hispanic origin can be of any race
Source: 1990 Census of Population and Housing, Summary Tape File 3C

School Enrollment by Type

| Area | Preprimary | | | | Elementary/High School | | | |
| | Public | | Private | | Public | | Private | |
	Enrollment	%	Enrollment	%	Enrollment	%	Enrollment	%
City	3,016	59.3	2,068	40.7	35,768	88.4	4,676	11.6
MSA[1]	17,848	52.0	16,451	48.0	244,416	89.0	30,326	11.0
U.S.	2,679,029	59.5	1,824,256	40.5	38,379,689	90.2	4,187,099	9.8

Note: figures shown cover persons 3 years old and over;
(1) Metropolitan Statistical Area - see Appendix A for areas included
Source: 1990 Census of Population and Housing, Summary Tape File 3C

School Enrollment by Race

Area	Preprimary (%)				Elementary/High School (%)			
	White	Black	Other	Hisp.[1]	White	Black	Other	Hisp.[1]
City	60.0	37.3	2.8	10.9	55.2	40.0	4.7	14.9
MSA[2]	82.6	14.6	2.8	6.4	80.0	16.0	4.0	8.9
U.S.	80.4	12.5	7.1	7.8	74.1	15.6	10.3	12.5

Note: figures shown cover persons 3 years old and over; (1) people of Hispanic origin can be of any race; (2) Metropolitan Statistical Area - see Appendix A for areas included
Source: 1990 Census of Population and Housing, Summary Tape File 3C

SAT/ACT Scores

Area/District	1997 SAT				1997 ACT	
	Percent of Graduates Tested (%)	Average Math Score	Average Verbal Score	Average Combined Score	Percent of Graduates Tested (%)	Average Composite Score
Hillsborough Co. SD	49	515	509	1,024	30	21.4
State	50	499	499	998	36	20.7
U.S.	42	511	505	1,016	36	21.0

Note: Math and verbal SAT scores are out of a possible 800; ACT scores are out of a possible 36
Caution: Comparing or ranking states/cities on the basis of SAT/ACT scores alone is invalid and strongly discouraged by the The College Board and The American College Testing Program as students who take the tests are self-selected and do not represent the entire student population.
Source: Hillsborough County Public Schools, Division of Instruction, Assessment, Accountability & Evaluation, 1997; American College Testing Program, 1997; College Board, 1997

Classroom Teacher Salaries in Public Schools

District	B.A. Degree		M.A. Degree		Ph.D. Degree	
	Min. ($)	Max ($)	Min. ($)	Max. ($)	Min. ($)	Max. ($)
Tampa	23,851	40,575	26,250	43,022	28,649	45,468
Average[1]	26,120	39,270	28,175	44,667	31,643	49,825

Note: Salaries are for 1996-1997; (1) Based on all school districts covered; n/a not available
Source: American Federation of Teachers (unpublished data)

Higher Education

Two-Year Colleges		Four-Year Colleges		Medical Schools	Law Schools	Voc/ Tech
Public	Private	Public	Private			
1	0	1	6	1	0	16

Source: College Blue Book, Occupational Education 1997; Medical School Admission Requirements, 1998-99; Peterson's Guide to Two-Year Colleges, 1997; Peterson's Guide to Four-Year Colleges, 1997; Barron's Guide to Law Schools 1997

MAJOR EMPLOYERS

Major Employers

Chase Manhattan Mortgage	Cigna Healthcare of Florida
GTE Data Services	GTE Florida
Hillsborough County Hospital Authority	Nutmeg Mills
Progressive Bayside Insurance	St. Joseph's Hospital
Tampa Electric	University Community Hospital

Note: companies listed are located in the city
Source: Dun's Business Rankings 1997; Ward's Business Directory, 1997

PUBLIC SAFETY

Crime Rate

Area	All Crimes	Violent Crimes				Property Crimes		
		Murder	Forcible Rape	Robbery	Aggrav. Assault	Burglary	Larceny -Theft	Motor Vehicle Theft
City	14,549.5	14.6	89.6	906.4	1,938.1	2,502.1	7,054.3	2,044.3
Suburbs[1]	n/a	n/a	n/a	n/a	n/a	n/a	n/a	n/a
MSA[2]	n/a	n/a	n/a	n/a	n/a	n/a	n/a	n/a
U.S.	5,078.9	7.4	36.1	202.4	388.2	943.0	2,975.9	525.9

Note: Crime rate is the number of crimes per 100,000 pop.; (1) defined as all areas within the MSA but located outside the central city; (2) Metropolitan Statistical Area - see Appendix A for areas incl.
Source: FBI Uniform Crime Reports 1996

RECREATION

Culture and Recreation

Museums	Symphony Orchestras	Opera Companies	Dance Companies	Professional Theatres	Zoos	Pro Sports Teams
9	1	1	1	2	1	3

Source: International Directory of the Performing Arts, 1996; Official Museum Directory, 1998; Chamber of Commerce/Economic Development 1997

Library System

The Tampa-Hillsborough County Public Library has 16 branches, holdings of 2,296,250 volumes and a budget of $17,252,648 (1994-1995). *American Library Directory, 1997-1998*

MEDIA

Newspapers

Name	Type	Freq.	Distribution	Circulation
Carrollwood News	General	1x/wk	Local	30,400
The Florida Dollar Stretcher	Black	1x/wk	State	8,000
Florida Sentinel-Bulletin	Black	2x/wk	Local	30,000
The Free Press	General	1x/wk	Area	1,500
La Gaceta	Hispanic	1x/wk	Local	18,000
Lake Area News	n/a	1x/wk	Area	30,000
The Laker	n/a	1x/wk	Area	21,300
Lutz Community News	General	1x/wk	Local	10,000
Nuevo Siglo	Hispanic	1x/wk	Area	22,000
Pennysaver Weekly News	General	1x/wk	Local	8,000
Sun Times of Canada	Native Canadian	1x/wk	National	13,500
Tampa Tribune	n/a	7x/wk	Area	268,876
Temple Terrace Beacon	General	1x/wk	Local	22,000
Town 'n Country News	General	1x/wk	Area	23,000
USF Oracle	n/a	5x/wk	Campus	community & alumni

Note: Includes newspapers with circulations of 1,000 or more located in the city; n/a not available
Source: Burrelle's Media Directory, 1998 Edition

AM Radio Stations

Call Letters	Freq. (kHz)	Target Audience	Station Format	Music Format
WRMD	680	Hispanic	M	Contemporary Top 40/Spanish
WBDN	760	General	T	n/a
WGUL	860	General	M	n/a
WFLA	970	General	N/T	n/a
WTMP	1150	Black	M/N/S	Adult Contemporary/Christian/Oldies/R&B
WDAE	1250	General	M	Adult Contemporary
WQBN	1300	Hispanic	M/N	Spanish
WWAB	1330	General	M/T	R&B/Urban Contemporary
WRBQ	1380	General	M/N/S	Urban Contemporary
WAMA	1550	Hispanic	M/N/S	Adult Contemporary/Spanish

Note: Stations included broadcast in the Tampa metro area; n/a not available
Station Format: E = Educational; M = Music; N = News; S = Sports; T = Talk
Source: Burrelle's Media Directory, 1998 Edition

FM Radio Stations

Call Letters	Freq. (mHz)	Target Audience	Station Format	Music Format
WMNF	88.5	General	M/N/S	Jazz/R&B
WUSF	89.7	General	M/N	Classical/Jazz
WBVM	90.5	General	M/N	Christian/Classical
WFLZ	93.3	General	M	Contemporary Top 40
WSJT	94.1	General	M/N/S	Jazz
WMTX	95.7	n/a	M	Adult Contemporary
WAKS	100.7	n/a	M/N	Adult Contemporary/Oldies
WDUV	103.5	General	M	Easy Listening
WRBQ	104.7	General	M/N/S	Country

Note: Stations included broadcast in the Tampa metro area; n/a not available
Station Format: E = Educational; M = Music; N = News; S = Sports; T = Talk
Source: Burrelle's Media Directory, 1998 Edition

Television Stations

Name	Ch.	Affiliation	Type	Owner
WEDU	3	PBS	Public	Florida West Coast Public Broadcasting
WFLA	8	NBC	Commercial	Media General Broadcasting Group Inc.
WTVT	13	Fox	Commercial	New World Communications of Tampa Inc.
WUSF	16	PBS	Public	University of South Florida
WFTS	28	ABC	Commercial	Scripps Howard Broadcasting
WWWB	32	WB	Commercial	WWWB-TV Company, Hearst Broadcasting
WTTA	38	Fox Children's Network	Commercial	Bay TV
WBHS	50	HSN	Non-Commercial	Silver King Communications Inc.
WRMD	57	Telemundo	Commercial	Telemundo Group Inc.
WVEA	61	Univision	Commercial	Latin Communications Group Television

Note: Stations included broadcast in the Tampa metro area
Source: Burrelle's Media Directory, 1998 Edition

CLIMATE

Average and Extreme Temperatures

Temperature	Jan	Feb	Mar	Apr	May	Jun	Jul	Aug	Sep	Oct	Nov	Dec	Ann
Extreme High (°F)	85	88	91	93	98	99	97	98	96	94	90	86	99
Average High (°F)	70	72	76	82	87	90	90	90	89	84	77	72	82
Average Temp. (°F)	60	62	67	72	78	81	82	83	81	75	68	62	73
Average Low (°F)	50	52	56	61	67	73	74	74	73	66	57	52	63
Extreme Low (°F)	21	24	29	40	49	53	63	67	57	40	23	18	18

Note: Figures cover the years 1948-1990
Source: National Climatic Data Center, International Station Meteorological Climate Summary, 3/95

Average Precipitation/Snowfall/Humidity

Precip./Humidity	Jan	Feb	Mar	Apr	May	Jun	Jul	Aug	Sep	Oct	Nov	Dec	Ann
Avg. Precip. (in.)	2.1	2.8	3.5	1.8	3.0	5.6	7.3	7.9	6.5	2.3	1.8	2.1	46.7
Avg. Snowfall (in.)	Tr	Tr	Tr	0	0	0	0	0	0	0	0	Tr	Tr
Avg. Rel. Hum. 7am (%)	87	87	86	86	85	86	88	90	91	89	88	87	88
Avg. Rel. Hum. 4pm (%)	56	55	54	51	52	60	65	66	64	57	56	57	58

Note: Figures cover the years 1948-1990; Tr = Trace amounts (<0.05 in. of rain; <0.5 in. of snow)
Source: National Climatic Data Center, International Station Meteorological Climate Summary, 3/95

Weather Conditions

Temperature			Daytime Sky			Precipitation		
32°F & below	45°F & below	90°F & above	Clear	Partly cloudy	Cloudy	0.01 inch or more precip.	0.1 inch or more snow/ice	Thunder-storms
3	35	85	81	204	80	107	< 1	87

Note: Figures are average number of days per year and covers the years 1948-1990
Source: National Climatic Data Center, International Station Meteorological Climate Summary, 3/95

AIR & WATER QUALITY

Maximum Pollutant Concentrations

	Particulate Matter (ug/m^3)	Carbon Monoxide (ppm)	Sulfur Dioxide (ppm)	Nitrogen Dioxide (ppm)	Ozone (ppm)	Lead (ug/m^3)
MSA[1] Level	81	4	0.087	0.011	0.11	n/a
NAAQS[2]	150	9	0.140	0.053	0.12	1.50
Met NAAQS?	Yes	Yes	Yes	Yes	Yes	n/a

Note: (1) Metropolitan Statistical Area - see Appendix A for areas included; (2) National Ambient Air Quality Standards; ppm = parts per million; ug/m^3 = micrograms per cubic meter; n/a not available
Source: EPA, National Air Quality and Emissions Trends Report, 1996

Pollutant Standards Index

In the Tampa MSA (see Appendix A for areas included), the Pollutant Standards Index (PSI) exceeded 100 on 2 days in 1996. A PSI value greater than 100 indicates that air quality would be in the unhealthful range on that day. *EPA, National Air Quality and Emissions Trends Report, 1996*

Drinking Water

Water System Name	Pop. Served	Primary Water Source Type	Number of Violations in Fiscal Year 1997	Type of Violation/ Contaminants
City of Tampa-Water Dept	475,000	Surface	None	None

Note: Data as of January 16, 1998
Source: EPA, Office of Ground Water and Drinking Water, Safe Drinking Water Information System

Tampa tap water is alkaline, moderately hard and not fluoridated.
Editor & Publisher Market Guide, 1998

Comparative Statistics

Population Growth: City

City	Population			% Change	
	1980	1990	1996[1]	1980-90	1990-96
Abilene	98,312	106,665	108,476	8.5	1.7
Atlanta	425,022	394,017	401,907	-7.3	2.0
Austin	345,544	465,577	541,278	34.7	16.3
Brownsville	84,997	98,962	132,091	16.4	33.5
Corpus Christi	231,999	257,453	280,260	11.0	8.9
Dallas	904,074	1,006,831	1,053,292	11.4	4.6
Ft. Lauderdale	153,279	149,377	151,805	-2.5	1.6
Ft. Worth	385,166	447,619	479,716	16.2	7.2
Houston	1,595,167	1,630,672	1,744,058	2.2	7.0
Jacksonville	540,920	635,230	679,792	17.4	7.0
Knoxville	175,030	165,121	167,535	-5.7	1.5
Miami	346,865	358,548	365,127	3.4	1.8
Mobile	200,396	196,278	202,581	-2.1	3.2
Nashville	455,663	488,518	511,263	7.2	4.7
New Orleans	557,515	496,938	476,625	-10.9	-4.1
Orlando	128,291	164,693	173,902	28.4	5.6
San Antonio	785,809	935,927	1,067,816	19.1	14.1
Tallahassee	81,548	124,773	136,812	53.0	9.6
Tampa	271,523	280,015	285,206	3.1	1.9
U.S.	**226,545,805**	**248,765,170**	**265,179,411**	**9.8**	**6.6**

Note: (1) Census Bureau estimate as of 7/96
Source: 1980 Census; 1990 Census of Population and Housing, Summary Tape File 3C

Population Growth: Metro Area

MSA[1]	Population			% Change	
	1980	1990	1996[2]	1980-90	1990-96
Abilene	(a)	119,655	122,130	(a)	2.1
Atlanta	2,138,231	2,833,511	3,541,230	32.5	25.0
Austin	536,688	781,572	1,041,330	45.6	33.2
Brownsville	209,727	260,120	315,015	24.0	21.1
Corpus Christi	326,228	349,894	384,056	7.3	9.8
Dallas	1,957,378	2,553,362	3,047,983	30.4	19.4
Ft. Lauderdale	1,018,200	1,255,488	1,438,228	23.3	14.6
Ft. Worth	(b)	1,332,053	1,526,578	(b)	14.6
Houston	2,735,766	3,301,937	3,791,921	20.7	14.8
Jacksonville	722,252	906,727	1,008,633	25.5	11.2
Knoxville	565,970	604,816	649,277	6.9	7.4
Miami	1,625,781	1,937,094	2,076,175	19.1	7.2
Mobile	443,536	476,923	518,975	7.5	8.8
Nashville	850,505	985,026	1,117,178	15.8	13.4
New Orleans	1,256,256	1,238,816	1,312,890	-1.4	6.0
Orlando	700,055	1,072,748	1,417,291	53.2	32.1
San Antonio	1,072,125	1,302,099	1,490,111	21.5	14.4
Tallahassee	190,329	233,598	259,380	22.7	11.0
Tampa	1,613,621	2,067,959	2,199,231	28.2	6.3
U.S.	**226,545,805**	**248,765,170**	**265,179,411**	**9.8**	**6.6**

Note: (1) Metropolitan Statistical Area - see Appendix A for areas included; (2) Census Bureau estimate as of 7/96;
(a) Abilene was not defined as an MSA in 1980; (b) Ft. Worth was part of the Dallas-Ft. Worth MSA in 1980
Source: 1980 Census; 1990 Census of Population and Housing, Summary Tape File 3C

Population Characteristics: City

| City | 1990 Percent of Total (%) | | | | | |
	White	Black	American Indian/ Esk./Aleut.	Asian/ Pacific Islander	Other	Hispanic Origin[1]
Abilene	82.6	7.0	0.4	1.3	8.9	15.1
Atlanta	31.1	67.1	0.2	0.8	0.9	1.9
Austin	70.7	12.4	0.4	3.0	13.5	22.6
Brownsville	84.6	0.2	0.3	0.3	14.5	90.1
Corpus Christi	76.3	4.8	0.4	0.9	17.7	50.0
Dallas	55.4	29.5	0.5	2.1	12.5	20.3
Ft. Lauderdale	69.6	28.1	0.3	0.8	1.2	7.1
Ft. Worth	63.9	22.0	0.4	1.9	11.7	19.2
Houston	52.8	28.1	0.3	4.0	14.9	27.2
Jacksonville	71.8	25.3	0.4	1.9	0.7	2.5
Knoxville	82.8	15.6	0.4	1.0	0.2	0.6
Miami	65.8	27.3	0.1	0.6	6.1	62.3
Mobile	59.5	39.0	0.3	1.0	0.2	1.1
Nashville	73.9	24.3	0.3	1.3	0.3	0.8
New Orleans	34.9	62.1	0.2	1.9	1.0	3.2
Orlando	68.6	26.9	0.3	1.5	2.7	8.6
San Antonio	72.3	7.0	0.4	1.1	19.2	55.3
Tallahassee	68.2	29.1	0.2	1.8	0.7	3.1
Tampa	71.0	25.0	0.4	1.4	2.3	14.7
U.S.	**80.3**	**12.0**	**0.8**	**2.9**	**3.9**	**8.8**

Note: (1) People of Hispanic origin can be of any race
Source: 1990 Census of Population and Housing, Summary Tape File 3C

Population Characteristics: Metro Area

| MSA[1] | 1990 Percent of Total (%) | | | | | |
	White	Black	American Indian/ Esk./Aleut.	Asian/ Pacific Islander	Other	Hispanic Origin[2]
Abilene	84.0	6.2	0.3	1.2	8.3	14.2
Atlanta	71.3	26.0	0.2	1.8	0.7	1.9
Austin	76.9	9.2	0.4	2.3	11.2	20.2
Brownsville	82.4	0.3	0.2	0.2	16.7	81.7
Corpus Christi	75.9	3.8	0.4	0.7	19.2	51.6
Dallas	72.7	16.1	0.5	2.6	8.1	14.1
Ft. Lauderdale	81.8	15.4	0.2	1.3	1.2	8.4
Ft. Worth	80.4	10.8	0.5	2.2	6.1	11.0
Houston	66.4	18.5	0.3	3.8	11.1	21.1
Jacksonville	77.4	20.0	0.4	1.6	0.6	2.4
Knoxville	92.9	5.9	0.3	0.7	0.1	0.6
Miami	73.1	20.6	0.1	1.3	4.9	49.0
Mobile	71.1	27.3	0.7	0.7	0.2	0.9
Nashville	83.1	15.5	0.3	0.9	0.2	0.7
New Orleans	62.2	34.8	0.3	1.7	1.0	4.2
Orlando	82.8	12.4	0.3	1.9	2.5	8.8
San Antonio	75.2	6.8	0.4	1.2	16.4	47.4
Tallahassee	67.8	30.1	0.2	1.2	0.6	2.5
Tampa	88.4	8.9	0.3	1.1	1.2	6.6
U.S.	**80.3**	**12.0**	**0.8**	**2.9**	**3.9**	**8.8**

Note: (1) Metropolitan Statistical Area - see Appendix A for areas included;
(2) People of Hispanic origin can be of any race
Source: 1990 Census of Population and Housing, Summary Tape File 3C

Age: City

City	Median Age (Years)	Age Distribution (%)						
		Under 5	Under 18	18-24	25-44	45-64	65+	80+
Abilene	29.6	8.3	27.1	14.0	31.1	16.2	11.6	3.0
Atlanta	31.4	7.6	24.1	13.0	34.7	16.8	11.3	2.9
Austin	28.9	7.5	23.1	17.2	38.7	13.6	7.4	1.8
Brownsville	25.9	9.0	36.6	11.7	28.0	15.1	8.6	1.6
Corpus Christi	30.5	8.2	30.1	9.7	32.8	17.4	10.0	1.9
Dallas	30.5	8.0	25.0	11.4	37.6	16.4	9.7	2.2
Ft. Lauderdale	37.1	6.0	18.8	8.1	34.8	20.4	17.9	5.0
Ft. Worth	30.3	8.6	26.6	11.7	34.7	15.9	11.2	2.6
Houston	30.3	8.3	26.7	11.6	36.4	17.1	8.2	1.6
Jacksonville	31.2	8.1	26.1	11.1	34.6	17.5	10.6	2.1
Knoxville	32.4	5.9	19.8	16.5	31.1	17.2	15.4	3.8
Miami	35.9	7.1	23.0	9.1	29.6	21.6	16.7	4.1
Mobile	32.5	7.5	26.3	10.9	31.1	17.9	13.7	3.1
Nashville	32.2	7.0	22.9	11.6	36.2	17.9	11.4	2.6
New Orleans	31.5	7.7	27.6	11.1	31.4	16.9	13.0	3.0
Orlando	30.2	6.8	21.0	16.1	36.4	15.2	11.4	2.9
San Antonio	29.8	8.4	29.1	11.5	32.4	16.7	10.4	2.2
Tallahassee	26.9	5.5	19.3	26.4	31.9	13.6	8.8	1.9
Tampa	33.2	7.4	22.9	10.8	33.0	18.7	14.6	3.4
U.S.	**32.9**	**7.3**	**25.6**	**10.5**	**32.6**	**18.7**	**12.5**	**2.8**

Source: 1990 Census of Population and Housing, Summary Tape File 3C

Age: Metro Area

MSA[1]	Median Age (Years)	Age Distribution (%)						
		Under 5	Under 18	18-24	25-44	45-64	65+	80+
Abilene	30.2	8.1	27.2	13.1	30.9	16.8	11.9	3.1
Atlanta	31.4	7.7	25.9	10.7	37.8	17.7	7.9	1.6
Austin	29.4	7.7	25.3	14.9	38.1	14.4	7.3	1.7
Brownsville	27.4	8.9	35.4	10.9	27.5	15.7	10.5	1.9
Corpus Christi	30.5	8.2	30.7	9.6	31.8	17.8	10.0	1.9
Dallas	30.4	8.4	27.2	10.7	37.7	16.7	7.7	1.7
Ft. Lauderdale	37.6	6.2	20.4	8.0	32.0	18.9	20.7	5.1
Ft. Worth	30.6	8.4	27.3	10.7	36.3	17.1	8.6	1.8
Houston	30.4	8.5	28.9	10.4	36.9	16.7	7.0	1.4
Jacksonville	32.0	7.8	26.0	10.6	34.2	18.3	10.9	2.2
Knoxville	34.5	6.2	22.9	11.4	32.0	20.5	13.3	2.8
Miami	34.2	7.1	24.2	9.7	31.6	20.5	14.0	3.5
Mobile	32.6	7.5	27.9	9.8	31.0	18.8	12.5	2.5
Nashville	32.4	7.1	25.1	10.7	35.0	18.5	10.6	2.3
New Orleans	31.8	7.7	27.9	10.1	32.8	18.1	11.0	2.2
Orlando	32.1	7.2	24.3	11.3	35.2	18.3	10.9	2.2
San Antonio	30.3	8.3	29.0	11.0	32.7	17.2	10.2	2.1
Tallahassee	29.3	6.6	23.9	18.4	33.2	15.6	8.8	1.8
Tampa	38.5	6.0	20.4	8.4	29.7	20.0	21.5	4.9
U.S.	**32.9**	**7.3**	**25.6**	**10.5**	**32.6**	**18.7**	**12.5**	**2.8**

Note: (1) Metropolitan Statistical Area - see Appendix A for areas included
Source: 1990 Census of Population and Housing, Summary Tape File 3C

Male/Female Ratio: City

City	Number of males per 100 females (all ages)	Number of males per 100 females (18 years old+)
Abilene	93.9	90.7
Atlanta	91.0	87.8
Austin	99.9	98.4
Brownsville	89.3	82.5
Corpus Christi	95.2	91.4
Dallas	97.0	94.5
Ft. Lauderdale	100.9	101.6
Ft. Worth	96.3	94.3
Houston	98.4	96.3
Jacksonville	95.4	92.9
Knoxville	86.7	83.7
Miami	92.6	90.1
Mobile	86.3	81.2
Nashville	90.2	86.5
New Orleans	86.6	81.6
Orlando	101.0	101.0
San Antonio	93.0	88.7
Tallahassee	90.8	88.3
Tampa	92.8	88.7
U.S.	**95.0**	**91.9**

Source: 1990 Census of Population, General Population Characteristics

Male/Female Ratio: Metro Area

MSA[1]	Number of males per 100 females (all ages)	Number of males per 100 females (18 years old+)
Abilene	94.1	91.0
Atlanta	94.7	91.5
Austin	99.8	97.8
Brownsville	91.8	86.6
Corpus Christi	96.0	92.2
Dallas	97.2	94.5
Ft. Lauderdale	91.7	88.8
Ft. Worth	97.8	95.4
Houston	98.8	96.6
Jacksonville	95.5	93.1
Knoxville	92.2	88.9
Miami	91.6	88.1
Mobile	91.3	86.2
Nashville	93.2	89.5
New Orleans	90.5	86.3
Orlando	97.3	95.3
San Antonio	94.6	90.7
Tallahassee	91.5	88.9
Tampa	91.0	87.8
U.S.	**95.0**	**91.9**

Note: (1) Metropolitan Statistical Area - see Appendix A for areas included
Source: 1990 Census of Population, General Population Characteristics

Educational Attainment by Race: City

City	High School Graduate (%)					Bachelor's Degree (%)				
	Total	White	Black	Other	Hisp.[1]	Total	White	Black	Other	Hisp.[1]
Abilene	76.0	78.8	73.5	49.2	46.9	22.0	24.3	9.7	7.9	5.6
Atlanta	69.9	86.7	59.8	62.1	54.4	26.6	51.9	11.1	34.6	21.7
Austin	82.3	88.7	69.6	58.4	57.9	34.4	40.0	16.5	18.4	13.8
Brownsville	45.5	46.4	60.9	40.3	39.1	12.2	12.7	45.3	9.2	8.7
Corpus Christi	70.9	74.3	61.8	56.1	54.4	17.8	20.2	8.0	8.5	7.8
Dallas	73.5	82.5	67.2	38.6	33.9	27.1	36.9	10.9	10.9	7.0
Ft. Lauderdale	74.2	83.1	41.6	68.0	61.3	21.9	26.5	4.7	21.2	14.6
Ft. Worth	71.6	79.2	62.6	39.6	37.4	21.5	27.0	8.8	9.7	6.3
Houston	70.5	79.1	66.3	45.0	36.6	25.1	33.0	13.4	14.8	7.3
Jacksonville	76.4	80.2	63.6	77.1	78.9	17.9	19.6	10.9	25.3	20.2
Knoxville	70.8	71.5	64.9	82.7	89.6	21.7	22.9	11.0	48.2	49.3
Miami	47.6	50.6	39.7	42.6	43.0	12.8	15.5	4.9	10.7	10.5
Mobile	74.8	82.2	61.1	69.9	71.2	21.4	27.0	10.7	25.5	17.2
Nashville	75.4	77.7	66.7	73.8	73.5	23.6	25.4	16.6	32.3	24.7
New Orleans	68.1	81.4	58.4	57.6	60.3	22.4	36.6	11.6	20.4	18.7
Orlando	78.1	85.2	56.5	69.3	67.0	22.6	26.6	9.8	21.2	17.0
San Antonio	69.1	72.5	72.8	53.4	52.8	17.8	20.6	13.0	7.8	7.1
Tallahassee	85.5	91.4	68.1	92.4	84.4	40.7	46.2	23.3	61.5	33.7
Tampa	70.6	74.7	57.1	61.5	54.4	18.7	21.7	8.0	15.1	11.3
U.S.	**75.2**	**77.9**	**63.1**	**60.4**	**49.8**	**20.3**	**21.5**	**11.4**	**19.4**	**9.2**

Note: Figures shown cover persons 25 years old and over; (1) people of Hispanic origin can be of any race
Source: 1990 Census of Population and Housing, Summary Tape File 3C

Educational Attainment by Race: Metro Area

MSA[1]	High School Graduate (%)					Bachelor's Degree (%)				
	Total	White	Black	Other	Hisp.[2]	Total	White	Black	Other	Hisp.[2]
Abilene	75.4	78.0	73.3	48.2	45.9	20.7	22.6	9.6	7.5	5.4
Atlanta	79.5	82.6	70.3	72.7	69.8	26.8	29.7	16.6	32.3	24.5
Austin	82.5	87.3	70.0	58.5	56.8	32.2	35.9	16.9	17.8	13.1
Brownsville	50.0	52.1	57.8	39.1	39.3	12.0	12.9	21.5	6.8	7.3
Corpus Christi	67.6	71.6	60.2	50.2	49.7	16.0	18.4	8.0	6.7	6.6
Dallas	79.0	84.1	70.1	50.0	41.7	27.6	31.5	13.5	16.5	8.9
Ft. Lauderdale	76.8	79.9	55.5	71.5	68.2	18.8	19.9	10.1	21.4	15.7
Ft. Worth	79.1	82.4	69.4	52.9	47.9	22.6	24.2	12.8	16.1	9.3
Houston	75.1	81.1	68.9	50.2	41.6	25.1	29.0	15.1	16.3	7.9
Jacksonville	77.4	80.6	62.5	76.6	78.5	18.6	20.1	10.8	25.0	20.3
Knoxville	70.3	70.3	66.8	80.1	80.8	19.2	19.2	13.5	42.5	33.7
Miami	65.0	67.6	56.0	57.0	55.1	18.8	20.8	9.9	17.1	14.1
Mobile	70.8	75.2	57.5	59.5	69.3	15.8	18.1	8.6	15.7	15.1
Nashville	74.0	75.6	64.4	75.2	74.2	21.4	22.3	15.1	31.2	23.4
New Orleans	72.3	78.8	58.4	64.5	68.3	19.7	23.6	10.8	21.3	17.5
Orlando	79.9	82.6	60.3	72.0	68.9	21.6	22.8	11.5	21.4	16.0
San Antonio	72.7	75.8	75.9	55.4	54.4	19.4	22.0	14.4	8.2	7.7
Tallahassee	80.3	87.7	59.8	84.8	79.4	32.4	37.6	16.6	53.4	31.3
Tampa	75.1	76.5	60.4	64.4	59.9	17.3	17.7	10.8	18.4	14.2
U.S.	**75.2**	**77.9**	**63.1**	**60.4**	**49.8**	**20.3**	**21.5**	**11.4**	**19.4**	**9.2**

Note: Figures shown cover persons 25 years old and over; (1) Metropolitan Statistical Area - see Appendix A for areas included; (2) people of Hispanic origin can be of any race
Source: 1990 Census of Population and Housing, Summary Tape File 3C

Per Capita/Median/Average Income: City

City	Per Capita ($)	Median Household ($)	Average Household ($)
Abilene	11,857	24,725	32,120
Atlanta	15,279	22,275	37,882
Austin	14,295	25,414	33,947
Brownsville	6,284	15,890	23,219
Corpus Christi	11,755	25,773	33,396
Dallas	16,300	27,489	40,299
Ft. Lauderdale	19,814	27,239	43,756
Ft. Worth	13,162	26,547	34,359
Houston	14,261	26,261	37,296
Jacksonville	13,661	28,305	35,281
Knoxville	12,108	19,923	27,960
Miami	9,799	16,925	26,507
Mobile	12,509	22,446	31,715
Nashville	14,490	27,821	35,188
New Orleans	11,372	18,477	29,283
Orlando	13,879	26,119	33,136
San Antonio	10,884	23,584	30,622
Tallahassee	13,247	23,453	32,019
Tampa	13,277	22,772	31,813
U.S.	**14,420**	**30,056**	**38,453**

Note: Figures are for 1989
Source: 1990 Census of Population and Housing, Summary Tape File 3C

Per Capita/Median/Average Income: Metro Area

MSA[1]	Per Capita ($)	Median Household ($)	Average Household ($)
Abilene	11,791	24,661	31,840
Atlanta	16,897	36,051	44,968
Austin	14,521	28,474	36,754
Brownsville	7,125	17,336	24,858
Corpus Christi	11,065	24,952	32,308
Dallas	16,455	33,277	43,582
Ft. Lauderdale	16,883	30,571	39,823
Ft. Worth	14,842	32,121	39,560
Houston	15,091	31,473	41,650
Jacksonville	14,141	29,514	36,739
Knoxville	12,984	25,134	32,693
Miami	13,686	26,909	37,903
Mobile	11,388	23,645	30,703
Nashville	14,567	30,223	37,811
New Orleans	12,108	24,442	32,569
Orlando	14,895	31,230	39,069
San Antonio	11,865	26,092	33,646
Tallahassee	13,122	26,209	34,215
Tampa	14,374	26,036	33,685
U.S.	**14,420**	**30,056**	**38,453**

Note: Figures are for 1989; (1) Metropolitan Statistical Area - see Appendix A for areas included
Source: 1990 Census of Population and Housing, Summary Tape File 3C

Household Income Distribution: City

City	\% of Households Earning								
	Less than $5,000	$5,000 -$9,999	$10,000 -$14,999	$15,000 -$24,999	$25,000 -$34,999	$35,000 -$49,999	$50,000 -$74,999	$75,000 -$99,999	$100,000 and up
Abilene	7.4	10.1	11.4	21.6	17.7	15.8	10.7	2.9	2.3
Atlanta	14.8	11.6	9.9	17.8	13.1	12.5	10.1	3.9	6.3
Austin	8.9	9.5	10.6	20.3	16.1	15.6	11.6	4.0	3.5
Brownsville	16.1	16.4	15.3	20.2	12.8	9.5	6.6	1.8	1.3
Corpus Christi	9.6	10.1	10.2	18.8	15.8	17.4	12.3	3.1	2.7
Dallas	7.3	8.2	9.2	20.2	16.7	15.7	11.8	4.6	6.2
Ft. Lauderdale	7.5	8.9	9.7	19.9	14.9	14.7	12.7	4.6	7.1
Ft. Worth	7.7	9.4	10.1	19.7	17.1	16.7	12.5	3.6	3.2
Houston	8.9	9.1	9.9	19.7	15.8	15.2	12.1	4.5	4.8
Jacksonville	6.9	8.3	9.1	19.3	17.3	18.9	13.4	4.0	2.7
Knoxville	11.7	14.7	12.8	20.4	15.0	13.1	8.0	2.0	2.3
Miami	17.1	15.0	13.3	19.5	12.7	10.6	6.9	2.4	2.6
Mobile	12.6	11.7	10.6	19.3	15.0	13.9	10.8	3.1	3.1
Nashville	7.6	8.3	9.0	19.6	17.3	17.9	13.5	3.7	3.1
New Orleans	18.0	13.4	11.9	17.9	12.6	11.4	8.6	2.8	3.6
Orlando	6.8	8.5	10.2	21.9	17.6	17.1	11.9	3.1	2.7
San Antonio	9.8	10.1	11.2	21.3	16.3	15.1	10.5	3.1	2.4
Tallahassee	11.3	11.8	10.1	19.5	14.5	13.3	12.5	4.2	2.7
Tampa	9.7	11.7	11.5	21.0	16.1	14.6	9.2	2.9	3.4
U.S.	**6.2**	**9.3**	**8.8**	**17.5**	**15.8**	**17.9**	**15.0**	**5.1**	**4.4**

Note: Figures are for 1989
Source: 1990 Census of Population and Housing, Summary Tape File 3C

Household Income Distribution: Metro Area

MSA[1]	\% of Households Earning								
	Less than $5,000	$5,000 -$9,999	$10,000 -$14,999	$15,000 -$24,999	$25,000 -$34,999	$35,000 -$49,999	$50,000 -$74,999	$75,000 -$99,999	$100,000 and up
Abilene	7.7	10.1	11.4	21.5	17.7	15.9	10.7	2.9	2.2
Atlanta	5.3	5.8	6.2	15.2	15.9	19.9	19.0	6.9	5.9
Austin	7.7	8.4	9.5	18.6	15.8	17.2	14.1	4.8	3.9
Brownsville	14.6	15.4	14.3	20.4	13.6	10.8	7.2	2.1	1.5
Corpus Christi	9.9	10.6	10.6	18.9	15.6	16.9	12.0	2.9	2.5
Dallas	5.3	6.4	7.4	17.1	16.2	18.6	16.9	6.3	5.9
Ft. Lauderdale	5.2	8.2	8.8	18.6	16.0	17.8	15.4	5.3	4.7
Ft. Worth	5.1	6.9	8.0	17.6	16.6	19.3	17.0	5.5	4.0
Houston	6.7	7.3	8.2	17.2	15.5	17.5	16.1	6.0	5.5
Jacksonville	6.2	7.9	8.8	19.0	17.3	18.9	14.4	4.3	3.2
Knoxville	7.9	11.4	10.8	19.7	16.3	15.9	12.1	3.3	2.7
Miami	9.4	9.9	9.6	17.7	15.0	15.7	13.0	4.7	4.9
Mobile	10.7	11.1	10.7	19.9	15.9	15.4	11.1	2.8	2.4
Nashville	6.7	7.8	8.3	18.1	17.1	19.0	14.9	4.4	3.7
New Orleans	11.6	10.7	10.4	18.2	15.1	15.5	11.8	3.5	3.3
Orlando	4.2	6.6	8.4	19.1	18.1	19.5	15.6	4.7	3.8
San Antonio	8.5	9.0	10.2	20.2	16.5	16.7	12.3	3.6	3.0
Tallahassee	9.5	10.4	9.4	18.6	15.5	15.5	13.6	4.3	3.2
Tampa	5.5	9.7	11.0	21.6	17.3	16.8	11.5	3.5	3.0
U.S.	**6.2**	**9.3**	**8.8**	**17.5**	**15.8**	**17.9**	**15.0**	**5.1**	**4.4**

Note: Figures are for 1989; (1) Metropolitan Statistical Area - see Appendix A for areas included
Source: 1990 Census of Population and Housing, Summary Tape File 3C

Effective Buying Income: City

City	Per Capita ($)	Median Household ($)	Average Household ($)
Abilene	12,708	27,010	35,710
Atlanta	16,720	26,038	42,362
Austin	17,494	31,362	42,133
Brownsville	7,361	19,372	27,978
Corpus Christi	13,909	30,976	40,284
Dallas	18,644	32,897	47,180
Ft. Lauderdale	20,401	29,292	46,104
Ft. Worth	15,063	30,943	40,209
Houston	16,632	31,794	44,389
Jacksonville	15,500	32,781	41,119
Knoxville	15,019	24,643	35,092
Miami	10,351	18,910	29,009
Mobile	15,296	28,292	39,295
Nashville	18,826	36,179	45,647
New Orleans	13,684	22,908	36,135
Orlando	15,798	29,982	39,662
San Antonio	12,566	27,690	36,061
Tallahassee	15,643	28,173	38,942
Tampa	15,312	27,031	37,528
U.S.	**15,444**	**33,201**	**41,849**

Note: Data as of 1/1/97
Source: Standard Rate & Data Service, Newspaper Advertising Source, 2/98

Effective Buying Income: Metro Area

MSA[1]	Per Capita ($)	Median Household ($)	Average Household ($)
Abilene	13,015	27,639	36,177
Atlanta	17,633	39,042	47,409
Austin	17,880	35,778	46,175
Brownsville	8,600	21,681	31,061
Corpus Christi	13,598	31,004	40,308
Dallas	19,075	40,337	51,436
Ft. Lauderdale	18,145	33,566	43,263
Ft. Worth	17,405	38,608	46,856
Houston	18,065	39,455	50,894
Jacksonville	16,757	35,504	44,623
Knoxville	16,583	31,837	41,476
Miami	14,582	29,945	41,546
Mobile	14,734	30,936	39,739
Nashville	19,141	39,910	49,810
New Orleans	14,569	30,096	39,531
Orlando	16,817	35,073	44,469
San Antonio	13,995	31,298	40,458
Tallahassee	16,078	32,532	42,642
Tampa	16,754	30,996	40,199
U.S.	**15,444**	**33,201**	**41,849**

Note: Data as of 1/1/97; (1) Metropolitan Statistical Area - see Appendix A for areas included
Source: Standard Rate & Data Service, Newspaper Advertising Source, 2/98

Effective Household Buying Income Distribution: City

City	% of Households Earning						
	$10,000 -$19,999	$20,000 -$34,999	$35,000 -$49,999	$50,000 -$74,999	$75,000 -$99,000	$100,000 -$124,999	$125,000 and up
Abilene	20.8	27.4	16.8	13.5	3.7	0.8	1.7
Atlanta	18.2	21.5	13.5	12.4	5.2	2.4	4.6
Austin	17.1	23.7	16.8	16.2	6.4	2.6	2.9
Brownsville	25.3	22.6	11.6	9.1	3.2	0.9	1.0
Corpus Christi	17.2	22.4	17.7	17.0	6.0	1.7	2.2
Dallas	15.9	24.7	17.0	15.4	6.5	2.9	5.0
Ft. Lauderdale	18.6	24.5	15.1	14.4	5.3	2.5	4.7
Ft. Worth	17.6	24.5	17.6	16.3	5.7	1.9	2.3
Houston	16.6	23.5	16.4	15.5	6.9	2.8	3.9
Jacksonville	16.2	24.6	19.3	17.7	6.0	1.8	1.9
Knoxville	21.9	23.4	15.2	12.2	4.1	1.2	2.0
Miami	23.7	21.9	11.4	8.5	3.0	1.1	1.7
Mobile	17.9	22.9	15.6	14.9	5.5	1.8	2.6
Nashville	13.9	22.9	18.3	19.6	8.0	2.7	2.9
New Orleans	19.7	20.6	12.7	11.7	4.7	1.8	2.9
Orlando	17.9	27.2	18.4	15.5	4.8	1.6	1.8
San Antonio	19.2	25.4	16.6	14.0	4.9	1.6	1.7
Tallahassee	18.0	22.6	14.9	14.6	7.2	2.2	2.0
Tampa	20.0	24.7	16.3	13.2	4.4	1.6	2.7
U.S.	**16.5**	**23.4**	**18.3**	**18.2**	**6.4**	**2.1**	**2.4**

Note: Data as of 1/1/97
Source: Standard Rate & Data Service, Newspaper Advertising Source, 2/98

Effective Household Buying Income Distribution: Metro Area

MSA[1]	% of Households Earning						
	$10,000 -$19,999	$20,000 -$34,999	$35,000 -$49,999	$50,000 -$74,999	$75,000 -$99,000	$100,000 -$124,999	$125,000 and up
Abilene	20.2	26.6	17.4	14.0	4.0	0.9	1.7
Atlanta	12.4	22.5	19.9	21.6	8.2	2.8	3.1
Austin	14.9	21.9	17.2	18.8	8.3	3.2	3.3
Brownsville	23.7	22.9	13.1	10.4	3.9	1.3	1.3
Corpus Christi	17.3	22.2	17.1	17.3	6.4	1.8	2.2
Dallas	12.5	21.4	18.1	20.9	9.6	3.7	4.6
Ft. Lauderdale	16.6	23.9	17.9	18.1	6.7	2.4	2.9
Ft. Worth	13.6	22.2	18.7	21.0	9.1	3.1	3.0
Houston	13.1	20.8	17.1	19.9	9.8	3.9	4.6
Jacksonville	14.8	23.6	19.4	19.2	7.2	2.3	2.6
Knoxville	17.6	23.0	17.2	16.9	6.8	2.2	2.4
Miami	17.6	22.5	15.9	15.7	6.0	2.3	3.3
Mobile	17.0	23.3	16.9	17.1	6.1	1.9	2.1
Nashville	12.6	20.7	18.5	21.3	9.4	3.4	3.9
New Orleans	17.1	22.3	16.4	16.4	6.0	2.0	2.5
Orlando	15.6	25.0	19.2	18.6	7.2	2.4	2.7
San Antonio	17.0	24.3	17.5	16.7	6.1	2.0	2.2
Tallahassee	16.1	21.9	16.6	16.8	7.9	2.7	2.6
Tampa	18.5	26.1	17.9	15.9	5.7	2.0	2.3
U.S.	**16.5**	**23.4**	**18.3**	**18.2**	**6.4**	**2.1**	**2.4**

Note: Data as of 1/1/97; (1) Metropolitan Statistical Area - see Appendix A for areas included
Source: Standard Rate & Data Service, Newspaper Advertising Source, 2/98

Poverty Rates by Race and Age: City

City	Total (%)	By Race (%)				By Age (%)		
		White	Black	Other	Hisp.[1]	Under 5 years old	Under 18 years old	65 years and over
Abilene	15.3	12.0	24.6	33.7	32.4	22.7	19.3	14.7
Atlanta	27.3	9.8	35.0	35.5	30.5	47.1	42.9	25.1
Austin	17.9	13.5	26.5	30.2	27.4	23.4	21.5	11.7
Brownsville	43.9	44.3	16.4	42.0	47.3	54.0	54.3	34.5
Corpus Christi	20.0	16.8	34.8	29.4	27.9	30.3	27.2	19.1
Dallas	18.0	9.5	29.1	27.2	27.8	27.8	27.3	14.6
Ft. Lauderdale	17.1	8.8	38.1	17.3	21.0	33.2	31.0	10.8
Ft. Worth	17.4	10.8	31.3	25.4	25.9	26.0	24.9	14.4
Houston	20.7	12.4	30.7	29.3	30.7	31.4	30.0	17.8
Jacksonville	13.0	7.5	28.6	12.3	15.0	19.9	18.6	16.1
Knoxville	20.8	17.4	38.6	25.3	34.4	32.0	29.8	16.2
Miami	31.2	25.0	46.0	32.0	28.5	46.9	44.1	32.2
Mobile	22.4	9.3	41.9	30.1	19.3	35.4	33.4	17.8
Nashville	13.4	8.6	27.9	18.1	14.3	22.5	20.4	15.1
New Orleans	31.6	11.8	42.2	37.4	26.1	48.8	46.3	24.6
Orlando	15.8	8.2	33.9	20.6	21.6	29.0	27.1	16.1
San Antonio	22.6	19.1	30.3	32.3	30.8	35.4	32.5	19.1
Tallahassee	22.3	16.7	34.8	31.5	38.3	24.8	21.6	13.5
Tampa	19.4	12.2	39.8	21.0	20.6	35.0	30.9	19.4
U.S.	**13.1**	**9.8**	**29.5**	**23.1**	**25.3**	**20.1**	**18.3**	**12.8**

Note: Figures show the percent of people living below the poverty line in 1989. The average poverty threshold was $12,674 for a family of four in 1989; (1) People of Hispanic origin can be of any race
Source: 1990 Census of Population and Housing, Summary Tape File 3C

Poverty Rates by Race and Age: Metro Area

MSA[1]	Total (%)	By Race (%)				By Age (%)		
		White	Black	Other	Hisp.[2]	Under 5 years old	Under 18 years old	65 years and over
Abilene	15.4	12.5	24.5	34.1	32.8	23.1	19.4	16.1
Atlanta	10.0	5.4	22.4	14.4	16.2	15.5	13.9	14.3
Austin	15.3	11.8	26.2	27.7	26.3	19.1	17.4	13.0
Brownsville	39.7	38.7	24.1	44.4	45.9	50.9	50.7	26.9
Corpus Christi	21.6	17.9	35.9	32.7	30.5	32.6	29.1	20.4
Dallas	12.0	7.2	26.7	22.7	24.0	17.2	16.2	13.1
Ft. Lauderdale	10.2	7.0	26.8	13.2	13.7	15.5	15.0	9.0
Ft. Worth	11.0	7.7	27.0	21.8	22.2	16.5	14.7	12.2
Houston	15.1	9.4	27.9	24.8	26.6	21.6	20.2	16.0
Jacksonville	11.8	7.4	29.2	12.0	13.9	18.6	16.8	14.5
Knoxville	14.2	12.9	33.6	19.7	18.7	21.8	18.7	16.1
Miami	17.9	14.2	30.3	21.5	19.5	24.9	24.3	20.0
Mobile	19.9	10.8	42.9	31.1	17.4	30.4	28.6	17.9
Nashville	11.3	8.4	27.2	16.1	12.1	17.1	15.0	16.6
New Orleans	21.2	10.1	40.8	25.9	18.7	31.5	30.3	19.2
Orlando	10.0	7.3	26.4	15.0	15.9	14.8	14.0	10.7
San Antonio	19.5	16.2	26.4	30.5	29.3	30.3	27.7	17.2
Tallahassee	18.9	12.2	33.5	30.7	32.7	22.8	20.9	18.0
Tampa	11.4	9.0	33.1	20.4	19.4	20.2	17.6	9.4
U.S.	**13.1**	**9.8**	**29.5**	**23.1**	**25.3**	**20.1**	**18.3**	**12.8**

Note: Figures show the percent of people living below the poverty line in 1989. The average poverty threshold was $12,674 for a family of four in 1989; (1) Metropolitan Statistical Area - see Appendix A for areas included; (2) People of Hispanic origin can be of any race
Source: 1990 Census of Population and Housing, Summary Tape File 3C

Major State and Local Tax Rates

City	State Corp. Income (%)	State Personal Income (%)	Residential Property (effective rate per $100)	Sales & Use State (%)	Sales & Use Local (%)	State Gasoline (cents/ gallon)	State Cigarette (cents/ 20-pack)
Abilene	None[a]	None	n/a	6.25	2.0	20	41
Atlanta	6.0	1.0 - 6.0	2.04	4.0	3.0	7.5	12
Austin	None[a]	None	n/a	6.25	2.0	20	41
Brownsville	None[a]	None	n/a	6.25	2.0	20	41
Corpus Christi	None[a]	None	n/a	6.25	1.5	20	41
Dallas	None[a]	None	n/a	6.25	2.0	20	41
Fort Lauderdale	5.5[b]	None	n/a	6.0	None	12.8[c]	33.9
Fort Worth	None[a]	None	n/a	6.25	2.0	20	41
Houston	None[a]	None	2.61	6.25	2.0	20	41
Jacksonville	5.5[b]	None	1.11	6.0	0.5	12.8[c]	33.9
Knoxville	6.0	6.0[d]	n/a	6.0	2.25	21[e]	13[f]
Miami	5.5[b]	None	n/a	6.0	0.5	12.8[c]	33.9
Mobile	5.0	2.0 - 5.0	n/a	4.0	5.0	18[g]	16.5[h]
Nashville	6.0	6.0[d]	n/a	6.0	2.25	21[e]	13[f]
New Orleans	4.0 - 8.0	2.0 - 6.0	1.61	4.0	5.0	20	20
Orlando	5.5[b]	None	n/a	6.0	None	12.8[c]	33.9
San Antonio	None[a]	None	n/a	6.25	1.5	20	41
Tallahassee	5.5[b]	None	n/a	6.0	1.0	12.8[c]	33.9
Tampa	5.5[b]	None	n/a	6.0	1.0	12.8[c]	33.9

(a) Texas imposes a franchise tax of 4.5% of earned surplus; (b) 3.3% Alternative Minimum Tax. An exemption of $5,000 is allowed; (c) Rate is comprised of 4 cents excise and 8.8 cents motor carrier tax; (d) Applies to interest and dividend income only; (e) Rate is comprised of 20 cents excise and 1 cent motor carrier tax. Does not include a 1 cent local option tax; (f) Counties and cities may impose an additional tax of 1 cent per pack; (g) Rate is comprised of 16 cents excise plus 2 cents motor carrier tax. Rate does not include 1 - 3 cents local option tax; (h) Counties and cities may impose an additional tax of 1 - 6 cents per pack
Source: Source: Federation of Tax Administrators, www.taxadmin.org; Washington D.C. Department of Finance and Revenue, Tax Rates and Tax Burdens in the District of Columbia: A Nationwide Comparison, June 1997

Employment by Industry

MSA[1]	Services	Retail	Gov't.	Manuf.	Finance/ Ins./R.E.	Whole- sale	Transp./ Utilities	Constr.	Mining
Abilene	34.1	21.7	17.9	5.7	4.3	4.8	4.4	4.1	3.0
Atlanta	29.6	18.6	12.8	10.9	6.5	8.3	8.3	4.9	0.1
Austin	28.7	17.8	22.2	13.4	5.2	4.0	3.3	5.3	0.2
Brownsville	28.2	20.3	23.4	12.2	3.6	4.2	4.4	3.6	(a)
Corpus Christi	31.1	19.7	20.0	8.5	4.1	3.8	4.1	7.1	1.5
Dallas	30.7	16.9	11.1	13.7	7.8	7.6	6.9	4.7	0.6
Ft. Lauderdale	34.6	22.4	13.2	6.2	7.1	6.3	4.9	5.2	0.0
Ft. Worth	26.7	20.7	12.8	15.2	4.5	5.4	9.4	4.8	0.6
Houston	30.0	16.9	13.0	11.0	5.3	6.4	7.0	6.8	3.6
Jacksonville	32.5	19.4	13.0	7.2	10.0	5.6	7.0	0.1	(a)
Knoxville	27.1	21.6	17.1	15.3	4.3	5.1	4.4	4.8	0.2
Miami	32.2	18.7	13.9	7.6	7.0	8.5	8.7	3.5	0.0
Mobile	27.2	21.4	15.7	12.5	4.5	5.4	6.0	7.3	(a)
Nashville	30.9	18.7	13.1	15.1	6.2	6.0	5.0	4.9	(a)
New Orleans	30.8	19.0	17.2	7.9	5.1	5.8	6.8	5.0	2.4
Orlando	41.2	19.9	10.5	6.5	5.8	5.5	5.2	0.0	(a)
San Antonio	31.5	20.2	19.9	7.4	6.6	4.4	4.6	5.2	0.3
Tallahassee	25.8	17.8	39.5	3.4	3.8	2.8	2.9	0.1	(a)
Tampa	38.9	18.7	12.3	8.0	7.1	5.7	4.5	4.9	0.0
U.S.	**29.0**	**18.5**	**16.1**	**15.0**	**5.7**	**5.4**	**5.3**	**4.5**	**0.5**

Note: Figures cover non-farm employment as of 12/97 and are not seasonally adjusted; (1) Metropolitan Statistical Area - see Appendix A for areas included; (a) Mining is included with construction
Source: Bureau of Labor Statistics, http://stats.bls.gov

Labor Force, Employment and Job Growth: City

Area	Civilian Labor Force			Workers Employed		
	Dec. '95	Dec. '96	% Chg.	Dec. '95	Dec. '96	% Chg.
Abilene	53,903	53,630	-0.5	51,879	51,920	0.1
Atlanta	216,314	222,211	2.7	201,998	211,163	4.5
Austin	354,750	356,386	0.5	342,933	346,014	0.9
Brownsville	46,450	48,057	3.5	40,580	41,784	3.0
Corpus Christi	136,195	135,863	-0.2	125,789	127,830	1.6
Dallas	642,910	659,571	2.6	614,681	633,958	3.1
Ft. Lauderdale	90,552	93,681	3.5	85,383	88,451	3.6
Ft. Worth	256,691	263,985	2.8	246,141	253,873	3.1
Houston	986,035	998,579	1.3	929,435	950,619	2.3
Jacksonville	347,615	359,408	3.4	335,607	347,361	3.5
Knoxville	92,712	91,615	-1.2	89,425	88,537	-1.0
Miami	179,578	181,432	1.0	161,848	164,547	1.7
Mobile	103,442	107,809	4.2	99,120	103,271	4.2
Nashville	294,593	297,900	1.1	286,962	290,338	1.2
New Orleans	203,096	203,502	0.2	190,033	191,841	1.0
Orlando	103,146	108,383	5.1	99,616	104,867	5.3
San Antonio	509,509	519,826	2.0	489,275	500,305	2.3
Tallahassee	78,855	80,669	2.3	76,420	78,121	2.2
Tampa	157,781	163,166	3.4	151,425	156,998	3.7
U.S.	**134,583,000**	**136,742,000**	**1.6**	**127,903,000**	**130,785,000**	**2.3**

Note: Data is not seasonally adjusted and covers workers 16 years of age and older
Source: Bureau of Labor Statistics, http://stats.bls.gov

Labor Force, Employment and Job Growth: Metro Area

Area	Civilian Labor Force			Workers Employed		
	Dec. '95	Dec. '96	% Chg.	Dec. '95	Dec. '96	% Chg.
Abilene	60,896	60,603	-0.5	58,713	58,759	0.1
Atlanta	2,015,113	2,091,518	3.8	1,941,078	2,029,140	4.5
Austin	640,276	643,741	0.5	621,407	626,991	0.9
Brownsville	123,355	127,539	3.4	109,840	113,098	3.0
Corpus Christi	180,604	180,374	-0.1	166,812	169,519	1.6
Dallas	1,787,077	1,836,829	2.8	1,727,171	1,781,340	3.1
Ft. Lauderdale	737,842	763,545	3.5	704,192	729,497	3.6
Ft. Worth	843,922	868,132	2.9	817,088	842,756	3.1
Houston	2,034,311	2,064,833	1.5	1,939,278	1,983,477	2.3
Jacksonville	515,041	532,507	3.4	498,165	515,612	3.5
Knoxville	347,731	343,762	-1.1	335,309	331,979	-1.0
Miami	1,034,502	1,047,201	1.2	963,771	979,842	1.7
Mobile	259,203	269,529	4.0	249,797	260,259	4.2
Nashville	624,666	631,251	1.1	607,199	614,344	1.2
New Orleans	610,785	610,508	-0.0	576,686	582,172	1.0
Orlando	786,133	825,864	5.1	760,769	800,868	5.3
San Antonio	733,657	748,785	2.1	707,779	723,734	2.3
Tallahassee	142,470	145,695	2.3	138,511	141,593	2.2
Tampa	1,105,649	1,144,836	3.5	1,068,275	1,107,594	3.7
U.S.	**134,583,000**	**136,742,000**	**1.6**	**127,903,000**	**130,785,000**	**2.3**

Note: Data is not seasonally adjusted and covers workers 16 years of age and older;
(1) Metropolitan Statistical Area - see Appendix A for areas included
Source: Bureau of Labor Statistics, http://stats.bls.gov

Unemployment Rate: City

Area	1997											
	Jan.	Feb.	Mar.	Apr.	May	Jun.	Jul.	Aug.	Sep.	Oct.	Nov.	Dec.
Abilene	4.5	4.6	4.8	4.2	4.4	5.0	4.6	4.2	3.8	3.6	3.7	3.2
Atlanta	6.3	6.4	6.4	5.5	5.7	6.7	6.2	6.0	6.3	5.6	4.9	5.0
Austin	3.8	3.6	3.6	3.1	3.1	3.8	3.6	3.6	3.4	3.3	3.2	2.9
Brownsville	14.9	14.9	14.4	14.0	13.7	16.3	16.3	14.0	13.4	13.4	14.2	13.1
Corpus Christi	8.7	8.5	8.4	7.5	7.4	8.8	8.1	7.3	7.1	6.5	6.3	5.9
Dallas	5.1	5.3	5.1	4.6	4.7	5.5	5.2	5.0	4.8	4.5	4.4	3.9
Ft. Lauderdale	6.6	5.9	5.9	6.2	6.3	6.5	5.9	6.0	6.4	6.0	6.1	5.6
Ft. Worth	5.2	5.4	5.0	4.5	4.6	5.4	5.1	4.8	4.7	4.3	4.3	3.8
Houston	6.8	6.6	6.7	6.2	6.1	7.3	6.6	6.1	5.9	5.5	5.4	4.8
Jacksonville	4.3	3.8	3.8	3.8	4.0	4.3	3.9	3.8	3.9	3.6	3.7	3.4
Knoxville	4.6	4.5	4.6	4.3	4.0	5.0	4.9	4.5	4.1	4.2	4.3	3.4
Miami	11.2	10.0	10.1	10.5	10.8	11.4	10.3	10.0	10.5	10.0	10.1	9.3
Mobile	4.7	5.0	4.6	4.5	4.6	6.1	5.5	6.0	5.6	5.4	4.8	4.2
Nashville	3.2	3.0	3.1	3.1	3.0	4.0	3.7	3.7	3.5	3.4	3.1	2.5
New Orleans	6.8	5.3	5.6	5.2	5.9	7.6	7.4	6.9	6.6	6.5	6.3	5.7
Orlando	4.1	3.5	3.5	3.5	3.6	3.8	3.7	3.7	3.8	3.4	3.5	3.2
San Antonio	4.7	4.7	4.6	4.1	4.3	5.6	5.1	4.9	4.6	4.3	4.3	3.8
Tallahassee	3.8	3.3	3.4	3.4	3.9	4.2	3.7	3.4	3.6	3.4	3.5	3.2
Tampa	4.8	4.3	4.2	4.3	4.4	4.6	4.3	4.2	4.4	4.0	4.0	3.8
U.S.	**5.9**	**5.7**	**5.5**	**4.8**	**4.7**	**5.2**	**5.0**	**4.8**	**4.7**	**4.4**	**4.3**	**4.4**

Note: All figures are percentages, are not seasonally adjusted and covers workers 16 years of age and older
Source: Bureau of Labor Statistics, http://stats.bls.gov

Unemployment Rate: Metro Area

Area	1997											
	Jan.	Feb.	Mar.	Apr.	May	Jun.	Jul.	Aug.	Sep.	Oct.	Nov.	Dec.
Abilene	4.3	4.4	4.6	4.0	4.2	4.7	4.4	4.0	3.7	3.4	3.5	3.0
Atlanta	3.6	3.8	3.7	3.3	3.4	4.0	3.8	3.6	3.8	3.4	3.0	3.0
Austin	3.4	3.3	3.3	2.9	2.9	3.5	3.3	3.2	3.1	2.9	2.9	2.6
Brownsville	12.9	13.0	12.5	12.1	11.9	14.2	14.2	12.1	11.6	11.7	12.3	11.3
Corpus Christi	8.8	8.6	8.5	7.6	7.6	9.0	8.3	7.5	7.2	6.6	6.4	6.0
Dallas	3.9	4.0	3.9	3.6	3.6	4.3	4.0	3.8	3.7	3.5	3.4	3.0
Ft. Lauderdale	5.3	4.7	4.7	4.9	5.1	5.2	4.7	4.8	5.1	4.8	4.9	4.5
Ft. Worth	4.0	4.1	3.8	3.5	3.5	4.2	3.9	3.7	3.5	3.3	3.3	2.9
Houston	5.5	5.5	5.4	5.1	5.0	6.0	5.4	5.0	4.8	4.5	4.4	3.9
Jacksonville	4.1	3.6	3.6	3.6	3.7	4.0	3.7	3.5	3.6	3.4	3.5	3.2
Knoxville	5.5	5.4	5.1	4.3	3.7	4.5	4.1	3.8	3.4	3.5	3.9	3.4
Miami	7.8	6.9	7.0	7.3	7.5	7.9	7.2	6.9	7.3	6.9	7.0	6.4
Mobile	4.5	4.8	4.2	4.2	4.1	5.3	4.8	5.0	4.7	4.6	4.0	3.4
Nashville	3.5	3.2	3.3	3.2	3.0	3.9	3.7	3.8	3.7	3.4	3.2	2.7
New Orleans	5.8	4.6	4.8	4.4	4.9	6.5	6.3	5.6	5.4	5.4	5.1	4.6
Orlando	3.9	3.4	3.4	3.4	3.4	3.7	3.6	3.6	3.6	3.3	3.3	3.0
San Antonio	4.2	4.2	4.1	3.7	3.8	5.0	4.6	4.4	4.1	3.8	3.8	3.3
Tallahassee	3.4	3.0	3.0	3.0	3.3	3.6	3.1	3.0	3.2	2.9	3.0	2.8
Tampa	4.0	3.5	3.4	3.5	3.6	3.8	3.6	3.5	3.7	3.4	3.4	3.3
U.S.	**5.9**	**5.7**	**5.5**	**4.8**	**4.7**	**5.2**	**5.0**	**4.8**	**4.7**	**4.4**	**4.3**	**4.4**

Note: All figures are percentages, are not seasonally adjusted and covers workers 16 years of age and older
(1) Metropolitan Statistical Area - see Appendix A for areas included
Source: Bureau of Labor Statistics, http://stats.bls.gov

Average Wages: Selected Professional Occupations

MSA[1] (Month/Year)	Accountant III	Attorney III	Computer Program. II	Engineer III	Systems Analyst II	Systems Analyst Supv./Mgr. II
Abilene (12/93)	672	-	-	842	-	-
Atlanta (3/96)	789	1,158	591	942	892	1,342
Austin (8/95)	-	-	653	-	908	-
Brownsville	-	-	-	-	-	-
Corpus Christi (9/95)	656	809	584	936	756	-
Dallas (3/96)	831	1,183	637	939	909	1,350
Ft. Lauderdale (5/95)	-	-	676	-	923	-
Ft. Worth (10/93)	-	-	633	-	827	-
Houston (3/96)	881	1,430	703	985	1,021	1,455
Jacksonville (3/95)	-	-	596	-	829	-
Knoxville (11/93)	-	-	603	-	802	-
Miami (11/96)	811	1,386	599	1,049	929	-
Mobile (6/96)	-	-	-	-	807	-
Nashville (5/96)	746	1,072	539	876	838	-
New Orleans (1/96)	751	1,129	573	954	905	-
Orlando (4/96)	763	-	551	963	828	-
San Antonio (8/96)	-	-	645	-	946	-
Tallahassee (5/96)	-	-	-	-	-	-
Tampa (7/96)	759	1,255	-	983	925	-

Notes: Figures are average weekly earnings; Dashes indicate that data was not available;
(1) Metropolitan Statistical Area - see Appendix A for areas included
Source: Bureau of Labor Statistics, Occupational Compensation Surveys

Average Wages: Selected Technical and Clerical Occupations

MSA[1] (Month/Year)	Accounting Clerk III	General Clerk II	Computer Operator II	Key Entry Operator I	Secretary III	Switchboard Operator/ Receptionist
Abilene (12/93)	-	349	-	-	488	256
Atlanta (3/96)	462	-	469	351	551	372
Austin (8/95)	442	387	407	294	517	325
Brownsville	-	-	-	-	-	-
Corpus Christi (9/95)	393	295	441	294	388	306
Dallas (3/96)	442	401	459	305	529	337
Ft. Lauderdale (5/95)	412	465	464	337	495	334
Ft. Worth (10/93)	442	469	388	305	498	316
Houston (3/96)	493	479	453	341	573	363
Jacksonville (3/95)	389	369	391	317	517	327
Knoxville (11/93)	336	344	369	295	460	305
Miami (11/96)	435	486	452	304	524	343
Mobile (6/96)	423	338	-	-	541	290
Nashville (5/96)	418	341	427	314	495	354
New Orleans (1/96)	407	362	403	282	500	302
Orlando (4/96)	428	331	402	317	519	340
San Antonio (8/96)	404	395	-	-	500	301
Tallahassee (5/96)	497	361	-	297	521	268
Tampa (7/96)	407	354	404	284	516	320

Notes: Figures are average weekly earnings; Dashes indicate that data was not available;
(1) Metropolitan Statistical Area - see Appendix A for areas included
Source: Bureau of Labor Statistics, Occupational Compensation Surveys

Average Wages: Selected Health and Protective Service Occupations

MSA[1] (Month/Year)	Corrections Officer	Firefighter	Lic. Prac. Nurse II	Registered Nurse II	Nursing Assistant II	Police Officer I
Abilene (12/93)	-	-	-	-	-	-
Atlanta (3/96)	391	532	-	-	-	521
Austin (8/95)	-	-	-	722	-	-
Brownsville	-	-	-	-	-	-
Corpus Christi (9/95)	403	658	-	-	-	595
Dallas (3/96)	417	616	-	-	-	647
Ft. Lauderdale (5/95)	-	-	-	-	-	-
Ft. Worth (10/93)	-	-	-	-	-	-
Houston (3/96)	441	617	-	-	-	603
Jacksonville (3/95)	-	-	-	-	-	-
Knoxville (11/93)	-	-	-	-	-	-
Miami (11/96)	614	837	-	-	-	790
Mobile (6/96)	-	-	-	-	-	-
Nashville (5/96)	-	537	-	-	-	556
New Orleans (1/96)	-	423	463	756	218	413
Orlando (4/96)	518	-	-	-	-	-
San Antonio (8/96)	-	-	-	-	-	-
Tallahassee (5/96)	-	-	-	-	-	-
Tampa (7/96)	-	573	-	-	-	665

Notes: Figures are average weekly earnings; Dashes indicate that data was not available;
(1) Metropolitan Statistical Area - see Appendix A for areas included
Source: Bureau of Labor Statistics, Occupational Compensation Surveys

Average Wages: Selected Maintenance, Material Movement and Custodial Occupations

MSA[1] (Month/Year)	General Maintenance	Guard I	Janitor	Maintenance Electrician	Motor Vehicle Mechanic	Truckdriver (Trac. Trail.)
Abilene (12/93)	7.75	6.50	4.96	-	-	9.30
Atlanta (3/96)	10.68	6.62	6.58	-	17.17	15.59
Austin (8/95)	8.39	6.26	5.42	17.77	15.03	10.52
Brownsville	-	-	-	-	-	-
Corpus Christi (9/95)	7.70	6.49	6.46	14.50	12.06	-
Dallas (3/96)	8.74	6.79	-	15.49	15.66	-
Ft. Lauderdale (5/95)	8.69	5.56	-	16.03	15.20	15.86
Ft. Worth (10/93)	7.91	5.33	5.85	-	16.92	12.61
Houston (3/96)	9.22	6.55	5.34	18.67	14.63	13.30
Jacksonville (3/95)	9.83	5.45	5.33	17.77	14.20	14.35
Knoxville (11/93)	9.81	-	6.81	16.60	13.32	9.72
Miami (11/96)	8.93	5.97	6.22	15.61	14.49	16.94
Mobile (6/96)	6.91	4.88	4.94	15.93	13.37	9.64
Nashville (5/96)	9.50	6.60	6.66	15.48	14.34	17.97
New Orleans (1/96)	8.58	5.66	5.24	15.74	13.05	12.21
Orlando (4/96)	8.40	7.61	7.45	14.74	13.40	12.20
San Antonio (8/96)	8.03	5.68	5.36	14.31	12.98	11.12
Tallahassee (5/96)	7.44	5.05	5.92	-	14.44	-
Tampa (7/96)	9.06	5.78	6.26	-	14.02	12.06

Notes: Figures are average hourly earnings; Dashes indicate that data was not available;
(1) Metropolitan Statistical Area - see Appendix A for areas included
Source: Bureau of Labor Statistics, Occupational Compensation Surveys

Means of Transportation to Work: City

| City | Car/Truck/Van | | Public Transportation | | | Bicycle | Walked | Other Means | Worked at Home |
	Drove Alone	Car-pooled	Bus	Subway	Railroad				
Abilene	80.9	11.7	0.5	0.0	0.0	0.5	3.1	1.1	2.3
Atlanta	61.2	11.6	16.7	2.9	0.1	0.3	3.8	1.2	2.4
Austin	73.6	13.3	4.8	0.0	0.0	0.8	3.3	1.3	2.8
Brownsville	67.0	22.6	2.3	0.0	0.0	0.3	3.8	1.6	2.5
Corpus Christi	75.8	16.9	1.8	0.0	0.0	0.2	1.9	1.4	1.8
Dallas	72.5	15.2	6.4	0.0	0.0	0.2	2.4	1.2	2.2
Ft. Lauderdale	73.6	13.3	4.4	0.0	0.2	1.1	3.3	1.6	2.6
Ft. Worth	76.7	16.3	1.6	0.0	0.0	0.2	2.3	1.2	1.8
Houston	71.7	15.5	6.3	0.0	0.0	0.4	3.0	1.2	2.0
Jacksonville	75.5	14.2	2.5	0.0	0.0	0.6	2.7	1.7	2.7
Knoxville	77.1	13.1	1.8	0.0	0.0	0.2	4.8	1.0	1.9
Miami	60.9	18.0	11.8	0.6	0.2	0.6	4.2	1.8	1.9
Mobile	81.8	12.2	1.5	0.0	0.0	0.2	1.8	1.0	1.4
Nashville	78.1	13.4	2.8	0.0	0.0	0.1	2.6	0.8	2.2
New Orleans	58.6	15.4	15.6	0.0	0.0	0.9	5.2	2.3	1.9
Orlando	68.3	12.6	3.5	0.0	0.0	0.8	11.9	1.5	1.3
San Antonio	73.4	15.5	4.8	0.0	0.0	0.1	3.1	1.1	1.9
Tallahassee	75.0	13.5	2.7	0.0	0.0	0.8	5.0	1.3	1.7
Tampa	74.8	14.3	3.2	0.0	0.0	0.9	3.4	1.5	1.9
U.S.	**73.2**	**13.4**	**3.0**	**1.5**	**0.5**	**0.4**	**3.9**	**1.2**	**3.0**

Note: Figures shown are percentages and only include workers 16 years old and over
Source: 1990 Census of Population and Housing, Summary Tape File 3C

Means of Transportation to Work: Metro Area

| MSA[1] | Car/Truck/Van | | Public Transportation | | | Bicycle | Walked | Other Means | Worked at Home |
	Drove Alone	Car-pooled	Bus	Subway	Railroad				
Abilene	80.7	11.9	0.5	0.0	0.0	0.5	3.0	1.0	2.4
Atlanta	78.0	12.7	3.5	1.0	0.1	0.1	1.5	1.0	2.2
Austin	75.3	13.9	3.2	0.0	0.0	0.5	2.9	1.2	3.0
Brownsville	69.3	21.4	1.1	0.0	0.0	0.3	3.3	1.6	3.0
Corpus Christi	75.6	17.0	1.5	0.0	0.0	0.3	2.1	1.5	2.0
Dallas	77.6	14.0	3.1	0.0	0.0	0.1	1.9	1.0	2.3
Ft. Lauderdale	79.7	12.8	1.8	0.0	0.1	0.7	1.8	1.2	1.9
Ft. Worth	80.9	13.5	0.6	0.0	0.0	0.1	1.7	0.9	2.2
Houston	75.7	14.6	4.0	0.0	0.0	0.3	2.2	1.1	2.1
Jacksonville	76.2	14.3	1.9	0.0	0.0	0.7	2.6	1.7	2.6
Knoxville	80.5	13.2	0.6	0.0	0.0	0.1	2.3	0.8	2.5
Miami	72.4	15.6	4.8	0.7	0.1	0.5	2.5	1.3	2.0
Mobile	80.6	13.8	0.9	0.0	0.0	0.2	1.7	1.2	1.7
Nashville	79.1	13.8	1.6	0.0	0.0	0.1	1.9	0.9	2.6
New Orleans	70.9	15.3	6.6	0.0	0.0	0.5	3.1	1.8	1.7
Orlando	78.1	13.3	1.4	0.0	0.0	0.6	3.5	1.2	2.0
San Antonio	74.6	14.8	3.6	0.0	0.0	0.2	3.6	1.0	2.3
Tallahassee	75.2	16.4	1.8	0.0	0.0	0.5	3.2	1.1	1.9
Tampa	78.8	13.3	1.3	0.0	0.0	0.7	2.3	1.3	2.3
U.S.	**73.2**	**13.4**	**3.0**	**1.5**	**0.5**	**0.4**	**3.9**	**1.2**	**3.0**

Note: Figures shown are percentages and only include workers 16 years old and over;
(1) Metropolitan Statistical Area - see Appendix A for areas included
Source: 1990 Census of Population and Housing, Summary Tape File 3C

Cost of Living Index

Area	Composite	Groceries	Health	Housing	Misc.	Transp.	Utilities
Abilene	93.5	88.4	99.2	87.3	95.2	104.8	101.6
Atlanta	100.5	100.8	106.9	98.9	101.7	99.2	97.8
Austin	98.9	88.1	108.1	103.2	102.1	97.8	86.3
Brownsville	94.1	95.1	101.4	77.6	100.1	103.6	108.9
Corpus Christi	n/a	n/a	n/a	n/a	n/a	n/a	n/a
Dallas[1]	98.2	97.6	106.4	94.2	98.9	105.2	95.9
Fort Lauderdale	n/a	n/a	n/a	n/a	n/a	n/a	n/a
Fort Worth	95.9	106.1	97.8	82.9	100.6	95.7	99.9
Houston[1]	94.3	93.6	102.4	82.5	98.2	106.1	101.0
Jacksonville[3]	94.4	101.6	88.7	85.6	95.5	106.3	97.1
Knoxville	95.5	95.1	95.2	91.4	101.4	91.6	90.5
Miami[1]	106.4	101.1	111.9	108.1	103.0	117.6	108.8
Mobile	96.0	100.5	91.1	82.0	102.6	102.6	105.2
Nashville[2]	95.6	99.2	94.5	94.9	95.3	97.4	91.2
New Orleans	95.3	99.0	76.1	84.1	94.4	98.8	141.6
Orlando	99.6	102.9	106.4	94.1	100.5	99.9	103.7
San Antonio	91.8	88.4	95.0	91.5	95.5	95.4	77.6
Tallahassee	104.1	106.5	110.0	101.8	105.0	105.7	97.9
Tampa[3]	97.7	100.6	110.0	89.8	96.1	100.7	113.5
U.S.	**100.0**	**100.0**	**100.0**	**100.0**	**100.0**	**100.0**	**100.0**

Note: n/a not available; (1) Metropolitan Statistical Area (MSA) - see Appendix A for areas included;
(2) Nashville-Davidson; (3) 2nd Quarter 1997
Source: ACCRA, Cost of Living Index, 3rd Quarter 1997 unless otherwise noted

Median Home Prices and Housing Affordability

MSA[1]	Median Price[2] 3rd Qtr. 1997 ($)	HOI[3] 3rd Qtr. 1997	Affordability Rank[4]
Abilene	n/a	n/a	n/a
Atlanta	125,000	73.1	65
Austin	127,000	57.1	160
Brownsville	n/a	n/a	n/a
Corpus Christi	n/a	n/a	n/a
Dallas	130,000	59.6	151
Ft. Lauderdale	112,000	71.9	80
Ft. Worth	100,000	71.1	87
Houston	107,000	63.4	130
Jacksonville	97,000	73.5	63
Knoxville	85,000	76.8	40
Miami	102,000	59.7	150
Mobile	n/a	n/a	n/a
Nashville	118,000	69.1	99
New Orleans	92,000	67.8	107
Orlando	100,000	73.1	65
San Antonio	92,000	63.5	128
Tallahassee	96,000	76.3	45
Tampa	88,000	72.4	75
U.S.	**127,000**	**63.7**	**–**

Note: (1) Metropolitan Statistical Area - see Appendix A for areas included; (2) U.S. figures calculated from the sales of
625,000 new and existing homes in 195 markets; (3) Housing Opportunity Index - percent of homes sold that were within
the reach of the median income household at the prevailing mortgage interest rate; (4) Rank is from 1-195 with 1 being
most affordable; n/a not available
Source: National Association of Home Builders, Housing News Service, 3rd Quarter 1997

Average Home Prices

Area	Price ($)
Abilene	118,800
Atlanta	136,627
Austin	130,220
Brownsville	101,300
Corpus Christi	n/a
Dallas[1]	117,498
Fort Lauderdale	n/a
Fort Worth	105,550
Houston[1]	105,031
Jacksonville[3]	107,180
Knoxville	120,740
Miami[1]	139,900
Mobile	113,500
Nashville[2]	126,000
New Orleans	109,160
Orlando	126,729
San Antonio	125,200
Tallahassee	132,592
Tampa[3]	107,000
U.S.	**135,710**

Note: Figures are based on a new home with 1,800 sq. ft. of living area on an 8,000 sq. ft. lot; n/a not available;
(1) Metropolitan Statistical Area (MSA) - see Appendix A for areas included; (2) Nashville-Davidson; (3) 2nd Quarter 1997
Source: ACCRA, Cost of Living Index, 3rd Quarter 1997 unless otherwise noted

Average Apartment Rent

Area	Rent ($/mth)
Abilene	497
Atlanta	589
Austin	843
Brownsville	483
Corpus Christi	n/a
Dallas[1]	745
Fort Lauderdale	n/a
Fort Worth	617
Houston[1]	646
Jacksonville[3]	654
Knoxville	572
Miami[1]	725
Mobile	445
Nashville[2]	624
New Orleans	578
Orlando	591
San Antonio	563
Tallahassee	644
Tampa[3]	607
U.S.	**569**

Note: Figures are based on an unfurnished two bedroom, 1-1/2 or 2 bath apartment, approximately 950 sq. ft. in size,
excluding all utilities except water; n/a not available; (1) Metropolitan Statistical Area (MSA) - see Appendix A for areas
included; (2) Nashville-Davidson; (3) 2nd Quarter 1997
Source: ACCRA, Cost of Living Index, 3rd Quarter 1997 unless otherwise noted

Average Residential Utility Costs

Area	All Electric ($/mth)	Part Electric ($/mth)	Other Energy ($/mth)	Phone ($/mth)
Abilene	107.85	-	-	15.19
Atlanta	-	57.38	39.77	22.75
Austin	-	61.81	28.08	15.06
Brownsville	117.03	-	-	14.47
Corpus Christi	n/a	n/a	n/a	n/a
Dallas[1]	-	76.65	23.53	16.33
Fort Lauderdale	n/a	n/a	n/a	n/a
Fort Worth	-	73.85	30.27	17.33
Houston[1]	-	77.69	27.58	17.50
Jacksonville[3]	102.47	-	-	16.22
Knoxville	-	44.16	47.05	19.47
Miami[1]	115.52	-	-	16.27
Mobile	-	68.71	37.12	22.85
Nashville[2]	92.53	-	-	18.85
New Orleans	148.64	-	-	23.23
Orlando	106.15	-	-	20.29
San Antonio	-	54.29	24.23	16.38
Tallahassee	101.33	-	-	17.77
Tampa[3]	112.15	-	-	19.63
U.S.	**109.40**	**55.25**	**43.64**	**19.48**

Note: Dashes indicate data not applicable; n/a not available;
(1) Metropolitan Statistical Area (MSA) - see Appendix A for areas included; (2) Nashville-Davidson; (3) 2nd Quarter 1997
Source: ACCRA, Cost of Living Index, 3rd Quarter 1997 unless otherwise noted

Average Health Care Costs

Area	Hospital ($/day)	Doctor ($/visit)	Dentist ($/visit)
Abilene	398.25	48.86	60.00
Atlanta	343.40	51.67	73.60
Austin	389.33	48.20	75.00
Brownsville	380.50	49.20	65.40
Corpus Christi	n/a	n/a	n/a
Dallas[1]	457.50	51.10	63.40
Fort Lauderdale	n/a	n/a	n/a
Fort Worth	342.60	44.40	64.80
Houston[1]	414.11	48.20	62.50
Jacksonville[3]	327.60	45.40	50.40
Knoxville	368.80	51.20	53.00
Miami[1]	466.00	68.00	53.00
Mobile	211.40	47.60	60.00
Nashville[2]	275.60	53.14	56.20
New Orleans	366.00	36.00	41.20
Orlando	497.70	53.00	59.60
San Antonio	365.60	48.20	54.00
Tallahassee	443.00	60.20	60.80
Tampa[3]	374.60	46.40	55.20
U.S.	**392.91**	**48.76**	**60.84**

Note: n/a not available; Hospital - based on a semi-private room. Doctor - based on a general practitioner's routine exam of an established patient. Dentist - based on adult teeth cleaning and periodic oral exam; (1) Metropolitan Statistical Area (MSA) - see Appendix A for areas included; (2) Nashville-Davidson; (3) 2nd Quarter 1997
Source: ACCRA, Cost of Living Index, 3rd Quarter 1997 unless otherwise noted

Distribution of Office-Based Physicians

MSA[1]	General Practitioners	Specialists		
		Medical	Surgical	Other
Abilene	32	61	66	44
Atlanta	532	2,155	1,708	1,670
Austin	290	501	428	460
Brownsville	44	111	79	46
Corpus Christi	88	197	177	154
Dallas	516	1,453	1,339	1,408
Ft. Lauderdale	239	1,062	684	616
Ft. Worth	299	513	518	470
Houston	851	2,066	1,747	1,883
Jacksonville	263	576	455	454
Knoxville	220	447	366	357
Miami	747	1,769	1,220	1,228
Mobile	109	279	269	209
Nashville	207	857	711	719
New Orleans	206	1,060	905	893
Orlando	332	699	617	523
San Antonio	362	753	622	725
Tallahassee	92	117	112	106
Tampa	466	1,436	1,019	1,067

Note: Data as of 12/31/96; (1) Metropolitan Statistical Area - see Appendix A for areas included
Source: Physician Characteristics & Distribution in the U.S. 1997-98

Educational Quality

City	School District	Education Quotient[1]	Graduate Outcome[2]	Community Index[3]	Resource Index[4]
Abilene	Abilene	82.0	90.0	87.0	68.0
Atlanta	Atlanta City	106.0	52.0	116.0	149.0
Austin	Austin	96.0	103.0	126.0	59.0
Brownsville	Brownsville	70.0	51.0	51.0	109.0
Corpus Christi	Corpus Christi	72.0	71.0	64.0	80.0
Dallas	Dallas	79.0	57.0	111.0	68.0
Fort Lauderdale	Fort Lauderdale	70.0	68.0	92.0	51.0
Fort Worth	Fort Worth	85.0	66.0	121.0	69.0
Houston	Houston	89.0	62.0	109.0	95.0
Jacksonville	Jacksonville	97.0	69.0	94.0	129.0
Knoxville	Knox County	96.0	100.0	97.0	92.0
Miami	Miami	79.0	61.0	56.0	120.0
Mobile	Mobile County	81.0	63.0	60.0	119.0
Nashville	Nashville-Davidson Co.	96.0	63.0	108.0	116.0
New Orleans	Orleans Parish	66.0	56.0	54.0	87.0
Orlando	Orlando	92.0	73.0	101.0	102.0
San Antonio	San Antonio	86.0	52.0	72.0	134.0
Tallahassee	Tallahassee	n/a	n/a	n/a	n/a
Tampa	Tampa	107.0	96.0	92.0	132.0

Note: Nearly 1,000 secondary school districts were rated in terms of educational quality. The scores range from a low of 50 to a high of 150; (1) Average of the Graduate Outcome, Community and Resource indexes; (2) Based on graduation rates and college board scores (SAT/ACT); (3) Based on the surrounding community's average level of education and the area's average income level; (4) Based on teacher salaries, per-pupil expenditures and student-teacher ratios.
Source: Expansion Management, Ratings Issue 1997

School Enrollment by Type: City

City	Preprimary				Elementary/High School			
	Public		Private		Public		Private	
	Enrollment	%	Enrollment	%	Enrollment	%	Enrollment	%
Abilene	1,324	62.1	808	37.9	17,930	96.3	693	3.7
Atlanta	3,898	59.8	2,621	40.2	55,393	90.3	5,935	9.7
Austin	4,815	52.7	4,328	47.3	62,838	93.4	4,472	6.6
Brownsville	1,032	76.7	314	23.3	27,286	95.5	1,284	4.5
Corpus Christi	2,476	56.7	1,894	43.3	52,069	94.0	3,309	6.0
Dallas	8,029	52.2	7,349	47.8	147,967	90.2	16,105	9.8
Ft. Lauderdale	946	46.1	1,108	53.9	15,660	84.4	2,903	15.6
Ft. Worth	4,297	60.0	2,866	40.0	69,185	90.9	6,935	9.1
Houston	14,485	54.0	12,343	46.0	274,727	92.3	22,938	7.7
Jacksonville	6,877	55.5	5,519	44.5	92,698	87.5	13,236	12.5
Knoxville	1,461	68.5	673	31.5	19,991	94.3	1,216	5.7
Miami	2,688	61.0	1,720	39.0	53,740	90.3	5,750	9.7
Mobile	1,602	44.3	2,015	55.7	28,538	81.1	6,641	18.9
Nashville	3,671	51.4	3,472	48.6	61,254	84.7	11,083	15.3
New Orleans	4,980	53.7	4,290	46.3	75,984	79.7	19,309	20.3
Orlando	1,419	60.7	918	39.3	19,932	92.8	1,549	7.2
San Antonio	9,035	61.2	5,735	38.8	173,354	92.5	14,116	7.5
Tallahassee	1,297	53.2	1,141	46.8	14,252	91.1	1,393	8.9
Tampa	3,016	59.3	2,068	40.7	35,768	88.4	4,676	11.6
U.S.	2,679,029	59.5	1,824,256	40.5	38,379,689	90.2	4,187,099	9.8

Note: Figures shown cover persons 3 years old and over
Source: 1990 Census of Population and Housing, Summary Tape File 3C

School Enrollment by Type: Metro Area

MSA[1]	Preprimary				Elementary/High School			
	Public		Private		Public		Private	
	Enrollment	%	Enrollment	%	Enrollment	%	Enrollment	%
Abilene	1,444	62.6	863	37.4	20,549	96.3	799	3.7
Atlanta	28,793	49.6	29,303	50.4	437,891	92.0	37,989	8.0
Austin	8,688	52.4	7,888	47.6	119,826	94.2	7,318	5.8
Brownsville	3,016	78.3	834	21.7	67,669	96.3	2,573	3.7
Corpus Christi	3,591	61.8	2,216	38.2	73,649	95.2	3,729	4.8
Dallas	24,235	49.1	25,151	50.9	413,238	92.3	34,313	7.7
Ft. Lauderdale	9,740	43.6	12,606	56.4	146,453	87.1	21,625	12.9
Ft. Worth	13,513	55.4	10,874	44.6	216,997	92.6	17,279	7.4
Houston	34,923	52.8	31,273	47.2	607,238	93.9	39,303	6.1
Jacksonville	9,288	54.2	7,843	45.8	135,736	88.8	17,193	11.2
Knoxville	5,577	65.8	2,903	34.2	89,754	95.4	4,299	4.6
Miami	14,892	43.9	19,029	56.1	281,730	86.5	44,139	13.5
Mobile	4,123	50.8	3,999	49.2	79,476	86.1	12,784	13.9
Nashville	9,119	56.1	7,129	43.9	143,901	88.2	19,299	11.8
New Orleans	10,527	42.0	14,557	58.0	178,094	75.0	59,271	25.0
Orlando	9,698	49.2	9,997	50.8	154,434	91.4	14,467	8.6
San Antonio	12,989	59.1	8,978	40.9	240,288	92.4	19,686	7.6
Tallahassee	2,725	51.8	2,540	48.2	32,875	89.0	4,048	11.0
Tampa	17,848	52.0	16,451	48.0	244,416	89.0	30,326	11.0
U.S.	2,679,029	59.5	1,824,256	40.5	38,379,689	90.2	4,187,099	9.8

Note: Figures shown cover persons 3 years old and over;
(1) Metropolitan Statistical Area - see Appendix A for areas included
Source: 1990 Census of Population and Housing, Summary Tape File 3C

School Enrollment by Race: City

City	Preprimary (%)				Elementary/High School (%)			
	White	Black	Other	Hisp.[1]	White	Black	Other	Hisp.[1]
Abilene	78.7	9.9	11.4	14.9	75.2	9.1	15.7	24.5
Atlanta	26.6	71.9	1.5	1.5	13.8	84.6	1.6	1.9
Austin	73.9	11.0	15.1	20.9	58.1	18.2	23.8	33.8
Brownsville	86.1	0.4	13.4	90.1	84.5	0.3	15.3	94.6
Corpus Christi	75.8	7.2	17.0	43.2	70.5	5.2	24.3	61.7
Dallas	56.1	31.5	12.4	16.8	38.2	39.7	22.2	30.3
Ft. Lauderdale	59.2	39.5	1.3	3.0	41.2	55.4	3.4	8.8
Ft. Worth	66.5	23.3	10.3	14.9	50.6	28.9	20.5	27.9
Houston	54.6	29.7	15.6	22.8	40.2	33.3	26.5	38.1
Jacksonville	71.3	26.7	2.0	2.1	62.4	33.6	4.0	2.8
Knoxville	78.3	19.2	2.5	0.4	71.8	26.4	1.8	0.9
Miami	48.8	46.8	4.4	40.9	51.7	40.5	7.8	53.5
Mobile	64.4	33.9	1.7	1.0	45.8	52.5	1.6	1.1
Nashville	73.3	24.3	2.4	0.8	63.8	34.0	2.2	1.1
New Orleans	30.5	67.4	2.1	2.2	17.6	78.5	3.8	3.0
Orlando	60.2	37.5	2.3	10.9	49.0	44.6	6.4	11.9
San Antonio	71.9	7.5	20.6	51.9	67.0	6.8	26.2	68.2
Tallahassee	61.2	37.0	1.8	2.8	55.6	42.1	2.3	1.9
Tampa	60.0	37.3	2.8	10.9	55.2	40.0	4.7	14.9
U.S.	**80.4**	**12.5**	**7.1**	**7.8**	**74.1**	**15.6**	**10.3**	**12.5**

Note: Figures shown cover persons 3 years old and over; (1) People of Hispanic origin can be of any race
Source: 1990 Census of Population and Housing, Summary Tape File 3C

School Enrollment by Race: Metro Area

MSA[1]	Preprimary (%)				Elementary/High School (%)			
	White	Black	Other	Hisp.[2]	White	Black	Other	Hisp.[2]
Abilene	80.1	9.2	10.7	14.0	77.5	7.9	14.5	22.6
Atlanta	72.8	25.3	1.9	1.5	64.8	32.0	3.2	2.0
Austin	80.3	7.7	12.0	18.3	69.7	12.2	18.2	28.3
Brownsville	80.9	0.7	18.4	84.1	80.6	0.3	19.1	91.1
Corpus Christi	75.7	5.6	18.7	46.8	70.4	4.0	25.6	62.9
Dallas	76.1	15.8	8.2	10.6	64.7	20.3	15.0	19.3
Ft. Lauderdale	77.7	19.9	2.4	7.8	67.7	28.3	4.0	11.4
Ft. Worth	83.3	10.5	6.2	8.1	74.3	14.0	11.6	14.9
Houston	71.3	17.7	11.0	16.0	58.6	21.4	20.1	28.5
Jacksonville	76.9	21.2	1.9	2.1	69.8	26.6	3.5	2.9
Knoxville	91.3	6.5	2.2	0.8	90.4	8.2	1.4	0.8
Miami	66.7	28.6	4.6	35.5	62.4	30.2	7.4	47.6
Mobile	71.2	27.6	1.2	1.2	62.2	35.8	2.1	1.0
Nashville	83.9	14.4	1.7	1.0	79.0	19.3	1.7	1.0
New Orleans	63.6	34.1	2.3	3.1	51.1	45.3	3.6	4.2
Orlando	82.3	14.2	3.5	7.5	74.8	18.7	6.5	11.8
San Antonio	75.1	7.9	17.0	42.9	70.1	7.0	22.8	59.1
Tallahassee	67.5	30.8	1.8	2.0	56.1	42.1	1.8	2.0
Tampa	82.6	14.6	2.8	6.4	80.0	16.0	4.0	8.9
U.S.	**80.4**	**12.5**	**7.1**	**7.8**	**74.1**	**15.6**	**10.3**	**12.5**

Note: Figures shown cover persons 3 years old and over; (1) Metropolitan Statistical Area - see Appendix A for areas included; (2) People of Hispanic origin can be of any race
Source: 1990 Census of Population and Housing, Summary Tape File 3C

Crime Rate: City

City	All Crimes	Violent Crimes				Property Crimes		
		Murder	Forcible Rape	Robbery	Aggrav. Assault	Burglary	Larceny -Theft	Motor Vehicle Theft
Abilene	5,213.8	6.1	57.6	110.0	348.4	978.0	3,499.7	213.9
Atlanta	17,070.2	47.4	94.9	1,163.1	2,010.5	2,534.6	8,981.3	2,238.3
Austin	7,865.9	7.4	50.2	256.0	397.2	1,409.3	5,058.2	687.5
Brownsville	8,397.5	9.4	18.7	196.6	754.8	1,130.1	5,881.2	406.8
Corpus Christi	10,628.3	6.3	96.3	169.2	781.8	1,316.2	7,676.7	581.9
Dallas	9,466.6	20.5	69.8	577.2	867.5	1,693.4	4,621.8	1,616.4
Ft. Lauderdale	15,165.5	20.2	57.1	705.7	754.5	2,822.8	8,999.8	1,805.3
Ft. Worth	8,272.6	14.5	67.8	359.8	617.8	1,683.6	4,568.0	961.2
Houston	7,636.5	14.7	56.5	467.0	728.9	1,433.4	3,672.4	1,263.5
Jacksonville	8,623.5	12.3	98.6	404.4	899.1	1,907.8	4,613.8	687.5
Knoxville	6,186.0	13.2	38.5	340.7	484.9	1,345.0	3,047.3	916.4
Miami	13,745.8	32.2	52.2	1,334.9	1,695.2	2,546.7	6,086.4	1,998.3
Mobile	9,421.3	24.6	57.5	619.5	353.4	2,126.4	5,306.5	933.3
Nashville	11,218.9	16.8	91.9	549.0	1,232.9	1,514.0	6,262.5	1,551.9
New Orleans	11,042.2	71.9	79.9	1,167.3	937.9	2,038.5	4,663.9	2,082.7
Orlando	13,172.4	7.1	90.4	591.4	1,502.6	2,419.3	7,361.9	1,199.8
San Antonio	8,586.6	11.5	62.4	230.1	160.3	1,339.7	5,921.6	861.1
Tallahassee	10,157.9	7.2	68.8	263.0	792.7	1,563.0	6,887.6	575.4
Tampa	14,549.5	14.6	89.6	906.4	1,938.1	2,502.1	7,054.3	2,044.3
U.S.	**5,078.9**	**7.4**	**36.1**	**202.4**	**388.2**	**943.0**	**2,975.9**	**525.9**

Note: Crime rate is the number of crimes per 100,000 population;
Source: FBI Uniform Crime Reports 1996

Crime Rate: Suburbs

Suburbs[1]	All Crimes	Violent Crimes				Property Crimes		
		Murder	Forcible Rape	Robbery	Aggrav. Assault	Burglary	Larceny -Theft	Motor Vehicle Theft
Abilene	2,874.0	8.1	56.7	8.1	291.5	995.8	1,489.6	24.3
Atlanta	6,375.1	4.9	28.9	175.3	229.9	1,065.0	4,107.7	763.4
Austin	3,760.7	3.0	30.3	42.7	225.6	871.6	2,408.3	179.3
Brownsville	4,897.1	4.2	5.7	54.3	253.7	1,241.0	3,114.2	224.0
Corpus Christi	2,983.4	4.7	21.8	23.7	248.9	834.0	1,714.5	135.8
Dallas	4,564.3	3.7	29.2	72.2	249.1	818.8	3,072.3	319.0
Ft. Lauderdale	n/a	n/a	n/a	n/a	n/a	n/a	n/a	n/a
Ft. Worth	4,881.7	3.5	40.5	96.4	358.9	852.9	3,113.7	415.8
Houston	4,123.8	5.5	34.8	110.0	352.3	883.4	2,306.5	431.3
Jacksonville	n/a	n/a	n/a	n/a	n/a	n/a	n/a	n/a
Knoxville	n/a	n/a	n/a	n/a	n/a	n/a	n/a	n/a
Miami	n/a	n/a	n/a	n/a	n/a	n/a	n/a	n/a
Mobile	4,077.6	9.3	37.6	126.1	365.9	977.0	2,281.3	280.5
Nashville	4,222.1	4.4	27.9	55.6	372.2	833.7	2,666.7	261.6
New Orleans	6,638.6	8.4	32.3	215.1	523.4	1,086.8	4,116.8	655.7
Orlando	n/a	n/a	n/a	n/a	n/a	n/a	n/a	n/a
San Antonio	3,838.6	4.8	26.8	43.2	276.1	753.7	2,535.5	198.5
Tallahassee	n/a	n/a	n/a	n/a	n/a	n/a	n/a	n/a
Tampa	n/a	n/a	n/a	n/a	n/a	n/a	n/a	n/a
U.S.	**5,078.9**	**7.4**	**36.1**	**202.4**	**388.2**	**943.0**	**2,975.9**	**525.9**

Note: Crime rate is the number of crimes per 100,000 population; (1) Defined as all areas within the MSA but located outside the central city ; n/a not available
Source: FBI Uniform Crime Reports 1996

Crime Rate: Metro Area

MSA[1]	All Crimes	Violent Crimes				Property Crimes		
		Murder	Forcible Rape	Robbery	Aggrav. Assault	Burglary	Larceny -Theft	Motor Vehicle Theft
Abilene	4,986.0	6.3	57.5	100.1	342.9	979.7	3,304.0	195.5
Atlanta	7,647.7	9.9	36.8	292.8	441.8	1,239.9	4,687.7	938.9
Austin	5,960.0	5.4	41.0	157.0	317.6	1,159.7	3,827.9	451.5
Brownsville	6,228.1	6.1	10.7	108.4	444.3	1,198.8	4,166.3	293.5
Corpus Christi	8,574.8	5.9	76.3	130.1	638.6	1,186.7	6,075.1	462.1
Dallas	6,350.2	9.8	44.0	256.2	474.4	1,137.4	3,636.8	791.6
Ft. Lauderdale	n/a	n/a	n/a	n/a	n/a	n/a	n/a	n/a
Ft. Worth	5,865.3	6.7	48.4	172.8	434.0	1,093.8	3,535.6	574.0
Houston	5,761.0	9.8	44.9	276.4	527.8	1,139.8	2,943.1	819.2
Jacksonville	n/a	n/a	n/a	n/a	n/a	n/a	n/a	n/a
Knoxville	n/a	n/a	n/a	n/a	n/a	n/a	n/a	n/a
Miami	n/a	n/a	n/a	n/a	n/a	n/a	n/a	n/a
Mobile	6,211.3	15.4	45.5	323.1	360.9	1,435.9	3,489.2	541.2
Nashville	7,593.9	10.4	58.7	293.4	787.0	1,161.5	4,399.5	883.4
New Orleans	8,267.7	31.9	49.9	567.4	676.8	1,438.9	4,319.2	1,183.6
Orlando	n/a	n/a	n/a	n/a	n/a	n/a	n/a	n/a
San Antonio	7,080.7	9.4	51.1	170.8	197.0	1,153.9	4,847.7	651.0
Tallahassee	n/a	n/a	n/a	n/a	n/a	n/a	n/a	n/a
Tampa	n/a	n/a	n/a	n/a	n/a	n/a	n/a	n/a
U.S.	**5,078.9**	**7.4**	**36.1**	**202.4**	**388.2**	**943.0**	**2,975.9**	**525.9**

Note: Crime rate is the number of crimes per 100,000 population; n/a not available;
(1) Metropolitan Statistical Area - see Appendix A for areas included
Source: FBI Uniform Crime Reports 1996

Temperature & Precipitation: Yearly Averages and Extremes

City	Extreme Low (°F)	Average Low (°F)	Average Temp. (°F)	Average High (°F)	Extreme High (°F)	Average Precip. (in.)	Average Snow (in.)
Abilene	-7	53	65	76	110	23.6	5
Atlanta	-8	52	62	72	105	49.8	2
Austin	-2	58	69	79	109	31.1	1
Brownsville	16	65	74	83	106	25.8	Tr
Corpus Christi	13	63	72	81	103	29.9	0
Dallas	-2	56	67	77	112	33.9	3
Ft. Lauderdale	30	69	76	83	98	57.1	0
Ft. Worth	-1	55	66	76	113	32.3	3
Houston	7	58	69	79	107	46.9	Tr
Jacksonville	7	58	69	79	103	52.0	0
Knoxville	-24	48	59	69	103	46.7	13
Miami	30	69	76	83	98	57.1	0
Mobile	3	57	68	77	104	65.6	Tr
Nashville	-17	49	60	70	107	47.4	11
New Orleans	11	59	69	78	102	60.6	Tr
Orlando	19	62	72	82	100	47.7	Tr
San Antonio	0	58	69	80	108	29.6	1
Tallahassee	6	56	68	79	103	63.3	Tr
Tampa	18	63	73	82	99	46.7	Tr

Note: Tr = Trace
Source: National Climatic Data Center, International Station Meteorological Climate Summary, 3/95

Weather Conditions

City	Temperature			Daytime Sky			Precipitation		
	10°F & below	32°F & below	90°F & above	Clear	Partly cloudy	Cloudy	.01 inch or more precip.	1.0 inch or more snow/ice	Thunder-storms
Abilene	2	52	102	141	125	99	65	4	43
Atlanta	1	49	38	98	147	120	116	3	48
Austin	< 1	20	111	105	148	112	83	1	41
Brownsville	(a)	(b)	116	86	180	99	72	0	27
Corpus Christi	(a)	(b)	106	84	177	104	76	< 1	27
Dallas	1	34	102	108	160	97	78	2	49
Ft. Lauderdale	(a)	(b)	55	48	263	54	128	0	74
Ft. Worth	1	40	100	123	136	106	79	3	47
Houston	(a)	(b)	96	83	168	114	101	1	62
Jacksonville	< 1	16	83	86	181	98	114	1	65
Knoxville	3	73	33	85	142	138	125	8	47
Miami	(a)	(b)	55	48	263	54	128	0	74
Mobile	(a)	(b)	76	92	166	107	121	1	79
Nashville	5	76	51	98	135	132	119	8	54
New Orleans	0	13	70	90	169	106	114	1	69
Orlando	(a)	(b)	90	76	208	81	115	0	80
San Antonio	(a)	(b)	112	97	153	115	81	1	36
Tallahassee	< 1	31	86	93	175	97	114	1	83
Tampa	(a)	(b)	85	81	204	80	107	< 1	87

Note: Figures are average number of days per year; (a) Figures for 10 degrees and below are not available; (b) Figures for 32 degrees and below are not available
Source: National Climatic Data Center, International Station Meteorological Climate Summary, 3/95

Air Quality

MSA[1]	PSI>100[2] (days)	Ozone (ppm)	Carbon Monoxide (ppm)	Sulfur Dioxide (ppm)	Nitrogen Dioxide (ppm)	PM10 (ug/m3)	Lead (ug/m3)
Abilene	n/a	n/a	n/a	n/a	n/a	n/a	n/a
Atlanta	12	0.14	4	0.022	0.027	60	0.03
Austin	0	0.10	3	n/a	0.018	32	n/a
Brownsville	n/a	0.08	2	0.004	n/a	40	0.02
Corpus Christi	n/a	0.10	n/a	0.015	n/a	45	n/a
Dallas	6	0.14	6	0.046	0.019	102	0.17
Fort Lauderdale	0	0.10	4	0.008	0.010	48	0.05
Fort Worth	3	0.13	3	0.011	0.021	56	0.02
Houston	32	0.18	7	0.046	0.023	68	0.02
Jacksonville	0	0.10	4	0.030	0.015	61	0.02
Knoxville	1	0.11	3	0.058	0.014	78	n/a
Miami	1	0.10	5	0.005	0.016	62	0.01
Mobile	n/a	0.10	n/a	0.070	n/a	91	n/a
Nashville	2	0.12	5	0.076	0.012	66	0.07
New Orleans	1	0.11	4	0.035	0.018	64	0.09
Orlando	0	0.10	4	0.008	0.013	67	0.00
San Antonio	2	0.13	5	n/a	0.009	38	0.02
Tallahassee	n/a	n/a	n/a	n/a	n/a	33	n/a
Tampa	2	0.11	4	0.087	0.011	81	n/a
NAAQS[3]	-	**0.12**	**9**	**0.140**	**0.053**	**150**	**1.50**

Note: (1) Metropolitan Statistical Area - see Appendix A for areas included; (2) Number of days the Pollutant Standards Index (PSI) exceeded 100 in 1996. A PSI value greater than 100 indicates that air quality would be in the unhealthful range on that day; (3) National Ambient Air Quality Standard; ppm = parts per million; ug/m³ = micrograms per cubic meter; n/a not available
Source: EPA, National Air Quality and Emissions Trends Report, 1996

Water Quality

City	Tap Water
Abilene	Alkaline, hard and not fluoridated
Atlanta	Neutral, soft
Austin	Alkaline, soft and fluoridated
Brownsville	Alkaline and medium hard
Corpus Christi	Neutral, hard and fluoridated
Dallas	Moderately hard and fluoridated
Fort Lauderdale	Alkaline, very soft and fluoridated
Fort Worth	Alkaline, hard and fluoridated
Houston	Alkaline, hard
Jacksonville	Alkaline, very hard and naturally fluoridated
Knoxville	Alkaline, hard and fluoridated
Miami	Alkaline, soft and fluoridated
Mobile	Alkaline, very soft and fluoridated
Nashville	Alkaline, soft
New Orleans	Alkaline, soft and fluoridated
Orlando	Alkaline, hard and fluoridated
San Antonio	Not fluoridated and has moderate mineral content, chiefly sodium bicarbonate
Tallahassee	Alkaline, soft and fluoridated
Tampa	Alkaline, moderately hard and not fluoridated

Source: Editor & Publisher Market Guide 1998

Appendix A

Metropolitan Statistical Areas

Abilene, TX
Includes Taylor County

Atlanta, GA
Includes Barrow, Bartow, Carroll, Cherokee, Clayton, Cobb, Coweta, DeKalb, Douglas, Fayette, Forsyth, Fulton, Gwinnett, Henry, Newton, Paulding, Pickens, Rockdale, Spalding, and Walton Counties (as of 6/30/93)

Includes Barrow, Butts, Cherokee, Clayton, Cobb, Coweta, DeKalb, Douglas, Fayette, Forsyth, Fulton, Gwinnett, Henry, Newton, Paulding, Rockdale, Spalding, and Walton Counties (prior to 6/30/93)

Austin-San Marcos, TX
Includes Bastrop, Caldwell, Hays, Travis and Williamson Counties (as of 6/30/93)

Includes Hays, Travis and Williamson Counties (prior to 6/30/93)

Brownsville-Harlingen-San Benito, TX
Includes Cameron County

Corpus Christi, TX
Includes Nueces and San Patricio Counties

Dallas, TX
Includes Collin, Dallas, Denton, Ellis, Henderson, Hunt, Kaufman and Rockwall Counties (as of 6/30/93)

Includes Collin, Dallas, Denton, Ellis, Kaufman and Rockwall Counties (prior to 6/30/93)

Ft. Lauderdale, FL
Includes Broward County

Ft. Worth-Arlington, TX
Includes Hood, Johnson, Parker and Tarrant Counties (as of 6/30/93)

Includes Johnson, Parker and Tarrant Counties (prior to 6/30/93)

Houston, TX
Includes Chambers, Fort Bend, Harris, Liberty, Montgomery and Waller Counties (as of 6/30/93)

Includes Fort Bend, Harris, Liberty, Montgomery and Waller Counties (prior to 6/30/93)

Jacksonville, FL
Includes Clay, Duval, Nassau and St. Johns Counties

Knoxville, TN
Includes Anderson, Blount, Knox, Loudon, Sevier and Union Counties (as of 6/30/93)

Includes Anderson, Blount, Grainger, Jefferson, Knox, Sevier and Union Counties (prior to 6/30/93)

Miami, FL
Includes Dade County

Mobile, AL
Includes Baldwin and Mobile Counties

Nashville, TN
Includes Cheatham, Davidson, Dickson, Robertson, Rutherford, Sumner, Williamson and Wilson Counties

New Orleans, LA
Includes Jefferson, Orleans, Plaquemines, St. Bernard, St. Charles, St. James, St. John the Baptist and St. Tammany Parishes (as of 6/30/93)

Includes Jefferson, Orleans, St. Bernard, St. Charles, St. John the Baptist and St. Tammany Parishes (prior to 6/30/93)

Orlando, FL
Includes Lake, Orange, Osceola and Seminole Counties (as of 6/30/93)

Includes Orange, Osceola and Seminole Counties (prior to 6/30/93)

San Antonio, TX
Includes Bexar, Comal, Guadalupe and Wilson Counties (as of 6/30/93)

Includes Bexar, Comal and Guadalupe Counties (prior to 6/30/93)

Tallahassee, FL
Includes Gadsden and Leon Counties

Tampa-St. Petersburg-Clearwater, FL
Includes Includes Hernando, Hillsborough, Pasco and Pinellas Counties

Appendix B

Chambers of Commerce and Economic Development Organizations

Abilene

Abilene Chamber of Commerce
P.O. Box 2281
Abilene, TX 79604-2281
Phone: (915) 677-7241
Fax: (915) 677-0622

Abilene Industrial Foundation
1234 N. 4th Street
P.O. Box 2281
Abilene, TX 79604
Phone: (915) 673-7349
Fax: (915) 673-9193

Atlanta

Atlanta Chamber of Commerce
235 International Boulevard, N.W.
P.O. Box 1740
Atlanta, GA 30301
Phone: (404) 880-9000
Fax: (404) 586-8469

Atlanta Economic Development Corp.
230 Peachtree St. #210
Atlanta, GA 30303
Phone: (404) 658-7000
Fax: (404) 658-7734

Austin

Greater Austin
Chamber of Commerce
111 Congress Avenue
Plaza Level
P.O. Box 1967
Austin, TX 78767
Phone: (512) 478-9383
Fax: (512) 478-9615

Brownsville

Brownsville Economic Dev. Corp.
1205 N. Expressway
Brownsville, TX 78520-8622
Phone: (210) 541-1183
Fax: (210) 546-3938

Corpus Christi

Greater Corpus Christi
Business Alliance
1201 N. Shoreline
P.O. Box 640
Corpus Christi, TX 78403-0640
Phone: (512) 881-1888
Fax: (512) 882-8956

Dallas

City of Dallas
Economic Development Department
1500 Marilla
Room 5C South, City Hall
Dallas, TX 75201
Phone: (214) 670-1685
Fax: (214) 670-0158

Greater Dallas
Chamber of Commerce
1201 Elm Street, Suite 2000
Dallas, TX 75270
Phone: (214) 746-6600
Fax: (214) 746-6799

Fort Lauderdale

City of Ft. Lauderdale
Marketing & Public Information
100 N. Andrews Ave.
Ft. Lauderdale, FL 33301

Ft. Lauderdale
Chamber of Commerce
512 N.E. Third Ave.
P.O. Box 14516
Ft. Lauderdale, FL 33302-4516
Phone: (954) 462-6000
Fax: (954) 527-8766

Fort Worth

City of Fort Worth
Economic Development
Municipal Building
1000 Throckmorton Street
Ft. Worth, TX 76102
Phone: (817) 871-6103

Ft. Worth Chamber of Commerce
777 Taylor St. #900
Ft. Worth, TX 76102-4997
Phone: (817) 336-2491
Fax: (817) 877-4034

Houston

Greater Houston Partnership
1200 Smith St., Suite 700
Houston, TX 77002-4309
Phone: (713) 651-2100
Fax: (713) 651-2299

Jacksonville

Jacksonville Chamber of Commerce
3 Independent Drive
Jacksonville, FL 32202
Phone: (904) 366-6600
Fax: (904) 632-0617

Knoxville

Greater Knoxville
Chamber of Commerce
301 E. Church Ave.
Knoxville, TN 37915-2572
Phone: (423) 637-4550
Fax: (423) 523-2071

Miami

Greater Miami
Chamber of Commerce
Omni Complex
1601 Biscayne Blvd.
Miami, FL 33132-1260
Phone: (305) 350-7700
Fax: (305) 371-8255

The Beacon Council
One World Trade Plaza
Suite 2400
80 S.W. Eighth Street
Miami, FL 33130

Mobile

Mobile Area
Chamber of Commerce
P.O. Box 2187
Mobile, AL 36652-2187
Phone: (334) 433-6951
Fax: (334) 432-1143

Nashville

Nashville Area
Chamber of Commerce
161 Fourth Avenue, North
Nashville, TN 37219
Phone: (615) 259-4755
Fax: (615) 256-3074

New Orleans

City of New Orleans Partnership
Office of the Mayor
1300 Perdido Street, Room 2E10
New Orleans, LA 70112

New Orleans Metropolitan Convention
and Visitors Bureau, Inc.
1520 Sugar Bowl Drive#1100
New Orleans, LA 70112

Orlando

Greater Orlando
Chamber of Commerce
75 E. Ivanhoe Blvd.
P.O. Box 1234
Orlando, FL 32802
Phone: (407) 425-1234
Fax: (407) 839-5020

Metro Orlando Economic
Development Comm. of Mid-Florida
200 E. Robinson St., Suite 600
Orlando, FL 32801
Phone: (407) 422-7159
Fax: (407) 843-9514

San Antonio

San Antonio Economic
Development Department
P.O. Box 839966
San Antonio, TX 78283
Phone: (210) 207-8080

The Greater San Antonio
Chamber of Commerce
P.O. Box 1628
San Antonio, TX 78296
Phone: (210) 229-2100
Fax: (210) 229-1600

Tallahassee

Tallahassee Chamber of Commerce
100 N. Duval Street
P.O. Box 1639
Tallahassee, FL 32302
Phone: (904) 224-8116
Fax: (904) 561-3860

Tampa

Greater Tampa
Chamber of Commerce
P.O. Box 420
Tampa, FL 33601-0420
Phone: (813) 228-7777
Fax: (813) 223-7899

Appendix C

State Departments of Labor and Employment

Alabama

Department of Industrial Relations
649 Monroe St.
Montgomery, AL 36131

Florida

Florida Department of Labor &
Employment Security
Bureau of Labor Market Information
Suite 200, Hartman Bldg.
2012 Capitol Circle, SE
Tallahassee, FL 32399-2151

Georgia

Georgia Department of Labor
148 International Blvd., NE
Atlanta, GA 30303-1751

Louisiana

Louisiana Department of
Employment & Training
Research & Statistics
PO Box 94094
Baton Rouge, LA 70804-9094

Tennessee

Tennessee Department of
Employment Security
Research & Statistics Division
500 James Robertson Parkway
Nashville, TN 37245-1000

Texas

Texas Employment Commission
Economic Research & Analysis
101 E. 15th Street
Austin, TX 78778-0001